Lecture Notes in Computer Science   11469

Commenced Publication in 1973
Founding and Former Series Editors:
Gerhard Goos, Juris Hartmanis, and Jan van Leeuwen

More information about this series at http://www.springer.com/series/7410

Olivier Blazy · Chan Yeob Yeun (Eds.)

Information Security Theory and Practice

12th IFIP WG 11.2 International Conference, WISTP 2018
Brussels, Belgium, December 10–11, 2018
Revised Selected Papers

 Springer

Editors
Olivier Blazy 🆔
Université de Limoges
Limoges, France

Chan Yeob Yeun 🆔
Khalifa University
Abu Dhabi, United Arab Emirates

ISSN 0302-9743 ISSN 1611-3349 (electronic)
Lecture Notes in Computer Science
ISBN 978-3-030-20073-2 ISBN 978-3-030-20074-9 (eBook)
https://doi.org/10.1007/978-3-030-20074-9

LNCS Sublibrary: SL4 – Security and Cryptology

This Springer imprint is published by the registered company Springer Nature Switzerland AG
The registered company address is: Gewerbestrasse 11, 6330 Cham, Switzerland

Preface

The 12th WISTP International Conference on Information Security Theory and Practice attracted research contributions covering theoretical and practical aspects of security and privacy. Technical concepts from machine learning to real-world security, provide a global vision of current cybersecurity concerns.

This volume contains the papers presented at WISTP 2018 held during December 10–11 in Brussels.

There were 45 submissions. Each submission was reviewed on average by 3.1 Program Committee members. The reviewing was double-blind, with the identities of the authors not revealed to the reviewers of the papers and the identities of the reviewers not revealed to the authors, with some papers leading to intense discussions. The committee decided to accept 11 papers, yielding a 24% selection rate, together with two additional short papers. The program also included three invited talks by Amandine Jambert, Emil C. Lupu, and Damien Vergnaud.

Two papers received extra praised: "First Deep Learning Application in Security and Privacy – Theory and Practice: A Position Paper," received the best Student Paper Award, and "Efficient Information Theoretic Multi-Party Computation from Oblivious Linear Evaluation."

We would like to thank the General chairs (Jean-Michel Dricot, Olivier Markowitch, Yves Roggeman from ULB, Belgium) and the local organizers (Gaurav Sharma, Rajeev Anand Sahu, Dimitrios Sisiaridis, Suman Bala, Tania Ellinidou from ULB, Belgium).

We thank all the authors and participants who contributed to make this event a great success, the Technical Program Committee members and additional reviewers who worked on the program, and the volunteers who handled aspects of the organization behind the scenes. We greatly appreciate the input from members of the WISTP Steering Committee, whose help and advice was invaluable, and the support of IFIP WG 11.2: Pervasive Systems Security.

And we also want to thank our various sponsors (Centre for Cyber Security, Belgium; Fédération, Wallonie-Bruxelles, Belgium; IDfix), whose support helped to keep the registration costs as low as possible and at the same time allowed us to provide best paper awards and social activities to increase the networking opportunities. We also look forward to working together again in future WISTP events.

December 2018

Olivier Blazy
Chan Yeob Yeun

Organization

Program Committee

Mohamed Ahmed	SICS, Swedish ICT, Sweden
Raja Naeem Akram	ISG-Smart Card Centre, Royal Holloway, University of London, UK
Claudio Ardagna	Universitá degli Studi di Milano, Italy
Selcuk Baktir	Bahcesehir University, Turkey
Olivier Blazy	Université de Limoges, France
Samia Bouzefrane	CEDRIC Lab Conservatoire National des Arts et Métiers, France
Xavier Bultel	Université d'Auvergne, France
Céline Chevalier	ENS, France
Emmanuel Conchon	XLIM, France
Mauro Conti	University of Padua, Italy
José María De Fuentes	Universidad Carlos III de Madrid, Spain
Ruggero Donida Labati	Università degli Studi di Milano, Italy
Sara Foresti	Università degli Studi di Milano, Italy
Johann Groszschaedl	University of Luxembourg, Luxembourg
Yong Guan	Iowa State University, USA
Brahim Hamid	IRIT, University of Toulouse, France
Ben Hermann	Paderborn University, Germany
Julio Hernandez	University of Kent, UK
Sushil Jajodia	George Mason University, USA
Amandine Jambert	CNIL, France
Saqib A. Kakvi	Paderborn University, Germany
Süleyman Kardaş	Batman University, Turkey
Mehmet Sabir Kiraz	De Montfort University, UK
Ioannis Krontiris	Huawei Technologies, Germany
Andrea Lanzi	Università degli studi di Milano, Italy
Albert Levi	Sabanci University, Turkey
Olivier Levillain	French National and Information Security Agency, France
Javier Lopez	UMA, Spain
David M'Raihi	Pure Storage, USA
Vashek Matyas	Masaryk University, Czech Republic
Sjouke Mauw	University of Luxembourg, Luxembourg
Keith Mayes	ISG-Smart Card Centre, Royal Holloway, University of London, UK
Nele Mentens	Katholieke Universiteit Leuven, Belgium
Alessio Merlo	University of Genoa, Italy
Vladimir Oleshchuk	University of Agder, Norway

Jiaxin Pan	HGI, Ruhr University Bochum, Germany
Duong-Hieu Phan	University of Limoges, France
Joachim Posegga	University of Passau, Germany
Carla Ràfols	Universitat Pompeu Fabra, Spain
Kouichi Sakurai	Kyushu University, Japan
Pierangela Samarati	Università degli Studi di Milano, Italy
Siraj A. Shaikh	Coventry University, UK
Dave Singelee	Katholieke Universiteit Leuven, Belgium
Denis Trcek	University of Ljubljana, Slovenia
Umut Uludag	TUBITAK-BILGEM-UEKAE, Turkey
Anjia Yang	Jinan University, China
Stefano Zanero	Politecnico di Milano, Italy

Steering Committee

Angelos Bilas	FORTH-ICS and University of Crete, Greece
Ernesto Damiani	Universitá degli Studi di Milano, Italy
Gerhard Hancke	City University of Hong Kong, Hong Kong, SAR China
Konstantinos Markantonakis	ISG-SCC, Royal Holloway University of London, UK
Joachim Posegga	Institute of IT-Security and Security Law at the University of Passau, Germany
Jean-Jacques Quisquater	ICTEAM, Catholic University of Louvain, Belgium
Damien Sauveron	XLIM, University of Limoges, France

Additional Reviewers

Anada, Hiroaki	Longari, Stefano	Ramírez-Cruz, Yunior
Belgacem, Boutheyna	Marin, Eduard	Sauveron, Damien
Biondo, Andrea	Naccache, David	Sun, Bo
David, Michael	Nguyen, Hoang Nga	Tomlinson, Andrew
Gangwal, Ankit	Pogliani, Marcello	Trujillo, Rolando
Hary, Estelle	Polino, Mario	Xie, Fei
Kaliyar, Pallavi	Pöhls, Henrich C.	Xiong, Kaiya

Sponsors

Contents

Invited Papers

Blockchain and the GDPR: A Data Protection Authority Point of View

Amandine Jambert[✉]

C.N.I.L. - Commission Nationale de l'Informatique et des Libertés, Paris, France
ajambert@cnil.fr

Since the publication, in 2009, of the blockchain founding article by Nakamoto [3] more and more solutions rely on this architecture. In the process an increasing number of solution process personal data stored on this type of decentralized database. In this context the property of undeniability (i.e. once data is recorded, it cannot be altered or removed) of such solutions raise questions regarding how to assure compliance to GDPR. The French Data protection authority, the CNIL, received numerous requests from both the public and the private sector regarding blockchain projects and GDPR [1]. She thus addressed the matter in November 2018 through a publication on its website [2].

The objective of this talk was to give the main key points of the GDPR, to underline how they can apply in the blockchain context and finally to show how we hope for cryptographic techniques to solve part of the problems.

1 How Do the GDPR and Blockchain Interact?

When a blockchain contains personal data, such as public keys of individuals or personal data stored "within" a transaction, the GDPR may be applicable as it implies the processing of personal data. The second criteria for applicability will be whether the processing is performed by controllers or processors established in the EU or aiming at EU residents. Finally, this legal framework is applicable to any processing of personal data by a legal person or by a natural person not acting in the course of a purely personal or household activity. Thus, the GDPR is applicable to processing on blockchain in a wide array of cases.

Furthermore, some classical blockchain properties, especially transparency (i.e. all participants can view all data recorded) and undeniability, may have impacts on individual rights (namely, the right to privacy and the right to personal data protection) which calls for a specific analysis.

In consequence, the CNIL suggests the following initial analysis and recommendations to stakeholders who wish to use blockchain when carrying out personal data processing.

We consider in this short paper only the cases of processing on the blockchain using the payload to store personal data.

© IFIP International Federation for Information Processing 2019
Published by Springer Nature Switzerland AG 2019
O. Blazy and C. Y. Yeun (Eds.): WISTP 2018, LNCS 11469, pp. 3–6, 2019.
https://doi.org/10.1007/978-3-030-20074-9_1

2   Which Points Require Particular Attention?

Blockchains are a technology, not a processing in itself. In consequence the questions to be answered while processing data on a blockchain are similar to the questions that would have been raised for any others processing. However, the particular properties of the blockchain might interact with those obligations in positive or negative ways.

2.1   Responsibilities

The first point of attention will be to determine a clearly defined purpose for the processing using the blockchain and to clarify the responsibilities of the actors involved.

Regarding the responsibilities, the work carried out by the CNIL has revealed that, in many cases, the person deciding to register data on a blockchain can be considered as a data controller given that the participant determines the purpose (objectives pursued by the processing) and means of data processing (data format, use of a given blockchain technology, etc).

The miners, or validators, of transactions including personal data on a blockchain are not involved in the definition of the purpose, thus they would not be considered as controller by the CNIL. Nevertheless they are still processing data, they thus would be, at best, processors. Being a processor in the GDPR implies numerous obligation stated in article 28 which might be difficult in practice for public blockchain.

Thus for those last solutions, the CNIL is currently conducting an in-depth reflection on the matter and promotes the development of solutions to address contractual relations between participants/data controllers and miners.

2.2   Risk Minimization

The second point can be summed up as the minimization of risks for data subjects when their data are planned to be used in a processing carried out on a blockchain. In some cases, these technologies are likely to raise issues regarding the GDPR or to put unnecessary high risks on individuals. Therefore, it is necessary to balance, from an early stage, the needs of using a blockchain rather than another technology with the objectives and characteristics of each processing. In addition to questioning the use of a blockchain, the data controller must also question which type of blockchain, either a public or a permissioned blockchain (as defined in [5]) should be used and how it will be used to limit the risks on individuals.

f blockchain properties are not required in order to meet the purpose of the processing, the CNIL recommends favouring other solutions that allow for fullcompliance with the GDPR.-Permissioned blockchains should be favoured as they allow a better control over personal data governance, in particular as regards transfers outside of the EU.-The requirement for appropriate safeguards for transfers outside the EU, such as binding corporate rules or standard contractual clauses, are entirely applicable to permissioned blockchain.

2.3   Data Subject's Rights

The third point of attention concerns the exercise of rights. Some of them can be exercised effectively such as the right of access and the right to portability. Others, like the right to erasure, the right to rectification and the right to object to processing, are not straightforward. In those cases, the CNIL acknowledges the existence of technological solutions that should be evaluated.

2.4   Miscellaneous

Finally, while not covered here, actors need to be as cautious as possible regarding the implementation of obligations concerning sub-contracting and the rules governing international transfers of personal data, in particular for public blockchains.

3   What Are the Technical Solutions Considered?

We can define the data manipulated on a blockchain as two categories: the identifiers (i.e. the public keys of participants) and the payload which is used in numerous processing on blockchain.

The architecture of most blockchain needs the identifier to be visible to function, thus the CNIL considers that those data, in those cases, can not be further minimized and that their retention period will be in line with the blockchain life.

On the contrary, the payload format is chosen by participants independently to the blockchain architecture. The Privacy by Design principle (Article 25 of the GDPR) requires the data controller to choose the format with the least impact on individuals' rights and freedoms.

The CNIL considered different cryptological solutions to answer the challenge, from perfectly hiding commitment, as defined in [4], to secure encryption.

As the most protective format, the CNIL considers that personal data should be preferably registered on the blockchain as a commitment. The choice of a perfectly hiding commitment scheme would ensure that, upon erasure of the witness and the data committed (both kept off the blockchain), it would no longer be possible to prove or verify which information have been committed. The commit would be considered, by the CNIL, has anonymized in such a way that it can no longer be considered personal data.

If this is not possible, one may use a hash of the data generated using a keyed-hash function, or, at least, a ciphertext.

Excluding the specific case of perfectly hiding commitment, those solutions do not provide a perfect erasure of the data, insofar as the data would still exist in the blockchain and might be recovered in a distant future depending on cryptanalysis advances. However, the CNIL observes that they are partially answering the problem of giving an effective exercise of the right of erasure. Nevertheless, their acceptability for what concerns the requirements of the GDPR should still be evaluated.

The common feature underlying some of these solutions is to store any data in cleartext outside of the blockchain (such as, for example, on the data controller's information system) and to store on the blockchain only a proof of existence of the data (e.g. commitment, hash generated from a keyed hash function, etc.). It is technically impossible to grant the request for rectification or for erasure made by a data subject when cleartext or hashed data is recorded on a blockchain. It is therefore strongly recommended, from a GDPR point of view, not to register personal data in cleartext on a blockchain, and to use one of the others cryptographic solutions mentioned above.

Nevertheless, if no other solution is applicable, and when justified by its purpose, a DPIA can be carried out to evaluate whether the risk of storing the information either as a simple hash or in cleartext would be acceptable. If the conclusion are that risks on data subject are minimal then it can be exceptionally envisaged. For example when a data controller have the legal obligation to make some information public and accessible, without a retention period, the storage of personal data on a public blockchain can be envisaged, provided that the DPIA concludes that the risks for data subjects are minimal.

4   Conclusion

Blockchains raise numerous challenges in terms of compliance with human rights and fundamental freedoms that can be partially answered by technical solution. Nevertheless, it still call for a response at the European level. As one of the first authorities to officially address the matter, the CNIL will work cooperatively with its European counterparts to suggest a strong and harmonised approach.

References

1. Regulation (EU) 2016/679 of the European parliament and of the council of 27 April 2016 on the protection of natural persons with regard to the processing of personal data and on the free movement of such data, and repealing directive 95/46/EC (General Data Protection Regulation), April 2016
2. CNIL: Solutions for a responsible use of the blockchain in the context of personal data, November 2018. https://www.cnil.fr/sites/default/files/atoms/files/blockchain.pdf
3. Nakamoto, S.: Bitcoin: a peer-to-peer electronic cash system, May 2009
4. Pedersen, T.P.: Non-interactive and information-theoretic secure verifiable secret sharing. In: Feigenbaum, J. (ed.) CRYPTO 1991. LNCS, vol. 576, pp. 129–140. Springer, Heidelberg (1992). https://doi.org/10.1007/3-540-46766-1_9
5. Smith, J., Tennison, J., Wells, P., Fawcett, J., Harrison, S.: Applying blockchain technology in global data infrastructure. Open Data Institute, ODI Technical report (2016)

Secure Outsourcing in Discrete-Logarithm-Based and Pairing-Based Cryptography (Invited Talk)

Damien Vergnaud[1,2]([✉])

[1] CNRS, Laboratoire d'Informatique de Paris 6,
Sorbonne Université, LIP6, Paris, France
damien.vergnaud@lip6.fr
[2] Institut Universitaire de France, Paris, France

Abstract. Cryptographic operations are performed everywhere, from standard laptop to smart cards. Some devices computational resources can be very limited and it is natural to delegate costly operations to another device capable of carrying out cryptographic algorithms. In this setting, it is obviously important to ensure the limited device that the computation is carried out correctly and that the powerful device does not learn anything about what is actually computing (including the secret inputs and outputs). We briefly review the recent advances on secure outsourcing of group exponentiation (in groups of known prime order as well as in groups of unknown order) and pairing computation.

1 Introduction

Many widely used public-key cryptographic systems and protocols relies on the (supposed) computational hardness of the discrete-logarithm or the discrete-root problems. The core operation of these cryptosystems is group exponentiation in a finite Abelian group, i.e., computing u^a from a group element u and an exponent a. Besides, since their introduction in cryptography [4,15], *pairings* proved to be an amazingly flexible and useful tool for the construction of cryptosystems with unique features (*e.g.* efficient identity based cryptography [4]). In this setting, the core operation is the computation of pairings which is the most expensive operation in pairing-based cryptographic protocols.

We consider the problem of "outsourcing" group exponentiation and pairing computation from a weak computational device to a more powerful one. Indeed, some devices computational resources can be very limited and it is natural, as most of the devices are online or directly connected to a powerful device (like a SIM card in a smart phone) to securely delegate sensitive and costly operations to a device capable of carrying out cryptographic algorithms.Outsourcing cryptographic computations is a classical problem which was formalized in [13]

O. Blazy and C. Y. Yeun (Eds.): WISTP 2018, LNCS 11469, pp. 7–11, 2019.
https://doi.org/10.1007/978-3-030-20074-9_2

by Hohenberger and Lysyanskaya. In this scenario, the powerful device[1] can, potentially, be operated by a malicious adversary and it is obviously important to ensure the limited device that the computation is carried out correctly and that the powerful device does not learn anything about what is actually computing (including the secret inputs and outputs).

2   Group Exponentiation

In the last 30 years, the question of how a computationally limited device may outsource group exponentiation to another, potentially malicious, but much more computationally powerful device has been a very active research topic (e.g. [3, 6,7,17,18,26]). Many solutions have been proposed and then cryptanalyzed in follow-up papers (e.g. [7,14,21–24]). We briefly review the recent advances on secure outsourcing of group exponentiation.

Recently, Chevalier, Laguillaumie and Vergnaud [7] proposed a taxonomy of private exponentiation delegation protocols (to a single untrusted computational resource) in groups of *known prime* order. Their taxonomy covers all the practical situations: the group element u can be secret or public, variable or fixed, the exponent a can be secret or public, and the result of the exponentiation u^a can also be either public or secret. They provided simple constructions in all different settings and proved that these protocols cannot be significantly improved if one wants to use a single untrusted computational resource and to limit the computational cost of the delegating device to a small number of (generic) group operations. Aguilar-Melchor, Deneuville, Gaborit, Lepoint and Ricosset later showed [1] that using homomorphic encryption, it is sometimes possible to reduce the computational costs for privately delegating elliptic-curve operations (but at the cost of a very large communication complexity).

Another important use case is the setting of RSA exponentiation: a device wants to delegate the computation of a signature given a public key (N, e), a public message (or hash value of a message) m and the secret signing exponent d. By outsourcing some exponentiations to a powerful device, the delegation protocol outputs a (public) signature $\sigma = m^d \bmod N$. Most proposed protocols are variants of two protocols (named RSA-S1 and RSA-S2) that were proposed by Matsumoto, Kato and Imai in 1988 [18]. Both schemes use a random linear decomposition of the RSA private exponent d. Several attacks were proposed on the protocols RSA-S1 and its variants (e.g. [23]). Recently, Mefenza and Vergnaud [19] proposed an improved lattice-based attack on RSA-S1 and a simple variant of this protocol that provides better efficiency for the same security level. They also presented the first attacks on the protocol RSA-S2.

---

[1] Hohenberger and Lysyanskaya also considered delegation protocols to two devices that are physically separated (and do not communicate) that achieve security as long as one of them is honest. Since this separation of the two devices is a strong assumption hard to be met in practice, we consider only protocols to outsource cryptographic operations to a *single* untrusted server.

A cryptographic delegation protocol that does not ensure verifiability may cause severe security problems (in particular if the computation occurs in the verification algorithm of some authentication protocol). Di Crescenzo, Khodjaeva, Kahrobaei and Shpilrain [10] proposed recently private and verifiable protocols in a large class of cyclic groups. In the presented protocols, the probability that a cheating server convinces the client of an incorrect computation result can be proved to be exponentially small (whereas previous best results could only achieve a constant probability). Their protocols need some pre-computation depending on the base u and cannot be used easily in practice if this group element is variable. The different proposals for verifiable group exponentiation where pre-computation does not depend on the base u are very inefficient and it is actually better in practice to directly perform the computation on the restricted device rather than using these solutions. A challenging problem is to study secure and verifiable outsourcing protocols for group exponentiation that covers all the practical situations as in [7].

3 Pairings

Pairings (or bilinear maps) were introduced in cryptography in 2000 by Joux [15] and Boneh-Franklin [4]. A pairing is a bilinear, non-degenerate and computable map $e : \mathbb{G}_1 \times \mathbb{G}_2 \to \mathbb{G}_T$ where, in practice, $\mathbb{G}_1$ and $\mathbb{G}_2$ are subgroups (of prime-order r) of the group of points of an elliptic curve defined over a finite field $\mathbb{F}_q$ and some finite field extension $\mathbb{F}_{q^k}$ (respectively) and the so-called *target* group $\mathbb{G}_T$ is the order r subgroup of $\mathbb{F}_{q^k}$. The pairing computation is more resource consuming compared to a scalar multiplication on the elliptic curve $E(\mathbb{F}_q)$.

In 2005, Girault and Lefranc [11] introduced the first secure pairing delegation protocol via the notion of *Server-Aided Verification*, which consists in speeding up the verification step of an authentication/signature scheme. Chevallier-Mames, Coron, McCullagh, Naccache and Scott [8,9] introduced the security notions of verifiable pairing delegation protocol and proposed the first verifiable pairing delegation protocol. Later in 2014, Canard, Devigne and Sanders [5] improved their construction and proposed a much more efficient verifiable delegation protocol. Canard, Devigne and Sanders showed that their construction is more efficient for the client than computing a pairing himself on the so-called KSS-18 curve [16]. Later, Guillevic and Vergnaud [12] showed that Canard, Devigne and Sanders protocol is actually less efficient than computing a pairing for the state-of-the-art optimal Ate pairing on a Barreto-Naehrig curve [2] and it remains open to propose an efficient verifiable delegation protocol for pairing computation on these curves.

Due to the inefficiency of the known protocols for delegation of a unique pairing, another approach is to propose efficient protocols when the client wants to compute several pairings at the same time. In 2007, Tsang, Chow and Smith [25] introduced the security notion of *batch* pairing delegation protocols and propose the first verifiable batch pairing delegation protocols when the client wants to compute several pairings $e(P_i, Q_i)$ where $P_i \in \mathbb{G}_1$ and $Q_i \in \mathbb{G}_2$ for $i \in \{1, \dots, n\}$ and $n \geq 2$. In [20], Mefenza and Vergnaud recently proposed four new efficient batch pairing delegation protocols in different settings but it remains open to construct a generic verifiable batch pairing delegation protocol when both inputs of the pairing are variable and secret. Another interesting open problem is to provide lower bounds on the efficiency of verifiable pairing delegation protocols (as it was done in [7] for private delegation of group exponentiation).

Acknowledgments. The author would like to thank his co-authors on this active and interesting research area: Céline Chevalier, Aurore Guillevic, Fabien Laguillaumie and Thierry Mefenza. The author is supported in part by the French ANR ALAMBIC project (ANR16-CE39-0006) and the French ANR IDFIX project (ANR-16-CE39-0004).

References

1. Aguilar Melchor, C., Deneuville, J.-C., Gaborit, P., Lepoint, T., Ricosset, T.: Delegating elliptic-curve operations with homomorphic encryption. In: 2018 IEEE Conference on Communications and Network Security, CNS 2018, pp. 1–9. IEEE (2018)
2. Barreto, P.S.L.M., Naehrig, M.: Pairing-friendly elliptic curves of prime order. In: Preneel, B., Tavares, S. (eds.) SAC 2005. LNCS, vol. 3897, pp. 319–331. Springer, Heidelberg (2006). https://doi.org/10.1007/11693383_22
3. Béguin, P., Quisquater, J.-J.: Fast server-aided RSA signatures secure against active attacks. In: Coppersmith, D. (ed.) CRYPTO 1995. LNCS, vol. 963, pp. 57–69. Springer, Heidelberg (1995). https://doi.org/10.1007/3-540-44750-4_5
4. Boneh, D., Franklin, M.: Identity-based encryption from the weil pairing. In: Kilian, J. (ed.) CRYPTO 2001. LNCS, vol. 2139, pp. 213–229. Springer, Heidelberg (2001). https://doi.org/10.1007/3-540-44647-8_13
5. Canard, S., Devigne, J., Sanders, O.: Delegating a pairing can be both secure and efficient. In: Boureanu, I., Owesarski, P., Vaudenay, S. (eds.) ACNS 2014. LNCS, vol. 8479, pp. 549–565. Springer, Cham (2014). https://doi.org/10.1007/978-3-319-07536-5_32
6. Cavallo, B., Di Crescenzo, G., Kahrobaei, D., Shpilrain, V.: Efficient and secure delegation of group exponentiation to a single server. In: Mangard, S., Schaumont, P. (eds.) RFIDSec 2015. LNCS, vol. 9440, pp. 156–173. Springer, Cham (2015). https://doi.org/10.1007/978-3-319-24837-0_10
7. Chevalier, C., Laguillaumie, F., Vergnaud, D.: Privately outsourcing exponentiation to a single server: cryptanalysis and optimal constructions. In: Askoxylakis, I., Ioannidis, S., Katsikas, S., Meadows, C. (eds.) ESORICS 2016. LNCS, vol. 9878, pp. 261–278. Springer, Cham (2016). https://doi.org/10.1007/978-3-319-45744-4_13
8. Chevallier-Mames, B., Coron, J.-S., McCullagh, N., Naccache, D., Scott, M.: Secure delegation of elliptic-curve pairing. Cryptology ePrint Archive, Report 2005/150 (2005). http://eprint.iacr.org/2005/150
9. Chevallier-Mames, B., Coron, J.-S., McCullagh, N., Naccache, D., Scott, M.: Secure delegation of elliptic-curve pairing. In: Gollmann, D., Lanet, J.-L., Iguchi-Cartigny, J. (eds.) CARDIS 2010. LNCS, vol. 6035, pp. 24–35. Springer, Heidelberg (2010). https://doi.org/10.1007/978-3-642-12510-2_3
10. Di Crescenzo, G., Khodjaeva, M., Kahrobaei, D., Shpilrain, V.: Practical and secure outsourcing of discrete log group exponentiation to a single malicious server. In: Thuraisingham, B.M., Karame, G., Stavrou, A. (eds.) CCSW@CCS 2017, Dallas, TX, USA, 3 November 2017, pp. 17–28. ACM (2017)

11. Girault, M., Lefranc, D.: Server-aided verification: theory and practice. In: Roy, B. (ed.) ASIACRYPT 2005. LNCS, vol. 3788, pp. 605–623. Springer, Heidelberg (2005). https://doi.org/10.1007/11593447_33

12. Guillevic, A., Vergnaud, D.: Algorithms for outsourcing pairing computation. In: Joye, M., Moradi, A. (eds.) CARDIS 2014. LNCS, vol. 8968, pp. 193–211. Springer, Cham (2015). https://doi.org/10.1007/978-3-319-16763-3_12

13. Hohenberger, S., Lysyanskaya, A.: How to securely outsource cryptographic computations. In: Kilian, J. (ed.) TCC 2005. LNCS, vol. 3378, pp. 264–282. Springer, Heidelberg (2005). https://doi.org/10.1007/978-3-540-30576-7_15

14. Jakobsson, M., Wetzel, S.: Secure server-aided signature generation. In: Kim, K. (ed.) PKC 2001. LNCS, vol. 1992, pp. 383–401. Springer, Heidelberg (2001). https://doi.org/10.1007/3-540-44586-2_28

15. Joux, A.: A one round protocol for tripartite Diffie–Hellman. In: Bosma, W. (ed.) ANTS 2000. LNCS, vol. 1838, pp. 385–393. Springer, Heidelberg (2000). https://doi.org/10.1007/10722028_23

16. Kachisa, E.J., Schaefer, E.F., Scott, M.: Constructing brezing-weng pairing-friendly elliptic curves using elements in the cyclotomic field. In: Galbraith, S.D., Paterson, K.G. (eds.) Pairing 2008. LNCS, vol. 5209, pp. 126–135. Springer, Heidelberg (2008). https://doi.org/10.1007/978-3-540-85538-5_9

17. Laih, C.-S., Yen, S.-M., Harn, L.: Two efficient server-aided secret computation protocols based on the addition sequence. In: Imai, H., Rivest, R.L., Matsumoto, T. (eds.) ASIACRYPT 1991. LNCS, vol. 739, pp. 450–459. Springer, Heidelberg (1993). https://doi.org/10.1007/3-540-57332-1_38

18. Matsumoto, T., Kato, K., Imai, H.: Speeding up secret computations with insecure auxiliary devices. In: Goldwasser, S. (ed.) CRYPTO 1988. LNCS, vol. 403, pp. 497–506. Springer, New York (1990). https://doi.org/10.1007/0-387-34799-2_35

19. Mefenza, T., Vergnaud, D.: Cryptanalysis of server-aided RSA protocols with private-key splitting, in submission (2017)

20. Mefenza, T., Vergnaud, D.: Verifiable outsourcing of pairing computations, in submission (2018)

21. Merkle, J.: Multi-round passive attacks on server-aided RSA protocols. In: Jajodia, S., Samarati, P., (eds.) ACM CCS 2000, pp. 102–107. ACM Press, November 2000

22. Merkle, J., Werchner, R.: On the security of server-aided RSA protocols. In: Imai, H., Zheng, Y. (eds.) PKC 1998. LNCS, vol. 1431, pp. 99–116. Springer, Heidelberg (1998). https://doi.org/10.1007/BFb0054018

23. Nguyen, P.Q., Shparlinski, I.E.: On the insecurity of a server-aided RSA protocol. In: Boyd, C. (ed.) ASIACRYPT 2001. LNCS, vol. 2248, pp. 21–35. Springer, Heidelberg (2001). https://doi.org/10.1007/3-540-45682-1_2

24. Pfitzmann, B., Waidner, M.: Attacks on protocols for server-aided RSA computation. In: Rueppel, R.A. (ed.) EUROCRYPT 1992. LNCS, vol. 658, pp. 153–162. Springer, Heidelberg (1993). https://doi.org/10.1007/3-540-47555-9_13

25. Tsang, P.P., Chow, S.S.M., Smith, S.W.: Batch pairing delegation. In: Miyaji, A., Kikuchi, H., Rannenberg, K. (eds.) IWSEC 2007. LNCS, vol. 4752, pp. 74–90. Springer, Heidelberg (2007). https://doi.org/10.1007/978-3-540-75651-4_6

26. Wang, Y., et al.: Securely Outsourcing exponentiations with single untrusted program for cloud storage. In: Kutyłowski, M., Vaidya, J. (eds.) ESORICS 2014. LNCS, vol. 8712, pp. 326–343. Springer, Cham (2014). https://doi.org/10.1007/978-3-319-11203-9_19

Real World

Bringing Kleptography to Real-World TLS

Adam Janovsky[1]([✉]), Jan Krhovjak[2], and Vashek Matyas[1]

[1] Masaryk University, Brno, Czech Republic
`adamjanovsky@mail.muni.cz`
[2] Invasys, a.s., Brno, Czech Republic

Abstract. Kleptography is a study of stealing information securely and subliminally from black-box cryptographic devices. The stolen information is exfiltrated from the device via a backdoored algorithm inside an asymmetricaly encrypted subliminal channel. In this paper, the kleptography setting for the TLS protocol is addressed. While earlier proposals of asymmetric backdoors for TLS lacked the desired properties or were impractical, this work shows that a feasible asymmetric backdoor can be derived for TLS. First, the paper revisits the existing proposals of kleptographic backdoors for TLS of version 1.2 and lower. Next, advances of the proposal by Gołębiewski et al. are presented to achieve better security and indistinguishability. Then, the enhanced backdoor is translated both to TLS 1.2 and 1.3, achieving first practical solution. Properties of the backdoor are proven and its feasibility is demonstrated by implementing it as a proof-of-concept into the OpenSSL library. Finally, performance of the backdoor is evaluated and studied as a tool for side-channel detection.

Keywords: Asymmetric backdoor · Cryptovirology · Kleptography · TLS

1 Introduction

Tamper-proof devices were proposed as a remedy for many security-related problems. Their advantage is undeniable since they are protected from physical attacks and it is difficult to change the executed code. However, they inherently introduce a trust into the manufacturer. It was shown that such devices are theoretically vulnerable to the presence of so-called subliminal channels [20]. Such channels can be used to exfiltrate private information from the underlying system covertly, inside cryptographic primitives. As a consequence, malware introduced by a manufacturer or a clever third-party adversary can utilise subliminal channels to break the security of black-box devices.

This paper concerns kleptography – the art of stealing information securely and subliminally – for the TLS protocol. The field of kleptography was established in the 1990s by Yung and Young [18]. Kleptographic backdoors for many

© IFIP International Federation for Information Processing 2019
Published by Springer Nature Switzerland AG 2019
O. Blazy and C. Y. Yeun (Eds.): WISTP 2018, LNCS 11469, pp. 15–27, 2019.
https://doi.org/10.1007/978-3-030-20074-9_3

protocols and primitives were proposed ever since. For instance, we mention the RSA key generation protocol [18] and the Diffie-Hellman (DH) protocol [19]. Using kleptography, an attacker can subvert a target cryptosystem to deny confidentiality and authenticity of transferred data. Thus, it is important to explore the feasibility of kleptographic backdoors for various protocols, alongside with the methods for defeating such backdoors.

Several challenges arise when inventing a kleptographic backdoor. First, one must assure that such backdoor cannot be detected by looking at inputs and outputs of an infected device. Furthermore, the exploited channel is often narrow-band and the computing performance of the device should not be overly affected. Last but not least, one must prove the security of both the original cryptosystem and the encrypted subliminal channel.

Previous work on kleptography in the TLS protocol [9,21] showed that it is possible to utilise a single random nonce to exfiltrate session keys. Both backdoors exploit a random field inside *ClientHello* message, 32-byte nonce that is sent to server by a client. The proposal [9] was rather a sketch of an asymmetric backdoor and it lacked few key properties. The work [21] was an important theoretical result and proven asymmetrical backdoor for the TLS protocol. Nonetheless, it remains impractical to implement. Also, neither of the papers addressed TLS of version 1.3. More insight into the related work follows in Sect. 5.

In this work we make the following contributions:

- We modify the backdoor [9] to achieve better security of the backdoor and also idistinguishability in a random oracle model.
- We prove that our proposal is an asymmetric backdoor for all versions of the TLS protocol, including TLS 1.3.
- We implement the backdoor as a proof-of-concept into the OpenSSL library, confirming its feasibility.
- We evaluate the performance of the backdoor and discuss its detectability.

The remainder of the paper is organized as follows. Section 2 gives basic background on kleptography. In Sect. 3 we show a design of our backdoor. Section 4 comments on how we implemented the backdoor and gives the exact results of our performance tests. It also shows how a timing channel can be used to detect our backdoor. Section 5 reviews related work and, finally, Sect. 6 concludes the paper.

2   Kleptography Background

The work on kleptography utilises cryptology and virology and naturally extends the study of subliminal channels [20]; those are further encrypted and embedded into the devices, creating so-called asymmetric backdoors. As of 2018, secretly embedded backdoor with universal protection (SETUP) is a supreme (and only) tool in the field of kleptography. One could therefore say that kleptography studies development of asymmetric backdoors and possible defenses against them at the same time. Kleptography concerns black-box environment exclusively, as in white-box setting scrutiny allows to detect such channel. The aim of this section is to introduce necessary techniques that are involved in an asymmetric backdoor design. We begin with a formal description of an asymmetric backdoor adopted from [20].

Definition 1. *Assume that C is a black-box cryptosystem with a publicly known specification. A SETUP mechanism is an algorithmic modification made to C to get C' such that:*

1. *The input of C' agrees with the public specifications of the input of C.*
2. *C' computes efficiently using the attacker's public encryption function E (and possibly other functions) contained within C'.*
3. *The attacker's private decryption function D is not contained within C' and is known only by the attacker.*
4. *The output of C' agrees with the public specifications of the output of C. At the same time, it contains published bits (of the user's secret key) which are easily derivable by the attacker (the output can be generated during key-generation or during system operation like message sending).*
5. *Furthermore, the output of C and C' are polynomially indistinguishable to everyone except the attacker.*
6. *After the discovery of the specifics of the SETUP algorithm and after discovering its presence in the implementation (e.g. reverse engineering of hardware tamper-proof device), user (except the attacker) cannot determine past (or future) keys.*

Consider that an asymmetric backdoor itself can be a subject of cryptanalysis. That is why the resulting subliminal channel must be encrypted according to good cryptographic practice. To keep the notation unambiguous, we call the person who attacks the backdoor an *inquirer*. We say that an asymmetric backdoor has (m, n) leakage scheme if it leaks m keys/secret messages over n outputs of the cryptographic device. The desired leakage bandwidth that asymmetric backdoor should achieve is (m, m), meaning that the whole private information is leaked within one execution of the protocol. Further, a publicly displayed value that also serves as an asymmetric backdoor is denoted a *kleptogram*.

2.1   Example of Asymmetric Backdoor

The paper continues with an example of RSA key generation SETUP [18] to illustrate the concept of asymmetric backdoors. The backdoor allows for efficient factorization of RSA modulus by evil Eve. First, Eve generates her public RSA key (N, E) and embeds it into the contaminated device of Alice together with a subverted key-generation algorithm:

1. The device selects two distinct primes p, q, computes the product $pq = n$ and Euler's function $\varphi(n) = (p - 1)(q - 1)$.
2. The public exponent is derived as $e = p^E \pmod{N}$. If e is not invertible modulo $\varphi(n)$, new p is generated.

3. Private exponent is computed as $d = e^{-1} \pmod{\varphi(n)}$.
4. Public key is (n, e), private key is (n, d).

After obtaining the kleptogram e contained in public key (n, e), Eve can use her private key (N, D) to compute

$$e^D = p^{ED} = p \pmod{N}.$$

Thus, Eve can factorize the modulus n, and compute the private exponent d just by eavesdropping the public key. The reader may notice that the backdoor requires e to be uniformly distributed on the group (otherwise the backdoor can be detected), which leaves it unsuitable for real use. Yet, this toy example illustrates the concept of asymmetric backdoors beautifully. It is not difficult to prove that the backdoor fullfils all conditions of SETUP, if e is to be picked uniformly in the clean system. Also, we note that this backdoor exhibits the ideal leakage bandwidth (m, m). However, this backdoor lacks perfect forward secrecy. Indeed, when the attacker's private key (N, D) is compromised, an inquirer can factorize all past and future keys from the particular key generating device.

2.2 Kleptography in the Wild

Recall that an asymmetric backdoor is a modification of already established algorithm. Detection of such modification therefore proves its malicious nature. In contrast, when an algorithm is designed to be kleptographic initially, its malevolence cannot be decided so easily. To illustrate this aspect, we briefly revisit the DUAL_EC_DRBG pseudorandom number generator invented by the NSA[1]. The generator was standardized in NIST SP 8000-90A [2]. Later, a bit predictor with advantage 0.0011 was presented in [8]. Despite this serious flaw we concentrate on a different problem. In particular, the paper [2] shows potential kleptographic tampering. To be exact, the generator requires two constants on an elliptic curve, i.e., $P, Q \in E(\mathbb{F}_p)$, and the security of the internal state relies on the intractability of discrete logarithm problem for these constants. Consequently, if one is able to find scalar k such that $P = kQ$, they are able to compute the inner state of the generator efficiently based on the output. This naturally breaks the security of the generator. Despite the fact that arbitrary P, Q can be used for the generator, NIST standard forces the use of fixed constants with unknown origin. Naturally, NSA is alleged to provided the backdoored constants. The practical exploitability of backdoored constants was shown in [17]. However, one cannot prove nor disprove that the constants for the standard are backdoored except for the NSA. This aspect suggests that not many SETUPs are likely to appear in the wild, but rather delicate modifications of otherwise secure algorithms are expected, such that their sensitivity to efficient cryptanalysis can be viewed as a coincidence.

---

[1] National Security Agency.

3   Attack Design

Our proposal is based on [9] by Gołębiewski et al. However, several drawbacks are eliminated by our construction, and properties of the backdoor are treated more rigorously. The needed improvements w.r.t. the proposal [9] were:

- To achieve indistinguishability of kleptogram from random bit string,
- to ensure that reverse-engineering of the infected device will not compromise security of any session,
- to allow recovery of master secret to attacker even if she misses to eavesdrop some sessions.

An additional goal was to minimize the computational overhead introduced by the backdoor to avoid possible detection by timing analysis.

3.1   Backdoor Description

During the TLS handshake, assuming no pre-shared key is involved and a new session is to be established, all traffic keys are derived from a pre-master secret and publicly available values. Thus, for an attacker, it suffices to obtain the pre-master secret to decrypt whole session. Additionally, the pre-master secret can be derived via DH method, eventually via RSA method in the case of TLS 1.2 and lower[2] (The removal of the RSA key exchange method from TLS 1.3 makes it more difficult to debug or inspect encrypted connections for the industry – for example in datacenters of intrusion detection systems. This led to two RFC drafts [10,11] that would mitigate this issue. The former allows for opt-in mechanism that allows a TLS client and server to explicitly grant access to the TLS session plaintext. The latter relies on introducing static DH key exchange method to TLS 1.3. Naturally, both drafts inherently weaken the TLS 1.3 protocol and did not become a part of the final TLS 1.3 RFC. A question arises, whether the stated motivation behind introducing such drafts was honest, as debugging and inspection of traffic is possible even with ephemeral DH, only at a cost of adjusting infrastructure.). In the case of DH method, a shared secret is established between the server and the client. In the case of RSA method, server's certificate is required and used to encrypt random bytes generated on the client device. Those bytes then serve as the pre-master secret. We exploit the 32-byte random nonce sent by the client during *ClientHello* message to derive a secret only the attacker can obtain. We further sanitize that secret and use it as a seed during the function that creates the client's contribution to the pre-master secret.

We begin with the presentation of the original kleptographic construction by Gołębiewski et al. The authors suggest to hardcode a DH public key $Y = g^X$ on an infected device. During the first handshake on the device, a random value k is

---

[2] By DH method we refer to DH modulo prime. Nowadays, Diffie-Hellman over elliptic curves (ECDH) is mostly used in TLS connections. We stick to the modular case, even though our method can be translated to elliptic curves easily.

selected and g^k is published as the *ClientHello* random nonce. During subsequent executions, the *ClientHello* random nonce is not subverted, but the PMS is then derived deterministically from $H(Y^k, i)$, where H denotes a hash function and i is a counter to ensure that the secrets will differ across sessions. Notice that when an attacker fails to eavesdropp the first handshake, she will not be able to recover any of subsequent sessions. At the same time, if an inquirer manages to capture the first handshake and any of k or X, it allows the inquirer for a decryption of all previous and subsequent sessions. Also, the value Y^k must be stored in non-volatile memory on the infected device and is prone to reverse engineering, thus violating condition 6 of SETUP. Last but not least, the published nonce g^k can be distinguished from a random bit string since it is an element of a group, see [6] – this violates condition 5 of SETUP. Our improvements aim to eliminate all of the presented drawbacks.

The exact design of our proposal is as follows. Prior to the deployment, a designer generates a DH key pair on the X25519 curve, denoted $Y = g^X$. The public key Y is then hard-coded into the infected device, together with the 128-bit key for AES, denoted K and the counter. The initial value of the counter is 1 and is incremented by 2 after each execution. Suppose that the infected device connects to the server and the handshake is initiated. When construction of the *ClientHello* message is triggered, the infected device generates 32 random bytes denoted k and computes the public key g^k. The value g^k is then encrypted with AES-CTR into $C = E_K(g^k)$ and published as a kleptogram inside the *ClientHello* random nonce. Meanwhile, value $S = Y^k$ is derived on the device as a shared secret between the attacker and the device. When the attacker eavesdropps the value C, she is able to derive $g^k = D_K(C)$ and then $S = g^{kX}$ using her private key X. After obtaining S, the attacker can replicate the computation of the infected device. When the pre-master secret is to be derived, we differentiate two cases:

1. If the RSA method is used, the value S is stretched to 46 bytes by the TLS 1.2 pseudorandom function (PRF) and sent as the pre-master secret.
2. If the DH method is used, the server first sends the DH parameters to the client, including the prime p. The value S is then stretched by the TLS 1.2 PRF to the string of the same length as prime p. This bit string is checked to fulfill requirements for DH private key (not being 0, 1 or $\geq p$) and is used as the client's private key. If the requirements are not met, the output of PRF is repeatedly used as an input to PRF until proper key is generated.

Once the pre-master secret is generated, the handshake continues ordinarily.

The backdoor is described by Algorithms 1 and 2. Algorithm 1 generates the *ClientHello* random nonce and the seed S. The latter is further processed by Algorithm 2 to derive the pre-master secret.

The paper [14] proves that the counter mode (CTR) is polynomially indistinguishable from random bit string on the assumption that the underlying cipher is a pseudorandom function (PRF). This holds when the value of the counter never repeats. We have selected the AES in the CTR mode with a key of 128 bits to achieve indistinguishability. Some properties of this selection must be

---

Algorithm 1. Generate kleptogram and seed

Input: A public key Y, AES-CTR key K with counter
Output: The kleptogram C and seed S
$k \leftarrow 32$ random bytes
$C \leftarrow E_K(g^k)$
$S \leftarrow Y^k$
delete value k securely
return (C, S)

Algorithm 2. Generate pre-master secret

Input: Key exchange method, DH parameters and public key of server if
       needed, seed S
Output: Pre-master secret PMS
if *key exchange method is RSA* **then**
  | PMS $\leftarrow$ PRF$(S, 46$ bytes$)$
else
  | $l \leftarrow$ length of DH prime in bits
  | $Z \leftarrow$ DH public key of server
  | $x \leftarrow S$
  | **do**
  | | $x \leftarrow$ PRF$(x, l$ bits$)$
  | **while** $x = 0$ *or* $x = 1$ *or* $x \geq p$
  | PMS $\leftarrow Z^x$
end
return *PMS*

---

further discussed. First, NIST recommends [2] to limit the number of calls of pseudorandom number generator (PRNG) keyed with hard-coded value to 2^{48} blocks. Since AES-CTR is essentially a PRNG, this recommendation should be respected. Consider that birthday collisions are likely to appear only after 2^{64} bits of output, so they are trivially treated by the NIST recommendation. Since the backdoor uses two blocks of AES-CTR for one handshake, this limits the functioning of the backdoor to 2^{47} handshakes. It is emphasized that once the backdoor is reverse engineered and the symmetric key is obtained, the indistinguishability is broken.

3.2 Properties of SETUP Proposal

Theorem 1. *Under the following assumptions, our proposal is a SETUP:*

- *A random oracle is used to generate the values k and to sanitize the values C instead of a TLS PRF.*
- *AES is a random permutation.*
- *Computational DH assumption holds.*

Proof. The reader can easily verify that properties 1–3 of SETUP hold for our backdoor. To prove property 4, we show how the attacker can obtain the seed S by eavesdropping on the handshake traffic. Notice that once the seed S is known, anyone can replicate the computation of the device that leads to the pre-master secret.

When the attacker obtains the *ClientHello* nonce, she can decrypt it with the AES key K, obtaining the public key of the device g^k. The attacker can further utilise her private key X to compute the shared value $S = g^{kX} = Y^k$. Consider that when the DH key exchange method is used, the attacker must also eavesdrop the public key of the server and the parameters of the exchange; but those are sent in plaintext. To conclude, property 4 holds as well.

We proceed with the property 5. If AES is a random permutation, then AES-CTR produces ciphertext indistinguishable from uniformly distributed bit string as shown in [14]. Thus, one cannot distinguish between the kleptogram C and random bit strings (unless the collisions occur, which was discussed earlier). Further, the resulting pre-master secrets (both for RSA and DH method) are uniformly distributed too, since we utilize the random oracle to sanitize C.

Recall that non-volatile memory of the infected device contains AES key K with the counter and the public key Y. Only the key Y is relevant to the confidentiality of the shared secret S. Notice that obtaining shared secret g^{kX} from g^k and g^X is equivalent to solving ECDH problem. We therefore conclude that the property 6 holds.   □

To summarize, properties 1, 2, 3, 4 hold unconditionally for our proposal. The property 6 requires a computational DH assumption. Moreover, the property 5 requires a random oracle and AES to be a random permutation. This seems sufficient, as for the practical deployment, speed is more pressing than provable indistinguishability.

Regarding the perfect forward secrecy, an inquirer is not able to recover past session secrets if she obtains the private key of the device, k. However, after obtaining the key X, the inquirer can break all past (and future) sessions.

4   Attack Implementation

We have implemented the asymmetric backdoor into the OpenSSL library of version 1.1.1-pre2. Choosing this library allowed us to reveal whether the backdoor can pose as a regular malware, without the requirements of a black-box environment. When one designs malware in black-box setting, she is allowed to change both implementation and header files of the infected library. On the contrary, only the compiled binaries are infected in case of regular malware. The OpenSSL does not expose many low-level functions from a cryptographic library to high-level functions that are used in the TLS handshake. Our work shows that the proposal can be embedded into the compiled binary, leaving the header files untouched.

The pre-release version of the library was chosen because it provides certain functions for computations on the X25519 curve not available in previous releases. The X25519 is implemented in a different way than other elliptic curves in OpenSSL and older releases did not allow for the creation of specific keys on this curve; only random keys could be created. We decided to expose some low-level functions for direct use to achieve simpler implementation. This resulted into modification of the header files. Nevertheless, high-level interfaces could be used instead and the backdoor could be deployed as a compiled library. We faced no serious obstacles that would prevent the backdoor installation to the library.

4.1   Attack Detection

We have also studied the possible detections of the infected library via side channels. As we worked in the desktop environment, we limit our attention to the timing channel. Nonetheless, a power side channel could be a viable detection mechanism on different platforms. Several code snippets of both infected and clean version of OpenSSL were isolated and their performance was evaluated and compared. This creates a possible detection mechanism of the backdoor, yet, with certain limitations. As expected, the backdoor performs slower than the clean version. Nevertheless, this does not necessarily create a distinguisher. Suppose that all devices of a certain kind are infected. Then there exists no reference to how the uninfected version should perform. The inquirer must therefore somehow guess the expected performance and measure deviations based on this estimate. Also, the library could be used on various hardware and outperform clean versions when running on faster hardware.

Three code snippets were measured for the infected algorithm. In particular, those were the RSA pre-mater secret generation snippet, the DH private key generation snippet, and the *ClientHello* nonce generation snippet. The last snippet was measured in two versions. The first version contained only one exponentiation (computation of the public-key presented as kleptogram). The second version was expanded by shared-secret derivation between the attacker and the device. As the backdoor does not require any initialization except for loading the AES counter (other keys can be hard-coded in the binary), this aspect was ignored in the experiments (Table 1).

4.2   Average Execution Times

Our measurements show that the whole subverted version runs by 0.248 ms (0.282 ms) slower than the clean version when RSA (DH) key exchange method is used. The subverted RSA key exchange method runs slower by the factor of 2.28 over the clean version. On the contrary, the subverted DH key exchange method runs slower only by the factor of 1.01. This is because in the case of RSA, the newly introduced computations take relatively much more time to the overall key exchange method cost. It also can be seen that such an increase in time cannot be spotted just by using the device. The interaction over the network creates the opportunity for obfuscating the computation times. The exponentiations, or even parts of them, could be precomputed once the handshake is initiated, stored, and only loaded from memory when needed. The more

Table 1. Average execution times of code snippets.

Code snippet	Average computation time in μs
Timer overhead	0.312
g^k on X25519	171.132
ClientHello clean	4.726
ClientHello subverted	176.293
ClientHello subverted[a]	246 843
RSA PMS clean	4.887
RSA PMS subverted	11.185
DH private key gen. clean	3178.587
DH private key gen. subverted	3218.496
TLS context builder	374.5

[a]Version with the shared secret precomputation.

complex the underlying protocol is, the larger is the space for obfuscations. It is also questionable whether the inquirer will be able to isolate the corresponding snippets on a tamper-proof device to obtain precise measurements.

To conclude, the timing-channel method is not reliable and most likely could be evaded by a skilled adversary. Nevertheless, the proposal can be detected when a clean version of the OpenSSL is at hand and benchmarking is available on the same hardware on which the suspected version is running. As the highest increase in time is seen when the *ClientHello* nonce is generated, this could be the sweet spot for malware detection. Recall that the execution time of the *ClientHello* nonce function should correspond to the time in which the library generates 32 random bytes. If the function takes substantially larger amount of time, the backdoor is likely to be present.

We do not release the source code for the reason that it could be easily misused as a malware.

5   Related Work

Our work is based on the concept [9]. In contrast to the original backdoor, our solution cannot fullfils the conditions 5 and 6 of the SETUP mechanism. The paper [22] by Young and Yung presents how to generate shared secret with ECDH that is polynomially indistinguishable from random bit string. Furthermore, they also mention its applicability to the TLS protocol and provide first asymmetric backdoor for TLS. However, the proposal is rather impractical as to execute a single backdoored handshake more than 300 ECDH key exchanges are required. Injective mappings of strings on elliptic curve points [1,6] could have interesting applications for kleptography, as their inversion could map ECDH keys to strings that are polynomially indistinguishable from random strings. Regarding the detection of backdoors via side channels, the paper [12] presents a method that studies variance in execution times of functions which might reveal newly introduced exponentiations to the protocol – a common facet of kleptography.

In recent years, major advances came in the field of defenses against klepto-graphic adversaries. Most of them were published in [16]. The work achieves a general technique for preserving semantic security of a cryptosystem, if put into the kleptographic setting. Also, the paper classifies already proposed defenses into three categories:

- Abandoning the randomness in favour of deterministic computation [3–5],
- use of a trusted module that can re-randomize subverted primitives [7, 13],
- hashing the subverted randomness [15].

6 Conclusions

TLS is an essential protocol for securing data on the transport layer. As such, TLS is omnipresent in an era of computer networks, having applications in https, VPN, payment gateways and many others. The widespread use of TLS motivated us to study its vulnerability in the kleptographic setting. We aimed to answer whether a kleptographic backdoor can be practically implemented into the TLS libraries.

Our efforts resulted into a design of an asymmetric backdoor for all versions of the TLS protocol. Such backdoor can be used to exfiltrate session keys from a captured handshake by a passive eavesdropper, leading to a denial of confi-dentiality and authenticity of the whole session. We also demonstrated that it is fairly simple to implement the backdoor into an open source TLS library while maintaining a reasonable performance of the library. We stress that to install our backdoor, an adversary must have access to the target device. In such cases, other dangerous scenarios arise – we mention ransomware as an example. How-ever, the important property of our backdoor is that it may stay unnoticed for a long time on the target device. Also, it may be endorsed into a particular hardware by its manufacturer or organizations with sufficient resources. We also showed that timing analysis may prove as an effective defense, depending on the powers of an inquirer.

For future work, we suggest to study whether an effective defense could be derived for TLS on a protocol level, for instance, in the form of a protocol exten-sion. Regarding the offensive techniques, if mappings [1,6] could be combined with a cryptographic key, they would allow for ECDH secrets indistinguishable from a random noise.

References

1. Aranha, D.F., Fouque, P.-A., Qian, C., Tibouchi, M., Zapalowicz, J.-C.: Binary elligator squared. In: Joux, A., Youssef, A. (eds.) SAC 2014. LNCS, vol. 8781, pp. 20–37. Springer, Cham (2014). https://doi.org/10.1007/978-3-319-13051-4_2
2. Barker, E.B., Kelsey, J.M.: Recommendation for Random Number Generation Using Deterministic Random Bit Generators. Technical report (2015)

3. Bellare, M., Hoang, V.T.: Resisting randomness subversion: fast deterministic and hedged public-key encryption in the standard model. In: Oswald, E., Fischlin, M. (eds.) EUROCRYPT 2015. LNCS, vol. 9057, pp. 627–656. Springer, Heidelberg (2015). https://doi.org/10.1007/978-3-662-46803-6_21

4. Bellare, M., Jaeger, J., Kane, D.: Mass-surveillance without the state: strongly undetectable algorithm-substitution attacks. In: Proceedings of the 22nd ACM SIGSAC Conference on Computer and Communications Security - CCS 2015, pp. 1431–1440. ACM, New York (2015)

5. Bellare, M., Paterson, K.G., Rogaway, P.: Security of symmetric encryption against mass surveillance. In: Garay, J.A., Gennaro, R. (eds.) CRYPTO 2014. LNCS, vol. 8616, pp. 1–19. Springer, Heidelberg (2014). https://doi.org/10.1007/978-3-662-44371-2_1

6. Bernstein, D.J., Hamburg, M., Krasnova, A., Lange, T.: Elligator: elliptic-curve points indistinguishable from uniform random strings. In: Proceedings of the 2013 ACM SIGSAC Conference on Computer and Communications Security - CCS 2013, pp. 967–980. ACM, New York (2013)

7. Dodis, Y., Mironov, I., Stephens-Davidowitz, N.: Message transmission with reverse firewalls—secure communication on corrupted machines. In: Robshaw, M., Katz, J. (eds.) CRYPTO 2016. LNCS, vol. 9814, pp. 341–372. Springer, Heidelberg (2016). https://doi.org/10.1007/978-3-662-53018-4_13

8. Gjøsteen, K.: Comments on Dual-EC-DRBG/NIST SP 800-90, Draft December 2005. Technical report

9. Gołębiewski, Z., Kutyłowski, M., Zagórski, F.: Stealing secrets with SSL/TLS and SSH – kleptographic attacks. In: Pointcheval, D., Mu, Y., Chen, K. (eds.) CANS 2006. LNCS, vol. 4301, pp. 191–202. Springer, Heidelberg (2006). https://doi.org/10.1007/11935070_13

10. Green, M., Droms, R., Housley, R., Turner, P., Fenter, S.: Data Center use of Static Diffie-Hellman in TLS 1.3. RFC Draft (2017). https://tools.ietf.org/html/draft-green-tls-static-dh-in-tls13-01

11. Housley, R., Droms, R.: TLS 1.3 Option for Negotiation of Visibility in the Datacenter. RFC Draft (2018). https://tools.ietf.org/html/draft-rhrd-tls-tls13-visibility-01

12. Kucner, D., Kutyłowski, M.: Stochastic kleltography detecion. In: Public-Key Cryptography and Computational Number Theory, pp. 137–149. De Gruyter (2001)

13. Mironov, I., Stephens-Davidowitz, N.: Cryptographic reverse firewalls. In: Oswald, E., Fischlin, M. (eds.) EUROCRYPT 2015. LNCS, vol. 9057, pp. 657–686. Springer, Heidelberg (2015). https://doi.org/10.1007/978-3-662-46803-6_22

14. Rogaway, P.: Evaluation of some blockcipher modes of operation. Technical report, Cryptography Research and Evaluation Committees (CRYPTREC) for the Government of Japan (2011)

15. Russell, A., Tang, Q., Yung, M., Zhou, H.-S.: Cliptography: clipping the power of kleptographic attacks. In: Cheon, J.H., Takagi, T. (eds.) ASIACRYPT 2016. LNCS, vol. 10032, pp. 34–64. Springer, Heidelberg (2016). https://doi.org/10.1007/978-3-662-53890-6_2

16. Russell, A., Tang, Q., Yung, M., Zhou, H.S.: Generic semantic security against a kleptographic adversary. In: Proceedings of the 2017 ACM SIGSAC Conference on Computer and Communications Security - CCS 2017, pp. 907–922. ACM, New York (2017)

17. Checkoway, S., et al.: On the practical exploitability of dual EC in TLS implementations. In: SEC 2014 Proceedings of the 23rd USENIX conference on Security Symposium, pp. 319–335 (2014)

18. Young, A., Yung, M.: The dark side of "Black-Box" cryptography or: should we trust capstone? In: Koblitz, N. (ed.) CRYPTO 1996. LNCS, vol. 1109, pp. 89–103. Springer, Heidelberg (1996). https://doi.org/10.1007/3-540-68697-5_8

19. Young, A., Yung, M.: Kleptography: using cryptography against cryptography. In: Fumy, W. (ed.) EUROCRYPT 1997. LNCS, vol. 1233, pp. 62–74. Springer, Heidelberg (1997). https://doi.org/10.1007/3-540-69053-0_6

20. Young, A., Yung, M.: Malicious Cryptography: Exposing Cryptovirology. Wiley, Hoboken (2004)

21. Young, A.L., Yung, M.M.: Space-efficient kleptography without random oracles. In: Furon, T., Cayre, F., Doërr, G., Bas, P. (eds.) IH 2007. LNCS, vol. 4567, pp. 112–129. Springer, Heidelberg (2007). https://doi.org/10.1007/978-3-540-77370-2_8

22. Young, A., Yung, M.: Kleptography from standard assumptions and applications. In: Garay, J.A., De Prisco, R. (eds.) SCN 2010. LNCS, vol. 6280, pp. 271–290. Springer, Heidelberg (2010). https://doi.org/10.1007/978-3-642-15317-4_18

Generic Architecture for Lightweight Block Ciphers: A First Step Towards Agile Implementation of Multiple Ciphers

Etienne Tehrani[✉], Jean-Luc Danger, and Tarik Graba

LTCI, Télécom ParisTech,
Université Paris-Saclay, 75 013 Paris, France
{etienne.tehrani,jean-luc.danger,tarik.graba}@telecom-paristech.fr

Abstract. Lightweight cryptography is at the heart of today's security needs for embedded systems. The standardised cryptographic algorithms, such as the Advanced Encryption Standard (AES), hardly fits the resource restrictions of those small and pervasive devices. From this observation a plethora of Lightweight Block Ciphers have been proposed. Every algorithm has its own advantages in terms of security, complexity, latency, performances. This paper presents first a classification of some popular Substitution-Permutation-Networks (SPN) class of lightweight ciphers according to their architecture and features which share many common operators. From this last point, we studied a round-based generic hardware architecture that allows a security architect to dynamically change the lightweight cryptographic algorithms to be executed. The results of the ASIC implementation show that the configuration part of the proposed flexible architecture adds significant complexity. If compared with the parallel implementation of several algorithms, the complexity ratio becomes interesting when the number of algorithms (or the level of agility) increases. For instance, if we consider 6 SPN ciphers, the configurable architecture provides a complexity reduction of 62.5%, whereas there is no reduction with 4 algorithms.

Keywords: Lightweight cryptography · SPN · ASIC · Configurable architecture

1 Introduction

With the intense development of small and pervasive computing devices, as IoTs and their ability to communicate through insecure networks, it becomes essential to add security features. Indeed, from connected homes to connected vehicles or medical devices, security is at the heart of tomorrow's issues as it will affect our private lives as much as our health. Hence, all these devices need to be protected using sound cryptography in order to get a good level of confidentiality, integrity and privacy. Such devices are constrained by a low complexity with restricted

© IFIP International Federation for Information Processing 2019
Published by Springer Nature Switzerland AG 2019
O. Blazy and C. Y. Yeun (Eds.): WISTP 2018, LNCS 11469, pp. 28–43, 2019.
https://doi.org/10.1007/978-3-030-20074-9_4

chip area, memory and energy, while still needing communication channels. The security of these devices and the sensitive data they process have to be addressed by a new generation of Lightweight Cryptography algorithms which provide a good compromise between security and complexity in terms of area, latency and energy.

The most common standard symmetric-key cryptographic algorithm used to secure digital information is the Advanced Encryption Standard (AES) [22]. However, AES does not fit the strong restrictions of small embedded systems. This observation led to the development of Lightweight Block Ciphers. Plethora of such ciphers are available in the literature [7]. The NIST has started a project [19] to develop a strategy for the standardisation of lightweight cryptographic algorithms. Some of these algorithms are based on the same basic computation steps as AES since they use a Substitution Permutation Network (SPN) structure [17], some others use Feistel networks as DES [24]. Out of these numerous algorithms, none have emerged as a clear favorite in terms of becoming a NIST standard. PRESENT [8] has been accepted as an ISO standard [15], but the impact of standardisation was not as significant as AES. Actually, this means first, that the security of these algorithms is not officially recognised by an authority. Second, that some industrial may use modified versions of those algorithms, loosing interoperability and eventually weakening the algorithm. Third, since the demand for such algorithms is increasing and the maturity of some of them is becoming evident, the NIST might eventually standardise one of them rendering obsolete actual devices or protocol implementations. From these three last points, it appears that the possibility to use a flexible architecture allowing the user to change afterwords the cryptographic algorithm is an interesting feature. Moreover, this "agility" characteristic increases the security level as the attacker is thwarted by the unsteady nature of the cryptographic computing. The point is to know if such flexible architecture is feasible in terms of complexity and other physical constraints.

We could think this objective could be made possible thanks to the common operators of SPN algorithms. But the cryptographic algorithms were developed focussing on different features and the SPN operators have thus been implemented in different manners Most algorithms focus on area, others such as PRINCE [9] and MANTIS [6] focus on latency thanks to a specific structure, inspired by SPN, called $\alpha - reflection$. The objective of low energy consumption is tackled by MIDORI [3] and PICCOLO [23]. It arises the question of how similar those algorithms are, and if these similarities can be used to design a unique hardware to implement them. This would permit the deployment of those block ciphers, while being ready to switch as soon as a standard emerges. This Generic Architecture would also have the advantage of allowing algorithms to be slightly modified or tweaked if necessary. The basic idea to develop such an architecture is that the SPN structured algorithms share similar functions. Those functions can be grouped within *steps* which have the same function but do not work in the same way. These *steps* are further detailed in Sect. 2.

An original fine-grain FPGA [20] has already been proposed. It is based on the utilization of Full-adder configurable cells. Other flexible cryptographic architectures have been proposed [12,25] or [18] which focuses on an agile permutation layer but none of these targeted specifically lightweight cryptography. We propose in this paper to study a coarse-grain approach by taking into account the common operators found in the Lightweight algorithms. However, even if some operators are very close, the Feistel class of algorithms are too far from the SPN in terms of scheduling. Therefore, the study targets the SPN class only.

Our Contributions. In this paper, we first propose a classification of lightweight cryptographic algorithms according to their internal scheduling and functions. From this classification and a detailed study of the differences between the selected SPN algorithms, a generic round-based hardware architecture has been proposed. It can be configured for different levels of agility in order to handle some or all families of ciphers. The permutation layer (P-layer) which is quite specific to each algorithm has been deeply investigated. A third contribution is the evaluation of the generic architecture and the comparison with implementations of independent lightweight cryptographic ciphers.

The paper is organised as follows. Section 2 presents the classification of the different families of SPN lightweight algorithms. It focuses on the different functions which require specific hardware modules. Section 3 describes the design of the generic architecture. The overall architecture alongside the design of each *step*. Section 4 justifies the different design choices of the P-Layer, as the architectural optimisations in the P-Layer are strongly related to the requirements of each family of algorithms. Section 5 discusses the results of the architectural implementations. The hardware resources usage for different levels of agility are presented and compared to direct implementation of the algorithms. Finally, Sect. 6 concludes the paper.

2   Classification of the Algorithms

There are multiple ways to classify symmetric cryptographic algorithms, the main category used is the structure of the algorithm. An algorithm has either a Feistel structure (SIMON and SPECK [5]), an SPN structure (AES) or a structure derived from SPN (PRINCE [9], PICCOLO [23]).

Our study focuses on implementing SPN and SPN-like algorithms, as their functions are similar enough to be handled by the same hardware, and a large proportion of lightweight cryptographic algorithms use this structure. The SPN algorithms are composed of three *steps*:

– The Sbox: **S**, which corresponds to the confusion
– The P-Layer: **P**, which corresponds to the diffusion
– The AddKey: **K**, which corresponds to the addition of the secret

SPN Algorithms can differ by the order in which they execute those *steps*. This allow to classify them into three families based on the relative order of these *steps.* The first type is the SKP-type (SKINNY [6]), for which **S** is followed by **K**, itself followed by the P-layer. The second type is the SPK-type (MIDORI [3], GIFT [4], PRESENT [8]), for which **S** is followed by the P-layer, itself followed by **K**. On the one hand, each family can be implemented without changing the order, simply by changing the first *step* of the algorithm. On the other hand, the two families are not coherent and require extra modules to be handled by the same architecture. Note that it is also possible to handle both these families by adding computation to the key since the **P** and **K** are both linear layers. The last family is that of the $\alpha - reflective$ algorithms (PRINCE [9], MANTIS [6]) which change the order of the *steps* during the encryption.

Table 1 presents a classification proposal.

Table 1. Classification of lightweight ciphers sub-blocs

Algorithms			GIFT	PRESENT	SKINNY	MANTIS	PRINCE	MIDORI
		SKP			X			
Step order		SPK	X	X				X
		α reflection				X	X	
	Permutation	bit-level	X	X				
		nibble-level			X	X	X	X
P-Layer	Matrix	None	X	X				
	Multiplication	4 × 4 matrix			X	X		X
		64 × 64 matrix					X	
		Sub key extraction	A	B		C	C	C
Key Scheduling		Rotation	X	X	X			
		Sbox		X				
		Round constant	X	X	X	X	X	X

The P-layer **P** has two main types of permutations, either at the bit-level (PRESENT [8], GIFT [4]) or at the nibble-level (SKINNY [6], PRINCE [9]). These two different approaches require more or less complex permutation modules and implementing one but not the other has an influence over the cost of the permutation. An additional matrix multiplication can be used. It can be a 4×4 multiplication of the nibbles (SKINNY [6], MANTIS [6]) or a 64×64 multiplication on the whole word (PRINCE [9]). PRESENT [8], GIFT [4] do not use matrix multiplication. Each type represents different levels of complexity, especially if we consider the resources to store the matrix values. Finally, though most algorithms only use one Sbox, $\alpha - reflective$ algorithms (PRINCE [9], MANTIS [6]) use two Sboxes: the Sbox and its inverse.

The **Key Scheduling** block is in charge of generating the round keys. Key Scheduling is done in very different ways from one algorithm to the other. Despite basic operations such as rotation or the use of round constants, the Key scheduling uses different functions applied to different parts of the key. Indeed, the sub-key generation is rather complex to unify as extracting different groups of bits of variety of size is hard to achieve in hardware without great increase in the design size. For example, GIFT [4] divides the entire key in 16-bit words and extracts two of them (A type), PRESENT [8] extracts two nibbles (B type) and use the Sbox. In other algorithms such as PRINCE [9] and MANTIS [6] the key is divided into two parts (C type) used separately. For these reasons, and because making the key scheduling generic in hardware would be complex and costly, we have decided to use a buffer that will contain pre-computed round keys. The round keys will be generated by software in the configuration phase.

Table 2 presents a selection of Lightweight Block Cipher and their implementations results from the literature.

Table 2. Comparison of area, latency and throughput for implementations of 64-bit block size lightweight block ciphers

Cipher	Ref.	Tech (nm)	Architecture (cycle/round)	Area (GE)	Latency (ns)	TPmax (Gbps)	TP@100kHz (kbps)
Block size : 64-bit							
PRINCE	[9]	90	1/32	7996	13.9	4.56	-
	[9]	90	11/32	3286	58.3	1.10	-
PRESENT	[4]	90	32/32	1560	52.16	1.23	-
Midori64	[3]	90	16/16	2450	33.92	1.89	-
SKINNY 64	[6]	180	32/32	1696	59.84	0.95	177.78
	[6]	180	1/32	17454	51.59	1.24	6400
	[6]	180	128/32	1399	121.60	0.09	8.12
	[6]	180	2048/32	1172	2170.88	0.02	2.03
	[4]	90	32/32	1477	58.88	0.96	-
Mantis7	[6]	180	1/14	11209	20.5	3.12	-
	[6]	180	1/14	23926	11.0	5.82	-
GIFT-64	[4]	90	28/28	1345	51.24	1.25	-
	[4]	90	112/28	1113	239.68	0.06	-
	[4]	90	2048/32	930	4784.64	0.01	-

3   Generic Architecture

In order to handle multiple algorithms with the same hardware, the architecture is designed to be configurable.

The overall architecture is divided between the key scheduling and the configurable SPN structure. Each cipher computes the three steps of the SPN structure in a specific order, and can skip some of them (completely or at a specific round). In our design, this is achieved through the use of four 3-way multiplexers (see Fig. 1) which are controlled using configuration bits. These configuration bits need also to be different from one round to another.

For the desired functionality, there are only 15 different possible options to order the three steps, therefore all the multiplexers can be configured with only

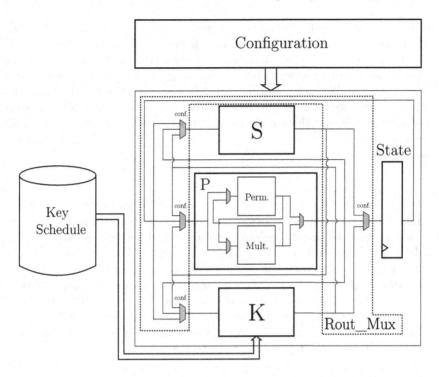

Fig. 1. Overall organisation of the generic architecture

4 bits per round. Thus, the number of necessary configuration bits is 4× the maximum number of rounds that the implemented ciphers need. This can be further reduced if we store a unique configuration for all the rounds that use the same configuration.

3.1   Key Scheduling

Initially, as with the rest of the architecture, the key scheduling of each algorithm was studied in order to identify similarities between each of them. The issue is that unlike the algorithm itself, which uses a set SPN structure and is broadly similar to the standardised AES, key scheduling is achieved through a plethora of methods. Each of these methods applies calculation specific to the algorithm. An example would be isolating parts of the key, a few bits long, apply a certain processing such as an LFSR or the algorithm's Sbox to them, then each part is reordered and the result is shifted. Not only does this general description not fit most of the key scheduling but even if it were, being able to isolate different amounts of different-sized sample represents a real challenge and requires an important amount of hardware no matter the solution.

Once it had been made obvious that the variety of key scheduling does not allow a unified implementation at a reasonable cost, a different path had to be considered in order to obtain the used round keys. Using a configurable architecture means this architecture would most likely not work independently and thereby require to be included within a processor system. Computing the round keys could be done by software, prior to or in parallel with the configuration phase and the unrolled key could be stored in a specific buffer. Obviously this processor system, used for security applications, would have to ensure a secure way to store and handle the unrolled key. Moreover, as the key is generally not changed at each encryption, handling the Key Scheduling through software is not an issue.

3.2 The Sbox: S

The **S** module is rather straight forward, for each of the 16 possible nibble inputs there is an output defined through information stored within a RAM bloc. This module is therefore similar to a LUT. The substitution of each of the 16 nibbles is done in parallel and therefore requires 16 actual Sboxes. Most algorithms use the same Sbox throughout the entire encryption process but some of them require two different Sboxes. This is the case with $\alpha - reflective$ algorithms which use both an Sbox and its inverse, such as PRINCE [9] and Mantis [6]. Including a second Sbox means having to store twice as much information and add a mechanism to switch from one Sbox to the other.

3.3 The Key Addition: K

Each algorithm uses a different key for each round, called a round key, which is computed during the key scheduling. The *round key* considered here is not necessarily what algorithms call their round key, it also encompasses the round constant if any. Thereby, the **K** *step* is simply composed of 64 Xor gates in parallel to add the state to the software precomputed round key. The main security issue is that the round keys need to be stored in a secure environment, which is coherent with the natural use of encryption where the key needs to be stored securely. This mechanism also echoes the fact that the **K** needs to access this secure memory once per round, therefore once per cycle. Memory does not usually have this feature but this can be handled by using a bypass between this section of the memory and the **K** module. That part was not implemented and is a theoretical solution.

3.4 The P-Layer: P

The permutation bloc **P** for an SPN structured algorithm can include two different parts. The first part, equivalent to the MixColumn function of AES, is a matrix multiplication.

This matrix multiplication (see Fig. 2) uses the same four bits of the input with four different bit sets of the matrix to compute four bits of the output. This means that the matrix multiplication uses four times 64 bits values or a unique

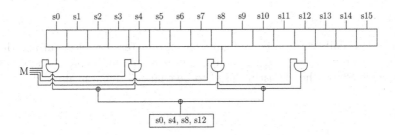

Fig. 2. The generic matrix multiplication

256 bits value. This seems like a lot but it is still smaller then a full 64×64 matrix.

The second part of the **P** bloc is equivalent to the Shift Row function of the AES cipher. This part required a lot of attention for multiple reasons. First, in a classic Lightweight Bloc Cipher, this part generally implemented as a simple reordering of wires and uses no specific hardware. Second, the algorithms which do not use a matrix multiplication require permutation at a bit level rather than the at the nibble level as with AES's Shift Row. Third, designing a configurable permutation meant being able to route a signal through a crossbar-like module, but crossbars are expensive in terms of both area and configuration memory. It was therefore essential to find a lighter solution. The most efficient solution to optimise those crossbars was using Banyan switches [13].

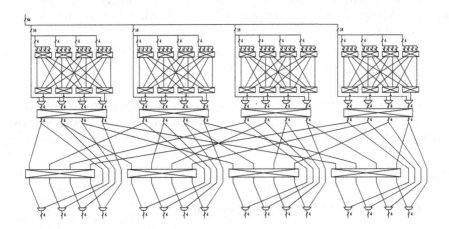

Fig. 3. The generic permutation function

The chosen solution (see Fig. 3) was based on a thorough study of each algorithms' requirements in terms of permutation flexibility and the crossbar-like modules were optimised to better fit the situation (these optimised crossbar-like modules will be referred to as Banyan switches for the rest of the paper). More details on **P** will be given in Sect. 4.

3.5   The Configuration

The generic architecture uses configuration parameters to select an algorithm. These parameters are set during the configuration phase, before the encryption begins. This allows the algorithm used to be changed dynamically.

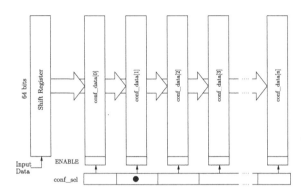

Fig. 4. The configuration scheme

The configuration memory bits are distributed throughout the architecture. A shift register mechanism is used (see Fig. 4) to limit the complexity of the external configuration interface. Once the shift register's content is valid, the configuration data is written by bloc in a configuration register chosen by a selection signal.

4   Detailed Analysis of the P-Layer

Each module of the Generic Architecture has been designed to allow several levels of agility depending on the acceptable area overhead. This was achieved by identifying the common characteristics of different algorithms and designing the architecture accordingly. The most key part in unifying the architecture to each algorithm was **P**.

4.1   Unifying the Matrix Multiplication

The matrices used for the matrix multiplication are of two types. The first type is considering a 4×4 matrix composed of nibbles whose value is either F or 0 (SKINNY [6]). They are represented as 4×4 matrix but the multiplication actually applies to each bit of the state's 4×4 matrix of nibbles, they can therefore be considered as 4×4 matrix of *nibbles*. The second type is a 64×64 bit matrix which is mostly filled with 0s but has 4 16×16 sub-matrices composed of 1s and 0s (Prince [9]). The latter matrix are themselves composed of 16 4×4

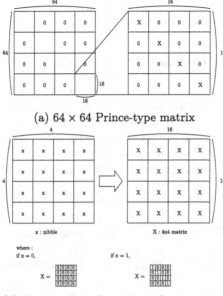

(a) 64 × 64 Prince-type matrix

(b) Turning the information of a 4 × 4 matrix to the information of a 16 × 16 matrix

Fig. 5. Unifying the different types of matrix multiplication

diagonal matrices, therefore the 16 × 16 matrix can only have 1s placed along the 4 × 4 matrix's diagonals (see Fig. 5a).

This property makes it possible to reduce the 64 × 64 matrix to the information on the 4 × 4 matrix's diagonal which compose the 16 × 16 sub-matrix. There are 16 4 × 4 matrix in each of the 4 16 × 16 sub-matrices, each of which have 4 bits on their diagonal, which amount to a total of $4 \times 16 \times 4 = 256bits$ of useful information. The first type only consists of a 4 × 4 matrix of nibbles with a single bit either at 1 or 0. In this type of matrix, the value of a bit is the same as the other bits of the same nibble, in other word the $4 \times 4 \times 4 = 64bits$ of the matrix can be summed up as $4 \times 4 = 16bits$ of useful information.

This meant that either some algorithms were discarded in order to maintain a lower amount of required information, or they had to be harmonised. Doing so meant turning 16 bits of information into 256 bits without changing the result of the multiplication. This was achieved by changing every nibble of the 4 × 4 matrix into a 4 × 4 matrix, either filled with 0s if the nibble was a 0 or the 4 × 4 identity matrix if the nibble was a 1 (see Fig. 5b). The result is a 16 × 16 matrix with $4 \times 4 \times 16 = 64bits$ of useful information, which is the same as one of the 16 × 16 sub matrix of the 64 × 64 matrix. The 16 × 16 matrix thereby obtained was then duplicated four times in order to have the 256 bits of useful information as with the 64 × 64 matrix. This choice is still costly as 256 bits is meaningful but is much less than the $64 \times 64 = 2048bits$ of the entire matrix.

The question remains nonetheless on whether adding the second type of matrix is worth the cost, this will be discussed later.

4.2 Minimizing the Cost of the Permutation

Permutation was a key issue as it is usually achieved by just reordering the wires. The overhead of making this bloc configurable could thus be significant. The simplest way to go is to consider a 64 × 64 crossbar which would allow any permutation but would be incredibly costly both in terms of area and in terms of the size of configuration memory. It was therefore essential to identify similarities between the different permutations in order to limit the area of this module.

The result was two levels of permutations, as explained beforehand, the bit-level permutation and the nibble-level permutation. The bit-level permutation (PRESENT [8], GIFT [4]) allows any layer-input bit to end up as any layer-output bit within the same 16-bit word, the restriction being that two bits from the same input nibble may not end up in the same output nibble. This restriction is coherent with the diffusion properties of a cipher as a bit level permutation needs to spread the information as much as possible in order to ensure the security. It requires four sets of Banyan switches each using the same parameters, which apply to each of the four 16-bit words of the 64-bits state.

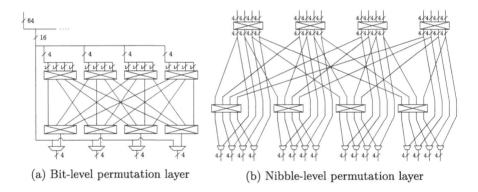

(a) Bit-level permutation layer   (b) Nibble-level permutation layer

Fig. 6. Detailed permutation design

It is composed of two layers (see Fig. 6a). Between these layers, the connection wires are fixed and cannot be configured. They link each bit of a nibble to a different nibble. The first layer defines which bit of each nibble will be connected to which nibble of the second layer, through the use of a 4 × 4 Banyan switch for each nibble. The second layer reorders the bits within each nibble with a 4 × 4 Banyan switch for each nibble.

Nibble-level permutation (see Fig. 6b) works similarly and therefore, once again, any layer-input nibble may end up as any layer-output nibble and the restriction is that two nibbles of the same 16-bit input may not end in the same 16-bit word output. There is an exception to this rule in the case of an actual Shift Register where each nibble is reordered but every nibble stays within the same 16-bit word. It also requires two layers of Banyan switches separated with transition wires, which can be configured. There is a set of multiplexers which allows either to connect the four nibbles of a 16-bit word to four different 16-bit words or to keep each nibble within the same 16-bit word, which is needed for the Shift Row function. The first layer defines which nibble goes to which 16-bit word, and the second layer reorders each 16-bit word. They each use four 4-bit 4×4 Banyan switches.

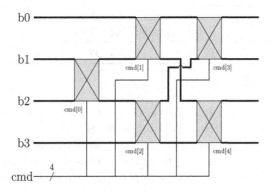

Fig. 7. Optimised crossbar-like module, the Banyan switch

Finally, the Banyan Switches are composed of a set of five switches (see Fig. 7). Each switch allows the reordering of two inputs and is controlled by a single configuration bit. The 4×4 Banyan Switch can thus be configured to reorder its 4 inputs to get any permutation at the output. The $4 \times 3 \times 2 = 24$ permutations can be controlled with only 5 configuration bits. This structure allows to reduce the area in terms of logic and configuration memory.

5   Implementation Results

The architecture was implemented targeting the Cadence Free45PDK standard cells library. Post synthesis results are used to evaluate the area and complexity of our design.

First the generic architecture complexity is evaluated for different levels of agility. Second the generic architecture is compared to the cost of implementation of classic Lightweight Block Ciphers to identify the gain of using such an architecture.

The Generic architecture can be divided in multiple sub-parts which have been presented in detail in chapter 3. The results of Table 3 show the cost of each of these parts. Making the architecture agile has important over-costs. For

Table 3. Cost of architecture's sub-parts for the level of agility III

Sub-part		Cost		Area percentage
		Area	GE	
Configuration	Route_Mux	695	678	26.9
	Sbox	348	339	
	Permutation	956	932	
	Multiplication	1390	1355	
	Other	87	85	
	Route_Mux	2791	2720	21.6
	S	1784	1739	13.8
P	Permutation	2059	2007	21.7
	Multiplication	744	725	
	K	175	171	1.4

instance, Permutation is usually free in terms of area but making it configurable will obviously make it costly. It is also true for **S** which requires a configurable table and could not be optimised through the use of specific logic functions. The other two main parts are also new to such an architecture as they do not exist in a non-agile implementation of cryptographic algorithms. The Route_Mux allows to order each *step* at each round and therefore uses an important amount of multiplexers in order to select the path for the entire state. Finally, the most costly sub-part is the configuration which gathers all the parameters used to select which algorithm is implemented within the architecture. This last sub-part is divided between the different aspects which need configuration. It appears that the Multiplication requires the most important part of the parameters. Indeed, configuration of the Matrix multiplication has a cost of 256 bits (see Sect. 4.1) which is a lot more that the 64 bits required for **S** or the 176 bits used to define the algorithm's route at each round. The overhead of the generic architecture is therefore important but most of it is due to the very nature of the architecture whose agility has a minimal cost which cannot be canceled. It would therefore seem that this architecture is not efficient when compared to a single algorithm but, the more algorithms it implements, the more interesting it becomes.

The next step was thereby comparing different levels of agility in order to identify how much adding new algorithms costs. This will then lead to a comparison between the cost of the generic architecture and the cost of implementing multiple algorithms.

Each level of agility, **I**, **II**, **III** and **IV** from Table 4 allows the implementation of a certain set of algorithms. Each of these levels is compared to the cost of each of the algorithms it can handle in Table 5.

Table 4. Different levels agility for the architecture

Algorithm	Level of Agility			
PRESENT				
GIFT	I			
SKINNY		III		
MIDORI	II		IV	
PRINCE				
MANTIS				

Table 5. Comparison between different levels of agility and the sum of the algorithms it can implement

Level of agility	Area of the generic architecture (in GE)	Sum of the implementations (complexity ratio)
I	8494	1.72
II	8245	1.96
III	9212	1
IV	9631	0.625

Figure 8 illustrates the complexity reduction provided by the generic architecture when the level of agility increases. It shows that balance is achieved around an agility of four algorithms and that once this limit is exceeded, the generic architecture offers a real gain.

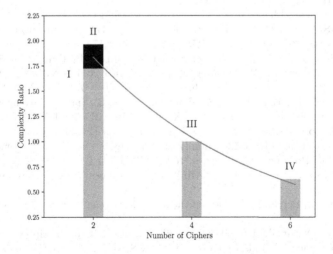

Fig. 8. Complexity ratio for different levels of agility

6   Conclusion

An implementation of a round-based generic architecture of SPN lightweight ciphers has been presented. The results showed it was possible to compound multiple algorithms within the same architecture to provide agility features. The proposed architecture has the advantage of allowing to easily change the configuration at a round level and thus implementing the majority of SPN Lightweight algorithms.

However, the proposed architecture has a significant complexity cost, mainly due to the configuration logic. Compared to the complexity of a parallel implementation of different algorithms, we observe a complexity reduction if more than 4 ciphers are considered. The reduction can reach 62.5% if 6 different algorithms are considered. These results are promising if agility requirement is more important than complexity.

Apart from optimizing the design complexity by finding more optimal implementations for each sub bloc, a prospect is to search for ways to implement countermeasures against physical attacks. Indeed, specific countermeasures have to be implemented as they have to take into account the flexibility of our architecture without significantly increasing the global complexity.

References

1. Cryptographic technology guideline - lightweight cryptography (cryptrec-gl-0001-2016). Technical report, CRYPTREC Cryptographic Technology Guideline (2017)
2. Badel, S., et al.: ARMADILLO: a multi-purpose cryptographic primitive dedicated to hardware. In: Mangard, S., Standaert, F.-X. (eds.) CHES 2010. LNCS, vol. 6225, pp. 398–412. Springer, Heidelberg (2010). https://doi.org/10.1007/978-3-642-15031-9_27
3. Banik, S., et al.: Midori: a block cipher for low energy. In: Iwata, T., Cheon, J.H. (eds.) ASIACRYPT 2015. LNCS, vol. 9453, pp. 411–436. Springer, Heidelberg (2015). https://doi.org/10.1007/978-3-662-48800-3_17
4. Banik, S., Pandey, S.K., Peyrin, T., Sasaki, Y., Sim, S.M., Todo, Y.: GIFT: a small present. In: Fischer, W., Homma, N. (eds.) CHES 2017. LNCS, vol. 10529, pp. 321–345. Springer, Cham (2017). https://doi.org/10.1007/978-3-319-66787-4_16
5. Beaulieu, R., Treatman-Clark, S., Shors, D., Weeks, B., Smith, J., Wingers, L.: The SIMON and SPECK lightweight block ciphers. In: 2015 52nd ACM/EDAC/IEEE Design Automation Conference (DAC), pp. 1–6. IEEE (2015)
6. Beierle, C., et al.: The SKINNY family of block ciphers and its low-latency variant MANTIS. In: Robshaw, M., Katz, J. (eds.) CRYPTO 2016. LNCS, vol. 9815, pp. 123–153. Springer, Heidelberg (2016). https://doi.org/10.1007/978-3-662-53008-5_5
7. Biryukov, A., Perrin, L.P.: State of the art in lightweight symmetric cryptography (2017)
8. Bogdanov, A., et al.: PRESENT: an ultra-lightweight block cipher. In: Paillier, P., Verbauwhede, I. (eds.) CHES 2007. LNCS, vol. 4727, pp. 450–466. Springer, Heidelberg (2007). https://doi.org/10.1007/978-3-540-74735-2_31

9. Borghoff, J., et al.: Prince-a low-latency block cipher for pervasive computing applications. Cryptology ePrint Archive, Report 2012/529 (2012). https://eprint.iacr.org/2012/529.pdf

10. Borghoff, J., et al.: PRINCE – a low-latency block cipher for pervasive computing applications. In: Wang, X., Sako, K. (eds.) ASIACRYPT 2012. LNCS, vol. 7658, pp. 208–225. Springer, Heidelberg (2012). https://doi.org/10.1007/978-3-642-34961-4_14

11. Daemen, J., Peeters, M., Van Assche, G., Rijmen, V.: Nessie proposal: NOEKEON. In: First Open NESSIE Workshop, pp. 213–230 (2000)

12. Elbirt, A.J., Paar, C.: An instruction-level distributed processor for symmetric-key cryptography. IEEE Trans. Parallel Distrib. Syst. 16(5), 468–480 (2005)

13. Goke, L.R., Lipovski, G.J.: Banyan networks for partitioning multiprocessor systems. In: ACM SIGARCH Computer Architecture News, vol. 2, pp. 21–28. ACM (1973)

14. Guo, J., Peyrin, T., Poschmann, A., Robshaw, M.: The LED block cipher. In: Preneel, B., Takagi, T. (eds.) CHES 2011. LNCS, vol. 6917, pp. 326–341. Springer, Heidelberg (2011). https://doi.org/10.1007/978-3-642-23951-9_22

15. Hanley, N., ONeill, M.: Hardware comparison of the ISO/IEC 29192-2 block ciphers. In: 2012 IEEE Computer Society Annual Symposium on VLSI (ISVLSI), pp. 57–62. IEEE (2012)

16. Jean, J., Nikolić, I., Peyrin, T.: Tweaks and keys for block ciphers: The TWEAKEY framework. In: Sarkar, P., Iwata, T. (eds.) ASIACRYPT 2014. LNCS, vol. 8874, pp. 274–288. Springer, Heidelberg (2014). https://doi.org/10.1007/978-3-662-45608-8_15

17. Kam, J.B., Davida, G.I.: Structured design of substitution-permutation encryption networks. IEEE Trans. Comput. 10, 747–753 (1979)

18. Lee, R.B., Shi, Z., Yang, X.: Efficient permutation instructions for fast software cryptography. IEEE Micro. 21(6), 56–69 (2001)

19. McKay, K.A., Bassham, L.E.: Meltem Sonmez Turan Report on lightweight cryptography (nist interagency/internal report (nistir) - 8114). Technical report, NIST Interagency/Internal Report (NISTIR) (2017)

20. Mentens, N., Charbon, E., Regazzoni, F.: Rethinking secure FPGAs: towards a cryptography-friendly configurable cell architecture and its automated design flow. In: 2018 IEEE 26th Annual International Symposium on Field-Programmable Custom Computing Machines (FCCM), pp. 215–215. IEEE (2018)

21. AES NIST: Advanced encryption standard. FIPS Publication, 197 (2001)

22. Rijmen, V., Daemen, J.: The Design of Rijndael: AES. The Advanced Encryption Standard. Springer, Heidelberg (2002). https://doi.org/10.1007/978-3-662-04722-4

23. Shibutani, K., Isobe, T., Hiwatari, H., Mitsuda, A., Akishita, T., Shirai, T.: *Piccolo*: an ultra-lightweight blockcipher. In: Preneel, B., Takagi, T. (eds.) CHES 2011. LNCS, vol. 6917, pp. 342–357. Springer, Heidelberg (2011). https://doi.org/10.1007/978-3-642-23951-9_23

24. Data Encryption Standard: Federal information processing standards publication 46. National Bureau of Standards, US Department of Commerce, 23 (1977)

25. Taylor, R.R., Goldstein, S.C.: A high-performance flexible architecture for cryptography. In: Koç, Ç.K., Paar, C. (eds.) CHES 1999. LNCS, vol. 1717, pp. 231–245. Springer, Heidelberg (1999). https://doi.org/10.1007/3-540-48059-5_20

Generating a Real-Time Constraint Engine for Network Protocols

Mohamed Sami Rakha[1], Fahim T. Imam[2(✉)], and Thomas R. Dean[2]

[1] School of Computing, Queen's University, Kingston, Ontario, Canada
m.rakha@queensu.ca
[2] Department of Electrical and Computer Engineering, Queen's University,
Kingston, Ontario, Canada
{fahim.imam,tom.dean}@queensu.ca

Abstract. In this paper, we present a practical approach to generate the constraint engine for an effective constraint-based intrusion detection system (IDS). The IDS framework was designed for safety-sensitive networks that involve limited-access closed networks such as the networks for command and control systems or Air Traffic Control (ATC) systems. The constraint engine generated by the framework supports real-time performance while ensuring the intended, normal behaviour of its target networks. We present the IDS framework in terms of its internal DSL representation as well as its transformation mechanisms to generate the constraint engine code. Comparing the autogenerated version against a manually implemented, optimized version of the constraint engine indicates no significant difference in terms of their performance.

Keywords: Intrusion detection · Domain-specific language ·
Network security · Real-time systems · Source code generation

1 Introduction

As part of a cybersecurity project, we designed an effective framework to generate a robust constraint-based Intrusion Detection System (IDS) [9] for limited-access closed networks. The IDS was designed to support real-time detection of intrusions for safety-sensitive networks while keeping the intended, normal behaviour of the networks intact for its authentic systems and agents. The IDS framework is envisaged to generate efficient executable code for all of its components, including the constraint engine, from a single specification document. The framework, therefore, supports practical usability for its constraint engine, allowing only limited human interventions for its code maintenance and change management. The key strength of the IDS framework is its realization of three levels of abstractions as follows:

1. The high-level description of the network protocols along with their constraints that can be written by the IDS users like Network Engineers;

ⓒ IFIP International Federation for Information Processing 2019
Published by Springer Nature Switzerland AG 2019
O. Blazy and C. Y. Yeun (Eds.): WISTP 2018, LNCS 11469, pp. 44–60, 2019.
https://doi.org/10.1007/978-3-030-20074-9_5

2. The mid-level specification of the constraints represented in an internal DSL that can be transformed from the high-level description;
3. The low-level abstraction representing the executable constraint engine code that can be autogenerated from the internal DSL.

In this paper, we present the current state of our IDS framework in terms of its internal DSL representation that corresponds to the mid-level abstraction above. We also present the transformation mechanism of the internal DSL that we have implemented to generate the low-level, executable code for the constraint engine. The DSL allows expressing different protocol-specific constraints in terms of their internal data structures and other computational details. Essentially, the DSL was designed to ensure optimal memory management and real-time performance for the constraint engine code. Extending based on our previous work [9], the DSL presented in this paper allows generalizing its mechanism to accommodate complex constraints that involve multiple valid sequences of packets with arbitrary order and length.

Prior to proposing the original DSL, we have also presented an optimization approach for the constraint engine which was manually implemented in C with promising results [9]. The manual version of the constraint engine code was used as a guide for our automatic code generation framework presented in this paper. Evaluating the generated constraint engine on a set of test cases with different constraints validates the correctness of the autogenerated code. Comparing the performance of the autogenerated constraint engine against the manually implemented version shows that there is no significant performance penalty to our autogenerated code.

The focus of our constraint engine is to achieve real-time performance when inspecting the network packets against a set of constraints and successfully detect any intrusion. The subsequent response to a detected intrusion, however, is outside the scope of our current research. We are currently working on implementing the high-level language to specify different constraints which will be used to autogenerate the internal DSL code discussed in this paper. We will present the high-level language along with its transformation mechanism in our next article.

2   Background

The scope of our research is an anomaly-based IDS for limited-access, closed networks such as industrial control networks or command and control systems such as the Air Traffic Control (ATC) systems. A key feature of these systems is that they all involve a limited number of known protocols with restrictive operations. The network traffic of these systems therefore involve much less variability than that of a conventional network. The queries, responses, and commands involved in these networks tend to have regular patterns that can be predefined and specified as a set of logical constraints. These constraints can then be used to characterize the traffic in terms of their normal, predefined patterns. The IDS can detect potential intrusions based on traffic that deviates from the specified constraints.

The IDS Framework. Figure 1 presents the high-level architecture of our IDS framework. The two main components of the framework are the packet parser

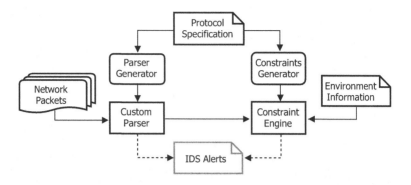

Fig. 1. The IDS framework.

and the constraint engine. Both of these components are automatically generated from the protocol specification document at the top. The specification document is meant to be written by the Network Engineers in a language called SCL [13] using their familiar ASN.1-based notations. SCL allows modular description of multiple protocols in terms of the syntax and semantics of their network traffic packets. The generated parser [6] reads the network packets and converts them into an internal structure for the constraint engine to use. In the process, the parser also validates the internal structure of the packets [6].

The main task of the constraint engine is to validate different constraints among the network packets. The engine is responsible for storing constraint-specific information from the incoming packets that can be used to check the validity of the later packets. The engine also supports the mechanism of automatically deleting the stored information when no longer needed. The interface between the parser and the constraint engine consists of dedicated callback entries for each of the protocol-specific packet type recognized by the parser.

As presented in Fig. 1 our IDS framework only requires minimal human intervention for its change management and code maintenance. Any changes to the network such as the addition of new systems or protocols simply require updating the protocol specification at the top. The underlying framework of the IDS will then take care of generating the new executable code for the parser and the constraint engine based on the updated specification.

The Evaluation Framework. While our IDS framework was designed to support any kind of network protocol, in order to demonstrate our approach we consider the Real Time Publish and Subscribe (RTPS) protocol [16] along with the Internet Group Message Protocol (IGMP) [3] as part of our evaluation framework. The RTPS protocol is a real-time implementation of the Data Distribution Service (DDS) framework [15], where some systems publish data (e.g. radar tracks) while the other systems subscribe to the data (e.g., air traffic control terminal, flight service station). RTPS protocol has been used in many critical domains and real-time applications such as NASA's Launch Control Networks and the Canadian Automated Air Traffic Management System [1]. One of the key concepts in DDS is that of a *topic* which refers to a particular message type and a quality of service. An example might be a radar track, or flight plan information. RTPS is a UDP protocol which uses both multicast and unicast messages. Multicast messages allow a publisher to send a single message that can be received by all subscribers. However, to track which systems are listening to multicast packets means we must also analyze the IGMP protocol, which is used to manage multicast UDP messages. Our IDS framework is being extended to support other UDP protocols such as the NTP [14], TFTP [21], and NFS [4].

The Threat Model. Our threat model is that the attacker has compromised one or more nodes of the network through an alternate channel such as USB and is looking to infect another node or to compromise the network function at some point in the future. In our case, the IDS must treat each of the incoming network packets as a suspicious entity. The contents of an incoming packet as well as its arriving sequence must be evaluated against a set of protocol-specific constraints in order to validate the packet's right to exist in the network traffic as a safe entity. The constraint engine for the anomaly-based IDS, therefore, requires a set of constraints for each of the protocol-specific packet types that collectively specify the normal behaviour of its target network.

There are three types of constraints that we are interested in. The first type involves the constraints specified by the protocol parser to validate the well-formedness of the network packets. The second type involves describing the constraints between the incoming packets and the network environment. For example, radar data and ADS-B [2] data may only originate from a specific set of systems. Finally, the third type of constraints involves describing the constraints among multiple packets along with their valid sequences. Three examples of constraints for the RTPS protocol are: RTPS packets have the correct format and structure, application data packets originate from the correct source addresses, and that an intruder has not introduced a new topic in order to suborn the DDS framework to provide communication between malware components.

3   Generating Constraint Engine Code

Each of the packet types within a network stream must have a set of associated constraints. A packet type refers to the protocol-specific type of the packet such as the `RTPS DATA` message packet. In our approach, the constraints are considered to be independent from each other. Each of the multipacket constraints must specify a set of *Packet Types*, $P = \{P_o, P_1, .., P_n, P_t, P_f\}$ that must exist in a particular order; where, P_o is the type of the `Initial Packet` of the sequence, $P_1, .., P_n$ are the types of the `Intermediate Packets` leading up to the `Target Packet` type, P_t, and the `Final Packet` type P_f after the P_t marks the closure of the packet sequence relevant to the constraint.

Each instance of the network constraints corresponds to a tree data structure, which is referred to as the *constraint tree* in this paper. Such a tree gradually collects data for its nodes from the stream of network packets. A constraint tree can be expressed using the prefix notation: `AND(OP(a, b), OP(c, d))`; where,

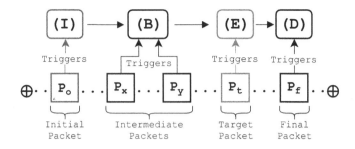

Fig. 2. Sequence of packets with constraint tree phases.

AND refers to the logical conjunction, OP is a logical operator such as equality (EQ) or non-equality (NEQ), and a, b, c, and d represent the leaf node data from different packets that must be evaluated. Hasan et al. [9] proposes a life-cycle model for the constraint trees with four consecutive phases: *Instantiate* (I), *Bind* (B), *Evaluate* (E) and *Destroy* (D). It is the life-cycle model of the constraint trees that dictates the overall memory management and the optimization of the constrain engine in order to achieve the real-time performance of our IDS.

3.1   The Constraint Tree Life-Cycle Model

Based on its corresponding constraint specification, each phase of the constraint tree is triggered by the arrival of a particular packet type within a stream of network packets. Figure 2 illustrates a generic scenario of a constraint that involves different packet types with a particular arriving sequence. In between the initial packet, P_o and the final packet, P_f, there could be many intermediate packets of different types; however, within those packets, the constraint is specific about the existence of three particular types of packets, P_x, P_y, and the target packet P_t, that must arrive in the specified order. The constraint tree phases along with their internal memory management processes are described below.

Instantiate is the first phase of a constraint tree instance which is triggered by the arrival of the initial packet type, P_o from a predefined sequence. In this phase, a memory space is allocated for the constraint tree and a reference to the tree is cached in a hash table that can be used by the later phases. The common values between the initial packet and the consecutive packet(s) are used as the keys for the hash table. Any data needed from the initial packet to evaluate the constraint are stored in the tree instance.

Bind is the second phase of a multi-packet constraint that has more than two packets. This phase involves the following tasks: validate the sequence of the arriving packets and fill out the empty leaves in the constraint tree. While our original approach [9] only allowed a single bind phase, the approach currently allows multiple bind phases to be defined for a constraint. Figure 2 illustrates that scenario by multiple intermediate packet types between the initial and the target packet types. In the first bind phase, the constraint engine retrieves the

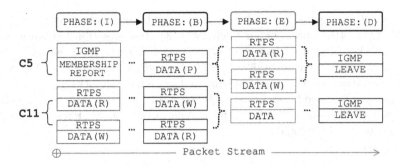

Fig. 3. The constraint tree phases in 2 different constraints.

tree from the instantiate hash table. In the case of more than one bind phases, the constraint tree will be passed from one bind phase to the next through one or more hash tables.

Evaluate is the phase in which the validity of the target packet P_t is evaluated. The triggering packet type P_t of this phase should provide the data for any remaining leaf nodes of the constraint tree. A security violation occurs if the evaluate phase fails to retrieve the tree from the hash table of the previous phase or the tree evaluates to a false value. The evaluate phase for the same tree instance can be executed every time a triggering packet arrives.

Destroy is the final phase of the life cycle which is triggered by the arrival of the final packet, P_f in the predefined packet sequence. As a result of this phase, the constraint tree is deleted from all the hash tables to free up memory.

3.2   The DSL Representation of Network Constraints

It should be noted that for the single-packet constraints, the life-cycle model only involves the evaluate phase for the P_t contents against a known set of environmental values. For two-packet constraints, the model simply involves the instantiate phase for the P_o and the evaluate phase for the P_t. The life-cycle model presented above is particularly useful for those constraints that involve more than two packets in a sequence with multiple alternative valid orders. In this section, we describe the internal DSL representation using two such constraints namely the $C5$ and $C11$. Figure 3 illustrates the possible sequences of packets involved in these two constraints in terms of their constraint tree phases.

> **Constraint** $C5$. All subscribers and publishers must be valid members of an IGMP multicast group. These participants must send their membership reports to specific group addresses before showing their interests in a topic.
>
> **Constraint** $C11$. The data of a certain topic is considered valid if it is produced from a valid publisher and consumed by a valid subscriber.

As reflected in Fig. 3, the target packet type to evaluate constraint $C5$ is
RTPS.DATA(W) (the publisher) or RTPS.DATA(R) (the subscriber) submessage of
an RTPS packet. The previous packet types, in order, are an RTPS packet containing a participant submessage, RTPS.DATA(P), and an IGMP membership report
packet. The IDS parser that we implemented can parse callbacks not only for the
entire packets but also for the meaningful parts of the packets such as the RTPS
submessages. Therefore, the constraint engine can use the RTPS submessage as
a trigger for its phase logic.

```
 1 CONSTRAINT C5 /* Constraint ID */
 2 /* Constraint Tree Expression for C5 */
 3 V(AND(EQ(SrcIPAddressNewJoin, SrcIPParticipant),
 4       EQ(GroupDestIPToBeJoined, DestIPParticipant)))
 5 INSTANTIATE
 6 IGMP Packet.Type is V2Report
 7  if not SEARCH Packet.srcIP, IGMP.groupaddr :Hash=hashIC5
 8       Tree.SrcIPAddressNewJoin = Packet.srcIP
 9       Tree.GroupDestIPToBeJoined = IGMP.groupaddr
10       Key = Packet.srcIP, IGMP.groupaddr
11       HashInstantiate = hashIC5
12  endif
13 BIND
14 RTPS FULL_RTPS.Type is DATAPSUB
15       REPEAT
16       HashInstantiate = hashIC5
17       KeyInstantiate = Packet.srcIP, Packet.dstIP
18       Tree.SrcIPParticipant = Packet.srcIP
19       Tree.DestIPParticipant = Packet.dstIP
20       Key = Packet.srcIP
21       HashBind = hashBC5
22 EVALUATE
23 RTPS FULL_RTPS.Type is DATARSUB Or FULL_RTPS.Type is DATAWSUB
24       HashBind = hashBC5
25   if SEARCH Packet.srcIP :Hash=hashBC5
26       EVAL Packet.srcIP
27   endif
28 DESTROY
29 IGMP Packet.Type is V2Leave
30   if SEARCH Packet.srcIP:Hash=hashBC5
31       HashBind = hashBC5
32       Key = Packet.srcIP
33   endif
34 END
```

Listing 1.1. The DSL Code for Constraint $C5$

Listing 1.1 shows the DSL representation for the constraint $C5$. The first line
of the code specifies the constraint ID (line 1). The constraint ID is a unique
identifier value that is used as a suffix in the generated code for each constraint.
Next, in line 3–4, we have the constraint tree expression in prefix notation. The
keywords INSTANTIATE, BIND, EVALUATE, and DESTROY correspond to the life-
cycle phases of the constraint tree, each followed by a triggering packet type as
specified in Fig. 3. For instance, the instantiate phase is triggered when reporting
the multi-cast group address of a network; i.e., arrival of the IGMP Membership
Report packet. The V2REPORT in line 6 refers to the Membership Report packet
from the IGMP version 2 specification. The packet type DATAPSUB in line 14
refers to an RTPS participant submessage, RTPS.DATA(P) which triggers the
bind phase. The packet types DATARSUB and DATAWSUB in lines 23 correspond to

the RTPS subscriber and publisher submessages. In line 29, the V2Leave packet type corresponds to the leave submessage from the IGMP version 2 specification.

Tree Instance Hashing. The DSL proposed by Hasan et al. [9] had two implicit hash tables to hold the constraint tree between the instantiate and bind phase, and between the bind and evaluate phase. In our DSL, each of the instantiate and bind phase can have an unlimited number of defined hash tables. In Listing 1.1, line 10 shows an example of assigning key fields from the packet while line 11 defines the hash table name hashIC5. During the bind phase, the constraint engine should be able to find the constraint tree in the instantiate hash table. The constraint engine uses key fields from the triggering packet to lookup the constraint tree instance created in the instantiate phase. In Listing 1.1, the hash table name for the instantiate is defined in line 16 while the necessary key fields are defined in line 17.

The bind phase updates the constraint tree by filling the empty leaves with the appropriate packet fields as in lines 18–19 of Listing 1.1. The bind phase stores the updated constraint tree in the bind hash table. In Listing 1.1, the hash table name and key fields for bind phase are defined in lines 20–21. The hash table name and key fields used by the evaluate phase are defined in lines 24 and 26. Finally, the destroy phase deallocates the constraint tree from the defined hash tables. Based on the constraint specification, the autogenerated constraint engine may have an unlimited number of hard-coded definitions of hash tables for the instantiate and bind phases.

Hash Table Naming. In our current DSL, each hash table should have a unique name throughout the constraint engine code. In Listing 1.1, the variable HashInstantiate holds the hash table name for the instantiate phase of constraint $C5$. While the variable HashBind holds the hash table name for the bind phase. The constraint phases should access any of the hash tables by their unique names. For example, the bind phase should be able to find the constraint tree allocated previously at the instantiate phase. Therefore, the HashInstantiate is specified twice in the DSL of Listing 1.1 - first in the instantiate clause and the next in the bind clause. The DSL grammar allows the naming of multiple hash tables when the phase clause holds multiple cases. Listing 1.2 shows an example of multiple hash tables within the same phase clause for constraint $C11$. In $C11$ example, the instantiate phase has two hash tables: hashIC11_DATARSUB and hashIC11_DATAWSUB. Each one of these hash tables is accessed at different cases based on the logical sequence.

Hash Table Management. Figure 4 summarizes the hashing mechanism among the four phases of a constraint tree. During the instantiate phase, the constraint engine instantiates a tree for the constraint C_x and inserts its reference to a hash table. The location of the tree reference in the hash table is determined by the hash key value. The packet fields used to calculate the key value should be specified in the DSL. For example, Listing 1.1 for $C5$ defines srcIP and groupaddr as the key fields for its hash table hashIC5. Based on these two fields, a reference to constraint tree is located in the hash table hashIC5. In

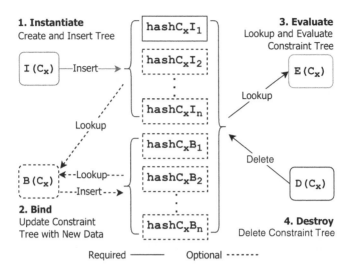

Fig. 4. The constraint tree phases and hashing.

some cases, the calculated key value may point to an already existing hashing slot causing a collision [23]. In such a case of collision, the old tree is deleted and the hash slot is updated with a new tree instance. At the bind phase, the instantiate tree reference is copied from the instantiate hash table into the bind hash table. In $C5$ example, the bind hash table is `hashBC5`. At the end of the bind phase, the copied tree reference is deleted from the instantiate hash table to free up space. However, the DSL allows disabling this deletion by adding the keyword `SPLIT` in the bind clause. In case of collision, the tree update can be ignored by adding the keyword `REPEAT`. For example, Listing 1.1 for $C5$ has the keyword `REPEAT` at line 15. During the evaluate phase, the constraint tree is retrieved from the hash table specified by the name in variable `HashBind`, if available. Otherwise, the constraint engine should report a security violation. The evaluate phase does not change the content of the hash tables. In our approach, the generated hashing uses the linear probing algorithm with a relatively prime step size [7]. However, other hashing algorithms that support deletion can be used.

Constraint Generalization. The automatic generation approach takes into consideration the generality of constraint specifications. One of the challenging generalizations is the cross scenarios handling. The cross scenarios happen when the constraint specification permits the same triggering packets for more than one phase. For instance, the constraint $C11$ in Listing 1.2. The target of the constraint determines if a data message of a given RTPS topic is produced by a valid publisher and consumed by a valid subscriber. Both the instantiate and bind phases can be triggered by a `DATA(W)` or a `DATA(R)` as depicted in Fig. 3. For such a case, the generated constraint engine must conform to the accurate scenario by checking if the other packet has already arrived. We use the `SEARCH` function (in Line 8 and Line 24) to check if the other packet has arrived by the availability of constraint tree in hash table.

In Listing 1.2, we added the `if` condition at the start of each phase case to handle the cross scenario generalization. Another example of generalization is the multiple triggering packets for the same phase. We can observe that $C11$ specification handles such a case by applying a `switch` block. Each packet type in such case will represent a triggering packet type. The same approach can be applied to extend the $C5$ specifications. In $C5$ instantiate and destroy phases, we add switch statements to handle older versions of `IGMP Report` packets. Listing 1.3 shows the two phases after generalization.

```
 1 CONSTRAINT C11
 2 V(AND(EQ(SrcIPPublisher, DesIPfromSubscriber), EQ(PublisherSrtPort),
 3       EQ(entityIDPublisher), EQ(SrcIPSubscriber)))
 4 INSTANTIATE
 5 RTPS FULL_RTPS.Type is DATAWSUB Or FULL_RTPS.Type is DATARSUB
 6 switch (FULL_RTPS.Type)
 7  case DATAWSUB:
 8     if not SEARCH HashKey(.pidtopicname_rtps.topicname.name
 9         IN Protoco~serializeddata~topicdata:type,
10         PIDTOPICNAME_RTPS_VAL), Packet.srcIP, Packet.dstIP
11         :Hash=hashIC11_DATARSUB
12     endif
13  case DATARSUB:
14     if not SEARCH HashKey(.pidtopicname_rtps.topicname.name
15         IN Protocol~serializeddata~topicdata:type,
16         PIDTOPICNAME_RTPS_VAL), Packet.dstIP, Packet.srcIP
17         :Hash=hashIC11_DATAWSUB
18     endif
19 endswitch
20 BIND
21 RTPS FULL_RTPS.Type is DATAWSUB Or FULL_RTPS.Type is DATARSUB
22 switch (FULL_RTPS.Type)
23 case DATARSUB:   /* Case Logic */
24     if SEARCH HashKey(.pidtopicname_rtps.topicname.name IN Protocol~
        serializeddata~topicdata:type,PIDTOPICNAME_RTPS_VAL), Packet.dstIP,
        Packet.srcIP :Hash=hashIC11_DATAWSUB
25     endif
26 case DATAWSUB:   /* Case Logic */
27     if SEARCH  HashKey(.pidtopicname_rtps.topicname.name IN Protocol~
        serializeddata~topicdata:type,PIDTOPICNAME_RTPS_VAL), Packet.srcIP,
        Packet.dstIP:Hash=hashIC11_DATARSUB
28     endif
29 endswitch
```

Listing 1.2. The DSL Code for Constraint $C11$

```
 1 INSTANTIATE
 2 IGMP Packet.Type is V2Report Or Packet.Type is V3Report
 3 switch (Packet.Type)
 4 case V2Report: /* Case Logic */
 5     if  not SEARCH Packet.srcIP, IGMP.groupaddr :Hash=hashIC5
 6     endif
 7 case V3Report: /* Case Logic */
 8     loop for groupaddr in IGMP.grouprecordinfo
 9         if not SEARCH Packet.srcIP, Iterator.groupaddr :Hash=hashIC5
10         endif
11     endloop
12 endswitch
13 /* The Bind phase followed by the Evaluate phase [Same as Listing 1] */
14 DESTROY
15 IGMP Packet.Type is V2Leave Or Packet.Type is V3Leave
```

```
16 switch (Packet.Type)
17 case V2Leave:   /* Case Logic */
18    if SEARCH Packet.srcIP:Hash=hashBC5
19    endif
20 case V3Leave:   /* Case Logic */
21        if SEARCH Packet.srcIP:Hash=hashBC5
22        endif
23 endswitch
24 END
```

Listing 1.3. DSL Code for Generalized Constraint C5

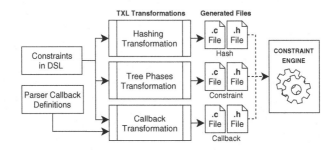

Fig. 5. Automatic generation of the constraint engine code.

3.3 Implementation

An overview of our implemented autogeneration framework for the constraint engine code is presented in Fig. 5. Based on the constraints specified in the DSL input, the framework requires three kinds of transformations to generate the necessary C files for the constraint engine. These include the transformations for the hashing, the constraint tree phases, and the parser callbacks, as depicted in the figure. We used the TXL [5] as the transformation language between the DSL and the constraint engine code. After the transformations, all the generated C files of the IDS are compiled to build a binary executable file. The binary file includes the parser and the autogenerated constraint engine.

Four snippets of the generated code for constraint $C5$ are presented in this section. First is the example of **hash.h** file in Listing 1.4 that includes the function prototypes of the generated hashing operations for the $C5$ constraint tree. Next, in Listing 1.5, we have the generated code for **constraint.h** which includes the function prototypes of the constraint tree phases. Notice how the function parameters correspond to the $C5$ DSL in Listing 1.1. For example, the function **instantiateC5_V2Report(..)** in Line 1 requires a pair of key fields, followed by a pair of leaf node values based on lines 8–10 of the instantiate clause in $C5$ DSL 1.1. Listing 1.6 presents the generated implementation of the $C5$ bind function for the **constraint.c** file. The bind implementation calls different hash functions to retrieve and update each tree instance.

```
 1 typedef struct {
 2     uint32_t SrcIPAddressNewJoin;
 3     uint32_t SrcIPParticipant;
 4     uint32_t GroupDestIPToBeJoined;
 5     uint32_t DestIPParticipant;
 6 } treeHashC5;
 7 int insertIValueC5V2Report (uint32_t key1, uint32_t key2, uint32_t
       SrcIPAddressNewJoin, uint32_t GroupDestIPToBeJoined);
 8 int deleteValueIhashIC5 (uint32_t key1, uint32_t key2);
 9 treeHashC5* GetValuefromfhashIC5 (uint32_t key1, uint32_t key2);
10 int insertIValueC5V3Report (uint32_t key1, uint32_t key2, uint32_t
       SrcIPAddressNewJoin, uint32_t GroupDestIPToBeJoined);
11 int insertBValueC5hashBC5 (uint32_t key1, uint32_t SrcIPParticipant,
       uint32_t DestIPParticipant, treeHashC5* treeInst);
12 int deleteValueBhashBC5 (uint32_t key1);
13 treeHashC5* GetValuefromfhashBC5 (uint32_t key1);
14 void clearC5 ();
```

Listing 1.4. Generated Code in **hash.h** for $C5$.

```
 1 int instantiateC5_V2Report (uint32_t key1, uint32_t key2, uint32_t
       SrcIPAddressNewJoin, uint32_t GroupDestIPToBeJoined, unsigned long
       pktCount);
 2 int instantiateC5_V3Report (uint32_t key1, uint32_t key2, uint32_t
       SrcIPAddressNewJoin, uint32_t GroupDestIPToBeJoined, unsigned long
       pktCount);
 3 int bind1C5 (uint32_t instatiate_key1, uint32_t instatiate_key2, uint32_t
       key1, uint32_t SrcIPParticipant, uint32_t DestIPParticipant, unsigned
       long pktCount);
 4 int evaluateC5 (uint32_t key1, unsigned long pktCount);
 5 int destroyC5_V2Leave (uint32_t key1, unsigned long pktCount);
 6 int destroyC5_V3Leave (uint32_t key1, unsigned long pktCount);
```

Listing 1.5. Generated Code in **constraint.h** for $C5$.

```
 1 int bind1C5 (uint32_t instantiate_key1, uint32_t instantiate_key2, uint32_t
       key1, uint32_t SrcIPParticipant, uint32_t DestIPParticipant, unsigned
       long pktCount){
 2 if (true){
 3   treeHashC5* insTree=GetValuefromfhashIC5(instantiate_key1,
       instantiate_key2);
 4   if (insTree==NULL){iC5f++; iC5bindf++; return -1;}
 5    else {}
 6   treeHashC5* bindTree=GetValuefromfhashBC5(key1);
 7   bool noRepeat=false;
 8   if (bindTree!=NULL){if (!noRepeat) return 1;}
 9   bool split=false;
10   if (split){
11     treeHashC5* splitedTree=malloc(sizeof(treeHashC5));
12     memcpy (splitedTree, insTree, sizeof(treeHashC5));
13     bindTree=splitedTree;}
14     else if (!noRepeat){
15     treeHashC5* splitedTree=malloc(sizeof(treeHashC5));
16     memcpy (splitedTree, insTree, sizeof(treeHashC5));
17     bindTree=splitedTree;}
18       else {bindTree=insTree;}
19   if (insertBValueC5hashBC5 (key1, SrcIPParticipant, DestIPParticipant,
       bindTree) == -1)
20     {iC5f++; iC5bindf++; return -1;}
21   if (noRepeat){if (!split){if (deleteValueIhashIC5 (instantiate_key1 ,
       instantiate_key2) == -1){
22       iC5f++; iC5bindf++; return -1;}}}
23   iC5bind++; return 1;}
24 else return 1;}
```

Listing 1.6. Snippet of Generated Code in **constraint.c** for $C5$

```
1 void V2Report_IGMP_callback(V2Report_IGMP *v2report_igmp, PDU *thePDU){
2     struct HeaderInfo *Packet = thePDU->header;
3     instantiateC5_V2Report (Packet->srcIP,
4         v2report_igmp->groupaddr, Packet->srcIP,
5         v2report_igmp->groupaddr, Packet->pktCount);}
```

Listing 1.7. IGMP V2Report with a trigger call to $C5$ Instantiate Phase.

Finally, Listing 1.7 shows an example of triggering the $C5$ instantiate phase within the generated callback function of IGMP V2Report based on the instantiate phase of the $C5$ DSL in Listing 1.1. The callback function headers are predefined in the parser and used as inputs for the callback transformation. The callback functions passes the triggering packets defined in the constraint specifications and fills the required parameters of the tree phases. The transformation keeps appending the callback functions into the callback.c file for different triggering packets based on the constraint tree phases.

4   Results and Evaluation

The generated IDS has been tested against four different constraints with the test cases listed in Table 1. Each of the cases in the table was intentionally induced in separate packet capture (pcap) files. As shown in Table 1, each of the four constraints has a normal scenario where the IDS should pass with no violations, along with a set of abnormal cases with anomalous packets. The violation checks reported by the generated constraint engine are consistent with the test case expectations, proving the correctness of the constraint engine code.

Table 1. Test cases with four constraints.

	$C5$ Tests	$C8$ Tests
✓	Normal	Normal
✗	Missing IGMP Packet in the Sequence	Wrong Topic Name in DATA(W)
✗	Wrong Group Address in IGMP Report	-
	$C11$ Tests	$C12$ Tests
✓	Normal	Normal
✗	Wrong SrcIP in IGMP DATA(W)	Wrong SrcIP in IGMP DATA(W)
✗	Wrong DestIP in IGMP DATA(W)	Wrong SrcIP in IGMP DATA

Figure 6 shows the performance results on the run-time averages of the two IDS versions on three pcap files. For our evaluation, we used the same set of pcap files used by Hasan et al. [9] against the same three constraints: $C5$, $C11$ and $C8$. We run each IDS 10 times for each pcap file. Each of the IDS was ran on an Ubantu Linux 64-bit VM with Intel core i7 processor using 2 GB of RAM.

As we can observe in Fig. 6, the autogenerated IDS is slower with a maximum drop of less than 6%. The results indicate that there is a slight drop in the

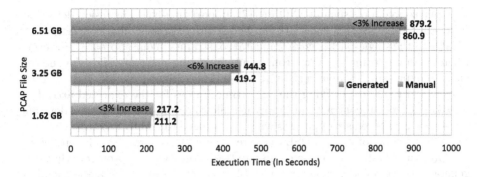

Fig. 6. Performance comparison between the constraint engines.

performance for the autogenerated IDS in contrast to the manually implemented version. However, the performance difference is insignificant. These results highlight that the automatic generation of the constraint engine presented in this paper does not lead to a significant performance penalty.

5   Related Work and Discussion

While there exist various approaches to develop an IDS [12], the premise of our approach is an anomaly-based IDS [8] for limited-access closed-networks which involve a limited number of protocols. Various anomaly-based approaches have been studied that apply Machine Learning (ML) techniques [22] to identify suspicious patterns in the network traffic. However, the ML-based approaches are typically useful for conventional public networks that involve a broad variety of protocols with variable traffic patterns that are hard to prognosticate. Since the target networks of our IDS solely involve a limited number of protocols with restrictive operational patterns, we did not consider any ML-based technique for our approach. Our approach is based on the idea of inspecting each of the network packets against a finite set of protocol-specific constraints that are already known. We considered achieving real-time performance and automatic generation of our constraint-based IDS [9] to be the key challenges for our approach.

Satisfying network constraints can be considered similar to finding frequent patterns in the data stream. Various tree-based approaches have been considered in literature for different applications [11,18,20]. A key limitation of these approaches is that they require maintaining large constraint trees to express their desired patterns. Against streaming data in large scale, even with efficient pruning algorithms, traversing and updating such constraint trees would require continuous memory operation which is bound to cause major bottlenecks in performance. In our approach, using the constraint tree life-cycle model we instantiate a simple tree for each of the individual constraints with optimized memory management. Using the hashing mechanism presented in this paper, our approach allows accessing the required tree nodes in the memory or removing a tree from memory, both in constant time.

Open source tools such as SNORT [17] support rule-based intrusion detection techniques. The SNORT rules [10] can be used to express similar concerns comparable to the single-packet environmental constraints in our approach. However, when it comes to multi-packet constraints involving a set of valid sequence of packets, expressing them using SNORT-based rules are not feasible. Writing such rules would require specifying the exact time frames for the expected arrival of related packets. In contrast, our approach allows defining the partial-order patterns on the required set of packets without the need to specify any time window. In a related effort of using a DSL to express network constraints, Salgueiro et al. [19] present a DSL to describe common attacks on TCP/IP protocols that can generate solution code. However, the DSL was not designed to handle the kind of multi-packet constraints that we needed for the DDS networks.

Generating automated code has been used in various Model-Driven Engineering projects. These projects usually involve generating operational code from a model specifying the system to be created. Our code generation approach is distinct in that we are generating the code to validate the network data against the models. The generated constraint engine code by our IDS framework checks the validity of the traffic data against a set of protocol-specific behavioural models of the target networks.

6   Conclusion and Future Work

In this paper, we have presented an effective approach to autogenerate a constraint engine through a practical IDS framework. The approach implements and extends our earlier DSL proposed by Hasan et al. [9] and generalizes its representation to accommodate any kind of complex multi-packet constraints that involve alternative sequences of packets with arbitrary length and order. We have successfully implemented a mechanism to transform the internal DSL into executable constraint engine code using TXL.

Comparing the performance of the autogenerated constraint engine against the manually implemented version displays no significant performance overhead. The correctness of the generated constraint engine was evaluated based on four different test cases. For our next evaluation, we plan to involve a third-party Red team to incorporate a comprehensive collection of malicious activities on our simulation environment for an ATC network.

We are currently working on generating the internal DSL from an SCL-based high-level constraint specification language suitable for the Network Engineers to use. The SCL language, already being used to generate the parser for our IDS framework, is modular, which allows easy specification of multiple protocols for a given network. Finally, since the IDS framework only allows autogenerating its constraint engine from a high-level specification, the approach requires minimum human interventions. The intricate implementation details of the constraint engine are not needed to be coded or managed by humans which eliminates the possibility of having human-induced errors and heavy maintenance overhead when adapting a new set of protocols and systems for the IDS.

Acknowledgements. This research is supported by the Department of National Defence (DND), Canada, The Natural Sciences and Engineering Research Council of Canada (NSERC), and The Ontario Research Foundation (ORF), Canada.

References

1. NAV CANADA. The Canadian Automated Air Traffic System. https://takecharge.navcanada.ca/. Accessed 11 May 2018
2. Baud, O., Honore, N., Taupin, O.: Radar/ADS-B data fusion architecture for experimentation purpose. In: 2006 9th International Conference on Information Fusion, pp. 1–6. IEEE (2006)
3. Cain, B., Deering, S., Kouvelas, I., Fenner, B., Thyagarajan, A.: Internet group management protocol, version 3. Technical report (2002)
4. Callaghan, B., Pawlowski, B., Staubach, P.: NFS version 3 protocol specification. Technical report (1995)
5. Cordy, J.R.: The TXL source transformation language. Sci. Comput. Program. **61**(3), 190–210 (2006)
6. ElShakankiry, A., Dean, T.: Context sensitive and secure parser generation for deep packet inspection of binary protocols. In: 2017 15th Annual Conference on Privacy, Security and Trust (PST), Calgary, Canada, pp. 77–7709. IEEE (2017). https://doi.org/10.1109/PST.2017.00019
7. Flajolet, P., Poblete, P., Viola, A.: On the analysis of linear probing hashing. Algorithmica **22**(4), 490–515 (1998)
8. Garcia-Teodoro, P., Diaz-Verdejo, J., Maciá-Fernández, G., Vázquez, E.: Anomaly-based network intrusion detection: techniques, systems and challenges. Comput. Secur. **28**(1–2), 18–28 (2009)
9. Hasan, M.S., Dean, T., Imam, F.T., Garcia, F., Leblanc, S.P., Zulkernine, M.: A constraint-based intrusion detection system. In: Proceedings of the 5th European Conference on the Engineering of Computer-Based Systems, ECBS 2017, pp. 12:1–12:10. ACM, New York (2017). https://doi.org/10.1145/3123779.3123812
10. Khamphakdee, N., Benjamas, N., Saiyod, S.: Improving intrusion detection system based on SNORT rules for network probe attack detection. In: 2014 2nd International Conference on Information and Communication Technology (ICoICT), pp. 69–74. IEEE (2014)
11. Kurien, L.S., Sreekumar, K., Minu, K.K.: Survey on constrained based data stream mining. Int. J. Comput. Appl. **107**(16), 12–15 (2014)
12. Liao, H.J., Lin, C.H.R., Lin, Y.C., Tung, K.Y.: Intrusion detection system: a comprehensive review. J. Netw. Comput. Appl. **36**(1), 16–24 (2013)
13. Marquis, S., Dean, T.R., Knight, S.: SCL: a language for security testing of network applications. In: Proceedings of the 2005 Conference of the Centre for Advanced Studies on Collaborative Research, pp. 155–164. IBM Press (2005)
14. Mills, D., Martin, J., Burbank, J., Kasch, W.: Network time protocol version 4: Protocol and algorithms specification. Technical report (2010)
15. Pardo-Castellote, G.: OMG data-distribution service: architectural overview. In: 2003 Proceedings of the 23rd International Conference on Distributed Computing Systems Workshops, pp. 200–206. IEEE (2003)
16. Object Management Group: The Real-time Publish-Subscribe Protocol (RTPS) DDS Interoperability Wire Protocol Specification OMG Document Number: formal/2014-09-01. http://www.omg.org/spec/DDSI-RTPS/2.2. Accessed April 2019

17. Park, W., Ahn, S.: Performance comparison and detection analysis in SNORT and Suricata environment. Wirel. Pers. Commun. **94**(2), 241–252 (2017)
18. Potharst, R., Feelders, A.J.: Classification trees for problems with monotonicity constraints. In: Special Interest Group (SIG) on Knowledge Discovery and Data Mining Explorations (SIGKDD), vol. 4, pp. 1–10 (2002)
19. Salgueiro, P., Abreu, S.: On using constraints for network intrusion detection. In: INForum (2010)
20. Silva, A., Antunes, C.: Pushing constraints into data streams. In: Proceedings of the 2nd International Workshop on Big Data, Streams and Heterogeneous Source Mining: Algorithms, Systems, Programming Models and Applications, pp. 79–86. ACM (2013)
21. Sollins, K.: The TFTP protocol (revision 2) (1992)
22. Tsai, C.F., Hsu, Y.F., Lin, C.Y., Lin, W.Y.: Intrusion detection by machine learning: a review. Expert Syst. Appl. **36**(10), 11994–12000 (2009)
23. Wolper, P., Leroy, D.: Reliable hashing without collision detection. In: Courcoubetis, C. (ed.) CAV 1993. LNCS, vol. 697, pp. 59–70. Springer, Heidelberg (1993). https://doi.org/10.1007/3-540-56922-7_6

Cryptography

Principles of Discontinuous Dynamical Systems

Principles of Discontinuous Dynamical Systems

Marat Akhmet

Middle East Technical University, Ankara, Turkey

 Springer

Marat Akhmet
Middle East Technical University
Department of Mathematics
06531 Ankara, Turkey
Marat@metu.edu.tr

ISBN 978-1-4899-9956-6   ISBN 978-1-4419-6581-3 (eBook)
DOI 10.1007/978-1-4419-6581-3
Springer New York Dordrecht Heidelberg London

Mathematics Subject Classification (2010): 34-01, 34-02, 34A12, 34A37, 34C23, 34C25, 34C28, 34D09, 34D20, 34D45, 34E05, 37G15, 37D45, 37D99, 37N05

Printed on acid-free paper

Springer is part of Springer Science+Business Media (www.springer.com)

To my beloved mother, wife and daughters:
Zhanar and Laila

Preface

The main subject of this book is discontinuous dynamical systems. These have played an extremely important role theoretically, as well as in applications, for the last several decades. Still, the theory of these systems seems very far from being complete, and there is still much to do to make the application of the theory more effective. This is especially true of equations with trajectories discontinuous at moments that are not prescribed.

The book is written not only on the basis of research experience but also, importantly, on the basis of the experience of teaching the course of Impulsive differential equations for about 10 years to the graduate students of mathematics. It is useful for a beginner as we try not to avoid any difficult instants in delivering the material. Delicate questions that are usually ignored in a research monograph are thoroughly addressed. The standard material on equations with fixed moments of impulses is presented in a compact and definitive form. It contains a large number of exercises, examples, and figures, which will aid the reader in understanding the enigmatic world of discontinuous dynamics. The following peculiarity is very important: the material is built on the basis of close parallelism with ordinary differential equations theory. For example, even higher order differentiability of solutions, which has never been considered before, is presented with a full definition and detailed proofs. At the same time, the definition of the derivatives as coefficients of the expansion is fruitfully used, which is very rare in the theory of ordinary differential equations. Moreover, the description of stability, continuous and differentiable dependence of solutions on initial conditions, and right-hand side, chaotic ingredients is given on a more strong functional basis than that of ordinary differential equations.

The book is attractive to an advanced researcher, since a strong background for the future analysis of all theoretical and application problems is built. It will benefit scientists working in other fields of differential equations with discontinuities of various types, since it reflects the experience of the author in working on these subjects. We would like to emphasize that the basics of discontinuous flows are for the first time rigorously laid out so that all the attributes of dynamical systems are present. Hence, there is plenty of room for extending all the results of continuous, smooth and analytic dynamics to the systems with discontinuities.

The content of the book is a good background for the application in vibro-mechanisms theory, mechanisms with friction, biology, molecular biology, physiology, pharmacology, secure communications, neural networks, and other real world problems involving discontinuities.

Chapters 5–10 contain the core research contributions. Chapters 1–4 present preliminaries for the theory and elements of differential equations with fixed moments of discontinuity. Chapters 1–8 provide sufficient material for a standard one-semester graduate course. It is natural to finalize a general theory with more specific results. For this reason, in the last two chapters (9 and 10) we discuss Hopf bifurcation of periodic discontinuous solutions, Devaney's chaos, and the Shadowing property for discontinuous dynamical systems.

The author expresses his gratitude to his students who have contributed to the preparation of this book: Duygu Arugaslan, Cemil Buyukadali, Mehmet Turan, and Enes Yilmaz.

Contents

Chapter 1
Introduction

Nowadays, many mathematicians agree that discontinuity as well as continuity should be considered when one seeks to describe the real world more adequately. The idea that, besides continuity, discontinuity is a property of motion is as old as the idea of motion itself. This understanding was strong in ancient Greece. For example, it was expressed in paradoxes of Zeno. Invention of calculus by Newton and Leibniz in its last form, and the development of the analysis adjunct to celestial mechanics, which was stimulating for the founders of the theory of dynamical systems, took us away from the concept of discontinuity. The domination of continuous dynamics, and also smooth dynamics, has been apparent for a long time. However, the application of differential equations in mechanics, electronics, biology, neural networks, medicine, and social sciences often necessitates the introduction of discontinuity, as either abrupt interruptions of an elsewhere continuous process (impulsive differential equations) or in the form of discrete time setting (difference equations). If difference equations may be considered as an instrument of investigation of continuous motion through, for example, Poincaré maps, impulsive differential equations seem appropriate for modeling motions where continuous changes are mixed with impact type changes in equal proportion. Recently, it is becoming clear that to discuss real world systems that (1) exist for a long period of time, or (2) are multidimensional, with a large number of dependent variables, researchers resort to differential equations with: (1) discontinuous trajectories (impulsive differential equations); (2) switching in the right-hand side (differential equations with discontinuous right-hand side); (3) some coordinates ruled by discrete equations (hybrid systems); (4) disconnected domains of existence of solutions (time scale differential equations), where these properties may be combined in a single model.

The theory of equations with discontinuous trajectories has been developed through applications [14, 16, 38, 41, 43, 50, 52, 53, 56, 57, 70, 71, 75, 79, 89, 91, 99, 101, 103, 107–109, 115, 121, 123, 125–127, 130, 144, 145, 155, 158–160, 162] and theoretical challenges [4–9, 19, 32–36, 65, 69, 75, 85, 95–97, 99–101, 103, 110, 111, 118–124, 135–142, 151–153].

We give a limited number of references, since this work was written as a textbook rather than a research monograph, and secondly, sources related to systems with nonfixed moments of discontinuity were preferentially presented.

M. Akhmet, *Principles of Discontinuous Dynamical Systems*,
DOI 10.1007/978-1-4419-6581-3_1, © Springer Science+Business Media, LLC 2010

Our main objective is to present the theory of differential equations with solutions that have discontinuities either at the moments when the integral curves reach certain surfaces in the extended phase space (t, x), as time t increases (decreases), or at the moments when the trajectories enter certain sets in the phase space x. That is, the moments when the solutions have discontinuities are not prescribed. Notably, the systems with nonprescribed times of discontinuity were first introduced in [91, 123, 124], manuscripts in applied mathematics, which underscores the practical importance of the theory of equations with variable moments of impulses. Differential equations with fixed moments of impulses were the next to be studied. These serve as an auxiliary instrument for the study of the above named systems in the same way as nonautonomous equations play a role in the analysis of autonomous systems through linearization. For that reason, we provide a more extensive discussion of the theory of equations with fixed moments of impulses, than might otherwise seem necessary. It takes the first four chapters of the manuscript. We thoroughly describe the solutions of these equations, consider the existence and uniqueness of solutions and their dependence on parameters. The problem of extension of a solution for both increasing and decreasing time is investigated. For example, we prove the Gronwall–Bellman Lemma for piecewise continuous functions, and the integral representation formulas, for decreasing time, as well as for increasing time. This extension of the results is obviously necessary to explore dynamical systems' properties in the fullest form, as required for applications. Since the moments of discontinuities are different for different solutions, the equations are nonlinear. Equations with nonfixed moments of discontinuity create a great number of opportunities for theoretical inquiry, as well as theoretical challenges. This is due to the structure of these systems, namely the three components: a differential equation, an impulsive action, and the surfaces of discontinuity which are involved in the process of governing the motion. Therefore, in addition to the features of the ordinary differential equations, we may vary the properties of the maps, which transform the phase point at the moment of impulse, and try various topological and differential characteristics of the surfaces of discontinuity to produce one or another interesting theoretical phenomenon, or satisfy a desired application property.

Effective methods of investigation of systems with nonfixed moments of impulsive action can be found in [2–4, 32–36, 65, 69, 95–97, 123, 124, 135, 136, 142, 152, 153]. Theoretical problems of nonsmooth dynamics and discontinuous maps [17, 19, 38, 48, 51, 66, 68, 86, 92, 93, 146] are also close to the subject matter of our book.

The present book plays its own modest role in attracting the attention of scientists, first of all mathematicians, to the symbiosis of continuity and discontinuity in the description of a motion.

The book presented to the attention of the reader is to be viewed first and foremost as a textbook on the theory of discontinuous dynamical systems. There is some similarity between the content of this book and that of the monographs on ordinary differential equations. Accordingly, we deliver some standard topics: description of the systems, definition of solutions, local existence and uniqueness theorems, extension of solutions, dependence of solutions on parameters. It is our conviction that many results of the theory of equations with impulses (if not all), that at the moment appear as very specific, in fact, have their counterparts in the theory of ordinary differential equations. We take up the task of extending the parallels with the theory of continuous (smooth) dynamical systems. It seems appropriate to place the results on the existence of periodic solutions and Hopf bifurcation of periodic solutions in the final part of the book. The last chapter is devoted to complex motions, in whose description we use ingredients of Devaney chaos. It is noteworthy that the method of creation of chaos through impulses does not have analogs in continuous dynamics yet. We bring up only a few examples to illustrate the possibilities for application.

We use a powerful analytical tool of B-equivalence, which was introduced and developed in our papers. The method was created especially for the investigation of systems with solutions that have discontinuities at variable moments of time [1–4, 25–37]. But it can also be applied to differential equations with discontinuous right-hand-side [13, 15, 27, 34] and differential equations on variable time scales with transition conditions [20]. The method is effective in the analysis of chaotic systems [8–11], as well.

In the last decades, the exceptional role of differential equations with impulses at variable times in dealing with problems of mechanisms with vibrations has been perceived. Collision-bifurcations, oscillations, and chaotic processes in this mechanisms have been investigated in many papers and books [67, 79, 118, 119, 144, 151, 156]. We are very confident that the content of this book will give a strong push to the development of this field, as well as other related areas of research, where a discontinuity appears.

Let us consider the following examples, which highlight the modeling role of discontinuous dynamics.

Example 1.1. Consider a mechanical model consisting of a bead B bouncing on a massive, sinusoidally vibrating table P (see Fig. 1.1). Such a system has been investigated in [71, 79, 89, 133, 158]. We assume that the table is so massive that

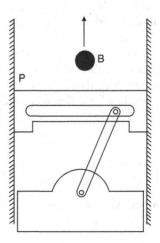

Fig. 1.1 A model consisting of a bead bouncing on a vibrating table

it does not react to collisions with the bead and moves according to the law $X = X_0 \sin \omega t$. The motion of the bead between collisions is given by the formula

$$x = \frac{-g(t - t_0)^2}{2} + x_0'(t - \phi) + x_0, \tag{1.1}$$

where x_0 and x_0' are, respectively, the values of the coordinate and the velocity of the bead at the instant $t = \phi$ immediately after collision, and $g = 9.8 \, m/s^2$ is the gravitational constant. The change of the velocity of the bead at the moment of the hit is given by the following relation:

$$R = \frac{X_+' - x_+'}{x_-' - X_-'}. \tag{1.2}$$

Here R is the restitution coefficient ($0 < R \leq 1$), $X_-', x_-', X_+',$ and x_+' are the velocities of the table and the bead before and after the strike, repectively, ($X_+' = X_-'$).

Among the results of investigation of the model, one can mention those in [71], where the period-doubling bifurcation, as well as chaos emergence, is discussed. If we write $x_1 = x, x_2 = x', \tau_i(x_1) = \arcsin(x_1/X_0) + (\pi/\omega)i$, where i are integers, then, using (1.1) and (1.2), one can construct a suitable mathematical model in the form of the following nonlinear system of differential equations with impulsive actions:

$$\begin{aligned} x_1' &= x_2, \\ x_2' &= -g, \\ \Delta x_2|_{t=\tau_i(x_1)} &= (1 + R)[x_0\omega \cos(\omega \tau_i(x_1)) - x_2]. \end{aligned} \tag{1.3}$$

Example 1.2. Consider a mechanical model of the oscillator consisting of a cart C (see Fig. 1.2), which can impact against a rigid wall W, and is subjected to an external force $H \sin(\omega t + \gamma)$. There is an elastic element S. The wall is at the distance B from the origin of the coordinate system, which is placed at the equilibrium point. The change of velocity of the cart at the moment of the hit against the wall is given by the relation $x_+' = -Rx_-'$, where R is the restitution coefficient ($0 < R \leq 1$), and x_-' and x_+' are the velocities of the cart before and after the strike, respectively. One can easily find a mathematical model of the system, which takes the form of the following differential equations with impulses:

$$\begin{aligned} x_1' &= x_2, \\ x_2' &= -cx_1 + H \sin(\omega t + \gamma), \\ \Delta x_2|_{x_1=-B} &= (1 + R)x_2, \end{aligned} \tag{1.4}$$

where $x_1 = x, x_2 = x'$.

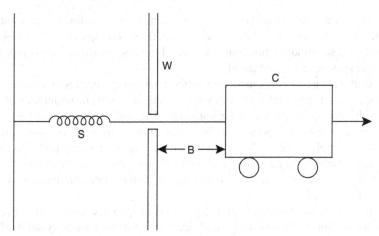

Fig. 1.2 A model of an oscillator consisting of a cart C, which can impact against a rigid wall W

Systems (1.3) and (1.4) are typical examples of differential equations with variable moments of impulses discussed in the book. The first system has solutions that exhibit discontinuity when they reach surfaces in the extended phase space. Solutions of the other system have jumps at the moments when they cross a set in the phase space of the equation.

The book is organized as follows:

We start with the description of differential equations with fixed moments of impulses in the second chapter. The characteristics of the sets of discontinuity moments are listed, and the spaces of piecewise continuous functions are introduced. The extension of solutions is presented in a very detailed manner. The theorems on local and global existence, and uniqueness of solutions are proved. The continuous dependence of solutions on initial conditions and the right-hand side are discussed.

The third chapter is devoted to the generalities of stability and periodic solutions of differential equations with fixed moments of impulses. Definitions of stability, the description of periodic systems, and illustrating examples are provided.

The basics of linear impulsive systems are the focus of the fourth chapter: Linear homogeneous systems; Linear nonhomogeneous systems; Linear periodic systems; Spaces of solutions; Stability of linear systems.

The next, fifth chapter is one of the main parts of the book. Nonautonomous differential equations with impulses at variable moments of time, whose solutions have jumps at the moments of intersection with surfaces in the extended phase space, are considered. In this chapter, we provide all conditions that make the investigation of these equations convenient. Namely, the conditions that guarantee the absence of beating of the solutions against the surfaces of discontinuity, and the conditions that preserve the ordering of the intersection with the surfaces. Moreover, we obtain conditions that allow the reduction to equations with fixed moments of impulses. It should be emphasized that the results concerning the dependence of solutions on the initial conditions and on the right-side, and stability are presented in the full form for the first time in the literature. Also, for the first time conditions for the extension of solutions to the left are formulated. The main auxiliary concepts are: the topology in the set of discontinuous functions. A general nonlinear case is considered, and quasilinear systems are investigated.

The sixth chapter is concerned with differentiability properties of solutions of nonautonomous differential equations with variable moments of impulses with respect to the initial conditions and parameters. The subject is relatively new for discontinuous dynamics, especially for higher order derivatives. What makes this investigation possible is the implementation of the B-equivalence method. The same can be said about the issue of the analyticity of solutions. We propose a uniform approach so that not only solutions themselves but also their discontinuity moments can be differentiated.

The results on smoothness from the previous chapter are used in the seventh chapter to develop the method of small parameter for quasilinear systems. Both critical and noncritical cases for the existence of periodic solutions are discussed. Practically useful algorithms are derived.

Chapter 8 is the central part of the book. We obtain conditions sufficient to shape a motion that is very similar to the flow of an autonomous ordinary differential equation so that all the properties of the dynamical system – extension of all solutions on $\mathbb{R}$, continuous dependence on the initial value, the group property and uniqueness – are preserved. Differentiability in the initial value is considered. In fact, B-smooth discontinuous flows are obtained.

The last two chapters revolve around more specific topics. The ninth chapter develops the mechanisms for discovering the Hopf bifurcation of a discontinuous dynamical system. Additionally, the question of the persistence of focus and the problems of distinguishing the focus and the center in the critical case are discussed as preliminaries.

We consider complex behavior of a discontinuous dynamics in the tenth chapter. For a special initial value problem, where moments of impulses are generated through map iterations, analogs of all Devaney's ingredients, as well as the shadowing property, are studied. Examples illustrating the existence of the chaotic attractor and the intermittency phenomenon are provided.

Chapter 2
Description of the System with Fixed Moments of Impulses and Its Solutions

2.1 Spaces of Piecewise Continuous Functions

Let $\mathbb{R}$, $\mathbb{N}$, and $\mathbb{Z}$ be the sets of all real numbers, natural numbers, and integers, respectively. Denote by $\theta = \{\theta_i\}$ a strictly increasing sequence of real numbers such that the set $\mathcal{A}$ of indexes i is an interval in $\mathbb{Z}$.

Definition 2.1.1. θ is a B-sequence, if one of the following alternatives is valid:

(a) $\theta = \emptyset$;
(b) θ is a nonempty and finite set;
(c) θ is an infinite set such that $|\theta_i| \to \infty$ as $|i| \to \infty$.

Example 2.1.1. θ with $\mathcal{A} = \{-1, 1, 2\}$, and $\theta_{-1} = -5, \theta_1 = \pi, \theta_2 = 7$, satisfies condition (b).

Example 2.1.2. $\theta_i = i + \frac{1}{3}$, where $i \geq -102$, is a B-sequence of type (c).

Example 2.1.3. $\theta_i = -i + \frac{1}{5}$, where $i \in \mathbb{Z}$, is not a B-sequence.

It is obvious that any B-sequence has no finite limit points.

Example 2.1.4. $\theta_i = 1 - \frac{1}{i+3}$, where $i = 1, 2, 3, \ldots$, is not a B-sequence.

Denote by Θ the union of all B-sequences.
  Fix a sequence $\theta \in \Theta$.

Definition 2.1.2. A function $\phi : \mathbb{R} \to \mathbb{R}^n$, $n \in \mathbb{N}$, is from the set $\mathcal{PC}(\mathbb{R}, \theta)$ if :

(i) it is left continuous;
(ii) it is continuous, except, possibly, points of θ, where it has discontinuities of the first kind.

The last definition means that if $\phi(t) \in \mathcal{PC}(\mathbb{R}, \theta)$, then the right limit $\phi(\theta_i+) = \lim_{t \to \theta_i+} \phi(t)$ exists and $\phi(\theta_i-) = \phi(\theta_i)$, where $\phi(\theta_i-) = \lim_{t \to \theta_i-} \phi(t)$, for each $\theta_i \in \theta$.
  Let $\mathcal{PC}(\mathbb{R}) = \cup_{\theta \in \Theta} \mathcal{PC}(\mathbb{R}, \theta)$.

M. Akhmet, *Principles of Discontinuous Dynamical Systems*,
DOI 10.1007/978-1-4419-6581-3_2, © Springer Science+Business Media, LLC 2010

Definition 2.1.3. A function $\phi : \mathbb{R} \to \mathbb{R}^n$ is from the set $\mathcal{PC}^1(\mathbb{R}, \theta)$ if $\phi(t), \phi'(t) \in \mathcal{PC}(\mathbb{R}, \theta)$, where the derivative at points of θ is assumed to be the left derivative.

In what follows, in this section, $T \subset \mathbb{R}$ is an interval in $\mathbb{R}$. For simplicity of notation, θ is not necessary a subset of T.

Definition 2.1.4. A function $\phi : T \to \mathbb{R}^n$ is from the set $\mathcal{PC}_r(T, \theta)$ if it has a continuation from $\mathcal{PC}(\mathbb{R}, \theta)$.

Definition 2.1.5. A function $\phi : T \to \mathbb{R}^n$ is from the set $\mathcal{PC}_r^1(T, \theta)$ if it has a continuation from $\mathcal{PC}^1(\mathbb{R}, \theta)$.

Exercise 2.1.1. Prove that Definitions 2.1.4 and 2.1.5 are equivalent to the following two Definitions 2.1.6 and 2.1.7, respectively.

Definition 2.1.6. A function $\phi : T \to \mathbb{R}^n$ is from the set $\mathcal{PC}_r(T, \theta)$ if:

(i) ϕ is left continuous;
(ii) ϕ is continuous, except, possibly, points of θ, where it has discontinuities of the first kind;
(iii) if an end point of T is finite, then there exists the one-sided limit of ϕ.

Definition 2.1.7. A function $\phi : T \to \mathbb{R}^n$ belongs to the set $\mathcal{PC}_r^1(T, \theta)$ if:

(i) $\phi \in \mathcal{PC}_r(T, \theta)$;
(ii) $\phi'(t) \in \mathcal{PC}_r(T, \theta)$, where the derivative at finite end points is a one-sided derivative and the derivative at points of θ is assumed to be the left derivative.

We shall use also the following definitions.

Definition 2.1.8. A function $\phi : T \to \mathbb{R}^n$ is from the set $\mathcal{PC}(T, \theta)$ if:

(i) ϕ is left continuous;
(ii) ϕ is continuous, except, possibly, points from θ, where it has discontinuities of the first kind.

Definition 2.1.9. A function $\phi : T \to \mathbb{R}^n$ belongs to the set $\mathcal{PC}^1(T, \theta)$ if:

(i) $\phi \in \mathcal{PC}(T, \theta)$;
(ii) $\phi'(t) \in \mathcal{PC}(T, \theta)$, where the derivative at finite end points is assumed to be a one-sided derivative, and the derivative at points of θ is assumed to be the left derivative.

Exercise 2.1.2. Assume that an interval T is one of the following types: the axis $\mathbb{R}$; a section $[a, b]$; a half-axis $[a, \infty)$; a half-axis $(-\infty, b], a, b \in \mathbb{R}$. Prove that $\mathcal{PC}_r(T, \theta) = \mathcal{PC}(T, \theta)$. Otherwise, $\mathcal{PC}_r(T, \theta) \subset \mathcal{PC}(T, \theta)$.

Exercise 2.1.3. Does the greatest integer function belong to $\mathcal{PC}(\mathbb{R})$?

2.2 Description of the System

Let $I \subseteq \mathbb{R}$ be an open interval, θ a nonempty B-sequence with set of indexes $\mathcal{A}$, and $G \subseteq \mathbb{R}^n$, $n \in \mathbb{N}$, an open connected set. Consider a function $f : I \times G \to \mathbb{R}^n$ and a map $J : \mathcal{A} \times G \to \mathbb{R}^n$, which we shall write as $f(t, x)$ and $J_i(x)$, respectively. Assume throughout this chapter that f is a continuous function.

For a fixed $i \in \mathcal{A}$, we introduce a *transition operator* $\Pi_i x \equiv x + J_i(x)$ on G.

Let $x(t)$ be a function defined in a neighborhood of a number $\xi \in \mathbb{R}$. We set $\Delta x|_{t=\xi} \equiv x(\xi+) - x(\xi)$, assuming that the limit $x(\xi+) = \lim_{t \to \xi+} x(t)$ exists. Applying the transition operator Π_i, define the following *equation of jumps*

$$\Delta x|_{t=\theta_i} = \Pi_i x(\theta_i) - x(\theta_i)$$

or

$$\Delta x|_{t=\theta_i} = J_i(x(\theta_i)). \tag{2.1}$$

Definition 2.2.1. We call the pair, which consists of the equation of jumps (2.1) and the ordinary differential equation

$$x' = f(t, x), \tag{2.2}$$

where the derivative at points of θ is assumed to be the left derivative, a discontinuous vector field.

Thus, the discontinuous vector field has the form

$$x' = f(t, x),$$
$$\Delta x|_{t=\theta_i} = J_i(x). \tag{2.3}$$

We shall call this field, (2.3), an *impulsive differential equation* . The domain of the equation is the set $\Omega = I \times \mathcal{A} \times G$.

In our book we make the following assumption, which is valid everywhere unless otherwise stated.

(M0) Each solution $\phi(t), \phi(t_0) = x_0, (t_0, x_0) \in I \times G$, of ordinary differential equation (2.2) exists and is unique on any interval of existence. It has an open maximal interval of existence, and any limit point of the set $(t, \phi(t))$, as t tends to an end point of the interval, is a boundary point of $I \times G$.

Let us remember that (M0) is valid if, for example, $f(t, x)$ satisfies a local Lipschitz condition.

Definition 2.2.2. [60] The function $f(t, x)$ satisfies a local Lipschitz condition, with respect to x, in $I \times G$ if for any compact subset K of $I \times G$ there exists a positive number L_K, such that

$$\|f(t, x) - f(t, y)\| \le L_K \|x - y\|$$

for any $(t, x), (t, y) \in K$.

2.3 Description of Solutions

Assume that $\phi : T \to \mathbb{R}^n$, where $T \subseteq I$ is an open interval, is a solution of (2.3). That is, it satisfies differential equation (2.2) and equation of jumps (2.1).

Theorem 2.3.1. *The solution ϕ belongs to $\mathcal{PC}^1(T, \theta)$.*

Proof. Indeed, by the differentiability of ϕ, it is continuous on $T \backslash \theta$. Consequently, as f is continuous, we have that ϕ' is continuous on the same set. The left differentiability implies that ϕ is a left-continuous function at the points from θ. Hence, ϕ is a left-continuous function on T. Now, ϕ' is a left-continuous function at all points of θ, since of the continuity of f. Further, the formula

$$\Delta \phi|_{t=\theta_i} = J_i(\phi(\theta_i))$$

yields that the right limit of the solution ϕ exists at the points of θ and

$$\phi(\theta_i+) = \phi(\theta_i) + J_i(\phi(\theta_i)).$$

Using the last equality in (2.2), one can obtain that the limit

$$\lim_{t \to \theta_i+} \phi'(t) = \phi'(\theta_i+)$$

exists. Thus, we can conclude that $\phi \in \mathcal{PC}^1(T, \theta)$. The theorem is proved. □

Exercise 2.3.1. Assume that a function $\phi : T \to \mathbb{R}^n$, where $T \subset I$ is a finite closed interval, is a solution of equation (2.3). Prove that $\phi \in \mathcal{PC}_r^1(T, \theta)$.

Example 2.3.1. Consider the following system:

$$\begin{aligned} x' &= 0, \\ \Delta x|_{t=i} &= (-1)^i, \end{aligned} \tag{2.4}$$

where $t, x \in \mathbb{R}$, and the function

$$\phi(t) = \begin{cases} 1, & \text{if } 2i < t \le 2i + 1, \\ 0, & \text{if } 2i - 1 < t \le 2i, i \in \mathbb{Z}. \end{cases} \tag{2.5}$$

It is easy to check that ϕ satisfies the differential equation. Moreover, $\Delta \phi|_{t=2k} = \phi(2k+) - \phi(2k) = 1 - 0 = 1$ and $\Delta \phi|_{t=2k-1} = 0 - 1 = -1$. That is, ϕ is a solution of (2.4). One can see that $\phi \in \mathcal{PC}^1(\mathbb{R}, \theta)$, if $\theta_i = i, i \in \mathbb{Z}$.

Exercise 2.3.2. Prove that the solution ϕ of (2.4) is a 2-periodic function.

In what follows, we consider existence and extension of a solution of the impulsive differential equation (2.3). Because of the singularity at moments of discontinuity, the procedure of extension is more complex than that of ordinary differential equations.

We shall use the following definitions, which are similar to those of ordinary differential equations [60, 77, 98].

Definition 2.3.1. A solution $x_1(t) : T_1 \to G$ of (2.3) is said to be a continuation of a solution $x(t) : T \to G$ on T_1, and $x(t)$ is said to be continuable on T_1, if $T \subset T_1$ and $x(t) = x_1(t)$ on T.

Definition 2.3.2. An interval T is called a right maximal interval of existence of a solution $x(t)$ of (2.3) if there is no continuation of the solution on an interval T_1 with right end point greater, than the end point of T.

Similarly one can give a definition of a left maximal interval of existence.

Definition 2.3.3. An interval T is said to be a maximal interval of existence of a solution $x(t)$ of (2.3) if it is both a right and left maximal interval of the solution.

Let a point $(t_0, x_0) \in I \times G$ be given. Denote by $x(t) = x(t, t_0, x_0)$ a solution of the initial value problem (2.3) and $x(t_0) = x_0$.

Extension over a maximal interval of existence. We will extend the solution, if:

(a) t is increasing, $t \geq t_0$;
(b) t is decreasing, $t \leq t_0$.

The case (a), in its own turn, consists of two sub-cases:

(a1) $t_0 \neq \theta_i, i \in \mathcal{A}$;
(a2) $t_0 = \theta_j$ for some $j \in \mathcal{A}$.

In the sequel, we denote by $\phi(t, \kappa, z), \kappa \in I, z \in G$, a solution of ordinary differential equation (2.2) such that $\phi(\kappa, \kappa, z) = z$.

Let us consider the sub-case $(a1)$. That is, the initial moment is not a discontinuity point. To be more concrete, suppose that $\theta_{j-1} < t_0 < \theta_j$, for a fixed $j \in \mathcal{A}$, (see Fig. 2.1). Denote by $[t_0, r), t_0 < r$, the right maximal interval of the solution $\phi(t, t_0, x_0)$. If $r \leq \theta_j$, then $[t_0, r)$ is the maximal interval of $x(t)$, and

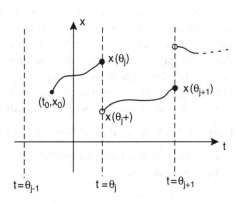

Fig. 2.1 Extension of a solution of system (2.3)

$x(t) = \phi(t, t_0, x_0)$. Otherwise, $r > \theta_j$, and if $\Pi_j x(\theta_j) \notin G$, then $x(t)$ is not continuable beyond $t = \theta_j$, and the right maximal interval of $x(t)$ is $[t_0, \theta_j]$. If $\Pi_j x(\theta_j) \in G$, then $x(t)$ can be extended to the right as $x(t) = \phi(t, \theta_j, x(\theta_j+))$, where $x(\theta_j+)) = \Pi_j x(\theta_j)$. Denote by $[\theta_j, r)$ the right maximal interval of $\phi(t, \theta_j, x(\theta_j+))$. If $r \le \theta_{j+1}$, then $[t_0, r)$ is the right maximal interval of $x(t)$, and $x(t) = \phi(t, \theta_j, x(\theta_j+)), t \in [\theta_j, r)$. If $r > \theta_{j+1}$, and $\Pi_{j+1} x(\theta_{j+1}) \notin G$, then the maximal interval of existence of $x(t)$ is $[t_0, \theta_{j+1}]$. If $r > \theta_{j+1}$ and $\Pi_{j+1} x(\theta_{j+1}) \in G$, then $x(t)$ can be continued as $\phi(t, \theta_{j+1}, x(\theta_{j+1}+))$, and so on.

If $\mathcal{A}$ is a finite set, then by using a finite number of steps we shall define the right maximal interval of $x(t)$, bounded or unbounded. Now, assume that the set $\mathcal{A}$ is unbounded on the right. There are two possibilities of the extension of the solution: either the number of steps is infinite, and the maximal interval is unbounded on the right or the number of admissible steps is finite and the right maximal interval is definitely bounded.

Now, consider the subcase $(a2), t_0 = \theta_j$ for some $j \in \mathcal{A}$. That is, the initial moment is a point of discontinuity. If $\Pi_j x(\theta_j) \notin G$, then $x(t)$ does not exist for $t > t_0$. If $\Pi_j x(\theta_j) \in G$, then $x(t_0+) = \Pi_j x(\theta_j)$. That is, the solution jumps at t_0, and the further discussion is the same as that of sub-case $(a1)$.

Consider the left extension of the solution. That is, the case (b). It is useful to start with the following exercise.

Exercise 2.3.3. Explain why an initial moment cannot be a discontinuity point for a left extension.

Fix $j \in \mathcal{A}$ such that $\theta_j < t_0 \le \theta_{j+1}$. Denote by $(l, t_0], l < t_0$, the left maximal interval of existence of the solution $\phi(t, t_0, x_0)$. If $l > \theta_j$, then $(l, t_0]$ is a left maximal interval of $x(t)$. If $l = \theta_j$ and the limit $\phi(\theta_j+, t_0, x_0)$ does not exist, then $(l, t_0]$ is a left maximal interval of existence of $x(t)$. Otherwise, if $l = \theta_j$ and the limit $\phi(\theta_j+, t_0, x_0)$ exists, or if $l < \theta_j$, then $x(\theta_j+) = \phi(\theta_j+, t_0, x_0)$. Now, if the equation

$$x(\theta_j+) = v + J_j(v) \tag{2.6}$$

is solvable with respect to v in G, then take the solution of this equation as $x(\theta_j)$, and continue $x(t) = \phi(t, \theta_j, x(\theta_j))$ at the right of θ_j. If (2.6) does not have a solution in G, then $(\theta_j, t_0]$ is a left maximal interval of existence of $x(t)$. Remark that (2.6) may have several solutions, and even infinitely many. We assume that one can be chosen, and we are not busy with the uniqueness problem this time. Proceeding in this way, one could finally construct a left maximal interval of $x(t)$.

Unite the left and right maximal intervals to obtain the maximal interval of $x(t)$.

Exercise 2.3.4. Solve the following six problems.

1. Complete the discussion of the left maximal interval similarly to that of the right maximal interval.

2. Explain why the solution $x(t, t_0, x_0)$ of (2.3) may have more than one maximal intervals.
3. Explain why the solution $x(t, t_0, x_0)$ of (2.3) may have more than one left maximal intervals.
4. Explain why the maximal interval of existence of the solution $\phi(t, t_0, x_0)$ of ordinary differential equation (2.2) is open.
5. Why a solution of (2.3) may have a right-closed maximal interval?
6. Why the left maximal intervals are not closed?

Exercise 2.3.5. Consider the system

$$x' = 0,$$
$$\Delta x|_{t=i} = x^{-1}, \tag{2.7}$$

where $t, x \in \mathbb{R}, i \in \mathbb{Z}$. Verify that the solution $x(t, 0, 2)$ of (2.7) exists and is unbounded on $[0, \infty)$.

Hint: To prove the unboundedness, use a contradiction.

Theorem 2.3.2. *(Local existence theorem) Suppose $f(t, x)$ is continuous on $I \times G$ and $\Pi_i G \subseteq G, i \in \mathcal{A}$. Then for any $(t_0, x_0) \in I \times G$ there is $\alpha > 0$ such that a solution $x(t, t_0, x_0)$ of (2.3) exists on $(t_0 - \alpha, t_0 + \alpha)$.*

Theorem 2.3.3. *Assume that condition (M0) is valid. Then each solution of (2.3) has a maximal interval of existence and for this interval the following alternatives are possible:*

(1) it is an open interval (α, β) such that any limit point of the set $(t, x(t))$ as $t \to \alpha$ or $t \to \beta$ belongs to the boundary of $I \times G$;
(2) it is a half-open interval $(\alpha, \beta]$, where β is a member of θ and any limit point of the set $(t, x(t))$ as $t \to \alpha$ belongs to the boundary of $I \times G$.
(3) it is a half-open interval $(\alpha, \beta]$, where α and β are elements of θ, the limit $x(\alpha+)$ exists and it is an interior point of G.
(4) it is an open interval (α, β) such that any limit point of the set $(t, x(t))$ as $t \to \beta$ belongs to the boundary of $I \times G$, the limit $x(\alpha+)$ exists and it is an interior point of G.

Theorem 2.3.4. *(Uniqueness theorem) Assume that $f(t, x)$ satisfies a local Lipschitz condition, and every equation*

$$x = v + J_i(v), \tag{2.8}$$

$i \in \mathcal{A}, x \in G$, *has at most one solution with respect to v. Then any solution $x(t, t_0, x_0), (t_0, x_0) \in I \times G$, of (2.3) is unique. That is, if $y(t, t_0, x_0)$ is another solution of (2.3), and the two solutions are defined at some $t \in I$, then $x(t, t_0, x_0) = y(t, t_0, x_0)$.*

Exercise 2.3.6. Prove the last three theorems.

Remark 2.3.1. The results of our book can be easily expanded for more general impulsive systems, if the function f in (2.3) is discontinuous and is of the following type. Without loss of generality assume that $I = \mathbb{R}$ and $\mathcal{A} = \mathbb{Z}$. Consider $f(t,x)$ such that it is continuous in each region $(\theta_i, \theta_{i+1}] \times G, i \in \mathbb{Z}$, and there exists a continuation $f_e^i(t,x)$ of this function on the set $[\theta_i, \theta_{i+1}] \times G$ for each $i \in \mathbb{Z}$. To demonstrate how the discussion should be arranged in this case, we consider the extension of the solution $x(t) = x(t, t_0, x_0)$ for $t \geq t_0$. Fix $j \in \mathbb{Z}$, such that $\theta_{j-1} < t_0 < \theta_j$. The beginning of the extension is identical to that of with continuous f. That is, assume that $x(t) = \phi(t, t_0, x_0), t \in [t_0, \theta_j]$ where ϕ is the solution of (2.2). Let $\Pi_j x(\theta_j) \in G$. Now, $x(t)$ is continuable to the right, and $x(t) = \psi(t, \theta_j, x(\theta_j+))$, where $x(\theta_j+) = \Pi_j x(\theta_j)$, and ψ is not the solution of (2.2) as it was above, but of the system

$$x' = f_e^j(t,x), \tag{2.9}$$

where $t \in [\theta_j, \theta_{j+1}]$. Proceeding in this way one can find the right maximal interval of $x(t)$.

Impulsive systems with the discontinuous right-hand side are needed for applications and investigation methods. For example, they emerge if one linearizes an impulsive system around a certain solution, (see, for instance, Chap. 6).

2.4 Equivalent Integral Equations

In this small section we construct an integral equation, which has the common set of solutions with the original impulsive differential equation (2.3). To prove the equivalence assertion, we shall need the result of the following exercise:

Exercise 2.4.1. Let ϕ and ψ be functions from $\mathcal{PC}^1(T, \theta)$ such that:

(1) $\phi(t_0) = \psi(t_0)$ for some $t_0 \in T$;
(2) $\phi'(t) = \psi'(t)$ for all $t \in T$, (the derivative is the left derivative at points of θ, and it is an one-sided derivative at the end points of T);
(3) $\Delta\phi|_{t=\theta_i} = \Delta\psi|_{t=\theta_i}, i \in \mathcal{A}$.

Prove that $\phi(t) = \psi(t)$ for all $t \in T$.

Theorem 2.4.1. *A function* $\phi(t) \in \mathcal{PC}^1(T, \theta), \phi(t_0) = x_0$, *is a solution of (2.3) if and only if*

$$\phi(t) = \begin{cases} x_0 + \int_{t_0}^t f(s, \phi(s))ds + \sum_{t_0 \leq \theta_i < t} J_i(\phi(\theta_i)), & t \geq t_0, \\ x_0 + \int_{t_0}^t f(s, \phi(s))ds - \sum_{t \leq \theta_i < t_0} J_i(\phi(\theta_i)), & t < t_0. \end{cases} \tag{2.10}$$

Proof. Necessity. Let $\phi(t)$ be a solution of (2.3) on T. Define a function

$$\psi(t) = \begin{cases} x_0 + \int_{t_0}^t f(s, \phi(s))ds + \sum_{t_0 \leq \theta_i < t} J_i(\phi(\theta_i)), & t \geq t_0, \\ x_0 + \int_{t_0}^t f(s, \phi(s))ds - \sum_{t \leq \theta_i < t_0} J_i(\phi(\theta_i)), & t < t_0. \end{cases} \tag{2.11}$$

We shall check that $\psi \in \mathcal{PC}^1(T, \theta)$ and show that functions ψ, ϕ satisfy all conditions of Exercise 2.4.1. Condition $\phi(t_0) = \psi(t_0)$ is obviously true. If $t \notin \theta$, and it is not an end point of T, then differentiating $\psi(t)$ we find that $\psi'(t) = f(t, \phi(t)) = \phi'(t)$. We verify conditions (2) and (3) of Exercise 2.4.1 only with $t \geq t_0$. For a fix $j \in \mathcal{A}$ one has that

$$\psi(\theta_j) = x_0 + \int_{t_0}^{\theta_j} f(s, \phi(s))ds + \sum_{t_0 \leq \theta_i < \theta_j} J_i(\phi(\theta_i))$$

and

$$\psi(\theta_j - h) = x_0 + \int_{t_0}^{\theta_j - h} f(s, \phi(s))d\,s + \sum_{t_0 \leq \theta_i < \theta_j - h} J_i(\phi(\theta_i)),$$

where $h > 0$. Next, we obtain that

$$\psi'_-(\theta_j) = \lim_{h \to 0+} \frac{\psi(\theta_j - h) - \psi(\theta_j)}{h} =$$

$$\lim_{h \to 0+} \frac{1}{h}\left[\int_{t_0}^{\theta_j - h} f(s, \phi(s))ds - \int_{t_0}^{\theta_j} f(s, \phi(s))ds\right] =$$

$$f(\theta_j, \phi(\theta_j)) = \phi'_-(\theta_j). \tag{2.12}$$

If α is the right end point of T and $\alpha \in T$, then similarly one can check that $\psi'_-(\alpha) = \phi'_-(\alpha)$. Consider condition 3). Fix $j \in \mathcal{A}$, then

$$\Delta\psi|_{t=\theta_j} = \psi(\theta_j+) - \psi(\theta_j) =$$

$$\left[x_0 + \int_{t_0}^{\theta_j+} f(s, \phi(s))ds + \sum_{t_0 \leq \theta_i < \theta_j+} J_i(\phi(\theta_i))\right] -$$

$$\left[x_0 + \int_{t_0}^{\theta_j} f(s, \phi(s))ds + \sum_{t_0 \leq \theta_i < \theta_j} J_i(\phi(\theta_i))\right] =$$

$$J_j(\phi(\theta_j)) = \Delta\phi|_{t=\theta_j}. \tag{2.13}$$

Thus, the conditions are verified if $t \geq t_0$.

Exercise 2.4.2. Verify that conditions (2), (3) of Exercise 2.4.1 are valid if $t < t_0$.

Thus, all the conditions of Exercise 2.4.1 are fulfilled and $\psi(t) = \phi(t)$. The necessity is proved. □

Sufficiency. Assume that $\phi(t)$ is a solution of (2.10). Then differentiate the expression and evaluate the discontinuities to check that it is as well a solution of (2.3). The theorem is proved. □

2.5 The Gronwall–Bellman Lemma for Piecewise Continuous Functions

Lemma 2.5.1. *Let* $u, v \in \mathcal{PC}(I, \theta), u(t) \geq 0, v(t) > 0, t \in I, \beta_i \geq 0, i \in \mathcal{A}, t_0 \in I$, *and* $c \in \mathbb{R}$ *is a nonnegative constant. From the inequality*

$$u(t) \leq c + \int_{t_0}^{t} v(s)u(s)ds + \sum_{t_0 \leq \theta_i < t} \beta_i u(\theta_i), t \geq t_0, \tag{2.14}$$

it follows that:

$$u(t) \leq c e^{\int_{t_0}^{t} v(s)ds} \prod_{t_0 \leq \theta_i < t} (1 + \beta_i), t \geq t_0. \tag{2.15}$$

Moreover, if additionally $\beta_i < 1, i \in \mathcal{A}$, *then the inequality*

$$u(t) \leq c + \int_{t_0}^{t} v(s)u(s)ds + \sum_{t \leq \theta_i < t_0} \beta_i u(\theta_i), t < t_0, \tag{2.16}$$

implies that

$$u(t) \leq c e^{-\int_{t_0}^{t} v(s)ds} \prod_{t \leq \theta_i < t_0} (1 - \beta_i)^{-1}, t < t_0. \tag{2.17}$$

Proof. The proof falls naturally in two parts. We first examine that (2.14) implies (2.15). Next, we will prove that (2.17) follows (2.16).

(a) Let $\theta_{j-1} < t_0 \leq \theta_j$, where $j \in \mathcal{A}$ is fixed. Introduce the following notations:

$$V(t) \equiv c + \int_{t_0}^{t} v(s)u(s)ds + \sum_{t_0 \leq \theta_i < t} \beta_i u(\theta_i);$$

$$W(t) \equiv c e^{\int_{t_0}^{t} v(s)ds} \prod_{t_0 \leq \theta_i < t} (1 + \beta_i).$$

To prove the assertion it is sufficient to check that

$$V(t) \leq W(t), t_0 \leq t. \tag{2.18}$$

On the interval $[t_0, \theta_j]$ inequality (2.18) is correct (see the Proof of the Gronwall–Bellman Lemma in [77]). We assume that (2.18) is true if $t \in [t_0, \theta_m]$

for some $m \in \mathcal{A}, m \geq j$, and will prove that it is fulfilled for $t \in (\theta_m, \theta_{m+1}]$. We have, for these t, the following inequalities:

$$V(t) = V(\theta_m) + \int_{\theta_m}^{t} v(s)u(s)ds + \beta_m u(\theta_m) \leq$$

$$(1 + \beta_m)V(\theta_m) + \int_{\theta_m}^{t} v(s)V(s)u(s)ds \leq$$

$$(1 + \beta_m)W(\theta_m) + \int_{\theta_m}^{t} v(s)V(s)u(s)ds.$$

Applying the Gronwall–Bellman Lemma [77] to the last inequality, one can obtain that

$$V(t) \leq (1 + \beta_m)W(\theta_m)e^{\int_{\theta_m}^{t} v(s)ds} = W(t).$$

Thus, (2.15) is true by the induction.

(b) Let $\theta_j < t_0 \leq \theta_{j+1}$, where $j \in \mathcal{A}$ is fixed. Assuming $t \leq t_0$, denote

$$\tilde{V}(t) \equiv c + \int_{t_0}^{t} v(s)u(s)ds + \sum_{t \leq \theta_i < t_0} \beta_i u(\theta_i),$$

$$\tilde{W}(t) \equiv ce^{-\int_{t_0}^{t} v(s)ds} \prod_{t \leq \theta_i < t_0} (1 - \beta_i)^{-1}.$$

Let us show that

$$\tilde{V}(t) \leq \tilde{W}(t), t \leq t_0, \tag{2.19}$$

to prove the assertion.

If $\theta_j < t \leq t_0$, then $u(t) \leq V(t)$, and assuming $c > 0$ (this restriction could be removed by the limit procedure), one can obtain that

$$-\frac{uv}{\tilde{V}} \geq -v.$$

Integrate the last inequality to prove

$$\tilde{V}(t) \leq \tilde{V}(t_0)e^{-\int_{t_0}^{t} v(s)ds} = \tilde{W}(t).$$

Now, assume that (2.19) is true for $t \in (\theta_m, t_0], m \in \mathcal{A}, m \leq j$. Then

$$\tilde{V}(\theta_m) \leq \tilde{V}(\theta_m+) + \beta_m u(\theta_m) \leq \tilde{V}(\theta_m+) + \beta_m \tilde{V}(\theta_m)$$

or

$$\tilde{V}(\theta_m) \leq (1 - \beta_m)^{-1}\tilde{V}(\theta_m+) \leq (1 - \beta_m)^{-1}\tilde{W}(\theta_m+) = \tilde{W}(\theta_m).$$

Consequently, if $\theta_{m-1} < t < \theta_m$, then

$$\tilde{V}(t) \le \tilde{V}(\theta_m) + \int_{t_0}^{t} v(s)u(s)ds \le \tilde{W}(\theta_m) + \int_{t}^{\theta_m} v(s)\tilde{V}(s)ds.$$

That is,

$$\tilde{V}(t) \le \tilde{W}(\theta_m)e^{\int_{t}^{\theta_m} v(s)ds} = \tilde{W}(t).$$

Now, induction on m proves the theorem. □

Notation. Let $T \subseteq \mathbb{R}$ be an arbitrary set and $\theta \in \Theta$ a sequence. For a symbol $i(T)$, one should understand the number of elements of the sequence θ in T. For example, if $\theta_j = j, j \in \mathbb{Z}$, then $i((0, 1)) = 0, i([0, 1]) = 2, i([-7.5, 15]) = 23$.

Let us formulate the following two lemmas without proving them.

Lemma 2.5.2. *[142] Let $u \in PC(I, \theta), t_0 \in I$, and the following inequality be valid*

$$u(t) \le \alpha + \int_{t_0}^{t} [\beta + \gamma u(s)]ds + \sum_{t_0 \le \theta_i < t} [\beta + \gamma u(\theta_i)], \qquad (2.20)$$

for all $t \ge t_0$, where $\alpha \ge 0, \beta \ge 0, \gamma > 0$, are constants. Then

$$u(t) \le (\alpha + \frac{\beta}{\gamma})(1 + \gamma)^{i([t_0, t])}e^{\gamma(t - t_0)} - \frac{\beta}{\gamma}. \qquad (2.21)$$

Lemma 2.5.3. *Let $u \in PC(I, \theta), t_0 \in I$, and the following inequality be valid:*

$$u(t) \le \alpha + \int_{t_0}^{t} [\beta + \gamma u(s)]ds + \sum_{t \le \theta_i < t_0} [\beta + \gamma u(\theta_i)], t \le t_0, \qquad (2.22)$$

where $\alpha \ge 0, \beta \ge 0, 0 < \gamma < 1$, are constants. Then

$$u(t) \le (\alpha + \frac{\beta}{\gamma})(1 - \gamma)^{-i([t, t_0])}e^{-\gamma(t - t_0)} - \frac{\beta}{\gamma}. \qquad (2.23)$$

Exercise 2.5.1. Prove Lemmas 2.5.2 and 2.5.3.

2.6 Existence and Uniqueness Theorems

Let us consider again the impulsive differential equation (2.3), which is defined on Ω, and described in Sect. 2.1, where we clarified the concept of a solution of impulsive differential equations, and the way of extension of solutions for increasing t as

well as for decreasing t. We want to determine conditions, which provide confidence
that a solution of the initial value problem exists and is unique on a certain interval.
Before solving this problem one should verify that the set of functions, where we
are looking for a solution is complete. That is, each Cauchy sequence of functions
from this set converges to a function of the same set.

Completeness of $\mathcal{PC}_r(\mathbf{T}, \boldsymbol{\theta})$. Assume that T is a bounded interval in $\mathbb{R}$. Introduce
the following norm. We set $\|\phi\|_0 = \sup_T \|\phi(t)\|$, if a function ϕ is bounded on T.
Consider a Cauchy sequence of functions $\{\phi_n\} \subset \mathcal{PC}_r(T, \theta), n \geq 1$. It is easily seen
that the sequence converges point-wise to a function $\phi^0(t)$ on T. Now, it is sufficient
to prove that the following assertion is valid.

Theorem 2.6.1. *If $\{\phi_n\} \subset \mathcal{PC}_r(T, \theta), n \geq 1$, and $\lim_{n \to \infty} \|\phi_n - \phi^0\|_0 = 0$, then
$\phi^0 \in \mathcal{PC}_r(J, \theta)$.*

Proof. Fix $i \in \mathcal{A}$ such that $(\theta_i, \theta_{i+1}] \subset T$. The functions ϕ_n are continuous on
$(\theta_i, \theta_{i+1}]$ and have the right limits at $t = \theta_i$. Hence, their continuous extensions
are uniformly convergent to the continuation of ϕ_0 on $[\theta_i, \theta_{i+1}]$. Consequently, the
function ϕ_0 is continuous on $(\theta_i, \theta_{i+1}]$ and has the right limit at $t = \theta_i$. Similarly we
can consider every interval of continuity in T. Thus, $\phi_0 \in \mathcal{PC}_r(T, \theta)$. The theorem
is proved. $\qquad\square$

Fix $(t_0, x_0) \in I \times G$, and let

$$I_0 = [t_0 - h, t_0 + h], G_0 = \{x \in \mathbb{R}^n : \|x - x_0\| < H\},$$

with some fixed positive numbers H and h.

Assume that the numbers are small such that $I_0 \times G_0 \subset I \times G$. Let $p_+ = i([t_0, t_0 + h]), p_- = i([t_0 - h, t_0]), A_0 = \{i \in \mathcal{A} : \theta_i \in I_0\}$ and $\theta^0 = \{\theta_i\}, i \in A_0$.

We will make the following assumptions:

(C1) $\|f(t, x) - f(t, y)\| \leq l\|x - y\|, \|J_i(x) - J_i(y)\| \leq l_1\|x - y\|$, for arbitrary
$\quad\quad x, y \in G$, uniformly in all $(t, i) \in I \times \mathcal{A}$;
(C2) $\sup_{J \times G} \|f(t, x)\| + \sup_{A \times G} \|J_i(x)\| = M < \infty.$

Theorem 2.6.2. *Let conditions (C1), (C2), and the inequalities*

$$M(h + \max(p_+, p_-)) < H, \tag{2.24}$$

$$lh + l_1 \max(p_+, p_-) < 1, \tag{2.25}$$

*be valid. Then the initial value problem (2.3) and $x(t_0) = x_0$ admit a unique
solution on I_0.*

Proof. Introduce the following norm $\|\phi\|_1 = \sup_{I_0} \|\phi\|$ for functions defined on
I_0. Let

$$S_H = \{\phi \in \mathcal{PC}_r(I_0, \theta^0) : \|\phi\|_1 < H\}.$$

Consider the operator $\mathcal{P}$ on S_H such that if $\phi \in S_H$, then

$$\mathcal{P}\phi(t) = \begin{cases} x_0 + \int_{t_0}^t f(s, \phi(s))ds + \sum_{t_0 \le \theta_i < t} J_i(\phi(\theta_i)), & t \ge t_0, \\ x_0 + \int_{t_0}^t f(s, \phi(s))ds - \sum_{t \le \theta_i < t_0} J_i(\phi(\theta_i)), & t < t_0. \end{cases} \qquad (2.26)$$

Exercise 2.6.1. Prove that $\mathcal{P} : S_H \to S_H$.

If two functions, ϕ and ψ are from S_H then

$$\|\mathcal{P}\phi - \mathcal{P}\psi\| \le l\|\phi - \psi\|_1 + l_1 \max(p_+, p_-)\|\phi - \psi\|_1$$
$$\le (lh + l_1 \max(p_+, p_-))\|\phi - \psi\|_1.$$

The last inequality in view of (2.25) proves that $\mathcal{P}$ is a contraction. Consequently, there exists a unique fixed point of $\mathcal{P}$, which is a unique solution of the initial value problem. The theorem is proved. $\square$

Exercise 2.6.2. Solve the following problems.

1. Why the completeness is needed to prove the last theorem?
2. Prove that each of the equations (2.6), where $x(t)$ is the solution determined in the last theorem, has at most one solution with respect to v.
3. Using the Schauder fixed point theorem prove that the following assertion is valid.

Theorem 2.6.3. *Assume that all conditions of the last theorem are true, except inequality (2.25). Then (2.3) admits a solution defined on I_0.*

2.7 Continuity

In this section we assume that $I \times G$ is a bounded set in $\mathbb{R} \times \mathbb{R}^n$, and fix a finite and closed interval $\tilde{I} = [a, b] \subset I$. We consider a solution $x(t) = x(t, t_0, x_0), t_0, t \in \tilde{I}$, of (2.3) with moments of discontinuity $\theta_i, a < \theta_m < \ldots < \theta_k < b$. That is, we suppose that the moments of discontinuity are interior points of the section. Denote by $G_{m-1} = \{(t, x) : a \le t \le \theta_m, x \in G\}, G_k = \{(t, x) : \theta_k < t \le b, x \in G\}$ and $G_i = \{(t, x) : \theta_i < t \le \theta_{i+1}, x \in G\}, i = m, \ldots, k - 1$.

Definition 2.7.1. The solution $x(t) = x(t, t_0, x_0)$ of (2.3) continuously depends on x_0 if to any $\epsilon > 0$ there corresponds $\delta > 0$ such that any other solution $\tilde{x}(t)$ with $\|x_0 - \tilde{x}(t_0)\| < \delta$ is continuable on $\tilde{I}$, and $\|x(t) - \tilde{x}(t)\| < \epsilon$ on this interval.

Denote by $d(x_0, \delta) = \{(t, x) \in \mathbb{R} \times \mathbb{R}^n : t_0 - \delta < t < t_0 + \delta, x = x_0\}$ the set, where δ is a positive real number, and fix j such that $(t_0, x_0) \in G_j$.

Definition 2.7.2. The solution $x(t) = x(t, t_0, x_0)$ of (2.3) continuously depends on t_0 if to any $\epsilon > 0$ there corresponds $\delta > 0$ such that any other solution $\tilde{x}(t) = x(t, \tilde{t}_0, x_0)$ is continuable on $\tilde{I}$, and $\|x(t) - \tilde{x}(t)\| < \epsilon$ on this interval, as soon as $\tilde{t}_0 \in d(x_0, \delta) \cap G_j$.

Consider the following system:

$$y' = f(t, y) + g(t, y),$$
$$\Delta y|_{t \neq \theta_i} = J_i(y) + W_i(y), \tag{2.27}$$

which is defined as well as (2.3) on Ω, and assume that function g is continuous, functions $W_i, i \in \mathcal{A}$, are defined on G, and

(C3) $\sup_{I \times G} ||g|| + \sup_{A \times G} ||W|| = \eta < \infty.$

Definition 2.7.3. The solution $x(t) = x(t, t_0, x_0)$ of (2.3) continuously depends on the right-hand side of the system if to any $\epsilon > 0$ there corresponds $\delta > 0$ such that any solution $y(t)$ of (2.27) with $y(t_0) = x_0$ is continuable on $\tilde{I}$, and $||x(t) - y(t)|| < \epsilon$ on this interval, whenever $\eta < \delta$.

Lemma 2.7.1. *Suppose functions f, J_i, satisfy condition (C1) with $l_1 = l$, functions g, W are such that (C3) is valid, and a solution $y(t) = y(t, t_0, y_0)$ of (2.27) exists on $\tilde{I}$.*

Then the inequality

$$||x(t) - y(t)|| \leq (||x_0 - y_0|| + \frac{\eta}{l})(1 + l)^{i([t_0, t])} e^{l(t-t_0)} - \frac{\eta}{l}, \tag{2.28}$$

is true, where $t \geq t_0$. Moreover, if $l < 1$, then

$$||x(t) - y(t)|| \leq (||x_0 - y_0|| + \frac{\eta}{l})(1 - l)^{-i([t, t_0])} e^{-l(t-t_0)} - \frac{\eta}{l}, \tag{2.29}$$

where $t \leq t_0$.

Proof. Consider (2.29). The case with $t \geq t_0$ could be discussed similarly. Let $y(t) = y(t, t_0, y_0)$ be a solution of (2.27) defined on $\tilde{I}$. Then for $t \leq t_0$ we have that

$$y(t) = y_0 + \int_{t_0}^{t} \left[f(s, y(s)) + g(s, y(s)) \right] ds - \sum_{t \leq \theta_i < t_0} J_i(y(\theta_i)). \tag{2.30}$$

Moreover,

$$x(t) = x_0 + \int_{t_0}^{t} f(s, x(s)) ds - \sum_{t \leq \theta_i < t_0} J_i(x(\theta_i)). \tag{2.31}$$

Finding difference of the last two equalities one can obtain, through conditions (C1), (C3), that

$$||x(t) - y(t)|| \leq ||x_0 - y_0|| + \int_{t_0}^{t} [\eta + l||x(s) - y(s)||] ds$$
$$+ \sum_{t \leq \theta_i < t_0} [\eta + l||x(\theta_i) - y(\theta_i)||].$$

Applying Lemma 2.5.1 to the last inequality, we find that (2.29) is true. The lemma is proved. □

Lemma 2.7.2. *Suppose* $||J_i(x) - J_i(y)|| \le l_1 ||x - y||$ *for all* $i \in \mathcal{A}, x, y \in G$. *If* $l_1 < 1$, *then the equation*

$$x = v + J_i(v),$$

$i \in \mathcal{A}, x \in G$, *has at most one solution* $v \in G$. *Moreover, if* $x_j = v_j + J_i(v_j), j = 1, 2$, *then*

$$||v_1 - v_2|| \le \frac{1}{1 - l_1} ||x_1 - x_2||. \tag{2.32}$$

Proof. Fix $i \in \mathcal{A}$. We have that $||x_1 - x_2|| = ||v_1 - v_2 + J_i(v_1) - J_i(v_2)|| \ge ||v_1 - v_2|| - l_1 ||v_1 - v_2|| = (1 - l_1) ||v_1 - v_2||$. Consequently, (2.32) is correct. The uniqueness follows this formula immediately. The lemma is proved. □

Theorem 2.7.1. *Suppose* f, J *satisfy (C1) and* $l_1 < 1$. *Then the solution* $x(t)$ *of (2.3) continuously depends on* x_0 *if* $t_0 = b$. *If* $\tilde{x}(t) = x(t, t_0, \tilde{x}_0)$ *is another solution of (2.3), and* $||x_0 - \tilde{x}_0||$ *is sufficiently small, then*

$$||x(t) - \tilde{x}(t)|| \le ||x_0 - \tilde{x}_0||(1 - l_1)^{-i([t,t_0])} e^{-l(t-t_0)}, \quad a \le t \le t_0. \tag{2.33}$$

Proof. Fix $\epsilon > 0$. One can take δ' sufficiently small such that the tube $\mathcal{T} = \{(t, x) : ||x - x(t)|| < \delta', t \in [a, t_0]\}$ is entirely in $I \times G$. Moreover, by Lemma 2.7.2, a number $\delta' > 0$ can be chosen such that the maps Π_i^{-1} are defined in the small neighborhoods of $x(\theta_i +)$.

Fix a positive δ such that $\delta(1 - l_1)^{-i([a,t_0])} e^{l(t_0-a)} < \min\{\delta', \epsilon\}$. Let $\tilde{x}(t) = x(t, t_0, \tilde{x}_0)$ be another solution of (2.3), and $||x_0 - \tilde{x}_0|| < \delta$. Applying Lemma 2.5.1 and formula (2.29), we obtain inequality (2.33). Since of Theorem 2.4.1, Lemma 2.7.2, and condition (M0), the solution $\tilde{x}(t)$ is continuable on $\tilde{I}$ and $||x(t) - \tilde{x}(t)|| < \epsilon$ for all $t \in [a, t_0]$. The theorem is proved. □

We will formulate several theorems on the continuous dependence without proving them.

Theorem 2.7.2. *Suppose functions* f, J *satisfy (C1). Then the solution* $x(t)$ *of (2.3) continuously depends on* x_0 *if* $t_0 = a$.

If $\tilde{x}(t) = x(t, t_0, \tilde{x}_0)$ *is another solution of (2.3), and* $||x_0 - \tilde{x}_0||$ *is sufficiently small, then*

$$||x(t) - \tilde{x}(t)|| \le ||x_0 - \tilde{x}_0||(1 + l_1)^{i([t_0,t))} e^{l(t-t_0)}, \quad t_0 \le t \le b. \tag{2.34}$$

Theorem 2.7.3. *Suppose* f, J *satisfy (C1), and* $l_1 < 1$. *Then every solution* $x(t) = x(t, t_0, x_0), (t_0, x_0) \in I \times G$, *of (2.3) continuously depends on* x_0 *on any closed and finite interval, where it is defined.*

By reduction to the dependence on the initial value one can prove that the following assertions are valid.

Theorem 2.7.4. *Assume that functions* f, J *satisfy (C1). Then the solution* $x(t)$ *of (2.3) continuously depends on* t_0 *if* $t_0 = a$.

Theorem 2.7.5. *Assume that* f, J *satisfy (C1) and* $l_1 < 1$. *Then the solution* $x(t) = x(t, t_0, x_0)$ *of (2.3) continuously depends on* t_0 *if* $t_0 = b$.

Theorem 2.7.6. *Assume that* f, J *satisfy (C1) and* $l_1 < 1$. *Then every solution* $x(t) = x(t, t_0, x_0), (t_0, x_0) \in I \times G$, *of (2.3) continuously depends on* t_0 *on each closed and finite interval, where it is defined.*

Exercise 2.7.1. Explain, why the set $d(x_0, \delta)$ in Definition 2.7.2 cannot be ignored in the last three theorems. Give a simple example, where a solution with initial discontinuity moment does not depend continuously on the initial moment despite the equation 'encourages' the continuity.

Hint: Consider the following system:

$$x' = 0,$$
$$\Delta x|_{t \neq i} = 1, \tag{2.35}$$

where $x, t \in \mathbb{R}, i \in \mathbb{Z}$, and the solution $x(t, 0, 0)$ of this system if $t > 0$.

Theorem 2.7.7. *Assume that* f, J *satisfy (C1),* $l_1 = l < 1$, *functions* g, W *satisfy (C2) and* $\|g(t, x) - g(t, y)\| + \|W_i(x) - W_i(y)\| \leq l_2\|x - y\|, l_2$ *is a positive constant, for arbitrary* $x, y \in G$ *uniformly in all* $(t, i) \in I \times \mathcal{A}$. *Then the solution* $x(t)$ *of (2.3) continuously depends on the right-hand side of the system.*

Exercise 2.7.2. Prove Theorems 2.7.2 to 2.7.7. Hint: To prove Theorem 2.7.7, use Lemma 2.7.1.

Remark 2.7.1. In Theorem 2.7.7 the Lipschitz condition for g, W can be replaced by the local existence assumption.

Remark 2.7.2. Assume that function $f(t, x)$ in (2.3) satisfies a Lipschitz condition, and all transition operators Π_i are homeomorphisms. Then one can see that the solution $x(t, t_0, x_0)$ of (2.3) continuously depends on the initial condition. Theorems with strong restrictions on the impulsive functions are important for applications as they provide exact evaluations of the dependence.

Notes

To the best of our knowledge, the history of mathematical treatment of discontinuous processes began in the middle of the last century. Various aspects of the theory and its applications can be found in pioneer papers and books [38, 42, 75, 78, 90, 91, 107, 116, 143, 147–149, 154]. In [111], the authors expressed the idea of general theory of differential equations with fixed moments of impulses. Papers [137–140] developed this idea, and first theorems, analogues to those for ordinary differential equations, were proved. The investigation was continued in [22, 30, 45, 102, 128] and many other papers. These results were summarized in the books [95, 141]. Further, extended version of [141] was published in English [142]. Some results of the present chapter can be found in [46, 95, 111, 137–140, 142]. The Gronwall–Bellman Lemma for piecewise continuous functions is published in [138], and in [46] the version with $t \leq t_0$ is proved. The importance of the transition operator for continuation of solutions was first mentioned in [111]. The local existence and uniqueness theorems, different versions of extension theorems, including assertions on maximal intervals of existence, continuous dependence of solutions on initial conditions are considered in [46, 111, 142]. In the present book, Theorems 2.3.3, 2.6.2, 2.6.3, 2.7.1, 2.7.5, 2.7.6, 2.7.7, of global existence and uniqueness, extension of solutions, maximal intervals of existence, continuous dependence on initial conditions and the right-hand side, when the time is increasing and decreasing, are formulated in the unified form, similarly to ordinary differential equations. The form is convenient for searching new sufficient conditions, which may provide the qualitative properties required by future applications. Theorems 2.3.1, 2.3.3, 2.4.1, 2.7.1, 2.7.3, 2.7.6, 2.7.7, as well as Definition 2.7.2, which uses the set-interval $d(x_0, \delta)$, are published for the first time.

In addition, we want to make the following two important remarks:

1. It is the first time that the differential equation with impulses is given in the form

$$
\begin{aligned}
x' &= f(t, x), \\
\Delta x|_{t=\theta_i} &= J_i(x),
\end{aligned}
\tag{2.36}
$$

in the present book. Commonly the system

$$
\begin{aligned}
x' &= f(t, x), t \neq \theta_i, \\
\Delta x|_{t=\theta_i} &= J_i(x),
\end{aligned}
\tag{2.37}
$$

has been used [95, 142]. The system (2.36) is more adequate to the motion with discontinuities than (2.37), since it does not ignore the existence of the left derivative at the points of discontinuity.

We should say to the reader that system (2.36) can be accepted as (2.37) and vise versa. So, one can read our book considering (2.36) as equation of the type (2.37), for convenience. That is, assuming that inequality $t \neq \theta_i$ is involved in the first line of (2.36). Moreover, introduction of the new form, (2.36), changes nothing in all proofs of the theory.

2. In [95] (see also [46]), the initial condition $x(t_0+) = x_0$ is considered. This excludes a jump at the initial moment, when a solution is continued to the right. In our book we keep the initial condition in its classical form $x(t_0) = x_0$, [142]. Thus, we have achieved the maximal parallelism with ordinary differential equations theory in proofs as well as in notations.

Chapter 3
Stability and Periodic Solutions of Systems with Fixed Moments of Impulses

3.1 Definitions of Stability

Let us consider a differential equation with impulses,

$$x'(t) = f(t, x),$$

$$\Delta x|_{t=\theta_i} = J_i(x), \tag{3.1}$$

which is defined on the set Ω. In this section we assume that $I = [0, \infty)$, and $\theta_i \to \infty$ as $i \to \infty$. Let $\phi(t)$ be a solution of (3.1) such that $\phi : I \to G$.

Definition 3.1.1. The solution $\phi(t)$ is stable if to any $\epsilon > 0$ and $t_0 \in I$ there corresponds $\delta(t_0, \epsilon) > 0$ such that for any other solution $\psi(t)$ of (3.1) with $||\phi(t_0) - \psi(t_0)|| < \delta(t_0, \epsilon)$ we have $||\phi(t) - \psi(t)|| < \epsilon$ for $t \geq t_0$.

Definition 3.1.2. The solution $\phi(t)$ is uniformly stable, if $\delta(t_0, \epsilon)$ from Definition 3.1.1 can be chosen independently of t_0.

Definition 3.1.3. The solution $\phi(t)$ is asymptotically stable if it is stable in the sense of Definition 3.1.1 and there exists a positive number $\kappa(t_0)$ such that if $\psi(t)$ is any other solution of (3.1) with $||\phi(t_0) - \psi(t_0)|| < \kappa(t_0)$, then $||\phi(t) - \psi(t)|| \to 0$ as $t \to \infty$.

Definition 3.1.4. The solution $\phi(t)$ is uniformly asymptotically stable if it is uniformly stable in the sense of Definition 3.1.2, and given $\epsilon > 0$ we can find $T(\epsilon) > 0$ such that for any other solution $\psi(t)$ of (3.1) with $||\phi(t_0) - \psi(t_0)|| < \kappa$, where κ is independent of t_0, we have $||\phi(t) - \psi(t)|| < \epsilon$ for $t \geq t_0 + T(\epsilon)$.

Definition 3.1.5. The solution $\phi(t)$ is unstable if there exist numbers $\epsilon_0 > 0$ and $t_0 \in I$ such that for any $\delta > 0$ there exists a solution $y_\delta(t)$, $||\phi(t_0) - y_\delta(t_0)|| < \delta$, of (3.1) such that either it is not continuable to ∞ or there exists a moment $t_1, t_1 > t_0$ such that $||y_\delta(t_1) - \phi(t_1)|| \geq \epsilon_0$.

M. Akhmet, *Principles of Discontinuous Dynamical Systems*,
DOI 10.1007/978-1-4419-6581-3_3, © Springer Science+Business Media, LLC 2010

Example 3.1.1. Consider the following system:

$$x' = -2x,$$
$$\Delta x|_{t=i} = \alpha x, \tag{3.2}$$

where $i \in \mathbb{Z}$.

Define the coefficient $\alpha \in \mathbb{R}$ such that the trivial solution $x \equiv 0$ of the system is: (a) stable; (b) asymptotically stable; (c) unstable.

Solution. Fix $j \in \mathbb{Z}$, $j \geq 0$. One can find that

$$x(j + 1) = x(j)e^{-2}(1 + \alpha).$$

Set $q = |e^{-2}(1 + \alpha)|$. Applying the last formula, we can obtain by recursion that

$$|x(i)| = |x_0|q^i, i \geq 1.$$

The last formula implies easily that:

(i) if $q = 1$ then $|x(i)| = |x_0|, i \geq 1$;
(ii) if $q < 1$ then $|x(i)| \to 0$ as $i \to \infty$;
(iii) if $q > 1$ then $|x(i)| \to \infty$ as $i \to \infty$.

Now, by using the cases (i)–(iii), we shall prove that the zero solution is stable if $\alpha = -1 \pm e^2$, asymptotically stable if $-1 - e^2 < \alpha < -1 + e^2$, and unstable if $\alpha < -1 - e^2$ or $\alpha > -1 + e^2$.

Indeed, if $\alpha = -1 \pm e^2$, then $q = 1$. Fix $\epsilon > 0$ and choose a positive δ such that $\delta < \frac{\epsilon}{|1+\alpha|}$.

Let us show that $|x_0| < \delta$ implies $|x(t, 0, x_0)| < \epsilon, t \geq 0$. Since $|e^{-2}(1 + \alpha)| = 1$, we have that $|1 + \alpha| > 1$ and, consequently,

$$|x(i)| = |x_0| < \delta < \frac{\epsilon}{|1 + \alpha|} < \epsilon, i \geq 0.$$

Moreover, the equality $x(i+) = x(i)(1+\alpha)$ implies that $|x(i+)| = |x(i)||1+\alpha| < \delta|1 + \alpha| < \epsilon$.

On each interval $(i, i + 1], i \geq 0$, the expression $|x(t)|$ is a decreasing function. Hence, $|x(t)| \leq |x(i+)| < \epsilon$ if $i < t \leq i + 1$. The stability of the trivial solution is proved.

Exercise 3.1.1. Prove that the trivial solution is stable if $q < 1$.

Assume, now, that $-1 - e^2 < \alpha < -1 + e^2$. Then $q < 1$. We have that $|x(i+)| = |x_0|q^i(1 + \alpha), i \geq 0$, and, hence, $x(i+) \to 0$ as $i \to \infty$. Moreover, $|x(t)|$ is a decreasing function on each interval $(i, i + 1], i \geq 0$. That is, $x(t) \to 0$ as $t \to \infty$. Since the last relation is valid for an arbitrary x_0, the zero solution is asymptotically stable in large.

If $\alpha < -1 - e^2$ or $\alpha > -1 + e^2$, then $q > 1$. Fix $\epsilon > 0$ and an arbitrary $\delta, \delta < \epsilon$. Consider the solution $x(t) = x(t, 0, x_0)$ such that $|x_0| = \frac{\delta}{2}$. If $i_0 = \left[\frac{\ln \frac{2\epsilon}{\delta}}{\ln q} \right] + 1$, where $[\cdot]$ is the greatest integer function, then $|x(i)| = \frac{\delta}{2} q^i$ implies that $|x(i)| \geq \epsilon$, $i \geq i_0$. Thus, the trivial solution is unstable.

3.2 Basics of Periodic Systems

Consider system (3.1) assuming that $I = \mathbb{R}, \mathcal{A} = \mathbb{Z}$, and $|\theta_i| \to \infty$ as $|i| \to \infty$. Fix positive $\omega \in \mathbb{R}, p \in \mathbb{Z}$.

We shall need the following additional conditions of periodicity:

(C4) $f(t + \omega, x) = f(t, x)$ for all $(t, x) \in \mathbb{R} \times G$;
(C5) $J_{i+p}(x) = J_i(x)$ for all $(i, x) \in \mathbb{Z} \times G$;
(C6) $\theta_{i+p} = \theta_i + \omega$ for all $i \in \mathbb{Z}$, (p-property).

If conditions (C4)–(C6) are valid, then (3.1) is called an (ω, p)-periodic system.

Exercise 3.2.1. Prove that the system

$$x' = -2\cos(\pi t)x^2,$$
$$\Delta x|_{t=\theta_i} = e^{2(-1)^i x}, \tag{3.3}$$

where $\theta_i = i + (-1)^{i+1}\frac{1}{3}, i \in \mathbb{Z}$, is $(2, 2)$-periodic.

A function $\phi(t) \in \mathcal{PC}(\mathbb{R}, \theta)$ is a piecewise continuous ω-periodic function (or just a periodic function) if

$$\phi(t + \omega) = \phi(t),$$

for all $t \in \mathbb{R}$. Denote by $\mathcal{PC}_p$, the set of all periodic functions from $\mathcal{PC}(\mathbb{R})$.

Exercise 3.2.2. If $\phi(t) \in \mathcal{PC}_p$ and the set of discontinuity moments θ of this function is not empty, then prove that there exist a positive real number ω and an integer p such that $(C6)$ is valid.

Exercise 3.2.3. Prove that every function $\phi(t) \in \mathcal{PC}_p$:

(a) is bounded on $\mathbb{R}$;
(b) is uniformly continuous on the union of intervals of continuity;
(c) satisfies $\phi(t + k\omega) = \phi(t)$, for all $(t, k) \in \mathbb{R} \times \mathbb{Z}$, if ω is its period.

Lemma 3.2.1. If $\phi(t) \in \mathcal{PC}(\mathbb{R}, \theta)$ is a solution of (ω, p)-periodic system (3.1), then $\phi(t + k\omega), k \in \mathbb{Z}$, also satisfies the system.

Proof. Denote $\psi(t) = \phi(t + k\omega), k \in \mathbb{Z}$. We have that

$$\frac{d\psi(t)}{dt} = \frac{d\phi(t + k\omega)}{d(t + k\omega)}\frac{d(t + k\omega)}{dt} = f(t + k\omega, \phi(t + k\omega)) = f(t, \psi(t)).$$

One can also see that the jump equation is satisfied. Indeed,

$$\Delta\psi|_{t=\theta_i} = \psi(\theta_i+) - \psi(\theta_i) = \phi(\theta_i + k\omega+) - \phi(\theta_i + k\omega) =$$

$$\phi(\theta_{i+kp}+) - \phi(\theta_{i+kp}) = J_{i+kp}(\phi(\theta_{i+kp})) = J_i(\phi(\theta_i + k\omega)) = J_i(\psi(\theta_i)).$$

The lemma is proved.   □

Theorem 3.2.1. *(Poincaré criterion) Assume that conditions (C4)–(C6) are valid and $f(t, x)$ satisfies a local Lipschitz condition. A solution $\phi(t) \in PC(\mathbb{R}, \theta)$ of (3.1) is ω-periodic if and only if $\phi(0) = \phi(\omega)$.*

Proof. Necessity of the theorem is obvious. Let us prove sufficiency. Write $\psi(t) = \phi(t + \omega)$. By Lemma 3.2.1, $\psi(t)$ is a solution of (3.1). Moreover, $\psi(0) = \phi(0) = \phi(\omega)$. That is, ψ and ϕ are solutions with one and the same initial values. Consequently, $\psi(t) = \phi(t), t \in \mathbb{R}$, i.e., $\phi(t + \omega) = \phi(t), t \in \mathbb{R}$. The theorem is proved.   □

Exercise 3.2.4. Explain, why we do not impose any conditions on the impulsive functions J in the last theorem.

Example 3.2.1. For system (3.2), find values of the coefficient α such that all solutions are 1-periodic. Investigate stability of these solutions.

Solution. Using the formula $x(i) = x_0 q^i, i \geq 0$, and the Poincaré criterion one can obtain that all solutions of (3.2) are 1-periodic functions if and only if

$$x_0 = x_0 e^{-2}(1 + \alpha).$$

That is, all solutions of the system

$$x' = -2x,$$
$$\Delta x|_{t=i} = (e^2 - 1)x \tag{3.4}$$

are 1-periodic.

Let $\phi(t)$ be a 1-periodic solution of (3.4) and $\psi(t)$ be another solution of the system. Verify that the difference $\phi(t) - \psi(t)$ is also a solution of (3.4). Since the trivial solution of (3.4) is stable, solution $\phi(t)$ is also stable.

Exercise 3.2.5. By using the periodicity of all solutions and the continuous dependence of solutions on the initial value prove that the solution $\phi(t)$ is stable.

Example 3.2.2. Investigate periodicity and stability of solutions of the following system:

$$x' = 0,$$
$$\Delta x|_{t=i} = -x + \frac{1}{x}, \tag{3.5}$$

where $(t, x) \in \mathbb{R} \times \mathbb{R}$.

Solution. It is not difficult to see that

$$x(i+1) = \frac{1}{x(i)}, \tag{3.6}$$

if $x(t)$ is a solution such that $x(i) \neq 0, i \in \mathbb{Z}$.

Let $x(t) = x(t, t_0, 0)$ be a solution of (3.6) with $j - 1 < t_0 \leq j$ for some $j \in \mathbb{Z}$. We have that $x(t) = 0$, if $t \in [t_0, j]$ and it is not continuable beyond $t = j$.

Consider solutions with a nonzero initial value. Fix $x_0 > 0$. One can verify that

$$x(t) = \begin{cases} x_0, & t_0 \leq t \leq j, \\ \frac{1}{x_0}, & j < t \leq j+1, \\ x_0, & j+1 < t \leq j+2. \end{cases} \tag{3.7}$$

is a solution such that $x(t_0) = x_0$. Proceeding, one can see that $x(t)$ is continuable as a 2-periodic solution, and

$$x(t) = \begin{cases} \frac{1}{x_0}, & j+2i < t \leq j+2i+1, \\ x_0, & j+2i+1 < t \leq j+2(i+1), \end{cases} \tag{3.8}$$

where $i \in \mathbb{Z}$.

Thus, every solution with a positive initial value is a 2-periodic function. Let us investigate stability of this solution. Assume that $\bar{x}(t) = x(t, 0, \bar{x}_0)$ is a neighbor solution. Fix $\epsilon > 0$, and choose

$$\delta = \min\{\epsilon, \frac{x_0}{2}, \frac{\epsilon x_0^2}{1 + \epsilon x_0}\}.$$

Let $|x_0 - \bar{x}_0| < \delta$. Then $\bar{x}_0 > x_0 - \delta > 0$.

1. If $t_0 \leq t \leq j$, then

$$|x(t) - \bar{x}(t)| = |x_0 - \bar{x}_0| < \delta \leq \epsilon.$$

2. If $j < t \leq j+1$, then

$$|x(t) - \bar{x}(t)| = |\frac{1}{x_0} - \frac{1}{\bar{x}_0}| = \frac{|x_0 - \bar{x}_0|}{x_0 \bar{x}_0} < \frac{\delta}{x_0(x_0 - \delta)} \leq \epsilon.$$

3. If $j+1 < t \leq t_0 + 2$, then again we have that

$$|x(t) - \bar{x}(t)| = |x_0 - \bar{x}_0| < \delta \leq \epsilon.$$

Now, the periodicity of $x(t)$ and $\bar{x}(t)$ implies that $|x(t) - \bar{x}(t)| < \epsilon$ for all $t \geq t_0$. That is, $x(t)$ is a stable solution.

Exercise 3.2.6. Verify that a solution $x(t) = x(t, t_0, x_0), x_0 < 0$, of (3.5) is continuable on $\mathbb{R}$, 2-periodic and stable.

Exercise 3.2.7. [141] Consider the following system:

$$x' = 1 + x^2,$$
$$\Delta x|_{t=\theta_i} = -1, \tag{3.9}$$

where $\theta_i = i\frac{\pi}{4}, i \in \mathbb{Z}$. Prove that:

(i) the solution $x(t, 0, 1)$ of (3.9) is $\frac{\pi}{4}$-periodic;
(ii) every solution of (3.9) is unstable.

Notes

The main results of the chapter were published in [137–141].

Chapter 4
Basics of Linear Systems

4.1 Linear Homogeneous Systems

We start discussion of linear impulsive systems with the following differential equation:

$$x' = A(t)x,$$
$$\Delta x|_{t=\theta_i} = B_i x, \qquad (4.1)$$

where $(t, x) \in \mathbb{R} \times \mathbb{R}^n$, $\theta_i, i \in \mathbb{Z}$, is a B-sequence, such that $|\theta_i| \to \infty$ as $|i| \to \infty$. We suppose that the entries of $n \times n$ matrix $A(t)$ are from $\mathcal{PC}(\mathbb{R}, \theta)$, real valued $n \times n$ matrices $B_i, i \in \mathbb{Z}$, satisfy

$$\det(\mathcal{I} + B_i) \neq 0, \qquad (4.2)$$

where $\mathcal{I}$ is the identical $n \times n$ matrix.

Theorem 4.1.1. *Every solution $x(t) = x(t, t_0, x_0), (t_0, x_0) \in \mathbb{R} \times \mathbb{R}^n$, of (4.1) is unique and continuable on $\mathbb{R}$.*

Proof. There exists $j \in \mathbb{Z}$ such that $\theta_{j-1} < t_0 \leq \theta_j$. Assume that $t_0 < \theta_j$. Since $A(t) \in \mathcal{PC}(\mathbb{R}, \theta)$, the matrix is continuous on $[t_0, \theta_j]$. That is why, the solution $x(t)$ exists and unique on this interval as the solution $\phi(t, t_0, x_0)$ of the linear homogeneous ordinary differential equation

$$x' = A(t)x. \qquad (4.3)$$

If $t_0 = \theta_j$, then the solution starts with a jump. Next, we have that $x(\theta_j+) = (\mathcal{I} + B_j)x(\theta_j)$. Construct the following system (see Remark 2.3.1):

$$x' = A_e(t)x, \qquad (4.4)$$

where $A_e(t) = A(t)$ if $t \neq \theta_i$, and $A_e(\theta_i) = A(\theta_i+), i \in \mathbb{Z}$.

M. Akhmet, *Principles of Discontinuous Dynamical Systems*,
DOI 10.1007/978-1-4419-6581-3_4, © Springer Science+Business Media, LLC 2010

Solution $x(t)$ is equal to the solution $\psi(t, \theta_j, x(\theta_j+))$ of (4.4) on the interval $(\theta_j, \theta_{j+1}]$. The solution exists, unique and continuable on $(\theta_j, \theta_{j+1}]$. Similarly we can obtain the proof for all $t \geq t_0$.

Let us consider $t \leq t_0$. Equation (4.3) has the unique solution $\phi(t, t_0, x_0)$ on the interval $(\theta_{j-1}, t_0]$, and $x(t) = \phi(t, t_0, x_0)$. Obviously, we have that $x(\theta_{j-1}+) = \phi(\theta_{j-1}, t_0, x_0)$. Solving the equation

$$x(\theta_{j-1}+) = (\mathcal{I} + B_{j-1})x(\theta_{j-1}),$$

one can find

$$x(\theta_{j-1}) = (\mathcal{I} + B_{j-1})^{-1}x(\theta_{j-1}+).$$

Next, we have that $x(t) = \phi(t, \theta_{j-1}, x(\theta_{j-1}))$ on the interval $(\theta_{j-2}, \theta_{j-1}]$, where $\phi(t, \theta_{j-1}, x(\theta_{j-1}))$ is the unique solution of (4.3). Proceeding in this way one can complete the proof for all $t \leq t_0$. The theorem is proved. □

Exercise 4.1.1. Consider system (4.1) with $A(t) \in \mathcal{PC}_r(J, \theta), J \subset \mathbb{R}$. Prove that every solution $x(t) = x(t, t_0, x_0), (t_0, x_0) \in J \times \mathbb{R}^n$, of (4.1) is unique, continuable on J, and $x(t) \in \mathcal{PC}_r^1(J, \theta)$.

Hint: Use Theorem 4.1.1, Definitions 2.1.4, 2.1.5, and Exercise 2.3.1.

Exercise 4.1.2. Suppose that the entries of $A(t)$ belong to $\mathcal{PC}(J, \theta), J \subset \mathbb{R}$. Prove that every solution $x(t) = x(t, t_0, x_0), (t_0, x_0) \in J \times \mathbb{R}^n$, of (4.1) is unique, continuable on J, and $x(t) \in \mathcal{PC}^1(J, \theta)$.

Lemma 4.1.1. *The set $\mathcal{X}$ of all solutions of (4.1) is a linear space.*

Proof. Let $x_1(t), x_2(t) : \mathbb{R} \to \mathbb{R}^n$, be two solutions of (4.1). We shall show that $\alpha x_1(t) + x_2(t), \alpha \in \mathbb{R}$, is also a solution of (4.1).

Indeed, we first have that

$$(\alpha x_1(t) + x_2(t))' = \alpha x_1'(t) + x_2'(t) = \alpha A(t)x_1(t) + A(t)x_2(t)$$
$$= A(t)(\alpha x_1(t) + x_2(t)).$$

It means that the linear combination satisfies the differential equation. Moreover, for a fixed $i \in \mathbb{Z}$ one can obtain that

$$\Delta(\alpha x_1 + x_2)|_{t=\theta_i} = \alpha x_1(\theta_i+) + x_2(\theta_i+) - \alpha x_1(\theta_i) - x_2(\theta_i) =$$

$$\alpha \Delta x_1|_{t=\theta_i} + \Delta x_2|_{t=\theta_i} = \alpha B_i x_1(\theta_i) + B_i x_2(\theta_i) = B_i(\alpha x_1(\theta_i) + x_2(\theta_i)).$$

Thus, the equation of jumps is also satisfied by the linear combination of solutions. The lemma is proved. □

Lemma 4.1.2. *The linear space $\mathcal{X}$ has dimension n.*

The proof of this lemma is the same as that of Theorem 4.2 [60].

Let $x_i(t), i = 1, 2, \ldots, n$, be a basis of the space $\mathcal{X}$. It is called a *fundamental system of solutions* of (4.1).

Set $x_i(t) := (x_i^1, x_i^2, \ldots, x_i^n), i = 1, 2, \ldots, n$, and consider the matrix

$$X(t) = \begin{pmatrix} x_1^1 & x_2^1 \ldots x_n^1 \\ x_1^2 & x_2^2 \ldots x_n^2 \\ \cdots \\ x_1^n & x_2^n \ldots x_n^n \end{pmatrix}.$$

The matrix $X(t)$ is called a *fundamental matrix of solutions* (a fundamental matrix) of (4.1).

Exercise 4.1.3. Prove the following theorem.

Theorem 4.1.2. *A set of solutions* $x_1(t), x_2(t), \ldots, x_n(t)$, *of (4.1) is a fundamental system if and only if* $\det X(t) \neq 0$, *for all* $t \in \mathbb{R}$.

Denote by $X(t, s), t, s \in \mathbb{R}$, a fundamental matrix of (4.1) such that $X(s, s) = \mathcal{I}$, $s \in \mathbb{R}$. We shall call it a *transition matrix*.

Exercise 4.1.4. Let $X(t)$ be a fundamental matrix of (4.1). Show that $X(t, s) = X(t)X^{-1}(s)$ for all $t, s \in \mathbb{R}$.

It is useful to to solve the following two problems.

Example 4.1.1. Construct a fundamental matrix of (4.1) using the transition matrix $U(t, s)$ of (4.3) and matrices $B_i, i \in \mathbb{Z}$.

Solution. Since all solutions of (4.1) are defined on $\mathbb{R}$ and the solution of the initial value problem is unique, assume, without loss of generality, that $t_0 = 0$ and fix $k \in \mathbb{Z}$ such that $\theta_{k-1} < 0 \leq \theta_k$. Denote $X_0 = X(0)$.

Using the extension procedure of solutions, which is described in Sect. 2.3, one can find that

$$X(t) = \begin{cases} X_0, \text{ if } t = 0, \\ U(t, \theta_p)(\mathcal{I} + B_p)U(\theta_p, \theta_{p-1}) \cdots \\ U(\theta_{k+1}, \theta_k)(\mathcal{I} + B_k)U(\theta_{k-1}, t_0)X_0, \text{ if } \theta_k \leq \theta_p < t \leq \theta_{p+1}, \\ U(t, t_0)X_0, \text{ if } t_0 \leq t \leq \theta_k, \\ U(t, \theta_l)(\mathcal{I} + B_l)^{-1}U(\theta_l, \theta_{l+1}) \cdots \\ U(\theta_{k-1}, \theta_{k-1})(\mathcal{I} + B_{k-1})^{-1}U(\theta_{k-1}, 0)X_0, \text{ if } \theta_{l-1} < t \leq \theta_l \leq \theta_{k-1}, \\ U(t, t_0)X_0, \text{ if } \theta_{k-1} < t \leq 0. \end{cases} \quad (4.5)$$

From the last formula it is not difficult to see that $\det X(t) \neq 0$ for all $t \in \mathbb{R}$.

Example 4.1.2. Construct the transition matrix $X(t, s)$ of (4.1), using the transition matrix $U(t, s)$ of (4.3) and matrices $B_i, i \in \mathbb{Z}$.

Solution. We have found above that $X(t,s) = X(t)X^{-1}(s)$, where $X(t)$ is a fundamental matrix that could be defined by (4.5). Obviously, there exist several possible situations for t and s in $\mathbb{R}$. Let us consider only one of them. Namely, assume that $\theta_k \leq \theta_p < t \leq \theta_{p+1}$ and $\theta_{l-1} < s \leq \theta_l \leq \theta_{k-1}$. Then, using (4.5) one can find that

$$X(t,s) = X(t)X^{-1}(s) = U(t,\theta_p)(\mathcal{I} + B_p)U(\theta_p, \theta_{p-1})\ldots$$

$$\ldots U(\theta_{k+1},\theta_k)(\mathcal{I} + B_k)U(\theta_{k-1},t_0)X_0[U(t,\theta_l)(\mathcal{I} + B_l)^{-1}U(\theta_l,\theta_{l+1})\ldots$$

$$\ldots U(\theta_{k-1},\theta_{k-1})(\mathcal{I} + B_{k-1})^{-1}U(\theta_{k-1},0)X_0]^{-1} =$$

$$U(t,\theta_p)(\mathcal{I} + B_p)U(\theta_p,\theta_{p-1})\ldots U(\theta_{k+1},\theta_k)(\mathcal{I} + B_k)U(\theta_{k-1},t_0)X_0 \times$$

$$X_0^{-1}U(0,\theta_{k-1})(\mathcal{I} + B_{k-1})\ldots U(\theta_l,s) = U(t,\theta_p)(\mathcal{I} + B_p)U(\theta_p,\theta_{p-1})\ldots$$

$$\ldots (\mathcal{I} + B_l)U(\theta_l,s).$$

Thus, we have obtained that

$$X(t,s) = U(t,\theta_p)(\mathcal{I} + B_p)U(\theta_p,\theta_{p-1})\ldots(\mathcal{I} + B_l)U(\theta_l,s). \qquad (4.6)$$

So, the transition matrix in this particular case is defined. We propose to the reader to derive the formula (4.6) directly, using the common procedure of extension of solutions of Sect. 2.3 and the condition $X(s,s) = \mathcal{I}$.

Example 4.1.3. Construct the fundamental matrix $X(t)$, $X(0) = \mathcal{I}$ of the system

$$\begin{aligned}
x_1' &= -x_2, \\
x_2' &= x_1, \\
\Delta x_1|_{t=i} &= kx_1, \\
\Delta x_2|_{t=i} &= kx_2.
\end{aligned} \qquad (4.7)$$

Solution. First, consider the case $t \geq 0$. It is known that

$$U(t,s) = \begin{pmatrix} \cos(t-s) & -\sin(t-s) \\ \sin(t-s) & \cos(t-s) \end{pmatrix},$$

is a transition matrix of the system

$$\begin{aligned}
x_1' &= -x_2, \\
x_2' &= x_1,
\end{aligned} \qquad (4.8)$$

for all $t, s \in \mathbb{R}$.

Using (4.6) one can find that

$$X(t,s) = \begin{pmatrix} \cos(t-\theta_p) & -\sin(t-\theta_p) \\ \sin(t-\theta_p) & \cos(t-\theta_p) \end{pmatrix} \begin{pmatrix} 1+k & 0 \\ 0 & 1+k \end{pmatrix} \times$$

$$\begin{pmatrix} \cos(\theta_p-\theta_{p-1}) & -\sin(\theta_p-\theta_{p-1}) \\ \sin(\theta_p-\theta_{p-1}) & \cos(\theta_p-\theta_{p-1}) \end{pmatrix} \begin{pmatrix} 1+k & 0 \\ 0 & 1+k \end{pmatrix} \times$$

$$\cdots \begin{pmatrix} \cos(\theta_k-) & -\sin(\theta_k-) \\ \sin(\theta_k-) & \cos(\theta_k-) \end{pmatrix}, \qquad (4.9)$$

where $\theta_{k-1} < 0 \le \theta_k, \theta_p < t \le \theta_{p+1}$.

The matrix

$$\begin{pmatrix} 1+k & 0 \\ 0 & 1+k \end{pmatrix}$$

commutes with any another matrix. Moreover,

$$\begin{pmatrix} \cos\alpha & -\sin\alpha \\ \sin\alpha & \cos\alpha \end{pmatrix} \begin{pmatrix} \cos\beta & -\sin\beta \\ \sin\beta & \cos\beta \end{pmatrix} = \begin{pmatrix} \cos(\alpha+\beta) & -\sin(\alpha+\beta) \\ \sin(\alpha+\beta) & \cos(\alpha+\beta) \end{pmatrix},$$

for arbitrary $\alpha, \beta \in \mathbb{R}$. Consequently,

$$X(t) = \begin{pmatrix} \cos t & -\sin t \\ \sin t & \cos t \end{pmatrix} (1+k)^{i([0,t))}. \qquad (4.10)$$

Similarly, one can find that if $t < 0$, then

$$X(t) = \begin{pmatrix} \cos t & -\sin t \\ \sin t & \cos t \end{pmatrix} (1+k)^{-i([t,0))}. \qquad (4.11)$$

Finally, we have that

$$X(t) = \begin{cases} \begin{pmatrix} 1 & 0 \\ 0 & 1 \end{pmatrix}, & t = 0, \\[2mm] \begin{pmatrix} \cos t & -\sin t \\ \sin t & \cos t \end{pmatrix} (1+k)^{i([0,t))}, & t > 0 \\[2mm] \begin{pmatrix} \cos t & -\sin t \\ \sin t & \cos t \end{pmatrix} (1+k)^{-i([t,0))}, & t < 0. \end{cases} \qquad (4.12)$$

Exercise 4.1.5. Apply (4.12)

(a) to verify that formula $X(t,s) = X(t)X^{-1}(s)$ is valid for all $t, s \in \mathbb{R}$;
(b) to analyze stability of the zero solution, varying the coefficient k.

Exercise 4.1.6. Consider a solution $x(t, 0, x_0)$ of the following linear system:

$$\begin{aligned}
x_1' &= -x_2, \\
x_2' &= x_1, \\
\Delta x_1|_{t=2\pi i} &= -x_1, \\
\Delta x_2|_{t=2\pi i} &= x_2.
\end{aligned} \tag{4.13}$$

Show that there are values of $x_0 \in \mathbb{R}^2$, such that the solution does not exist on $(-\infty, 0]$. Explain this result.

Example 4.1.4. [142] Consider the system

$$\begin{aligned}
x' &= Ax, \\
\Delta x|_{t=\theta_i} &= Bx,
\end{aligned} \tag{4.14}$$

where constant matrices A, B are such that $AB = BA$. Let λ be an eigenvalue of matrix A, and x_0 be the correspond eigenvector. Prove that $x(t) = e^{\lambda(t-t_0)}$ $(\mathcal{I} + B)^{i([t_0,t))}x_0, t \geq 0$, is a solution of (4.14), such that $x(t_0) = x_0$.

Solution. To verify that the proposed function is a solution, one should check that it satisfies the differential equation and equation of jumps. Let us begin with the differential equation. We have that

$$x'(t) = \lambda e^{\lambda(t-t_0)}(\mathcal{I} + B)^{i([t_0,t))}x_0 = e^{\lambda(t-t_0)}(\mathcal{I} + B)^{i([t_0,t))}\lambda x_0 =$$

$$e^{\lambda(t-t_0)}(\mathcal{I} + B)^{i([t_0,t))}Ax_0 = Ae^{\lambda(t-t_0)}(\mathcal{I} + B)^{i([t_0,t))}x_0 = Ax(t).$$

Now, fix $i \in \mathbb{Z}$. Then for the given function one can see that

$$\begin{aligned}
\Delta x|_{t=\theta_i} &= x(\theta_i+) - x(\theta_i) = e^{\lambda(\theta_i-t_0+)}(\mathcal{I} + B)^{i([t_0,\theta_i+))}x_0 - e^{\lambda(\theta_i-t_0)} \\
&\quad \times (\mathcal{I} + B)^{i([t_0,\theta_i))}x_0 \\
&= [e^{\lambda(\theta_i-t_0+)}(\mathcal{I} + B) - e^{\lambda(\theta_i-t_0)}\mathcal{I}](\mathcal{I} + B)^{i([t_0,\theta_i))}x_0 \\
&= [(\mathcal{I} + B) - \mathcal{I}]e^{\lambda(\theta_i-t_0)}(\mathcal{I} + B)^{i([t_0,\theta_i))}x_0 = Bx(\theta_i).
\end{aligned}$$

Thus, $e^{\lambda(t-t_0)}(\mathcal{I} + B)^{i([t_0,t))}x_0$ is a solution. The initial condition can be verified easily.

Exercise 4.1.7. Use the result of the last example to determine a real valued solution of (4.14) if the eigenvalue is a complex number.

Exercise 4.1.8. Assume that the real parts of all eigenvalues of the matrix $A + \ln(\mathcal{I} + B)$ are negative, and there exists a positive number τ such that $i\tau \leq \theta_i \leq (i + 1)\tau, i \in \mathbb{Z}$. Use the last two results to prove that there exist positive numbers N and ω, such that $||X(t, s)|| \leq Ne^{-\omega(t-s)}, t \geq s$, where $X(t, s)$ is the transition matrix of the system (4.14). Evaluate the numbers N and ω.

Example 4.1.5. Investigate asymptotic behavior of solutions of the system

$$x' = ax,$$
$$\Delta x|_{t=\theta_i} = bx, \tag{4.15}$$

where $t, x \in \mathbb{R}, i \in \mathbb{Z}$, coefficients a and b are real numbers, $b \neq -1, |\theta_i| \to \infty$ as $|i| \to \infty$.

Solution. Since the equation is linear, $x(t, 0, x_0) = x(t, 0, 1)x_0$. So, it is sufficient to consider the behavior of $x_1(t) = x(t, 0, 1)$, the fundamental solution of (4.15). We shall consider the following cases.

(a) First, let us discuss the problem with $\theta_i = i\omega, i \in \mathbb{Z}$, where ω is a fixed positive real number. Applying (4.5), one can find that

$$x_1(t) = \begin{cases} e^{at}(1+b)^{i([0,t))}, & t \geq 0, \\ e^{at}(1+b)^{-i([t,0))}, & t < 0. \end{cases} \tag{4.16}$$

Then

$$|x_1(t)| = \begin{cases} e^{(1-\{\frac{t}{\omega}\})\ln|1+b|}e^{(a+\frac{\ln|1+b|}{\omega})t}, & t \geq 0, \\ e^{-\{\frac{t}{\omega}\}\ln|1+b|}e^{(a+\frac{\ln|1+b|}{\omega})t}, & t < 0. \end{cases} \tag{4.17}$$

where $\{t\} = t - [t]$. Let $\kappa = a + \frac{\ln|1+b|}{\omega}$. From (4.17) it follows that there are positive numbers m and M such that

$$m e^{\kappa t} \leq |x_1(t)| \leq M e^{\kappa t}, t \in \mathbb{R} \tag{4.18}$$

and

$$\kappa = \lim_{t \to \infty} \frac{1}{t} \ln |x_1(t)|. \tag{4.19}$$

That is, κ is an exponent of $x_1(t)$ and, consequently, it is the exponent of (4.15). Using (4.17) one can make the following conclusions:

(i) if $\kappa > 0$, then every nonzero solution $x(t)$ of (4.15) satisfies $|x(t)| \to \infty$ as $t \to \infty$, and $|x(t)| \to 0$ as $t \to -\infty$;
(ii) if $\kappa < 0$, then every nonzero solution $x(t)$ of (4.15) satisfies $|x(t)| \to 0$ as $t \to \infty$, and $|x(t)| \to \infty$ as $t \to -\infty$;
(iii) if $\kappa = 0$, then all solutions of (4.15) are functions bounded on $\mathbb{R}$.

(b) Assume that $\theta_{i+1} - \theta_i = \omega, i \in \mathbb{Z}$, where ω is a positive real number. Prove yourself that the solution $x_1(t) = x(t, 0, 1)$ of (4.15) and the number $\kappa = a + \frac{\ln|1+b|}{\omega}$ satisfy relations (4.18) and (4.19).
(c) Assume that the sequence $\theta_i, i \in \mathbb{Z}$, satisfies a more general condition than in (a) and (b). Namely, assume that the following limit:

$$\lim_{t-s \to \infty} \frac{i((s,t))}{t-s} = q \geq 0$$

exists.

It is obvious that if $x(t) = x(t, s, x_0), x(s) = x_0$ is a solution of (4.15), then $x(t) = x(t, s)x_0$, where

$$x(t, s) = \begin{cases} e^{a(t-s)}(1+b)^{i([s,t))}, & t \geq s, \\ e^{a(t-s)}(1+b)^{-i([t,s))}, & t < s. \end{cases} \tag{4.20}$$

is the transition "matrix" of (4.15).

So, it is sufficient to analyze $x(t, s)$ if one wants to investigate the asymptotic behavior of solutions of (4.15).

Fix $\epsilon > 0$ and set $\epsilon_1 = \frac{\epsilon}{\ln|1+b|}$. There exists a positive number $T(\epsilon_1)$ such that if $t - s \geq T(\epsilon_1)$, then

$$q - \epsilon < \frac{i([s,t])}{t - s} < q + \epsilon.$$

That is, each interval with the length $T(\epsilon_1)$ has at most $[(q + \epsilon)T(\epsilon_1)]$ points of θ. Consequently, there exist

$$M(\epsilon) = \sup_{0 \leq t - s \leq T} e^{a(t-s)}|1 + b|^{i([s,t))}$$

and

$$m(\epsilon) = \inf_{0 \leq t - s \leq T} e^{a(t-s)}|1 + b|^{i([s,t))}.$$

Hence,

$$m(\epsilon)e^{(\alpha-\epsilon_1)(t-s)} \leq |x(t, s)| \leq M(\epsilon)e^{(\alpha+\epsilon_1)(t-s)}, \ t \geq s, \tag{4.21}$$

where $\alpha = a + q \ln|1 + b|$.

Exercise 4.1.9. Investigate asymptotic behavior of solutions of (4.15) if θ is a finite set.

Exercise 4.1.10. Solve the following problems.

1. Prove that (4.21) implies

$$\alpha = \lim_{t-s \to \infty} \frac{1}{t - s} \ln|x(t, s)|. \tag{4.22}$$

2. Prove analogs of (4.21) and (4.22) if $t - s < 0$.
3. Let the following relation be valid:

$$\sup_{s \in \mathbb{R}} \lim_{t-s \to \infty} \frac{i((s,t))}{t - s} = q \geq 0, \tag{4.23}$$

and set $\alpha = a + q \ln|1 + b|$.
   Prove that

$$\alpha = \lim_{t-s \to \infty} \frac{1}{t - s} \ln|x(t, s)|.$$

4. Assume that for some numbers $p \in \mathbb{N}, \omega \in \mathbb{R}, \omega > 0$, condition $(C6)$ of Chap. 3 is fulfilled. Applying the Poincaré criterion, find a sufficient condition for ω-periodicity of all solutions of (4.15).
5. Let the following system be given:

$$x' = ax,$$
$$\Delta x|_{t=\theta_i} = b_i x, \qquad (4.24)$$

where $t, x \in \mathbb{R}, a$ and b_i are real coefficients. Assume that there exist limits

$$\lim_{t-s\to\infty} \frac{i([s,t])}{t-s} = q, \quad \lim_{i\to\infty} |1 + b_i| = \beta.$$

Show that all solutions of the system tend to the zero as $t \to \infty$ if $a + q \ln \beta < 0$.

The adjoint system. Consider, besides (4.1), the linear system of impulsive differential equations

$$y' = P(t)y,$$
$$\Delta y|_{t=\theta_i} = Q_i y. \qquad (4.25)$$

where $(t, y) \in \mathbb{R} \times \mathbb{R}^n$, and the sequence $\theta_i, i \in \mathbb{Z}$, is the same as in (4.1). We suppose that entries of the matrix $P(t)$ belong to $\mathcal{PC}(\mathbb{R}, \theta)$, the real valued $n \times n$ matrices $Q_i, i \in \mathbb{Z}$, satisfy

$$\det(\mathcal{I} + Q_i) \neq 0. \qquad (4.26)$$

One can easily see that all solutions of system (4.25) exist on $\mathbb{R}$ and are unique.

Definition 4.1.1. Systems (4.1) and (4.25) are mutually adjoint if any two solutions $x(t)$ and $y(t)$ of these equations satisfy

$$< x(t), y(t) >= c, \qquad (4.27)$$

where $t \in \mathbb{R}, < \cdot, \cdot >$ is the scalar product and c is a real constant, which depends on these solutions.

Exercise 4.1.11. Prove that systems (4.1) and (4.25) are mutually adjoint if and only if any two solutions $x(t)$ and $y(t)$ of these systems satisfy conditions:

(a) $\frac{d<x(t),y(t)>}{dt} = 0$;
(b) $\Delta < x(t), y(t) > |_{t=\theta_i} \equiv < x(\theta_i+), y(\theta_i+) > - < x(\theta_i), y(\theta_i) >= 0$, $i \in \mathbb{Z}$.

Theorem 4.1.3. *Systems (4.1) and (4.25) are mutually adjoint if and only if* $P(t) = -A^T(t)$ *and* $Q_i = -(\mathcal{I} + B_i^T)^{-1}B_i^T$.

Proof. Sufficiency. It is easily seen that entries of matrix $-A^T(t)$ belong to $\mathcal{PC}(\mathbb{R}, \theta)$. Moreover, we have that $\mathcal{I} - (\mathcal{I} + B_i^T)^{-1}B_i^T = (\mathcal{I} + B_i^T)^{-1}$

$(\mathcal{I} + B_i^T - B_i^T) = (\mathcal{I} + B_i^T)^{-1}$ is not a singular matrix for an integer i. Consequently, each solution of the system exists on $\mathbb{R}$. Next, we will apply the results of the last exercise to prove the sufficiency. We have that

$$\frac{d < x(t), y(t) >}{dt} = < x'(t), y(t) > + < x(t), y'(t) > = < A(t)x(t), y(t) > +$$

$$< x(t), -A(t)^T y(t) > = < x(t), (A(t)^T - A(t)^T)y(t) > = < x(t), 0 > = 0.$$

Moreover, if $i \in \mathbb{Z}$, then

$$\Delta < x(t), y(t) > |_{t=\theta_i} = < x(\theta_i +), y(\theta_i +) > - < x(\theta_i), y(\theta_i) > =$$

$$< x(\theta_i +) - x(\theta_i), y(\theta_i +) > + < x(\theta_i), y(\theta_i +) - y(\theta_i) > =$$

$$< B_i x(\theta_i), y(\theta_i +) > + < x(\theta_i), -(\mathcal{I} + B_i^T)^{-1} B_i^T y(\theta_i) > =$$

$$< x(\theta_i), (B_i^T (\mathcal{I} - (\mathcal{I} + B_i^T)^{-1} B_i^T)) - (\mathcal{I} + B_i^T)^{-1} B_i^T) y(\theta_i) > = < x(\theta_i), 0 > = 0.$$

The sufficiency is proved.   □

Necessity. Assume that systems (4.1) and (4.25) are adjoint. Consider arbitrary solutions $x(t)$ and $y(t)$ of these systems. By Exercise 4.1.11 we have that $< x(t), y(t) >' = 0$ and $\Delta < x(t), y(t) > |_{t=\theta_i} = 0, i \in \mathbb{Z}$. Consequently, $< x, (A^T(t) + P(t))y > = 0, t \in \mathbb{R}$ and $< x, ((\mathcal{I} + B_i^T)^{-1} B_i^T + Q_i)y > = 0, i \in \mathbb{Z}$, for arbitrary $x, y \in \mathbb{R}^n$. The last two expressions imply that $P(t) = -A^T(t)$, and $Q_i = -(\mathcal{I} + B_i^T)^{-1} B_i^T$. Indeed, let us verify the second equation. Assume on the contrary, that $(\mathcal{I} + B_i^T)^{-1} B_i^T + Q_i \neq 0$, for some $i \in \mathbb{Z}$. Then one can find a vector $\bar{y} \in \mathbb{R}^n$ such that $((\mathcal{I} + B_i^T)^{-1} B_i^T + Q_i)\bar{y} \neq 0$. If $x = ((\mathcal{I} + B_i^T)^{-1} B_i^T + Q_i)\bar{y}$, then $< x, ((\mathcal{I} + B_i^T)^{-1} B_i^T + Q_i)\bar{y} > \neq 0$, and the last inequality contradicts the previous conclusion. Consequently, $(\mathcal{I} + B_i^T)^{-1} B_i^T + Q_i = 0$. The lemma is proved.   □

Exercise 4.1.12. Prove that $X^T(t)^{-1}$ is a fundamental matrix of the adjoint system (4.25) if $X(t)$ is a fundamental matrix of (4.1).

Linear exponentially dichotomous systems. Fix a natural number $m, 0 < m < n$. Suppose that there exist m and $(n - m)$-dimensional hyperplanes $X_+(t)$ and $X_-(t)$ of $\mathbb{R}^n$ respectively such that if $x(t)$ is a solution of (4.1) and $x(t) \in X_+(t)$, then $\|x(t)\| \leq a_1 \|x(s)\| e^{-\gamma_1 (t-s)}, -\infty < s \leq t < +\infty$ and, if $x(t) \in X_-(t)$, then $\|x(t)\| \geq a_2 \|x(s)\| e^{\gamma_2(t-s)}, -\infty < s \leq t < +\infty$. Here $a_j, \gamma_j, j = 1, 2$, are positive constants. Then (4.1) is said to be an *exponentially dichotomous* linear impulsive system.

Assume that the matrix $A(t)$ is bounded on $\mathbb{R}$. Let us show that by a piecewise-continuous Lyapunov transformation system (4.1) can be reduced to a box-diagonal system, i.e., a system splitting into two equations:

$$\frac{d\xi}{dt} = P_1(t)\xi, \quad \Delta\xi|_{t=\theta_i} = Q_i^1\xi, \tag{4.28}$$

and

$$\frac{d\eta}{dt} = P_2(t)\eta, \ \Delta\eta|_{t=\theta_i} = Q_i^2\eta. \tag{4.29}$$

By applying the Gram–Schmidt process one can obtain a linear transformation $x(t) = U(t)y(t), y = (\xi, \eta)$, which takes system (4.3) to the form

$$\frac{d\xi}{dt} = P_1(t)\xi, \ \frac{d\eta}{dt} = P_2(t)\eta, \tag{4.30}$$

on each interval of continuity $(\theta_i, \theta_{i+1}), i \in \mathbb{Z}$. Matrix $U(t)$ is continuous on the union of intervals $(\theta_i, \theta_{i+1}), i \in \mathbb{Z}$, and is uniformly bounded on the set together with matrices $dU(t)/dt, U^{-1}(t)$. For each θ_i one can continue $U(\theta_i) = U(\theta_i-)$. That is, $U(t)$ is a Lyapunov piecewise continuous matrix [142]. Since solutions of impulsive differential equations are left-continuous functions, $x(\theta_i) = U(\theta_i)y(\theta_i)$ for all i. Let $X(t)$ be the fundamental matrix of (4.1), which is used to define $U(t), U(t) = X(t)S(t), S(t) = diag(S_+, S_-)$. Then $U(\theta_i+) = X(\theta_i+)S(\theta_i+) = (I + B_i)X(\theta_i)S(\theta_i+)$ and $U(\theta_i) = X(\theta_i)S(\theta_i)$. Subtract from the first equality the second one to obtain $\Delta U|_{t=\theta_i} = (I + B_i) X(\theta_i)\Delta S + B_i U(\theta_i)$ or

$$U^{-1}(\theta_i+)[B_i U(\theta_i) - \Delta U] = U^{-1}(\theta_i+)(I + B_i)X(\theta_i)\Delta S.$$

It implies that

$$U^{-1}(\theta_i+)[B_i U(\theta_i) - \Delta U] = -S^{-1}(\theta_i+)\Delta S.$$

That is, $Q_i = U^{-1}(\theta_i+)[B_i U(\theta_i) - \Delta U], i \in \mathbb{Z}$, are box-diagonal matrices. Consequently, using the transformation $x = U(t)y$ in the equation $\Delta x|_{t=\theta_i} = B_i x$, we obtain that $\Delta y|_{t=\theta_i} = Q_i y$. Denoting $Q_i = diag(Q_i^1, Q_i^2)$, we arrive to the system of equations (4.28) and (4.29). Next, one can obtain that there exist positive constants K, γ such that

$$\|X_1(t, s)\| \le K \exp(-\gamma(t - s)), \ t \ge s, \tag{4.31}$$

and

$$\|X_2(t, s)\| \le K \exp(\gamma(t - s)), \ t \le s, \tag{4.32}$$

where $X_1(t, s)$ and $X_2(t, s)$ are transition matrices of (4.28) and (4.29) respectively.

4.2 Linear Nonhomogeneous Systems

Consider the following system:

$$\begin{aligned} y' &= A(t)y + f(t), \\ \Delta y|_{t=\theta_i} &= B_i y + J_i, \end{aligned} \tag{4.33}$$

where $(t, x) \in \mathbb{R} \times \mathbb{R}^n$, an infinite sequence θ_i satisfies $|\theta_i| \to \infty$ as $|i| \to \infty$. It is assumed that there exists a positive constant θ such that $\theta_{i+1} - \theta_i \leq \theta$. Moreover, real valued entries of the matrix $A(t)$ are from $\mathcal{PC}(\mathbb{R}, \theta)$, bounded on $\mathbb{R}$, and real valued $n \times n$ matrices $B_i, i \in \mathbb{Z}$, satisfy (4.2). Coordinates of the vector-function $f(t) : \mathbb{R} \to \mathbb{R}^n$ belong to $\mathcal{PC}(\mathbb{R}, \theta)$, and $J_i, i \in \mathbb{Z}$, is a sequence of vectors from $\mathbb{R}^n$. We assume that

$$\sup_t ||f|| + \sup_i ||J|| = \bar{M} < \infty. \tag{4.34}$$

Repeating identically the proof of Theorem 4.1.1, one can check that the following assertion is valid.

Theorem 4.2.1. *Every solution $x(t) = x(t, t_0, x_0)$, $(t_0, x_0) \in \mathbb{R} \times \mathbb{R}^n$, of (4.33) is unique and continuable on $\mathbb{R}$.*

The general solution of (4.33). Fix $(t_0, x_0) \in \mathbb{R} \times \mathbb{R}^n$. Let $X(t), X(t_0) = \mathcal{I}$, be a fundamental matrix of (4.1), associated with (4.33). Let us apply to system (4.33) the transformation $y = X(t)z$, where $z \in \mathbb{R}^n$ is a new variable, depending on t. We have that $X(t)z' + X'(t)z = A(t)X(t)z + f(t)$ or

$$z'(t) = X^{-1}(t)f(t). \tag{4.35}$$

If $t = \theta_i$, for some $i \in \mathbb{Z}$, then the substitution implies that

$$X(\theta_i+)z(\theta_i+) - X(\theta_i)z(\theta_i) = B_i X(\theta_i)z(\theta_i) + J_i,$$

and

$$X(\theta_i+)(z(\theta_i+) - z(\theta_i)) + (X(\theta_i+) - X(\theta_i))z(\theta_i) = B_i X(\theta_i)z(\theta_i) + J_i.$$

Since $X(\theta_i+) - X(\theta_i) = B_i X(\theta_i)$, the last formula yields that

$$\Delta z|_{t=\theta_i} = X^{-1}(\theta_i+)J_i, i \in \mathbb{Z}. \tag{4.36}$$

Thus, combining (4.35) with (4.36), $y(t)$ is a solution of (4.33) if and only if $z(t) = X^{-1}(t)y(t)$ is a solution of the system

$$\begin{aligned} z'(t) &= X^{-1}(t)f(t) \\ \Delta z|_{t=\theta_i} &= X^{-1}(\theta_i+)J_i. \end{aligned} \tag{4.37}$$

Exercise 4.2.1. Prove that the coordinates of $X^{-1}(t)f(t)$ belong to $\mathcal{PC}(\mathbb{R}, \theta)$.

A solution $z(t) = z(t, t_0, z_0)$ of (4.37) can be easily found, similarly to the results of Sect. 2.7,

$$z(t) = \begin{cases} z_0 + \int_{t_0}^t X^{-1}(s)f(s)ds + \sum_{t_0 \leq \theta_i < t} X^{-1}(\theta_i+)J_i, & t \geq t_0, \\ z_0 + \int_{t_0}^t X^{-1}(s)f(s)ds - \sum_{t \leq \theta_i < t_0} X^{-1}(\theta_i+)J_i, & t < t_0. \end{cases} \tag{4.38}$$

Now, taking into account that $y_0 = X(t_0)z_0 = z_0$, and making the inverse substitution one can derive that

$$x(t, t_0, x_0) = \begin{cases} X(t)x_0 + \int_{t_0}^{t} X(t)X^{-1}(s)f(s)ds + \sum_{t_0 \le \theta_i < t} X(t)X^{-1}(\theta_i+)J_i, & t \ge t_0, \\ X(t)x_0 + \int_{t_0}^{t} X(t)X^{-1}(s)f(s)ds - \sum_{t \le \theta_i < t_0} X(t)X^{-1}(\theta_i+)J_i, & t < t_0. \end{cases}$$

If the fundamental matrix is not necessarily the unit matrix at $t = t_0$, then one can write

$$x(t, t_0, x_0) = \begin{cases} X(t, t_0)x_0 + \int_{t_0}^{t} X(t,s)f(s)ds + \sum_{t_0 \le \theta_i < t} X(t, \theta_i+)J_i, & t \ge t_0, \\ X(t, t_0)x_0 + \int_{t_0}^{t} X(t,s)f(s)ds - \sum_{t \le \theta_i < t_0} X(t, \theta_i+)J_i, & t < t_0. \end{cases} \quad (4.39)$$

Last two formulas define the general solution of the linear nonhomogeneous system (4.33).

Example 4.2.1. Consider the following system:

$$y' = ay + f(t),$$
$$\Delta y|_{t=\theta_i} = by + w_i, \quad (4.40)$$

where $t, y \in \mathbb{R}, a$ and $b, b \ne -1$, are real constants, $f \in PC(\mathbb{R}, \theta), w_i \in \mathbb{R}, i \in \mathbb{Z}$. Assume that

$$\sup_{t} |f| + \sup_{i} |w_i| = M < \infty.$$

We suppose that θ is a B-sequence, and there exists the limit

$$\lim_{t-s \to \infty} \frac{i([s,t])}{t-s} = q \ge 0.$$

Write $\alpha = a + q \ln |1 + b|$, and assume that $\alpha \ne 0$.

Let us show that (4.40) admits a unique solution $y_0(t)$ bounded on $\mathbb{R}$. Consider $\alpha > 0$. Results of Example 4.1.5, (c) imply that there exist positive constants β, K such that

$$|x(t,s)| \le Ke^{\beta(t-s)}, t \le s, \quad (4.41)$$
$$|x(t,s)| \ge K^{-1}e^{\beta(t-s)}, t \ge s, \quad (4.42)$$

where $x(t,s)$ is the fundamental solution of (4.15). The solution $y(t) = y(t, 0, y_0)$ of (4.40) has the form

$$y(t) = x(t,0)y_0 + \int_0^t x(t,s)f(s)ds + \sum_{0 \le \theta_i < t} x(t, \theta_i+)w_i$$

or

$$y(t) = x(t, 0)[y_0 + \int_0^t x(0, s) f(s) ds + \sum_{0 \le \theta_i < t} x(0, \theta_i +) w_i].$$ (4.43)

The last formula and condition (4.42) imply that the solution is bounded only if

$$y_0 = - \int_0^\infty x(0, s) f(s) ds - \sum_{0 \le \theta_i < \infty} x(0, \theta_i +) w_i.$$ (4.44)

Let us show that the integral and sum in the last formula are convergent. Using (4.41) we have that

$$\left| \int_0^\infty x(0, s) f(s) ds \right| \le \frac{MK}{\beta} < \infty.$$

Further, one can obtain that

$$\left| \sum_{0 \le \theta_i < \infty} x(0, \theta_i +) w_i \right| \le MK \sum_{0 \le \theta_i < \infty} e^{-\beta \theta_i}.$$

Fix $\epsilon > 0$. Then $i([s, t]) \le (q + \epsilon)(t - s)$, if $t - s \ge T(\epsilon)$ for some positive $T(\epsilon)$.

Thus, every interval of the length $T(\epsilon)$ consists of not more than $[(q + \epsilon)(t - s)]$ elements of θ. Hence,

$$\sum_{0 \le \theta_i < \infty} e^{-\beta \theta_i} \le \sum_{i=0}^\infty (q + \epsilon) T(\epsilon) e^{-i\beta T(\epsilon)} = (q + \epsilon) T(\epsilon) \frac{1}{1 - e^{\beta T(\epsilon)}}.$$

Thus, the integral and sum are convergent. Using the value of y_0 in (4.43) one can find that

$$y_0(t) = - \int_t^\infty x(t, s) f(s) ds - \sum_{t \le \theta_i < \infty} x(t, \theta_i +) w_i.$$ (4.45)

If $\epsilon > 0$ is fixed, then one can obtain that

$$|y_0(t)| \le MK \left[\frac{1}{\beta} + (q + \epsilon) T(\epsilon) \frac{1}{1 - e^{\beta T(\epsilon)}} \right] < \infty,$$ (4.46)

for all $t \in \mathbb{R}$.

Exercise 4.2.2. Solve the following problems.

1. Verify that (4.46) is valid;
2. Show, directly, that $y_0(t)$ is a solution of (4.40);
3. Prove that $y_0(t)$ is a unique solution of (4.40) bounded on $\mathbb{R}$.

Exercise 4.2.3. Assume that $\alpha < 0$ in the last example. Prove that

$$y_0(t) = \int_{-\infty}^{t} x(t,s) f(s) ds + \sum_{t < \theta_i} x(t, \theta_i +) w_i$$

is a unique solution of (4.40) bounded on $\mathbb{R}$.

In the rest of this section, we shall develop the results of the last example and exercise to the most general case. Consider system (4.33) again assuming that associated homogeneous system (4.1) is exponentially dichotomous. That is, there exists a linear transformation $U(t)$, which reduces (4.1) to (4.28) and (4.29). Apply the substitution in (4.33) and obtain the following system of linear nonhomogeneous impulsive differential equations:

$$\frac{d\xi}{dt} = P_1(t)\xi + f_1(t),$$
$$\Delta\xi|_{t=\theta_i} = Q_i^1 \xi + J_i^1, \tag{4.47}$$

$$\frac{d\eta}{dt} = P_2(t)\eta + f_2(t),$$
$$\Delta\eta|_{t=\theta_i} = Q_i^2 \eta + J_i^2, \tag{4.48}$$

where $x = U(t)y$, $y = (\xi, \eta)$, matrices P_1, P_2, Q_i^1, Q_i^2, are defined in (4.28) and (4.29), and $(f_1, f_2) = U^{-1}(t) f$, $(J_i^1, J_i^2) = U^{-1}(\theta_i +) J_i$. On the basis of the assumptions made above, we have that

$$\sup_t \|(f_1, f_2)\| + \sup_i \|(J_i^1, J_i^2)\| = M < \infty.$$

Theorem 4.2.2. *If the associated linear homogeneous system (4.1) is exponentially dichotomous and (4.34) is valid, then there exists a unique solution of (4.33) bounded on $\mathbb{R}$.*

Proof. It is sufficient to show that functions

$$\xi(t) = \int_{-\infty}^{t} X_1(t,s) f_1(s) ds + \sum_{-\infty < \theta_i < t} X_1(t, \theta_i +) J_i^1, \tag{4.49}$$

and

$$\eta(t) = -\int_{t}^{\infty} X_2(t,s) f_2(s) ds - \sum_{t \le \theta_i < \infty} X_2(t, \theta_i +) J_i^2. \tag{4.50}$$

are components of a unique bounded solution of the system of equations (4.47) and (4.48).

(i). We start with (4.49). First of all one has that

$$\|\xi(t)\| \leq \int_{-\infty}^{t} Ke^{-\gamma(t-s)} M ds + \sum_{-\infty < \theta_i < t} Ke^{-\gamma(t-\theta_i)} M \leq KM[\frac{1}{\gamma} + \frac{1}{1-e^{-\gamma\theta}}].$$

That is, both the integral and infinite sum are convergent uniformly for all t, and the function ξ is bounded on $\mathbb{R}$. Differentiating, we have that

$$\xi'(t) = X_1(t,t) f_1(t) + \int_{-\infty}^{t} X_1'(t,s) f_1(s) ds + \sum_{-\infty < \theta_i < t} X_1'(t, \theta_i+) J_i^1 =$$

$$f_1(t) + \int_{-\infty}^{t} P_1(t) X_1(t,s) f_1(s) ds + \sum_{-\infty < \theta_i < t} P_1(t) X_1(t, \theta_i+) J_i^1 = P_1(t)\xi(t) + f_1(t).$$

Fix $j \in \mathbb{Z}$ and verify that

$$\Delta\xi|_{t=\theta_j} = \xi(\theta_j+) - \xi(\theta_j) = \int_{-\infty}^{\theta_j+} X_1(\theta_j+, s) f_1(s) ds + \sum_{-\infty < \theta_i < \theta_j+} X_1(\theta_j+, \theta_i+) J_i^1 -$$

$$\int_{-\infty}^{\theta_j} X_1(\theta_j, s) f_1(s) ds - \sum_{-\infty < \theta_i < \theta_j} X_1(\theta_j, \theta_i+) J_i^1 = \int_{-\infty}^{\theta_j} Q_i^1 X_1(\theta_j, s) f_1(s) ds +$$

$$\sum_{-\infty < \theta_i < \theta_j} Q_i^1 X_1(\theta_j, \theta_i+) J_i^1 + J_j^1 = Q_j^1 \xi(\theta_i) + J_j^1.$$

Thus, ξ is a solution of (4.49). Assume that the equation has another solution $\phi(t)$ bounded on $\mathbb{R}$. Then, the difference $\xi - \phi$ is a bounded solution of the system (4.28). The general solution of the equation is $X_1(t, t_0)\xi_0$. The inequality $1 = \|\mathcal{I}\| \leq \|X_1(t,s)\|\|X_1(s,t)\|$ implies that $\|X_1(s,t)\| \geq K^{-1}e^{\gamma(t-s)}, s \leq t$. That is, $\|X_1(t, t_0)\| \to \infty$, as $t \to -\infty$, and (4.28) admits a unique bounded solution, $\xi \equiv 0$. Hence, $\phi = \xi$.

(ii). Consider the function η, now. Evaluating

$$\|\eta(t)\| \leq \int_{t}^{\infty} Ke^{\gamma(t-s)} M ds + \sum_{t \leq \theta_i < \infty} Ke^{\gamma(t-\theta_i)} M \leq KM[\frac{1}{\gamma} + \frac{1}{1-e^{-\gamma\theta}}],$$

we obtain that η is a bounded function. To show that it is a solution of (4.50), substitute the function in the system. We have that

$$\eta'(t) = X_2(t,t)f_2(t) - \int_t^\infty X_2'(t,s)f_2(s)ds - \sum_{t \le \theta_i < \infty} X_2'(t,\theta_i+)J_i^2 =$$

$$f_2(t) - \int_t^\infty P_2(t)X_2(t,s)f_2(s)ds - \sum_{t \le \theta_i < \infty} P_2(t)X_2(t,\theta_i+)J_i^2 = P_2(t)\eta(t) + f_2(t).$$

Fix $j \in \mathbb{Z}$, and obtain that

$$\Delta\eta|_{t=\theta_j} = -\int_{\theta_j+}^\infty X_2(\theta_j+,s)f_2(s)ds - \sum_{\theta_j+ \le \theta_i < \infty} X_2(\theta_j+,\theta_i+)J_i^2 +$$

$$\int_{\theta_j}^\infty X_2(\theta_j,s)f_2(s)ds + \sum_{\theta_j \le \theta_i < \infty} X_2(\theta_j,\theta_i+)J_i^2 = -\int_{\theta_j}^\infty Q_i^2 X_2(\theta_j,s)f_2(s)ds -$$

$$\sum_{\theta_j \le \theta_i < \infty} Q_i^2 X_2(\theta_j,\theta_i+)J_i^2 - (-J_j) = Q_i^2\eta(\theta_i) + J_j.$$

That is, η is a solution of (4.50). Uniqueness of this solution can be verified in the same way as that of $\xi(t)$. The theorem is proved.   □

4.3 Linear Periodic Systems

In this section the basic information on the important subject, existence of periodic solutions and their stability is discussed. We investigate linear homogeneous and nonhomogeneous systems with periodic coefficients. Consider (4.1) assuming this time that it is (ω, p)-periodic system. That is, $A(t)$ is an ω-periodic matrix-function, B_i is a p-periodic sequence of matrices, and $\theta_{i+p} = \theta_i + \omega$ for all $i \in \mathbb{Z}$, that is the sequence θ has the p-property. If $\det(\mathcal{I} + B_i) \ne 0, i \in \mathbb{Z}$, then, by results of Sect. 4.1, there exists a fundamental matrix $X(t)$ of (4.1).

Exercise 4.3.1. Prove the following assertions.

1. If sequence θ has the p-property then for arbitrary $a \in \mathbb{R}$ there exist p numbers, $a \le \xi_1 < \xi_2 < \ldots < \xi_p < a + \omega$, such that for each $\theta_i \in \theta$ one can find uniquely an integer k and a number ξ_j, which satisfy $\theta_i = \xi_j + k\omega$;
2. The matrix $X(t + \omega)$ is also a fundamental matrix of (4.1) and

$$X(t + \omega) = X(t)X(\omega), \tag{4.51}$$

for all $t \in \mathbb{R}$;

3. It is true that

$$X(t + \omega)X^{-1}(s + \omega) = X(t)X^{-1}(s),\qquad(4.52)$$

for all $t, s \in \mathbb{R}$.

If $X(t)$ is a fundamental matrix with $X(0) = \mathcal{I}$, then $X(\omega)$ is called a *monodromy matrix* and the eigenvalues of the monodromy matrix are *multipliers*. Denote the multipliers by $\rho_i, i = 1, 2, \ldots, n$. The role of multipliers for linear periodic systems is identical to one of eigenvalues for linear systems with constant coefficients. To emphasize the role we can introduce the special numbers, *exponents*, which are equal to $\lambda_i = \frac{1}{\omega}\text{Ln}\rho_i, i = 1, 2, \ldots, n$.

Thus, multipliers are solutions of the equation

$$\det(X(\omega) - \rho\mathcal{I}) = 0,\qquad(4.53)$$

and exponents are solutions of the equation

$$\det(\frac{1}{\omega}\text{Ln}\,X(\omega) - \lambda\mathcal{I}) = 0.\qquad(4.54)$$

Theorem 4.3.1. *A number ρ is a multiplier of (4.1) if and only if there exists a solution $x(t)$ of the system such that $x(t + \omega) = \rho x(t)$.*

The proof of the last theorem replicates that of the similar theorem for ordinary differential equations [59].

Exercise 4.3.2. Prove that (ω, p)-periodic system (4.1) has a periodic solution with period $k\omega, k = 1, 2, \ldots$, if and only if the k-th power of a multiplier equals to one.

Exercise 4.3.3. Use the result of Exercise 4.1.12 to prove the following assertion.

Theorem 4.3.2. *[142] System (4.1) has $r, 1 \leq r \leq n$, linearly independent ω-periodic solutions if and only if the adjoint system*

$$\begin{aligned}
y' &= -A^T(t)y,\\
\Delta y|_{t=\theta_i} &= -(\mathcal{I} + B_i^T)^{-1}B_i^T y
\end{aligned}\qquad(4.55)$$

has $r, 1 \leq r \leq n$, linearly independent ω-periodic solutions.

Suppose systems (4.1) and (4.55) have $r, 1 \leq r \leq n$, linearly independent ω-periodic solutions. Denote those of (4.55) as $\psi_j(t), j = 1, 2, \ldots, r$. Consider the problem of existence of periodic solutions of the following (ω, p)-periodic non-homogeneous system:

$$\begin{aligned}
y' &= A(t)y + f(t),\\
\Delta x|_{t=\theta_i} &= B_i y + J_i.
\end{aligned}\qquad(4.56)$$

In what follows, we denote by $PC_\omega(\theta) \subset PC_p$ the set of all functions of fixed period ω and with sequence of discontinuity moments θ.

Exercise 4.3.4. Prove that the following assertion is valid.

Theorem 4.3.3. *[142] Assume that homogeneous system (4.1) has $r, 1 \leq r \leq n$, linearly independent ω-periodic solutions. System (4.56) admits an ω-periodic solution if and only if*

$$\int_0^\omega <\psi_j(t), f(t)> dt + \sum_{i=1}^p <\psi_j(\theta_i), J_i> = 0, \qquad (4.57)$$

for all $j = 1, 2, \ldots, r$. In this case, system (4.56) has r-parametric family of ω-periodic solutions.

Let us introduce matrices $P = \frac{1}{\omega}\mathrm{Ln}X(\omega)$ and $F(t) = X(t)e^{-Pt}$. By applying (4.51), we find that

$$F(t+\omega) = X(t+\omega)e^{-P(t+\omega)} = X(t)X(\omega)e^{-P(t+\omega)} = F(t).$$

That is, $F(t) \in PC_\omega(\theta)$.

Exercise 4.3.5. Prove that the following assertions are valid.

1. $F \in PC^1(\mathbb{R}, \theta)$.
2. $|\det F(t)| \geq m$, for some positive number m and all $t \in \mathbb{R}$.
3. $F^{-1}(t), t \in \mathbb{R}$, exists, and its entries are from $PC_\omega(\theta)$.

The following result is a basic one for the Floquet theory.

Theorem 4.3.4. *The substitution $x = F(t)y$ transforms (4.1) to the system with constant coefficients,*

$$\frac{dy}{dt} = Py. \qquad (4.58)$$

Proof. First, we have that

$$F(t)y' + F'(t)y = X(t)e^{-Pt}y' + [X'(t)e^{-Pt} + X(t)(-P)e^{-Pt}]y = A(t)X(t)e^{-Pt}y$$

or $X(t)e^{-Pt}y' = X(t)Pe^{-Pt}y$. Cancellations in both parts of the last equality give us

$$y' = Py.$$

Moreover,

$$F(\theta_i+)y(\theta_i+) - F(\theta_i)y(\theta_i) = B_i F(\theta_i)y(\theta_i),$$

or

$$F(\theta_i+)\Delta y|_{t=\theta_i} + (F(\theta_i+) - F(\theta_i))y(\theta_i) = B_i F(\theta_i)y(\theta_i),$$

for a fixed $i \in \mathbb{Z}$.

Since $F(\theta_i +) - F(\theta_i) = B_i F(\theta_i)$, the last formula yields that

$$\Delta y|_{t=\theta_i} = 0.$$

That is, $y(t)$ satisfies (4.58). The theorem is proved.   □

Exercise 4.3.6. Using the results of Exercise 4.3.5 prove that the following assertions are valid.

1. System (4.1) has a bounded solution if and only if (4.58) does.
2. System (4.1) is uniformly stable if and only if (4.58) is.
3. System (4.1) is uniformly asymptotically stable if and only if (4.58) is.
4. System (4.1) is unstable if and only if (4.58) is.
5. If system (4.1) is unstable then it has an unbounded solution.
6. If system (4.1) is stable then it is uniformly stable.
7. If system (4.1) is asymptotically stable then it is uniform asymptotically stable.

Exercise 4.3.7. Prove that the exponents $\lambda_i = \frac{1}{\omega}Ln\rho_i, i = 1,\ldots,n$, are eigenvalues of the matrix P.

Exercise 4.3.8. Using Exercises 4.3.6 and 4.3.7 prove that the following theorem is valid.

Theorem 4.3.5. *[142] The periodic system (4.1) is:*

(i) *uniformly stable if and only if all multipliers satisfy $|\rho_i| \leq 1, i = 1,\ldots,n$, and Jordan cells of the monodromy matrix, which correspond to multipliers with unit absolute values, have order one;*

(ii) *uniformly asymptotically stable if and only if all multipliers lie inside of the unite circle of the complex plane;*

(iii) *unstable if there exists a multiplier with absolute value larger than one.*

Consider the following linear nonhomogeneous system

$$\frac{dx}{dt} = A(t)x + f(t),$$
$$\Delta x|_{t=t_i} = B_i x + I_i, \tag{4.59}$$

where $A(t), f(t) \in \mathcal{PC}_\omega(\theta)$, $B_i, I_i, i \in \mathbb{Z}$, are p-periodic sequences. That is, (4.59) is an (ω, p)-periodic system. Let (4.1) be the linear homogeneous system associated with (4.59). Denote by $X(t,s)$ the transition matrix of this system, and let $\lambda_i, i = 1,\ldots,n$, be the exponents of system (4.1).

Theorem 4.3.6. *If the real parts of the exponents $\lambda_i, i = 1,\ldots,n$, do not vanish, then (4.59) has a unique ω-periodic solution, which is uniformly asymptotically stable as soon as all of the exponents have negative real parts.*

Proof. Apply the Floquet transformation $x = F(t)y$ to (4.59). Then one can easily find that

$$\frac{dy}{dt} = Py + F^{-1}(t)f(t),$$
$$\Delta y|_{t=\theta_i} = F^{-1}(\theta_i+)I_i. \tag{4.60}$$

Exponents $\lambda_i, i = 1, \ldots, n$, are eigenvalues of the matrix P. Therefore, there is a constant nonsingular matrix S such that the transformation $x = F(t)Sz$ reduces (4.59) to

$$\frac{dz}{dt} = \Lambda z + g(t),$$
$$\Delta z|_{t=\theta_i} = V_i, \tag{4.61}$$

where $\Lambda = \text{diag}(\Lambda_+, \Lambda_-)$ is a constant box-diagonal matrix, $\text{Re}\lambda_j(\Lambda_+) < 0, j = 1, \ldots, m, \text{Re}\lambda_j(\Lambda_+) > 0, j = m+1, \ldots, n$, the integer m satisfies $0 \le m \le n$, and

$$\Lambda = S^{-1}F^{-1}(t)[A(t) - \frac{dF(t)}{dt}F^{-1}(t)]F(t)S,$$
$$g(t) = S^{-1}F^{-1}(t)f(t), \quad V_i = S^{-1}F^{-1}(\theta_i+)I_i.$$

One can easily see that (4.61) is an (ω, p)-periodic system. Set $g = (g_+, g_-)$, $V_i = (V_i^+, V_i^-), z = (z^+, z^-)$, such that system (4.61) has the form

$$\frac{dz^+}{dt} = \Lambda_+ z^+ + g_+(t),$$
$$\Delta z^+|_{t=\theta_i} = V_i^+, \tag{4.62}$$

$$\frac{dz^-+}{dt} = \Lambda_- z^- + g_+(t),$$
$$\Delta z^-|_{t=\theta_i} = V_i^-, \tag{4.63}$$

If $\gamma = \min_{1 \le j \le n} |\text{Re}\lambda_j(\Lambda)| + \epsilon$, where ϵ is a positive number, then there exists a number $K = K(\epsilon), K > 1$, such that $\|e^{\Lambda_+ t}\| \le Ke^{-\gamma t}, t \ge 0$, and $\|e^{\Lambda_- t}\| \le Ke^{\gamma t}, t \le 0$. By Theorem 4.2.2, there is a unique bounded solution $z(t) = (z^+, z^-)$ of the system,

$$z^+(t) = \int_{-\infty}^{t} e^{\Lambda_+(t-s)}g_+(s)ds + \sum_{-\infty < \theta_i < t} e^{\Lambda_+(t-\theta_i)}V_i^+, \tag{4.64}$$

$$z^-(t) = -\int_{t}^{\infty} e^{\Lambda_-(t-s)}g_-(s)ds - \sum_{t \le \theta_i < \infty} e^{\Lambda_-(t-\theta_i)}V_i^-. \tag{4.65}$$

So, it is sufficient to check that $z(t)$ is ω-periodic. Consider the question only for z^+, as for z^- the verification is very similar. We have that

$$
z^+(t+\omega) = \int_{-\infty}^{t+\omega} e^{\Lambda_+(t+\omega-s)} g_+(s)ds + \sum_{-\infty<\theta_i<t+\omega} e^{\Lambda_+(t+\omega-\theta_i)} V_i^+ =
$$

$$
\int_{-\infty}^{t} e^{\Lambda_+(t+\omega-(s+\omega))} g_+(s+\omega)ds + \sum_{-\infty<\theta_i<t} e^{\Lambda_+(t+\omega-(\theta_i+\omega))} V_{i+p}^+ =
$$

$$
\int_{-\infty}^{t} e^{\Lambda_+(t-s)} g_+(s)ds + \sum_{-\infty<\theta_i<t} e^{\Lambda_+(t-\theta_i)} V_i^+ = z^+(t).
$$

The theorem is proved.   □

Next, let us consider the periodic systems applying the *Green's function* concept. Let (4.59) be again an (ω, p)-periodic system, and $X(t), X(0) = \mathcal{I}$, be the fundamental matrix of the associated homogeneous system (4.1). Without loss of generality we assume that $\theta_i \neq 0, i \in \mathbb{Z}$. Hence, $\theta_i \neq \omega, i \in \mathbb{Z}$. In what follows, we assume that $\det(\mathcal{I} - X(\omega)) \neq 0$ and introduce a Green's function

$$
G(t,s) = \begin{cases} X(t)[\mathcal{I} - X(\omega)]^{-1}X^{-1}(s), & 0 \leq s < t \leq \omega, \\ X(t+\omega)[\mathcal{I} - X(\omega)]^{-1}X^{-1}(s), & 0 \leq t \leq s \leq \omega. \end{cases} \tag{4.66}
$$

Theorem 4.3.7. *The following properties are valid.*

1. $G_t'(t,s) = A(t)G(t,s), t \neq s$;
2. $\Delta G(t,s)|_{t=\theta_j} = G(\theta_j+,s) - G(\theta_j,s) = B_j G(\theta_j,s), s \neq \theta_j, j \in \mathbb{Z}$;
3. $G(s+,s) - G(s,s) = \mathcal{I}, s \neq \theta_i, i = 1, 2, \ldots, p$;
4. $G(0,s) - G(\omega,s) = 0, s \in [0, \omega)$;
5. $G(0,\omega) - G(\omega,\omega) = \mathcal{I}$.

Exercise 4.3.9. Prove the last theorem.

Exercise 4.3.10. Using the last theorem, verify that the function

$$
x(t) = \int_0^\omega G(t,s) f(s)ds + \sum_{0<\theta_i<\omega} G(t, \theta_i+)I_i \tag{4.67}
$$

is an ω-periodic solution of (4.59).

Theorem 4.3.8. *If the associated homogeneous system (4.1) does not admit a nontrivial ω-periodic solution, then (4.59) has a unique ω-periodic solution equals (4.67).*

- (E_2, E_3) such that there is a cyclic group $G \subseteq E_0[\ell_2^{e_2}]$ of order $\ell_2^{e_2}$ and $E_2 \cong E_0/G$ and $E_3 \cong E_1/\phi(G)$.
- (E_2, E_3) where E_2 is chosen at random among the curves having the same cardinality as E_0, and $\phi' : E_2 \to E_3$ is a random $\ell_1^{e_1}$-isogeny.

As discussed in [10] and [12], the problems CSSI and DSSP are non-standard isogeny problems since they use special primes as *isogeny smooth prime*, use somewhat small isogeny degrees, and reveal auxiliary points. In general, the problems CSSI and DSSP are proven to be exponentially hard even under quantum attack [10], but it is known that revealing auxiliary points may be dangerous in certain context. Even with such concern on the underlying computational problems CSSI and DSSP, GPS signature is simple to describe and easy to implement which could be very important advantages in practice.

2.4 Non-repudiation of Signature Scheme and Key Substitution Attack

A digital signature scheme consists of three polynomial time algorithms

$$(\mathsf{KeyGen}, \mathsf{Sign}, \mathsf{Verify})$$

which are defined as follows:

$\mathsf{KeyGen}(1^\lambda)$: On a given security parameter λ, the algorithm KeyGen outputs a pair (pk, sk) of keys, where pk is a public key for signature verification and sk is a private key for signature generation. The private key sk is kept secret by the owner of the public key pk.

$\mathsf{Sign}(sk, m \in \{0,1\}^*)$: On a given message $m \in \{0,1\}^*$ and a private key sk, the algorithm Sign outputs a signature σ_m.

$\mathsf{Verify}(m, \sigma_m, pk)$: On a given input $((m, \sigma_m), pk)$, the algorithm Verify outputs $1(= \mathsf{valid})$ or $0(= \mathsf{invalid})$.

We say that a digital signature is correct if

$$\mathsf{Verify}(m, \mathsf{Sign}(sk, m \in \{0,1\}^*), pk) = 1$$

for any $(pk, sk) \leftarrow \mathsf{KeyGen}(1^\lambda)$ and message m. The existential unforgeability (EUF) of a signature requires that it is infeasible for anyone to compute a valid signature under a public key pk without knowing the private key sk. Generally, a secure signature scheme means EUF-CMA (existential unforgeable against chosen message attack) secure which is defined as follows.

Definition 2.8 *(EUF-CMA). A digital signature scheme* $(\mathsf{KeyGen}, \mathsf{Sign}, \mathsf{Verify})$ *is EUF-CMA secure if for all probabilistic polynomial-time algorithm $\mathcal{A}$ with access to a signing oracle $\mathsf{Sign}(\cdot, sk)$, there is a negligible function $\epsilon(\cdot)$ such that:*

$$\Pr\left[\begin{cases} (pk, sk) \leftarrow \mathsf{KeyGen}(1^\lambda) \\ (m^*, \sigma^*) \leftarrow \mathcal{A}^{\mathsf{Sign}(\cdot, sk)}(pk) \end{cases} : (m^* \notin Q) \wedge (\mathsf{Verify}(m^*, \sigma^*, pk) = 1) \right] \leq \epsilon(\lambda),$$

where Q is the set of queries which $\mathcal{A}$ has accessed to the signing oracle.

The non-repudiation of a signature requires that it is infeasible for the signer to repudiate his/her signing on a valid signature under the public key pk of the signer. For a digital signature scheme, unforgeability and non-repudiation are two main security requirements which seem to be closely related. The existence of a forged signature of a signature scheme lets the signer to claim his/her signed signature as a forged signature. Therefore, issue of non-repudiation of a signature is to be considered only for EUF-CMA secure signatures. It is known that unforgeability of signature may not guarantee the non-repudiation of the signature [1,6].

We focus on the non-repudiation of digital signatures in this paper. The most basic attack for the non-repudiation is the public key substitution attack. The goal of public key substitution attack is to compute a new public key pk' where a valid signature σ on a message m under a public key pk can be also validated under pk'. Therefore, any signer can repudiate his/her signing on a signature σ on a message by using the existence of a successful key substitution attack. More precisely, the signer, the owner of public key pk, computes pk' by using a key substitution attack and claims that the signature σ is signed by the owner of pk', not himself/herself. The key substitution attack has been formalized as follows.

Definition 2.9 *(**Key Substitution Attack**)* [6]. *Given a signature scheme* (KeyGen, Sign, Verify), *a key substitution attack is a probabilistic polynomial-time algorithm* $\mathcal{A}$ *which on input of valid domain parameters outputs two valid public keys pk and pk' and a message/signature pair (m,σ) where* Verify(m,σ,pk) *and* Verify(m,σ,pk') *each return* 1(= valid). *A digital signature scheme is key substitution secure if it is secure against key substitution attacks.*

Since the potential attacker for the non-repudiation of a signature scheme is the original signer, one can assume that the key substitution attacker for the non-repudiation of a signature knows the private key of the original signature and the private information, such as nonce, used during signing process. And this contrasts the potential attackers against the unforgeability of a signature scheme.

3   Results

3.1   GPS Signature Scheme

This section recalls a signature scheme in [12], which we call it as GPS signature. Let p be a large isogeny smooth prime, that is, $p = \ell_1^{e_1} \ell_2^{e_2} \cdot f \pm 1$, where ℓ_1, ℓ_2 are small primes (typically $\ell_1 = 2$ and $\ell_2 = 3$). We define a supersingular elliptic curve E_0 over $\mathbb{F}_{p^2}$ with $|E_0(\mathbb{F}_{p^2})| = \ell_1^{e_1} \ell_2^{e_2} \cdot f$ and a primitive $\ell_1^{e_1}$-torsion point $P_1 \in E_0$. Define $E_1 = E_0/\langle P_1 \rangle$ and denote the corresponding $\ell_1^{e_1}$-isogeny by $\phi : E_0 \to E_1$. In [12], Galbraith, Petit and Silva apply the Fiat-Shamir transform [2] to the De Feo-Jao-Plût identification scheme, and construct GPS signature which is described as follows.

KeyGen(1^λ): On input a security parameter λ, the algorithm proceeds the following steps:

- generate a prime $p = \ell_A^{e_1} \ell_B^{e_2} \cdot f \pm 1$ with at least 4λ bits for small ℓ_1, ℓ_2, f (ideally $f = 1, \ell_1 = 2, \ell_2 = 3$) and $\ell_1^{e_1} \approx \ell_2^{e_2}$.
- choose a supersingular elliptic curve E_0 with j-invariant j_0.
- compute points $R_2, S_2 \in E_0(\mathbb{F}_{p^2})[\ell_2^{e_2}]$ and a random primitive $\ell_1^{e_1}$-torsion point $P_1 \in E_0[\ell_1^{e_1}]$.
- compute an isogeny $\phi : E_0 \to E_1$ with kernel generated by P_1, and let j_1 be the j-invariant of the image curve.
- set $R_2' = \phi(R_2), S_2' = \phi(S_2)$.
- choose a hash function H with $t = t(\lambda)$ bits of output.
- output

$$pk = (p, j_0, j_1, R_2, S_2, R_2', S_2', H), \; sk = P_1.$$

Sign($sk = P_1, m \in \{0,1\}^*$): On the given input, the algorithm proceeds the following steps:

- for $i = 1, \ldots, t$,
  - choose random integers $0 \le \alpha_i < \ell_2^{e_2}$.
  - compute an isogeny $\psi_i : E_0 \to E_{2,i}$ with the kernel generated by $R_2 + [\alpha_i]S_2$ and let $j_{2,i} = j(E_{2,i})$.
  - compute an isogeny $\psi_i' : E_1 \to E_{3,i}$ with the kernel generated by $R_2' + [\alpha_i]S_2'$ and let $j_{3,i} = j(E_{3,i})$.
  - compute

$$h = H(m, j_{2,1}, \ldots, j_{2,t}, j_{3,1}, \ldots, j_{3,t}) = b_1 b_2 \cdots b_t \in \{0,1\}^t.$$

- for $i = 1, \ldots, t$,
  - if $b_i = 0$ then set $z_i = \alpha_i$.
  - if $b_i = 1$ then compute $\psi_i(P_1)$ and set $z_i = (j_{2,i}, \psi_i'')$ where $\psi_i'' : E_{2,i} \to E_{3,i}'$ is an isogeny with the kernel generated by $\psi_i(P_1)$.
- output

$$\sigma_m = (h = b_1 b_2 \cdots b_t, z_1, \ldots, z_t)$$

Verify(m, σ_m, pk): On the given input,

- from pk, recover the parameters p, E_0, E_1.
- for each $1 \le i \le t$, using the information provided by z_i, one recompute the j-invariants $j_{2,i}'$ and $j_{3,i}'$.
  - in the case $b_i = 0$ this is done by using $z_i = \alpha_i$ and computing $j_{2,i}'$ from the isogeny with kernel generated by $R_2 + [\alpha_i]S_2 \in E_0$ and $j_{3,i}'$ from the isogeny with the kernel generated by $R_2' + [\alpha_i]S_2' \in E_1$.
  - when $b_i = 1$ then the value $j_{2,i}$ and a description of the isogeny $\psi_i'' : E_{2,i} \to E_{3,i}'$ is provided in z_i. The verifier computes $j_{2,i}' = j_{2,i}$ and $j_{3,i}'$ as the j-invariant of the image curve of ψ_i'' which means that $j_{3,i}' = j(E_{2,i}/Ker(\psi_i'')) = j(E_{3,i}')$.
- compute $h' = H(m, j_{2,1}', \ldots, j_{2,t}', j_{3,1}', \ldots, j_{3,t}')$.
- output $1(= \text{valid})$ if and only if $h' = h$.

Theorem 3.1 ([12]). *If the problems CSSI (Computational Supersingular Isogeny) and DSSP (Decisional Supersingular Product) are computationally hard then the signature above, GPS signature, is secure in the random oracle model under a chosen message attack.*

3.2 Our Attack on the Non-repudiation of GPS Signature

Now we show that GPS signature fails to provide non-repudiation of the signature. In particular, we present a key substitution attack on GPS signature for a signer to repudiate his/her signature. We describe our attack in general and present an example.

3.2.1 A Description of Our Key Substitution Attack

Our attack uses isomorphism of elliptic curves. A legal but malicious user U creates two public keys

$$pk = (p, j_0, j_1, R_2, S_2, R_2', S_2', H), \text{ and } pk' = (p, j_0, j_1, \widetilde{R_2}, \widetilde{S_2}, \widetilde{R_2}', \widetilde{S_2}', H) \quad (1)$$

- $\eta_0(\widetilde{P_1}) = P_1, \eta_0(\widetilde{R_2}) = R_2, \eta_0(\widetilde{S_2}) = S_2$ and
- $\eta_1^{-1} \cdot \phi \cdot \eta_0(\widetilde{R_2}) = \widetilde{R_2}', \eta_1^{-1} \cdot \phi \cdot \eta_0(\widetilde{S_2}) = \widetilde{S_2}'$

for some isomorphisms $\eta_0 : E_0' \to E_0$ and $\eta_1 : E_1' \to E_1$ with the inverses $\eta_0^{-1} : E_0 \to E_0'$ and $\eta_1^{-1} : E_1 \to E_1'$, respectively.

The public key pk' is correctly formulated by using the isogeny $\eta_1^{-1} \cdot \phi \cdot \eta_0 : E_0' \to E_1'$ with kernel generated by $\widetilde{P_1}$. We set $\widetilde{\phi} = \eta_1^{-1} \cdot \phi \cdot \eta_0$.

The following commutative diagram explains the relations between pk and pk'.

$$
\begin{array}{ccc}
E_0' & \xrightarrow{\ \widetilde{\phi} = \eta_1^{-1} \cdot \phi \cdot \eta_0\ } & E_1' \\
\eta_0 \downarrow & & \downarrow \eta_1 \\
E_0 & \xrightarrow{\ \phi\ } & E_1 \\
\psi_i \downarrow & & \downarrow \psi_i' \\
E_{2,i} & \xrightarrow{\ \psi_i''\ } & E_{3,i}
\end{array}
$$

Now we prove that the user with the public key pk' succeed a key substitution attack on GPS signature scheme.

Theorem 3.2. *Let the public keys $pk = (p, j_0, j_1, R_2, S_2, R_2', S_2', H)$ and $pk' = (p, j_0, j_1, \widetilde{R_2}, \widetilde{S_2}, \widetilde{R_2}', \widetilde{S_2}', H)$ of GPS signature be given as in Eq. 1. For any valid signature $\sigma_m = (h = b_1 b_2 \cdots b_t, z_1, \ldots, z_t)$ on a message $m \in \{0,1\}^*$ under the public key pk, σ_m is a valid signature on the message $m \in \{0,1\}^*$ under the public key pk'.*

Proof. From the validity of $\sigma_m = (h = b_1 b_2 \cdots b_t, z_1, \ldots, z_t)$ as a signature on the message $m \in \{0,1\}^*$ under the public key pk, the followings hold,

- for the $i = 1, \ldots, t$ with $b_i = 0$, which implies that $z_i = \alpha_i$,
  - $j_{2,i} = j(E_0/\langle R_2 + [\alpha_i]S_2 \rangle)$ and $j_{3,i} = j(E_0/\langle R_2' + [\alpha_i]S_2' \rangle)$.
- for the $i = 1, \ldots, t$ with $b_i = 1$, which implies that $z_i = (j_{2,i}, \psi_i'' : E_{2,i} \to E_{3,i}')$,
  $j_{3,i} = j(E_{2,i}/\langle Ker(\psi_i'') \rangle) = j(E_{3,i}')$.
- $h = b_1 b_2 \cdots b_t = H(m, j_{2,1}, \ldots, j_{2,t}, j_{3,1}, \ldots, j_{3,t})$.

Now we show that σ_m is also a valid signature on m under pk'. From (m, σ_m), anyone can verify the validity of σ_m as a signature on m under pk' as follows:

- If $b_i = 0$, that is, $z_i = \alpha_i$, any verifier computes $(j_{2,i}', j_{3,i}')$ as follows by using pk' which turns out $(j_{2,i}', j_{3,i}') = (j_{2,i}, j_{3,i})$:
  - The verifier computes $j_{2,i}' = j(E_0'/\langle \widetilde{R_2} + [\alpha_i]\widetilde{S_2} \rangle)$ from an isogeny $\widetilde{\psi}_i : E_0' \to E_{2,i}'$ whose kernel is generated by $\widetilde{R_2} + [\alpha_i]\widetilde{S_2}$. We want to show that $j_{2,i}' = j_{2,i}$. Since $\eta_0 : E_0 \to E_0'$ is an isomorphism, we have

    $$j_{2,i}' = j(E_0'/\langle Ker(\widetilde{\psi}_i) \rangle) = j(E_0/\langle Ker(\widetilde{\psi}_i \cdot \eta_0^{-1}) \rangle).$$

    We also have that $Ker(\widetilde{\psi}_i \cdot \eta_0^{-1}) = \langle R_2 + [\alpha_i]S_2 \rangle$ from the fact

    $$\eta_0^{-1}(R_2 + [\alpha_i]S_2) = \eta_0^{-1}(R_2) + [\alpha_i]\eta_0^{-1}(S_2) = \widetilde{R_2} + [\alpha_i]\widetilde{S_2}.$$

    Therefore, $j_{2,i}' = j(E_0/Ker(\widetilde{\psi}_i \cdot \eta_0^{-1})) = j(E_0/\langle R_2 + [\alpha_i]S_2 \rangle) = j_{2,i}$
  - The verifier computes $j_{3,i}' = j(E_1'/\langle \widetilde{R_2}' + [\alpha_i]\widetilde{S_2}' \rangle)$ from an isogeny $\widetilde{\psi}_i' : E_1' \to E_{3,i}'$ whose kernel is generated by $\widetilde{R_2}' + [\alpha_i]\widetilde{S_2}'$. We want to show that $j_{3,i}' = j_{3,i}$. Since $\eta_1 : E_1 \to E_1'$ is an isomorphism, we have

    $$j_{3,i}' = j(E_1'/\langle Ker(\widetilde{\psi}_i') \rangle) = j(E_1/\langle Ker(\widetilde{\psi}_i' \cdot \eta_1^{-1}) \rangle).$$

    We also have that $Ker(\widetilde{\psi}_i' \cdot \eta_1^{-1}) = \langle R_2' + [\alpha_i]S_2' \rangle$ from the fact

    $$\eta_1^{-1}(R_2' + [\alpha_i]S_2') = \eta_1^{-1}(R_2') + [\alpha_i]\eta_1^{-1}(S_2') = \widetilde{R_2}' + [\alpha_i]\widetilde{S_2}'.$$

    Therefore, $j_{3,i}' = j(E_1/\langle Ker(\widetilde{\psi}_i' \cdot \eta_1^{-1}) \rangle) = j(E_1/\langle R_2' + [\alpha_i]S_2' \rangle) = j_{3,i}$.
- If $b_i = 1$, that is, $z_i = (j_{2,i}, \psi_i'' : E_{2,i} \to E_{3,i}')$, then any verifier computes $j_{3,i}'$ as follows

  $$j_{3,i}' = j(E_{2,i}/\langle Ker(\psi_i'') \rangle) = j_{3,i}.$$

- Since the verifier computes $(j_{2,i}', j_{3,i}')$ such that $(j_{2,i}', j_{3,i}') = (j_{2,i}, j_{3,i})$ for all i, it is clear to see that

  $$H(m, j_{2,1}', \ldots, j_{2,t}', j_{3,1}', \ldots, j_{3,t}') = H(m, j_{2,1}, \ldots, j_{2,t}, j_{3,1}, \ldots, j_{3,t}) = h.$$

Therefore, $\sigma_m = (h, z_1, \ldots, z_t)$ is a valid signature on $m \in \{0,1\}^*$ under the public key $pk' = (p, j_0, j_1, \widetilde{R_2}, \widetilde{S_2}, \widetilde{R_2}', \widetilde{S_2}', H)$. □

Theorem 3.2 implies that the signer U whose public key is pk can repudiate his/her signing of σ_m on m whenever he/she wants by submitting pk' as another public key that validates the signature σ_m on m. Moreover, we note that the public key pk' can be computed independently to any valid pair $(message, signature)$ under pk, the owner U of pk can register pk' as another legal user in the system a priori to prepare his/her future malicious actions. This concludes that GPS signature scheme does not provide the non-repudiation property.

Remark 3.3. *Unruh [5] has given a transform that converts a secure interactive identification scheme into a signature scheme that is secure against a quantum adversary. In [12] the authors presented a post-quantum version of GPS signature using the Unruh transform and prove that it is existentially unforgeable in the quantum random oracle model if CSSI and DSSP are computationally hard for a quantum computer. It is easy to see that our key substitution attack on the (classic) GPS signature scheme works exactly the same for the post-quantum version of GPS signature scheme, too. Therefore, we see that the post-quantum version of GPS signature scheme does not provide the non-repudiation property, too.*

3.2.2   An Example

In this section, we present a simple example of our key substitution attack on GPS signature for a clear view of isogenies and our attack. We compute our example using Sage with a small prime p for simplicity. We also use the hash function $MD5$ in our example, but our attack succeeds independently the underlying hash function.

(A Valid Key Generation)

- $p = 2^4 \cdot 3^3 \cdot 2 - 1 = 863$;
- $E_0 : y^2 = x^3 + x$, an elliptic curve over a finite field $\mathbb{F}_{p^2}$;
- a is generator of finite field $\mathbb{F}_{p^2}$;
- Choose points $P_1, R_2, S_2 \in E_0$ as follows:

$$P_1 = (197a + 648 : 758a + 405 : 1),$$
$$R_2 = (422a + 27 : 548a + 682 : 1), \quad S_2 = (164a + 7 : 478a + 586 : 1)$$

- Compute an isogeny $\phi : E_0 \to E_1$ of degree 16 with the kernel $\langle P_1 \rangle$ where $E_1 : y^2 = x^3 + (155a + 756)x + (18a + 470)$ and the isogeny ϕ is defined as follows:

$$\phi = (\frac{q_1(x)}{q_2(x)}, \frac{r_1(x,y)}{r_2(x)})$$

$$q_1(x) = x^{16} + (-36a - 343)x^{15} + (169a + 373)x^{14} + (312a + 388)x^{13}$$
$$+ (284a + 400)x^{12} + (-398a + 78)x^{11} + (330a - 125)x^{10}(-41a - 139)x^9$$
$$+ (-295a - 193)x^8 + (249a - 353)x^7 + (-321a - 224)x^6 + (-199a + 165)x^5$$
$$+ (-182a + 265)x^4 + (352a + 127)x^3 + (-31a + 257)x^2 + (-239a + 77)x$$
$$+ (174a + 150)$$

$$q_2(x) = x^{15} + (-36a - 343)x^{14} + (200a - 339)x^{13} + (143a + 351)x^{12}$$
$$+ (-65a - 311)x^{11} + (195a - 81)x^{10} + (23a + 395)x^9 + (-25a + 252)x^8$$
$$+ (340a - 422)x^7 + (329a - 325)x^6 + (-24a + 201)x^5 + 307a - 158)x^4$$
$$+ (242a - 368)x^3 + (-118a - 163)x^2 + (147a - 20)x + (48a + 133)$$

$$r_1(x,y) = x^{23}y + (-286a + 33)x^{22}y + (215a + 131)x^{21}y + (203a - 75)x^{20}y$$
$$+ (202a - 238)x^{19}y + (203a + 273)x^{18}y + (-348a - 351)x^{17}y$$
$$+ (-31a - 269)x^{16}y + (412a + 373)x^{15}y + (117a + 414)x^{14}y$$
$$+ (204a + 157)x^{13}y + (-203a - 363)x^{12}y + (290a - 250)x^{11}y$$
$$+ (-59a - 49)x^{10}y + (-189a + 349)x^9y + (-391a - 360)x^8y$$
$$+ (385a - 231)x^7y + (328a - 189)x^6y + (-142a - 283)x^5y$$
$$+ (76a + 398)x^4y + (-303a + 129)x^3y + (352a + 62)x^2y$$
$$+ (-16a - 397)xy + (366a + 237)y$$

$$r_2(x) = x^{23} + (-286a + 33)x^{22} + (184a - 20)x^{21} + (-60a - 208)x^{20}$$
$$+ (-235a + 431)x^{19} + (428a - 178)x^{18} + (-a + 378)x^{17} + (327a + 338)x^{16}$$
$$+ (-27a - 356)x^{15} + (77a + 351)x^{14} + (-385a - 137)x^{13} + (425a - 63)x^{12}$$
$$+ (226a + 372)x^{11} + (95a + 156)x^{10} + (118a - 425)x^9 + (-128a + 248)x^8$$
$$+ (344a + 299)x^7 + (310a - 417)x^6 + (184a + 337)x^5 + (371a - 154)x^4$$
$$+ (-105a + 307)x^3 + (11a + 243)x^2 + (79a + 327)x + (409a - 149)$$

- Compute j-invariants $j_0 = j(E_0) = 2$, $j_1 = j(E_1) = 465a + 831$.
- Compute $R_2', S_2' \in E_1$ as follows:

$$R_2' = \phi(R_2) = (347a + 480 : 357a + 737 : 1),$$
$$S_2' = \phi(S_2) = (712a + 662 : 268a + 204 : 1)$$

- Hash function $H = MD5 : \{0,1\}^* \to \{0,1\}^{128}$
- Output

$$pk = (p, j_0, j_1, R_2, S_2, R_2', S_2', H), \ sk = P_1.$$

(A Key Generation for Key Substitution Attack)

- For the given E_0 from the valid key generation, compute an isomorphism $\zeta_0 : E_0 \to E_0'$ defined by $\zeta_0(x, y) = (557x, (842a + 442)y)$ for the elliptic curve $E_0' : y^2 = x^3 + 2x$. Compute $\eta_0 = \zeta_0^{-1} : E_0' \to E_0$, then $\eta_0^{-1} = \zeta_0$. Note that $\eta_0(x, y) = (251x, (677a + 93)y)$ and $j(E_0') = j(E_0) = j_0$.
- For the given E_1 from the valid key generation, compute an isomorphism $\zeta_1 : E_1 \to E_1'$ defined by $\zeta_1(x, y) = (406x, (385a + 239)y)$ for $E_1' : y^2 = x^3 + (465a + 542)x + (349a + 291)$. Compute $\eta_1 = \zeta_1^{-1} : E_1' \to E_1$, then $\eta_1^{-1} = \zeta_1$. Note that $\eta_1(x, y) = (423x, (779a + 42)y)$ and $j(E_1') = j(E_1) = j_1$.

- Compute

  - $\widetilde{P_1} = \eta_0^{-1}(P_1) = (256a + 404 : 23a + 425 : 1)$
  - $\widetilde{S_2} = \eta_0^{-1}(S_2) = (603a + 31 : 164a + 224 : 1)$
  - $\widetilde{R_2} = \eta_0^{-1}(R_2) = (636a + 736 : 825a + 34 : 1)$

- Compute the isogeny $\widetilde{\phi} = \eta_1^{-1} \cdot \phi \cdot \eta_0 : E_0' \to E_1'$. Note that the kernel of $\widetilde{\phi}$ is $\langle \widetilde{P_1} \rangle$. Set

  - $\widetilde{S_2}' = \widetilde{\phi}(\widetilde{S_2}) = (830a + 379 : 680a + 602 : 1)$
  - $\widetilde{R_2}' = \widetilde{\phi}(\widetilde{R_2}) = (213a + 705 : 795a + 677 : 1)$

- Output

$$pk' = (p, j_0, j_1, \widetilde{R_2}, \widetilde{S_2}, \widetilde{R_2}', \widetilde{S_2}', H), \; sk = \widetilde{P_1}$$

(A Signature Generation using sk on a message $m = \mathsf{message}$)

A signature σ_m on the message $m = \mathsf{message}$ is computed as follows: First we compute the first part h of the signature as follows: For a randomly chosen $[\alpha_i]_{1 \le i \le t} = [15, 5, 6, 18, 2, \ldots]$, compute the following isogenies and j-invariants for each i:

- $\psi_i : E_0 \to E_{2,i}$ with the kernel $\langle R_2 + [\alpha_i]S_2 \rangle$ and $j_{2,i} = j(E_0/\langle R_2 + [\alpha_i]S_2 \rangle)$:

  $$j_2 = [j_{2,1}, j_{2,2}, j_{2,3}, j_{2,4}, \ldots] = [515a + 716, 473a + 144, 473a + 144, 451a + 551, \ldots]$$

- $\psi_i' : E_1 \to E_{3,i}$ with the kernel $\langle R_2' + [\alpha_i]S_2' \rangle$ and $j_{3,i} = j(E_1/\langle R_2' + [\alpha_i]S_2' \rangle)$:

  $$j_3 = [j_{3,1}, j_{3,2}, j_{3,3}, j_{3,4} \ldots] = [232a+541, 657a+665, 657a+665, 590a+114 \ldots]$$

For the two sequences j_2 and j_3 of j-invariants, compute the hash value

$$h = b_1 b_2 b_3 \cdots = H(\mathsf{message}, j_2, j_3) = 10111011 \ldots.$$

Now we compute the second part (z_i's) of the signature as follows:

- From the fact $b_1 = 1$, set $z_1 = (j_{2,1} = 515a + 716, \psi_1'')$, where

  - $\psi_1'' : E_{2,1} \to E_{3,1}'$ is an isogeny with the kernel generated by $\psi_1(P_1)$ for the elliptic curves $E_{2,1} : y^2 = x^3 + (285a + 129)x + (507a + 262)$ and $E_{3,1}' : y^2 = x^3 + (713a + 733)x + (70a + 235)$.

- $b_2 = 0$, and set $z_2 = \alpha_2 = 5$.

$$\vdots$$

Finally, we have a sequence $z = [z_1, z_2, z_3 \ldots] = [(515a + 716, \psi_1''), 5, (473a + 144, \psi_3''), \ldots]$, and the computed signature is $\sigma = ((h, z), \mathsf{message})$. This signature $\sigma_m = ((h, z), \mathsf{message})$ can be verified as a valid signature on $\mathsf{message}$ under the public key pk.

(Key Substitution Attack on σ_m using the public key pk')

Note that $pk' = (p, j_0, j_1, \widetilde{R_2}, \widetilde{S_2}, \widetilde{R_2}', \widetilde{S_2}', H)$. Suppose that a valid signature $\sigma = ((h, z), \mathsf{message})$ under pk is given as follows:

- $h = H(\text{message}, j_2, j_3) = 10111011\cdots$
- $z = [z_1, z_2, z_3, \ldots] = [(515a + 716, \psi_1''), 5, (473a + 144, \psi_3''), \ldots] = [(j_{2,1}, \psi_1'' : E_{2,1} \to E_{3,1}'), \alpha_2, (j_{2,3}, \psi_3'' : E_{2,3} \to E_{3,3}'), \ldots]$

For the verification, anyone compute the values of j-invariants ($j_2' = [j_{2,1}', j_{2,2}', \ldots], j_3' = [j_{3,1}', j_{3,2}', \ldots]$) for the pk' as follows:

From $b_1 = 1$ and $z_1 = (j_{2,1}, \psi_1'') = (515a + 716, \psi_1'' : E_{2,1} \to E_{3,1}')$:

- set $j_{2,1}' = j_{2,1}$ and
- compute the j-invariant $j_{3,1}' = j(E_{3,1}') = 232a + 541$, which turns out $j_{3,1}' = j_{3,1}$.

From $b_2 = 0$, that is, $z_2 = \alpha_2 = 5$:

- The verifier computes an isogeny $\widetilde{\psi}_2 : E_0' \to E_{2,2}'$ with the kernel $\widetilde{R_2} + 5\widetilde{S_2}$ and the j-invariant $j_{2,2}' = j(E_0'/\langle \widetilde{R_2} + 5\widetilde{S_2} \rangle) = 473a + 144$, which turns out $j_{2,2}' = j_{2,2}$.
- The verifier computes an isogeny $\widetilde{\psi}_2' : E_1' \to E_{3,2}'$ with the kernel $\widetilde{R_2}' + 5\widetilde{S_2}'$ and the j-invariant $j_{3,2}' = j(E_1'/\langle \widetilde{R_2}' + 5\widetilde{S_2}' \rangle) = 657a + 665$, which turns out $j_{3,2}' = j_{3,2}$.

Similarly, the values of j-invariants j_2', j_3' for the pk' such that $j_2 = j_2', j_3 = j_3'$ are computed. Clearly, $h = H(\text{message}, j_2, j_3) = H(\text{message}, j_2', j_3')$, therefore, the signature $\sigma = ((h, z), \text{message})$ is valid under pk'.

3.3   How to Prevent Our Attack

Our attack on GPS signature uses isomorphisms of the underlying elliptic curves and isomorphic elliptic curves have the same j-invariants. Therefore, if one restricts distinct j-invariants (j_0, j_1) for each public key, our key substitution attack can be prevented. However, our result is the first key substitution attack on isogeny based signature schemes under the consideration of the non-repudiation of the signature and one could expect a more advanced key substitution attack on isogeny based signature.

In general, there are two ways to prevent key substitution attacks on digital signature schemes. One is that the certificate authority (CA) for public keys requires that users to prove possession of user's private key before issuing certificates. This prevents the adversary mounts key substitution attacks without knowing the corresponding private key. However, this counter-measure is not suitable to prevent key substitution attack under consideration of non-repudiation, since the original signer is considered as a potential attacker and the original signer knows the related private keys. Another way to prevent key substitution attack is proposed by Menezes and Smart. They formalize the key substitution security as a security of signature schemes in multi-user setting and formatting messages specific to each public key, such as including the signer's public key to the message in some unambiguous way prior to signing (e.g., $pk\|message$) guarantees the key substitution security if the original signature scheme is proven unforgeable [1].

4   Conclusion

GPS signature [12] is an efficient isogeny based signature scheme which is proven EUF-CMA secure in the random oracle model under the assumption that the problems CSSI (Computational Supersingular Isogeny) and DSSP(Decisional Supersingular Product) are infeasible. In this paper, we show that the current version of GPS signature fails to provided non-repudiation by presenting a public key substitution attack on GPS signature. In [12], they also presented a post-quantum version of GPS signature which is proven EUF-CMA secure in the quantum random oracle model based on the hardness of CSSI and DSSP. It is easy to see that our key substitution attack on the (classic) GPS signature scheme works exactly the same against the post-quantum version of GPS signature scheme, too. We recommend to use distinct j-invariants (j_0, j_1) for each public key of GPS signature scheme to prevent our key substitution attack. Moreover, we suggest to format messages as specific to each public key, such as $pk\|message$, prior to signing according to the analysis of Menezes and Smart [1].

References

1. Alfred, M., Nigel, S.: Security of signature schemes in a multiuser setting. Des. Codes Cryptogr. **23**, 261–274 (2004)
2. Fiat, A., Shamir, A.: How to prove yourself: practical solutions to identification and signature problems. In: Odlyzko, A.M. (ed.) CRYPTO 1986. LNCS, vol. 263, pp. 186–194. Springer, Heidelberg (1987). https://doi.org/10.1007/3-540-47721-7_12
3. Jao, D., De Feo, L.: Towards quantum-resistant cryptosystems from supersingular elliptic curve isogenies. In: Yang, B.-Y. (ed.) PQCrypto 2011. LNCS, vol. 7071, pp. 19–34. Springer, Heidelberg (2011). https://doi.org/10.1007/978-3-642-25405-5_2
4. Jao, D., Soukharev, V.: Isogeny-based quantum-resistant undeniable signatures. In: Mosca, M. (ed.) PQCrypto 2014. LNCS, vol. 8772, pp. 160–179. Springer, Cham (2014). https://doi.org/10.1007/978-3-319-11659-4_10
5. Unruh, D.: Non-interactive zero-knowledge proofs in the quantum random oracle model. In: Oswald, E., Fischlin, M. (eds.) EUROCRYPT 2015. LNCS, vol. 9057, pp. 755–784. Springer, Heidelberg (2015). https://doi.org/10.1007/978-3-662-46803-6_25
6. Jens-Matthias, B., Stefan, R., Rainer, S.: Key substitution attacks revisited: taking into account malicious signers. Int. J. Inf. Secur. **5**, 30–36 (2006)
7. John, T.: Endomorphisms of abelian varieties over finite fields. Inven. Math **2**, 134–144 (1966)
8. Joseph, H.S.: The Arithmetic Elliptic Curves. Graduate Texts in Mathematics. Springer, New York (2009). ISBN 9780387962030
9. Lawrence, C.W.: Elliptic Curves: Number Theory and Cryptography, 2nd edn. CRC Press, London (2008). ISBN 978-1420071467
10. De Feo, L., Jao, D., Plût, J.: Towards quantum-resistant cryptosystems from supersingular elliptic curve isogenies. J. Math. Cryptol. **8**, 209–247 (2014)
11. Robin, H.: Algebraic Geometry. Graduate Texts in Mathematics, vol. 52. Springer, New York (1977). https://doi.org/10.1007/978-1-4757-3849-0

12. Galbraith, S.D., Petit, C., Silva, J.: Identification protocols and signature schemes based on supersingular isogeny problems. In: Takagi, T., Peyrin, T. (eds.) ASIACRYPT 2017. LNCS, vol. 10624, pp. 3–33. Springer, Cham (2017). https://doi.org/10.1007/978-3-319-70694-8_1

13. Velu, J.: Isogenies Entre Courbes Elliptiques. Communications de Academie royale des Sciences de Paris, pp. 305–347 (1971)

14. William, C.W.: Abelian varieties over finite fields. Annales scientifiques de l'É.N.S., pp. 521–560 (1969)

15. Xi, S., Haibo, T., Wang, Y.: Toward quantum-resistant strong designated verifier signature from isogenies. Int. J. Grid Util. Comput. **5**, 80–86 (2014)

Efficient Information Theoretic Multi-party Computation from Oblivious Linear Evaluation

Louis Cianciullo$^{(\boxtimes)}$ and Hossein Ghodosi

James Cook University, Townsville 4811, Australia
{louis.cianciullo,hossein.ghodosi}@jcu.edu.au

Abstract. Oblivious linear evaluation (OLE) is a two party protocol that allows a receiver to compute an evaluation of a sender's private, degree 1 polynomial, without letting the sender learn the evaluation point. OLE is a special case of oblivious polynomial evaluation (OPE) which was first introduced by Naor and Pinkas in 1999. In this article we utilise OLE for the purpose of computing multiplication in multi-party computation (MPC).

MPC allows a set of n mutually distrustful parties to privately compute any given function across their private inputs, even if up to $t < n$ of these participants are corrupted and controlled by an external adversary. In terms of efficiency and communication complexity, multiplication in MPC has always been a large bottleneck. The typical method employed by most current protocols has been to utilise Beaver's method, which relies on some precomputed information. In this paper we introduce an OLE-based MPC protocol which also relies on some precomputed information.

Our proposed protocol has a more efficient communication complexity than Beaver's protocol by a multiplicative factor of t. Furthermore, to compute a share to a multiplication, a participant in our protocol need only communicate with one other participant; unlike Beaver's protocol which requires a participant to contact at least t other participants.

1 Introduction

Oblivious polynomial evaluation (OPE) was first introduced by Naor and Pinkas [10] in 1999. An OPE protocol consists of two participants, a sender, S who holds a polynomial $f(x)$ and a receiver, R who has a value α. OPE allows R to learn $f(\alpha)$ without having S learn α and also keeping $f(x)$ private. A more formal definition, originally given in [5] is presented below:

Definition 1 [5]**.** *An OPE protocol is composed of two parties, S who has a polynomial $f(x)$ over a finite field $\mathbb{F}$ and R who has an input value $\alpha \in \mathbb{F}$.*

This research is supported by an Australian Government Research Training Program (RTP) Scholarship.

O. Blazy and C. Y. Yeun (Eds.): WISTP 2018, LNCS 11469, pp. 78–90, 2019.
https://doi.org/10.1007/978-3-030-20074-9_7

Correctness is achieved if, at the end of the protocol, R learns $f(\alpha)$. Security is guaranteed if the following two conditions are met after the protocol has been executed:

1. *S cannot reduce his uncertainty of α.*
2. *R does not learn any information relating to $f(x)$, other than $f(\alpha)$.*

In this article we focus on a special case of OPE, wherein $f(x)$ is of degree at most one, known as oblivious linear evaluation (OLE). Specifically, we utilise OLE for the purpose of performing multiplication in multi-party computation (MPC).

MPC allows a set of n mutually distrustful participants to compute any given function across their private inputs, without revealing any information relating to their private inputs. We focus on the threshold setting, where an MPC protocol is considered secure if a set of t or less participants, where $t < n$, cannot gain any information relating to another participant's private input, other than what the output of the protocol gives them. More formally:

Definition 2. *A (t, n) threshold MPC protocol allows a set of n participants, $P_1, \cdots, P_n$ with respective private inputs, $x_1, \cdots, x_n$ to compute a given function, $f(x_1, \cdots, x_n)$.*

Privacy is maintained if, after completion of the protocol, an adversary controlling any subset of up to t participants $(t < n)$, cannot learn more information (about other participant's private inputs) than what could be derived from each participant's individual, private input and the output of the protocol.

Traditionally, the adversary is classified as either passive or malicious. Participants under control of a passive adversary may share information with one another but do not deviate from the MPC protocol. Participants under control of a malicious adversary also share information but may act arbitrarily, i.e. they do not necessarily follow the protocol. Another aspect of the adversary considered in an MPC protocol is the resources it has at its command. Specifically, an unconditionally (information theoretic) secure MPC protocol is secure against a computationally unbounded adversary. Whilst a conditionally (computationally) secure MPC protocol is secure against a computationally bounded adversary.

In this article we focus on information theoretic (t, n) threshold MPC secure against a passive adversary. We show the construction of an efficient MPC scheme based on OLE. In the next section we give some background and motivation on this topic, following this we then discuss our contribution in depth.

1.1   Background

MPC is an extremely powerful tool that can be used to solve practically any given problem involving a set of distrustful parties. In classical, unconditionally secure protocols [2,6,11] each participant, P_i ($i = 1, \cdots n$) shares their private input, x_i by utilising Shamir's secret sharing scheme [12] to distribute shares to all participants. To compute a given function, $f(x_1, \cdots x_n)$, participants need simply perform all computations on the shares of each input value. For instance, if a participant wants to compute a share relating to the sum of two distributed input values he simply adds his two corresponding shares together. At the end of the protocol, a set of $t + 1$ or more participants then pool their information to reconstruct the output.

Due to the homomorphic nature of Shamir's scheme [3] participants can easily compute any linear operation by privately computing on their shares. However, since the inception of MPC [8] the largest limiting factor has been the high amount of resources required to compute a multiplication. Perhaps the most widely known and efficient method of computing a multiplication in an MPC protocol is known as Beaver's method (A.K.A Beaver's triples) [1]. For completeness we review this protocol below.

Beaver's Method. Beaver's method [1] for computing a multiplication in MPC relies on some pre-shared information known as a triple. Specifically, a triple is composed of three values, a, b and c where $a \cdot b = c$ and $a, b, c \in \mathbb{F}_q$ such that $q > n$ and q is a prime number. Each participant has a share of these triples, such that participant P_k ($k = 1, \cdots, n$) receives the shares a_k, b_k and c_k relating to (respectively) a, b and c.

Suppose we have participants P_i with input x_i and P_j with input x_j for $i, j = 1, \cdots, n$ and $i \neq j$. To compute shares of the multiplication $\gamma = x_i \cdot x_j$ we first have both P_i and P_j distribute shares of their private values among the other participants, where P_k gets x_{i_k} relating to x_i and x_{j_k} relating to x_j. To compute a share, γ_k relating to the product γ, a set of at least $t + 1$ participants execute the following steps:

1. Each participant, P_k, computes $z_k = x_{i_k} - a_k$ and $v_k = x_{j_k} - b_k$, where z_k is a share of the value $z = x_i - a$ and v_k is a share of $v = x_j - b$.
2. A set of at least $t + 1$ participants broadcast their shares, z_k and v_k amongst themselves.
3. Participants publicly reconstruct the values of z and v using the shares z_k and v_k, respectively.
4. P_k computes his share of γ as $\gamma_k = zv + zb_k + va_k + c_k$.
5. $t + 1$ or more participants can reconstruct $\gamma = x_i \cdot x_j$ by pooling their shares.

In order to construct z and v a set of $t + 1$ participants is required to cooperate. If all participants in this set wish to compute these values (and consequently, the multiplication) then each participant must both receive and send t messages. Since each message would consist of 2 elements from the field $\mathbb{F}_q$ (i.e. z_k and v_k) the communication complexity of this protocol can be given as $\mathcal{O}(qt^2)$.

Many recent MPC protocols utilise a resource intensive computationally secure offline phase to compute these multiplication triples. The actual MPC is then carried out in a faster information theoretic online phase. For our purposes, we focus solely on the information theoretic online phase. It suffices to assume that participants gain the shares of the triples via an external party known as an initialiser, who (after computing and distributing the shares of the triples) does not take part in the actual MPC protocol. In the next section we review the OLE based two-party protocol given by Döttling et al. [7].

TinyOLE. Recently Döttling et al. [7] proposed a two-party protocol ($n = 2$) in which the two participants, P_1 and P_2 use OLE to compute shares to a multiplication. Specifically, they use OLE to compute multiplication triples in an offline phase. Their scheme utilises a simple additive secret sharing scheme wherein a given value, a (for example), is represented as $a = a_1 + a_2$, across a finite field $\mathbb{F}$; where P_2 has the share a_2 and P_1 gets a_1. Addition in their scheme consists of simply adding shares together. Multiplication is achieved by utilising OLE in a black-box fashion.

To compute a multiplication of two distributed (and not necessarily known) values, a and b, they rely on the fact that: $ab = a_1b_1 + a_1b_2 + a_2b_1 + a_2b_2$. To compute the "troublesome" terms of the form $c = a_1b_2$ they utilise a black-box OLE. Essentially, P_1 acts as a sender and submits the polynomial $f(x) = a_1x - c_1$ where c_1 is a randomly chosen value. The second participant, P_2 acts as receiver and submits $\alpha = b_2$. Both participants send their values to a black-box OLE, with P_2 receiving back $f(\alpha) = a_1b_2 - c_1$. If we set $c_2 = f(\alpha)$ then each participant now holds a share of c as $c = c_1 + c_2$. To compute shares to the entire multiplication it is easy to see that at least 2 OLEs are needed.

Döttling et al. specifically use this method in a computationally secure offline phase to compute random multiplication triples, where the values of a and b are not actually known to either participant. Our proposed scheme differs to theirs in that we wish to utilise OLE in an information theoretic, online phase to compute the multiplication of known input values for a given MPC function.

1.2   Our Contribution

In this section we summarise our proposed MPC scheme which utilises OLE to compute shares to a given multiplication. In contrast to the methods discussed above our protocol obtains the following desirable properties:

1. Unlike Beaver's scheme [1] our proposed protocol only requires communication between two participants to compute a given share to a multiplication i.e. a participant may compute his share without the assistance of t other participants. We achieve this result by having one designated participant who acts as a sender in an OLE. The other participants need simply privately compute an OLE with this sender participant to compute a share to a multiplication. As a result of this, the communication complexity of our protocol is $\mathcal{O}(qt)$, which is more efficient than Beaver's (at $\mathcal{O}(qt^2)$) by a multiplicative factor of t.
2. We do not rely on a black-box method of OLE and instead provide a specific construction. Our OLE multiplication scheme is based on the information theoretic protocol given in [9,13]. This scheme, like Beaver's scheme, relies on some precomputed information which can be produced via an offline phase or

an initialiser. Since we wish to focus solely on the information theoretic OLE-based MPC scheme itself we will assume that the information is provided via an initialiser.

3. Our scheme only utilises one OLE per participant to compute a multiplication. In a two party protocol we would only need one OLE. So, for an individual participant to compute his share (in either a multi-party or two-party protocol) the complexity cost is just $\mathcal{O}(q)$. Using Beaver's scheme, this would be $\mathcal{O}(qt)$.

4. Lastly, unlike the TinyOLE scheme [7], our scheme is scalable, in that it extends to the multi-party case with n participants. In fact, computing n shares (one for each participant) to a single multiplication requires only $n-1$ OLEs, one for each individual participant to compute his share. We note that utilising all n participants is not actually necessary. We only really require a set of $t+1$ participants, enough to compute the output of a given multiplication at the end of the protocol.

1.3   Outline

The rest of the paper is organised as follows. In Sect. 2 we go over some of the sub protocols and tools used in our proposed MPC protocol. Section 3 gives a high level overview of our protocol as well as a model for security. The actual construction for our protocol is given in Sect. 4, along with an evaluation and proof of correctness and security.

2   Preliminaries

In this section we review Shamir's secret sharing scheme [12] and the information theoretic OPE originally given by Hanaoka et al. in [9]. Both of these protocols are fundamental building blocks of our proposed MPC protocol.

2.1   Shamir's Secret Sharing Scheme

Like all MPC schemes our proposed protocol utilises secret sharing to ensure privacy. In a secret sharing scheme a set of n participants are each privately sent a share of a given secret. An authorised subset of these participants can pool their shares to recover the secret, whilst an unauthorised subset should get no information. We note that our proposed OLE-based MPC scheme can potentially work with any linear secret sharing scheme. However, in order to show a specific implementation we will demonstrate our proposed protocol using Shamir's secret sharing scheme [12].

Shamir's scheme is a (t, n) threshold scheme, meaning that an authorised subset is any set of $t+1$ or more participants where $t < n$. This scheme operates over a finite field $\mathbb{F}_q$ where $q > n$ and q is a prime number. To demonstrate, suppose we have participant P_i $(i = 1, \cdots, n)$ who wishes to distribute his input value, x_i among the other participants. P_i computes a random polynomial,

$g(x)$ of degree at most t and sets $g(0) = x_i$. He then privately sends to each participant, P_k $(k = 1, \cdots n)$ the share $x_{i_k} = g(k)$. A set of $t + 1$ or more participants can reconstruct x_i by performing Lagrange interpolation across their shares to compute $g(x)$.

2.2 Information Theoretic OPE

Hanaoka et al. [9] introduced an unconditionally secure OPE protocol that utilises some pre-distributed information to achieve information theoretic security. Our proposed OLE-based MPC protocol utilises a modified variant of their OPE protocol to compute a multiplication. Therefore, for completeness, we display their full protocol in Fig. 1.

In the initial, setup phase of their protocol a third party, known as an initialiser assigns some random information to both $\mathcal{R}$ and $\mathcal{S}$. Following this the initialiser takes no further part in the protocol and $\mathcal{R}$ and $\mathcal{S}$ utilise the assigned information to compute an OPE in the computation phase of the protocol.

Input: $\mathcal{R}$ has a value α and $\mathcal{S}$ the polynomial $f(x)$ of degree at most t.
Output: $\mathcal{R}$ obtains $f(\alpha)$ and $\mathcal{S}$ gets nothing.

Setup The initialiser privately sends:

1. A random polynomial, $S(x)$, of degree at most t to $\mathcal{S}$.
2. A random value, d and the value $g = S(d)$ to $\mathcal{R}$.

Computation

1. $\mathcal{R}$ sends the value $l = \alpha - d$ to $\mathcal{S}$.
2. $\mathcal{S}$ then computes and sends to $\mathcal{R}$ the polynomial $V(x) = f(l + x) + S(x)$.
3. $\mathcal{R}$ computes $f(\alpha) = V(d) - g$.

Fig. 1. Information theoretic OPE [9,13]

3 Model

This section presents a high level overview of our protocol and a set of criteria for evaluating the security of our scheme. We use the traditional setting of MPC protocols. That is, each party P_j $(1 \le j \le n)$ distributes its private input, x_j amongst all participants, using a Shamir (t, n) threshold scheme. Linear functions can be computed by each participant privately. In order to perform multiplication, however, we must utilise OLE.

3.1   Overview

Suppose we have a set of n participants who wish to compute shares to the value $\gamma = x_i \cdot x_j$, where x_i and x_j are the respective private input values of participants P_i and P_j, for $1 \leq i,j \leq n$ and $i \neq j$. Further suppose, that P_j utilises the polynomial $f_j(x)$ to share x_j among all participants (via Shamir's secret sharing scheme), such that a given participant P_k $(k = 1, \cdots, n)$ receives the share $x_{j_k} = f_j(k)$ of x_j.

A simple method for computing shares of γ is to have each participant, P_k, simply send his share, x_{j_k}, to P_i who can then send back the value $\gamma_k = x_i x_{j_k}$. Due to the homomorphic nature of Shamir's secret sharing scheme the value γ_k is a share corresponding to the polynomial $\Gamma(x) = x_i f_j(x)$ with free term $x_i \cdot x_j$. The obvious problem with this simple protocol is that neither P_i's nor P_j's privacy is maintained.

To keep P_i's input, x_i, private we can have P_i introduce a random, private masking polynomial, $h_i(x)$, of degree at most t, with free term $h_i(0) = 0$. Now, when he receives a given share, x_{j_k}, we require P_i to send back $\gamma_k = x_i x_{j_k} + h_i(k)$. Each P_k now holds shares to the polynomial $\Gamma(x) = x_i f_j(x) + h_i(x)$. Intrinsically we can see that, due to Shamir's secret sharing scheme, the protocol is now t-private with respect to P_i, as a set of t participants with t shares cannot compute any information relating to the effectively random polynomial $\Gamma(x)$. It remains to ensure the privacy of P_j.

Surprisingly, ensuring that P_j's privacy is maintained is actually quite simple. Rather than having each P_k simply hand his share to P_i we instead have P_k and P_i utilise an OLE protocol, where P_k acts as the receiver and P_i as the sender. First P_i computes two polynomials, $f_i(x) = x_i \cdot x$ and $h_i(x)$ (the masking polynomial, as before). Each P_k $(1 \leq k \leq n)$ then acts as the receiver and executes an OPE protocol with P_i (who acts as the sender) to privately evaluate P_i's polynomial, $f_i(x)$ at the point x_{j_k}, as before P_i adds the masking polynomial to his computation.

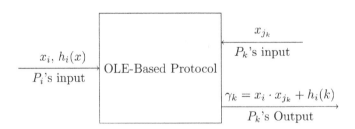

Fig. 2. Overview of the protocol

Since the OLE protocol does not allow P_i to learn the evaluation point then the protocol can now be considered t-private for both P_i and P_j. Specifically, P_i's privacy is maintained via the masking polynomial and P_j's privacy is maintained via Shamir's secret sharing scheme and the OLE protocol. An overview of this is given in Fig. 2. Note that P_i will also use his share from x_j and compute his own share of $\gamma = x_i \cdot x_j$ (of course, there is no need to perform OLE, as he plays the role of the sender and receiver at the same time).

3.2 Security and Correctness

In order to prove the security and correctness of our proposed scheme we will evaluate it against the following criteria specified below:

1. **Correctness** – Upon completion of the protocol each participant, P_k holds a share, γ_k of the polynomial $\Gamma(x)$, of degree at most t with free term $\Gamma(0) = x_i \cdot x_j$.
2. **Privacy** – A set of t or less participants, not including either P_i or P_j, cannot reduce their uncertainty of x_i or x_j.
3. **Privacy with respect to P_i** – A set of t or less participants, including P_j, cannot reduce their uncertainty of x_i.
4. **Privacy with respect to P_j** – A set of t or less participants, including P_i, cannot reduce their uncertainty of x_j.

We note that the last three criterion presented here simply encapsulate the notion of privacy given in Definition 2.

4 Proposed OLE-Based MPC Protocol

Similar to the OPE protocol given in Fig. 1, our proposed multiplication protocol consists of two phases:

1. **The Setup Phase:** Where the initialiser privately sends some (essentially random) information to each participant involved in the protocol.
2. **The Computation Phase:** Where participants are able to compute shares to the multiplication.

Where our scheme differs, however, is in the addition of a masking polynomial ($h_i(x)$) and the limiting of the receivers polynomial to a degree no greater than 1 (OLE).

As per Sect. 3.1 suppose we have a set of n participants $P_1, \cdots, P_n$, with respective private inputs $x_1, \cdots, x_n$, who wish to compute shares of the value $\gamma = x_i \times x_j$ where $i, j \in [1, n]$ and $i \neq j$. Participant P_j first privately distributes shares for x_j amongst all participants, using the polynomial $f_j(x)$, such that P_k $(1 \leq k \leq n)$ gets the share $x_{j_k} = f_j(k)$. To compute a share γ_k, of γ each P_k cooperates with P_i to execute our modified OLE protocol, with P_k essentially acting as the receiver and P_i acting as the sender for each P_k. Note that all computations are performed in the field $\mathbb{F}_q$ where q is a prime number such that $q > n$. The full protocol is given in Fig. 3.

In order to compute a share P_k and P_i exchange exactly 3 field elements (l and $V(x)$). This gives a communication complexity of $\mathcal{O}(q)$. Therefore, the overall communication complexity, required for each of the n participants to compute his share can be given as $\mathcal{O}(qn)$. However, since the protocol is based on Shamir's (t, n) secret sharing scheme [12] we actually only require $t + 1$ participants to ensure the output can be constructed. This gives a communication complexity of $\mathcal{O}(qt)$.

Input: P_i has x_i and P_k has the share x_{j_k}, of x_j.
Output: P_k obtains the share γ_k, of $\Gamma(x)$ where $\Gamma(0) = x_i \cdot x_j$.

Setup The initialiser privately sends:

1. A set of $n - 1$ random polynomials, $S_{i_k}(x)$, of degree at most 1 to P_i where $k = 1, \cdots, n$ and $k \neq i$.
2. A random value, d_k and the value $g_k = S_{i_k}(d_k)$ to every participant P_k.

Computation
P_i privately computes:

 - A masking polynomial, $h_i(x)$ of degree at most t with $f_i(0) = 0$.
 - The multiplication polynomial, $f_i(x) = x_i \cdot x$.

Each P_k then privately executes the following steps with P_i:

1. P_k sends the value $l_k = x_{j_k} - d_k$ to P_i.
2. P_i then computes and sends to P_k the polynomial $V_k(x)$ which is computed as:
$$V_k(x) = h_i(k) + f_i(x + l_k) + S_{i_k}(x)$$
3. P_k computes his share of γ as $\gamma_k = V_k(d_k) - g_k$.

Fig. 3. An information theoretic, OLE-based multiplication protocol for MPC

4.1 Evaluation

In this section we evaluate the proposed protocol against the set of security criteria given in Sect. 3.2. We note that all four of these criterion evaluate the specific multiplication protocol and not the actual MPC itself. That is, we evaluate the multiplication protocol only and assume that participants have not yet reconstructed the actual output of the MPC.

Correctness. At the end of our protocol each participant, P_k, will now have a share of the polynomial: $\Gamma(x) = h_i(x) + x_i f_j(x)$. Since the free term of $h_i(x)$ is equal to zero, we can say that $\Gamma(0) = x_i f_j(0)$. Now, $f_j(x)$ has the free term x_j and both $h_i(x)$ and $f_j(x)$ are of degree at most t. As a result of this we can conclude that correctness is achieved, as each P_k has a share to a polynomial, $\Gamma(x)$, of degree at most t, with free term equal to $x_i \cdot x_j$.

Privacy

Theorem 1. *A set of t participants, not including P_i or P_j, cannot compute any information relating to x_i or x_j.*

In order to prove this we must first show that the modified OLE protocol is secure. Following this, we need to prove that a set of t shares relating to the multiplication reveals no information.

Proof. Suppose that a given participant, P_k executes the multiplication protocol with P_i. After sending l_k to P_i he receivers the polynomial $V_k(x) = h_i(k) + f_i(x + l_k) + S_{i_k}(x)$ which we can simplify as $V_k(x) = v_k + z_k x$. Let $S_{i_k}(x) = \kappa_k + \omega_k x$ and recall that $f_i(x) = x_i \cdot x$, then we can rewrite the equation as $V(x) = h_i(k) + x_i l_k + \kappa_k(x_i + \omega_k)x$. This gives P_k the following information:

$$v_k = h_i(k) + x_i l_k + \kappa_k$$

$$z_k = x_i + \omega_k$$

Since the values ω_k and κ_k (as well as the coefficients of $h_i(x)$) are chosen at random, P_k cannot gain any information from the above equations. The next step in the protocol is for P_k to compute $\gamma_k = V(d_k) - g_k$, which can be written as $\gamma_k = h_i(k) + x_i x_{i_j}$. Individually, this gives no information to P_k as he does not know the value of either $h_i(k)$ or x_i, it remains to be seen if a coalition of participants can compute any information.

Without loss of generality suppose that the first set of t participants, $P_1, \cdots, P_t$ pool their information together. Let $h_i(x) = m_1 x + m_2 x^2 + \cdots + m_t x^t$, then the coalition can compute the following system:

$$\gamma_1 = x_i \cdot x_{i_1} + m_1 + m_2 + \cdots + m_t$$

$$\gamma_2 = x_i \cdot x_{i_2} + 2m_1 + 4m_2 + \cdots + 2^t m_t$$

$$\vdots$$

$$\gamma_t = x_i \cdot x_{i_t} + t m_1 + t^2 m_2 + \cdots + t^t m_t$$

Due to the perfectness of Shamir's secret sharing scheme [4,12] the above system does not reveal any information to the participants as they effectively have a set of t shares relating to a degree t polynomial. This becomes even more evident when we take into account that $x_{i_k} = f_j(k)$ meaning that each P_k has a share of the polynomial $\Gamma = x_i f_j(x) + h_i(x)$.

The end result being that a coalition of t participants cannot reduce their uncertainty of x_i. The same is also true for x_j, as collectively the coalition only has t shares of $f_j(x)$.

Privacy with Respect to P_i

Theorem 2. *A set of t participants, including P_j, cannot compute any information relating to x_i.*

Proof. The proof of this is similar to the proof of Theorem 1 along with some extra information. Namely, we now assume that the coalition of participants has the values of both $f_j(x)$ and, consequently x_j. The first, obvious ramification of this is that the coalition now know the shares of every other participant relating to x_j. This actually gives them no advantage, in regards to the OLE, as they do not know (and cannot compute) the values given to the other participants by the initialiser (namely d_k and g_k). We therefore only need to prove that knowing $f_j(x)$ reveals no information relating to x_i.

As before, at the end of the protocol each participant has a share to the polynomial $\Gamma(x) = x_i f_j(x) + h_i(x)$. It is easy to see that if the coalition can compute $\Gamma(x)$ or even $h_i(x)$ then they can easily compute x_i. However, the coalition do not hold direct shares to $h_i(x)$, so even knowing $h_i(0) = 0$ gives them nothing. Furthermore, to compute any information relating to $\Gamma(x)$ would require the coalition to compute a solution to the system given in the proof of Theorem 1.

Computing a solution to this system is analogous to solving a system of equations composed of $t + 1$ unknowns (x_i and the coefficients of $h_i(x)$) and t equations. We can therefore conclude that a set of participants, including P_j cannot reduce their uncertainty of x_i.

Privacy with Respect to P_j

Theorem 3. *A set of t participants, including P_i, cannot compute any information relating to x_j.*

Proof. In the proof of Theorem 1 it was shown that the modified OLE is secure, therefore to prove the above theorem we need to show that a coalition of t participants, including P_i, with t shares relating to $\Gamma(x) = x_i f_j(x) + h_i(x)$ and t shares of $f_j(x)$ cannot compute any information relating to x_j. First, let $f_j(x) = x_j + W_1 x + \cdots + W_t x^t$ and assume, as before, that a coalition composed of the first t participants (which includes P_i) pool their knowledge. They can construct the following system from their shares of $\Gamma(x)$:

$$\gamma_1 = x_i \cdot (x_j + W_1 + \cdots + W_t) + h_i(1)$$
$$\gamma_2 = x_i \cdot (x_j + 2W_1 + \cdots + 2^t W_t) + h_i(2)$$
$$\vdots$$
$$\gamma_t = x_i \cdot (x_j + tW_1 + \cdots + t^t W_t) + h_i(t)$$

From the shares of $f_j(x)$ we get:

$$x_{j_1} = x_j + W_1 + \cdots + W_t$$
$$x_{j_2} = x_j + 2W_1 + \cdots + 2^t W_t$$
$$\vdots$$
$$x_{j_t} = x_j + tW_1 + \cdots + t^t W_t$$

It is easy to see that the two systems are actually linearly dependent. Since the values of x_i and $h_i(x)$ are known to the coalition, this results in a system composed of $t + 1$ unknowns (the coefficients of $f_j(x)$) and only t linearly independent equations. The net result of this is that each value of x_j is, from the point of view of the coalition, equally likely. Meaning that they cannot compute any information relating to x_j.

References

1. Beaver, D.: Efficient multiparty protocols using circuit randomization. In: Feigenbaum, J. (ed.) CRYPTO 1991. LNCS, vol. 576, pp. 420–432. Springer, Heidelberg (1992). https://doi.org/10.1007/3-540-46766-1_34
2. Ben-Or, M., Goldwasser, S., Wigderson, A.: Completeness theorems for noncryptographic fault-tolerant distributed computation. In: Proceedings of the Twentieth Annual ACM Symposium on Theory of Computing, STOC 1988. ACM, New York (1988)
3. Benaloh, J.C.: Secret sharing homomorphisms: keeping shares of a secret secret (extended abstract). In: Odlyzko, A.M. (ed.) CRYPTO 1986. LNCS, vol. 263, pp. 251–260. Springer, Heidelberg (1987). https://doi.org/10.1007/3-540-47721-7_19
4. Corniaux, C.L.F., Ghodosi, H.: An entropy-based demonstration of the security of Shamir's secret sharing scheme. In: 2014 International Conference on Information Science, Electronics and Electrical Engineering, vol. 1, pp. 46–48, April 2014
5. Chang, Y.-C., Lu, C.-J.: Oblivious polynomial evaluation and oblivious neural learning. In: Boyd, C. (ed.) ASIACRYPT 2001. LNCS, vol. 2248, pp. 369–384. Springer, Heidelberg (2001). https://doi.org/10.1007/3-540-45682-1_22
6. Chaum, D., Crépeau, C., Damgård, I.: Multiparty unconditionally secure protocols. In: Proceedings of the Twentieth Annual ACM Symposium on Theory of Computing, STOC 1988, pp. 11–19. ACM, New York (1988)
7. Döttling, N., Ghosh, S., Nielsen, J.B., Nilges, T., Trifiletti, R.: TinyOLE: efficient actively secure two-party computation from oblivious linear function evaluation. In: Proceedings of the 2017 ACM SIGSAC Conference on Computer and Communications Security, CCS 2017, pp. 2263–2276. ACM, New York (2017)
8. Goldreich, O., Micali, S., Wigderson, A.: How to play any mental game. In: Proceedings of the Nineteenth Annual ACM Symposium on Theory of Computing, STOC 1987, pp. 218–229. ACM, New York (1987). https://doi.org/10.1145/28395.28420
9. Hanaoka, G., Imai, H., Mueller-Quade, J., Nascimento, A.C.A., Otsuka, A., Winter, A.: Information theoretically secure oblivious polynomial evaluation: model, bounds, and constructions. In: Wang, H., Pieprzyk, J., Varadharajan, V. (eds.) ACISP 2004. LNCS, vol. 3108, pp. 62–73. Springer, Heidelberg (2004). https://doi.org/10.1007/978-3-540-27800-9_6

10. Naor, M., Pinkas, B.: Oblivious transfer and polynomial evaluation. In: Proceedings of the Thirty-First Annual ACM Symposium on Theory of Computing, STOC 1999, pp. 245–254. ACM, New York (1999)
11. Rabin, T., Ben-Or, M.: Verifiable secret sharing and multiparty protocols with honest majority. In: Proceedings of the Twenty-First Annual ACM Symposium on Theory of Computing, STOC 1989. ACM, New York (1989)
12. Shamir, A.: How to share a secret. Commun. ACM 22(11), 612–613 (1979)
13. Tonicelli, R., et al.: Information-theoretically secure oblivious polynomial evaluation in the commodity-based model. Int. J. Inf. Secur. 14(1), 73–84 (2015)

Linear Depth Integer-Wise Homomorphic Division

Hiroki Okada[1(✉)], Carlos Cid[2], Seira Hidano[1], and Shinsaku Kiyomoto[1]

[1] KDDI Research, Inc., Saitama, Japan
ir-okada@kddi-research.jp
[2] Royal Holloway, University of London, Egham, Surrey, UK

Abstract. We propose a secure *integer-wise* homomorphic division algorithm on fully homomorphic encryption schemes (FHE). For integer-wise algorithms, we encrypt plaintexts as integers without encoding them into bit values, while in *bit-wise* algorithms, plaintexts are encoded into binary and bit values are encrypted one by one. All the publicly available division algorithms are constructed in bit-wise style, and to the best of our knowledge there are no known integer-wise algorithm for secure division. We derive some empirical results on the FHE library HElib and show that our algorithm is 2.45x faster than the fastest bit-wise algorithm. We also show that the multiplicative depth of our algorithm is $O(l)$, where l is the integer bit length, while that of existing division algorithms is $O(l^2)$. Furthermore, we generalise our secure division algorithm and propose a method for secure calculation of a general 2-variable function. The order of multiplicative depth of the algorithm, which is a main factor of the complexity of a FHE algorithm, is exactly the same as our secure division algorithm.

Keywords: Fully homomorphic encryption · HElib ·
Secure integer arithmetic · Circuit depth

1 Introduction

Fully Homomorphic Encryption. A fully homomorphic encryption (FHE) scheme presents a way to perform arbitrary calculations on encrypted data without the requirement of decryption. The first construction of FHE [11,12] was given by Gentry in 2009. Several improvements [4–6,10,13,14,25,27] have followed since then, developing a diversity of features and complexity assumptions. HElib [17–19] is a library for FHE widely used in applications, which implements the BGV scheme [3]. It allows for the "packing" of ciphertexts and single instruction multiple data (SIMD) computations, amortizing the cost for certain tasks.

There are numerous applications of FHE, but one of the most remarkable is privacy-preserving delegated computations, such as privacy-preserving machine learning as a service. In the service, users do not wish to reveal their sensitive

© IFIP International Federation for Information Processing 2019
Published by Springer Nature Switzerland AG 2019
O. Blazy and C. Y. Yeun (Eds.): WISTP 2018, LNCS 11469, pp. 91–106, 2019.
https://doi.org/10.1007/978-3-030-20074-9_8

data to the server, and the server does not want to reveal the cognitive model to users. FHE enables these scenarios in an elegant way with non-interactivity. However, because of the inefficiency of existing FHE schemes, most applications are constructed evading the *non-crypto-friendly* calculations such as comparison, division, and some non-linear functions.

Bit-Wise Encryption vs. Integer-Wise Encryption. Most FHE schemes, including the BGV scheme, feature *integer-wise* and *bit-wise* encryption; the size of the plaintext space in the scheme is variable. In bit-wise encryption the plaintext space is $\mathbb{Z}_2$, and in integer-wise encryption the plaintext space is $\mathbb{Z}_p$ where $p > 2$. Because the main libraries of FHE, including HElib, do not support some basic integer arithmetic operations such as division and comparison, several studies [8,9,28] have been performed on improved arithmetic. The proposed algorithms are primarily for bit-wise encryption, and they simply leverage the existing algorithms for such operations on the bit-wise circuit such as Ripple carry adder, long multiplication, and non-restoring division. Although bit-wise encryption can perform integer comparison very efficiently [7], integer addition and multiplication are not practical since they require homomorphic multiplication. On the other hand, integer-wise arithmetic can naturally perform integer addition and multiplication efficiently, and recent remarkable privacy-preserving machine learning such as [1,2,15,20] use integer-wise encryption. However, the algorithm for these applications evades arithmetic such as division and comparison, which are believed to be inefficient. While a concrete algorithm for secure integer-wise comparison has been recently proposed in [22], to the best of our knowledge there is no known concrete algorithm for secure integer-wise division algorithm. Emergence of efficient algorithms for basic arithmetic operations such as division and comparison will undoubtedly increase options to optimise higher level applications of secure computation.

Our Contribution. We present a new concrete algorithm for privacy preserving *integer-wise* division. Although several studies have been performed on privacy preserving *bit-wise* division algorithms [8,9,28], there is no known concrete algorithm for the *integer-wise* version. We implement our division algorithm using HElib, and test its performance. The experimental results show that our algorithm performs 2.45 times faster than the fastest bit-wise algorithm [8]. We also theoretically analyse the multiplicative depth, which is a barometer for the complexity for the FHE-based algorithm. While the order of the multiplicative depth of existing division algorithms [8,9,28] is $O(l^2)$ for l-bit size integers, we show that our algorithm can perform with $O(l)$.

Furthermore, we generalise our secure division algorithm and propose an algorithm for secure calculation of a *general 2-variable function*; the order of multiplicative depth of the algorithm is $O(l)$, which is the same as our secure division algorithm. This is the first result to construct a concrete algorithm for performing the general 2-variable function, expanding the FHE application diversity.

2 Preliminaries

2.1 Notation

In the FHE construction, a ring R is used, whose elements are written in lower case; for example, $r \in R$. For an integer q, we use R_q to denote R/qR. For $a \in R$, we use the notation $[a]_q$ to refer to $a \bmod q$, with coefficients reduced to the range $(-\frac{q}{2}, \frac{q}{2}]$. A concrete instantiation for our applications is the quotient polynomial ring $R_q = \mathbb{Z}_q[x]/\Phi_m(x)$, where q is a prime and $\Phi_m(x)$ is the m-th cyclotomic polynomial. We denote a ciphertext of r, which is encrypted with a FHE scheme, by C_r.

We denote the logarithm to base 2 and the natural logarithm as $\log(\cdot)$ and $\ln(\cdot)$, respectively. We denote vectors in bold. The notation $\boldsymbol{v}[i]$ refers to the ith coefficient of $\boldsymbol{v}$, while the scalar product of two vectors $\boldsymbol{u}, \boldsymbol{v} \in R^n$ is denoted as $\langle \boldsymbol{u}, \boldsymbol{v} \rangle = \sum_{i=1}^{n} \boldsymbol{u}[i] \cdot \boldsymbol{v}[i] \in R$. By $(\boldsymbol{a} \| \boldsymbol{b})$ we denote the concatenation of two vectors $\boldsymbol{a}$ and $\boldsymbol{b}$. We write $\boldsymbol{s} \xleftarrow{U} \mathcal{S}$ to denote the process of sampling $\boldsymbol{s}$ uniformly at random over $\mathcal{S}$; when the set $\mathcal{S}$ is clear from the context, we will write $e \leftarrow \chi$ to denote the process of sampling e according to the probability distribution χ over $\mathcal{S}$.

2.2 The BGV Scheme

A FHE scheme is a public-key cryptographic scheme that includes two operations $(+, \cdot)$ on ciphertexts such that: $\mathsf{Dec}(C_a + C_b) = a + b$, $\mathsf{Dec}(C_a \cdot C_b) = a \cdot b$. The BGV scheme [3] is a widely used FHE scheme for practical applications, which is implemented in the FHE library HElib [16]. The security of the scheme is based on the standard assumptions of the Learning with Error (LWE) problem [23] or Ring-LWE (RLWE) problem [21]. This is in contrast to the earlier FHE constructions [11,12] which were based on ad-hoc average-case assumptions on ideal lattice problems.

The Basic Encryption Scheme. BGV is a public-key cryptography scheme $\mathsf{E} = (\mathsf{E.Setup}, \mathsf{E.SecretKeyGen}, \mathsf{E.PublicKeyGen}, \mathsf{E.Enc}, \mathsf{E.Dec})$ defined as follows.

– Setup(1^λ). Given the security parameter λ as input, set an integer $m = m(\lambda)$ that defines the cyclotomic polynomial $\Phi_m(x)$, and the odd modulus $q = q(\lambda)$. If $R = \mathbb{Z}[x]/\Phi_m(x)$, the underlying working ring is $R_q = \mathbb{Z}_q[x]/\Phi_m(x)$. Set a plaintext modulus p that is relatively prime to q, with the plaintext space given by $R_p = \mathbb{Z}_p[x]/\Phi_m(x)$. Set a noise distribution $\chi = \chi(\lambda)$ over the underlying working ring, and $N = N(\lambda) = \mathrm{polylog}(q)$. Output $params = (R, m, q, p, \chi, N)$.
– SecretKeyGen($params$). Sample $s \leftarrow \chi$. Output the secret key $sk = \boldsymbol{s} := (1, s) \in R_q^2$.
– PublicKeyGen($params, sk$). Take as input the secret key $sk = \boldsymbol{s} = (1, s)$ and $params$. Sample $\boldsymbol{a} \xleftarrow{U} R_q^N$ and $\boldsymbol{e} \leftarrow \chi^N$. Set $\boldsymbol{b} := \boldsymbol{s}a + p\boldsymbol{e} \in R_q^N$, and output the public key defined as $pk = \boldsymbol{A} := (\boldsymbol{b}, -\boldsymbol{a}) \in R_q^{N \times 2}$. Notice that $\boldsymbol{A} \cdot \boldsymbol{s} = \boldsymbol{b} - \boldsymbol{s}a = p\boldsymbol{e}$, from the definition of $\boldsymbol{b}$.

- $\mathsf{Enc}(params, pk, m)$. To encrypt a message $m \in R_p$, set $\boldsymbol{m} = (m, 0) \in R_p^2$, sample $\boldsymbol{r} \xleftarrow{U} R_p^N$ and output the ciphertext $\boldsymbol{c} := \boldsymbol{m} + \boldsymbol{r}^\top \boldsymbol{A} \in R_q^2$.
- $\mathsf{Dec}(params, sk, \boldsymbol{c})$. Output the message $m := [[\langle \boldsymbol{c}, \boldsymbol{s} \rangle]_q]_p$.

The decryption works because

$$[[\langle \boldsymbol{c}, \boldsymbol{s} \rangle]_q]_p = [[(\boldsymbol{m} + \boldsymbol{r}^\top \boldsymbol{A}) \cdot \boldsymbol{s}]_q]_p = [[m + p\boldsymbol{r}^\top \boldsymbol{e}]_q]_p = [m + p\boldsymbol{r}^\top \boldsymbol{e}]_p = m,$$

where the third equality holds since $\boldsymbol{r}$ and $\boldsymbol{e}$ have small enough entries so that the value $m + p\boldsymbol{r}^\top \boldsymbol{e}$ is smaller than the modulus q.

The FHE Scheme. As a FHE scheme, the BGV scheme supports addition and multiplication over the plaintext and ciphertext spaces. Let $\boldsymbol{c}_a$ and $\boldsymbol{c}_b$ be ciphertexts of plaintexts a and b under the same key sk, respectively. The addition of two ciphertexts is simply a component-wise addition, i.e.

$$\boldsymbol{c}_a + \boldsymbol{c}_b = (\boldsymbol{c}_a[0], \boldsymbol{c}_a[1]) + (\boldsymbol{c}_b[0], \boldsymbol{c}_b[1]) = (\boldsymbol{c}_a[0] + \boldsymbol{c}_b[0], \boldsymbol{c}_b[1] + \boldsymbol{c}_a[1]) = \boldsymbol{c}_{a+b},$$

which is a ciphertext of $a+b \in R_p$. The homomorphic multiplication is performed by the tensor product of two ciphertexts. The tensor product of ciphertexts

$$\boldsymbol{c}_{a \cdot b} := \boldsymbol{c}_a \otimes \boldsymbol{c}_b := (\boldsymbol{c}_a[0]\boldsymbol{c}_b[0], \boldsymbol{c}_a[0]\boldsymbol{c}_b[1] + \boldsymbol{c}_a[1]\boldsymbol{c}_b[0], \boldsymbol{c}_a[1]\boldsymbol{c}_b[1]) \tag{1}$$

is a ciphertext of $a \cdot b \in R_p$ under the new secret key $\boldsymbol{s}' := \boldsymbol{s} \otimes \boldsymbol{s}$. In this way, the homomorphic multiplication increases the size of ciphertexts exponentially. In order to deal with this expanding ciphertext, the BGV scheme features *key switching*. The key switching function $\mathsf{SwitchKey}(\tau_{\boldsymbol{s}' \to \overline{\boldsymbol{s}}}, \boldsymbol{c}', q)$ takes the ciphertext $\boldsymbol{c}'$ under $\boldsymbol{s}'$ and outputs a new ciphertext $\overline{\boldsymbol{c}}$ that encrypts the same message under the secret new key $\overline{\boldsymbol{s}}$. Using this function, we can reduce the size of ciphertext $\boldsymbol{c}_{a \cdot b} \in R_q^3$ to $\overline{\boldsymbol{c}}_{a \cdot b} \in R_q^2 \leftarrow \mathsf{SwitchKey}(\tau_{\boldsymbol{s}' \to \overline{\boldsymbol{s}}}, \boldsymbol{c}_{a \cdot b})$. The BGV scheme also features *modulus switching* techniques, which reduce the magnitude of the noise of the ciphertext by switching the modulus from q to the smaller modulus q'. The modulus switching function $\mathsf{Scale}(\boldsymbol{c}, q, q', p)$, takes a ciphertext $\boldsymbol{c}$ for modulus q and outputs a ciphertext under same secret for modulus q'.

We now briefly describe the BGV FHE scheme. The scheme is a *levelled* FHE scheme.

- $\mathsf{FHE.Setup}(1^\lambda, 1^L)$. Takes as input the security parameter λ and a number of levels L. Set an integer $m = m(\lambda, L)$ that defines the cyclotomic polynomial $\Phi_m(x)$. Let $\mu = \mu(\lambda, L, b) = \theta(\log \lambda + \log L)$ be a parameter to define the bit size of the moduli. For $j = L$ (input level of circuit) to 0 (output level), run $params_j \leftarrow \mathsf{E.Setup}(1^\lambda, 1^{(j+1) \cdot \mu}, b)$ to obtain a list of parameters, including a list of moduli $\{q_L ((L+1) \cdot \mu \text{ bits}), q_{L-1}, \ldots, q_0 (\mu \text{ bits})\}$.
- $\mathsf{FHE.KeyGen}(params_j)$. For $j = L$ down to 0, do the following:
  1. Run the basic schemes $\boldsymbol{s}_j \leftarrow \mathsf{E.SecretKeyGen}(params_j)$, and $\boldsymbol{A}_j \leftarrow \mathsf{E.PublicKeyGen}(params_j, \boldsymbol{s}_j)$.
  2. Set $\boldsymbol{s}_j' \leftarrow \boldsymbol{s}_j \otimes \boldsymbol{s}_j$.

3. Run $\tau_{s'_j \to s_{j-1}} \leftarrow$ SwitchKeyGen(s'_j, s_{j-1}), where SwitchKeyGen is a generator function of auxiliary information $\tau_{s'_j \to s_{j-1}}$ that will be used for SwitchKey. (Note that we omit this step when $j = 0$.)

4. Output $sk := \{s_j\}_{j=0}^L$, $pk = \{A_j\}_{j=0}^L$.

- FHE.Enc$(params, pk, m)$. Take a message m in R_p. Run $c \leftarrow$ E.Enc$(params_L, A_L, m)$ of the basic scheme.

- FHE.Dec$(params, sk, c)$. Suppose that the input ciphertext c is under key s_j. Here, we know the level (the index j) of the ciphertext from its augmented information. Run E.Dec$(params_j, s_j, c)$.

- FHE.Eval$(pk, f, c_1, \ldots, c_l)$. Take as input a circuit f for ciphertexts $c_1, \ldots, c_l$. It is assumed that f is a levelled circuit composed of layers of alternating addition and multiplication gates. FHE.Eval will invoke FHE.Add and FHE.Mult, which is described next, to compute the circuit. The ciphertext refreshing procedure FHE.Refresh (described later) is invoked after every multiplication layer, in order to reduce the noise in the ciphertexts and move it to a different level.

  - FHE.Add(pk, c_1, c_2). Takes two ciphertexts encrypted under the same s_j. If they are not under the same key, use FHE.Refresh to make one of them, the level of which is higher than the other, to be encrypted under s_j. Output $c_3 \leftarrow c_1 + c_2 \mod q_j$.

  - FHE.Mult(pk, c_1, c_2). Takes two ciphertexts encrypted under the same s_j. If they are not under the same key, use FHE.Refresh to make one of them, the level of which is higher than the other, to be encrypted under s_j. Multiply the two ciphertexts, then obtain the new ciphertext c_3 under the long secret key $s'_j = s_j \otimes s_j$. c_3 is the coefficient vector of $\langle c \otimes c, x \otimes x \rangle$. Then, output $c_4 \leftarrow$ FHE.Refresh$(c_3, \tau_{s'_j \to s_{j-1}}, q_j, q_{j-1})$.

- FHE.Refresh$(c, \tau_{s'_j \to s_{j-1}}, q_j, q_{j-1})$. Takes a ciphertext encrypted under s'_j, the auxiliary information $\tau_{s'_j \to s_{j-1}}$ for key switching, and the current and next moduli q_j and q_{j-1}. Perform the following.

  1. (Key switching.) Set $c_1 \leftarrow$ SwitchKey$(\tau_{s'_j \to s_{j-1}}, c, q_j)$, a ciphertext under the key s_{j-1} for modulus q_j.

  2. (Moduli switching.) Set $c_2 \leftarrow$ Scale(c_1, q_j, q_{j-1}, p), a ciphertext under the key s_{j-1} for modulus q_{j-1}. Output c_2.

Multiplicative Depth and Level Parameter L. As mentioned in [3], we do not need to perform FHE.Refresh after addition. We do not perform SwitchKey after addition either, since addition does not increase the size of the ciphertext. Moreover, since addition increases the noise much more slowly than multiplication, we do not need to perform Scale after addition either. Finally we also note that in HElib, FHE.Refresh is performed only after FHE.Mult is performed.

The parameter L, which indicates the number of levels of arithmetic circuit that the scheme is capable of evaluating, is very important when we estimate the complexity of the FHE circuit. Every time we perform FHE.Mult, we perform SwitchKey and move the index j to $j - 1$. Thus, basically, we set the level parameter L according to the multiplicative depth of the circuit. The level L is

Table 1. Basic interfaces for homomorphic evaluation in HElib.

HElib interface	Abbreviation we use
`Ctxt::addCtxt`	FHE.Add(c, c')
`Ctxt::multiplyBy`	FHE.Mult(c, c')
`Ctxt::addConstant`	FHE.addConst(c, m')
`Ctxt::multByConstant`	FHE.multConst(c, m')

related with the complexity of FHE.Add or FHE.Add. Brakerski *et al.* [3] showed the order of complexity is $O(\lambda L^3)$.

2.3   HElib

HElib [16] is a software library that implements the BGV scheme in C++. HElib is based on the number theory library NTL [24]. In addition to the basic scheme, HElib also supports the SIMD feature proposed by Smart and Vercauteren [26]. The SIMD feature enables packing multiple plaintexts into a single element of R_p with the Chinese Remainder Theorem; it also enables parallel component-wise evaluation of the plaintexts in the SIMD "slots". It produces a much better amortised performance, due to parallelisation.

HElib has an interface for the "constant" evaluation, where addition or multiplication by a plaintext is performed for ciphertext. Note that Table 1 shows basic interfaces for homomorphic evaluation in the HElib. These constant evaluations are efficient when the addend or multiplier are not encrypted values. In particular, constant multiplication is quite efficient compared to the homomorphic multiplication; the constant multiplication does not increase the dimension of the ciphertext, and we do not need to perform SwitchKey after the constant multiplication.

2.4   Polynomial Interpolation and Integer-Wise Secure Comparison

The first integer-wise homomorphic comparison algorithm was proposed in [22]. We refer to the algorithm as Algorithm 1, which is based on the polynomial interpolation technique.

Polynomial interpolation is a process of constructing a polynomial $f(x)$ of degree at most n which satisfies $y_i = f(x_i), i \in \{0, 1, \ldots, n\}$, where $\{x_i, y_i\}$ is given for $n + 1$ data points such that $x_i \neq x_j$ when $i \neq j$. We can calculate the polynomial $f(x)$ by

$$f(x) = \sum_{i=0}^{n} \left(\prod_{0 \leq j \leq n, j \neq i} \frac{x - x_j}{x_i - x_j} \right) y_i. \tag{2}$$

Note that in Algorithm 1, the polynomial intepolation technique is used to construct the Heaviside step function (i.e, comparison with 0). Our sub-algorithms

---

Algorithm 1. $\mathsf{Comp}(C_a, C_b)$: Integer-wise Homomorphic Comparison [22]

Input: Ciphertexts C_a, C_b.

Output: $C_{(a \geq b)}$, such that $C_{(a \geq b)} = \begin{cases} C_0 & (a \geq b), \\ C_1 & (a < b). \end{cases}$

1: (Precomputation): Using the polynomial interpolation algorithm, find polynomial $f(x) \in \mathbb{Z}_p[x]$ that satisfies

$$f(x) = \begin{cases} 0 & (x = 0, 1, 2, \ldots, \lfloor \frac{p}{2} \rfloor), \\ 1 & (x = -\lfloor \frac{p}{2} \rfloor, \ldots, -2, -1). \end{cases}$$

For example, with plaintext modulus $p = 7$, the interpolation polynomial $f(x)$ of degree 6 is calculated such that

$$f(-3) = 1, f(-2) = 1, f(-1) = 1, f(0) = 0, f(1) = 0, f(2) = 0, f(3) = 0.$$

For this example, $f(x) = 4x^6 - x^5 - 6x^3 - 4x \in \mathbb{Z}_7[x]$.

2: Homomorphically computes $C_{a-b} = C_a - C_b$.

3: Calculate and output $C_{(a \geq b)} = f(C_{a-b})$.

$\mathsf{ConstDiv}$ and $\mathsf{ConstEq}$ are also constructed based on the polynomial interpolation, as discussed in the next section.

3   Our Algorithm for Integer-Wise Homomorphic Division

In this section we present our integer-wise secure division algorithm. In the algorithm, the polynomial interpolation technique is used as a precomputation, similar to the integer-wise comparison algorithm from [22] (Algorithm 1).

In the following, we present in Sect. 3.1 the overview of the algorithms employed in our secure homomorphic division. We describe the algorithms in detail in Sect. 3.2. Finally, we analyse their complexity and provide empirical results in Sect. 3.3.

3.1   Overview

Our integer-wise homomorphic division algorithm $\mathsf{Div}(C_a, C_d)$ is given in Algorithm 2, and is constructed based on the following subroutines:

- (Algorithm 3) $\mathsf{Pows}(C_a)$: Computes powers of a ciphertext C_a.
- (Algorithm 4) $\mathsf{ConstDiv}(C_a^{\mathsf{pow}}, y)$: Integer-wise division by public divisor y.
- (Algorithm 5) $\mathsf{ConstEq}(C_d^{\mathsf{pow}}, y)$: Integer-wise equality check with a public input y.

$\mathsf{ConstDiv}(C_a^{\mathsf{pow}}, y)$ homomorphically computes the ciphertext of a quotient $\lfloor a/y \rfloor$ denoted as $C_{\lfloor a/y \rfloor}$, from the ciphertext of $a \in \mathbb{Z}_p$ denoted as C_a, and public

---

Algorithm 2. $\mathsf{Div}(C_a, C_d)$: Integer-wise Homomorphic Division

---
Input: Ciphertexts C_a, C_d.
Output: $C_{\lfloor a/d \rfloor}$
1: $C_{\mathsf{sum}} = 0$
2: $\boldsymbol{C}_a^{\mathsf{pow}} = \mathsf{Pows}(C_a)$ $\triangleright \boldsymbol{C}_a^{\mathsf{pow}} := \{C_a, C_a^2, C_a^3, \dots, C_a^{p-1}\}$
3: $\boldsymbol{C}_d^{\mathsf{pow}} = \mathsf{Pows}(C_d)$ $\triangleright \boldsymbol{C}_d^{\mathsf{pow}} := \{C_d, C_d^2, C_d^3, \dots, C_d^{p-1}\}$
4: **for** $i = 0$ to $(p-1)$ **do**
5:      $C_{\lfloor a/i \rfloor} = \mathsf{ConstDiv}(\boldsymbol{C}_a^{\mathsf{pow}}, i)$
6:      $C_{(d=i)} = \mathsf{ConstEq}(\boldsymbol{C}_d^{\mathsf{pow}}, i)$
7:      $C_{\mathsf{sum}} = C_{\mathsf{sum}} + \mathsf{FHE.Mult}(C_{\lfloor a/i \rfloor}, C_{(d=i)})$ $\triangleright$ $\mathsf{FHE.Mult}(C_{\lfloor a/i \rfloor}, C_{(i=d)}) =$
8: **end for** $\triangleright$ $C_{\lfloor a/d \rfloor}$ if $i = d$; C_0 otherwise
9: Output $C_{\lfloor a/d \rfloor} = C_{\mathsf{sum}}$

---

divisor $y \in \mathbb{Z}_p$. $\mathsf{ConstEq}(C_d^{\mathsf{pow}}, y)$ homomorphically computes the ciphertext of the Boolean value $(y = d)$ denoted as $C_{(y=d)}$, where

$$C_{(y=d)} := \begin{cases} C_1 & \text{if } y = d; \\ C_0 & \text{otherwise.} \end{cases}$$

Note that given C_a, C_d for unknown $a, d \in \mathbb{Z}_p$, then for an arbitrary public value $y \in \mathbb{Z}_p$, we have

$$C_{\lfloor a/y \rfloor} * C_{(y=d)} = \begin{cases} C_{\lfloor a/d \rfloor} & \text{if } y = d; \\ C_0 & \text{otherwise.} \end{cases}$$

Our main algorithm for homomorphic division of a by d is then based on a simple idea: calculate $C_{\lfloor a/y \rfloor} * C_{(y=d)}$ for all public values y and sum them:

$$C_{\mathsf{sum}} := \sum_{y \in \mathbb{Z}_p} C_{\lfloor a/y \rfloor} * C_{(y=d)} = C_{\lfloor a/d \rfloor}.$$

3.2 Algorithms

Main Algorithm. Algorithm 2 shows the integer-wise secure division algorithm $\mathsf{Div}(C_a, C_d)$. The algorithm takes two ciphertexts C_a and C_d, which are ciphertexts of a and d, respectively, then homomorphically calculates a ciphertext $C_{\lfloor a/d \rfloor}$, the decryption of which gives $\lfloor a/d \rfloor$.

The algorithm first calls Pows for both inputs C_a and C_d, to obtain the list of powers $\boldsymbol{C}_a^{\mathsf{pow}}$ and $\boldsymbol{C}_d^{\mathsf{pow}}$. This part performs a high number of homomorphic multiplications, but we store these values and can reuse them. Next, in the `for` loop, for all $i \in \{0, 1, 2, \dots, p-1\}$, we exhaustively calculate $C_{\lfloor a/i \rfloor}$ and $C_{(d=i)}$ with $\mathsf{ConstDiv}$ and $\mathsf{ConstEq}$, then perform the homomorphic multiplication of $C_{\lfloor a/i \rfloor} * C_{(i=d)} := \mathsf{FHE.Mult}(C_{\lfloor a/i \rfloor}, C_{(i=d)})$. Recall that $C_{\lfloor a/i \rfloor} * C_{(i=d)}$ equals to $C_{\lfloor a/d \rfloor}$ if $y = d$, and C_0 otherwise. Thus, at the end of the algorithm we obtain $C_{\lfloor a/d \rfloor} = C_{\mathsf{sum}}$.

Algorithm 3. $\mathsf{Pows}(C_a)$: Computation of powers of C_a

---

Input: Ciphertexts C_a
Output: $C_a^{\mathsf{pow}} := (C_a, C_a^2, C_a^3, \ldots, C_a^{p-1})$
 1: Let $l := \lfloor \log p \rfloor$.
 2: **for** $i = 0$ to $(l - 1)$ **do**
 3:     **for** $j = 1$ to 2^i **do**
 4:         Calculate $C_a^{(2^i + j)} := \mathsf{FHE.Mult}(C_a^{(2^i)}, C_a^j)$.
 5:     **end for**
 6: **end for**   ▷ Here, we have $C_a, C_a^2, C_a^3 \ldots, C_a^{2^l}$.
 7: **if** $2^l < p - 1$ **then**
 8:     **for** $j = 1$ to $p - 1 - 2^l$ **do**
 9:         Calculate $C_a^{(2^l + j)} := \mathsf{FHE.Mult}(C_a^{(2^l)}, C_a^j)$.
10:     **end for**
11: **end if**   ▷ Here, we obtain $C_a^{2^l + 1}, \ldots, C_a^{p-1}$.
12: Output $C_a^{\mathsf{pow}} := (C_a, C_a^2, C_a^3, \ldots, C_a^{p-1})$.

$\mathsf{Pows}(C_a)$. Algorithm 3 shows the sub-algorithm $\mathsf{Pows}(C_a)$. The algorithm takes a ciphertext C_a as an input and homomorphically calculates the powers of C_a, returning the list of powers $C_a^{\mathsf{pow}} := (C_a, C_a^2, C_a^3, \ldots, C_a^{p-1})$. This sub-algorithm is the most complex part of the main division algorithm Div. In Div, this algorithm is called only once per ciphertext. Note that the multiplicative depth of $\mathsf{Pows}(C_a)$ is $\lceil \log(p - 1) \rceil$. For example, when $p = 17$, since $C_a^2 = \mathsf{FHE.Mult}(C_a, C_a)$, $C_a^4 = \mathsf{FHE.Mult}(C_a^2, C_a^2)$, $C_a^8 = \mathsf{FHE.Mult}(C_a^4, C_a^4)$, and $C_a^{16} = \mathsf{FHE.Mult}(C_a^8, C_a^8)$, multiplicative depth is $\log(16) = 4$. See Sect. 3.3 for a more detailed complexity analysis.

$\mathsf{ConstDiv}(C_a^{\mathsf{pow}}, d)$. Algorithm 4 shows the sub-algorithm $\mathsf{ConstDiv}(C_a^{\mathsf{pow}}, d)$. The algorithm takes a list of powers of ciphertext $C_a^{\mathsf{pow}} := (C_a, C_a^2, C_a^3, \ldots, C_a^{p-1})$ and a plaintext divisor d as input, then homomorphically calculates a ciphertext $C_{\lfloor a/d \rfloor}$, the decryption of which gives $\lfloor a/d \rfloor$. Note that this algorithm does not perform homomorphic multiplication, it only requires multiplication by constant $\mathsf{multConst}$, which can be performed efficiently without increasing the size of the ciphertexts and $\mathsf{SwitchKey}$. Moreover we note that line 1 of Algorithm 4 is performed before the algorithm start, i.e. we precompute coefficient vectors $\{a_{f_d}\}_{d \in \mathbb{Z}_p}$, which appear in (3), of the interpolation polynomial.

$\mathsf{ConstEq}(C_a^{\mathsf{pow}}, y)$. Algorithm 5 shows the sub-algorithm $\mathsf{ConstEq}(C_a^{\mathsf{pow}}, y)$. The algorithm takes a list of powers of ciphertext $C_a^{\mathsf{pow}} := (C_a, C_a^2, C_a^3, \ldots, C_a^{p-1})$ and a plaintext input y as inputs, then homomorphically calculates a ciphertext $C_{(a=y)}$, the decryption of which gives 1 when $a = y$, or 0 when $a \neq y$. This algorithm is similar to $\mathsf{ConstDiv}$, except that the values of the precomputed coefficient vectors a_{f_y} are different. Thus, the complexity of the algorithm is almost the same as the $\mathsf{ConstDiv}$, and there is no homomorphic multiplication.

Algorithm 4. ConstDiv(C_a^{pow}, d): Integer-wise Constant Division

---

Input: C_a^{pow}: Powers of ciphertexts C_a. d: public divisor.
Output: $C_{\lfloor a/d \rfloor}$
1: (Precomputing): We define a function for dividing by the fixed constant d as

$$g_d(x) := \left\lfloor \frac{x}{d} \right\rfloor.$$

Given points $\{g_d(x)\}_{x \in \mathbb{Z}_p}$, calculate the interpolation polynomial $f_d(x)$ that satisfies $\forall x \in \mathbb{Z}_p$, $f_d(x) = g_d(x)$. For example, when plaintext modulus $p = 7$ and public divisor $d = 2$, an interpolation polynomial $f_d(x)$ is calculated given that

$$f_d(0) = 0, \ f_d(1) = 0, \ f_d(2) = 1, \ f_d(3) = 1, \ f_d(4) = 2, \ f_d(5) = 2, \ f_d(6) = 3.$$

And we obtain $f_d(x) = -2x + 3x^3 + x^5 - 2x^6$. We define $a_{f_d}^{\mathsf{ConstDiv}} := (a_1, \ldots, a_{p-1}) = (-2, 0, 3, 0, 5, -2)$ as a coefficient vector of $f_d(x)$.
2: Output

$$C_{\lfloor a/d \rfloor} := (a_{f_d}^{\mathsf{ConstDiv}})^\top C_a^{\mathsf{pow}} := \sum_{i=1}^{p-1} \mathsf{FHE.multConst}(C_a^i, a_i). \tag{3}$$

Note. We note that $a_{f_d}^{\mathsf{ConstDiv}}$ is dependent on d, and we precompute $a_{f_d}^{\mathsf{ConstDiv}}$ for all $d \in \mathbb{Z}_p$: We have a list of coefficient vector $\{a_{f_0}^{\mathsf{ConstDiv}}, \ldots, a_{f_{p-1}}^{\mathsf{ConstDiv}}\}$ as constant.

Algorithm 5. ConstEq(C_a^{pow}, y): Integer-wise Constant Equality test

---

Input: C_a^{pow}: Powers of ciphertexts C_a. y: public constant.
Output: $C_{(a=y)}$
1: (Precomputing): We define a function for testing the equality to the fixed constant y as

$$g_y(x) := \begin{cases} 1 & (x = y), \\ 0 & (x \neq y). \end{cases}$$

Given points $\{g_y(x)\}_{y \in \mathbb{Z}_p}$, calculate the interpolation polynomial $f_y(x)$ that satisfies $\forall y \in \mathbb{Z}_p$, $f_y(x) = g_y(x)$. For example, when $p = 7$ and $y = 3$, an interpolation polynomial $f_y(x)$ is calculated given that

$$f_y(0) = 0, \ f_y(1) = 0, \ f_y(2) = 0, \ f_y(3) = 1, \ f_y(4) = 0, \ f_y(5) = 0, f_y(6) = 0.$$

And we obtain $f_y(x) = 2x + 3x^2 + x^3 - 2x^4 - 3x^5 - x^6$, the coefficient vector of which is $a_{f_y}^{\mathsf{ConstEq}} := (a_1, \ldots, a_{p-1}) = (2, 3, 1, -2, -3, -1)$.
2: Output

$$C_{(a=y)} := (a_{f_y}^{\mathsf{ConstEq}})^\top C_a^{\mathsf{pow}} := \sum_{i=1}^{p-1} \mathsf{FHE.multConst}(C_a^i, a_i).$$

Note. Note that, as with ConstDiv, we precompute the first step and we have a list $\{a_{f_0}^{\mathsf{ConstEq}}, \ldots, a_{f_{p-1}}^{\mathsf{ConstEq}}\}$ as constant.

Table 2. The multiplicative depth and the number of calls of Mult, Add and multConst in our algorithms for l-bit size input.

	Multiplicative depth	Mult	Add	multConst
Pows	$O(l)$	$O(2^l)$	0	0
ConstEq	0	0	$O(2^l)$	$O(2^l)$
ConstDiv	0	0	$O(2^l)$	$O(2^l)$
Div	$O(l)$	$O(2^l)$	$O(2^{2l})$	$O(2^{2l})$

3.3   Complexity Analysis and Experiments

Complexity. Although Algorithm 2 might seem exhaustive and inefficient due to its for loop, this homomorphic computation can be performed efficiently. This is mainly because:

- ConstDiv and ConstEq do not include FHE.Mult, but include FHE.multConst. Thus, ConstDiv and ConstEq do not increase the multiplicative depth.
- The most complex part Pows is executed only once for each input ciphertext C_a and C_d before the for loop.

In the following, we analyse the multiplicative depth and the total complexity of our algorithm Div. Table 2 shows a summary. In our analysis we denote by l the bit length of the input integers.

Multiplicative Depth. The multiplicative depth of Pows is $O(\log p) = O(l)$, as shown in Sect. 3.2. The multiplicative depth of Div is also $O(l)$, because we perform only one FHE.Mult after Pows in one loop in the Div algorithm, and ConstDiv and ConstEq do not include FHE.Mult. Chen *et al.* showed that the multiplicative depth of their bit-wise division algorithm [9] is $O(l^2)$. The other bit-wise division algorithms [8,28] are the same as that of [9], the idea of which is based on the non-restoring division, since their improvements are mainly for bit-wise addition and multiplication. Therefore, our algorithm provides quadratic improvement in regard to the multiplicative depth of homomorphic division.

Total Complexity. It is not trivial to adequately analyse the total complexity of the FHE circuit, because the cost of the homomorphic calculation depends on the level parameter L: the order of the cost of the homomorphic calculation is $O(\lambda L^3)$, as we mentioned in Sect. 2.2. Moreover, as mentioned in FHE.Setup, the level L also defines the parameter m. The parameter m defines the cyclotomic polynomial $\Phi_m(x)$, which in turn defines the ciphertext space. HElib has a bound on the value L, and HElib halts if we set L too high because of the bound on the size of the cyclotomic polynomial, as noted in [9,28]. Probably based on this fact, the existing works [8,9,28] do not show the results on higher (>4) bits input integers (see Table 3).

Although ConstDiv and ConstEq do not include homomorphic multiplication and do not increase the multiplicative depth, we perform them exhaustively

Table 3. Performance comparison.

l (bits)	p	L	nslots	Time (s)	Type	Method
4	2	21	720	67.94	Bit-wise	[9]
4	2	21	720	14.63		[28]
4	2	21	720	7.74		[8]
4	17	9	108	3.15	Integer-wise	Our (Div)
5	37	11	340	15.11		
6	67	13	165	51.34		
7	131	15	138	198.92		
8	257	17	396	795.84		

in the `for` loop (from $i = 0$ to $p - 1$), and thus we cannot ignore their cost. However, since this `for` loop is parallelisable, this issue could be decreased by parallelisation. In contrast, existing secure division algorithms are not suitable for parallelisation because of their full-adder circuit (e.g. Ripple Carry adder), as discussed in [8].

We also note that the memory complexity of our algorithm is relatively high. In the precomputation of polynomial interpolation, we generate the coefficient vectors and store them as a matrix, the space for which is $\mathbb{Z}_p^{p \times p}$.

Experiments. We implemented our secure division algorithm on HElib [16], and compared timings with existing secure division algorithms based on FHE schemes. We can compare the results only for 4-bit size input, since all the existing works report only for 4-bit integer division. We also implement for higher bit values $l = 5, \ldots, 8$, and observe that the results follow our complexity analysis.

Parameters. We set the security parameter $\lambda = 80$, following the existing works of the secure division algorithm [8,9,28]. Let l be a the bit size of the input integer. Since our algorithm is integer-wise and stores an input integer in $\mathbb{Z}$ into $\mathbb{Z}_p$, we define the size p of the plaintext space R_p as $p = \text{nextprime}(2^l)$. We set the Hamming weight of the secret vector $w = 64$. For the level parameter L, which is related to the multiplicative depth of the circuit, we search the minimum level by trial and error. As L is the lower level, we can perform the circuit faster. However, setting L too small leads to incorrectness of the outputs. For the rest of the parameter including "nslots", which means the number of the SIMD slots, we use the default values automatically calculated by HElib. For further details, we refer the reader to [16].

Results. Table 3 shows our timing results, in addition to results given in existing work for bit-wise integer division. All timings were generated on a PC with a 3.4 GHz Intel Core i5 and 16 GB RAM. To the best of our knowledge, the work by Chen *et al.* [8] provides the fastest results for 4-bit size input integers;

Algorithm 6. ConstFunc($C_a^{\text{pow}}, y, g(\cdot, \cdot)$): Integer-wise Constant Function

---

Input: C_a^{pow}: Powers of ciphertexts C_a. y: public constant. $g(\cdot, \cdot)$: 2-variable function.

Output: $C_{g(a,y)} = g(C_a, y)$

1: (Precomputing): In this algorithm, fix y. Thus, we consider the input 2-variable function $g(x, y) : \mathbb{Z}_p \times \mathbb{Z}_p \to \mathbb{Z}_p$ as 1-variable function $g_y(x) := g(x, y)$. For a fixed y, an interpolation polynomial $f_y(x)$ for $g_y(x)$ is calculated given the values $g(0, y), g(1, y), \ldots, g(p-1, y)$. And we can write the interpolation polynomial as follows: $f_y(x) = a_{\{1,y\}} \cdot x + a_{\{2,y\}} \cdot x^2 + a_{\{3,y\}} \cdot x^3 + \cdots + a_{\{p-1,y\}} \cdot x^6 \bmod p$.

2: Calculate $C_{g(a,y)} = f_y(C_a) = \boldsymbol{a}_{f_y}^{\top} \boldsymbol{C}_a^{\text{pow}} \bmod p$, where $\boldsymbol{a}_{f_y} = \{a_{\{1,y\}}, a_{\{2,y\}}, a_{\{3,y\}}, \ldots, a_{\{p-1,y\}}\}$.

---

thus our algorithm is the fastest secure division algorithm. While existing works report only for $l = 4$, we implemented our algorithm also for the higher bit sizes $l = 5, \ldots, 8$. We can observe that our algorithm requires only $L = O(l)$, following our analysis given in Sect. 3.3. Moreover, we can observe that required L of our algorithm is lower than that of the bit-wise algorithm for $l = 4$. Based on this fact, and that the bit-wise algorithm requires $L = O(l^2)$, we can expect that L of our algorithm is globally less than that of the bit-wise algorithm.

We also note that nslots of our algorithm, which are automatically calculated by HElib depending on the other parameters, is lower than in bit-wise algorithms. This means that the amortised cost of our algorithm might be larger than existing algorithms.

4 Integer-Wise Homomorphic Evaluation of Arbitrary 2-variable Function

We show that our secure division algorithm can be generalised to integer-wise secure computation of any 2-variable function with the same computation cost.

4.1 Algorithms

Our integer-wise homomorphic evaluation algorithm of any (predefined) 2-variable function Func(C_a, C_d) given in Algorithm 7 is constructed based on Div, by replacing ConstDiv with ConstFunc($C_a^{\text{pow}}, y, g(\cdot, \cdot)$) (Algorithm 6), which performs 1-variable function $g_y(x) := g(x, y)$ over a ciphertext C_a.

ConstFunc. Algorithm 6 shows the ConstFunc algorithm. The algorithm takes a list of powers of ciphertext $C_a^{\text{pow}} := (C_a, C_a^2, C_a^3, \ldots, C_a^{p-1})$, a plaintext y and a 2-variable function $g(\cdot, \cdot)$ (i.e., coefficient vectors of its interpolation polynomial), and then homomorphically calculates a ciphertext $C_{g(a,y)}$, the decryption of which gives $g(a, y)$. Recall that, in the ConstDiv(C_a^{pow}, d), we used polynomial interpolation to construct a function $f_d(x) = \lfloor \frac{x}{d} \rfloor$ for all $d \in \mathbb{Z}_p$, giving data points $\{f_d(0), f_d(1), \ldots, f_d(p-1)\}$. We can simply generalise ConstDiv as a general function: in ConstFunc, we use polynomial interpolation to construct a required function $g_y(x)$ defined by given data points $\{g_y(0), g_y(1), \ldots, g_y(p-1)\}$,

---

Algorithm 7. $\mathsf{Func}(C_a, C_b, g(\cdot, \cdot))$: Integer-wise Homomorphic 2-variable function

---

Input: Ciphertexts C_a, C_b. 2-variable function g.
Output: $C_{g(a,b)} = g(C_a, C_b)$
1: $C_{\mathsf{sum}} = 0$
2: $\boldsymbol{C}_a^{\mathsf{pow}} = \mathsf{Pows}(C_a)$ ▷ $\boldsymbol{C}_a^{\mathsf{pow}} := \{C_a, C_a^2, C_a^3, \ldots, C_a^{p-1}\}$
3: $\boldsymbol{C}_b^{\mathsf{pow}} = \mathsf{Pows}(C_b)$ ▷ $\boldsymbol{C}_b^{\mathsf{pow}} := \{C_b, C_b^2, C_b^3, \ldots, C_b^{p-1}\}$
4: **for** $i = 1$ to $(p-1)$ **do**
5:    $C_{g(a,i)} = \mathsf{ConstFunc}(\boldsymbol{C}_a^{\mathsf{pow}}, i, g)$ ▷ $C_{g(a,i)} = g(C_a, i)$
6:    $C_{(i=b)} = \mathsf{ConstEq}(\boldsymbol{C}_b^{\mathsf{pow}}, i)$ ▷ $C_{(i=b)} = C_1$ if $i = b$, $C_{(i=b)} = C_0$ otherwise.
7:    $C_{\mathsf{sum}} = C_{\mathsf{sum}} + \mathsf{FHE.Mult}(C_{g(a,i)}, C_{(i=b)})$ ▷ $\mathsf{FHE.Mult}(C_{g(a,i)}, C_{(i=b)}) = C_{g(a,b)}$ if $i = b$, C_0 otherwise.
8: **end for**
9: Output $C_{g(a,b)} = C_{\mathsf{sum}}$

---

for all $y \in \mathbb{Z}_p$. Only the data points (or, coefficient vectors) are different between ConstDiv and ConstFunc. Thus, the order of multiplicative depth of ConstFunc is exactly the same as ConstDiv. Note that we precompute the coefficient vectors $\boldsymbol{a}_{f_y}$ for all $y \in \mathbb{Z}_p$ using the polynomial interpolation, as with ConstDiv.

Func. Algorithm 7 shows our algorithm for integer-wise homomorphic evaluation of the arbitrary 2-variable function, Func. The algorithm takes two ciphertexts C_a and C_b, which are ciphertexts of a and b, respectively, and a 2-variable function $g(\cdot, \cdot)$ (i.e., coefficient vectors of its interpolation polynomial) as inputs. It then homomorphically calculates a ciphertext $C_{g(a,b)}$, which decrypts to $g(a, b)$. This algorithm is almost the same as Div (Algorithm 2), except that ConstDiv is replaced by ConstFunc. Since the order of multiplicative depth of ConstFunc is exactly the same as ConstDiv, that of Func is exactly the same as Div.

5   Conclusion

We propose a first secure integer-wise homomorphic division algorithm on fully homomorphic encryption schemes. We implemented the algorithm on HElib, and show that our algorithm is over twice as fast as the fastest existing algorithm given in [8]. We also showed that the multiplicative depth of our algorithm is $O(l)$ for l-bit size integer, while that of existing division algorithms is $O(l^2)$.

Furthermore, we generalise our secure division algorithm and propose an algorithm for secure calculation of general 2-variable functions. We showed that the complexity of the algorithm is the same as our division algorithm. This means that the homomorphic calculation of any 2-variable functions taking integer inputs can be performed with multiplicative depth $O(l)$.

References

1. Bost, R., Popa, R.A., Tu, S., Goldwasser, S.: Machine learning classification over encrypted data. In: NDSS Symposium 2015, p. 04_1_2. Internet Society (2015). https://doi.org/10.14722/ndss.2015.23241
2. Bourse, F., Minelli, M., Minihold, M., Paillier, P.: Fast homomorphic evaluation of deep discretized neural networks. In: Shacham, H., Boldyreva, A. (eds.) CRYPTO 2018. LNCS, vol. 10993, pp. 483–512. Springer, Cham (2018). https://doi.org/10. 1007/978-3-319-96878-0_17
3. Brakerski, Z., Gentry, C., Vaikuntanathan, V.: (Leveled) fully homomorphic encryption without bootstrapping. In: Proceedings of the 3rd Innovations in Theoretical Computer Science Conference, ITCS 2012, pp. 309–325. ACM (2012). https://doi.org/10.1145/2090236.2090262
4. Brakerski, Z., Vaikuntanathan, V.: Efficient fully homomorphic encryption from (standard) LWE. In: Proceedings of the 2011 IEEE 52nd Annual Symposium on Foundations of Computer Science, FOCS 2011, pp. 97–106. IEEE Computer Society (2011). https://doi.org/10.1109/FOCS.2011.12
5. Brakerski, Z., Vaikuntanathan, V.: Fully homomorphic encryption from ring-LWE and security for key dependent messages. In: Rogaway, P. (ed.) CRYPTO 2011. LNCS, vol. 6841, pp. 505–524. Springer, Heidelberg (2011). https://doi.org/10. 1007/978-3-642-22792-9_29
6. Brakerski, Z., Vaikuntanathan, V.: Lattice-based FHE as secure as PKE. In: Proceedings of the 5th Conference on Innovations in Theoretical Computer Science, ITCS 2014, pp. 1–12. ACM (2014). https://doi.org/10.1145/2554797.2554799
7. Çetin, G.S., Doröz, Y., Sunar, B., Savaş, E.: Depth optimized efficient homomorphic sorting. In: Lauter, K., Rodríguez-Henríquez, F. (eds.) LATINCRYPT 2015. LNCS, vol. 9230, pp. 61–80. Springer, Cham (2015). https://doi.org/10.1007/978-3-319-22174-8_4
8. Chen, J., Feng, Y., Liu, Y., Wu, W.: Faster binary arithmetic operations on encrypted integers. In: The 7th International Workshop on Computer Science and Engineering (2017)
9. Chen, Y., Gong, G.: Integer arithmetic over ciphertext and homomorphic data aggregation. In: 2015 IEEE Conference on Communications and Network Security (CNS), pp. 628–632, September 2015. https://doi.org/10.1109/CNS.2015.7346877
10. van Dijk, M., Gentry, C., Halevi, S., Vaikuntanathan, V.: Fully homomorphic encryption over the integers. In: Gilbert, H. (ed.) EUROCRYPT 2010. LNCS, vol. 6110, pp. 24–43. Springer, Heidelberg (2010). https://doi.org/10.1007/978-3-642-13190-5_2
11. Gentry, C.: A fully homomorphic encryption scheme. Ph.D. thesis, Stanford University (2009). crypto.stanford.edu/craig
12. Gentry, C.: Fully homomorphic encryption using ideal lattices. In: Proceedings of the 41st Annual ACM Symposium on Theory of Computing, STOC 2009, pp. 169–178. ACM (2009). https://doi.org/10.1145/1536414.1536440
13. Gentry, C., Halevi, S., Smart, N.P.: Homomorphic evaluation of the AES circuit. In: Safavi-Naini, R., Canetti, R. (eds.) CRYPTO 2012. LNCS, vol. 7417, pp. 850–867. Springer, Heidelberg (2012). https://doi.org/10.1007/978-3-642-32009-5_49
14. Gentry, C., Sahai, A., Waters, B.: Homomorphic encryption from learning with errors: conceptually-simpler, asymptotically-faster, attribute-based. In: Canetti, R., Garay, J.A. (eds.) CRYPTO 2013. LNCS, vol. 8042, pp. 75–92. Springer, Heidelberg (2013). https://doi.org/10.1007/978-3-642-40041-4_5

15. Gilad-Bachrach, R., Dowlin, N., Laine, K., Lauter, K., Naehrig, M., Wernsing, J.: CryptoNets: applying neural networks to encrypted data with high throughput and accuracy. In: Balcan, M.F., Weinberger, K.Q. (eds.) Proceedings of The 33rd International Conference on Machine Learning. Proceedings of Machine Learning Research, vol. 48, pp. 201–210. PMLR, 20–22 June 2016. http://proceedings.mlr.press/v48/gilad-bachrach16.html

16. Halevi, S., Shoup, V.: HElib - An Implementation of homomorphic encryption. https://github.com/shaih/HElib/

17. Halevi, S., Shoup, V.: Algorithms in HElib. In: Garay, J.A., Gennaro, R. (eds.) CRYPTO 2014. LNCS, vol. 8616, pp. 554–571. Springer, Heidelberg (2014). https://doi.org/10.1007/978-3-662-44371-2_31

18. Halevi, S., Shoup, V.: Bootstrapping for HElib. In: Oswald, E., Fischlin, M. (eds.) EUROCRYPT 2015. LNCS, vol. 9056, pp. 641–670. Springer, Heidelberg (2015). https://doi.org/10.1007/978-3-662-46800-5_25

19. Halevi, S., Shoup, V.: Faster homomorphic linear transformations in HElib. In: Shacham, H., Boldyreva, A. (eds.) CRYPTO 2018. LNCS, vol. 10991, pp. 93–120. Springer, Cham (2018). https://doi.org/10.1007/978-3-319-96884-1_4

20. Juvekar, C., Vaikuntanathan, V., Chandrakasan, A.: GAZELLE: a low latency framework for secure neural network inference. In: 27th USENIX Security Symposium (USENIX Security 2018), Baltimore, MD, pp. 1651–1669. USENIX Association (2018). https://www.usenix.org/conference/usenixsecurity18/presentation/juvekar

21. Lyubashevsky, V., Peikert, C., Regev, O.: On ideal lattices and learning with errors over rings. In: Gilbert, H. (ed.) EUROCRYPT 2010. LNCS, vol. 6110, pp. 1–23. Springer, Heidelberg (2010). https://doi.org/10.1007/978-3-642-13190-5_1

22. Narumanchi, H., Goyal, D., Emmadi, N., Gauravaram, P.: Performance analysis of sorting of FHE data: integer-wise comparison vs bit-wise comparison. In: 2017 IEEE 31st International Conference on Advanced Information Networking and Applications (AINA), pp. 902–908, March 2017. https://doi.org/10.1109/AINA.2017.85

23. Regev, O.: On lattices, learning with errors, random linear codes, and cryptography. J. ACM **56**(6), 34:1–34:40 (2009). https://doi.org/10.1145/1568318.1568324

24. Shoup, V.: NTL: A Library for doing Number Theory. http://shoup.net/ntl/

25. Smart, N.P., Vercauteren, F.: Fully homomorphic encryption with relatively small key and ciphertext sizes. In: Nguyen, P.Q., Pointcheval, D. (eds.) PKC 2010. LNCS, vol. 6056, pp. 420–443. Springer, Heidelberg (2010). https://doi.org/10.1007/978-3-642-13013-7_25

26. Smart, N.P., Vercauteren, F.: Fully homomorphic SIMD operations. Des. Codes Cryptogr. **71**(1), 57–81 (2014). https://doi.org/10.1007/s10623-012-9720-4

27. Stehlé, D., Steinfeld, R.: Faster fully homomorphic encryption. In: Abe, M. (ed.) ASIACRYPT 2010. LNCS, vol. 6477, pp. 377–394. Springer, Heidelberg (2010). https://doi.org/10.1007/978-3-642-17373-8_22

28. Xu, C., Chen, J., Wu, W., Feng, Y.: Homomorphically encrypted arithmetic operations over the integer ring. In: Bao, F., Chen, L., Deng, R.H., Wang, G. (eds.) ISPEC 2016. LNCS, vol. 10060, pp. 167–181. Springer, Cham (2016). https://doi.org/10.1007/978-3-319-49151-6_12

Artificial Learning

Prediction-Based Intrusion Detection
System for In-Vehicle Networks
Using Supervised Learning
and Outlier-Detection

Khaled Karray[1,4(✉)], Jean-Luc Danger[1,2], Sylvain Guilley[1,2,3],
and Moulay Abdelaziz Elaabid[4]

[1] Telecom Paristech, Paris, France
khaled.karray@telecom-paristech.fr
[2] Secure-IC, Paris, France
[3] École Normale Supérieure, Info dpt, Paris, France
[4] PSA-GROUPE, Paris, France

Abstract. Modern connected vehicles are composed of multiple electronic control units (ECUs) holding sensors, actuators but also wired and wireless connection interfaces, all communicating over shared internal communication buses. The cyber-physical architecture based on this ECU network has been proven vulnerable to multiple types of attacks leveraging remote, direct and indirect physical access. Attacks initiated from these access vectors go through the internal communication buses and spread over the whole network of ECUs. For this reason it is important to detect, and if possible to mitigate, attacks on the internal buses of the vehicle.

In this article, a novel intrusion detection system is developed to monitor vehicle state from information collected on internal buses. Based on supervised machine learning techniques, a normal behavior is learned and used as a reference to detect deviations. The principle is to learn how to predict the next state of the vehicle based on information and sensor values sent over communication buses. Experimental validation is conducted using data collected from different drivers. Results show that the approach is able to learn the nominal behavior with high accuracy for a single driver as well as for a set of different drivers. Results also demonstrate its ability to predict attacks with low false negative rate. This motivates the approach to be used for indirect and remote attacks intrusion detection as well as for safety purposes to detect sensor failures, lost connection with the sensor, etc.

Keywords: Automotive · Intrusion detection · Machine learning

1 Introduction

Two important requirements of today's cars are a high level of safety and connectivity with the outside world. This involves the use of advanced technologies

© IFIP International Federation for Information Processing 2019
Published by Springer Nature Switzerland AG 2019
O. Blazy and C. Y. Yeun (Eds.): WISTP 2018, LNCS 11469, pp. 109–128, 2019.
https://doi.org/10.1007/978-3-030-20074-9_9

based on a computing infrastructure composed of numerous electronic components –named Electronic Control Units (ECUs)– embedded inside the vehicle. These ECUs are in charge of processing sensed data through embedded sensors, and transforming them into commands for the actuators. For this purpose, ECUs share communication buses. These are used for periodic and event-based messages that allows the ECUs to monitor the vehicle state through the control and supervision of sensors and actuators states. The communication bus mostly used in the automotive domain is the Controller Area Network (CAN, ISO 11898), which connects together many ECUs.

Recently, the CAN protocol has become the center of multiple cyber-security issues [2,4]. In this context, Hoppe et al. [7] were the first researchers to point out the weaknesses of the CAN bus. These findings were further investigated and confirmed by Koscher et al. [11] and Checkoway et al. [2] who performed frame replay and frame injection attacks on a real vehicle. In these attacks, the attacker physically connects to the CAN network and replays or injects messages on the CAN bus. Miller and Valasek [15] showed that physical access to the communication bus was not necessary and showcased an attack granting remote control over a vehicle. In their experiments, the attacker remotely takes control of a legitimate ECU and use that ECU to send legitimate messages.

To protect against these attacks, multiple solutions have been proposed:

– Protecting the messages payload can be a good approach against an attacker that has physical access to the communication bus. Nilsson et al. [18] proposed to send message authentication codes over consecutive CAN frames to authenticate the messages. Hartkopp et al. [6] proposed to use Cipher based Message Authentication Code (CMAC) as a symmetric authentication measure between the sender and the receiver. These types of solution allow the receiving ECU to verify the integrity and/or the authenticity of the messages and to filter out forged information sent by the attacker (which is unauthentic).
– A second family of protection solutions is known as in-vehicle network Intrusion Detection and Prevention Systems. The role of these systems is to monitor the in-vehicle network for suspicious behavior like frame(s) injection and replay attacks and either physically kill suspicious frames by causing a frame error or by filtering them out. Examples of such detection mechanisms are presented for instance in the work of Taylor et al. [20], and the work of Marchetti et al. [14]. In general, state-of-the-art detection mechanisms can be categorized into two main classes: *rule-based* detection mechanisms and *statistical* detection mechanisms. We investigate more in details these types of solutions in Sect. 2.1.
– Another type of protection solution, specific to the CAN bus focuses on protecting the identifier. These solutions are useful to protect against reverse engineering, replay and injection attacks for an attacker that has physical access to the CAN network. For instance Humayed et al. [8] presented a solution that can change a message identifier when an attack is detected, thereby stopping the targeted attack dead. Han et al. [5,12] proposed an identifier randomization function for the same purpose.

In the sequel we focus on in-vehicle intrusion detection techniques. State-of-the-art *rule-based* intrusion detection uses mechanisms known as identifier filtering, identifier timing and syntax check. Some of them also focus on payload content and implement what is known as *deep packet inspection* techniques.

Contributions. In this paper, we tackle the problem of deep packet inspection of in-vehicle networks from a practical viewpoint. For an attacker that gains control over an ECU, we consider that her capacity evolves from simply injecting an extra message on the communication bus, to being capable of modifying the content (payload) of a legitimate message. This evolution makes the classical detection mechanisms, based on identifier timing and syntax check, merely obsolete. In order to detect these kinds of attacks, a novel detection mechanism is developed. We formulate the problem in a way that allows to learn the normal behaviour of the system in terms of message payload content. Bad behaviour and bad payload content are flagged with outlier detection techniques. The method thus described can be adopted not only as an intrusion detection mechanism, but also as an *online monitoring failure detection* and a *sensor rationality check* safety mechanisms as described by the "Road vehicles – Functional safety" standard ISO-26262 [9]. We validate in practice the model with real CAN traces collected from drive tests. We show that the approach is able to learn the nominal behavior with high accuracy and low false positives, for three different driving behaviors separately. Then we show that it is also able to learn a unified nominal behavior with high accuracy and low false positives, that can accommodate different driving behaviors. Finally we run an attack campaign in order to test the robustness of the detection rules, and demonstrate its ability to predict attacks with low false negative rate.

Outline. The remainder of the paper is structured as follows. Section 2 gives some background on CAN intrusion detection mechanisms, machine learning techniques and the related work. Section 3 gives details about data collection and feature engineering. Section 4 presents practical validation results on real CAN traces. Section 5 concludes.

2 Background

2.1 Intrusion Detection Systems over CAN

Detecting intrusions on the in-vehicle communication buses is important as it can prevent attacks from spreading to other ECUs. It can be considered as the last line of defense after protecting ECUs interfaces from the outside world. Many mechanisms have been proposed to detect possible intrusion on the CAN bus. Figure 1 gives a high level overview of these mechanisms.

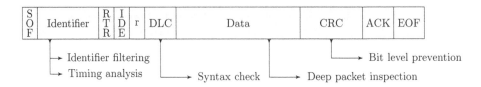

Fig. 1. High level synthesis of detection mechanisms applied to the CAN frame

Using the frame identifier, an intrusion detection system can establish a list of *allowed* and *forbidden* identifiers, based on which it can decide which frames to filter. This technique is best known as *identifier filtering* or *identifier white-listing* [15,16]. Such white list can also depend on the context of the vehicle: for instance the intrusion detection system may allow certain identifiers when the vehicle is on parking state, and reject them when the vehicle is moving. This technique is used in particular to enforce the diagnostic security policy by allowing diagnostic messages only in certain vehicle states.

Another detection mechanisms that uses identifiers is *timing analysis* [3,7, 16]. It is a very popular technique that works well with periodic messages. It consists in setting an acceptance time-window for each periodic message. If the same message is received outside of its acceptance time-window, the system shall consider it as an intrusion and shall filter it out.

Besides the identifier of the messages, the data length code (DLC) can also be exploited to detect bad behaviour [16]. In fact, each manufacturer sets-up a proprietary protocol over the CAN standard. This protocol consists in creating a mapping between identifiers and payload information (sensor values for instance), also called signals, shared across all ECUs. This mapping defines a syntax that can be checked based on the payload length of each message. Messages that violate this syntax (i.e., messages sent with the wrong DLC) are then flagged as intrusions.

In this paper we distinguish between two attacker models (Fig. 2). Figure 2a shows an attacker model that has direct physical access to the CAN bus. Since modification of a message on the fly is rather difficult (the message being protected with CRC mechanism), this attacker instead injects *extra* messages on the CAN bus. These messages will modify the proprietary communication protocol defined on top of CAN for instance by modifying the syntax of the message or its periodicity. These anomalies are caught by the classical detection mechanisms described previously. Therefore, an advanced attacker who has indirect and even remote access over a legitimate ECU (Fig. 2b), might aim at modifying sensor information and commands directly on the payload without disrupting the defined protocol. Thus will not be detected by above-mentioned classical detection mechanisms. Consequently, we need to build mechanisms able to detect bad behaviour inside the payload. These mechanisms are referred to as *deep packet inspection*. The latter encompasses most safety checks. For instance, duplicated signals, process counters, checksum ... In this paper, we focus on *deep packet inspection* type of detection, as this detection mechanism is well adapted to sophisticated attacker model. Supervised machine learning techniques are used in order to build a nominal behaviour based on received signals; then outlier detection flags deviations from the previously built behavioral model.

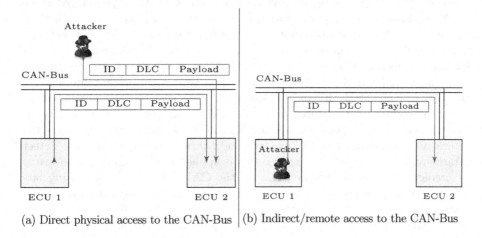

(a) Direct physical access to the CAN-Bus | (b) Indirect/remote access to the CAN-Bus

Fig. 2. Attacker models. (a) State-of-the-art model. (b) Model investigated in this paper

2.2   Machine Learning Algorithms and Their Application

In practice there are multiple application domains where machine learning algorithms excel in prediction tasks. They are generally used to study correlation between different inputs (also called features), to approximate an output function and/or to discover interesting data structures. For these reasons we decided to explore the use of machine learning techniques in the context of vehicle cyberphysical attacks and intrusion detection.

Machine learning algorithms can be divided into two main categories depending on the learning strategy:

1. *Supervised learning:* a machine learning algorithm is said to be using supervised learning strategy when the training set includes both the input data and the output data of the algorithm. In that sense the algorithm is training to learn a mapping function by minimizing a pre-defined cost function. The trained algorithm is then tested on some other examples that were not included in the training set. It is said to be generalizing well if the performance of the trained algorithm on the test set is comparable to its performance on the training set.
2. *Unsupervised learning:* a machine learning algorithm is said to be using unsupervised learning strategy if the training only includes the input data but not the expected output. In that sense, the machine learning algorithm is trying to discover interesting data structures.

Machine learning techniques have been used previously in the context of *deep packet inspection* for intrusion detection. Kang et al. [10] train a deep neural network structure to classify normal *versus* attack packets using probability-based feature vectors of packet payload bits. Training data were generated by the *Open Car Test-bed and Network Experiments (OCTANE)* packet generator [1]. Normal and attacked packets were necessary in order to train the algorithm. Loukas et al. [13] use sensor input features along with recurrent neural network (RNN) to detect attacks on vehicles. The detection mechanism also consists in learning to classify whether the vehicle is under attack or not with a training data that included both attacked and normal packets. An important limitation of the work of Kang et al. [10] and Loukas et al. [13] is that the intrusion detection system is trained to recognize specific attacks. An important effort is devoted to generate attacked packets in order for the detection module to learn the attack profile. Taylor et al. [21] use long short-term memory networks to detect attacks on the CAN bus. The approach was applied to the identifier, and learns to predict the next packet identifier on the CAN bus. Highly surprising bits are then flagged as anomalous. This method draws its strength from repetitive periodic sequences. This is why it is applied to the identifier field. Nevertheless, this is hardly the case for payload information that holds sensor information. Narayanan et al. [17] propose to build Hidden Markov Model of the normal behaviour of the car based on sensor values (or signals). Their work shows that it is possible to detect data manipulation attacks like speed discontinuity. In their work, Narayanan et al. focus on signal changes rather than signal values, i.e., gradients of signals. As a result, the built model can serve to detect *signal jumps* types of anomalies and cannot be used for prevention. Besides, their work does not evaluate the True Positive Rate and False Positive Rate of the detection principle.

An important limitation of the previous approaches is that during training, data representing both attacked and non-attacked states is needed to learn to recognize attacks. In order to produce this kind of data we need to select and perform multiple attacks on the vehicle. Thus it is challenging to generate the data for a large range of attacks. Besides, the intrusion detection system learns only to recognize performed attacks included in the training set. Another downside is that the approach allows only to predict whether the vehicle is under attack or not but does not deliver more detailed information useful to investigate on the cause of the attack.

In order to overcome these limitations, we propose a different formulation of the problem. In fact, instead of predicting whether the vehicle is under attack (or not) based on payload inputs, we break down the payload information into signals according to the manufacturer proprietary protocol and we train a machine learning algorithm to predict the next signal value based on other signals. The idea is then to compare the predicted signal and the received signal. Under the assumption that the predictor is *accurate enough*, we assume the following as a security metric: if the difference between the prediction and the received value is *large enough*, then, with a high probability, the vehicle is being attacked and that the predicted signal is the potential cause of the attack.

Input signals are sensor values sent from one ECU to the other ones. They can either be real-valued or categorical signals:

- An example of real-valued signal is the speed of the vehicle (Fig. 3a). It is sent over 2 bytes of payload information. The received value is then an integer between 0 and 65535. A multiplication by 0.01 is necessary to recover the actual measurement of the sensor to make speed range in [0, 655.35] km/h.
- An example of categorical signal is the brake lights command signal (Fig. 3b). It is sent over 1 bit of payload data. The received value is a binary information (0/1) indicating whether to activate the brake lights (1) or not (0).

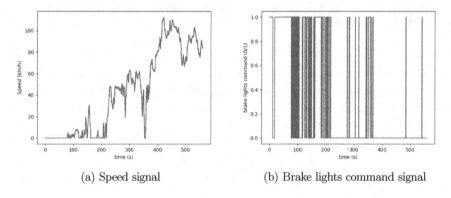

(a) Speed signal   (b) Brake lights command signal

Fig. 3. Example of real-valued and categorical signals

2.3   Problem Formulation

In what follows we formulate our problem as a supervised machine learning problem. Let $\mathcal{D} = \{(x_i, y_i)\}_{i \in [1,N]}$ be the set of input-output pairs. Here $\mathcal{D}$ is the collected Data set, and N is the number of observed examples. Each training input $(x_i)_{i \in [1,N]}$ is a d-dimensional vector of components representing signal values/states $(s_i^{(1)}, s_i^{(2)}, \ldots, s_i^{(d)})$. These are called features and are stored in an $(N \times d)$ matrix X (Fig. 4). The output $(y_i)_{i \in [1,N]}$ is stored in a 1-dimensional vector y and represents the target signal that we want to predict. It can be either real-valued (in this case we will talk about *regression*) or a categorical value (in which case we will talk about *classification*), depending on the signal type.

The object of supervised machine learning is to assume the existence of some unknown function $<f>$ that maps the inputs to the outputs, as in (1):

$$f(x) = y, \quad \forall (x, y) \in \mathcal{D}. \tag{1}$$

The goal of the learning process is to estimate the function $<f>$ given a labeled training set and then to make predictions on unseen data x_u using the estimated function $\hat{y} = \hat{f}(x_u)$. We denote the probability distribution over possible labels, given the input vector x_u and the training data set $\mathcal{D}_{train}$ by $p(y|x_u, \mathcal{D}_{train})$. This probability is conditional on the input vector x_u and the training set $\mathcal{D}_{train}$. When approximating the function $<f>$, we will use a machine learning model M_θ, where M is the model, and θ denotes the parameters of the model. The probability distribution over possible labels becomes also conditioned by the chosen model, $p(y = \hat{y}|x_u, \mathcal{D}_{train}, M_\theta)$.

When using regression parametric models, we assume that the estimated function used for the prediction introduces a residual error ϵ between the predictions and the ground truth:

$$y = \hat{y} + \epsilon. \tag{2}$$

We make the assumption that the residual error term ϵ has a Gaussian normal distribution, $\epsilon \sim \mathcal{N}(\mu, \sigma^2)$. More explicitly we will assume that the probability distribution over possible labels is as follows:

$$p(y|x_u, \mathcal{D}_{train}, M_\theta) = \mathcal{N}(\mu_\theta(x_u), \sigma^2). \tag{3}$$

In order to estimate the model parameters $<\theta>$, we use the maximum likelihood estimator that maximizes $p(\mathcal{D}_{train}|\theta) = \prod_{i=1}^{N} p(y_i|x_i, \theta)$. It is equivalent to finding the model parameters $\hat{\theta}$ that minimizes the negative log-likelihood which is the sum of residual errors $\sum_{i=1}^{N}(y_i - \hat{y}_i)^2 = \sum_{i=1}^{N} \epsilon_i^2$:

$$\hat{\theta} = \underset{\theta}{\operatorname{argmin}} \sum_{i=1}^{N}(y_i - \hat{f}_\theta(x_i))^2. \tag{4}$$

Once optimal parameters $\hat{\theta}$ are estimated, the prediction model outputs a predicted signal estimation $\hat{y}_u = \hat{f}_{\hat{\theta}}(x_u)$ for an unseen input vector x_u. The received signal value y is then compared to the estimated signal value. An alert is raised if the two signals are *not similar*

$$Alert = 1 \iff |\hat{y} - y| \geq t_p. \tag{5}$$

When using classification parametric models, where the output is one out of C classes, we model the probability over possible labels with a categorical distribution. Let $y_{ij} = I(y_i = j)$ be the one-hot encoding of y_i:

$$p(y|x_u, \mathcal{D}_{train}, M_\theta) = \prod_{j=1}^{C} \mu_{\theta,j}(x_u)^{I(y=j)}. \tag{6}$$

In order to estimate the model parameters $<\theta>$, we use the maximum likelihood estimator that maximizes $p(\mathcal{D}_{train}|\theta) = \prod_{i=1}^{N} p(y_i|x_i, \theta) = \prod_{i=1}^{N} \prod_{j=1}^{C} \mu_{\theta,j}(x_i)^{I(y_i=j)}$. This is equivalent to minimizing the negative log-likelihood which is the cross entropy function:

$$\hat{\theta} = \underset{\theta}{\operatorname{argmin}} \sum_{i=1}^{N} \sum_{j=1}^{C} y_{ij} \log(\mu_{\theta,j}(x_i)). \tag{7}$$

Once we have the optimal model parameters $\hat{\theta}$, for each unseen input vector x_u, we make a prediction in favor of the class where the probability distribution is the highest: $\hat{y}_u = \underset{j\in[1,C]}{\mathrm{argmax}}(\mu_{\hat{\theta},j}(x_u))$.

Once optimal parameters $\hat{\theta}$ are estimated, the prediction model outputs a predicted signal estimation $\hat{y}_u = \hat{f}_{\hat{\theta}}(x_u)$ for an unseen input vector x_u. The received signal value y is then compared to the estimated signal value. An alert is raised if the two signals are *not similar*:

$$Alert = 1 \quad \Longleftrightarrow \quad \hat{y} \neq y. \tag{8}$$

3 Data Collection and Feature Engineering

3.1 Data Collection

In order to provide training vectors, the best way is to collect data directly from a real vehicle. For this purpose we prepared a CAN acquisition device. The device is composed of a Raspberry Pi with additional CAN-Bus hardware module running a Linux kernel with *SocketCAN* drivers. We equipped a vehicle with the acquisition device connected directly to different CAN buses in order to have direct access to *all* sensor information, although not all of them will be used during training. We collected CAN traces from <u>one</u> vehicle for <u>three</u> different drivers, driving in different circuits for about 90 min each. Circuits consisted of multiple driving conditions including city driving, vehicle parking, highway driving, etc. During those data collections, drivers were asked to drive normally but also to perform rare but legitimate scenarios like activating cruise control, activating lane keep assist, activating emergency breaking, etc. For safety reasons no attacks were performed during data collections step.

3.2 Feature Engineering

After raw data acquisition, the second step consists in preparing the data for processing. In this step, the goal is to select and arrange the features in a form that would be useful during training step. Each CAN identifier sent over the CAN bus has a payload that is composed of one or multiple signals. A signal is an information (sensor value, ECU state, counter, checksum, ...) that can occupy one or multiple bits or bytes depending on the nature of the information. Extraction of signals requires the knowledge of the proprietary protocol of the car manufacturer. Signals included in the payload for safety reasons, like checksums, process counters, duplicated signals, are checked by safety functions and problems with those signals, if any, would be handled by appropriate safety mechanisms. Thus, they are not relevant for this task and therefore are not selected. Typically we are interested in physical sensor values like speed, acceleration, RPM, etc. The set of those signals defines the state of the vehicle and constitutes the input features that are relevant for learning the normal behaviour and evolution of the car states. The second selection criteria is the relevance with respect to the target signal. In fact, the dimensionality of the training vectors equals the number of selected signals. However, in general, machine learning algorithms do not work well with high dimensional inputs. Indeed, as input vectors dimensions grow, the performance deteriorates, due to the curse of dimensionality. As a result, we choose to select only signal with high correlation with the target signal. For instance, the engine oil temperature has no influence on the vehicle speed, thus would not be selected when building a predictor for the speed signal. On the other hand, the acceleration of the vehicle is highly correlated to the speed of the vehicle, thus will be selected as an input to predict the speed. Using this selection criteria we can guarantee that signals that can *explain the most* the target signal are used for prediction. Signals are featured in the form of a matrix where columns represent signals and lines represent signal values evolution over time. For each received CAN message that holds selected signal, a new line is added to the matrix where all signals keep their previous values/states except the one that has just been received. Figure 4 gives more details about how to construct the features matrix.

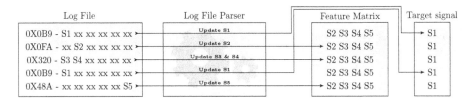

Fig. 4. Parsing the log file and building the training data.

4   Experimental Validation and Discussion

In order to validate the approach, we conduct some experiments to predict two target signals, one of each type (categorical and real-valued), using five selected input signals. To this end, a total of six signals are extracted. For each target signal, the remaining five are used as input features.

- Speed, is a real-valued signal sent from the Electronic Stability Program (ESP) and that is generated by an embedded speed sensor.
- Acceleration, is real-valued signal that is sent from the Electronic Stability Program (ESP) and generated by an acceleration sensor.
- Engine rotational speed expressed in revolutions per minute (RPM), is a real-valued signal sent by the Engine Control Module (ECM).
- Torque, is a real-valued signal sent by the Engine Control Module (ECM) that contains the engine torque.
- Gearbox position, is a categorical signal sent by the Electronic Shifter Module (ESM), that indicates the gear lever position.
- Brake lights command is a categorical signal that is sent from the Electronic Stability Program (ESP) module to control brake lights.

Experimental validation is conducted in two steps. First we train and evaluate the detection rules using collected data and without performing any attacks. This step gives us the True Negative rate, that we define hereafter as the accuracy (*Acc*) of the supervised learning algorithm, which will be formally introduced in the Sect. 4.1. The False Positive rate is then derived from the accuracy and equals $(1 - Acc)$. Then we conduct an attack campaign and measure how many of the performed attacks are detected. This step gives us the True Positive rate and the False Negative rate. Table 1 defines the metrics that will be used in the sequel.

Table 1. Detection metrics

	Detected	Not-detected
No-attack	$FP = 1 - Acc$	$TN = Acc$
Attack	TP	FN

4.1 Validation Metrics

Regression Metrics for Real-Valued Signals: The *accuracy* (denoted as *Acc*) of a machine learning prediction algorithm is generally measured using the coefficient of determination R^2. The R^2 coefficient of determination is a statistical measure of how well the regression predictions approximate the observed target values. The closer it is to 1, the more accurate the prediction is. An R^2 of 1 indicates that the regression predictions perfectly fit the data. We can express the prediction accuracy with the following:

$$Acc = R^2 = 1 - \frac{\sum(\hat{y}_i - y_i)^2}{\sum(y_i - E(y_i))^2} = 1 - \frac{\sigma_\epsilon^2 + \mu_\epsilon^2}{\sigma_y^2}, \tag{9}$$

where $\sum(\hat{y}_i - y_i)^2$ is the residual sum of squares, $\sum(y_i - E(y_i))^2$ is the total sum of squares, σ_ϵ^2 and μ_ϵ^2 are respectively, the standard deviation and mean of the error term, and σ_y^2 is the standard deviation of the target signal y.

Intuitively, comparing the quality of the predictors can be based on the mean and variance of the prediction error ϵ. Ideally the error has to be centered around zero (unbiased predictor) with the smallest possible variance.

To define an intrusion detection system based on the predictor we need to define an *acceptable deviation* of the prediction that can be tolerated. Beyond this *acceptable deviation*, the received signal can be considered way off compared to the prediction and an alarm should be raised. This *acceptable deviation* or detection threshold t_p for the predictor defines the false positives statistically generated by the predictor (red bars in Fig. 6). More formally we can define the *false prediction*, as follows:

$$FP_{t_p}(y, \hat{y}) = \begin{cases} 1 \text{ if } |y - \hat{y}| \geq t_p, \\ 0 \text{ if } |y - \hat{y}| < t_p. \end{cases} \tag{10}$$

Tweaking this parameter t_p helps increase/decrease the false positives probability of the intrusion detection rule that will be defined based on this predictor. The new accuracy measure with respect to t_p becomes $Acc_{t_p} = P(|\epsilon| < t_p)$ (Fig. 5).

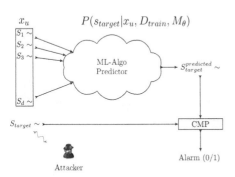

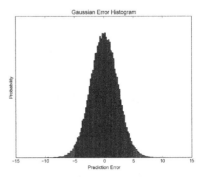

Fig. 5. Prediction principle

Fig. 6. Gaussian shaped prediction error (Color figure online)

Classification Metrics for Categorical Signals: The default accuracy metrics used in machine learning classification tasks is the correct classification ratio:

$$Acc = \frac{\# \text{ correct predictions}}{\# \text{ use-cases}} \tag{11}$$

Unlike regression, for classification it is straightforward to define a false prediction which in this case is simply a mis-classification. More formally we can define the mis-classification function as the following:

$$MC(s, p) = \begin{cases} 1 \text{ if } class(s) \neq class(p), \\ 0 \text{ if } class(s) = class(p). \end{cases} \tag{12}$$

4.2   Predicting a Real-Valued Signal: Speed

For regression problems, we chose to validate the approach we described in previous sections on a signal that is important from a safety standpoint. The speed information is sent by the Electronic Stability Program over the CAN bus for the other ECUs to be used in other functions. Besides being displayed for user-information, it is used to compute the effort to be applied on brakes when emergency brakes are activated, to decide when to activate airbags in case of an accident, also to decide if the car doors should be open or closed, and whether or not to accept diagnostics commands and a lot of other functions. In the performed experiments, the goal is to compare between different machine learning algorithms, as each algorithm has a different way of capturing dependencies between input features and the target signal. We used a data set of 10^6 input vectors from each drive test. The data set was split into a training set and a test set of 0.7 and 0.3 size ratio respectively. All experiments are done with the `scikit-learn` library [19].

In the first experiment, we train and evaluate detection rules for each driver separately. We used four types of machine learning algorithms: k-nearest neighbors (KNN), Decision Tree, neural network with logistic perceptron and neural network with rectified linear unit (Relu) perceptron. For each type of machine learning algorithms, we used different tuning parameters to progressively give them the ability to capture more complex dependencies, but also that increase the complexity of the learning algorithm. For instance, this consists in increasing the depth of a decision tree or in increasing the number of neurons and layers for neural networks. Table 2 reports evaluation metrics of the tested algorithms.

First, we note that the results of KNN is merely provided as a baseline. In fact using KNN is advantageous as it gives a very precise local approximation for dense and uniformly distributed training set. It is nevertheless not useful in the context of embedded systems as it needs all the training data in memory in order to make a prediction. Second, each algorithm performs approximately similarly on the three drivers. Third, for a given algorithm, we note that as we increase the complexity (tuning parameters) of the learning algorithm, the accuracy improves. The rule becomes progressively able to capture more dependencies. As a result, it becomes necessary to take into consideration the added complexity compared to the gain in accuracy. For the decision tree algorithm, changing the tree depth from 20 to 40 does not improve significantly the accuracy. Similarly increasing the number of neurons in the Logistic-Neural-Network up to 80 neurons, and increasing the number of layers in the Relu-Neural-Network up to 10 layers does not have a significant effect on the accuracy for all three drivers. We conclude that as the complexity of the algorithm increases, its ability of capturing more dependencies also increases, but reaches a a certain limit beyond which it is no longer advantageous to increase the complexity. Overall, and for all three drivers, we can establish that the best results were reported for the decision tree algorithm tuned with depth parameter equals to 40.

4.3   Predicting a Categorical Signal: Brake Lights Command

For classification problem, we choose to validation the approach on the *brake-lights-command* categorical signals. In order for the accuracy metric to make sense, test data should be balanced, i.e., the number of test vectors should be roughly the same for each class. Results are reported in Table 3.

Table 2. Prediction accuracy of detection rules for $tp = \pm 5\,\mathrm{km/h}$ trained and tested with data captures from three different drive tests

ML-Algorithm	Tuning	Driver 1		Driver 2		Driver 3	
		$Acc\,(\%)$	Acc_{t_p}	$Acc\,(\%)$	Acc_{t_p}	$Acc\,(\%)$	Acc_{t_p}
KNN regression	$k = 1$	99.97	99.66	99.97	99.77	99.66	99.22
KNN regression	$k = 2$	99.97	99.78	99.97	99.82	99.71	99.40
KNN regression	$k = 3$	99.97	99.76	99.97	99.78	99.71	99.40
Linear Regression	Null	79.88	23.28	83.47	22.61	74.42	59.89
Decision Tree	Depth = 10	99.71	98.19	99.67	98.39	98.58	96.17
Decision Tree	Depth = 20	99.97	99.89	99.97	99.93	99.67	99.29
Decision Tree	Depth = 40	99.97	99.92	99.97	99.96	99.77	99.59
Neural Net (Logistic)	1 Layer, 30 neurons	98.97	94.74	98.22	88.52	75.67	84.94
Neural Net (Logistic)	1 Layer, 35 neurons	98.96	94.90	98.35	88.95	80.38	83.02
Neural Net (Logistic)	1 Layer, 40 neurons	99.01	94.76	98.62	88.66	82.10	84.97
Neural Net (Logistic)	1 Layer, 80 neurons	99.15	94.74	99.07	92.58	97.54	94.20
Neural Net (Relu)	1 Layer, 10 neurons	99.31	92.82	99.11	87.91	97.26	92.52
Neural Net (Relu)	1 Layer, 20 neurons	99.25	92.44	99.35	93.58	97.32	92.55
Neural Net (Relu)	1 Layer, 40 neurons	99.36	93.75	99.29	92.42	97.61	93.65
Neural Net (Relu)	5 Layer, 10 neurons	99.53	95.19	99.46	94.52	97.67	94.11
Neural Net (Relu)	10 Layers, 10 neurons	99.55	95.36	99.55	95.37	98.37	95.90

A similar test procedure was also used for the *brake-lights-command* signal. We notice that there are small differences in the accuracy for the same rule when comparing between different drivers. In fact, practically all the tested rules perform better on the first and second driver than on the third driver. An explanation of this result might be that the third drive test contained singular use-cases that did not appear frequently enough, thus the rules did not train well enough in order to recognize them. An easy solution to overcome this limitation is to collect more data for these specific use-cases. We also notice that the decision tree algorithm tuned with depth parameter equals to 40, reported the best performance for all three drivers.

4.4   Unification of Detection Rule

In the previous section, we reported results on the accuracy of the predictors trained and evaluated for each driver separately. The resulting detection rules could be influenced by the driving behaviour of the driver. In this section we investigate the possibility of building one single detection rule that can accommodate all three drivers. According to the previous results, the Decision Tree algorithm outperforms the rest of the algorithms for both predicted signals. Thus, we use Decision Tree algorithm to build the detection rules in this section. In order to train the algorithm we combine the data sets collected during the three drive tests and we split the resulting data set into 0.7 and 0.3 ratio training set and

Table 3. Prediction accuracy of detection rules for the *brake-lights-command* signal

ML-Algorithm	Tuning	Driver 1 Acc (%)	Driver 2 Acc (%)	Driver 3 Acc (%)
KNN classification	$k = 1$	98.96	98.45	97.27
KNN classification	$k = 2$	98.70	98.11	96.14
KNN classification	$k = 3$	98.89	98.34	97.22
Logistic Regression	Null	93.68	93.01	90.62
Decision Tree	Depth = 10	96.72	95.80	94.65
Decision Tree	Depth = 20	99.10	98.63	97.12
Decision Tree	Depth = 40	99.36	99.00	97.77
Neural Net (Logistic)	1 Layer, 30 neurons	95.86	94.23	94.56
Neural Net (Logistic)	1 Layer, 35 neurons	95.82	94.11	94.48
Neural Net (Logistic)	1 Layer, 40 neurons	96.01	93.88	94.57
Neural Net (Logistic)	1 Layer, 80 neurons	95.97	94.15	94.55
Neural Net (Logistic)	5 Layer, 30 neurons	95.22	93.43	94.80
Neural Net (Relu)	1 Layer, 10 neurons	96.25	94.59	94.23
Neural Net (Relu)	1 Layer, 20 neurons	96.56	95.26	94.33
Neural Net (Relu)	1 Layer, 40 neurons	96.70	95.38	94.48
Neural Net (Relu)	5 Layer, 10 neurons	96.70	95.49	94.49
Neural Net (Relu)	10 Layers, 10 neurons	96.72	95.67	94.70

test sets. We report results of the accuracy on the test set as well as on the three data sets separately for the speed signal in Table 4 and for *brake-lights-command* in Table 5. Results show that, for both signals, the resulting detection rules have a high accuracy level on the combined data set as well as on data from each individual driver. This shows that it is possible to build a single detection rule that can accommodate the three drivers.

Table 4. Prediction accuracy of the unified detection rules for the speed

ML-Algorithm	Tuning	All		Driver 1		Driver 2		Driver 3	
		Acc (%)	Acc_{t_p}	Acc (%)	Acc_{t_p}	Acc (%)	Acc_{t_p}	Acc (%)	Acc_{t_p}
Decision Tree	Depth = 40	99.95	99.66	99.97	99.77	99.98	99.77	99.76	99.43

Table 5. Prediction accuracy of the unified detection rules for the *brake-lights-command*

ML-Algorithm	Tuning	All Acc (%)	Driver 1 Acc (%)	Driver 2 Acc (%)	Driver 3 Acc (%)
Decision Tree	Depth = 40	98.16	99.37	98.16	97.97

4.5   Evaluation Against Attacks

In order to evaluate the effectiveness of the detection rule, we conduct a test campaign against simulated attacks. Since we claim that our model can detect attacker that has full control over one of the ECUs (Fig. 2b), the simulated attacks consist in replacing the data content of the messages with an attacked content. Thus the attacker is showcasing a *Man-in-the-middle attack* between the signal generator (sensor) and the receiver ECU on which we install the intrusion detection system.

Attacks Against Real-Valued Signal: For the speed signal monitoring we perform three types of attacks:

– Random speed injection: in this attack, the attacker substitutes the real sensor value with a random value.
– Speed offset injection: in this attack, the attacker adds to the real speed sensor value an offset value.
– Speed Denial of service (signal drop): in this attack, the attacker interrupts the sending of the frame causing the speed signal to freeze at the last sent value.

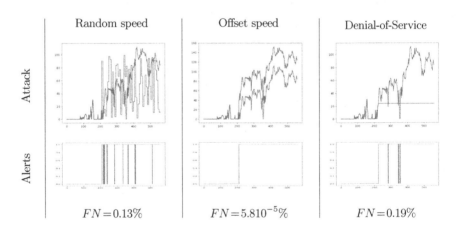

Fig. 7. Alerts raised by the decision tree (depth $= 40$) detection rule tested on three different attacks on the *speed* signal. On top is the ground truth and attacked signals: the blue signal represents the ground truth sensor value, the red signal is the attack signal. On the bottom is the alerts raised by the detection rule when receiving the attack signal. (Color figure online)

Figure 7 shows the attack use-cases on the speed signal. Note that the detection rule is set to raise an Alert as long as the received speed value (injected by the attacker) is outside the acceptance interval of ± 5 km/h of the predicted speed value. Thus we consider that an attack is happening if the injected speed signal is outside of this acceptance interval. We can see from the Alerts raised by the detection rule that:

- For the random speed injection attack: as long as the injected speed value is outside the acceptance window, alerts are raised. The alert is not raised when the injected speed value is close to the ground truth value. We obtained 0.13% of false negatives when performing this attack.
- For the speed offset attack, we can see that, the alert is raised as soon as the attack started. In fact, since the speed offset of the attack is set to +40 km/h, the received signal is always outside the acceptance window. The detection in this case is perfect and we obtained 5.810^{-5}% of false negatives.
- For the Denial of service attack, the same reasoning applies. The injected speed is frozen at around 20 km/h, which means that most of the time the alarm is raised as the received speed is outside the acceptance window. But as soon as the ground truth speed value approaches the injected value, the alarm turns off. We obtained 0.19% of false negatives on this attack.

Attacks Against Categorical Signal: For the *brake-lights-command* signal monitoring we perform three types of test:

- Random command injection: in this the attack, the attacker substitutes the real command with a (0/1) random command.
- Inverse command injection: in this attack, the attacker inverts to the real command.
- Denial of service (force to 0): in this attack, the attacker always sends the 0 command value.

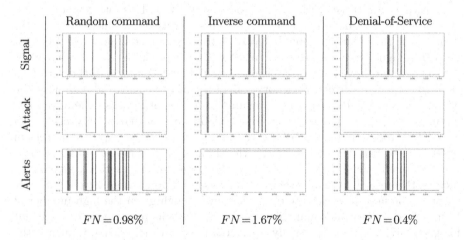

Fig. 8. Alerts raised by the decision tree (depth = 40) detection rule tested on three different attacks on the *brake-lights-command* signal. On top is the ground truth command, in the middle is the attack command and on the bottom is the Alerts raised by the detection rule when receiving the attack signal.

Figure 8 shows the attack use-cases on the *brake-lights-command* signal. Note that the detection rule is set to raise an Alert as long as the received command value (injected by the attacker) differs from the predicted command. Thus we consider that an attack is happening if the injected command signal is different from the real *brake-lights-command* signal. We can see from the Alerts raised by the detection rule that:

- For the random command injection: as long as the injected command differs from the ground truth command, alerts are raised. The alert is not raised when the injected and ground truth commands are the same. We obtained a false negative rate of 0.98%.
- For the Inverse command attack, we can see that, the alert is raised as soon as the attack started. In fact, since the injected command is always the opposite of the ground truth command, the predicted signal is always different from the received signal. Thus an attack is detected from the start, and we obtained a false negative rate of 1.67%.
- For the Denial of service attack, the injected command is set to 0. The ground truth *brake-lights-command* have occurrences of about 70% and 30% for 0 and 1 respectively. Thus, we consider that there is an attack only 30% of the time. Similarly, the alerts were raised when the injected command differs from the ground truth command. We obtained a false negative rate of 0.4%.

5 Conclusion

In this article we introduced a novel in-vehicle intrusion detection system capable of detecting an attacker with full control over an ECU. This intrusion detection system is based on detection rules built with supervised machine learning techniques. The rules learn nominal behavior of the system and make predictions for individual signal value. Alarms are raised when the predicted signal value is not similar to the received value. We showed first the effectiveness of the detection rules for separate drivers, then for a small set of drivers. We also showed the effectiveness of the detection rules against examples of attacks. The advantage of the proposed method relatively to previous work is that it only needs collected data to learn nominal behavior, and does not need examples of attacks in order to recognize them. Plus, it gives the ability to target individual signals (for instance most safety critical). Since the detection rules are actually signal predictors, theoretically the approach could be used for prevention as well. One may consider the false positive rate of 1% not low enough given the high number of frames used within the communication buses. For this purpose we can account for successive alerts as a remedy. In fact, in order to effectively influence the behavior of the car, the attacker needs to send successive attack frames. Thus, we can consider that an isolated detection alert could be ignored, and focus on successive alerts. This technique can tremendously reduce the number of false positives.

References

1. Borazjani, P., Everett, C., McCoy, D.: OCTANE: an extensible open source car security testbed. In: Proceedings of the Embedded Security in Cars Conference (2014)
2. Checkoway, S., et al.: Comprehensive experimental analyses of automotive attack surfaces. In: USENIX Security Symposium, San Francisco (2011)
3. Cho, K.-T., Shin, K.G.: Fingerprinting electronic control units for vehicle intrusion detection. In: 25th USENIX Security Symposium, USENIX Security 2016, pp. 911–927. USENIX Association (2016)
4. Foster, I.D., Prudhomme, A., Koscher, K., Savage, S.: Fast and vulnerable: a story of telematic failures. In: WOOT (2015)
5. Han, K., Weimerskirch, A., Shin, K.G.: Automotive cybersecurity for in-vehicle communication. In: IQT Quarterly, vol. 6, pp. 22–25 (2014)
6. Hartkopp, O., Reuber, C., Schilling, R.: MaCAN – message authenticated CAN. In: ESCAR Conference, Berlin, Germany (2012)
7. Hoppe, T., Kiltz, S., Dittmann, J.: Security threats to automotive CAN networks – practical examples and selected short-term countermeasures. In: Harrison, M.D., Sujan, M.-A. (eds.) SAFECOMP 2008. LNCS, vol. 5219, pp. 235–248. Springer, Heidelberg (2008). https://doi.org/10.1007/978-3-540-87698-4_21
8. Humayed, A., Luo, B.: Using ID-hopping to defend against targeted DoS on CAN. In: Proceedings of the 1st International Workshop on Safe Control of Connected and Autonomous Vehicles, pp. 19–26. ACM (2017)
9. ISO: ISO 26262–5: road vehicles - functional safety - part 5: product development at the hardware level. International Organization for Standardization (2011)
10. Kang, M.-J., Kang, J.-W.: Intrusion detection system using deep neural network for in-vehicle network security. PloS One 11(6), e0155781 (2016)
11. Koscher, K., et al.: Experimental security analysis of a modern automobile. In: 2010 IEEE Symposium on Security and Privacy (SP), pp. 447–462. IEEE (2010)
12. Han, K., Weimerskirch, A., Shin, K.G.: A practical solution to achieve real-time performance in the automotive network by randomizing frame identifier. In: Embedded Security in Cars, ESCAR Europe (2015)
13. Loukas, G., Vuong, T., Heartfield, R., Sakellari, G., Yoon, Y., Gan, D.: Cloud-based cyber-physical intrusion detection for vehicles using deep learning. IEEE Access 6, 3491–3508 (2018)
14. Marchetti, M., Stabili, D.: Anomaly detection of CAN bus messages through analysis of ID sequences. In: 2017 IEEE on Intelligent Vehicles Symposium (IV), pp. 1577–1583. IEEE (2017)
15. Miller, C., Valasek, C.: Remote exploitation of an unaltered passenger vehicle. Black Hat USA 2015 (2015)
16. Müter, M., Groll, A., Freiling, F.C.: A structured approach to anomaly detection for in-vehicle networks. In: 2010 Sixth International Conference on Information Assurance and Security (IAS), pp. 92–98. IEEE (2010)
17. Narayanan, S.N., Mittal, S., Joshi, A.: OBD_SecureAlert: an anomaly detection system for vehicles. In: 2016 IEEE International Conference on Smart Computing (SMARTCOMP), pp. 1–6. IEEE (2016)
18. Nilsson, D.K., Larson, U.E., Jonsson, E.: Efficient in-vehicle delayed data authentication based on compound message authentication codes. In: 2008 IEEE 68th Vehicular Technology Conference, VTC 2008-Fall, pp. 1–5. IEEE (2008)

19. Pedregosa, F., et al.: Scikit-learn: machine learning in python. J. Mach. Learn. Res. **12**(Oct), 2825–2830 (2011)
20. Taylor, A., Japkowicz, N., Leblanc, S.: Frequency-based anomaly detection for the automotive CAN bus. In: 2015 World Congress on Industrial Control Systems Security (WCICSS), pp. 45–49. IEEE (2015)
21. Taylor, A., Leblanc, S., Japkowicz, N.: Anomaly detection in automobile control network data with long short-term memory networks. In: 2016 IEEE International Conference on Data Science and Advanced Analytics (DSAA), pp. 130–139. IEEE, October 2016

Deep Learning Application in Security and Privacy – Theory and Practice: A Position Paper

Julia A. Meister[✉], Raja Naeem Akram[✉],
and Konstantinos Markantonakis[✉]

Information Security Group, Smart Card and IoT Centre,
Royal Holloway, University of London, Egham, UK
julia.a.meister@gmail.com, {r.n.akram,k.markantonakis}@rhul.ac.uk

Abstract. Technology is shaping our lives in a multitude of ways. This is fuelled by a technology infrastructure, both legacy and state of the art, composed of a heterogeneous group of hardware, software, services, and organisations. Such infrastructure faces a diverse range of challenges to its operations that include security, privacy, resilience, and quality of services. Among these, cybersecurity and privacy are taking the centre-stage, especially since the General Data Protection Regulation (GDPR) came into effect. Traditional security and privacy techniques are over-stretched and adversarial actors have evolved to design exploitation techniques that circumvent protection. With the ever-increasing complexity of technology infrastructure, security and privacy-preservation specialists have started to look for adaptable and flexible protection methods that can evolve (potentially autonomously) as the adversarial actor changes its techniques. For this, Artificial Intelligence (AI), Machine Learning (ML), and Deep Learning (DL) were put forward as saviours. In this paper, we look at the promises of AI, ML, and DL stated in academic and industrial literature and evaluate how realistic they are. We also put forward potential challenges a DL based security and privacy protection system has to overcome. Finally, we conclude the paper with a discussion on what steps the DL and the security and privacy-preservation community have to take to ensure that DL is not just going to be hype, but an opportunity to build a secure, reliable, and trusted technology infrastructure on which we can rely on for so much in our lives.

Keywords: Security · Privacy · Machine Learning · Deep Learning · Application

1 Introduction

Computing technology is an integral part of our lives and has many facets ranging from supercomputing (used in weather prediction, cutting-edge research, and

© IFIP International Federation for Information Processing 2019
Published by Springer Nature Switzerland AG 2019
O. Blazy and C. Y. Yeun (Eds.): WISTP 2018, LNCS 11469, pp. 129–144, 2019.
https://doi.org/10.1007/978-3-030-20074-9_10

business automation) to embedded devices (like smartphones, electronic devices in a home, and intelligent transport systems). Among many, security and privacy are considered to be two distinct and unique challenges. In the security and privacy domain, any protection system has to match a constantly evolving adversarial actor. According to the Symantec cybercrime report [1], the overall number of vulnerabilities has increased by 13% in 2018. Similarly, according to Cybersecurity Ventures [2], zero-day exploits seen in the wild will grow from one per week (in 2015) to one per day by 2021. It is practically impossible for a human to keep pace with the sheer number of cybersecurity events (and related activities) on a daily basis on top of an already daunting threat landscape [3].

In this paper, and as a matter of fact in any context, security and privacy are relative terms. It is not discussed as an absolute state, but rather as a state with potential and/or accepted risks. The global cost of data breaches has increased by 6.4% [4] and has the potential to severely damage an organisation's bottom-line, even without taking the potential penalties imposed by the General Data Protection Regulation (GDPR) into account [5]. As per the GDPR, an organisation can be fined up to €10 million or 2% of the firm's global turnover for a small offence (whichever is greater). For a serious offence, an organisation can be fined up to €20 million or 4% of a firm's global turnover (whichever is greater) [5].

Furthermore, there is a crisis of skilled cybersecurity practitioners. According to Ciccone, the cybersecurity job market will grow by approximately 6 million USD globally by 2019 – with potential shortages of trained professionals up to 25% [6]. Automation of decisions and actions based on network and system generated alerts has the potential to help overcome the challenges related to security and privacy – both in a technological and a business-operations (e.g. labour shortages) dimension.

Artificial Intelligence (AI) is seen as a potential solution towards the cybersecurity automation challenge in some academic and industrial circles. Machine Learning (ML) has been successfully deployed in a number of domains including but not limited to: image classification [7], object detection and recognition [8], language translation, and voice synthesis [9]. In many cases, Deep Learning (DL), a type of Machine Learning (ML) method, does not require prior expert knowledge for its learning (an obvious exception is Neuro-Fuzzy techniques). Therefore, it generally needs less manually engineered feature extraction and specialist knowledge [10]. DL can detect patterns in raw data by transforming it into higher and more abstract level representations - a function that is very interesting for cybersecurity zero-day vulnerability/exploit detection. Similarly, DL is used to abstract malware's behavioural features and anomalous activities and can then be used to detect its existence in a system [11,12].

AI as a cybersecurity tool is expected to capture a large market and it is clear that AI has the potential to impact the cybersecurity space [13]. Furthermore, there is sufficient market interest in both commercial (financial incentives) and academic research. In this paper, we discuss the challenges of deploying AI-based techniques (ML/DL) to security domains as a general security tool and highlight the difference between the theory and practice. The discussed challenges come from the technical development and exploration of DL methods in the context of cybersecurity – showcasing the fact that DL techniques in themselves are not the panacea but mearly a tool that requires a number of correct (and in some cases trustworthy) features to be effective. It is understood that there is a potential to mislead an ML/DL deployment as discussed in existing literature [14,15], which is not the focus of this paper.

The robustness of DL is stated in [14] as inversely proportional to the potential of an attacker's ability to find adversarial examples, which can impact the accuracy of detection and classification of a threat. However, we argue that robustness, no doubt an important feature, is not just dependent on the attacker's ability to find adversarial examples. It is also affected by the interdependent relationship of input data, its accuracy and trustworthiness, its feature-richness, how representative the data is of all possible case scenarios, and the potential of adversarial samples. We will discuss these features in further detail throughout the paper. Furthermore, we examine ML/DL not only from the view of theoretical and feature/ability specific limitations but also from the view of practical challenges related to implementation and deployment. For the most part, existing papers focus on discussing a specific model's success rate and implementation/deployment challenges. They do not include discussions on the general challenges related to ML/DL deployed as security and privacy mechanisms.

1.1 Structure of the Paper

Section 2 elaborates on the existing academic work that has shown the promise of ML/DL as an automation tool for security and privacy practices. In Sect. 3, we dive into the technical discussion of DL and how automation based on it is designed and developed. The discussion is derived from the author's first impressions and practical experience coming from a security background. Section 4 articulates the practical considerations that a security practitioner has to take into account when working on DL deployment. Section 5 is a list of DL features that would make the technology a useful security tool for cybersecurity practitioners.

2 Security and Privacy by Deep Learning

In this section, we survey the types of security and privacy services and applications in which DL has been deployed successfully – as represented by academic literature.

2.1 Deep Learning for Security and Privacy

The set of security and privacy services that are being explored in academic literature to be the target deployment scenarios for DL are as follows:

1. *Malware Detection*: Efficient pattern recognition in large datasets is what ML/DL is purpose built for. A number of proposals are put forward in academic literature that identify malware with high accuracy [16,17]. In most of these proposals, pattern recognition is based on a particular behaviour (communication, syscall and resource usage/utilisation patterns, etc.). For an adversarial entity, the objective is to hide or exhibit its behaviour within the scope of genuine applications to avoid detection.

2. *Anomaly Detection or Network Intrusion Detection*: Both anomaly and network intrusion detection by ML/DL rely on network traffic analysis to find usage and communication patterns that represent an abnormal behaviour. It is important to keep in mind that anomalous behaviour is not necessarily a set of activities that are prohibited by system policies (security/privacy). It is just an out-of-the-ordinary activity that can be genuine or malicious. For example, user A has access to client records. Usually, user A only accesses one record a day, but today user A accesses the entire list of clients. If the access control policy only focused on access (may user A access client records?) and not on frequency (how many client records can user A access?), accessing all client records would be a permitted action and not suspicious. However, this action might be anomalous. Such classification and detection of out-of-pattern usages fits nicely within the current capabilities of ML/DL technology [18–20].

3. *Distributed Denial of Service (DDoS) Detection*: DDoS can be viewed as an anomalous request to access a particular resource. Therefore, ML/DL can efficiently identify out-of-pattern access requests based on the access patterns to a particular resource (e.g. a website or an application) [21,22].

From the above list, we can ascertain that DL is not widely used for privacy-preservation techniques. There is a potential for exposing data on user access patterns based on the user connection graph, especially in the context of data flow analysis. These domains might have unique patterns that can be useful for an effective DL deployment but an academic literature search for applications of DL in these fields did not yield substantial results. Below, we explain some of the identified privacy related services that might be suitable for DL deployment but limited work has been carried out in academic literature:

1. *Data Flow Analysis*: The flow of data between any two entities can reveal data consumption in an organisation. For example, the flow of data between the consumer database and marketing teams can represent potential value to consumer profiling, targeted marketing, and campaign analysis. The data flow and usage in a specific enterprise have a set pattern, even when only looking at individual features such as 'data flow' and the actual 'contents of the data'. Therefore, ML/DL can be used to identify anomalies in the usage of data based on its analysis, and the resulting anomalous data flow patterns could be very useful for an Intrusion Detection System (IDS) or Intrusion Detection Prevention (IDP) but not as a privacy preservation function.

2. *Data Exposure Potential*: Whether in an enterprise environment or in personal settings, individuals have a circle of other individuals with whom they

communicate. A community map for each individual can be constructed based on these communication patterns which can represent not only 'with whom' individuals share information but also 'what information' is being shared with their community. For example, an individual shares one type of information with only a subset of the individuals in his/her community. This is easily classifiable and based on the patterns, ML/DL can predict whether information accessible to an individual at a particular point in time has a high probability of being shared with certain other individuals. This analysis can be used to build a data exposure prediction which could be a useful tool for privacy-preservation and assessment. Furthermore, in the event of an information leakage, an analysis of the data flows and the probability of data exposure can be incorporated into the forensic investigation to quickly find any potential points (individuals) that could have leaked the information. The potential of ML/DL has not been fully explored in the context of data exposure in current academic literature. We believe that the application of ML/DL for such analysis shows a lot of promise.

Most of the existing literature about privacy and DL is focused on how to design DL methods in a manner that does not violate the users' privacy [23–25]. Another application of DL in privacy is to build recommendation systems for users. For example, Yu et al. [26] put forward a privacy setting recommendation system (iPhoto) for photo sharing based on image analysis. Most dimensions related to DL and privacy are beyond the scope of the this paper. The scope of the paper is how DL itself can be used as a privacy-protection mechanism.

3   Deep Learning - A Deeper Look at Its Application

In this section, we explore the technical aspects of understanding and deploying DL. The discussion revolves around the pre-requisites for DL deployment, the tools that can be used, and DL optimisation. Readers are referred to consult the survey by Fadlullah et al. [27] for an in-depth analysis of DL structures and methodologies.

3.1   Representation Learning

DL uses representation learning algorithms to automatically identify complex hidden structures in large datasets [10]. Relations between parameters can be more or less hidden depending on the features present in the data. Representation learning works to solve this problem by transforming raw data into a more useful representation for detection and classification predictors by highlighting the important dependencies [28]. The challenge is to generalise as much as possible while also preserving most of the information in the original dataset.

DL implements the learning technique in the form of a model, a concatenation of multiple, relatively simple layers that each perform a transformation on the data [28]. The layers' input is either raw data (input layer) or the previous layer's learned representation of its input (hidden and output layers). This leads to automatically identified, hierarchical levels of abstraction, also called feature extraction, with higher level features defined as a composition of lower-level features [29, 30]. During the training phase, the model adjusts the internal parameters used to transform the data to achieve a more useful result [10].

3.2   Data Normalisation

DL models rely heavily on data as it is the basis of the pre-training and training phases, which in turn underlie the specialisation of a model to a task.

DL does not need a perfectly curated dataset due to its learning scheme. Semi-supervised techniques have been shown to alleviate problems, however, a new training strategy and a better cost function could make training on incomplete and noisy data sets more efficient [31]. Whitening data is a known way of speeding up training convergence, readers are referred to [32] for details on how to transform the input data.

Ioffe and Szegedy [33] describe batch normalisation, where normalisation is embedded in the model architecture as another method to reduce training-times. It works towards fixing the distribution of the layer's inputs and thereby solves the problems introduced by internal covariate shift. Internal covariate shift describes the fact that the layers' input distribution continuously changes during training due to the internal parameters updating [33]. The difficulty in changing the dataset in any way is to preserve as much of the original information as possible. This can be achieved by normalising the training examples relative to the entire training data [33]. Other, less efficient ways of combating covariate shift include lowering the training rate and careful parameter initialisation. Using DL in combination with Big Data is a popular concept in the industry, however, there are many challenges that need to be overcome. The three V's model identifies them as volume, variety, and velocity.

Chen and Lin [31] provides the authors' thoughts on how to solve these problems. According to the authors, the large volume of Big Data (number of inputs, number of represented classes and high dimensionality of the entries) cannot be accommodated by a single machine due to its limited memory and computing capacity. A distributed framework would be more suited to the task. DL has been successfully utilised for the integration of heterogeneous data, e.g. [34] and [35]. Therefore, the authors believe that DL methods can be applied to Big Data's large variety of data structures with further optimisation work. They propose online learning to combat the velocity (how quickly data is generated).

There are many large datasets ranging across a wide selection of categories publicly available which can be used in training and testing networks. Examples are the MNIST database[1] of handwritten digits and the Google Audioset[2], which includes thousands of labelled audio clips. Kaggle[3] is a platform that hosts ML competitions and maintains public datasets.

---

[1] http://yann.lecun.com/exdb/mnist.

[2] https://research.google.com/audioset.

[3] https://www.kaggle.com.

3.3   Designing Deep Learning Models

There are different *neural network architectures* used in DL, each with their own advantages and disadvantages. Convolutional networks are a type of feedforward network that are designed to process multidimensional signals such as images and video [36], whereas recurrent networks are adapted to work with sequence data which makes them more difficult to train but applicable to natural language processing (NLP) challenges [37]. Deep Belief Networks (DBNs) are made up of several layers of restricted Boltzmann Machines (RBMs) and are useful for when the training data set is made up of both labelled and unlabelled entries. They often perform better than networks trained only with backpropagation [36].

The *training distribution and structure* can be an important factor in the choice of model and learning method. Supervised learning methods require labelled data and tend to have good results when large quantities of data are available [29]. They adjust the model's internal parameters based on the training loss, calculated by comparing the predicted output to the expected output as defined by the data entry's label. When it comes to unsupervised learning, the ultimate goal is to abstract the raw data in a way that identifies the important factors of variation that apply to all classes. Bengio has had success applying a transductive strategy by using linear models such as Principal Component Analysis (PCA), among others, as some of the network's layers [30]. Semi-supervised learning makes use of both labelled and unlabelled data. The RBMs that make up a DBN are pre-trained with an unsupervised greedy layer-by-layer algorithm and the whole model is then fine-tuned with labelled data and backpropagation. DBNs often perform better than networks trained solely with backpropagation [36], as the combination of non-linear layers in a model can be sensitive to the initialisation values. Pre-training, as used with DBNs, can mitigate this sensitivity [29].

When it comes to optimising a model's accuracy, tuning the *hyperparameters* is an important step. They are values that directly influence the training of a neural network by configuring a model's complexity and the learning process [38], both of which are critical to the model's performance. However, finding the ideal values for these parameters can be very difficult as fine-tuning is often based on experience. According to Bengio, there are two common ways of optimising a model's performance through the choice of hyperparameters: manual trial and error and a grid search. Both approaches run into problems when the number of parameters is too large [30]. Readers are referred to [30] and [39] for a more efficient optimisation based on random search and greedy exploration. The number and type of parameters differ between models and learning algorithms. Some of the most common include the learning rate, momentum, number of hidden units, number of epochs and batch size.

Training large, distributed networks is slow, as the use of parallel resources is very inefficient. Denil et al. introduce a way to reduce the number of free parameters without dropping the accuracy, as many parameters can be predicted and are, therefore, redundant [40].

Over- and underfitting describe situations where a neural network has not learned the ideal generalisation of the training data which leads to poor performance when new data is introduced. This can also be described as the bias/variance dilemma, a trade-off between high bias and high variance [41]. Common metrics such as training and test error are used to analyse the accuracy of a model can help identify over- and underfitting.

High variance means that a model fails to differentiate between the signal (the general, underlying pattern) and the noise (dataset-specific randomness) of a dataset. In other words, an *overfit model* has failed to sufficiently generalise the features of its specific training distribution and therefore performs poorly on previously unseen data, as it has no general knowledge it can apply. Overfitting can occur with a complex model whose learning algorithm has a low bias and a high variance. Cross validation is a proven method of preventing overfitting by stopping training before the specification becomes to high [42]. The point in time at which to stop training is identified by comparing the model's accuracy on the training data to its accuracy on the unseen testing data. Training is stopped if the difference starts growing or is deemed too large, also called early stopping. Reducing the number of parameters is another method of combating overfitting [42]. Dropout layers have also been shown to be successful because they prevent the co-adaption of a network's hidden units [29]. They introduce unpredictable noise into the data by dropping random parameters in each training iteration.

Bias describes the difference between the model's expected output and the correct values. High bias occurs when the model is oversimplified and does not have enough flexibility to capture the underlying relations of features present in the data or when there are insufficient parameters. A model is said to be *underfit* if it has a low variance but a high bias and this can be identified by a high error on both the training and the test data. A possible solution to this problem is changing the model's structure and parameters so that it better fits the problem to be solved.

Bias and variance are inversely related. The ideal model minimises the expected total error of a learning algorithm, which is defined as the sum of squared bias, variance and irreducible error. While bias and variance are reducible, the irreducible error comes from modelling the problem itself.

3.4   Deploying Deep Learning Methods

There are many open-source tools and frameworks that support DL which can vary greatly in overhead, running speed and number of pre-made DL components. Following are short descriptions of a small selection of them.

TensorFlow[4] is a Python-based library with automatic differentiation capabilities that supports both ML and DL. The high-performance numerical computations, modelled as data flow graphs, can be applied to other domains as well. TensorFlow is used by companies such as Google, Uber, and AMD.

---

[4] https://www.tensorflow.org.

PyTorch[5] is another such library which enables rapid research on ML networks. The focus lies on extensibility and low overhead, which is possible because the core logic is written in C++. It also supports reverse mode automatic differentiation, which is the most important type of differentiation for DL applications [43] and distributed training. In 2017, Uber AI Labs released Pyro[6], a deep probabilistic programming language (PPL) based on PyTorch.

Caffe[7] is a C++ library that provides interfaces for Python and MAT-LAB [44]. It is a clean and modifiable framework, due to the fact that the model's representation is separate from the model's implementation [45]. It is very fast in training convolutional networks and allows for seamless switching between devices (CPU and GPU).

MATLAB[8] can be used for DL among other things and allows users to build and analyse models, even with little expert knowledge in DL. It provides access to models such as GoogLeNet and AlexNet and is compatible with models from Caffe and TensorFlow-Keras. MATLAB also supports collaboration with the PyTorch and MXNet frameworks.

MXNet[9] is a very versatile DL framework which supports imperative and symbolic programming as well as multiple languages, such as C++, Python, R, Scala, MATLAB and JavaScript. Its running speed is similar to Caffe and significantly faster than TensorFlow. It is used by both AWS and Azure, among others [44].

4   Practical Considerations of Deep Learning Deployment

In this section, we discuss the challenges related to deploying DL as part of the cyber security and privacy-preservation mechanism. We discuss three major issues related to the DL, which is in no way an exhaustive list. However, the problems listed in this section have a significant impact on current DL implementations.

4.1   Training Data Set

Any DL technique requires training to achieve specialisation for a task, therefore the training data set and its structure are very important. There are two crucial elements about the training data set: (a) feature-richness and (b) trustworthiness.

Feature-richness means that the training data should include an extensive collection of information so that the DL model can identify as many features as possible, which will help it differentiate between genuine and malicious behaviours accurately once it is deployed. Features have to be as extensive as possible; For example, data related to an activity should cover as much information about that

---

[5] https://pytorch.org.

[6] http://pyro.ai.

[7] http://caffe.berkeleyvision.org.

[8] https://uk.mathworks.com.

[9] https://mxnet.apache.org.

activity as possible so a malicious entity has as very little room to manoeuvre and trick the deployed DL system. Furthermore, the training data should include a diverse set of behaviours. If a training data set is representative of a behaviour set, the algorithm has a better chance of accurately classifying features in it. If the behaviour set is not comprehensive, any behaviour that is not part of the set might be miscategorised because the DL model could fail to differentiate between a genuine and malicious behaviour correctly. This failure is due to the fact that DL builds its knowledge base of genuine and malicious behaviour from the training dataset during the training phase. One of many learning techniques is re-enforced learning. Many learning techniques can open up a potential avenue for an adversary to modify the behaviour classification of an ML/DL system.

The second crucial element is the data's trustworthiness. As one of the most important elements of DL, data should be sourced from a trusted environment and this is also true for malicious activities captured (and tagged) for the training data set. The challenge is to capture malicious activities in a trusted manner from a real environment or a lab simulation that accurately depict how an attacker could behave. As a note, training is carried out on a data set that represents 'past' attacks (known attack patterns) and will not necessarily be representative of 'future' attacks (unknown vulnerability and attack patterns). The challenges related to new and unknown attacks are further discussed in Sect. 5.

4.2 Adversarial Samples

There is extensive work in academic literature that discusses the impact and limitation of ML/DL against adversarial samples [46]. From a deployment point of view, security and privacy practitioners have to keep in mind that a deployed DL system can be susceptible to adversarial samples. This means that an attacker could influence the DL model's training to learn malicious activities as genuine. By doing so, attackers are enabled to accomplish their goal without DL detecting and flagging them. The challenge related to adversarial samples is crucial, as organisations deploying DL based security and privacy mechanism would prefer for them to evolve over time, thereby accommodating the increasing sophistication in the threat landscape. However, allowing the evolution of a DL model after initial training opens it up to adversarial samples. On the other hand, a DL technique restricted to the initial training is not flexible and extensible, two of the important functions DL needs to cope with the challenges of cybersecurity and privacy. A potential middle ground could be to select a DL technique that is the least susceptible and designed to withstand adversarial samples. Unfortunately, even with such methodologies, the likelihood of adversarial samples cannot be completely removed. Therefore, adversarial samples are a threat vector that will see more sophistication in the future as more and more organisations deploy ML/DL based cybersecurity and privacy-preservation mechanisms.

4.3   General Data Protection Regulation (GDPR)

Organisations dealing with EU citizens' data have to comply with GDPR regulations. GDPR gives a number of rights to consumers, among which are the two that we are going to discuss in this section: Right-to-Know (RtK) and Right-to-Rectification (RtR).

When it comes to processing user data, the Right-to-Know (RtK, Article 15.1.h) states that data subjects have the right to know about the "the existence of automated decision-making, including profiling, referred to in Article 22(1) and (4) and, at least in those cases, meaningful information about the logic involved, as well as the significance and the envisaged consequences of such processing for the data subject" [5]. This article requires the availability of meaningful information about the processing method used to process users' data. As discussed before, DL is chaotic in many instances and the steps taken to reach a particular decision might have limited traceability or support for reverse-engineering. As an example, a user is in his or her rights to request information on why they received a certain result from an organisation. The organisation then has to explain how the user's data was processed by the company's AI to generate that particular result. GDPR also holds firms accountable for bias and discrimination in their automated decisions. The challenge of explaining how DL has reached a specific decision becomes paramount – an aspect of DL that has not been extensively investigated. To what extent DL's choice can be explained and whether that is an acceptable and, more importantly, meaningful explanation to the regulatory-authorities and consumer needs to be further researched.

The Right-to-Rectification (RtR, Article 16) states that "[t]he data subject shall have the right to obtain from the controller without undue delay the rectification of inaccurate personal data concerning him or her" [5]. If a user exercises RtR, they request changes to their personal data stored in the system. How these change in the data will impact previous processing and leaning, which are now based on incorrect data, is still a big question. The challenge is to make DL rectify its input data selectively post-processing in a manner that does not require a complete retraining.

On a side note, depending on how DL is deployed, the Right-to-Forget (RtF, GDPR Article 17) might have an impact if a sufficient number of consumers/users request their data to be deleted. At that point, the knowledge set reflecting the behaviour of an organisation's consumers/users will not be accurate anymore. How this impacts DL's subsequent decisions is still unclear and requires further investigation.

As a cybersecurity and privacy practitioner, a clear view of the needs and visions for a DL deployment are necessary. There are plenty of unanswered questions related to DL in terms of research (Sect. 5), operation, and legislation (GDPR). It is safe to say that this technology has the potential to be beneficial by improving security and privacy-preservation. However, the pertinent question is whether it is ready and mature enough to be deployed extensively as a security and privacy mechanism. The answer to this is complex and depends on multiple factors, including:

1. Organisational requirements and the prioritised security objectives.
2. How the organisation envisions using ML/DL, keeping in mind that ML/DL are not silver bullets.
3. Understanding the limitations of ML/DL and complimenting these techniques with traditional security and privacy measures.
4. Accepting that ML/DL are in the early stage of development and might go through many developments and improvements in the next few years, therefore deployed systems will have to keep up with rapid change (flexibility, extensibility, and scalability).

5   Research Challenges for Deep Learning

In this section, we put forward list of relevant topics and questions for ML/DL research from the perspective of a cybersecurity practitioner.

1. *Policy change impact analysis*: In an enterprise environment, policies change regularly, and can be related to the security and privacy aspects of the enterprise. The impact assessment of such policies on the enterprise environment is based on human experts' knowledge. If the enterprise has deployed ML/DL as a security and privacy measure, policy changes need to be reflected in the ML/DL method's learning and execution. To the authors' knowledge, there is no evaluation of how dynamic policies will impact currently deployed ML/DL implementations. Therefore, predictive impact analysis of policy changes on DL based security and privacy mechanism would be a important step forward.
2. *Defining a new policy*: An organisation's security and privacy objectives are specified by policies and rule-sets. In existing DL, these policies and rule-sets are represented in the labelling of individual records in the training data set. If the policy changes after the deployment of a DL based system, the available option is to generate a new training dataset based on the new policies and retraining the DL model. Generating the training data set and retraining can be considered costs in terms of performance and time. The challenge is to cut down this cost and make policy changes as similar to traditional security mechanisms like firewall, access control and IDS, to name a few.
3. *Preparing DL to cope with the 'future'*: The cybersecurity and privacy landscape is constantly evolving. To cope with this change, DL has to be flexible and have the ability to learn new patterns even after deployment. Furthermore, prior knowledge already learned by a particular instance of DL is valuable, and the ability to transfer it to other instances (for example among multiple organisations) would vastly improve the readiness of the collective cybersecurity field. A potential path forward could be to develop DL techniques with lifelong learning capabilities.
4. *Isolated or Collaborative Learning*: Isolated learning has its pros and cons. The positive side is that as an organisation, the training set will include behaviours specific to your organisation. However, this also means that unless you experience a cyber attack, you will not be able to profile it. With collaborative learning, if a single instance of the collaboration experiences a cyber

attack, its profiling can then be shared with the other instances in the group. This has the potential to rapidly improve security countermeasures against new and previously unknown attacks. Collaborative learning introduces some additional challenges, such as:

- *Knowledge based collaboration*: In collaborative learning, should algorithms share their learned knowledge or simply share the raw records of the out-of-profile observations? It also requires a method for sharing prior knowledge between multiple DL instances.
- *Raw records based collaboration*: Sharing raw records seems simple, as each instance can run its own learning process over it. However, this could leak security sensitive data and violate privacy requirements. For raw records based collaboration, efficient and strong anonymisation techniques have to be developed. This anonymisation technique has to protect privacy and security sensitive data but at the same retain sufficient features so that it is still useful for training other DL instances.

5. *Making deep learning forget*: There are a number of situations where it is preferable to make the DL de-profile specific records from its knowledge base. For example, (a) the discovery of malicious data in the training data set that is now required to be re-labelled as malicious, (b) removing adversarial samples from the DL knowledge and (c) if a consumer/user exercises RtR (Right-to-Rectification) or RtF (Right-to-Forget) under GDPR. In such situations, DL techniques need to 'forget' about certain records. How to achieve this seems to be an open question that will be crucial in a future with increased awareness about privacy in the general public and adversaries successfully training DL implementations with adversarial samples.

6 Conclusion

In this paper, we briefly explore the potential, practicality, implications, and shortcomings of DL mechanisms in fields such as security and privacy preservation mechanisms. There are numerous proposals in academic literature that advocate the success of DL as an effective mechanism for cybersecurity. We do not evaluate their claims in this paper. We view DL as a mature domain and evaluate how a security practitioner would go about deploying it, what challenges and issues they would have to overcome, and what options are available to resolve some of these issues. We are of the opinion that DL has come a long way and can potentially be applied to security and privacy functions with a defined set of static behaviours. In such situations, DL can efficiently detect any behavioural violations with high accuracy. However, it is too early to consider it an extensively useable security measure in its own right. DL has a long way to go before it is mature enough to be deployed as a standalone Unified Threat Management (UTM) environment. In this paper, we have discussed the aspects an organisation should keep in mind when deploying a DL based solution. In addition, we have also included a list of features that would be useful to security practitioners if they can be provided by the DL base mechanisms.

In conclusion, DL has a lot of promise and with the right features, it could become an impactful tool in the security and privacy arsenal. With the increase of sophistication and complexity of future technology in the current infrastructure, AI-based security and privacy countermeasures (ML/DL) might be the next logical step. For this reason, cybersecurity researchers have to become active participants in the ML/DL evolution, rather then just deploying them to security and privacy problems as off-the-shelf kits.

References

1. "Internet security threat report": Symantec Corporation, Annual Report - Online Volume 23 (2018)
2. Morgan, S.: 2017 Cybercrime report, cybercrime damages will cost the world us$6 trillion by 2021. Cybersecurity Ventures, Herjavec Group, Online Report (2017)
3. Trull, J.: Top 5 best practices to automate security operations. Microsoft Secure, Enterprise Cybersecurity Group, Online Blog, August 2017
4. "2018 Cost of a Data Breach Study: Global Overview": Ponemon Institute - Benchmark research sponsored by IBM Security, Online Report, July 2018
5. "Regulation (EU) 2016/679 of the European Parliament and of the Council of 27 April 2016 on the protection of natural persons with regard to the processing of personal data and on the free movement of such data, and repealing Directive 95/46/EC (General Data Protection Regulation)," Official Journal of the European Union, vol. L119/59, May 2016. [Online]. http://eur-lex.europa.eu/legal-content/EN/TXT/?uri=OJ:L:2016:119:TOC
6. Ciccone, S.: Cybersecurity: More threats, but also more opportunities, Paloalot Networks, Online, June 2016
7. Krizhevsky, A., Sutskever, I., Hinton, G.E.: Imagenet classification with deep convolutional neural networks. In: Advances in Neural Information Processing Systems, pp. 1097–1105 (2012)
8. Ren, S., He, K., Girshick, R., Sun, J.: Faster R-CNN: towards real-time object detection with region proposal networks. In: Advances in Neural Information Processing Systems, pp. 91–99 (2015)
9. Xiong, W., Wu, L., Alleva, F., Droppo, J., Huang, X., Stolcke, A.: The Microsoft 2017 conversational speech recognition system. In: 2018 IEEE International Conference on Acoustics, Speech and Signal Processing (ICASSP), pp. 5934–5938. IEEE (2018)
10. Hinton, G., LeCun, Y., Bengio, Y.: Deep learning, pp. 436–444 (2015)
11. Yuan, Z., Lu, Y., Wang, Z., Xue, Y.: Droid-Sec: deep learning in android malware detection. In: ACM SIGCOMM Computer Communication Review, vol. 44, no. 4, pp. 371–372. ACM (2014)
12. Saxe, J., Berlin, K.: Deep neural network based malware detection using two dimensional binary program features. In: 2015 10th International Conference on Malicious and Unwanted Software (MALWARE), pp. 11–20. IEEE (2015)
13. Armstrong, M.: The future of a.i. Statista Infographics, Statista, Online Report, November 2016
14. Carlini, N., Wagner, D.: Towards evaluating the robustness of neural networks. In: 2017 IEEE Symposium on Security and Privacy (SP), pp. 39–57. IEEE (2017)
15. Carlini, N., et al.: Hidden voice commands. In: 25th USENIX Security Symposium (USENIX Security 16), Austin, TX (2016)

Proof. The solution $x(t)$ 0f the initial value problem (4.59) and $x(t_0) = x_0$ is equal to

$$x(t) = X(t)x_0 + \int_0^t X(t)X^{-1}(s)f(s)ds + \sum_{0<\theta_i<t} X(t)X^{-1}(\theta_i+)I_i.$$

The Poincaré criterion implies that $x(t)$ is a unique ω-periodic solution of (4.59) if and only if x_0 satisfies the equation

$$[\mathcal{I} - X(\omega)]x_0 = \int_0^\omega X(\omega)X^{-1}(s)f(s)ds + \sum_{0<\theta_i<\omega} X(\omega)X^{-1}(\theta_i+)I_i$$

uniquely. That is,

$$x_0 = [\mathcal{I} - X(\omega)]^{-1}[\int_0^\omega X(\omega)X^{-1}(s)f(s)ds + \sum_{0<\theta_i<\omega} X(\omega)X^{-1}(\theta_i+)I_i].$$

Use the vector to obtain

$$x(t) = X(t)(\mathcal{I} - X(\omega))^{-1}[\int_0^\omega X(\omega)X^{-1}(s)f(s)ds + \sum_{0<\theta_i<\omega} X(\omega)X^{-1}(\theta_i+)I_i]$$

$$+ \int_0^t X(t)X^{-1}(s)f(s)ds + \sum_{0<\theta_i<t} X(t)X^{-1}(\theta_i+)I_i.$$

Now, use the periodicity of the solution and write

$$x(t) = X(t)[\int_0^\omega X(\omega)X^{-1}(s)f(s)ds + \sum_{0<\theta_i<\omega} X(\omega)X^{-1}(\theta_i+)I_i]+$$

$$\int_0^t X(t)X^{-1}(s)f(s)ds + \sum_{0<\theta_i<t} X(t)X^{-1}(\theta_i+)I_i =$$

$$\int_0^t [X(t)(\mathcal{I} - X(\omega))^{-1}X(\omega)X^{-1}(s) + X(t)X^{-1}(s)]f(s)ds+$$

$$\sum_{0<\theta_i<t} [X(t)(\mathcal{I} - X(\omega))^{-1}X(\omega)X^{-1}(\theta_i+) + X(t)X^{-1}(\theta_i+)]I_i+$$

$$\int_t^\omega X(t)(\mathcal{I} - X(\omega))^{-1}X^{-1}(s)f(s)ds + \sum_{t\le\theta_i<\omega} X(t)(\mathcal{I} - X(\omega))^{-1}X^{-1}(\theta_i+)I_i =$$

$$\int_0^t [X(t+\omega)(\mathcal{I} - X(\omega))^{-1}X^{-1}(s) + X(t)X^{-1}(s)]f(s)ds+$$

$$\sum_{0<\theta_i<t} [X(t+\omega)(\mathcal{I}-X(\omega))^{-1}X^{-1}(\theta_i+) + X(t)X^{-1}(\theta_i+)]I_i +$$

$$\int_t^\omega X(t)(\mathcal{I}-X(\omega))^{-1}X^{-1}(s)f(s)ds + \sum_{t\le\theta_i<\omega} X(t)(\mathcal{I}-X(\omega))^{-1}X^{-1}(\theta_i+)I_i =$$

$$\int_0^\omega G(t,s)f(s)ds + \sum_{0<\theta_i<\omega} G(t,\theta_i+)I_i.$$

The theorem is proved.   □

Notes

Basics of linear impulsive systems and periodic equations were investigated in [78, 111, 138–142]. Linear nonhomogeneous systems with impulses, existence of periodic and almost periodic solutions using reduction to discrete equations and theory of generalized functions were investigated in [75]. Gram–Schmidt orthonormalization method for impulsive linear systems was applied in [33].

Chapter 5
Nonautonomous Systems with Variable Moments of Impulses

5.1 Description of Systems

Let $G \subset \mathbb{R}^n$ be an open and connected set, I an open interval in $\mathbb{R}$, and $\mathcal{A}$ an interval in $\mathbb{Z}$. We consider the following system:

$$x' = f(t, x),$$
$$\Delta x|_{t=\tau_i(x)} = J_i(x), \tag{5.1}$$

where $(t, i, x) \in I \times \mathcal{A} \times G$, the function $f(t, x)$ is continuous on $I \times G$, functions J_i are defined on G, and $\tau_i(x), i \in \mathcal{A}$, are continuous on G functions.

The system combines the differential equation

$$x' = f(t, x), \tag{5.2}$$

and the equation of jumps

$$\Delta x|_{t=\tau_i(x)} = J_i(x). \tag{5.3}$$

The differential equation (5.2) satisfies the condition (M0), Chap. 2. Moreover, the following assumptions are fulfilled:

(N1) there exist positive numbers $\underline{\theta}, \bar{\theta}$ such that $\underline{\theta} < \tau_{i+1}(x) - \tau_i(x) < \bar{\theta}$ for all $i \in \mathcal{A}, x \in G$;
(N2) for all $i \in \mathcal{A}$ and $x \in G$, there exist real numbers $\alpha_i, \beta_i \in I$ such that $\alpha_i \leq \tau_i(x) \leq \beta_i$;
(N3) $\tau_i(x + J_i(x)) \leq \tau_i(x)$ for all $i \in \mathcal{A}$ and $x \in G$;
(N4) if $\xi(t, \tau_i(c), c + J_i(c)), c \in G, i \in \mathcal{A}$, is a solution of (5.2), then $t \neq \tau_i(\xi(t, \tau_i(c), c + J_i(c)))$ for all $t > \tau_i(c)$.
(N5) if $\eta(t, \tau_i(c), c), c \in G, i \in \mathcal{A}$, is a solution of (5.2), then $t \neq \tau_i(\eta(t, \tau_i(c), c))$ for all $t < \tau_i(c)$.

For simplicity of notation, denote by $\Gamma_i \subset I \times G$ the surface $t = \tau_i(x)$, and G_i subregion of $I \times G$ between Γ_i and $\Gamma_{i+1}, i \in \mathcal{A}$. More precisely, $G_i = \{(t, x) : \tau_i(x) < t \leq \tau_{i+1}(x), x \in G\}$.

M. Akhmet, *Principles of Discontinuous Dynamical Systems*,
DOI 10.1007/978-1-4419-6581-3_5, © Springer Science+Business Media, LLC 2010

The last five conditions are important for the next analysis. The condition (N1) guarantees that discontinuity moments of any solution of (5.1) format a B-sequence. Conditions (N1) with (N2) imply that each solution which intersects surfaces Γ_j and Γ_k, $j < k - 1$, must intersect all surfaces Γ_i, $j < i < k$, between the two. By condition (N4), each solution of (5.1) may intersect every surface of discontinuity Γ_i at most once. Indeed, if θ_i is the first meeting moment of the solution $x(t)$ with the surface, then for $t > \theta_i$ the solution is equal to the solution $\xi(t, \theta_i, x(\theta_i) + J_i(x(\theta_i)))$ of (5.2), and it cannot intersect the surface again, since of (N4). The phenomenon, when each solution meets every surface of discontinuity at most once is called the "absence of beating", and we will discuss the concept in the next section. Conditions (N1),(N3) imply that the point $(t, x(t))$ after a meeting with a surface $t = \tau_i(x)$ jumps in the region between surfaces $t = \tau_i(x)$ and $t = \tau_{i+1}(x)$. In general, (N1)–(N4) produce circumstances which allow us to keep the order of intersection of the surfaces of discontinuity by a solution. This order helps us to have well-formulated assertions as well as comprehensive proofs of the theory. We shall need condition (N5) for the left extension of solutions. Condition (N1) can be weakened for some special cases. For example, condition $\inf_G \tau_i(x) \to \infty$, as $i \to \infty$, is sufficient if we consider the increasing t.

The equation of jumps (5.3) is different from that of Chap. 2 since the solutions have discontinuities not at moments of intersection with the planes $t = \theta_i$, but at moments of intersection with surfaces $t = \tau_i(x), i \in \mathcal{A}$. That is, the moments are not prescribed, and not known until one starts to look for a certain solution of the impulsive system. That is why, we shall call system (5.1) a system with variable moments of impulses. Obviously, different solutions of the system have, in general, different moments of discontinuities.

5.2 Existence, Uniqueness, and Extension

In this section, we consider extension of solutions of the impulsive system, local existence, and uniqueness theorems. It is useful if the reader remembers the definitions of maximal intervals and the extension of solutions made in the Sect. 2.1 as it helps to understand the next discussion. To shorten it, in the sequel, we denote by $\phi(t, \kappa, z), (\kappa, z) \in I \times G$, a solution of ordinary differential equation (5.2) with $\phi(\kappa, \kappa, z) = z$, and let $x(t) = x(t, t_0, x_0)$ be a solution of (5.1) with $x(t_0) = x_0$. Suppose the point (t_0, x_0) does not belong to any of the surfaces of discontinuity. Let us say, it is lying between the surfaces Γ_j and Γ_{j+1}, for a fixed $j \in \mathcal{A}$ (see Fig. 5.1).

Similarly to the equation with fixed moments of impulses, we consider both directions of the extension:

(a) t is increasing and $t \geq t_0$;
(b) t is decreasing and $t \leq t_0$.

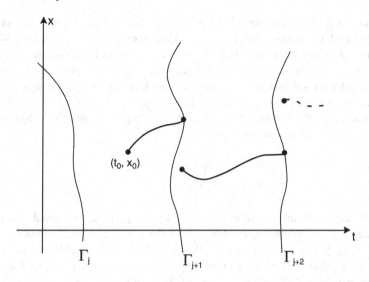

Fig. 5.1 Extension of a solution of system (5.1)

Consider the case (a). Let $[t_0, r), r \in \mathbb{R}$ or $r = \infty$, be the maximal right interval of existence of the solution $\phi(t, t_0, x_0)$. If $t \neq \tau_{j+1}(\phi(t, t_0, x_0))$ for all $t \in [t_0, r)$, then $[t_0, r)$ is the maximal interval of existence of $x(t)$. Otherwise, there exist solutions of equation $t = \tau_{j+1}(\phi(t, t_0, x_0))$. Denoting the least of them θ_{j+1}, we have that $x(t) = \phi(t, t_0, x_0)$ for $t \in [t_0, \theta_{j+1}]$. Particularly, $x(\theta_{j+1}) = \phi(\theta_{j+1}, t_0, x_0)$. Further, if $\Pi_{j+1} x(\theta_{j+1}) \in G$, then $x(\theta_{j+1}+) = \Pi_{j+1} x(\theta_{j+1})$. Taking into account that $(\theta_{j+1}, x(\theta_{j+1}+))$ is an interior point of $I \times G$, we can proceed the solution $\phi(t, \theta_{j+1}, x(\theta_{j+1}+))$ on some maximal interval $[\theta_{j+1}, r)$. Since of (N4), the last solution cannot meet the surface Γ_{j+1} again. There are two alternatives now. If $t \neq \tau_{j+2}(\phi(t, t_0, x_0)), t \in [t_0, r)$, then $[t_0, r)$ is the maximal right interval of existence of $x(t)$. Otherwise, we denote by θ_{j+2} the least solution of the equation $t = \tau_{j+2}(\phi(t, t_0, x_0))$, and $x(t) = \phi(t, \theta_{j+1}, x(\theta_{j+1}+))$ on $[\theta_{j+1}, \theta_{j+2}]$. Proceeding in this way one can find the right maximal interval of existence for $x(t)$.

Consider the case (b) now. That is, $t \leq t_0$. The point (t_0, x_0) lies, with a neighborhood, in G_j. By condition (M0), there is the left maximal interval of existence of $\phi(t, t_0, x_0)$. Denote by $(l, t_0]$ the interval. Consider the system

$$\Pi_j z = \phi(t+, t_0, x_0),$$
$$t = \tau_j(z), \tag{5.4}$$

where $\phi(t+, t_0, x_0)$ is the right limit at the moment t, if it exists. If (5.4) is not solvable with respect to $t \in (l, t_0]$ and $z \in G$, and $t \neq \tau_j(\phi(t, t_0, x_0))$ for all t, $l < t \leq t_0$, then $(l, t_0]$ is a left maximal interval of $x(t)$. Otherwise, we denote by s the maximal among numbers t such that $t = \tau_j(\phi(t, t_0, x_0))$ and $t \in (l, t_0]$. Now, if

(5.4) is not solvable with respect to $t \in [s, t_0]$ and $z \in G$, then $(s, t_0]$ is a left maximal interval of $x(t)$. Otherwise, if (5.4) has a solution, (it may have several solutions, and even infinitely many solutions), then choose one of them and denote it by $\theta_j, x(\theta_j)$. We set $x(t) = \phi(t, t_0, x_0)$ for all $t \in (\theta_j, t_0]$. Particularly, $x(\theta_j+) = \phi(\theta_j, t_0, x_0)$. Next, consider the solution $\phi(t, \theta_j, x(\theta_j))$ to the left of $t = \theta_j$. This solution will not meet the surface Γ_j again. (Why?) Let $(l, \theta_j], l \in \mathbb{R}$ or $l = \infty$, be the left maximal interval of existence of $\phi(t, \theta_j, x(\theta_j))$. If $t \neq \tau_{j-1}(\phi(t, \theta_j, x(\theta_j)))$ for all $t, l < t \leq \theta_j$, and the equation

$$\Pi_{j-1} z = \phi(t+, \theta_j, x(\theta_j)),$$
$$t = \tau_{j-1}(z), \tag{5.5}$$

does not have a solution $t \in (l, \theta_j], z \in G$, then $(l, t_0]$ is a left maximal interval of existence of $x(t)$. Otherwise, we denote by s the maximal among numbers t such that $t = \tau_{j-1}(\phi(t, \theta_j, x(\theta_j)))$ and $t \in (l, \theta_j]$. If (5.5) is not solvable with respect to $t, z, t \in [s, t_0]$, then a left maximal interval of existence of $x(t)$ is $(s, t_0]$. Otherwise, (5.5) has solutions, and we choose one of them and denote it by $\theta_{j-1}, x(\theta_{j-1})$. Moreover, $x(t) = \phi(t, \theta_j, x(\theta_j)), t \in (\theta_{j-1}, \theta_j]$. Proceeding the discussion in this way, we shall determine a left maximal interval of $x(t)$.

Unite the left and right maximal intervals to obtain the maximal interval of $x(t)$.

Example 5.2.1. Discuss the problem of a maximal interval of $x(t) = x(t, t_0, x_0)$ if (t_0, x_0) belongs to one of the surfaces Γ_i.

Solution. Fix i such that $t_0 = \tau_i(x_0)$. If t is increasing, and $x_0 + J_i(x_0) \in G$, then the solution starts with the jump $x(t_0+) = x_0 + J_i(x_0)$. So, the solution is continuable to the right, as it was described above, in the case (a). Otherwise, $x_0 + J_i(x_0) \notin G$, and the right end-point of the maximal interval of existence is t_0. If t decreases, then conditions (N1),(N2) imply that the solution exists for $t < t_0$, and the further discussion is the same as that of case (b).

From the last discussion it follows that each solution $x(t)$ of (5.1) is a function from $\mathcal{PC}(J, \theta)$, where J is the interval of existence of this solution, and $\theta \subset J$ is the sequence of discontinuity moments of the solution.

Remark 5.2.1. The moment of intersection of a solution $x(t)$ and a surface Γ_i is a moment of discontinuity. Even if $J_i(x(\theta_i)) = 0$.

Next three assertions are generalized versions of Theorems 2.3.2, 2.3.3, and 2.3.4, and they can be proved easily if one yields the analysis just made above.

Theorem 5.2.1. *(Local existence theorem) Suppose the function $f(t, x)$ is continuous on $I \times G$, and $\Pi_i G \subseteq G, i \in \mathcal{A}$. Then for each $(t_0, x_0) \in I \times G$, there is a number $\alpha > 0$, such that a solution $x(t, t_0, x_0)$ of (5.1) exists in the open interval $(t_0 - \alpha, t_0 + \alpha)$.*

Theorem 5.2.2. *Suppose conditions (M0),(N1)–(N5) are valid. Then each solution of (5.1) has a maximal interval of existence and for this interval the following alternatives are possible:*

(1) it is an open set (α, β) such that any limit point of the set $(t, x(t))$ as t tends to an end point of the maximal interval is a boundary point of $I \times G$;

(2) it is a half-open interval $(\alpha, \beta]$, where $\beta = \tau_j(x(\beta))$ for some $j \in \mathcal{A}$, and any limit point of the set $(t, x(t))$ as $t \to \alpha$ is a boundary point of $I \times G$;

(3) it is a half-open interval $(\alpha, \beta]$, where $\alpha = \tau_i(x(\alpha))$ and $\beta = \tau_j(x(\beta))$ for some $i, j \in \mathcal{A}$. The limit $x(\alpha+)$ exists and it is an interior point of G.

(4) it is an open set (α, β) such that any limit point of the set $(t, x(t))$ as $t \to \beta$ belongs to the boundary of $I \times G, \alpha = \tau_i(x(\alpha))$, the limit $x(\alpha+)$ exists and it is an interior point of G.

In the sequel, the following condition plays an important role.

(N6) If $x(t)$ is a solution of (5.1) and $\theta_j, j \in \mathcal{A}$, is a discontinuity moment, then the system

$$\Pi_{j-1} z = \phi(t+, \theta_j, x(\theta_j)),$$
$$t = \tau_{j-1}(z), \tag{5.6}$$

has at most one solution $(t, z), t < \theta_j, z \in G$. If θ_k is the maximal discontinuity moment of $x(t)$, then the system

$$\Pi_k z = \phi(t+, s, x(s)),$$
$$t = \tau_k(z), \tag{5.7}$$

where $s > \theta_k$, has at most one solution $(t, z), t < s, z \in G$.

Theorem 5.2.3. *(Uniqueness theorem) Suppose $f(t, x)$ satisfies a local Lipschitz condition, and $x(t)$ is a solution of (5.1), which satisfies condition (N6). If $y(t)$ is a solution of (5.1) such that $y(\tau) = x(\tau)$ for some $\tau \in I$, then $x(t) = y(t)$ for all t, where both $x(t)$ and $y(t)$ are defined.*

Exercise 5.2.1. Prove the last three theorems.

Summarizing, one can conclude that the following assertion is valid.

Theorem 5.2.4. *Assume that conditions (M0),(N1)–(N5) are fulfilled. Then every solution $x(t) = x(t, t_0, x_0), (t_0, x_0) \in I \times G$, of (5.1) has a maximal interval of existence. The solution is unique if condition (N6) is valid. The interval is left-open and either right-open or right-closed.*

5.3 Beating Phenomena and Related Properties

The task of investigation of the global behavior of solutions for equations with non-fixed moments of impulses is more complex than that of systems with impulses acting at prescribed moments. A reason for this is the possibility of the 'beating' of solutions against the surfaces of discontinuity.

Let $x(t)$ be a solution of (5.1). Fix an integer j and assume that $x(t)$ meets the surface Γ_j more than once. In other words, assume that equation $t = \tau_j(x(t))$ has several solutions with respect to t. They are not equal to each other. It is obvious that if we try to find an integral equation equivalent to (5.1), then the expression $J_j(x(t))$, where j is fixed, will be involved in that equation more than one time with various values of t. This will create certain difficulties in the analysis, exceptionally if the number of the members is not predictable. The number is important if we analyze stability problems, periodicity of solutions, almost periodicity, etc. That is why it is necessary to find conditions which will provide possibility for solutions to meet the surfaces of discontinuity not more than once, or, more precisely, exactly once. Conditions (N1),(N3) imply that the point $(t, x(t))$ after the first meeting with a surface $t = \tau_i(x)$ jumps inside the region between surfaces $t = \tau_i(x)$ and $t = \tau_{i+1}(x)$. By (N4), the integral curve does not intersect the surface Γ_i again. Obviously, there should be easily verifiable conditions, which guarantee (N4). There exist several results on the subject of absence of beating [63, 142]. We are going to consider simple and effective one, which is useful in applications, and which enables to understand the essence of the phenomena easily.

Let us formulate the following additional conditions:

(N7)
$$\|f(t, x) - f(t, y)\| \le l_f \|x - y\| \quad \text{for all} \quad x, y \in G;$$

(N8)
$$\|J_i(x) - J_i(y)\| \le l_J \|x - y\| \quad \text{for all} \quad i \in \mathcal{A}, x, y \in G;$$

(N9)
$$|\tau_i(x) - \tau_i(y)| \le l_\tau \|x - y\| \quad \text{for all} \quad i \in \mathcal{A}, x, y \in G.$$

In (N7)–(N9), l_f, l_J, l_τ are positive constants.

(N10) The inequality
$$l_\tau M_f < 1$$
is valid, where $M_f = \sup\limits_{(t,x) \in I \times G} \|f(t, x)\| < \infty$.

Lemma 5.3.1. *Suppose the surfaces $\Gamma_i, i \in \mathcal{A}$, and the function $f(t, x)$ satisfy conditions (N9) and (N10). Then conditions (N4) and (N5) are valid.*

Proof. Let us prove that $(N4)$ is valid. Assume on the contrary that there is a solution $\xi(t) = \xi(t, s, c + J_j(c)), c \in G, s = \tau_j(c), j \in \mathcal{A}$, of (5.2), which intersects surface Γ_j at a moment $s_1, s < s_1$. We have that

$$0 < s_1 - s = \tau_j(x(s_1)) - \tau_j(x(s)) \le$$

$$l_\tau \left\| \int_s^{s_1} f(t, \xi(t)) dt \right\| \le M_f l_\tau (s_1 - s).$$

The last inequality contradicts (N9).

Exercise 5.3.1. Prove that (N5) is valid, similarly to that of (N4).

The lemma is proved. □

Lemma 5.3.2. *Assume that conditions (N1) and (N2) are fulfilled and $x(t) : I \rightarrow G$ is a solution of (5.1). Then $x(t)$ intersects every surface $\Gamma_i, i \in \mathcal{A}$.*

Proof. Assume on the contrary that $x(t)$ does not intersect Γ_j for some $j \in \mathcal{A}$. Condition (N1) implies, without loss of generality, that we may assume the surface as a unique surface of discontinuity. In other words, $\mathcal{A} = \{j\}$. Introduce a new function $r(t) = t - \tau_j(x(t))$. As (N2) is valid, there exist $\alpha, \beta, \alpha < \alpha_j \leq \beta_j < \beta$, such that $r(\alpha) < 0 < r(\beta)$, and by the continuity of $r(t)$ there exists a point $\zeta \in (\alpha, \beta)$ such that $r(\zeta) = 0$. That is, $\zeta = \tau_j(x(\zeta))$. The lemma is proved. □

Using the last two lemmas one can formulate the following assertion.

Theorem 5.3.1. *Assume that conditions (N1)–(N3), (N8), and (N9) are fulfilled. Then every solution $x(t) : I \rightarrow G$ of (5.1) intersects each of the surfaces $\Gamma_i, i \in \mathcal{A}$ exactly once.*

Besides the last theorem the following general assertion can be formulated.

Theorem 5.3.2. *Assume that conditions (N1)–(N4) are fulfilled. Then every solution $x(t) : I \rightarrow G$ of (5.1) intersects each of the surfaces $\Gamma_i, i \in \mathcal{A}$, exactly once.*

Remark 5.3.1. In this book we discuss only systems, which satisfy conditions of absence of the beating, that is, each solution of a system intersects every surface of discontinuity not more than once.

Exercise 5.3.2. Solve the following problems.

1. Consider the impulsive system

$$x' = 0,$$
$$\Delta x|_{t=i+l|x|} = -\frac{1}{2}x, \qquad (5.8)$$

where $t, x \in \mathbb{R}, i \in \mathbb{Z}, l$ is a fixed positive number. Prove that there is no beating of solutions against the surfaces of discontinuity.

2. Let a solution $\phi(t) : I \rightarrow G, \phi(t_0) = x_0$, of (5.1) intersects each of the surfaces $\Gamma_i, i \in \mathcal{A}$, exactly once at the moment $t = \theta_i$. Prove that

$$\phi(t) = \begin{cases} x_0 + \int\limits_{t_0}^{t} f(s, \phi(s))ds + \sum\limits_{t_0 \leq \theta_i < t} J_i(\phi(\theta_i)), & t \geq t_0, \\ x_0 + \int\limits_{t_0}^{t} f(s, \phi(s))ds - \sum\limits_{t \leq \theta_i < t_0} J_i(\phi(\theta_i)), & t < t_0. \end{cases} \qquad (5.9)$$

3. Assume that conditions of Theorem 5.3.1 are valid and a function $\phi(t) : I \rightarrow G$ satisfies (5.9), where θ_i are all points of I such that $\theta_i = \tau_i(\phi(\theta_i))$. Prove that $\phi(t)$ is a solution of (5.1) on I.

On the basis of results of the last two exercises, one can formulate the following assertion.

Theorem 5.3.3. *Assume that conditions (N1)–(N5) are fulfilled. A function* $x(t)$:
$I \to G, x(t_0) = x_0, (t_0, x_0) \in I \times G,$ *with the sequence of discontinuity moments*
$\{\theta_i\} \subset I, i \in \mathcal{A},$ *is a solution of (5.1) on* I *if and only if it satisfies the following integral equation:*

$$x(t) = \begin{cases} x_0 + \int\limits_{t_0}^{t} f(s, x(s))ds + \sum\limits_{t_0 \le \theta_i < t} J_i(x(\theta_i)), & t \ge t_0, \\ x_0 + \int\limits_{t_0}^{t} f(s, x(s))ds - \sum\limits_{t \le \theta_i < t_0} J_i(x(\theta_i)), & t < t_0. \end{cases} \tag{5.10}$$

Remark 5.3.2. Obviously, that investigation of the system (5.1) through integral equations (5.10) is a complex work as the moments of discontinuity are not prescribed. In the next sections, we provide a method which will help to investigate (5.1) on the basis of an integral equation.

Theorem 5.3.4. *Assume that conditions (N8),(N9) are fulfilled and*

$$l_J < 1, \qquad M_f l_\tau < 1 - l_J. \tag{5.11}$$

Then (N6) is valid.

Proof. Assume on the contrary that (N6) is not valid for a solution $x(t)$ and some $j \in \mathcal{A}$. Then there exist vectors $z_1, z_2, z_1 \ne z_2$, and moments $t_1, t_2, t_2 \ge t_1$, such that $z_1 + J_j(z_1) = x(t_1), t_1 = \tau_j(z_1),$ and $z_2 + J_j(z_2) = x(t_2), t_2 = \tau_j(z_2).$ If $t_2 > t_1,$ then

$$\|z_1 - z_2\|(1 - l_J) \le \|z_1 - z_2 + J_j(z_1) - J_j(z_2)\| = \|\int_{\tau_j(z_1)}^{\tau_j(z_2)} f(s, x(s))ds\|$$
$$\le l_\tau M_f \|z_1 - z_2\|.$$

The last inequality contradicts (5.11). If $t_2 = t_1,$ then

$$\|z_1 - z_2\|(1 - l_J) \le \|z_1 - z_2 + J_j(z_1) - J_j(z_2)\| = \|x(t_1) - x(t_2)\| = 0.$$

We have another contradiction. The theorem is proved. □

5.4   The Topology on the Set of Discontinuous Functions

A difficulty of investigation of system (5.1) is that the moments of discontinuity of distinct solutions do not, in general, coincide. To investigate neighborhoods of solutions of differential equations with impulses at variable moments, we introduce the following concepts of closeness for piecewise continuous functions. Various metrics and topologies for discontinuous functions are described in [7, 32, 75, 90, 142, 147].

Denote by $\widehat{[a,b]}, a, b \in \mathbb{R}$, the interval $[a, b]$, whenever $a \leq b$ and $[b, a]$, otherwise.

Definition 5.4.1. Solutions $x_1(t) \in \mathcal{PC}(T_1, \theta^1)$ and $x_2(t) \in \mathcal{PC}(T_2, \theta^2)$ are said to be ϵ-equivalent if:

(1) the measure of the symmetric difference of the domains T_1 and T_2 does not exceed ϵ;
(2) $|\theta_i^1 - \theta_i^2| < \epsilon$ for all i;
(3) the inequality $\|x_1(t) - x_2(t)\| < \epsilon$ is valid for all t, which satisfy $t \notin \widehat{[\theta_i^1, \theta_i^2]}$ for all i.

Definition 5.4.2. A solution $x_1(t)$ is in the ϵ-neighborhood, $\epsilon > 0$, of a solution $x_2(t) \in \mathcal{PC}(T_2, \theta^2)$, if either it is continuable on an interval T_1, or can be restricted to an interval, such that the two are ϵ-equivalent.

If $x_1(t)$ and $x_2(t)$ are ϵ-equivalent then $x_1(t)$ is in the ϵ-neighborhood of $x_2(t)$, and vice versa.

The equivalence of two piecewise continuous functions, when ϵ is small, means roughly that they have close discontinuity points, and the values of the functions are close at points that do not lie on intervals between the corresponding discontinuity points of these functions.

The topology defined with the aid of ϵ-neighborhoods is called the B-topology. One can easily see that it is Hausdorff and it can be considered also if two solutions x_1 and x_2 are defined on a semi-axis or on the entire real axis.

5.5 B-Equivalence: General Case

Consider (5.1), assuming that conditions (N1)–(N3), (N7)–(N10), are valid, $\tau_i(x) = \theta_i + \kappa_i(x)$, with $|\kappa_i(x)| < \nu$, for some positive number ν and for all $x \in G, i \in \mathcal{A}$. Fix a number i. Let $x_0(t), x_0(\theta_i) = x$, be a solution of the system

$$x' = f(t, x). \tag{5.12}$$

Denote by ξ_i the meeting moment of the solution with the surface of discontinuity so that $\xi_i = \theta_i + \kappa_i(x_0(\xi_i))$. Let also, $x_1(t)$ be a solution of (5.12) such that $x_1(\xi_i) = x_0(\xi_i) + J_i(x_0(\xi_i))$. Assume that it exists on the interval $\widehat{[\theta_i, \xi_i]}$ and define the following map (see Fig. 5.2),

$$W_i(x) = \int_{\theta_i}^{\xi_i} f(u, x_0(u))du + J_i(x + \int_{\theta_i}^{\xi_i} f(u, x_0(u))du) +$$
$$\int_{\xi_i}^{\theta_i} f(u, x_1(u))du. \tag{5.13}$$

The map W_i defined for each i is called the B-map.

Fig. 5.2 Construction
of the map W_i

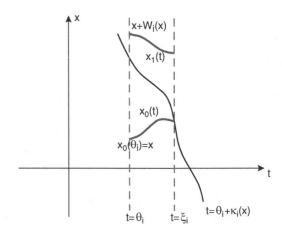

Beside (5.1) consider the following system:

$$x' = f(t, x),$$
$$\Delta x|_{t=\theta_i} = W_i(x). \tag{5.14}$$

We say that systems (5.1) and (5.14) are *B-equivalent* in $G \subset \mathbb{R}^n$ if there exists a set $G_1 \subset G$ such that for each solution $x(t)$ of (5.1) defined on an interval U, with discontinuity moments ξ_i and $x(t) \in G_1, t \in U$, there exists a solution $y(t) : U \to G$ of (5.14), satisfying

$$x(t) = y(t), t \notin \widehat{(\xi_i, \theta_i]} \tag{5.15}$$

if $\xi_i \neq \theta_i$, and

$$x(\xi_i) = y(\theta_i) \tag{5.16}$$

if $\xi_i = \theta_i$, for all i. In particular,

$$x(\theta_i) = y(\theta_i+), x(\xi_i) = y(\xi_i) \text{ if } \theta_i > \xi_i, \tag{5.17}$$

$$x(\theta_i) = y(\theta_i), x(\xi_i+) = y(\xi_i) \text{ if } \theta_i < \xi_i. \tag{5.18}$$

Conversely, for each solution $y(t)$ of (5.14) with $y(t) \in G_1, t \in U$, there exists a solution $x(t), t \in U$, of (5.1) such that (5.15)–(5.18) are valid.

Remark 5.5.1. To define W_i it is sufficient if the solution $x_1(t)$ is defined on the left-open interval $\widehat{(\theta_i, \xi_i]}$.

Suppose

$$\sup_{I \times G} \| f(t, x) \| + \sup_{\mathcal{A} \times G} \| J_i(x) \| = M < \infty. \tag{5.19}$$

Fix a vector $x_0 \in G$, and real positive numbers $h, H = h + vM, \bar{H} = h + (1 + 2v)M$. We assume that the set $\|x - x_0\| \leq \bar{H}$ is included in G.

Theorem 5.5.1. *Suppose (5.1) satisfies all conditions listed above. Then:*

(1) functions $W_i, i \in \mathcal{A}$, are defined on the set $G_h = \{x \in \mathbb{R}^n : \|x - x_0\| \leq h\}$;
(2) for arbitrary $x, y \in G_h$ and every $i \in \mathcal{A}$ it is true that

$$\|W_i(x) - W_i(y)\| \leq k(l_f, l_J, l_\tau)\|x - y\|, \tag{5.20}$$

where

$$k(l_f, l_J, l_\tau) = l_f v[(1 + l_J)e^{vl_f} + e^{2vl_f}(1 + l_J(1 - Ml_\tau))(1 - Ml_\tau)^{-1}] +$$

$$l_J + l_\tau(2 + l_J)e^{vl_f}M(1 - Ml_\tau)^{-1};$$

(3) systems (5.1) and (5.14) are B-equivalent in $G_H = \{x \in \mathbb{R}^n : \|x - x_0\| \leq H\}$, such that if a solution of (5.1) or (5.14) get values in G_h, then the corresponding solution get values in G_H.

Proof. Fix i, and let $x_0(t)$ and $x_1(t)$ be solutions of (5.12), which are mentioned in (5.13). We have

$$x_0(t) = x + \int_{\theta_i}^t f(u, x_0(u))du, \quad t \in [\widehat{\theta_i, \xi_i}].$$

Assuming $x \in G_h$, and then using the last equation one can find that $\|x_0(t) - x_0\| < h + vM = H$, if $t \in [\widehat{\theta_i, \xi_i}]$. Similarly, one check that $\|x_1(t) - x_0\| < \bar{H}$. Thus, W_i is defined on G_h and part (1) of the theorem is proved. □

We fix $y \in G_h$, and next, determine $W_i(y)$. Denote by $y_0(t), y_0(\theta_i) = y$, the solution of (5.12), and η_i the meeting moment of $y_0(t)$ with Γ_i. Let $y_1(t)$ be the solution of (5.12), which satisfies $y_1(\eta_i) = y_0(\eta_i) + J_i(y_0(\eta_i)), t \in [\theta_i, \eta_i]$. Then

$$W_i(y) = \int_{\theta_i}^{\eta_i} f(u, y_0(u))du + J_i(y + \int_{\theta_i}^{\eta_i} f(u, y_0(u))du) +$$

$$\int_{\eta_i}^{\theta_i} f(u, y_1(u))du. \tag{5.21}$$

Without loss of generality assume that $\theta_i \leq \xi_i \leq \eta_i$. Using the Gronwall–Bellman Lemma, one can find that

$$\|x_0(t) - y_0(t)\| \leq e^{vl_f}\|x - y\|, \tag{5.22}$$

if $t \in [\theta_i, \xi_i]$. Then, applying (5.22) and condition (N10) we obtain

$$\eta_i - \xi_i \leq l_\tau e^{vl_f}(1 - Ml_\tau)^{-1}\|x - y\|. \tag{5.23}$$

Moreover, using definition of solutions x_1 and y_1, we get that

$$\|x_1(t) - y_1(t)\| \le e^{2\nu l_f}(1 + l_J(1 - Ml_\tau))(1 - Ml_\tau)^{-1}\|x - y\|, \qquad (5.24)$$

if $t \in [\theta_i, \xi_i]$.

Now, subtracting (5.21) from (5.13) yields

$$W_i(x) - W_i(y) = \int_{\theta_i}^{\xi_i} f(u, x_0(u))du - \int_{\theta_i}^{\eta_i} f(u, y_0(u))du +$$

$$J_i\left(x + \int_{\theta_i}^{\xi_i} f(u, x_0(u))du\right) - J_i\left(y + \int_{\theta_i}^{\eta_i} f(u, y_0(u))du\right) +$$

$$\int_{\xi_i}^{\theta_i} f(u, x_1(u))du - \int_{\eta_i}^{\theta_i} f(u, y_1(u))du =$$

$$\int_{\theta_i}^{\xi_i} [f(u, x_0(u)) - f(u, y_0(u))]du + \int_{\xi_i}^{\eta_i} f(u, y_0(u))du +$$

$$J_i\left(x + \int_{\theta_i}^{\xi_i} f(u, x_0(u))du\right) - J_i\left(y + \int_{\theta_i}^{\eta_i} f(u, y_0(u))du\right) +$$

$$\int_{\theta_i}^{\xi_i} [f(u, x_1(u)) - f(u, y_1(u))]du + \int_{\xi_i}^{\eta_i} f(u, y_1(u))du,$$

and, using (5.22)–(5.24), we have that

$$\|W_i(x) - W_i(y)\| \le \int_{\theta_i}^{\xi_i} \|f(u, x_0(u)) - f(u, y_0(u))\|du + \int_{\xi_i}^{\eta_i} \|f(u, y_0(u))\|du +$$

$$l_J[\|x - y\| + \int_{\theta_i}^{\xi_i} \|f(u, x_0(u)) - f(u, y_0(u))\|du + \int_{\xi_i}^{\eta_i} \|f(u, y_0(u))\|du] +$$

$$\int_{\theta_i}^{\xi_i} \|f(u, x_1(u)) - f(u, y_1(u))\|du + \int_{\xi_i}^{\eta_i} \|f(u, y_1(u))\|du \le$$

$$\int_{\theta_i}^{\xi_i} l_f\|x_0(u) - y_0(u)\|du + M(\eta_i - \xi_i) + l_J[\|x - y\|$$

$$+ \int_{\theta_i}^{\xi_i} l_f\|x_0(u) - y_0(u)\|du + M(\eta_i - \xi_i)] +$$

$$\int_{\theta_i}^{\xi_i} l_f\|x_1(u) - y_1(u)\|du + M(\eta_i - \xi_i) \le k(l_f, l_J, l_\tau)\|x - y\|.$$

That is, (5.20) is valid. B-equivalence of the systems follows immediately from the definition of W_i.

Now, let us prove that $x(t) \in G_h, t \in I$, implies $y(t) \in G_H, t \in I$. Indeed, for all $t \notin \widehat{[\xi_i, \eta_i]}$, we have $y(t) = x(t)$. Hence, it is sufficient to consider an interval $\widehat{[\xi_i, \eta_i]}$, for some fixed i. Assume, for the sake of simplicity, that $\xi_i < \eta_i$. Then $y(\xi_i) = x(\xi_i)$ and $y(t) = x(\xi_i) + \int_{\xi_i}^t f(u, y(u)) du, t \in (\xi_i, \eta_i]$. Finally,

$$\|y(t)\| \leq \|x(\xi_i)\| + \int_{\xi_i}^t M du \leq h + Mv = H,$$

if $t \in (\xi_i, \eta_i]$.

Similarly one can check that $y(t) \in G_h, t \in I$, implies $x(t) \in G_H$, for all $t \in I$. The theorem is proved. □

Exercise 5.5.1. Interpret results of the last theorem with $v = 0$ and $l_\tau = 0$: evaluate $k(l_f, l_J, l_\tau)$ and W_i.

Example 5.5.1. Determine a B-equivalent system for the following impulsive equation:

$$x' = 2x,$$
$$\Delta x|_{t \neq i + x} = -\sin^2(x), \tag{5.25}$$

where $t, x \in \mathbb{R}, i \in \mathbb{Z}$.

Solution. Fix $i \in \mathbb{Z}$. We have that $x_0(t) = x(t, i, x) = xe^{2(t-i)}$ is a solution of

$$x' = 2x. \tag{5.26}$$

The moment of intersection of this solution with the line $t = i + x$ has to be found from $t = i + xe^{2(t-i)}$. It is equal to $\zeta_i = i + \phi(x)$, where $u = \phi(x)$ is an implicit function such that

$$u = xe^{2u}. \tag{5.27}$$

One can easily see that ϕ is a continuously differentiable function. Thus, we have that $x_0(\zeta_i) = xe^{2\phi(x)}$. Similarly, one can evaluate the solution $x_1(t) = x(t, \zeta_i, x_0(\zeta_i) - \sin^2(x_0(\zeta_i))) = (x_0(\zeta_i) - \sin^2(x_0(\zeta_i)))e^{2(t-\zeta_i)}$ of (5.26). Finally, one can find that $W_i(x) = x_1(i) - x = -\sin^2(xe^{2\phi(x)}))e^{-2\phi(x)}$, and the equivalent system is

$$y' = 2y,$$
$$\Delta y|_{t \neq i} = -\sin^2(ye^{2\phi(y)})e^{-2\phi(y)}. \tag{5.28}$$

Remark 5.5.2. The method of investigation of qualitative properties of a differential equation by a reduction to a more simple system is very fruitful for any kind of equations. One can mention, for instance, the Floquet–Lyapunov transformation of linear periodic systems, or the method of the first approximation, which not necessarily must be the approximation by a linear system. Generally speaking, the B-equivalence considered in our book is a first approximation. To describe our approach better, let us start with a more general case. Consider beside system (5.1), another one,

$$
\begin{aligned}
y' &= g(t, y), \\
\Delta y|_{t \neq \upsilon_i(y)} &= W_i(y).
\end{aligned} \tag{5.29}
$$

Assuming that system (5.29) has a specified quality, and differences $f - g$, $\upsilon - \tau$, $W - J$, are small in some sense, one may make conclusion about that property for system (5.1). One can call (5.29) a *first approximation system*. If we restrict ourself on asymptotic features of the equation, then one can say about *comparison method* for systems (5.1) and (5.29) as usually it is named for ordinary differential equations. We shall use the first approximation systems not only to investigate asymptotic properties but also for periodic and bounded solutions, smoothness of solutions, and even chaotic behavior of discontinuous dynamics. Since the equations with fixed moments of impulses have been well-investigated, it is beneficial to use them for the approximation. Moreover, we suppose that it will be possible to consider approximations of higher order in future. So, it is natural to call the approach the method of reduction to systems with fixed moments of impulses.

Assume that $\upsilon_i(y) \equiv \theta_i$ in (5.29), where θ_i is a sequence of ordered real numbers, and consider the following equation:

$$
\begin{aligned}
y' &= g(t, y), \\
\Delta y|_{t \neq \theta_i} &= W_i(y).
\end{aligned} \tag{5.30}
$$

Let us show, how one may choose the sequence θ. If (5.1) has the zero solution, then $\theta_i = \tau_i(0)$. If one investigates stability of a solution $\phi(t)$ of (5.1), then it is convenient to set the moments of discontinuity of this solution as θ_i, and rewrite the surfaces of discontinuity as $\tau_i(x) = \theta_i + \kappa_i(x)$, where $\kappa_i(x) = \tau_i(x) - \theta_i$.

5.6 Continuity Properties

In this section, we discuss the continuous dependence by using the B-equivalence method and the topology in the set of piecewise continuous functions.

Consider system (5.1) on the set $\Omega = I \times \mathcal{A} \times G$ of points (t, i, x), where $G \subset \mathbb{R}^n$ is an open and connected set, I is an open interval in $\mathbb{R}$, and $\mathcal{A}$ is an interval in $\mathbb{Z}$. Denote by $\tilde{I} = [a, b] \subset I$ a closed finite interval and fix it. Let $x(t)$ be a solution of (5.1) such that $x(t) : \tilde{I} \to G$, $x(t_0) = x_0$, $(t_0, x_0) \in \tilde{I} \times G$, and let $\theta_i, i = m, \dots, k$, be moments of discontinuity of the solution, that is, $\theta_i = \tau_i(x(\theta_i)), i = m, \dots, k$. Assume that for all $x \in G, a < \tau_m(x) < \dots < \tau_k(x) < b$, and denote $G_i = \{(t, x) : \tau_i(x) < t \leq \tau_{i+1}(x), x \in G\}, i = m, \dots, k - 1, G_{m-1} = \{(t, x) : a < t \leq \tau_m(x), x \in G\}, G_k = \{(t, x) : \tau_k(x) < t \leq b, x \in G\}$. The conditions imply that there are small neighborhoods of points $(\theta_i, x(\theta_i))$, where the surfaces of discontinuity have the form $\tau_i(x) = \theta_i + \kappa_i(x)$, where $\kappa_i(x) = \tau_i(x) - \theta_i$ and $\kappa_i(x(\theta_i)) = 0$. There exists a positive number ν such that $|\kappa_i(x)| < \nu$ for all i, and the number ν is arbitrary small if the neighborhoods are chosen sufficiently small. Thus, we can claim that all conditions of the last section needed for the reduction to the system with fixed moments of impulses, that is, $\theta_i, i \in \mathcal{A}$, are valid.

Let $D(t_0, \delta) = \{(t_0, x) : \|x - x_0\| < \delta\}$ be a disc centered at (t_0, x_0), and $d(x_0, \delta) = \{(t, x_0) : t_0 - \delta < t < t_0 + \delta\}$ be an interval centered at (t_0, x_0) with the radius $\delta > 0$. Fix a number j such that $(t_0, x_0) \in G_j$. We shall need the following definitions.

Definition 5.6.1. The solution $x(t)$ of (5.1) continuously depends on x_0 if for an arbitrary $\epsilon > 0$ there exists $\delta > 0$ such that any other solution $\tilde{x}(t)$ of (5.1) is in the ϵ-neighborhood of $x(t)$, as soon as $(t_0, \tilde{x}(t_0)) \in D(t_0, \delta) \cap G_j$.

Definition 5.6.2. The solution $x(t)$ of (5.1) continuously depends on t_0 if to any $\epsilon > 0$ there corresponds $\delta > 0$ such that any other solution $\tilde{x}(t), \tilde{x}(\tilde{t}_0) = x_0$, of (5.1) is in the ϵ-neighborhood of $x(t)$, as soon as $(\tilde{t}_0, x_0) \in d(x_0, \delta) \cap G_j$.

Using Theorems 2.7.1, 2.7.2, and reduction to the equation with fixed moments of impulses, one can easily prove that the following assertions, Theorems 5.6.1–5.6.4, are valid.

Theorem 5.6.1. *Suppose conditions (N1)–(N3), (N7)–(N10), are fulfilled. Then the solution $x(t)$ of (5.1) continuously depends on t_0 and x_0, if $t_0 = a$.*

Theorem 5.6.2. *Suppose conditions (N1)–(N3), (N7)–(N10), (5.11) are fulfilled, and $k(l_f, l_J, l_\tau) < 1$. Then each solution $x(t) = x(t, t_0, x_0), (t_0, x_0) \in I \times G$, of (5.1) is continuous in t_0 and x_0 on each closed finite interval, where it is defined.*

Remark 5.6.1. Conditions $(t_0, \tilde{x}_0) \in D(t_0, \delta) \cap G_j$ and $(\tilde{t}_0, x_0) \in d(x_0, \delta) \cap G_j$ in Definitions 5.6.1 and 5.6.2 are important. That is, assumptions $(t_0, \tilde{x}_0) \in D(t_0, \delta)$ or $(\tilde{t}_0, x_0) \in d(x_0, \delta)$ are not sufficient for the constructive description of the dependence. Indeed, consider the following simple system,

$$x' = 0,$$
$$\Delta x|_{t=x^{1/2}} = -5, \tag{5.31}$$

where $x, t \in \mathbb{R}$. Fix solutions $x(t) = x(t, 2, 4)$ and $x_1(t) = x(t, 2, 4 - \kappa), 0 < \kappa < 4$. One can easily see that the distance between $x(t)$ and $x_1(t)$ near $t = 2$ tends to 5 as $\kappa \to 0$.

Exercise 5.6.1. Show that the solution $x(t) = x(t, 2, 4)$ of (5.31) is continuously dependent on the initial value in the sense of Definition 5.6.1.

The last example demonstrates that a careful analysis of 'closeness' of solutions must be done, if one considers equations with variable moments of impulses. We must be attentive exceptionally, if one considers continuous dependence of a solution on the right-hand side.

Beside the (5.1), consider another system

$$x' = f(t, x) + \phi(t, x),$$
$$\Delta x|_{t=\tau_i(x)+\omega_i(x)} = J_i(x) + V_i(x), \tag{5.32}$$

where functions ϕ, ω, and V are all continuous.

Definition 5.6.3. The solution $x(t)$ of (5.1) continuously depends on the right-hand side of the equation if for an arbitrary $\epsilon > 0$ there exists $\delta > 0$ such that every solution $y(t) = y(t, t_0, x_0)$, of (5.32) is in the ϵ-neighborhood of $x(t)$, whenever $\|\phi(t, x)\| < \delta, \|V_i(x)\| < \delta, |\omega_i(x)| < \delta$ for all t, i, x.

Theorem 5.6.3. *Suppose (N1)–(N3),(N7)–(N9), and inequalities (5.11), are fulfilled, $k(l_f, l_J, l_\tau) < 1$, and functions g, W, ω satisfy $\|g(t, x) - g(t, y)\| + \|W_i(x) - W_i(y)\| + |\omega_i(x) - \omega_i(y)| \leq l_2 \|x - y\|$, where l_2 is a positive constant, for all $x, y \in G$ and $(t, i) \in I \times \mathcal{A}, \omega_i(x) \geq 0$ if $i \geq j$, and $\omega_i(x) \leq 0$ if $i < j$, for all $x \in G$. Then the solution $x(t)$ of (5.1) continuously depends on the right-hand side of the equation.*

Theorem 5.6.4. *Suppose (N1)–(N3),(N7)–(N9), and inequalities (5.11), are fulfilled, $k(l_f, l_J, l_\tau) < 1$, and functions g, W, ω are such that $\omega_i(x) \equiv 0, \|g(t, x) - g(t, y)\| + \|W_i(x) - W_i(y)\| \leq l_2 \|x - y\|$, where l_2 is a positive constant, for all $x, y \in G, (t, i) \in I \times \mathcal{A}$. Then each solution $x(t) = x(t, t_0, x_0), (t_0, x_0) \in I \times G$, of (5.1) continuously depends on the right-hand side of the equation on each closed finite interval, where it is defined.*

Exercise 5.6.2. Prove Theorems 5.6.3 and 5.6.4.

Remark 5.6.2. There exists another way of investigation of the continuity in parameters and the right-hand side. Indeed, if we suppose that conditions (N1)–(N3),(N7)–(N9), and inequalities (5.11) are fulfilled, and maps Π_i are homeomorphisms on G for all i, then one can prove that the continuous dependence on initial conditions of the solution $x(t)$ presents.

5.7 Generalities of Stability

Let us consider system (5.1) again, and assume that conditions (N1)–(N4) are valid, and $I = [0, \infty), \mathcal{A} = \{1, 2, \ldots\}, 0 < \tau_1(x) < \tau_2(x) < \ldots$. Let $x(t)$ be a solution of (5.1) such that $x(t) : [0, \infty) \to G$. Denote $G_0 = \{(t, x) : 0 \leq t \leq \tau_1(x), x \in G\}$, and $G_i, i \geq 1$, has the sense assigned above, that is, $G_i = \{(t, x) : \tau_i(x) < t \leq \tau_{i+1}(x), x \in G\}, i \geq 1$. Moreover, let $D(t_0, \delta) = \{(t_0, x) : \|x - x(t_0)\| < \delta\}$, where $t_0 \in I$ is fixed, be the disc with the center at $(t_0, x(t_0))$ and the radius $\delta > 0$. If $(t_0, x(t_0)) \in I \times G$, then it belongs to some $G_j, j \geq 0$. Fix this j.

Definition 5.7.1. The solution $x(t)$ is said to be B-stable if to any $\epsilon > 0$ there corresponds $\delta(t_0, \epsilon) > 0$ such that any other solution $y(t)$ is in the ϵ-neighborhood of $x(t)$ on $[t_0, \infty)$, as soon as $(t_0, y(t_0)) \in D(t_0, \delta) \cap G_j$.

Definition 5.7.2. The solution $x(t)$ is said to be uniformly B-stable if δ from Definition 5.7.1 can be chosen independently of $t_0 \in I$.

Definition 5.7.3. The solution $x(t)$ is called B-asymptotically stable, if it is B-stable, and there is $\nu > 0$ such that to any $\epsilon > 0$ there corresponds $t_1(\epsilon) > 0$ such that any other solution $y(t)$ is in the ϵ-neighborhood of $x(t)$ on $[t_0 + t_1, \infty)$, as soon as $(t_0, y(t_0)) \in D(t_0, \nu) \cap G_j$.

Definition 5.7.4. The solution $x(t)$ is called uniformly B-asymptotically stable, if it is uniformly B-stable, and the numbers ν and t_1 from the last definition can be chosen independently of $t_0 \in I$.

The reader can see that the last definitions can be easily transformed to definitions of stability for equations with fixed moments of impulses in Sect. 3.1, if $\tau_i(x) \equiv \theta_i = const, i \geq 1$. Moreover, they are essentially different from those of ordinary differential equations.

Example 5.7.1. Consider the following scalar system (scalar, since the variable x is one-dimensional, and a system, since it consists of two equations)

$$x' = 0,$$
$$\Delta x|_{t=x} = -1, \tag{5.33}$$

where $t, x \in \mathbb{R}$. It has a unique surface of discontinuity $\Gamma = \{(t, x) : t = x\}$. Consider solution $x(t) = x(t, 1, 1)$. Since $(1, 1) \in \Gamma$, it starts with a jump so that $x(1+) = 0$, and $x(t) \equiv 0$ on $(1, \infty)$. Let $x_1(t) = x(t, 1, z)$, be another solution, with $z < 1$. The initial value, z, can be chosen arbitrarily close to 1, but the solution does not have a jump for $t \geq 1$, and $x_1(t) \equiv z$ on $[1, \infty)$. So, we have paradoxical situation: the closer z to 1, the larger the distance between $x(t)$ and $x_1(t)$ on $(1, \infty)$. Despite the system has "good" properties. The reason of this awkward state of deal is that $x(t)$ starts on the surface of discontinuity. Hence the initial conditions for the stability discussion should be chosen more carefully. In this example, the neighbor (t_0, y_0) must be taken such that $y_0 \geq t_0$.

Consider now, beside (5.1), the perturbed system (5.32) again.

Definition 5.7.5. The solution $x(t)$ of (5.1) is totally stable (or stable under persistent disturbances), if given $\epsilon > 0$ one can find $\delta > 0$ such that if $(t_0, x(t_0)) \notin \Gamma_i$, and $\|\phi(t, x)\| < \delta, \|V_i(x)\| < \delta, |\omega_i(x)| < \delta$ for all t, i, x, then $y(t), y(t_0) = x(t_0)$, a solution of (5.32), is in the ϵ-neighborhood of $x(t)$ on $[t_0, \infty)$.

We have special circumstances, when discussing stability of the zero solution. Assume that $f(t, 0) = 0, J_i(0) = 0$, for all $i \geq 1$ in (5.1), and consider the following definitions.

Definition 5.7.6. The zero solution of (5.1) is stable if to any $\epsilon > 0$ and $t_0 \in I$, there corresponds $\delta(t_0, \epsilon) > 0$ such that if $\psi(t)$ is a solution of (5.1) with $||\psi(t_0)|| < \delta(t_0, \epsilon)$, then $||\psi(t)|| < \epsilon$ for $t \geq t_0$.

Definition 5.7.7. The zero solution is uniformly stable, if the δ in the last definition is independent of t_0.

Definition 5.7.8. The zero solution is asymptotically stable if it is stable and if there exists $v(t_0) > 0$ such that if $\psi(t)$ is a solution of (5.1) with $||\psi(t_0)|| < v(t_0)$, then $||\psi(t)|| \to 0$ as $t \to \infty$.

Definition 5.7.9. The zero solution is uniformly asymptotically stable if it is uniformly stable, and to any positive ϵ there corresponds $T(\epsilon) > 0$ such that if $\psi(t)$ is a solution of (5.1) with $||\psi(t_0)|| < \gamma_0$, γ_0 is independent of t_0, then $||\psi(t)|| < \epsilon$, for all $t \geq t_0 + T(\epsilon)$.

Definition 5.7.10. The zero solution is asymptotically stable in large if it is asymptotically stable and each solution $\psi(t)$ satisfies $\psi(t) \to 0$ as $t \to \infty$.

Definition 5.7.11. The zero solution is unstable at $t_0 \in I$ if there exists a number $\epsilon_0 > 0$ such that to any $\delta > 0$ there corresponds a solution $y_\delta(t)$, $||y_\delta(t_0)|| < \delta$, of (5.1) such that either the solution is not continuable to ∞ or there exists a moment $t_1, t_1 > t_0$ with $||y_\delta(t_1)|| \geq \epsilon_0$.

Example 5.7.2. Prove that the zero solution of the system

$$x' = kx,$$
$$\Delta x|_{t \neq i + x} = -x^2, \tag{5.34}$$

where $t, x \in \mathbb{R}, i \in \mathbb{Z}$, is asymptotically stable, if the constant k is a negative real number.

Solution. First, we construct a system, which is B-equivalent to (5.34) on $\mathbb{R}$. Fix $i \in \mathbb{Z}$. We have that $x_0(t) = x(t, i, x) = xe^{k(t-i)}$, the solution of

$$x' = kx. \tag{5.35}$$

Consider the equation $t = i + xe^{k(t-i)}$ to find the intersection moment of $x_0(t)$ with the surface $t = i + x$. It is equal to $\zeta_i = i + \phi(x)$, where $u = \phi(x)$ is an implicit function defined by the equation

$$u = xe^{ku}. \tag{5.36}$$

Thus, $x_0(\zeta_i) = xe^{k\phi(x)}$. Similarly, $x_1(t) = x(t, \zeta_i, x_0(\zeta_i) - x_0^2(\zeta_i)) = (x_0(\zeta_i) - x_0^2(\zeta_i))e^{k(t-\zeta_i)}$. Now, $W_i(x) = x_1(i) - x = -x^2e^{k\phi(x)}$, and the equivalent system has the form

$$y' = -2y,$$
$$\Delta y|_{t \neq i} = -y^2 e^{k\phi(y)}. \tag{5.37}$$

One can easily see that ϕ is a continuously differentiable function and, consequently, W_i are smooth functions. It is easily seen that $W_i(0) = 0$. Hence, for $h > 0$ there exists a Lipschitz constant $l(h) > 0, l(h) \to 0$, as $h \to 0$. For an arbitrary solution $y(t) = y(t, t_0, y_0)$ of (5.37) one has that

$$y(t) = e^{k(t-t_0)}y_0 + \Sigma_{t_0 \le i < t} W_i(y(i)).$$

By using the Gronwall–Bellman Lemma for discontinuous functions, we have that

$$|y(t)| \le |y_0|e^{k(t-t_0)} \Pi_{t_0 \le i < t}(1 + l(h)).$$

The last inequality implies immediately that the zero solution is asymptotically stable if $k + \ln(1 + l(h)) < 0$. The truth of the last inequality is obvious if h is sufficiently small.

5.8 B-Equivalence: Quasilinear Systems

In this section, we want to see the use of the reduction method for investigation of the following system with impulse actions:

$$\frac{dx}{dt} = A(t)x + f(t, x),$$
$$\Delta x|_{t=\theta_i + \tau_i(x)} = B_i x + I_i(x), \tag{5.38}$$

where $t \in \mathbb{R}, x \in \mathbb{R}^n, \theta = \{\theta_i\}, i \in \mathbb{Z}$, is a B-sequence, the entries of the $n \times n$ matrix $A(t)$ are continuous real valued functions, B_i are real valued square matrices of order n, and $\tau_i(x)$, are positive real valued continuous functions defined on $\mathbb{R}^n, i \in \mathbb{Z}$.

We may assume additionally that:

(Q1) there exists a positive constant κ such that $\theta_{i+1} - \theta_i \ge \kappa, i \in \mathbb{Z}$;
(Q2) there exists a positive constant $l < \kappa/4$ such that for all $t \in \mathbb{R}, x, y \in \mathbb{R}^n$, $i \in \mathbb{Z}$, the following inequality is valid

$$\|f(t, x) - f(t, y)\| + \|I_i(x) - I_i(y)\| + |\tau_i(x) - \tau_i(y)| \le l\|x - y\|, \tag{5.39}$$

and $|\tau_i(x)| < l$;
(Q3) $\det(\mathcal{I} + B_i) \ne 0, i \in \mathbb{Z}$;
(Q4) for a fixed positive number H,

$$\sup_{-\infty < t < +\infty, \|x\| < H} \|f(t, x)\| + \sup_{-\infty < i < +\infty, \|x\| < H} \|I_i(x)\| = M < +\infty.$$

and

$$\sup_{-\infty < t < +\infty} \|A(t)\| + \sup_{-\infty < i < +\infty} \|B_i\| = N < +\infty;$$

(Q5) $\tau_i(x) \geq \tau_i(x + I_i(x)), i \in \mathbb{Z}$, if $\|x\| \leq H$, and $l[NH + M] < 1$.

By virtue of Lemma 5.3.1 and assumption $(Q5)$ every solution $x(t), \|x(t)\| < H$, of (5.38) intersects each surface $\Gamma_i : t = \theta_i + \tau_i(x), i \in \mathbb{Z}$, at most once. Moreover, the solution intersects a surface if the range of the surface is a subset of the domain of the solution. Following the proof of Theorem 5.2.4, continuation of solutions of ordinary differential equation

$$\frac{dx}{dt} = A(t)x + f(t, x), \tag{5.40}$$

and the condition $|\theta_i| \to \infty$ as $|i| \to \infty$, one can find that every solution $x(t) = x(t, t_0, x_0), (t_0, x_0) \in \mathbb{R} \times \mathbb{R}^n$, of (5.38) is continuable on to $\mathbb{R}$, and intersect every surface of discontinuity exactly once.

We will start with a basic theorem, which is a specific form of Theorem 5.5.1 for the quasilinear case.

Fix $i \in \mathbb{Z}$. Let $x_0(t)$ be the solution of (5.40) with $x_0(\theta_i) = x$, and ξ_i the solution of the equation $t = \theta_i + \tau_i(x_0(t))$, that is, the intersection moment with Γ_i, and let $x_1(t)$ be the solution of system (5.40) with the initial condition $x_1(\xi_i) = B_i x_0(\xi_i) + I_i(x_0(\xi_i))$. Obviously, both of these two solutions exist. Similar to W_i in (5.13) one can construct the following B-map,

$$J_i(x) = (\mathcal{I} + B_i) \int_{\theta_i}^{\xi_i} (A(\tau)x(\tau) + f(\tau, x(\tau)))d\tau +$$

$$I_i(x(\xi_i)) + \int_{\xi_i}^{\theta_i} (A(\tau)x_1(\tau) + f(\tau, x_1(\tau)))d\tau, \tag{5.41}$$

and the system

$$\frac{dy}{dt} = A(t)y + f(t, y),$$
$$\Delta y|_{t=\theta_i} = B_i y + J_i(y). \tag{5.42}$$

Exercise 5.8.1. Prove that $J_i(x) = I_i(x)$ if $\tau_i(x) = 0$, that is (θ_i, x) is a point belonging to the discontinuity surface.

Let $b(l) = l[NH + M]$, and assume that $b(l) < \min(1, H)$. Moreover, set $h = H - b(l), c(l) = b(l)(1 + N + \|\mathcal{I}\|) + M, k(l) = e^{l(N+l)}\{(1 + N)(N + l) + [(NH + M)(N + 2) + (N + l)(1 + l + b(l))e^{l(N+l)} + 1](1 - b(l))^{-1}\}$.

Theorem 5.8.1. *Assume that (5.38) satisfies conditions* $(Q1)–(Q5)$.
Then:

(1) functions $J_i, i \in \mathbb{Z}$, *are defined on* $\mathbb{R}^n$;
(2) systems (5.38) and (5.42) are B-equivalent in $G_H = \{x \in \mathbb{R}^n : \|x\| \le H\}$,
such that if a solution of (5.38) or (5.42) get values in G_h, *then the correspond-
ing solution of (5.42)or (5.38) get values in* $G_H = \{x \in \mathbb{R}^n : \|x\| \le H\}$;
(3) the following inequalities are valid

$$\|J_i(x) - J_i(y)\| \le lk(l)\|x(\theta_i) - y(\theta_i)\|, \tag{5.43}$$

uniformly with respect to all $i \in \mathbb{Z}$, *for all* x, y *such that* $\|x(\xi_i, \theta_i, x)\| < h$ *and*
$\|y(\phi_i, \theta_i, y)\| < h$, *where* $x(t, \theta_i, x)$ *and* $y(t, \theta_i, y)$ *are solutions of (5.40), and*
ξ_i, ϕ_i, *are their meeting moments with the surface* Γ_i.

Proof. The first part of the theorem is verified above, since solutions $x_0(t)$ and $x_1(t)$
of (5.40) in (5.41) always exist.

To verify Part (2) we should remark that for a given $x \in \mathbb{R}^n$, the value $J_i(x)$ is
given by $J_i(x) = x_1(\theta_i) - x = x(\theta_i, \xi_i, x_0(\xi_i)) - x$, where all considered solutions
are of (5.40). Let $x(t)$ be a solution of (5.38), $\|x(t)\| < h$, and ξ_i the moment of
discontinuity of this solution. Assume that $x(\theta_i) = y(\theta_i) = x_0(\theta_i)$, where $y(t)$
is a solution of (5.42). We should prove that $x(\xi_i+) = y(\xi_i) = x_1(\xi_i)$. Indeed,
equality $y(\xi_i) = x_1(\xi_i)$ follows from the definition of J_i, and $x(\xi_i+) = x_0(\xi_i) +$
$I_i(x_0(\xi_i)) = x_1(\xi_i)$ since $x(t)$ is the solution of (5.38). By employing integral
equations corresponding to (5.40), we find that $\|y(t)\| < H$ if t is between θ_i
and ξ_i. Since inside of intervals of continuity the solutions satisfy the same equation
(5.40), one can see that the equivalence is proved in one direction. Similarly we can
discuss, if begin with $y(t)$ as a solution of (5.42), $\|y(t)\| < h$. Thus, the equivalence
is proved.

We next prove inequality (5.43). Let $\|x\| \le h$. By employing integral equations
corresponding to (5.40), again, we find that the solutions $x_0(t)$ and $x_1(t)$ determined
above satisfy the inequalities $\|x_0(t)\| < H$ and $\|x_1(t)\| < H$ on $[\theta_i, \xi_i]$. Let $y_0(t)$
be a solution of (5.40) for which $y_0(\theta_i) = y$ and $\|y\| \le h$. Let $\phi_i \ge \xi_i$ be a solution
of the equation $t = \theta_i + \tau_i(y_0(t))$, and let $y_1(t)$ be the solution of (5.40) with the
initial condition $y_1(\phi_i) = B_i y_0(\phi_i) + I_i(y_0(\phi_i))$. We have that

$$x_0(t) = x + \int_{\theta_i}^t [A(s)x_0(s) + f(s, x_0(s))]ds,$$

$$y_0(t) = y + \int_{\theta_i}^t [A(s)y_0(s) + f(s, y_0(s))]ds.$$

Subtract the second equation from the first one, and apply the Lipschitz condition
and the Gronwall–Bellmann Lemma to obtain

$$\|x_0(t) - y_0(t)\| \le e^{(N+l)l}\|x - y\|, t \in [\xi_i, \phi_i]. \tag{5.44}$$

Next, one can write that

$$\phi_i - \xi_i = \tau_i(y_0(\phi_i)) - \tau_i(x_0(\xi_i)) \le l\|y_0(\phi_i) - x_0(\xi_i)\| \le$$

$$l[\|y_0(\phi_i) - x_0(\phi_i)\| + \|x_0(\phi_i) - x_0(\xi_i)\|] \le le^{(N+l)l}\|x - y\| +$$

$$l\|\int_{\xi_i}^{\phi_i} [A(s)y_0(s) + f(s, y_0(s))]ds\| \le le^{(N+l)l}\|x - y\| + b(l)(\phi_i - \xi_i).$$

The last inequality implies

$$\phi_i - \xi_i \le \frac{le^{(N+l)l}}{1 - b(l)}\|x - y\|. \tag{5.45}$$

Now, we have

$$x_1(\xi_i+) - y_1(\xi_i) = x_0(\xi_i) + I_i(x_0(\xi_i)) - y_0(\xi_i) - \int_{\xi_i}^{\phi_i} [A(s)y_0(s)$$

$$+ f(s, y_0(s))]ds - I_i(y_0(\xi_i) +$$

$$\int_{\xi_i}^{\phi_i} [A(s)y_0(s) + f(s, y_0(s))]ds) + \int_{\xi_i}^{\phi_i} [A(s)y_1(s) + f(s, y_1(s))]ds,$$

and

$$\|x_1(\xi_i+) - y_1(\xi_i)\| \le \frac{(1 + l + b(l))e^{(N+l)l}}{1 - b(l)}\|x - y\|.$$

Consequently,

$$\|x_1(t) - y_1(t)\| \le \frac{(1 + l + b(l))e^{2(N+l)}}{1 - b(l)}\|x - y\|. \tag{5.46}$$

Finally, subtracting the expression

$$J_i(y) = (\mathcal{I} + B_i)\int_{\theta_i}^{\phi_i} (A(\tau)y_0(\tau) + f(\tau, y_0(\tau)))d\tau + I_i(y_0(\phi_i)) +$$

$$\int_{\phi_i}^{\theta_i} (A(\tau)y_1(\tau) + f(\tau, y_1(\tau)))d\tau$$

from (5.41) and using (5.44), (5.45), and (5.46), we conclude that (5.43) holds. The theorem is proved.   □

Bounded Solutions. Using the transformation $y = U(t)z$, which has been defined in Sect. 4.1, such that matrices $U(t), U^{-1}(t)$, are bounded on $\mathbb{R}$, one can reduce (5.42) to the system

$$\frac{d\xi}{dt} = P_1(t)\xi + f_1(t,z),$$

$$\Delta\xi|_{t=\theta_i} = Q_i^1\xi + I_i^1(z),$$

$$\frac{d\eta}{dt} = P_2(t)\eta + f_2(t,z),$$

$$\Delta\eta|_{t=\theta_i} = Q_i^2\eta + I_i^2(z), \tag{5.47}$$

where $z = (\xi, \eta), \xi \in \mathbb{R}^m, \eta \in \mathbb{R}^{n-m}$.

In what follows, without loss of generality, we assume that the system (5.42) has the form (5.47).

Theorem 5.8.2. *Assume that conditions $(Q1)$–$(Q5)$ are satisfied, associated with (5.38) system (4.1) is exponentially dichotomous and*

$(Q6)$ $2KM[\frac{1}{\gamma} + \frac{c(l)e^{2\gamma\kappa}}{1-e^{-\frac{\gamma\kappa}{2}}}] + b(l) < H;$

$(Q7)$ $2Kl[\frac{1}{\gamma} + \frac{k(l)e^{2\gamma\kappa}}{1-e^{-\frac{\gamma\kappa}{2}}}] < 1.$

Then (5.38) has a unique solution bounded on $\mathbb{R}$.

Proof. Consider the following system of integral equations:

$$\xi(t) = \int_{-\infty}^{t} X_1(t,\tau)f_1(\tau,z)d\tau + \sum_{\theta_i < t} X_1(t,\theta_i+)J_i^1(z),$$

$$\eta(t) = -\int_{t}^{\infty} X_2(t,\tau)f_2(\tau,z)d\tau - \sum_{\theta_i \geq t} X_2(t,\theta_i+)J_i^2(z), \tag{5.48}$$

and the sequence of approximations $z_k = (\xi_k, \eta_k), k \geq 0, \xi_0 \equiv 0, \eta_0 \equiv 0,$

$$\xi_{k+1}(t) = \int_{-\infty}^{t} X_1(t,\tau)f_1(\tau,z_k)d\tau + \sum_{\theta_i < t} X_1(t,\theta_i+)J_i^1(z_k),$$

$$\eta_{k+1}(t) = -\int_{t}^{\infty} X_2(t,\tau)f_2(\tau,z_k)d\tau - \sum_{\theta_i \geq t} X_2(t,\theta_i+)J_i^2(z_k).$$

Using $(Q6)$ one can check that all approximations satisfy $\|z_k(t)\| < h$, if $t \in \mathbb{R}$. Indeed, we have that $\|z_0\| = 0, t \in \mathbb{R}$. Assume that $\|z_k\| < h$. Then applying (4.31), we have

$$\|\xi_{k+1}(t)\| \leq \int_{-\infty}^{t} Ke^{-\gamma(t-\tau)}Md\tau + \sum_{t_i < t} Ke^{-\gamma(t-\theta_i)}M < KM[\frac{1}{\gamma} + \frac{c(l)e^{2\gamma\kappa}}{1-e^{-\frac{\gamma\kappa}{2}}}].$$

Similar evaluation can be made for $\eta_{k+1}(t)$. So, finally, we have that $\|z_{k+1}(t)\| \leq 2K[\frac{M}{\gamma} + \frac{c(l)}{1-e^{-\frac{\gamma\kappa}{2}}}] < H - b(l) = h$. That is, $\|z_k(t)\| < h, k \geq 0$, if $t \in \mathbb{R}$, by the induction.

Analogously, condition $(Q7)$ implies that the sequence z_k is convergent over $\mathbb{R}$. Thus, the integral equation has a solution $z_0(t)$, with $\|z_0(t)\| \le h$ for $t \in \mathbb{R}$. The uniqueness can be verified easily. The theorem is proved.   □

Exercise 5.8.2. Explain, why we do not use an analogue of condition (N6) in the last theorem. Discuss uniqueness of solutions of system (5.38), and the uniqueness of the solution bounded on $\mathbb{R}$.

5.9 Poincaré Criterion and Periodic Solutions of Quasilinear Systems

Theorem 5.9.1. *Assume that conditions (M0),(N1)–(N4) are fulfilled, (5.1) is an (ω, p)-periodic system, there exist a moment $t_0 \in \mathbb{R}$ and a solution $x(t)$ of (5.1) with $x(t_0 + \omega) = x(t_0)$. Then there exists an ω-periodic solution of the system.*

Proof. The necessity can be verified easily: if $x(t)$ is an ω-periodic solution, then $x(t_0 + \omega) = x(t_0)$ for all $t_0 \in \mathbb{R}$. Let us prove sufficiency. Assume that $x(t_0 + \omega) = x(t_0)$ is true for a fixed $t_0 \in \mathbb{R}$ and a solution $x(t)$. Without loss of generality, assume that t_0 is not a point of discontinuity of $x(t)$, and (t_0, x_0) lies between two consecutive surfaces Γ_i and Γ_{i+1}. Then $(t_0 + \omega, x_0)$ is between Γ_{i+p} and Γ_{i+1+p}. Consider $t \ge t_0$. The theorem on periodic systems of ordinary differential equations [59] implies that $x(t + \omega)$ is a solution of (5.2), and $x(t) = x(t + \omega)$ near t_0 while both solutions are continuous. More precisely, solutions of (5.2), which represent $x(t)$ and $x(t + \omega)$ on the intervals of continuity are equal to each other. The nearest moments of discontinuity from the right are defined by equations $t = \tau_{i+1}(x(t))$ and $t = \tau_{i+1+p}(x(t + \omega))$. The first of these equations has the solution $t = \theta_i$. Denote the solution of the second one as $t = \theta'_{i+1+p}$. We have that $\theta'_{i+1+p} = \tau_{i+1+p}(x(\theta'_{i+1+p} + \omega)) = \tau_{i+1+p}(x(\theta'_{i+1+p})) = \tau_{i+1}(x(\theta'_{i+1+p})) + \omega$. The absence of beating and $x(t) = x(t + \omega)$ imply that $\theta'_{i+1+p} = \theta_{i+1+p}$ and $\theta_{i+1+p} = \theta_{i+1} + \omega$. Next, we have that $x(\theta_{i+1}+) = J_{i+1}(x(\theta_{i+1+p})) = J_{i+1+p}(x(\theta_{i+1+p} + \omega)) = x(\theta_{i+1+p} + \omega+)$. Consequently, the two solutions are equal to each other while both solutions are continuous, near $t = \theta_{i+1+p}$, for increasing t, and $x(t + \omega)$ is a solution of (5.1) for these values of the argument. One can proceed in this way such that, finally, we obtain that $x(t + \omega)$ is a solution of (5.1), and, moreover, $x(t + \omega) = x(t)$, if $t \in [t_0, t_0 + \omega]$. The assertion is proved.   □

Suppose that (5.38) is an (ω, p)-periodic system, i.e., $A(t)$ and $f(t, x)$ are ω-periodic functions of t, there exists an integer p related to ω by the condition $\theta_{i+p} = \theta_i + \omega$, $i \in \mathbb{Z}$, and $B_{i+p} = B_i$, $\tau_{i+p}(x) = \tau_i(x)$ for all $i \in \mathbb{Z}, x \in \mathbb{R}^n$. Since (5.38) has the uniqueness property, it can be shown that the following result holds.

Lemma 5.9.1. *Assume that (5.38) is an (ω, p)-periodic system. Then the sequence of maps $J_i(x)$ is p-periodic in i, and (5.42) is an (ω, p)-periodic system.*

Exercise 5.9.1. Prove Lemma 5.9.1.

Hint: Use the technique of the last proof.

Theorem 5.9.2. *If conditions (Q1)–(Q7) are satisfied, and associated with (5.38) system (4.3) is exponentially dichotomous, then the (ω, p)-periodic system (5.38) has a unique ω-periodic solution.*

Proof. By Theorem 5.8.2 system (5.47) has a unique bounded solution $z^0(t)$, which satisfies (5.48). Let us prove that it is ω-periodic. Following the proof of Theorem 5.8.2, we only need to show that the approximations are ω-periodic functions. Let us apply the induction method. We have that $z_0(t) \equiv 0$. Assume that the approximation $z_k(t)$ is ω-periodic function. Consider the approximation z_{k+1}. We will check the periodicity of ξ_{k+1}, since that for the second component η_{k+1} is very similar.

$$
\xi_{k+1}(t + \omega) = \int_{-\infty}^{t+\omega} X_1(t + \omega, \tau) f_1(\tau, z_k(\tau)) d\tau
$$
$$
+ \sum_{t_i < t+\omega} X_1(t + \omega, \theta_i) J_i^1(z_k(\theta_i)) =
$$
$$
\int_{-\infty}^{t} X_1(t + \omega, \tau + \omega) f_1(\tau + \omega, z_k(\tau + \omega)) d\tau
$$
$$
+ \sum_{t_i < t} X_1(t + \omega, \theta_i + \omega) J_{i+p}^1(z_k(\theta_i + \omega)) =
$$
$$
\int_{-\infty}^{t} X_1(t, \tau) f_1(\tau, z_k(\tau)) d\tau + \sum_{t_i < t} X_1(t, \theta_i) J_i^1(z_k(\theta_i)) = \xi_k(t)
$$

The theorem is proved. □

Let us denote $\bar{M} = \max_{t,s \in [0,\omega]} \|G(t, s)\|$, where $G(t, s)$ is the Green's function (4.66). The following theorem is valid.

Theorem 5.9.3. *Suppose conditions (Q1)–(Q5) are satisfied, associated system (4.1) is exponentially dichotomous and*

(Q8) $\bar{M} M(T + p) < h$;
(Q9) $\bar{M} l(1 + lk(l)) < 1$.

Then (5.38) has a unique ω-periodic solution.

Exercise 5.9.2. Prove Theorem 5.9.3.

Notes

The problem of investigation of differential equations with solutions, which have discontinuities on surfaces placed in (t, x)-space is one of the most difficult and interesting subjects of the theory [2, 4, 14, 20, 32–36, 69, 82, 85, 95–97, 102, 138, 141,

142, 144, 145, 153, 161]. It was emphasized in early stage of theory's development in [111]. Conditions of "absence of beating" of solutions against surfaces of discontinuity were firstly defined in [138]. The theoretical importance caused further research of the beating phenomena [63, 82]. Another complexity in the analysis of the systems, except the beating of solutions, is description of the closeness of solutions with different moments of discontinuity. The problem was considered earlier in theory of functions [90, 147]. In implicit form, the description was done for impulsive differential equations in three cases: for stability of solutions of equations with variable moments of impulses; continuous dependence of solutions on parameters, when moments of impulses are not fixed; analysis of almost periodicity of discontinuous solutions in both cases of systems with fixed and nonfixed moments of impulses [30, 75, 95, 97, 138, 141, 142] . By using basic ideas of our predecessors [75, 141, 147], we introduce a special topology [2–4, 4–7, 7, 8, 32, 33, 35, 36] in a set of piecewise continuous functions having, in general, points of discontinuity, which do not coincide. Thus, we operate with the concepts of B-topology, B-equivalence, and ϵ-neighborhoods, when we investigate systems with variable moments of impulses [2–8, 32, 33, 35, 36] or consider almost periodicity of solutions of impulsive systems [7, 31]. In [90], it was explored that a topology in spaces of piecewise continuous functions can be metricized. We specify this result in [31] for investigation of almost periodic discontinuous nonautonomous systems. It is not surprising that the topology begins to be useful for other differential equations with discontinuities of different types [7, 17, 20, 27]: Filippov's type differential equations; differential equations on variable time scales. The most important concept used in the chapter is the method of reduction to systems with fixed moments of impulses, i.e., the B-equivalence method. It was introduced and developed in [1–4, 13, 15, 20, 21, 25–32]. The material of the chapter lies fully on results obtained by B-equivalence method. One must say that some of these results are published for the first time in the present book. Let us list these results: condition (N3) as a general source of the absence of beating; content of Sects. 5.5, 5.7, 5.9; Theorems 5.2.1–5.2.4 of existence and uniqueness; condition (N5), which provides uniqueness to the left extension, and Theorem 5.3.4, which guarantees the condition. Condition (N6) cancels many difficulties of the left continuation. Definitions 5.7.1–5.7.4 of stability for differential equations, where the importance of discs $D(t_0, \delta)$ is emphasized, are newly given. Lemmas 5.3.1, 5.3.2 and Theorems 5.3.1, 5.3.2 are due to [28]. Results of Sect. 5.8 are published in [33]. Let us point out that the B-equivalence method is effective not only in bounded domains but it can also be applied successfully if impulsive equations are considered with unbounded domains [37]. Exceptionally, it is important for existence of global manifolds. Linearization in the neighborhood of the nontrivial solution, the central auxiliary result of the stability theory is solved in [2]. The problem of controllability of boundary-value problems for quasilinear impulsive system of integro–differential equations is investigated in [18]. Finally, the method also proves its effectiveness to indicate chaos and shadowing property of impulsive systems [9, 11].

Chapter 6
Differentiability Properties of Nonautonomous Systems

In this chapter, we investigate the fundamental properties of differential equations with variable moments of impulses: differential and analytic dependence of solutions on initial conditions and parameters. Differentiability of solutions is the property, which is of underestimated importance for differential equations. One needs the conditions, which provide the smoothness of solutions if a system is to be linearized around a certain solution, to prove the existence of periodic and almost periodic solutions in critical and noncritical cases by using the method of small parameter [105, 107], to investigate problems of synchronization and bifurcation theory.

We consider the following system of impulsive differential equations:

$$x' = f(t, x),$$
$$\Delta x|_{t=\tau_i(x)} = J_i(x). \tag{6.1}$$

The system is defined on the set $\Omega = I \times \mathcal{A} \times G$ of points (t, i, x), where $G \subset \mathbb{R}^n$ is an open and connected set, I an open interval of $\mathbb{R}$, and $\mathcal{A}$ an interval of $\mathbb{Z}$. We assume that $f(t, x)$ is a continuous function, J_i are functions on G, and $\tau_i(x)$ are continuous functions on G, $i \in \mathcal{A}$. Condition (M0), Chap. 2, and conditions (N1)–(N6) of Chap. 5 are valid. Moreover, we assume that

(N11) the derivatives $\partial f(t, x)/\partial x_j$, $\partial J_i(x)/\partial x_j$, $\partial \tau_i(x)/\partial x_j$, are continuous on G, uniformly for all $t \in I, i \in \mathcal{A}$.

It is required that the vector functions f, J, x, and their derivatives are column-vectors, and the derivatives of the functions τ are assumed to be vector-rows. Products of vectors and matrices are the products of rectangle matrices. The following condition will be needed throughout this chapter:

(N12) the inequality $\tau_{ix}(x) f(\tau_i(x), x) \neq 1$, is fulfilled for all $(i, x) \in \mathcal{A} \times G$.

The condition means that each solution of (6.1) may meet a surface of discontinuity only transversally.

Results of the preceding chapter imply that if $(t_0, x_0) \in I \times G$, then there exists a unique solution $x(t) = x(t, t_0, x_0), x_0 = (x_0^1, \ldots, x_0^n)$, of (6.1) on some interval $[t_0, T], T > t_0$, with points of discontinuity $t = \theta_i, i \in \mathcal{A}$. We will discuss

M. Akhmet, *Principles of Discontinuous Dynamical Systems*,
DOI 10.1007/978-1-4419-6581-3_6, © Springer Science+Business Media, LLC 2010

differentiability properties assuming that $t \geq t_0$, since it is sufficient for application needs. For the sake of simplicity, we denote the moments $t_0 \leq \theta_m < \ldots < \theta_k < T$, and assume that $(t_0, x_0) \in G_{m-1} = \{(t, x) : \tau_{m-1}(x) < t \leq \tau_m(x), x \in G\}$.

6.1 Differentiability with Respect to Initial Conditions

Consider the disc $D(t_0, \delta) = \{(t_0, x) : \|x - x_0\| < \delta\}$ with the center at (t_0, x_0) and with the radius $\delta > 0$, and the interval $d(x_0, \delta) = \{(t, x_0) : t_0 - \delta < t < t_0 + \delta\}$ with the center at (t_0, x_0) and with the radius $\delta > 0$.

Denote by $x^j(t), j = 1, 2, \ldots, n$, the solution of (6.1) with $x^j(t_0) = (x_0^1, \ldots, x_0^j + \xi, \ldots, x_0^n)$, and by $\eta_i^j, i = 1, 2, \ldots, k$, the points of discontinuity of this solution.

Definition 6.1.1. The solution $x(t)$ is B-differentiable with respect to $x_0^j, j = 1, 2, \ldots, n$, on $[t_0, T]$ if there exists $\delta > 0$, such that if $(t_0, x^j(t_0)) \in D(t_0, \delta) \cap G_{m-1}$, then:

(1) there exist real constants $v_{ij}, i = 1, 2, \ldots, k$, such that

$$\theta_i - \eta_i^j = v_{ij}\xi + o(|\xi|); \tag{6.2}$$

(2) for all $t \notin \widehat{(\theta_i, \eta_i^j]}, i = 1, 2, \ldots, k$, it is true that

$$x^j(t) - x(t) = u_j(t)\xi + o(|\xi|), \tag{6.3}$$

where function $u_j(t) \in \mathcal{PC}([t_0, T], \theta)$.

The pair $\{u_j(t), \{v_{ij}\}\}$, which consists of the function u_j and the sequence $\{v_{ij}\}$, is called a B-derivative of the solution $x(t)$ with respect to x_0^j.

In a similar manner, we shall define B-derivatives with respect to t_0. Denote by $x^0(t)$ a solution of (5.45) such that $x^0(t_0 + \xi) = x_0$, where ξ is a fixed real number. If $|\xi|$ is sufficiently small then $x^0(t)$ exists on $[t_0 + \xi, T]$. Denote by $\eta_i^0, i = 1, 2, \ldots, k$, the points of discontinuity of this solution in this interval.

Definition 6.1.2. The solution $x(t)$ is B-differentiable with respect to t_0 if there exists $\delta > 0$, such that if $(t_0 + \xi, x_0) \in d(x_0, \delta) \cap G_m$, then:

(1) there exist real constants $v_{i0}, i = 1, 2, \ldots, k$, which satisfy

$$\theta_i - \eta_i^0 = v_{i0}\xi + o(|\xi|); \tag{6.4}$$

(2) for all $t \notin \widehat{(\theta_i, \eta_i^0]}, i = 1, 2, \ldots, k$, it is true that

$$x^0(t) - x(t) = u_0(t)\xi + o(|\xi|), \tag{6.5}$$

where $u_0(t) \in \mathcal{PC}([t_0, T], \theta)$, and $\theta = \{\theta_i\}_{i=1,2,\ldots,k}$.

The pair $\{u_0(t), \{v_{i0}\}\}$, which consists of the function u_0 and the sequence $\{v_{i0}\}$, is called a B-derivative of the solution $x(t)$ with respect to t_0.

In the sequel, we shall write values of functions and their derivatives at points $(\theta_i, x(\theta_i))$ and $(\theta_i, x(\theta_i+))$ without mentioning the values of the arguments, and distinct the second case by the subscript $+$. To denote derivatives with respect to x and t we apply subscripts. Let us start with some auxiliary maps and results. Consider the system of ordinary differential equations

$$x' = f(t, x), \tag{6.6}$$

which is the part of (6.1), and maps $J, \tau : G \to \mathbb{R}^n, \tau : G \to \mathbb{R}$, being continuously differentiable in x. Choose a point $(\kappa, x) \in I \times G$, and keep κ fixed next. Let $t = \theta, \theta = \theta(x)$, be a moment of meeting of $x(t) = x(t, \kappa, x)$, the solution of (6.6), with the surface $t = \tau(x)$ transversally. Moreover, assume that the solution $\bar{x}(t) = x(t, \theta, x(\theta) + I(x(\theta)))$ of (6.6) exists on $\overline{[\theta, \kappa]}$. Define the B-map $W : x \to \bar{x}(\kappa)$ such that

$$W(x) = \int_\kappa^\theta f(u, x(u))du + J\left(x + \int_\kappa^\theta f(u, x(u))du\right) +$$
$$\int_\theta^\kappa f(u, \bar{x}(u))du. \tag{6.7}$$

Denote by $\tilde{G} \subset G$, a domain of the map. Set $A(t) = f_x(t, x(t))$, and let $U(t), U(\kappa) = \mathcal{I}$, be the fundamental matrix of the system $u' = A(t)u$.

Lemma 6.1.1. $\theta(x) \in C^{(1)}(\tilde{G})$, and

$$\theta'(x) = \frac{\tau_x(x(\theta))U(\theta)}{(1 - \tau_x(x(\theta))f(\theta, x(\theta)))}. \tag{6.8}$$

Proof. The solution $x(t)$ meets the surface $t = \tau(x)$ transversally at a moment $t = \theta$, that is, $\tau_x(x(\theta))f(\theta, x(\theta)) \neq 1$. Obviously, the inequality is valid for all x in a neighborhood of $x(\theta)$. By conditions of the lemma, the solution $x(t)$ is differentiable in the initial value x. The moment of intersection with $t = \theta(x)$ satisfies $t = \tau(x(t))$. More precisely, $t = \tau(x(t, \kappa, x))$. Now, we use the implicit function theorem in a neighborhood of $(\theta, x(\theta))$. We have that

$$\frac{d\theta(x)}{dx} = -\frac{-\frac{d\tau(z)}{dz}\frac{\partial x(t, \kappa, x)}{\partial x}}{1 - \frac{d\tau(z)}{dz}\frac{dx(t, \kappa, x)}{dt}}\bigg|_{t=\theta, z=x(\theta)} = \frac{\tau_x(x(\theta))U(\theta)}{(1 - \tau_x(x(\theta))f(\theta, x(\theta)))}.$$

The differentiability of $\theta(x)$ implies that it is continuous at x. Consequently, the last formula and continuity of functions τ_x, f, U complete the proof of the lemma. $\quad\square$

Corollary 6.1.1. $\theta(x)$ is a continuous function.

Lemma 6.1.2. $W(x) \in C^{(1)}(\tilde{G})$.

Proof. By continuous differentiability of functions involved in (6.7) and the last lemma, one can find that

$$W_x(x) = (f(\theta, x(\theta)) - f(\theta, x(\theta) + J(x(\theta)))\theta_x(x) + J_x(\mathcal{I} + f(\theta, x(\theta))\theta_x), \tag{6.9}$$

and W_x is a continuous matrix. The lemma is proved. $\qquad\square$

Corollary 6.1.2. $W(x)$ *is a continuous function.*

Assume that there is an integer $r > 1$ such that the functions f, τ, and J are r times continuously differentiable in x, and the function f is $r - 1$ times continuously differentiable in t in a h-neighborhood of the surface $t = \tau(x)$, where h is a positive number.

The next lemma can be proved easily just by several differentiation of the expression in the right-hand side of (6.8), but we prefer another way, which can enrich our technique of investigation.

Lemma 6.1.3. $\theta(x) \in C^{(r)}(\tilde{G})$.

Proof. Beside the solution $x(t) = x(t, \kappa, x)$, let us consider a solution $\bar{x}(t) = x(t, \kappa, x + \Delta x)$ of (6.6). Denote by $t = \bar{\theta} = \theta(x + \Delta x)$ the meeting moment of this solution with the surface $t = \tau(x)$. Without loss of generality, assume that $\bar{\theta} \geq \theta \geq \kappa$.

We shall prove the lemma if the equality

$$\theta(x + \Delta x) - \theta(x) = \sum_{i=0}^{n} \phi_{1i}(x)\xi_i + \ldots +$$

$$\sum_{i,j,\ldots s=0}^{n} \phi_{rij\ldots s}(x)\xi_i\xi_j \ldots \xi_s + o(||\Delta x||^r), \tag{6.10}$$

where coefficients ϕ are continuous and symmetric with respect to permutation of indices, will be verified. Let us denote $Q_r(\cdot)$- an r-degree polynomial with respect to a vector $(\cdot)$. Applying the differentiability of $\tau(x)$, we can find that

$$\theta(x + \Delta x) - \theta(x) = Q_r(x(\bar{\theta}, \kappa, x + \Delta x) - x(\theta)) + o(||x(\bar{\theta}, \kappa, x + \Delta x) - x(\theta)||^r). \tag{6.11}$$

Moreover, differentiability of f, and consequently, smoothness of solutions of (5.2) imply that

$$\int_{\theta}^{\bar{\theta}} f(u, x(u, \kappa, x + \Delta x))du = Q_r(\bar{\theta} - \theta, \Delta x) + o(||\bar{\theta} - \theta, \Delta x||^r). \tag{6.12}$$

Now, applying equality

$$x(\bar{\theta}, \kappa, x + \Delta x) - x(\theta) = \int_{\theta}^{\bar{\theta}} f(u, x(u, \kappa, x + \Delta x)) du + x(\theta, \kappa, x + \Delta x) - x(\theta)$$

we obtain that

$$\bar{\theta} - \theta = \sum_{i=0}^{n} \psi_{1i}(x(\theta)) \{ f(\theta, x(\theta)) \}_i (\bar{\theta} - \theta) +$$

$$\sum_{i=0}^{n} L_i(\Delta x)(\bar{\theta} - \theta)^i + o(\|\xi\|^r), \tag{6.13}$$

where $\{a\}_i$ means the i-th coordinate of a vector $a = (a_1, a_2, \ldots, a_n)$, $L_i, i = 1, 2, \ldots, n$, are polynomials and $L_1 = o(\|\Delta x\|)$. The result of Lemma 6.1.1 is the relation

$$\bar{\theta} - \theta = \sum_{i=0}^{n} \phi_{1i}(x)\xi_i + o(\|\Delta x\|).$$

It implies that the inequality

$$1 - \sum_{i=0}^{n} \psi_{1i}(x(\theta)) \{ f(\theta, x(\theta)) \}_i - L_1(\Delta x) \neq 0$$

is true if $\|\Delta x\|$ is sufficiently small. Hence,

$$\bar{\theta} - \theta = \sum_{i=0}^{n} \phi_{1i}(x)\xi_i + \sum_{i,j=0}^{n} \phi_{2ij}(x)\xi_i\xi_j + o(\|\Delta x\|^2). \tag{6.14}$$

Substitute the last expression in (6.13) and proceed the procedure to obtain (6.10). The lemma is proved. $\qquad\square$

Lemma 6.1.4. $W(x) \in C^{(r)}(\tilde{G})$.

Proof. The last lemma imply that expression (6.9) is $r - 1$ times differentiable. The lemma is proved. $\qquad\square$

To investigate differentiability of solutions, we begin with the following auxiliary impulsive system of differential equations

$$\frac{dy}{dt} = f(t, y),$$

$$\Delta y|_{t=\theta_i} = W_i(y), \tag{6.15}$$

where moments of impulses θ_i are fixed, and W_i are functions defined on G. Assume that a solution $y(t) = y(t, t_0, x_0)$ of this system exists and is defined on the interval $[t_0, T]$.

Lemma 6.1.5. *If functions f and W_i are continuous and have continuous partial derivatives in coordinates of $y \in G$, then the solution $y(t) = y(t, t_0, x_0)$ of (6.15) is B-differentiable with respect to initial conditions. The first components of the B-derivatives, u_j, $j = 0, 1, 2, \ldots, n$, are solutions of the linear impulsive system*

$$\frac{du}{dt} = f_y(t, y(t))u,$$

$$\Delta u|_{t=\theta_i} = W_{iy}(y(\theta_i))u, \tag{6.16}$$

with initial values $-f(t_0, x_0)$ *if* $j = 0$, *and* $e_j = \underbrace{(0, \ldots, 0, 1, 0, \ldots, 0)}_{j}, j =$

$1, 2, \ldots, n$. *Constants* v_{ij} *in (6.2) and (6.4) are zeros for all i and j.*

Proof. Let us prove the theorem for x_0^1. For all other x_0^j, $j = 2, \ldots, n$, and t_0 the proof is similar.

Let $u_1(t), u_1(t_0) = e_1$, be the solution of (6.16). By the theorem of differentiability [77], we have that $y(t, t_0, x_0 + \xi e_1) - y(t, t_0, x_0) = u_1(t)\xi + p_1(\xi)$, where $p_1(\xi) = o(|\xi|)$. Let m be one of the numbers $1, 2, \ldots, k$. We assume that $y(\theta_m, t_0, x_0 + \xi e_1) - y(\theta_m, t_0, x_0) = u_1(\theta_m)\xi + p_m(\xi)$, $p_m = o(|\xi|)$, and will show that

$$y(\theta_m+, t_0, x_0 + \xi e_1) - y(\theta_m+, t_0, x_0) = u_1(\theta_m+)\xi + \bar{p}_m(\xi), \tag{6.17}$$

where $\bar{p}_m = o(|\xi|)$. Indeed, the conditions of the lemma imply that

$$y(\theta_m+, t_0, x_0 + \xi e_1) - y(\theta_m+, t_0, x_0) = y(\theta_m, t_0, x_0 + \xi e_1) -$$
$$y(\theta_m, t_0, x_0) + W_m(y(\theta_m, t_0, x_0 + \xi e_1)) - W_m(y(\theta_m, t_0, x_0)) =$$
$$u_1(\theta_m)\xi + p_m(\xi) + W_{mx}(y(\theta_m, t_0, x_0))(y(\theta_m, t_0, x_0 + \xi e_1) -$$
$$y(\theta_m, t_0, x_0)) + \tilde{p}(\xi) = (\mathcal{I} + W_{mx}(y(\theta_m, t_0, x_0)))y(\theta_m, t_0, x_0)\xi +$$
$$p_m(\xi) + W_{mx}(y(\theta_m, t_0, x_0))p_m(\xi) + \tilde{p}(\xi). \tag{6.18}$$

Then, as $\tilde{p} = o(|\xi|)$, the formula (6.17) is true. Denote by $U(t), U(\theta_m) = \mathcal{I}$, the fundamental matrix of (6.16) and use (6.18) to obtain that for all $t \in (\theta_m, \theta_{m+1}]$

$$y(t, t_0, x_0 + \xi e_1) - y(t, t_0, x_0) = U(t)[y(\theta_m+, t_0, x_0 + \xi e_1) - y(\theta_m+, t_0, x_0)]$$
$$+ p(u_1(\theta_m+)\xi + p_{m+1}(\xi)) = U(t)y(\theta_m+, t_0, x_0) + U(t)\bar{p}_{m+1}(\xi))$$
$$+ p(u_1(\theta_m+)\xi + p_{m+1}(\xi)) = u_1(t)\xi + p_{m+1}(\xi),$$

where $p_{m+1} = o(|\xi|)$. Thus, we obtain that

$$y(t, t_0, x_0 + \xi e_1) - y(t, t_0, x_0) = u_1(t)\xi + p(\xi), \quad p(\xi) = o(|\xi|).$$

The lemma is proved. □

Lemma 6.1.6. *If (N1)–(N6),(N11),(N12) are valid, then the solution* $x(t) = x(t, t_0, x_0)$ *of (6.1) is continuous in initial conditions in B-topology on* $[t_0, T]$.

Proof. We consider the continuity in x_0. The dependence on t_0 can be considered similarly. Denote by $\bar{x}(t) = x(t, t_0, x_0 + \Delta x)$, another solution of the equation. Our aim is to show that for an arbitrary $\epsilon > 0$ one can find $\delta > 0$ such that $\|\Delta x\| < \delta$ implies $\bar{x}(t)$ is in the ϵ-neighborhood of $x(t)$ in B-topology on $[t_0, T]$. Fix $\epsilon > 0$. For a positive number $\alpha \in R$ we shall construct a set G^α in the following way. Let $F_\alpha = \{(t, x) | t \in [t_0, T], \|x - x(t)\| < \alpha\}$, and $G_i(\alpha), i = 0, 1, 2, \dots, k + 1$, be α-neighborhoods of points (t_0, x_0), $(\theta_i, x(\theta_i))$, $i = 1, 2, \dots, k$, $(T, x(T))$ in $\mathbb{R} \times \mathbb{R}^n$ respectively, and $\bar{G}_i(\alpha)$, $i = 1, 2, \dots, k$, be α-neighborhoods of points $(\theta_i, x^0(\theta_i+))$, $i = 1, 2, \dots, k$, respectively. Let

$$G^\alpha = F_\alpha \cup \left(\cup_{i=0}^{k+1} G_i(\alpha)\right) \cup \left(\cup_{i=1}^{k} \bar{G}_i(\alpha)\right).$$

Take $\alpha = h$ sufficiently small that sets $G^h \subset I \times G$ and $\bar{G}_i(h)$, $i = 1, 2, \dots, k$, do not intersect any surface of discontinuity, except Γ_i. Fix $\epsilon, 0 < \epsilon < h$.

1. In view of the theorem on continuity of solutions [77], there exists $\bar{\delta}_k \in \mathbb{R}$, $0 < \bar{\delta}_k < \epsilon$, such that every solution $x_k(t)$ of (6.6), which starts in $\bar{G}_k(\bar{\delta}_k)$, is continuable to $t = T$, does not intersect any surface of discontinuity, except Γ_k, and
$$\|x_k(t) - x(t)\| < \epsilon.$$

2. The continuity of J and condition (N3) imply that there exists $\delta_k \in \mathbb{R}$, $0 < \delta_k < \epsilon$, such that $(\kappa, x) \in G_k(\delta_k)$ implies $(\kappa, x + J(x)) \in \bar{G}_k(\bar{\delta}_k)$.

3. Using continuity of solutions and condition (N3), one can find $\bar{\delta}_{k-1}, 0 < \bar{\delta}_{k-1} < \epsilon$, such that a solution $x_{k-1}(t)$ of (6.6), which starts in $\bar{G}_{k-1}(\bar{\delta}_{k-1})$, intersects Γ_k in $G_k(\delta_k)$ (we continue the solution $x_{k-1}(t)$ only to the moment of the intersection) and $\|x_{k-1}(t) - x(t)\| < \epsilon$ for all t from the common domain of $x_{k-1}(t)$ and $x(t)$.

Continue the process for $k - 2, k - 3, \dots, 1, 0$, to obtain a sequence of families of solutions of (6.6) $x_i(t), i = 1, 2, \dots, m$, and a number $\delta \in \mathbb{R}, 0 < \delta < \epsilon$, such that a solution $\bar{x}(t) = x(t, t_0, x_0 + \Delta x)$, which starts in $G_0(\delta)$, coincides with one of the solutions $x_0(t)$ on the first interval of continuity, except possibly, the δ_1-neighborhood of θ_1. Then on the interval $[\theta_1, \theta_2]$, it coincides with one of the solutions $x_1(t)$, except possibly, the δ_1-neighborhood of θ_1 and the δ_2-neighborhood of θ_2, etc. Finally, one can see that the integral curve of $\bar{x}(t)$ belongs to G^ϵ, it has exactly k meeting points with the surfaces Γ_i, θ_i^1, $i = 1, 2, \dots, k$, $|\theta_i^1 - \theta_i| < \epsilon$ for all i and is continuable to $t = T$. The lemma is proved. □

Theorem 6.1.1. *Suppose conditions (N1)–(N6),(N11),(N12) are valid. Then the solution $x(t)$ of (6.1) has B-derivatives with respect to initial conditions, $(u_j(t), v_{ij}), j = 0, 1, 2, \ldots, n$, which satisfy the following variational equation:*

$$\frac{du}{dt} = A(t)u,$$

$$\Delta u|_{t=\theta_i} = P_i u,$$

$$v_i = m_i u(\theta_i), \tag{6.19}$$

with initial value $-f(t_0, x_0)$ *if* $j = 0$ *and* $e^j = \underbrace{(0, \ldots, 0, 1, 0, \ldots, 0)}_{j}, j =$

$1, 2, \ldots, n$. *In (6.19)*

$$A(t) = f_x(t, x(t)), P_i = (f - f^+)\tau_{ix}(1 - \tau_{ix}f)^{-1} +$$

$$J_{ix}(\mathcal{I} + f\tau_{ix}(1 - \tau_{ix}f)^{-1})), m_i = (1 - \tau_{ix}f)^{-1}\tau_{ix}.$$

Proof. Consider differentiability in x_0. We use the last lemma and take $\delta > 0$ sufficiently small such that a solution $\bar{x}(t) = x(t, t_0, x_0 + \Delta x), \|\Delta x\| < \delta$, exists on the interval $[t_0, T]$, intersects each surface $\Gamma_i, i = 1, 2, \ldots, k$, once at moments $\theta_i^1, t_0 < \theta_1^1 < \ldots < \theta_k^1 < T$, which are near the moments of discontinuity of $x(t)$. One can choose small $\epsilon > 0$ such that (6.1) is B-equivalent to the system

$$\frac{dy}{dt} = f(t, y),$$

$$\Delta y|_{t=\theta_i} = W_i(y), \tag{6.20}$$

in G^ϵ, where $W_i(x)$ are defined by using the map (6.7) in neighborhoods of points $x(\theta_i)$. Applying Lemma 6.1.2, one can find that $W_i(x)$ are continuously differentiable functions. Consequently, by Lemma 6.1.5, the solution $y(t, t_0, x_0)$ is continuously differentiable in initial data. The B-equivalence implies immediately that the corresponding solution $x(t, t_0, x_0)$ is also B-differentiable. We can easily find P_i and m_i, using equalities $P_i = W_{ix}(x(\theta_i))$ and formulas (6.8), (6.9). The theorem is proved.   □

6.2 Differentiability with Respect to Parameters

Consider the following system of impulsive differential equations:

$$\frac{dx}{dt} = f(t, x, \mu),$$

$$\Delta u|_{t=\tau_i(x,\mu)} = J_i(x, \mu), \tag{6.21}$$

where $(t, i, x) \in I \times \mathcal{A} \times G \subset \mathbb{R} \times \mathbb{Z} \times \mathbb{R}^n, \mu = (\mu_1, \ldots, \mu_m) \in G_\mu \subset \mathbb{R}^m$, where G_μ is an open set, m and n are fixed positive integers. Functions f, J_i, and τ_i are continuous and continuously differentiable in x and μ. We assume that conditions (N1)–(N6),(N11),(N12), accepted above for system (6.1), as well as inequalities $\tau_i(x, \mu) < \tau_{i+1}(x, \mu), i \in \mathcal{A}$, are valid for (6.21) uniformly with respect to μ in G_μ. Moreover, assume that $J_i, \tau_i \in C^{(r,r)}(G \times G_\mu)$, $f \in C^{(0,r,r)}(I \times G \times G_\mu) \cap C^{(r-1,r,r)}(N_h)$, where r is a positive integer, and N_h is a union of h-neighborhoods of surfaces $t = \tau(x, \mu), i \in \mathcal{A}$, in $I \times G \times G_\mu$.

Consider the system of ordinary differential equations

$$x' = f(t, x, \mu), \tag{6.22}$$

which is the differential part of (6.21), and maps $J(x, \mu) : G \times G_\mu \to \mathbb{R}^n, \tau(x, \mu) : G \times G_\mu \to \mathbb{R}$, which are continuously differentiable in x. Choose a point $(\kappa, x) \in I \times G$ and keep κ fixed. Let $t = \theta, \theta = \theta(x, \mu)$ be a meeting moment of $x(t) = x(t, \kappa, x, \mu)$, the solution of (6.22), with the surface $t = \tau(x, \mu)$. Moreover, assume that the solution $\bar{x}(t) = x(t, \theta, x(\theta) + I(x(\theta)), \mu)$ of the system exists on $\widehat{[\theta, \kappa]}$. Define the following B-map:

$$W(x, \mu) = \int_\kappa^\theta f(u, x(u), \mu)du + J(x + \int_\kappa^\theta f(u, x(u))du, \mu) + \int_\theta^\kappa f(u, \bar{x}(u), \mu)du. \tag{6.23}$$

Denote by $\tilde{G} \times \tilde{G}_\mu \subset G \times G_\mu$, the set of all points such that the map $W : x \to \bar{x}(\kappa)$ is defined. Similarly to Lemmas 6.1.3 and 6.1.4, the following assertion can be proved.

Lemma 6.2.1. $W(x, \mu), \theta(x, \mu) \in C^{(r,r)}(\tilde{G} \times \tilde{G}_\mu)$.

For a fixed $\mu_0 \in G_\mu$, there exists a unique solution $x(t, t_0, x_0, \mu_0)$, of (6.1) on some interval $[t_0, T], T > t_0$. Denote by $\theta_i, i = m, m + 1, \ldots, k$ the moments of discontinuity of the solution. We assume that $t_0 \leq \theta_m < \ldots < \theta_k < T, (t_0, x_0) \in G_m(\mu_0) = \{(t, x, \mu_0) : \tau_m(x, \mu_0) < t \leq \tau_{m+1}(x, \mu_0), x \in G\}$. By introducing a new space variable μ, that is adding the equation $\mu' = 0$ to the system (6.21), we can find that the continuous dependence on the parameter is also valid.

Consider the disc $D((t_0, x_0), \delta) = \{(t_0, x_0, \mu) : \|\mu - \mu_0\| < \delta\}$ with the center (t_0, x_0, μ_0) and with the radius $\delta > 0$.

Denote by $x^j(t) = x(t, t_0, x_0, \mu_0 + \xi e_j), j = 1, 2, \ldots, m$, a solution defined on $[t_0, T]$, and $\eta_i^j, i = 1, 2, \ldots, k$, the moments of discontinuity of this solution.

Definition 6.2.1. The solution $x(t)$ is B-differentiable in $\mu_j, j = 1, 2, \ldots, m$, if there exists $\delta > 0$ such that $(t_0, x_0, \mu_0 + \xi e_j) \in D((t_0, x_0), \delta) \cap G_m(\mu_0)$ implies that:

(1) there exist real constants $\beta_{ij}, i = 1, 2, \ldots, k$, which satisfy

$$\theta_i - \eta_i^j = \beta_{ij}\xi + o(|\xi|); \tag{6.24}$$

(2) for all $t \notin \overparen{(\theta_i, \eta_i^j]}, i = 1, 2, \ldots, k$, it is true that

$$x^j(t) - x(t) = v_j(t)\xi + o(|\xi|), \tag{6.25}$$

where $v_j(t) \in \mathcal{PC}([t_0, T], \theta), \theta = \{\theta_i\}_{i=1,2,\ldots,k}.$

The pair $\{v_j(t), \{\beta_i^j\}\}$ is called a B-derivative of $x(t)$ with respect to μ_j.

Assume that the solution $x(t)$ meets each surface of discontinuity transversally, that is,

$$\tau_{ix}(x(\theta_i), \mu_0) f(\theta_i, x(\theta_i), \mu_0) \neq 1, \tag{6.26}$$

for all $i = m, m + 1, \ldots, k$. Denote

$$A(t) = f_x(t, x(t), \mu_0), \ P_i = (f - f^+)\tau_{ix}(1 - \tau_{ix} f)^{-1} + J_{ix}(\mathcal{I} + f \tau_{ix}(1 - \tau_{ix} f)^{-1})),$$

$$g_j(t) = f_{\mu_j}(t, x(t), \mu_0), \ Q_j^i = J_{i\mu_j} + \tau_{i\mu_j}(f^+ - (\mathcal{I} + J_{ix})f)(1 - \tau_{ix} f)^{-1}, \ k_j^i$$
$$= (1 - \tau_{ix} f)^{-1} \tau_{i\mu_j},$$

where values of functions are evaluated either at $(\theta_i, x(\theta_i), \mu_0)$ or $(\theta_i, x(\theta_i+), \mu_0)$, and the last case is indicated with the upper index $+$.

Similarly to Theorem 6.1.1, by using the map $W(x, \mu)$, we can show that the following assertion is valid.

Theorem 6.2.1. *Suppose that conditions (N1)–(N6),(N11),(N12), accepted above for system (6.1) are valid for (6.21) uniformly with respect to μ in G_μ. Moreover, there exists a number $\kappa > 0$ such that $\tau_{m+1}(x_0, \mu) \geq \tau_{m+1}(x_0, \mu_0)$ for all $\|\mu - \mu_0\| < \kappa$.*

Then the solution $x(t)$ has the B-derivative with respect to $\mu_j, j = 1, 2, \ldots, m$, which satisfies the following variational system

$$\frac{dv}{dt} = A(t)v + g_j(t),$$
$$\Delta v|_{t=\theta_i} = P_i v + Q_j^i,$$
$$\beta_i = k_j^i v(\theta_i), \tag{6.27}$$

with $v_j(t_0) = 0$.

6.3 Higher Order B-Derivatives

In this section, we assume that surfaces $\Gamma_i, i \in \mathcal{A}$, are placed in $I \times G$ with their h-neighborhoods for some fixed positive number h. Let us denote the union of the neighborhoods by N_h. We assume that $J_i, \tau_i \in C^{(r)}(G), f \in C^{(0,r)}$

$(I \times G) \cap C^{(r-1,r)}(N_h)$, where r is a positive integer. That is, functions $J_i, \tau_i, i \in \mathcal{A}$, are r times continuously differentiable in G. The function f is continuous in t, and r times continuously differentiable in $x \in G$, and additionally it is $r - 1$ times continuously differentiable in t if the point (t, x) is in N_h. Consider the solution $x(t) = x(t, t_0, x_0)$ of system (5.45) again. In what follows, assume that the solution $x(t)$ meets each surface of discontinuity transversally, that is, (6.26) is valid. Denote by $\bar{x}(t) = x(t, t_0 + \xi_0, x_0 + \Delta x), \Delta x = (\xi_1, \xi_2, \ldots, \xi_n), \xi = (\xi_0, \xi_1, \xi_2, \ldots, \xi_n)$ another solution of (6.1). Denote by $\eta_i, i \in \mathcal{A}$, the moments of discontinuity of this solution, and $B((t_0, x_0), \delta)$ the ball in $\mathbb{R} \times \mathbb{R}^n$ with the center at (t_0, x_0) and the radius δ.

Definition 6.3.1. The solution $x(t)$ has B-derivatives of up to r-th order, inclusive, with respect to t_0 and $x_0^j, j = 1, 2, \ldots, n$, if there exist functions $u_{1i}(t)$, $u_{2ij}(t), \ldots, u_{rij\ldots s}(t) \in \mathcal{PC}^1([t_0, T], \theta), \theta = \{\theta_i\}_{i=1,2,\ldots,k}$ and constants $v_{1i}^l, v_{2ij}^l, \ldots, v_{rij\ldots s}^l, l = 1, 2, \ldots, k$, which are symmetric with respect to permutation of indices, such that if $(t_0 + \xi, x_0 + \Delta x) \in B((t_0, x_0)\delta) \cap G_m$, for sufficiently small $\delta > 0$, then:

(1)

$$\theta_l - \eta_l = \sum_{i=0}^{n} v_{1i}^l \xi_i + \ldots + \sum_{i,j,\ldots s=0}^{n} v_{rij\ldots s}^l \xi_i \xi_j \ldots \xi_s + o(\|\xi\|^r), \quad (6.28)$$

where $l = 1, 2, \ldots, k$;

(2) for all $t \notin \widehat{(\theta_i, \eta_i]}, i = 1, 2, \ldots, k$, it is true that

$$\bar{x}(t) - x(t) = \sum_{i=0}^{n} u_{1i}(t)\xi_i + \ldots +$$

$$\sum_{i,j,\ldots s=0}^{n} u_{rij\ldots s}(t)\xi_i \xi_j \ldots \xi_s + o(\|\xi\|^r). \quad (6.29)$$

The pairs $\{u_{1i}(t), \{v_{1i}^l\}\}, \ldots, \{u_{rij\ldots s}(t), \{v_{rij\ldots s}^l\}\}$ are called the B-derivatives of the solution $x(t)$ with respect to initial conditions.

Lemma 6.3.1. *Suppose* $f \in C^{(0,r)}(I \times G), W_i \in C^{(r)}(G)$. *Then the solution* $y(t, t_0, x_0)$ *of system (6.15) has B-derivatives of up to r-th order, inclusive, with respect to $t_0, x_0^j, j = 1, 2, \ldots, n$, on the interval $[t_0, T]$. The formulas (6.29) are valid for all $t \in [t_0, T]$. That is, constants v in (6.28) are all equal to zero.*

Proof. By Lemma 6.1.5, solution $y(t, t_0, x_0)$ has B-derivatives of the first order, which are solutions of the variational system (6.16). The right-hand side of the system satisfies the conditions of Lemma 6.1.5. Hence, there exist B-derivatives for $y(t, t_0, x_0)$ of the second order, $(v = 0)$. Repeat similar discussion $r - 1$ times to obtain the complete proof of the lemma.

Theorem 6.3.1. *Suppose conditions (N1)–(N6), (N12) are valid, and $J_i, \tau_i \in C^{(r)}(G)$, $f \in C^{(0,r)}(I \times G) \cap C^{(r-1,r)}(N_h)$, where r is a positive integer. Then the solution $x(t)$ of (6.1) has B-derivatives of up to r-th order, inclusive, with respect to $t_0, x_0^j, j = 1, 2, \ldots, n$.*

Proof. Let us consider (6.1) in the domain G^h, where systems (6.1) and (6.15) are B-equivalent. One can show that the map $W_i, i = 1, 2, \ldots, k$, is defined in a neighborhood G_i of the point $x(\theta_i)$. Without loss of generality we assume that $G_i = G$ for all i. By Lemma 6.1.4, one has $W_i \in C^{(r)}(G), i = 1, 2, \ldots, k$. Consequently, by the last lemma there exist B-derivatives of $y(t, t_0, x_0)$ to r-th order, inclusive. It is obvious that the first components, u, of the B-derivatives is the first component of the B-derivatives of $x(t, t_0, x_0)$. By using (6.10), one can verify (6.28). The theorem is proved. □

Consider the solutions $x(t) = x(t, t_0, x_0, \mu_0)$ and $\bar{x}(t) = x(t, t_0, x_0, \mu_0 + \Delta\mu)$ of system (6.21), again. Denote by $\eta_i, i = 1, 2, \ldots, k$, the moments of discontinuity of $\bar{x}(t)$.

Definition 6.3.2. The solution $x(t)$ has B-derivatives of up to r-th order, inclusive, with respect to parameters $\mu_j, j = 1, 2, \ldots, m$, on $[t_0, T]$ if there exist functions $v_{1i}(t), v_{2ij}(t), \ldots, v_{rij\ldots s}(t) \in \mathcal{PC}^1([t_0, T], \theta), \theta = \{\theta_i\}_{i=1,2,\ldots,k}$ and constants $\beta_{1i}^l, \beta_{2ij}^l, \ldots, \beta_{rij\ldots s}^l, l = 1, 2, \ldots, k$, which are symmetric with respect to permutation of indices, such that if $(t_0, x_0, \mu) \in D((t_0, x_0), \delta) \cap G_m(\mu_0)$ for some $\delta > 0$, then:

(1)

$$\theta_l - \eta_l = \sum_{i=1}^n \beta_{1i}^l \xi_i + \ldots + \sum_{i,j,\ldots s=1}^n \beta_{rij\ldots s}^l \xi_i \xi_j \ldots \xi_s + o(\|\xi\|^r), \quad (6.30)$$

where $l = 1, 2, \ldots, k$;
(2) for all $t \notin \overline{(\theta_i, \eta_i]}, i = 1, 2, \ldots, k$, it is true that

$$\bar{x}(t) - x(t) = \sum_{i=1}^n v_{1i}(t)\xi_i + \ldots +$$

$$\sum_{i,j,\ldots s=1}^n v_{rij\ldots s}(t)\xi_i \xi_j \ldots \xi_s + o(\|\xi\|^r). \quad (6.31)$$

The pairs $\{v_{1i}(t), \{\beta_{1i}^l\}\}, \ldots, \{v_{rij\ldots s}(t), \{\beta_{rij\ldots s}^l\}\}$ are called B-derivatives of the solution $x(t)$ in $\mu_j, j = 1, 2, \ldots, m$.

Using Lemma 6.2.1, similar to the proof of Theorem 6.3.1, one can prove that the following theorem is valid.

Theorem 6.3.2. *Suppose conditions (N1)–(N6), (N12) are valid uniformly with respect to* $\mu \in G_\mu$, *and* $J_i, \tau_i \in C^{(r,r)}(G \times G_\mu)$, $f \in C^{(0,r,r)}(I \times G \times G_\mu) \cap C^{(r-1,r,r)}(N_h)$, *where* r *is a positive integer. Then the solution* $x(t)$ *of (6.21) has B-derivatives of up to* r*-th order, inclusive, with respect to* $\mu_j, j = 1, 2, \ldots, m$, *if there exists a number* $\kappa > 0$ *such that* $\tau_{m+1}(x_0, \mu) \geq \tau_{m+1}(x_0, \mu_0)$ *for all* $\|\mu - \mu_0\| < \kappa$.

6.4 B-Analyticity Property

In this part of the book, assume that in addition to conditions (N1)–(N6), (N12), which are valid for all $\mu \in G_\mu$, functions J_i, τ_i, and f are holomorphic in x and μ on $G \times G_\mu$, and f is holomorphic in t, x, and μ in the region N_h. Let us choose a point $(\kappa, x_0, 0)$ in $I \times G \times G_\mu$, and fix κ. Denote by $t = \theta$ a meeting moment of a solution $x(t, \kappa, x_0, 0)$ of (6.6) and the surface $t = \tau(x, 0)$ transversally. Assume that there exists a number $\kappa > 0$ such that $\tau(x_0, \mu) \geq \tau(x_0, 0)$ for all $\|\mu\| < \kappa$. Moreover, f is holomorphic in t in a neighborhood of $(\theta, x(\theta+), 0)$. Consider a solution $\bar{x}(t) = x(t, \kappa, x, \mu)$ of (6.6). If $\|\mu\|$ and $\|x - x_0\|$ are sufficiently small, then $\bar{x}(t)$ intersects the surface Γ transversally at moment $\bar{\theta} = \theta(x, \mu)$ near to θ. We assume also that (6.6) admits a solution $x_1(t) = x(t, \bar{\theta}, \bar{x}(\bar{\theta}) + I(\bar{x}(\bar{\theta}), \mu))$, defined on $\widehat{[\kappa, \bar{\theta}]}$, and introduce the map $W : (x, \mu) \to x_1(\kappa) - x$.

Lemma 6.4.1. $\theta(x, \mu)$ *is holomorphic at* $(x_0, 0)$.

Proof. Apply Poincaré's expansion theorem [98] to show that if t is near $t = \theta$ then the expansion

$$x(t) = \sum C_{p\alpha\ldots\lambda a\ldots l}(t - \theta)^p (x - x_1^0)^\alpha \ldots (x - x_n^0)^\lambda \mu_1^a \ldots \mu_m^l \quad (6.32)$$

is valid. Since the solution meets the surface of discontinuity transversally, if $\|x - x_0\|$ and $\|\mu\|$ are sufficiently small there exists a unique solution of the equation $\bar{\theta} = \tau(\bar{x}(\bar{\theta}), \mu)$. The function $\bar{\theta} = \theta(x, \mu)$ is defined as an implicit function, from the equation $\Psi(\bar{\theta}, \mu) \equiv \bar{\theta} - \tau(\bar{x}(\bar{\theta}), \mu) = 0$, where $\Psi_\theta(\theta, 0) \neq 0$. Using the theorem on the holomorphic implicit function [98], one can find

$$\bar{\theta} = \sum B_{p\alpha\ldots\lambda a\ldots l}(t - \theta)^p (x - x_1^0)^\alpha \ldots (x - x_n^0)^\lambda \mu_1^a \ldots \mu_m^l$$

such that $\bar{\theta}(x_0, 0) = \theta$. The lemma is proved. $\qquad\square$

By using $W(x, \mu) = x(\kappa, \bar{\theta}, x(\bar{\theta}, x, \mu) + I(x(\bar{\theta}, x, \mu), \mu)) - x$, Lemma 6.4.1, and the theorem on substitution of a series into a series [59] one can prove that the following assertion is valid.

Lemma 6.4.2. $W(x, \mu)$ *is holomorphic at* $(x_0, 0)$.

Let us consider the main subject of our discussion. Denote by $x(t) = x(t, t_0, x_0, 0)$ a solution of (6.21) with $\mu = 0$, and assume that it exists on an interval $[t_0, T], T > t_0$, with points of discontinuity $t_0 < \theta_1 < \ldots < \theta_k < T$. From the previous discussion, it implies that a solution $\bar{x}(t) = x(t, t_0, x, \mu)$ with sufficiently small $||x - x_0||$ and $||\mu||$ exists on the interval $[t_0, T]$. Denote by $\eta_i, i = 1, 2, \ldots, k$, the points of discontinuity of this solution. One can find a neighborhood of the integral curve of $x(t)$ on $[t_0, T]$ such that system (6.21) and

$$\frac{dy}{dt} = f(t, y, \mu),$$
$$\Delta y|_{t=\theta_i} = W_i(y, \mu), \tag{6.33}$$

are B-equivalent there. Since functions W_i are specified W for $\kappa = \theta_i$, by Lemma 6.4.2, they are analytic at points $(\theta_i, x(\theta_i), 0)$. There exists a solution $\phi(t) = y(t, t_0, x_0, 0)$ of system

$$\frac{dy}{dt} = f(t, y, 0),$$
$$\Delta y|_{t=\theta_i} = W_i(y, 0), \tag{6.34}$$

such that $\phi(t) = x(t)$ for all $t \in [t_0, T]$.

Definition 6.4.1. The solution $y(t) = y(t, t_0, x, \mu)$ of (6.33) is expanded in power series of coordinates $x - x_0$ and μ if

$$y(t) = \sum A_{\alpha \ldots \lambda a \ldots l}(t)(x - x_1^0)^\alpha \ldots (x - x_n^0)^\lambda \mu_1^a \ldots \mu_m^l, t \in [t_0, T],$$

where coefficients $A \in \mathcal{PC}_r([t_0, T], \theta)$.

Lemma 6.4.3. *The solution* $y(t) = y(t, t_0, x, \mu)$ *of system (6.33) is expanded in power series of coordinates of* $x - x_0$ *and* μ.

Proof. By continuity, if $||x - x_0||$ and $||\mu||$ are sufficiently small, then solution $y(t)$ exists on $[t_0, T]$. Let us show that

$$y(t) = \sum A_{\alpha \ldots \lambda a \ldots l}(t)(x - x_1^0)^\alpha \ldots (x - x_n^0)^\lambda \mu_1^a \ldots \mu_m^l,$$

where coefficients A are piecewise continuous functions with discontinuities at points θ_i. Indeed, apply the Poincaré' expansion theorem to obtain a series on the interval $[t_0, \theta_1]$. Now, using analyticity of J_1 one can find that the value $y(\theta_i+) = y(\theta_i) + W_1(y(\theta_1), \mu)$ has also a series expansion. Consequently, considering the solution of (6.6) with initial condition $(\theta_i, x(\theta_i))$ on $[\theta_1, \theta_2]$ and using the lemma on substitution of a series into a series, we find that the expansion is valid on $(\theta_1, \theta_2]$. Proceeding for all i, one comes to the complete proof of the assertion. The lemma is proved. □

Definition 6.4.2. The solution $\bar{x}(t) = x(t, t_0, x, \mu)$ of (6.21), with discontinuity moments $\eta_i, i = 1, 2, \ldots, k$, is expanded in power series of coordinates $x - x_0$ and μ (or it B-analytically depends on x and μ) if for all $t \notin \widehat{(\theta_i, \eta_i]}$ it is true that

$$\bar{x}(t) = \sum A_{\alpha \ldots \lambda a \ldots l}(t)(x - x_1^0)^\alpha \ldots (x - x_n^0)^\lambda \mu_1^a \ldots \mu_m^l,$$

and

$$\theta_i - \eta_i = \sum D^i_{\alpha \ldots \lambda a \ldots l}(x - x_1^0)^\alpha \ldots (x - x_n^0)^\lambda \mu_1^a \ldots \mu_m^l,$$

where coefficients $A \in \mathcal{PC}_r([t_0, T], \theta)$ and D are real numbers.

From the last lemma and the B-equivalence it follows that the next theorem is valid.

Theorem 6.4.1. *The solution $\bar{x}(t) = x(t, t_0, x, \mu)$ of system (6.21) is expanded in power series of coordinates $x - x_0$ and μ.*

The following assertion is an easy corollary of the last theorem.

Theorem 6.4.2. *For each fixed $\bar{t} \in [t_0, T]$ the function $x(\bar{t}, t_0, x, \mu)$ is an analytic function of x and μ in a neighborhood of the point $(x_0, 0)$.*

6.5 B-Asymptotic Approximation of Solutions

In this part of the chapter, we investigate the problem of asymptotic approximation with respect to the small parameter of solutions of impulsive differential equations with impulses on surfaces. The results obtained here are development of previous parts of the present chapter. Consider system (6.21), assuming this time that the dimension of the parameter space μ is one, $m = 1$. We assume that for all $\mu \in (-\mu_0, \mu_0)$, where μ_0 is a fixed positive number, conditions (N1)–(N6),(N11),(N12), are valid, and the following higher order differentiability is fulfilled, $J_i, \tau_i \in C^{(r,r)}(G \times G_\mu), f \in C^{(0,r,r)}(I \times G \times G_\mu) \cap C^{(r-1,r,r)}(N_h)$, where r is a positive integer, and N_h is a union of h-neighborhoods of surfaces $t = \tau(x, \mu), i \in \mathcal{A}$, in $I \times G \times G_\mu$.

Denote by $x_0(t) = x(t, t_0, x_0, 0)$ a solution of (6.21), where $\mu = 0$, that is, $x_0(t)$ is a solution of the system

$$\frac{dx}{dt} = f(t, x, 0),$$
$$\Delta x|_{t = \tau_i(x,0)} = J_i(x, 0), \tag{6.35}$$

and assume that it exists on an interval $[t_0, T], T > t_0$, with points of discontinuity $t = \theta_i, t_0 < \theta_1 < \ldots < \theta_k < T$.

From the earlier discussion, it implies that a solution $x(t, \mu) = x(t, t_0, x_0, \mu)$ with sufficiently small $|\mu|$ exists on the interval $[t_0, T]$. Denote by $\eta_i, i = 1, 2, \ldots, k$, the points of discontinuity of this solution.

We say that the solution $x(t, \mu)$ has a B-asymptotic approximation if for sufficiently small $|\mu|$ and for all $t \in [t_0, T]$ outside the intervals $\widehat{[\theta_i, \eta_i]}, i = 1, 2, \ldots, k$, the following equality is valid,

$$x(t, \mu) = \sum_{j=1}^{r} x_j(t)\mu^j + O(\mu^{r+1}), \tag{6.36}$$

where $x_j(t)$ are piecewise continuous vector-valued functions from $\mathcal{PC}([t_0, T], \theta)$, $\theta = \{\theta_i\}_{i=1,2,\ldots,k}$. Moreover, for all $i = 1, 2, \ldots, k$,

$$\eta_i - \theta_i = \sum_{j=1}^{r} \kappa_{ij}\mu^j + O(\mu^{r+1}), \tag{6.37}$$

where κ_{ij} are real constants.

By the B-equivalence, $x_0(t)$ is a solution of (6.35) and (6.34). Moreover, one can find a sufficiently small neighborhood of the integral curve of $x_0(t)$ on $[t_0, T]$, where systems (6.21) and (6.33) are B-equivalent. The existence of the expansions (6.36) and (6.37) is proved in Theorem 6.3.2. We consider here the problem of determining the coefficients $x_j(t)$ and κ_{ij}. By virtue of the correspondence established between solutions $x(t, \mu)$ and $y(t, \mu)$ of systems (6.21) and (6.33) above, it suffices to determine the x_j beginning with (6.33), taking into account the fact that the asymptotic formula

$$y(t, \mu) = \sum_{j=1}^{r} x_j(t)\mu^j + O(\mu^{r+1}), \tag{6.38}$$

holds for all points in $[t_0, T]$.

Substituting the last expression into (6.33) and using the smoothness of f and W_i, we find that for each $j = 1, 2, \ldots, r$, the coefficient $x_j(t)$ is a solution of the Cauchy problem $x_j(t_0) = 0$ for the equation

$$\frac{dx}{dt} = \frac{f(t, x_0(t), 0)}{dx}x + F(t, x_0, x_1, \ldots, x_{j-1}),$$

$$\Delta x|_{t=\theta_i} = \frac{W_i(x, 0)}{dx}x + G_i(x_0, x_1, \ldots, x_{j-1}), \tag{6.39}$$

where functions F and G_i are completely determined by $x_0, x_1, \ldots, x_{j-1}$ and the partial derivatives of f and V_i of order up and including j, evaluated for $x = x_0(t)$ and $\mu = 0$.

Let us determine the partial derivatives of the W_i at the points $(x_0(\theta_i), 0)$. Fix i and for brevity we omit the index i in what follows. We let $\theta_i = \theta$, and if $x = x_0(\theta), t = \theta$, and $\mu = 0$, or if $x = x_0(\theta+), t = \theta$, and $\mu = 0$, then all functions used below will be written without showing the values of the arguments, and we will distinguish between these two cases by using a $+$ superscript in the second case.

Also, we use the subscripts $x, t,$ and μ to indicate partial derivatives. We will assume that $x, f, J,$ and W and their derivatives are column vectors, and that derivatives of τ and θ are row vectors. We define the product of vectors and matrices according to the usual rule of multiplying rectangular matrices.

The moment of discontinuity $t = \eta$ of the solution $x(t, \mu)$ is determined from the equation $t = \tau(x(t, \mu), \mu)$ as a function $\eta = \eta(x, \mu)$, where $x = x(\eta, \mu)$. Therefore, applying the known implicit function theorem and passing to the limit as $\mu \to 0$, we get

$$
\begin{aligned}
\eta_x &= \tau_x (1 - \tau_x f)^{-1}, \eta_\mu = \tau_x (1 - \tau_x f)^{-1} \tau_\mu, \\
\eta_{x\mu} &= \tau_{x\mu} (1 - \tau_x f)^{-1} + \tau_x (\tau_{x\mu} f + \tau_x f_\mu)(1 - \tau_x f)^{-2}, \\
\eta_{\mu\mu} &= \tau_\mu (1 - \tau_x f)^{-1} + \tau_\mu (\tau_{x\mu} f + \tau_x f_\mu), \\
\eta_{xx_j} &= 2\tau_{xx_j} (1 - \tau_x f)^{-1} + \tau_x (2\tau_{xx_j} f + \tau_x f_{x_j})(1 - \tau_x f)^{-2}. \quad (6.40)
\end{aligned}
$$

Applying the resulting expressions in a similar way, starting from (6.23), we find that

$$
\begin{aligned}
W_x &= \eta_x (f - f^+) + J_x (\mathcal{I} + \eta_x f), W_\mu = (f - f^+)\eta_\mu + J_x f \eta_\mu + J_\mu, \\
W_{x\mu} &= \eta_x (f_t - f_t^+)\eta_\mu + \eta_{x\mu} (f - f^+) + (f_x - f_x^+ (\mathcal{I} + J_x))\eta_\mu + \\
&\quad (\sum_{k=1}^{n} J_{xx_k} f_k \eta_\mu + J_{x\mu})(\mathcal{I} + \eta_x f) + J_x (\eta_x f_\mu + f_x \eta_\mu + \eta_{x\mu} f), \\
W_{xx_j} &= \eta_x ((f_t - f_t^+)\eta_{x_j}^{\cdot} + f_{x_j} - f_{x_j}^+) + \eta_{xx_j} (f - f^+) + \\
&\quad \eta_{x_j} (f_x - f_x^+ - f_x^+ J_x) + \sum_{k=1}^{n} J_{xx_k} (\delta_{kj} + f_k \eta_{x_j})(\mathcal{I} + \eta_x f) + \\
&\quad J_x (\eta_x (f_{x_j} + f_t \eta_{x_j}) + \eta_{xx_j} f + \eta_{x_j} f_x), \\
W_{\mu\mu} &= (f_t - f_t^+)\eta_\mu^2 + (f - f^+)\eta_{\mu\mu} + (f_\mu + J_{x\mu} f)\eta_\mu + \\
&\quad \sum_{k=1}^{n} J_{xx_k} f_k \eta_\mu (f \eta_\mu + J_\mu) + J_x (f_t \eta_\mu^2 + 2f_\mu \eta_\mu + f \eta_{\mu\mu}) + \\
&\quad \sum_{k=1}^{n} J_{\mu x_k} f_k + J_{\mu\mu}. \quad (6.41)
\end{aligned}
$$

where δ_{ij} is the Kronecker symbol. It is clear that in this way it is possible to calculate the derivatives of W up to and including order r at the point $(x(\theta_i), 0)$ from the values of the derivatives of $f, J,$ and τ at points $(\theta, x_0(\theta), 0)$ and $(\theta, x_0(\theta+), 0)$. In addition, the coefficients in (6.37) can be determined by starting from (6.40).

Notes

Some results on differentiable dependence of first order for solutions of impulsive
systems on initial conditions and parameters can be found in [45, 64, 74, 141, 142].
All definitions of differentiability of solutions, higher order differentiable dependence, and analyticity of solutions of differential equations with nonfixed moments
of impulses were given in papers [24, 25, 32, 34, 35] for the first time, as well as corresponding theorems and their proofs. Further applications and development of the
results for autonomous equations and Filippov's differential equations were made in
[1, 3, 4, 14, 27, 36]. The results of the chapter show that the method of B-equivalence
is suitable to realize any type of smoothness for differential equations with variable moments of discontinuities. The variational equations are presented for the
first time with the second component of the B-derivatives.

Chapter 7
Periodic Solutions of Nonlinear Systems

In this part of the book, we investigate, by applying methods developed in the previous chapters, existence and stability of periodic solutions of quasilinear systems with variable moments of impulses.

7.1 Quasilinear Systems: the Noncritical Case

Consider the following (ω, p)-periodic system of differential equations with impulses on surfaces

$$x' = A(t)x + f(t) + \mu\phi(t, x, \mu),$$

$$\Delta x|_{t=\theta_i + \mu\tau_i(x,\mu)} = B_i x + I_i + \mu\Psi_i(x, \mu), \qquad (7.1)$$

where $(t, x) \in \mathbb{R} \times \mathbb{R}^n, \mu \in (-\mu_0, \mu_0)$, μ_0 is a fixed positive number, real valued elements of $n \times n$ matrix $A(t)$ are continuous functions, and constant real valued $n \times n$ matrices $B_i, i \in \mathbb{Z}$, satisfy condition (4.2). Coordinates of $f(t) : \mathbb{R} \to \mathbb{R}^n$ are continuous functions, and $J_i, i \in \mathbb{Z}$, is a sequence of vectors from $\mathbb{R}^n$. Being an (ω, p)-periodic system means that there exist a positive real number ω and a positive integer p such that $A(t+\omega) = A(t), f(t+\omega) = f(t), \phi(t+\omega, x, \mu) = \phi(t, x, \mu)$, for all $t \in \mathbb{R}, x \in \mathbb{R}^n, \mu \in (-\mu_0, \mu_0)$, and $B_{i+p} = B_i, I_{i+p} = I_i, \Psi_{i+p}(x, \mu) = \Psi_i(x, \mu), \theta_{i+p} = \theta_i + \omega, \tau_{i+p}(x, \mu) = \tau_i(x, \mu)$, for all $i \in \mathbb{Z}, x \in \mathbb{R}^n$, $\mu \in (-\mu_0, \mu_0)$. We assume also that $\phi \in C^{(0,1,1)}(\mathbb{R} \times \mathbb{R}^n \times (-\mu_0, \mu_0)), \tau_i,$ $\Psi_i \in C^{(1,1)}(\mathbb{R}^n \times (-\mu_0, \mu_0)), i \in \mathbb{Z}$.

It is obvious that θ is a B-sequence. That is, the infinite sequence satisfies $|\theta_i| \to \infty$ as $|i| \to \infty$. Beside the system (7.1), consider the nonperturbed system

$$x' = A(t)x + f(t),$$

$$\Delta x|_{t=\theta_i} = B_i x + I_i. \qquad (7.2)$$

M. Akhmet, *Principles of Discontinuous Dynamical Systems*,
DOI 10.1007/978-1-4419-6581-3_7, © Springer Science+Business Media, LLC 2010

Theorem 7.1.1. *Assume that (7.2) has a unique nontrivial ω-periodic solution $x_0(t)$. If $|\mu|$ is sufficiently small, then (7.1) admits an ω-periodic solution that converges in the B-topology to $x_0(t)$ as $\mu \to 0$.*

Proof. Without loss of generality, we assume that the periodic solution $x_0(t) = x(t, 0, x_0, 0)$ has moments of discontinuity θ_i such that $0 < \theta_1 < \ldots < \theta_p < \omega$. Let $x(t) = x(t, 0, \xi, \mu)$ be a solution of (7.1), $x(0) = \xi$. If $|\mu|$ is sufficiently small, then from results of the last chapter it follows that $x(t)$ has moments of discontinuity η_i such that $0 < \eta_1 < \ldots < \eta_p < \omega$, and there is a neighborhood of the point $(0, x_0)$, which does not intersect all surfaces of discontinuity $t = \theta_i + \mu\tau(x, \mu)$. By the Poincaré criterion, the solution $x(t)$ is a periodic function if and only if the equation

$$\Phi(y, \mu) \equiv x(\omega, 0, y, \mu) - y = 0 \tag{7.3}$$

is satisfied with $y = \xi$. It follows, from the implicit function theorem that (7.3) has a solution if $\det \Phi_y(x_0, 0) \neq 0$, and the matrix is continuous in a neighborhood of $(x_0, 0)$. By Theorem 6.1.1, B-derivatives of $x(t)$ in $\xi_j, j = 1, 2, \ldots, n$, form a fundamental matrix $Z(t, y, \mu), Z(0, y, \mu) = \mathcal{I}$, of the variational system. If $\mu = 0$, then the variational system has the form

$$\begin{aligned} x' &= A(t)x, \\ \Delta x|_{t=\theta_i} &= B_i x. \end{aligned} \tag{7.4}$$

The uniqueness of the periodic solution $x_0(t)$ implies that

$$\det \Phi_y(x_0, 0) = \det(Z(\omega, y, 0) - \mathcal{I}) \neq 0.$$

Hence, (7.3), for sufficiently small $|\mu|$, has a unique solution in a small neighborhood of x_0, and this solution is as much near x_0 as μ is close to 0. By Lemma 6.1.6, we have that the ω-periodic solution $x(t)$ converges to $x_0(t)$ as $\mu \to 0$. The theorem is proved.   □

Fix positive h such that N_h, the union of h-neighborhoods of points $\theta_i, i = 1, 2, \ldots, p$, is placed in $[0, \omega]$. Similarly to the proof of the last theorem, one can verify that the following assertion is valid.

Theorem 7.1.2. *Assume that (7.2) has a unique nontrivial ω-periodic solution $x_0(t)$, functions ϕ, Ψ, τ_i are analytic in $x \in G$, and, moreover, functions A, f, ϕ are analytic in $t \in N_h$. Then for a sufficiently small $|\mu|$ system (7.1) admits an ω-periodic solution that converges in the B-topology to $x_0(t)$, as $\mu \to 0$. The solution is analytic at $\mu = 0$.*

Let us formulate the following assertion without proving it.

Theorem 7.1.3. *Suppose all multipliers of (7.4) are inside the unit disc. If $|\mu|$ is sufficiently small, then the ω-periodic solution of (7.1) is B-asymptotically stable.*

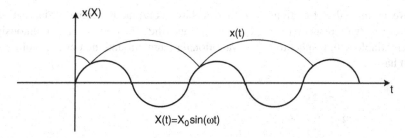

Fig. 7.1 The first coordinate, $x(t)$, of the periodic solution $\psi(t)$

Example 7.1.1. Consider system (1.3), which is constructed in Example 1.1 as a model of a mechanical system consisting of a bead bouncing on a table. In [89], it is proven that the mechanical model considered with the condition

$$\omega^2 \geq \frac{\pi g}{X_0} \frac{1 - R}{1 + R} \tag{7.5}$$

admits a periodic discontinuous motion $\psi(t)$ with period $T = \frac{2\pi}{\omega}$ (see Fig. 7.1).

The solution has the initial value $x_0 = X_0\sqrt{1 - \cos^2(\phi)}$, $x_0' = \frac{\pi g}{X_0\omega}$ at the moment of the impact $t = \phi$, which is defined by the relation

$$\cos(\phi) = \frac{\pi g}{X_0\omega^2} \frac{1 - R}{1 + R}. \tag{7.6}$$

Applying the Poincaré map, it was shown that the periodic motion is asymptotically stable if

$$\frac{\pi g}{X_0} \frac{1 - R}{1 + R} < \omega^2 < \{[\frac{\pi g}{X_0} \frac{1 - R}{1 + R}]^2 + [\frac{2g(1 + R^2)}{X_0(1 + R)^2}]^2\}^{\frac{1}{2}}. \tag{7.7}$$

It is obvious that (1.3) is a highly idealized model. It takes no account of drag in the medium, the unavoidable perturbations of the table, and possible elastic couplings. Hence, it is natural to consider a system of the form

$$x_1' = x_2,$$
$$x_2' = -g + \mu f(t, x, \mu),$$
$$\Delta x_2|_{t=\tau_i(x_1)+\mu\kappa_i(x,\mu)} = (1 + R)[x_0\omega \cos(\omega\tau_i(x_1)) - x_2] + \mu I_i(x, \mu), \tag{7.8}$$

where μ is a small parameter.

We assume that functions f, I, and κ have continuous second-order partial derivatives with respect to x_1, x_2, and μ, and the function f is continuously differentiable with respect to t. The variational system around the periodic solution $\psi(t)$ has the form

$$u_1' = u_2,$$
$$u_2' = 0,$$
$$\Delta u_2|_{t=\phi} = \frac{\omega}{2}\left[\frac{(1+R)^2}{\pi} - b(1-R)^2)\right]u_1 - (1+R)u_2, \qquad (7.9)$$

where $b = \sqrt{\cos^{-2}(\phi) - 1}$. The characteristic equation for (7.9) is

$$\rho^2 + (\pi b(1 - R^2) - (1 + R^2))\rho + R^2 = 0.$$

We have from the last equation that (7.9) does not have a unique multiplier provided

$$R = 1 \quad \text{or} \quad \omega^2 \neq \frac{\pi g}{X_0}\frac{1 - R}{1 + R}.$$

A necessary and sufficient condition for the multipliers to be situated inside the unit circle is the inequality (7.7).

Assume that $R \neq 1$, and suppose that the function f is periodic with period $T = \frac{2\pi}{\omega}$ with respect to t, and for all $x, \mu, i \in \mathbb{Z}$, the equalities $I_{i+1} = I_i, \kappa_{i+1} = \kappa_i$ are satisfied. Then one can see that the system is $(T, 1)$-periodic, and from relations (7.5) and (7.7), we find, according to Theorems 7.1.1 and 7.1.3, that for a sufficiently small μ system (7.8) admits a unique T-periodic B-asymptotically stable solution, which converges to $\psi(t)$, as $\mu \to 0$.

In the sequel, we proceed with the investigation of system (5.38) and find the conditions for the existence of a unique bounded solution, a periodic solution, and asymptotical stability of these solutions. In this part of the section, we want to see the use of the reduction method for this system. Beside it, we consider the following equations with impulse actions at fixed moments

$$\frac{dx}{dt} = A(t)x + f(t, x),$$
$$\Delta x|_{t=\theta_i} = B_i x + I_i(x), \qquad (7.10)$$

where $t \in \mathbb{R}, x \in \mathbb{R}^n, \theta = \{\theta_i\}, i \in \mathbb{Z}$, is a B-sequence, entries of $n \times n$ matrix $A(t)$ are continuous real valued functions, $B_i, i \in \mathbb{Z}$, are constant real valued square matrices of order n. That is, system (7.10) differs from (5.38) only by absence of perturbations $\tau_i(x)$.

For the convenience of discussion we will reformulate conditions $(Q1)$–$(Q5)$ of Sect. 5.8.

So, we assume that for system (7.10) the following conditions are valid:

(P1) there exists a positive constant κ such that $\theta_{i+1} - \theta_i \geq \kappa, i \in \mathbb{Z}$;
(P2) there exists a positive constant l such that for all $t \in \mathbb{R}, x, y \in \mathbb{R}^n, i \in \mathbb{Z}$, the following inequality is valid

$$\|f(t, x) - f(t, y)\| + \|I_i(x) - I_i(y)\| \leq l\|x - y\|; \qquad (7.11)$$

(P3) $\det(\mathcal{I} + B_i) \neq 0, i \in \mathbb{Z}$;
The transition matrix $X(t, s)$ of the associated homogeneous system

$$x' = A(t)x,$$
$$\Delta x|_{t \neq \theta_i} = B_i x, \qquad (7.12)$$

satisfies the following inequality
(P4)

$$\|X(t, s)\| \leq Ke^{-\gamma(t-s)}, s \leq t, \qquad (7.13)$$

where K and γ are positive real numbers;
(P5) $Kl[\frac{1}{\gamma} + \frac{e^{\kappa\gamma}}{1-e^{-\kappa\gamma}}] < 1$;
(P6) there exists a positive number H such that

$$\sup_{-\infty < t < +\infty, \|x\| < H} \|f(t, x)\| + \sup_{-\infty < i < +\infty, \|x\| < H} \|I_i(x)\| = M < +\infty,$$

and

$$KM[\frac{1}{\gamma} + \frac{e^{\kappa\gamma}}{1 - e^{-\kappa\gamma}}] < H;$$

(P7) $\sup_{\mathbb{R}} \|A(t)\| + \sup_{\mathbb{Z}} \|B_i\| = N < +\infty$;
(P8) $-\gamma + Kl + \frac{\ln(1+Kl)}{\kappa} < 0$.

Since (7.10) belongs to the class of equations (5.38), the discussion made in Sect. 5.8 on extension of solutions of (5.38) is also valid for (7.10). Consequently, each solution $x(t) = x(t, t_0, x_0), (t_0, x_0) \in \mathbb{R} \times \mathbb{R}^n$ of (7.10) exists and is unique on $\mathbb{R}$.

Theorem 7.1.4. *If conditions $(P1) - (P7)$ are valid, then:*

(1) there exists a unique bounded solution $\phi(t) \in PC^1(\mathbb{R}, \theta)$ of (7.10), and $\|\phi(t)\| < H$ for all $t \in \mathbb{R}$;
(2) if in addition condition $(P8)$ is fulfilled then $\phi(t)$ is a globally asymptotically stable solution;
(3) if (7.10) is an (ω, p)-periodic system, then $\phi(t)$ is an ω-periodic solution.

Proof. The proof falls naturally into following three parts.

1. Let us introduce a set of functions $\mathcal{H} = \{x \in \mathcal{PC}^1(\mathbb{R}, \theta) : \|x(t)\| < H, t \in \mathbb{R}\}$. Define in $\mathcal{H}$ an operator E such that, if $\xi \in \mathcal{H}$, then

$$E\xi(t) = \int_{-\infty}^{t} X(t, \tau) f(\tau, \xi) d\tau + \sum_{\theta_i < t} X(t, \theta_i +) I_i(\xi(\theta_i)). \quad (7.14)$$

Let us show that $E : \mathcal{H} \to \mathcal{H}$. Indeed, it is easy to see that $\xi \in \mathcal{PC}^1(\mathbb{R}, \theta)$. See, for example, the proof of Theorem 2.4.1. Moreover, we have that

$$\|E\xi(t)\| \leq \int_{-\infty}^{t} K e^{-\gamma(t-\tau)} M d\tau + \sum_{\theta_i < t} K e^{-\gamma(t-\theta_i)} M < H.$$

Show now, that E is a contraction. If $\xi_1(t), \xi_2(t) \in \mathcal{H}$, then

$$\|E\xi_1(t) - E\xi_2(t)\| \leq \int_{-\infty}^{t} K l e^{-\gamma(t-\tau)} \|\xi_1(\tau) - \xi_2(\tau)\| d\tau +$$

$$\sum_{\theta_i < t} K l e^{-\gamma(t-\theta_i)} \|\xi_1(\theta_i) - \xi_2(\theta_i)\| <$$

$$K l [\frac{1}{\gamma} + \frac{e^{\gamma}}{1 - e^{-\kappa\gamma}}] \sup_{\mathbb{R}} \|\xi_1(\tau) - \xi_2(\tau)\|.$$

That is E is a contraction and the sequence $\xi^k(t), \xi^0(t) \equiv 0, \xi^{k+1}(t) = E\xi^k(t), k = 0, 1, \ldots$, converges to a unique bounded solution $\phi(t)$ of system (7.10) such that $\|\phi(t)\| < H$.

2. Assume that condition $(P8)$ besides $(P1) - -(P7)$ is valid, and $\psi(t)$ is another solution of system (7.10). Then

$$\phi(t) = X(t, t_0)\phi(t_0) + \int_{t_0}^{t} X(t, \tau) f(\tau, \phi(\tau)) d\tau + \sum_{t_0 \leq \theta_i < t} X(t, \theta_i +) I_i(\phi(\theta_i))$$

and

$$\psi(t) = X(t, t_0)\psi(t_0) + \int_{t_0}^{t} X(t, \tau) f(\tau, \psi(\tau)) d\tau + \sum_{t_0 \leq \theta_i < t} X(t, \theta_i +) I_i(\psi(\theta_i)).$$

Now, we have that

$$\|\phi(t) - \psi(t)\| \leq K e^{-\gamma(t-t_0)} \|\phi(t_0) - \psi(t_0)\| + \int_{t_0}^{t} K l e^{-\gamma(t-\tau)} \|\phi(\tau) - \psi(\tau)\| d\tau +$$

$$\sum_{t_0 \leq \theta_i < t} K l e^{-\gamma(t-\theta_i)} \|\phi(\theta_i) - \psi(\theta_i)\|.$$

Denote by $u(t) = \|\phi(t) - \psi(t)\|e^{\gamma t}$ in the last formula and apply Lemma 2.5.1 to obtain

$$\|\phi(t) - \psi(t)\| \leq K e^{\kappa \gamma} e^{-(\gamma - Kl - \frac{\ln(1+Kl)}{\kappa})(t-t_0)} \|\phi(t_0) - \psi(t_0)\|.$$

The stability is proved.   □

3. Assume that conditions $(P1) - -(P7)$ are valid, (7.10) is an (ω, p)-periodic system and prove, very similarly to Theorem 5.9.2, periodicity of the bounded solution $\phi(t)$, yourself.
   The theorem is proved.   □

Let us consider other conditions:

(S1) each interval $[id, (i+1)d), i \in \mathbb{Z}$, where d is a positive fixed number, contains at most one element of the sequence θ;

(S2) $Kl[\frac{1}{\gamma} + \frac{e^{\gamma d}}{1-e^{-\gamma d}}] < 1$;

(S3) there exists a positive number H such that

$$\sup_{-\infty < t < +\infty, \|x\| < H} \|f(t,x)\| + \sup_{-\infty < i < +\infty, \|x\| < H} \|I_i(x)\| = M < +\infty,$$

and

$$KM[\frac{1}{\gamma} + \frac{e^{\gamma d}}{1-e^{-\gamma d}}] < H;$$

(S4) $-\gamma + Kl + \frac{\ln(1+Kl)}{d} < 0.$

We may formulate a new theorem, useful in Chap. 10, which can be proved similarly to the last assertion.

Theorem 7.1.5. *Assume that conditions* $(P2) - (P4), (P7), (S1)–(S3)$, *are valid. Then:*

(1) there exists a unique bounded solution $\phi(t)$ of (7.10), and $\|\phi(t)\| < H$ for all $t \in \mathbb{R}$;

(2) if additionally condition (S4) is fulfilled then $\phi(t)$ is an asymptotically stable solution;

(3) if (7.10) is an (ω, p)-periodic system, then $\phi(t)$ is an ω-periodic solution.

Now, introduce the following assumptions:

(Q10) $K[\frac{M}{\gamma} + \frac{c(l)e^{2\gamma\kappa}}{1-e^{-\frac{\gamma\kappa}{2}}}] + b(l) < H$;

(Q11) $Kl[\frac{1}{\gamma} + \frac{k(l)e^{2\gamma\kappa}}{1-e^{-\frac{\gamma\kappa}{2}}}] < 1$;

(Q12) $-\gamma + Kl + \frac{\ln(1+Klk(l))}{\kappa} < 0,$

and consider the following assertion.

Theorem 7.1.6. *If conditions* $(P4), (Q1) - (Q5), (Q10), (Q11),$ *are valid, then:*

(1) there exists a unique bounded solution $\phi(t)$ of (5.38), and $\|\phi(t)\| < H$ for all $t \in \mathbb{R}$;

(2) if in addition condition $(Q12)$ is fulfilled then $\phi(t)$ is an asymptotically stable solution;

(3) if (5.38) is an (ω, p)-periodic system, then $\phi(t)$ is an ω-periodic solution.

The proof of the last theorem follows immediately Theorem 7.1.4 and the results of Sect. 5.8. Moreover, assertions (1), (2), (3) of the last theorem can be considered as corollaries of the results in Sects. 5.8, 5.9.

7.2 The Critical Case

Consider the (ω, p)-periodic system (7.1), assuming this time that we have a critical case. That is, the associated linear homogeneous system (7.4) admits a maximal set of linearly independent ω-periodic solutions $\phi_j(t), j = 1, 2, \ldots, k, 0 < k \le n$. Then, by Theorem 4.3.2, the system adjoint to (7.4),

$$y' = -A^T(t)y,$$
$$\Delta y|_{t=\theta_i} = -(\mathcal{I} + B_i^T)^{-1} B_i^T y, \tag{7.15}$$

(where T denotes transposition), has k linearly independent ω-periodic solutions $\psi_j(t), j = 1, 2, \ldots, k$. Compose these solutions as the $n \times k$ matrix $H_1(t)$.

Suppose that the following condition is satisfied,

$$\int_0^\omega H_1^T(t) f(t) dt + \sum_{i=1}^p H_1^T(\theta_i) I_i = 0. \tag{7.16}$$

Then, by Theorem 4.3.3, (7.2) has the family of ω-periodic solutions $x(t, \alpha) = \alpha_1 \phi_1(t) + \alpha_2 \phi_2(t) + \ldots + \alpha_k \phi_k(t) + \phi_0(t)$, where $\phi_0(t)$ is an ω-periodic particular solution of (7.2).

We assume that the smoothness of system (7.1) is of higher order. That is, the matrix $A(t)$ and the function $f(t)$ are $l - 1$ times, $l \ge 2$, continuously differentiable in ϵ-neighborhoods of the points $\theta_i, i \in \mathbb{Z}$. Denote the union of the neighborhoods as G_ϵ and assume that $\phi \in C^{(l-1,l,l)}(G_\epsilon \times \mathbb{R}^n \times (-\mu_0, \mu_0)) \cap C^{(0,l,l)}(\mathbb{R} \times \mathbb{R}^n \times (-\mu_0, \mu_0)), \tau_i, \Psi_i \in C^{(l,l)}(\mathbb{R}^n \times (-\mu_0, \mu_0))$.

Theorem 7.2.1. *Suppose system (7.1) satisfies the conditions discussed, (7.2) admits a family of ω-periodic solutions $x(t, \alpha)$. Let α_0 be a solution of the equation $h(\alpha) = 0$, where*

$$h(\alpha) = \int_0^\omega H_1^T(t) \phi(t, x(t, \alpha), 0) dt + \sum_{i=1}^p H_1^T(\theta_i) \{ \Psi_i(x(\theta_i, \alpha), 0) +$$

$$\tau_i(x(\theta_i, \alpha), 0)[((\mathcal{I} + B_i)A(\theta_i) - A(\theta_i)B_i)x(\theta_i, \alpha) - A(\theta_i)I_i]\},$$

such that

$$\det[\frac{\partial h}{\partial \alpha}|_{\alpha=\alpha_0}] \neq 0.$$

Then system (7.1) has an ω-periodic solution, if $|\mu|$ is sufficiently small. The solution converges in the B-topology to $x(t, \alpha_0)$ as $\mu \to 0$.

Proof. To prove the assertion, we will use the B-equivalence method. Consider the system of ordinary differential equations

$$x' = A(t)x + f(t) + \mu\phi(t, x, \mu), \tag{7.17}$$

which is the part of system (7.1).

Fix $i \in \mathbb{Z}$ and $x \in \mathbb{R}^n$. Let $x_0(t)$ be the solution of (7.17) such that $x_0(\theta_i) = x$, and ξ_i be a solution of the equation $t = \theta_i + \mu\tau_i(x_0(t))$. That is, ξ_i is the meeting moment of $x_0(t)$ with Γ_i. Let $x_1(t)$ be the solution of system (7.17) with the initial condition $x_1(\xi_i) = B_i x_0(\xi_i) + I_i + \mu\Psi_i(, \mu)x_0(\xi_i)$. Consider the following map:

$$J_i(x, \mu) = (\mathcal{I} + B_i) \int_{\theta_i}^{\xi_i} (A(\tau)x_0(\tau) + f(\tau) + \mu\phi(\tau, x_0(\tau), \mu))d\tau +$$

$$+I_i + \mu\Psi_i(x(\xi_i), \mu) + \int_{\xi_i}^{\theta_i} (A(\tau)x_0(\tau) + f(\tau) + \mu\phi(\tau, x_0(\tau), \mu))d\tau +$$

$$+I_i + \int_{\xi_i}^{\theta_i} (A(\tau)x_1(\tau) + f(\tau) + \mu\phi(\tau, x_1(\tau), \mu))d\tau. \tag{7.18}$$

We can verify that $J_i(x, \mu) = \mu\Omega_i(x, \mu)$, where $\Omega_i(x, \mu)$ is a continuously differentiable function such that $\Omega_i(x, 0) = \Psi_i(x, 0) + (\tau_i(x, 0)[((\mathcal{I} + B_i)A(\theta_i) - A(\theta_i)B_i)x - A(\theta_i)I_i]$. One can show that systems (7.1) and

$$y' = A(t)y + f(t) + \mu\phi(t, y, \mu),$$

$$\Delta y|_{t=\theta_i} = B_i y + I_i + \mu\Omega_i(y, \mu), \tag{7.19}$$

are B-equivalent in $\mathbb{R} \times \mathbb{R}^n \times (-\mu_0, \mu_0)$. That is, the problem of existence of periodic solutions of system (7.1) can be reduced to the problem for (7.19) with fixed moments of impulsive action.

Complete the matrix $H_1(t)$ by solutions $\psi_j, j = k+1, \ldots, n$, of the adjoint system to build a fundamental matrix of solutions $H(t)$. Substitute $z = H^T(0)y$ in (7.19) and obtain the system

$$z' = P(t)z + g(t) + \mu\mathcal{F}(t, z, \mu),$$

$$\Delta z|_{t=\theta_i} = S_i z + K_i + \mu\mathcal{O}_i(z, \mu), \tag{7.20}$$

where

$$P(t) = H^T(0)A(t)H^T(0)^{-1}, g(t) = H^T(0)f(t),$$

$$S_i = H^T(0)B_i H^T(0)^{-1}, K_i = H^T(0)I_i,$$

$$\mathcal{F}(t, y, \mu) = H^T(0)\phi(t, H^T(0)^{-1}y, \mu), \mathcal{O}_i(y, \mu) = H^T(0)\Omega_i(H^T(0)^{-1}y, \mu).$$

Denote $z(t, \alpha) = H^T(0)x(t, \alpha), \beta = (\beta_{k+1}, \ldots, \beta_n)$ and let $v(t) = z(t, \alpha, \beta)$ be a solution of system (7.20) with initial condition $v(o) = z(0, \alpha) + (0, \beta)$. Further, let $L(t) = H^{-1}(0)H(t), L_1(t) = H^{-1}(0)H_1(t), L_2(t)$ be the matrix composed of the entries of the last $n - k$ columns and $n - k$ rows of $L(t)$, and $L_3(t)$ be the matrix composed of the entries of the last $n - k$ rows of $L(t)$. Let

$$U(\alpha, \beta, \mu) = \int_0^\omega L_1^T(t)\mathcal{F}(t, v(t), \mu)dt + \sum_{i=1}^p L_1^T(\theta_i)\mathcal{O}_i(v(\theta_i), \mu),$$

$$V(\alpha, \beta, \mu) = (L_2^T(\omega) - \mathcal{I})\beta - \mu \int_0^\omega L_3^T(t)\mathcal{F}(t, v(t), \mu)dt - \mu \sum_{i=1}^p L_3^T(\theta_i)\mathcal{O}_i(v(\theta_i), \mu).$$

Theorem 4.3.3 implies that the ω-periodicity condition for the solution $v(t)$ has the form of the following two equations:

$$U(\alpha, \beta, \mu) = 0, \tag{7.21}$$

$$V(\alpha, \beta, \mu) = 0. \tag{7.22}$$

If in (7.22) one takes $\mu = 0$, we obtain $\beta = 0$, and then (7.21) has the form

$$U(\alpha, 0, 0) = \int_0^\omega L_1^T(t)\mathcal{F}(t, z(t, \alpha), 0)dt + \sum_{i=1}^p L_1^T(\theta_i)\mathcal{O}(z(\theta_i, \alpha), 0) = 0. \tag{7.23}$$

Let $\alpha_0 = (\alpha_1^0, \ldots, \alpha_k^0)$ be a solution of (7.23). Since the function U has continuous partial derivatives with respect to $\alpha_j, j = 1, \ldots, k$, in a sufficiently small neighborhood of the point $(\alpha_0, 0,)$, it follows under the assumption:

$$\det[\frac{\partial U}{\partial \alpha}|_{\alpha=\alpha_0}] \neq 0$$

that the system of equations (7.21), (7.22) is solvable with respect to α and β so that the functions $\alpha_j(\mu)$ and $\beta_s(\mu), j = 1, \ldots, k, s = k+1, \ldots, n$, are continuous and $\alpha_j(\mu) \to \alpha_j^0, \beta_s(\mu) \to 0$ as $\mu \to 0$.

Thus, we have established that for sufficiently small $|\mu|$ system, (7.20) admits an ω-periodic solution, which converges to the solution $x(t, \alpha_0)$ of system (7.2), as $\mu \to 0$. The solution has the form $x(t, \alpha_0) = \alpha_1^0\phi_1(t) + \ldots + \alpha_r^0\phi_r(t)$, where $\phi_1(t), \ldots, \phi_r(t)$, are linearly independent ω-periodic solutions of (7.2).

To complete the proof, one should apply the equivalence of (7.20) and (7.1). The theorem is proved.   □

Next, we discuss the problem of asymptotic representation of the periodic solutions, whose existence has been proved in the last theorem.

Theorem 7.2.2. *Assume that system (7.1) satisfies all conditions of the last theorem, and it is smooth with order $l \geq 3$. Then, if $|\mu|$ is sufficiently small, the periodic solution $x(t)$ of this system admits the following B-asymptotic representation:*

$$x(t) = x(t, \alpha_0) + \mu x_1(t) + \ldots + \mu^{l-1} x_l(t, \mu), \qquad (7.24)$$

which is valid for all $t \in \mathbb{R}$, except those $t \in \widehat{(\theta_i, \eta_i]}, i \in \mathbb{Z}$, where η_i are points of discontinuity of $x(t)$, such that $\eta_i \to \theta_i$ as $\mu \to 0$, for all $i \in \mathbb{Z}$. The functions $x_j, j = 1, \ldots, l$, belong to $\mathcal{PC}_\omega(\mathbb{R}, \theta)$.

Proof. Present the ω-periodic solution $y(t)$ of (7.19) in the form $y(t) = x(t, \alpha_0) + \mu \zeta(t, \mu)$. One can easily check that the function ζ satisfies

$$\zeta' = A(t)\zeta + \phi(t, x(t, \alpha_0) + \mu \zeta, \mu),$$
$$\Delta \zeta|_{t=\theta_i} = B_i \zeta + \Omega_i(x(\theta_i, \alpha_0) + \mu \zeta, \mu). \qquad (7.25)$$

We shall show that the last system has an ω-periodic solution if $|\mu|$ is sufficiently small. Denote $e(t) = \phi(t, x(t, \alpha_0), 0), m_i = \Omega_i(x(\theta_i, \alpha_0), 0), \pi(t, \zeta, \mu) = \mu^{-1}[\phi(t, x(t, \alpha_0) + \mu \zeta, \mu) - \phi(t, x(t, \alpha_0), 0)], \Pi_i(\zeta, \mu) = \mu^{-1}[\Omega_i(x(\theta_i, \alpha_0) + \mu \zeta, \mu) - \Omega_i(x(\theta_i, \alpha_0), 0)]$. Then ζ is a solution of the following system:

$$\zeta' = A(t)\zeta + e(t) + \mu \pi(t, \zeta, \mu),$$
$$\Delta \zeta|_{t=\theta_i} = B_i \zeta + m_i + \mu \Pi_i(\zeta, \mu). \qquad (7.26)$$

Since $h(\alpha_0) \neq 0$, the system

$$\zeta' = A(t)\zeta + e(t),$$
$$\Delta \zeta|_{t=\theta_i} = B_i \zeta + m_i, \qquad (7.27)$$

admits r-parametric family of ω-periodic solutions $x_1(t, \bar{\alpha}) = \bar{\alpha}_1 \phi_1 + \ldots + \bar{\alpha}_r \phi_r + \phi_0$, where $\phi_0(t)$ is a particular solution of (7.27). Hence, by Theorem 7.2.1, the problem is reduced to the investigation of the expression

$$v_1(\bar{\alpha}) = \int_0^\omega H_1^T(t)\pi(t, x_1(t, \bar{\alpha}), 0)dt + \sum_{i=1}^p H_1^T(\theta_i)\Pi_i(x_1(\theta_i, \bar{\alpha}), 0). \qquad (7.28)$$

It is a linear equation with respect to $\bar{\alpha} = (\bar{\alpha}_1, \ldots, \bar{\alpha}_r)$. The matrix of coefficients of the system is $\frac{\partial h}{\partial \alpha}|_{\alpha=\alpha_0}$. Indeed, we have

$$\pi(t, \zeta, 0) = \phi_\mu(t, x(t, \alpha_0) + \mu\zeta, \mu)|_{\mu=0} = \sum_{j=1}^{n} \phi_{x_j}(t, x(t, \alpha_0), 0)\zeta_j + \phi_\mu(t, x(t, \alpha_0), 0),$$

$$\Pi_i(\zeta, 0) = \sum_{j=1}^{n} \Omega_{ix_j}(x(\theta_i, \alpha_0), 0)\zeta_j + \Omega_{i\mu}(x(\theta_i, \alpha_0), 0).$$

Consequently, (7.28) can be written as

$$\int_0^\omega H_1^T(t) \sum_{j=1}^{n} \phi_{x_j}(t, x(t, \alpha_0), 0)(\sum_{j=1}^{n} \alpha_j \phi_j$$

$$+ \phi_0)dt + \int_0^\omega H_1^T(t)\phi_\mu(t, x(t, \alpha)_0, 0)dt +$$

$$\sum_{i=1}^{p} H_1^T(\theta_i) \sum_{j=1}^{n} \Omega_{ix_j}(x(\theta_i, \alpha_0), 0)(\sum_{j=1}^{n} \alpha_j \phi_j(\theta_i) + \phi_0(\theta_i))$$

$$+ \sum_{i=1}^{p} H_1^T(\theta_i)\Omega_{i\mu}(x(\theta_i, \alpha_0), 0).$$

The last expression proves the assertion. Then the equation $v_1(\bar{\alpha}) = 0$ has a unique solution $\bar{\alpha}_0$, and $\det(v_{1\alpha}(\bar{\alpha}_0)) \neq 0$ is true. Thus for system (7.27), all conditions of the last theorem are valid, and consequently, $\zeta(t, \mu) = x_1(t, \bar{\alpha}_0) + \zeta_1(t, \mu)$, where ζ_1 is convergent to 0 as $\mu \to 0$. It follows that denoting $x_0(t) = x(t, \alpha_0), x_1(t) = x_1(t, \bar{\alpha}_0)$, one can obtain $y(t) = x_0(t) + \mu x_1(t) + \mu \zeta_1(t, \mu)$. One can show that ζ_1 is a solution of the system

$$\zeta' = A(t)\zeta + e(t) + \mu\pi(t, x_1(t, \bar{\alpha}_0) + \mu\zeta, \mu),$$
$$\Delta\zeta|_{t=\theta_i} = B_i\zeta + m_i + \mu\Pi_i(x_1(\theta_i, \bar{\alpha}_0) + \mu\zeta, \mu). \tag{7.29}$$

Next, assuming that $l \geq 4$, we can check that $\zeta_1 = x_2(t, \bar{\alpha}_0) + \zeta_2(t, \mu)$, where $\zeta_2 \to 0$, as $\mu \to 0$, and x_2 is a solution of the (ω, p)-periodic equation

$$x' = A(t)x + \pi_1(t, x_1(t), 0),$$
$$\Delta x|_{t=\theta_i} = B_i x + m_i + \Pi_i^1(x_1(\theta_i), 0), \tag{7.30}$$

$\bar{\alpha}_0$ is a solution of the equation $v_2(\alpha) = 0$, where

$$v_2(\alpha) = \int_0^\omega H_1^T(t)\pi_1(t, x_2(t, \alpha), 0)dt + \sum_{i=1}^{p} H_1^T(\theta_i)\Psi_i^1(x_1(\theta_i, \alpha), 0),$$

$$\pi_1 = \mu^{-1}[\pi(t, x_1 + \mu x, \mu) - \pi(t, x_1(t), 0)], |pi_i^1$$
$$= \mu^{-1}[\Pi_i(x_1(\theta_i) + \mu x, \mu) - \Pi_i(x_1(\theta_i), 0)],$$

$$x_2(t, \alpha) = \alpha_1 \phi_1 + \ldots \alpha_r \phi_r + \bar{\phi},$$

and $\bar{\phi}$ is a particular periodic solution of (7.30). In this way one can obtain the representation of $y(t)$ up to l-th order. The expansion is valid for the solution $x(t)$ of B-equivalent system (7.1). The theorem is proved.   □

Notes

The Poincaré method of small parameter [132], with Lyapunov's stability [104] development was applied in [105] for intensive investigation of the existence of periodic solutions. In [112], the problem of existence of periodic solutions for strongly nonlinear systems with analytic members and nonfixed moments of impulses, was considered by using method of generalized functions. Asymptotic expansion along the powers of a small parameter for solutions of differential equations with fixed moments of impulses is discussed in [47]. We have obtained the results for a quasilinear system, considering critical and noncritical cases, by using B-equivalence method. More results on the subject can be found in [23, 26, 29, 34, 36]. The approach considered in our results allows to achieve higher order approximations. Significant development of the mechanics with impacts [41, 43, 50, 56, 57, 79, 103, 109, 113, 115, 116, 121, 125–127, 130, 162] provides an opportunity for applications. In Example 7.1.1, we consider a simple mechanical model just with an illustrative goal. Some interesting results of impacts theory [113, 126, 127] form a basis for further development of the equations considered in this Chapter. The method of small parameter can be applied to synchronization of systems with discontinuities [44, 53, 81, 94, 108, 114, 129].

Chapter 8
Discontinuous Dynamical Systems

8.1 Generalities

The book [39] edited by D.V. Anosov and V.I. Arnold considers two fundamentally different dynamical systems: flows and cascades. Roughly speaking, flows are dynamical systems with continuous time and cascades are dynamical systems with discrete time. One of the most important theoretical problems is to consider *Discontinuous Dynamical Systems* (*DDS*). That is, the systems whose trajectories are piecewise continuous curves. Analyzing the behavior of the trajectories, we can conclude that *DDS* combine features of vector fields and maps. They cannot be reduced to flows or cascades but are close to flows since time is continuous. That is why we propose to call them also as *Discontinuous Flows* (*DF*). One must emphasize that *DF* are not differential equations with discontinuous right side, which often have been accepted as *DDS* [68]. One should also agree that nonautonomous impulsive differential equations, which were thoroughly described in previous chapters are not discontinuous flows.

Let us remind the definition of a continuous dynamical system. Denote by X a complete metric space, with a countable base, and with ρ a metric function. A dynamical system on X is defined to be a mapping $\phi : \mathbb{R} \times X \to X$, such that

1. $\phi(0, x) = x$ for all $x \in X$, (Identical property);
2. $\phi(t + s, x) = \phi(t, \phi(s, x))$ for all $x \in X$, and $t, s \in \mathbb{R}$, (Group property);
3. $\phi(t, x)$ is a continuous function.

Definitely, one may expect that systems with similar properties can be defined for processes with discontinuities. Present chapter is devoted to the problem of identification of such kind of systems, one of the most interesting and difficult problems for impulsive differential equations.

To motivate the reader, we may propose the following simple example, where an autonomous system with even linear elements is not a dynamical system.

Example 8.1.1. Let us study the motion of the following system

$$\ddot{x} + \omega^2 x = 0,$$
$$\Delta \dot{x}|_{x=x_0} = k,$$

where ω, k, and x_0 are positive constants.

M. Akhmet, *Principles of Discontinuous Dynamical Systems*, DOI 10.1007/978-1-4419-6581-3_8, © Springer Science+Business Media, LLC 2010

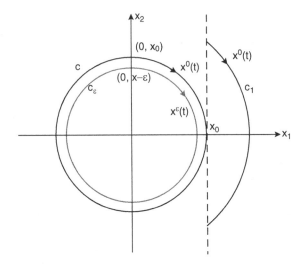

Fig. 8.1 Trajectories of the system (8.1), (8.2)

Denote $x_1 = x$ and $x_2 = \frac{1}{\omega}\dot{x}$. By using this substitution, the system can be rewritten in the form:

$$\dot{x}_1 = \omega x_2, \tag{8.1}$$
$$\dot{x}_2 = -\omega x_1, \quad x_1 \neq x_0,$$
$$x_2^+ = k_1 + x_2^-, \quad x_1 = x_0, \tag{8.2}$$

where $k_1 = \frac{k}{\omega}$. A solution of the system (8.1) is $x_1(t) = r \sin \omega t$ and $x_2(t) = r \cos \omega t$, where r is a fixed real number.

Let us observe the behavior of solutions of the system (8.1), (8.2) in Fig. 8.1. Consider the solution $x^0(t) = x(t, 0, (0, x_0))$. The point moves along the circle **c** until it meets the line $x_1 = x_0$ at the point $(x_0, 0)$. Then it jumps and continues to move along the arc of the circle c_1. Then, it meets the line $x_1 = x_0$ again and jumps.

One may examine that the solution is not continuous in the initial value. Indeed, let us take another solution $x^\epsilon(t) = x(t, 0, (0, x_0 - \epsilon))$ of this system, which starts at the point $(0, x_0 - \epsilon)$, where ϵ is a fixed positive real number. The solution $x^0(t)$ jumps at the point $(x_0, 0)$ and continues along the arc c_1, as explained above. However, the solution $x^\epsilon(t)$ continues its motion along the circle c_ϵ without any jump. So, as it is seen in Fig. 8.1, the distance between these two trajectories cannot be less than $\sqrt{x_0^2 - k_1^2} - x_0$, despite the initial points of these two solutions can be chosen arbitrarily close. This example demonstrates that the solution $x^0(t)$ of the system (8.1), (8.2) does not depend continuously on the initial value. Obviously, we cannot accept the system as a dynamical system. We may remark that this type of "irregularity" in models with impacts causes many interesting phenomena, for instance, collision bifurcation [51, 118].

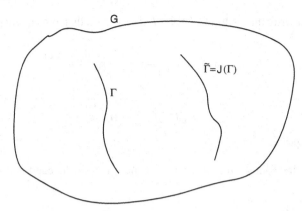

Fig. 8.2 A domain of a discontinuous dynamical system

Let $G = \bigcup G_j$ where G_j, $j = 1, 2, \ldots, m$, are disjoint open connected subsets of $\mathbb{R}^n$. Denote by G_r, an r-neighborhood of G in $\mathbb{R}^n$ for a fixed $r > 0$. Let $\Phi : G_r \longrightarrow \mathbb{R}$ be a function from $C^1(G_r)$ and assume that the surface $\Gamma = \Phi^{-1}(0)$ is a closed subset of $\bar{G}$, where $\bar{G}$ is the closure of G. Denote by Γ_r, the r-neighborhood of Γ in $\mathbb{R}^n$, and define a function $J : \Gamma_r \to G_r$, such that $J(\Gamma) \subset \bar{G}$ is a closed set. We shall need the following assumptions:

(C1) $\nabla\Phi(x) \neq 0$ for all $x \in \Gamma$;
(C2) $J \in C^1(\Gamma_r)$ and $\det[\frac{\partial J(x)}{\partial x}] \neq 0$, for all $x \in \Gamma_r$,

where $\nabla\Phi(x)$ denotes the gradient vector of Φ with respect to x. Let $\tilde{\Gamma} = J(\Gamma)$, (see Fig. 8.2), $\tilde{\Phi}(x) = \Phi(J^{-1}(x))$. One can verify that $\tilde{\Gamma} = \{x \in G | \tilde{\Phi}(x) = 0\}$. Condition (C1) implies that for every $x_0 \in \Gamma$ there exists a number j and a function $\varphi_{x_0}(x_1, \ldots, x_{j-1}, x_{j+1}, \ldots, x_n)$ such that Γ is the graph of the function $x_j = \varphi_{x_0}(x_1, \ldots, x_{j-1}, x_{j+1}, \ldots, x_n)$ in a neighborhood of x_0. The same is true for every $x_0 \in \tilde{\Gamma}$.

Sets Γ and $\tilde{\Gamma}$ consist of disjoint manifolds. These manifolds are with or without boundaries. We shall denote unions of all these boundaries as $\partial\Gamma$ and $\partial\tilde{\Gamma}$. One may recommend to the reader books [58, 73] to recall definitions of manifolds. It is easily seen that restrictions $J|_\Gamma$, $\tilde{J}|_{\tilde{\Gamma}}$ are one-to-one functions.

Remark 8.1.1. It is natural to consider domains of continuous dynamical systems as connected sets [157]. Otherwise, each region of a partition can be discussed as a domain of a continuous dynamical system. A trajectory of a discontinuous dynamical system may jump from one component to another, such that only the union of the disjoint regions is a domain.

Lemma 8.1.1. $\nabla\tilde{\Phi}(x) \neq 0, \forall x \in \tilde{\Gamma}$.

Proof. We can write that $\nabla \tilde{\Phi}(x) = \nabla \Phi \left(J^{-1}(x) \right)$, and then the equality

$$\nabla \Phi \left(J^{-1}(x) \right) = \frac{\partial \Phi(y)}{\partial y}\Big|_{y=J^{-1}(x)} \frac{\partial J^{-1}(x)}{\partial x}$$

implies that

$$\nabla \Phi \left(J^{-1}(x) \right) \neq 0.$$

The lemma is proved.   □

We make the following assumptions which will be needed throughout the chapter.

(C3) $f \in C^1(G_r)$,
(C4) $\Gamma \cap \tilde{\Gamma} = \emptyset$,
(C5) $\langle \nabla \Phi(x), f(x) \rangle \neq 0$ if $x \in \Gamma$,
(C6) $\langle \nabla \tilde{\Phi}(x), f(x) \rangle \neq 0$ if $x \in \tilde{\Gamma}$.

Consider the following impulsive differential equation:

$$\begin{aligned} x' &= f(x), \\ \Delta x|_{x \in \Gamma} &= W(x), \end{aligned} \tag{8.3}$$

where $W(x) = J(x) - x$, in the domain $D = \left[G \cup \Gamma \cup \tilde{\Gamma} \right] \setminus \left[\partial \Gamma \cup \partial \tilde{\Gamma} \right]$.

If $\phi(t) : I \to \mathbb{R}^n$, where I is an interval, is a solution of (8.3), then it is required that it belongs to $\mathcal{PC}(I, \theta)$, where $\theta \subset I$ is a B-sequence. The solution must satisfy $\phi'(t) = f(\phi(t))$, if $t \notin \theta$, and $\phi(\theta_i+) = J(\phi(\theta_i))$, $\phi(\theta_i) \in \Gamma, \phi(\theta_i+) \in \tilde{\Gamma}$, for each $\theta_i \in \theta$. Sets Γ and $\tilde{\Gamma}$ may have common points with the boundary of the domain D, and the boundary points of these sets, Γ and $\tilde{\Gamma}$, do not belong to D, as they may cause a violence of the continuous dependence on initial value. If the boundary points are in the domain, then one needs specific additional conditions. For instance, if $x \in \partial \Gamma$, then we may request $J(x) = 0$.

Now, we continue with examples, where conditions (C1)–(C6) are satisfied.

Example 8.1.2. Let us consider the following system:

$$\begin{aligned} x_1' &= -x_1 - 3x_2, \\ x_2' &= 3x_1 - x_2, \\ \Delta x_1|_{x \in \Gamma} &= x_1 \\ \Delta x_2|_{x \in \Gamma} &= x_2, \end{aligned} \tag{8.4}$$

where $x = (x_1, x_2)$, and

$$\Gamma = \left\{ (x_1, x_2)| \quad x_1^2 + x_2^2 = 1, \quad x_1, x_2 \in \mathbb{R} \right\},$$

$$\tilde{\Gamma} = \left\{ (x_1, x_2)| \quad x_1^2 + x_2^2 = 4, \quad x_1, x_2 \in \mathbb{R} \right\}.$$

Cybersecurity Behaviour: A Conceptual Taxonomy

Thulani Mashiane$^{(\boxtimes)}$ and Elmarie Kritzinger

School of Computing, University of South Africa, UNISA,
PO Box 392, Pretoria 0003, South Africa
tmashiane@csir.co.za, kritze@unisa.ac.za

Abstract. User cybersecurity behaviour is a concern for organisations as well as home users. This is because cyber-criminals have made a shift from targeting security systems to targeting the users of the systems. As a result, an increasing number of studies have been conducted in efforts to understand user cybersecurity behaviour. The advantage in understanding user behaviour is that researchers and security practitioners can apply this knowledge and begin to change behaviour to benefit cybersecurity. Different studies have categorised similar cybersecurity behaviours, however the naming conventions differ across studies. This brings out the first contribution of the paper, unified terminology for the cybersecurity behaviour. Secondly, most studies were conducted in an organisational setting. User behaviour in other environments is yet to be identified and categorised. The second contribution of this study is the identification and categorisation of home user cybersecurity behaviour. The identification and classification of more cybersecurity behaviour is aimed to have a positive impact in the creation of strategic interventions to change and maintain good cybersecurity behaviour.

Keywords: Cybersecurity behaviour · Classification · Taxonomy · Cybersecurity

1 Introduction

To decrease the number of cyber incidents, it is key that users, especially user behaviours, are understood to understand how to change user behaviour [1–3]. An initial step is the identification and classification of user cybersecurity behaviour (CSB).

1.1 Cybersecurity Behaviour (CSB)

Human behaviour refers to an individual's actions, reactions, mannerisms and conduct within different environments [4]. CSB is therefore defined, by the current research, as an individual's actions, reactions, mannerisms, and general conduct in the cyber domain. The goal of studying user CSB is to promote good CSB while decreasing malicious or bad CSB.

© IFIP International Federation for Information Processing 2019
Published by Springer Nature Switzerland AG 2019
O. Blazy and C. Y. Yeun (Eds.): WISTP 2018, LNCS 11469, pp. 147–156, 2019.
https://doi.org/10.1007/978-3-030-20074-9_11

1.2 Cybersecurity Behaviour Context

Researchers [5,6] have noted that users act differently in different settings. But, the categorisation of CSB has been focused mainly on behaviour in organisations. Numerous targets of cybersecurity attacks fall outside the context of the organisation [7]. Therefore, a gap exists in literature, where other cybersecurity contexts have been left out. The importance of including different contexts is the ability to accurately categories CSB.

1.3 Cybersecurity Behaviour Taxonomy

To understand a system, it is necessary to understand the components that make up that system. A taxonomy is a tool used to classify components in a domain. Making use of a taxonomy allows for the structural organisation of concepts that make up the system. CSB have been expressed in the form of taxonomies. More recently, Bitton et al. presented a taxonomy for mobile cybersecurity awareness [8]. The current study builds on previously published taxonomies in the classification of users' CSB.

The remainder of the paper is presented as follows. Section 2 presents a literature review and Sect. 3 presents the proposed conceptual taxonomy. The conclusion and future work is presented in Sect. 4.

2 Literature Review

The following section presents literature that focuses on user CSB in the workplace as well as at home.

2.1 Cybersecurity Behaviour

Context is made up of the circumstances surrounding a behaviour. Context has an influence on behaviour [10]. An example related to CSB is: social engineering attacks may be more effective at certain times of the year, such as the festive season. In this section, the CSB in the work and home context are discussed.

Cybersecurity Behaviour at Work. The CSB of employees is mostly governed by policies and regulations. Employees are held accountable for misconduct or not adhering to the organisational rules [1,11,12]. Furthermore, ICT departments assist users in adhering to policy by sending reminders about software updates, information on new threats, information best practices, and blocking dangerous or inappropriate sites [9].

Blythe strived to understand CSB in an organisational setting [13]. In an organisational setting, cybersecurity is usually evaluated as a function of compliance [14,15]. In an organisation, bad CSB is seen as noncompliance to the set policies. Blythe contended that behaviour is more entailed than this. The study argued that the evaluation of compliance is limited in that it tests a small scope of policies and procedures. Among other behavioural determinants, the behaviour is a function of interior and exterior influences. Interior influences include self-motivation or drive, similar to intentions mentioned in [9], while exterior influences are features such as the environment [13].

To categorise CSB in organisations, a six-element taxonomy was developed by Stanton et al. The dependent variables used to group the behaviours were (1) the amount of expertise required to carry out the behaviour, and (2) the intention towards the organisation when carrying out the behaviour. The six categories of the taxonomy where: *intentional destruction, dangerous tinkering, aware assurance, detrimental misuse, naïve mistakes,* and *basic hygiene* [9].

Intentional destruction, detrimental misuse, dangerous tinkering, and naïve mistakes are examples of bad CSB and aware assurance and basic hygiene are examples of good CSB. To visualise the taxonomy, the categories of the taxonomy were put on a two-dimensional plane. On the x-axis, the intention of the user is plotted; intentions range from malicious to unintentional. On the y-axis, the user expertise ranging from expert to novice are plotted (see Fig. 1).

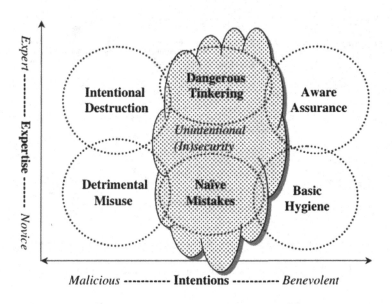

Fig. 1. End user security behaviours [9]

Taking and expanding on the work by Stanton et al., Djajadikerta et al. made use of the four classifications (Intentional Destruction, Dangerous Tinkering, Detrimental Misuse and Naïve Mistakes) to further investigate bad information security behaviour [16]. The four classifications were verified by placing organisational CSB concerns into each group.

Guo observed the disparities in the conclusions of information systems behaviour research. The different, often contradicting results were hypothesised to be due to methodological issues or the ill definition of information system's behaviour. The study realised the need for more clear definitions of information systems behaviours. Through the review and synthesis of previous studies, a conceptual framework was designed which incorporates four categorisations of organisational behaviour: *security assurance behaviour, security compliant behaviour, security risk-taking behaviour,* and *security damaging behaviour* [17].

Chu, Chau, and So developed a typo-logical theory for information security deviant behaviour in an organisational setting [18]. The result of the study categorised cybersecurity into four categories: *Misuse of information systems resources, Information security carelessness, System protection deviance* and *Access control deviance.*

In terms of CSB at work, Fig. 2 presents a graph with the cybersecurity categories taken from the studies presented in Sect. 2. The categories are plotted on the same graph that was used in the research by Stanton et al. [9].

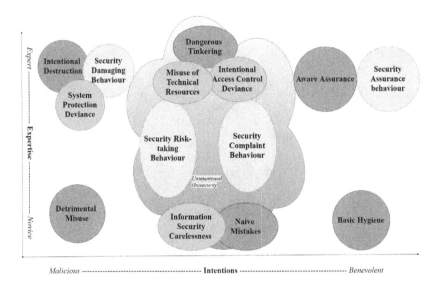

Fig. 2. Cybersecurity behaviour in organisations [9,17,18].

The graph shows most of the categories identified require some level of cybersecurity expertise. This implies that users in organisations, generally, have the expertise in cybersecurity. An inference can be made that CSB in organisations is not hindered by the lack of cybersecurity expertise.

The next important observation is that a majority of the security behaviour categories are not intended on malicious or benevolent behaviour. This neutral attitude towards cybersecurity is a risk because users, then show no interest in improving or applying their skills.

Currently, through the graph in Fig. 2, it is not clear what the intentional difference between Security Risk taking behaviour and Security Compliance behaviour is. It is therefore a need that a clear distinction in intentions is derived. This distinction must also be represented, though the graph.

Cybersecurity Behaviour at Home. Home users are individuals of different ages that make use of computers or mobile devices that connect to the Internet. In the home context, users are typically solely responsible for managing their CSB [22,23]. It is assumed that cybersecurity knowledge, awareness and skills are much lower for home users, as they are not exposed to training programs [19]. This assumption was later proven false by [20] where it was found that home users do have cybersecurity knowledge and skills. The knowledge may be gained from other environments such as work, but the behaviour at home is different [11,21,22,24].

Lastly, there are home users that do follow cybersecurity principals at home. Cybercitizens is a term found in the study by Catherine et al. Cybercitizens describe home users that are proactive in being cybersecurity aware and applying cybersecurity skills in their environments [19]. The study focuses on the intentions of cybercitizens and presents interventions to encourage more users to become cybercitizens. The type of behaviours that a cybercitizen exhibits are installing and updating antivirus software, be cautious of emails as well as email attachments, and lastly choosing strong and easy to remember passwords [19].

3 Proposed Conceptual Cybersecurity Behaviour Taxonomies

The proposed CSB taxonomy addresses the two points: (1) Ambiguity in cybersecurity intentions, and (2) Completeness in the introducing of context as an independent variable when categorising CSB.

3.1 Updated Work Cybersecurity Behaviour Taxonomy

The current section proposes an updates CSB taxonomy for the work environment. The contribution in this section is the division of behaviour intentions into four categories.

Figure 3 presents the CSBs at work with the derived intentions. This new graph offers the advantage of clearly showing the intentions associated with the categories of behaviours. Headings should be numbered. Lower level headings remain unnumbered; they are formatted as run-in headings.

Intentions. Intentions are plans for performing a behaviour. The literature on CSB intentions can be divided into intentional and unintentional CSB [25].

Intentional Cybersecurity Behaviour. Intentional CSB refers to instances where the user purposefully wants to harm systems or disregard cybersecurity principals. Opposite to this, users can purposefully uphold or/and promote cybersecurity principals.

Intentional Bad (IB) Cybersecurity Behaviour. This category of users shows dysfunctional CSB. The categorisation is adapted from research done by

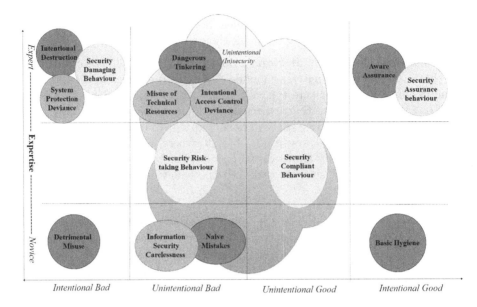

Fig. 3. Work CS behaviour with segmented intentions adapted from [9,17,18].

Stanton et al. were categories such as intentional destruction and detrimental misuse where used to describe users' dysfunctional CSB [9,16]. Users that show this type of harmful CSB are called cybercriminals, hackers, crackers and script kiddies. Examples of behaviour include website defacement, spamming, unauthorised system access, malware and malware distribution and vulnerability exploitation.

Intentional Good (IG) Cybersecurity Behaviour. There exist instances where the user purposefully upholds cybersecurity principles [9]. This category is adopted from Stanton et al. where aware assurance and basic hygiene are collapsed into intentional good CSB. An example of users performing intentional good CSB are users that create good passwords to protect information belonging to them or an organisation. Literature has developed terms such as good cybersecurity hygiene and conscious care behaviour to describe this category of users [9,26].

Unintentional Cybersecurity Behaviour. Unintentional CSB refers to instances where the user does not intend on disregarding nor upholding cybersecurity principals. In these instances, good or bad CSB is a by-product of other actions or intentions.

Unintentional Bad (UB) Cybersecurity Behaviour. Behaviours categorised as unintentional bad CSB are those where the user does not intend to cause malicious harm or purposefully disregard cybersecurity principals. Ifinedo referred to these behaviours as counterproductive computer security behaviours [27], while Stanton et al. referred to it as dangerous tinkering and naïve mistakes [9] and Chu et al. refers to it as information security deviant behaviour [18]. An example of unintentional bad CSB is a user that writes their password down or recycles their password [28].

Unintentional Good (UG) Cybersecurity Behaviour. Behaviours categorised as unintentional good CSB are behaviours where users preserve cybersecurity because of other intentions or actions. The study by Virginia Tech found that even though users complied with password change policies, the users still felt that cybersecurity is an obstacle. In this case, the intention of the behaviour is to comply, and it is not to practice good CSB [29]. Unintentional good CSB is not ideal, because for a behaviour to be repeated the user must be intentional in repeating as well as sustaining the behaviour.

3.2 Home Cybersecurity Behaviour Taxonomy

Categories captured in Fig. 3's graph focus on CSB that occur at work. In the interest of completeness, the next section of the study aims to categorise CSBs of home users. To do so, different CSBs were extracted from literate. These behaviours were plotted on a similar graph as used in Fig. 4. However, the y-axis had to be adjusted. According to the literature presented, home users do have cybersecurity knowledge and skills. In the home environment the application of these knowledge and skills is more distinguishing of the behaviours as opposed to having the knowledge and skills. Therefore, the y-axis is divided into *None or Limited Knowledge and Skills, Knowledge and Skills but No Implementation* and finally, *Knowledge and Skills with Implementation.*

Eight CSB categories were derived for the home user behaviour taxonomy: *Hacking, Aggravative, Disrupting, Unconcerned, Cognitive Laziness, Convenience, Proactive* and *Knowledge Gaining.* The categories are a result of plot-

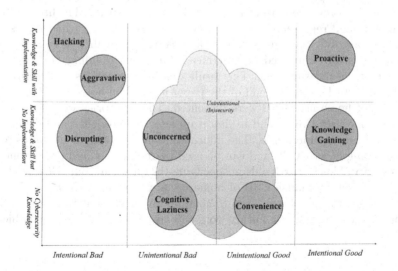

Fig. 4. Home users' cybersecurity behaviour categories

ting 95 CSBs on a graph similar to Fig. 4. CSB plotted close together were then grouped together to form the resulting graph in Fig. 4.

In Fig. 4 in the Knowledge and Skills with Implementation there are three behaviour categories, namely Hacking, Aggravating and Proactive. Hacking and Aggravating behaviours are intentional bad behaviours, while Proactive is intentional good behaviour. Hacking are behaviours that seek out to cause harm to other systems and people though technical expertise, while aggravate behaviours are targeted at other people especially on social media sites.

In the Knowledge and Skills with no Implementation there are three behaviour categories, namely Disrupting, Unconcerned and Knowledge Gaining. Disrupting behaviours are intentional bad CSBs. The behaviours under this category show neglecting of cybersecurity principals through the reckless actions such as downloading torrents from peer-to-peer networks. The category Unconcerned describes careless CSBs. However, the intention of these behaviours in not to intentionally cause harm. Knowledge gaining CSB is intentionally good behaviour. However, without applying the knowledge and skills these behaviours have little use in maintaining cybersecurity.

In the No or Limited Knowledge row there are two behaviour categories, namely Cognitive Laziness and Convenience. These terms were taken from [30]. Cognitive Laziness is unintentional bad CSB. This category of behaviours describes behaviour that is done mindlessly without consideration of any cybersecurity. Finally, the Convenience category describes unintentional good CSB. These behaviours are done only if the cybersecurity related task is convenient.

4   Conclusion

The aim of the paper was to provide a clear representation and visualisation of CSB. The study reviewed literature on CSB in the workplace. The literature was consolidated and represented on one graph. Previous research had represented user intentions of CSB on an ordinal scale ranging from malicious to benevolent. The current study improved on this measurement by dividing intentions into smaller units of measurement. The result was four categories to describe user CSB intentions. The second half of the paper focused on home user CSB. Eight categories of home user CSB were presented. The categories were obtained by plotting home user CSB found in literature against knowledge and skill implementation and user intentions. The information in this study contributes to the understanding of user CSB and can be used by researchers and practitioners of cybersecurity. This research aids in specifying the question from "How to change CSB?" to "How to change CSB of home users who exhibit *Cognitive Laziness* behaviour". Future work will need to conduct an experiment to verify the conclusions found in this study. Future work will also need to address the influences of CSBs.

References

1. Abrams, M., Weiss, J.: Malicious control system cyber security attack case study-Maroochy Water Services, Australia. The MITRE Corporation, McLean, VA (2008)
2. Smith, S.N., et al.: The impact of monetary value gains and losses on cybersecurity behavior (2017)
3. Anwar, M., et al.: Gender difference and employees' cybersecurity behaviors. Comput. Hum. Behav. **69**, 437–443 (2017)
4. Scheflen, A.E.: How Behavior Means. Gordon and Breach New York (1973)
5. Liang, H., Xue, Y.: Understanding security behaviors in personal computer usage: a threat avoidance perspective. J. Assoc. Inf. Syst. **11**(7), 394–413 (2010)
6. Kruger, H.A., et al.: An assessment of the role of cultural factors in information security awareness. In: 2011 Information Security South Africa (ISSA). IEEE (2011)
7. Bjørnhaug, T.: Internet of Things-Cybersecurity at Home. NTNU (2017)
8. Bitton, R., et al.: Taxonomy of mobile users' security awareness. Comput. Secur. **73**, 266–293 (2018)
9. Stanton, J.M., et al.: Analysis of end user security behaviors. Comput. Secur. **24**(2), 124–133 (2005)
10. Acquisti, A., Brandimarte, L., Loewenstein, G.: Privacy and human behavior in the age of information. Science **347**(6221), 509–514 (2015)
11. Kritzinger, E., von Solms, S.H.: Cyber security for home users: a new way of protection through awareness enforcement. Comput. Secur. **29**(8), 840–847 (2010)
12. Safa, N.S., Von Solms, R., Furnell, S.: Information security policy compliance model in organizations. Comput. Secur. **56**, 70–82 (2016)
13. Blythe, J.: Cyber security in the workplace: understanding and promoting behaviour change. In: Proceedings of CHItaly 2013 Doctoral Consortium, vol. 1065, pp. 92–101 (2013)
14. Bulgurcu, B., Cavusoglu, H., Benbasat, I.: Information security policy compliance: an empirical study of rationality-based beliefs and information security awareness. MIS Q. **34**(3), 523–548 (2010)
15. Deibert, R.J., Rohozinski, R.: Risking security: policies and paradoxes of cyberspace security. Int. Polit. Sociol. **4**(1), 15–32 (2010)
16. Djajadikerta, H.G., Roni, S.M., Trireksani, T.: Dysfunctional information system behaviors are not all created the same: challenges to the generalizability of security-based research. Inf. Manag. **52**(8), 1012–1024 (2015)
17. Guo, K.H.: Security-related behavior in using information systems in the workplace: a review and synthesis. Comput. Secur. **32**, 242–251 (2013)
18. Chu, A.M., Chau, P.Y., So, M.K.: Developing a typological theory using a quantitative approach: a case of information security deviant behavior. CAIS **37**, 25 (2015)
19. Anderson, C.L., Agarwal, R.: Practicing safe computing: a multimedia empirical examination of home computer user security behavioral intentions. MIS Q. **34**(3), 613–643 (2010)
20. Edwards, K.: Examining the security awareness, information privacy, and the security behaviors of home computer users (2015)
21. Talib, S., Clarke, N.L., Furnell, S.M.: An analysis of information security awareness within home and work environments. In: ARES 2010 International Conference on Availability, Reliability, and Security. IEEE (2010)

22. Li, Y., Siponen, M.T.: A call for research on home users' information security behaviour. In: PACIS (2011)
23. Sharma, K.: Impact of framing and priming on users' behavior in cybersecurity (2017)
24. Bada, M., Sasse, A.: Cyber security awareness campaigns: why do they fail to change behaviour? (2014)
25. Safa, N.S., Von Solms, R., Futcher, L.: Human aspects of information security in organisations. Comput. Fraud Secur. **2016**(2), 15–18 (2016)
26. Safa, N.S., et al.: Information security conscious care behaviour formation in organizations. Comput. Secur. **53**, 65–78 (2015)
27. Ifinedo, P.: Effects of organizational citizenship behavior and social cognitive factors on employees' non-malicious counterproductive computer security behaviors: an empirical analysis. In: CONF-IRM (2015)
28. Nthala, N., Flechais, I.: "If it's urgent or it is stopping me from doing something, then I might just go straight at it": a study into home data security decisions. In: Tryfonas, T. (ed.) HAS 2017. LNCS, vol. 10292, pp. 123–142. Springer, Cham (2017). https://doi.org/10.1007/978-3-319-58460-7_9
29. Virginia Tech: When users resist: how to change management and user resistance to password security (2011)
30. Rughiniş, C., Rughiniş, R.: Nothing ventured, nothing gained. Profiles of online activity, cyber-crime exposure, and security measures of end-users in European Union. Comput. Secur. **43**, 111–125 (2014)

Remote Credential Management with Mutual Attestation for Trusted Execution Environments

Carlton Shepherd$^{(\boxtimes)}$, Raja Naeem Akram, and Konstantinos Markantonakis

Information Security Group, Royal Holloway,
University of London, Egham, UK
{carlton.shepherd.2014,r.n.akram,k.markantonakis}@rhul.ac.uk

Abstract. Trusted Execution Environments (TEEs) are rapidly emerging as a root-of-trust for protecting sensitive applications and data using hardware-backed isolated worlds of execution. TEEs provide robust assurances regarding critical algorithm execution, tamper-resistant credential storage, and platform integrity using remote attestation. However, the challenge of remotely managing credentials *between* TEEs remains largely unaddressed in existing literature. In this work, we present novel protocols using mutual attestation for supporting four aspects of secure remote credential management with TEEs: *backups*, *updates*, *migration*, and *revocation*. The proposed protocols are agnostic to the underlying TEE implementation and subjected to formal verification using Scyther, which found no attacks.

Keywords: Credential management · TEEs · Security protocols

1 Introduction

Trusted computing offers robust, on-device protection of security-critical data and the ability to securely report evidence of platform integrity, which has culminated in efforts such as the Trusted Platform Module (TPM). Until recently, however, such technologies were relatively restricted: neither arbitrary application execution nor secure input/output (I/O) are realisable with TPMs without substantially increasing the hardware-software Trusted Computing Base (TCB), say, through the use of virtual machines [11]. Trusted Execution Environments (TEEs), discussed further in Sect. 2, have emerged as the forerunner for addressing these shortcomings, particularly for constrained devices [19]. Unlike TPMs, TEEs provide hardware-enforced isolated execution of critical applications and data on the same underlying hardware. TEEs aim to thwart sophisticated software adversaries from a conventional Operating System (OS) irrespective of its protection mode, e.g. Rings 0–3. Modern Intel and ARM chipsets offer Intel

© IFIP International Federation for Information Processing 2019
Published by Springer Nature Switzerland AG 2019
O. Blazy and C. Y. Yeun (Eds.): WISTP 2018, LNCS 11469, pp. 157–173, 2019.
https://doi.org/10.1007/978-3-030-20074-9_12

Software Guard eXtensions (SGX) and ARM TrustZone respectively for instantiating a TEE from the CPU or System-on-Chip (SoC).

Despite widespread availability, managing TEE data credentials throughout their life-cycle has received little attention by the community. Such credentials, whether derived from a public-key certificate, password or another value, are typically used to authenticate sensitive actions and transmitted data. Challenges arise, however, when credentials require migrating, revoking, updating or backing-up in a secure and trusted manner with bi-directional assurances between both end-points. Firstly, large numbers of TEEs must be administered, thus limiting the feasibility of human intervention, potentially over a multitude of communication mediums. Secondly, heterogeneous TEEs must be accommodated: Intel SGX, for example, is confined to Intel CPUs on more powerful devices, while ARM TrustZone is limited to ARM-based SoCs. Hence, for the first time, we address four key challenges when managing heterogeneous TEE credentials over its lifetime with bi-directional trust assurances for remote *migration* (Sect. 3), *revocation* (Sect. 4), *backups* (Sect. 5), and *updates* (Sect. 6). This paper presents the following contributions:

- An examination of existing smart card and TPM work relating to each credential management challenge and their applicability to TEEs.
- A suite of proposed protocols for facilitating TEE credential management with mutual attestation. The protocols are agnostic of the TEE and communication medium, and employ a Trusted Service Manager (TSM) in line with the GlobalPlatform TEE specifications [10].
- The proposed protocols are subjected to formal symbolic verification using Scyther, which found no attacks. We publicly release the verification specifications for further research[1].

2   Trusted Execution Environments (TEEs)

GlobalPlatform defines a TEE as an isolated execution environment that *"protects from general software attacks, defines rigid safeguards as to the data and functions a program can access, and resists a set of defined threats"* [9]. TEEs aim to isolate applications from integrity and confidentiality attacks from the untrusted OS, e.g. Android, or Rich Execution Environment (REE), by allocating distinct memory regions with accesses controlled by hardware. We summarise the foremost commercial TEEs for Intel and ARM chipsets; the reader is referred to [22] for a detailed survey of secure and trusted execution environments.

Intel Software Guard eXtensions (SGX) is an extension to the x86-64 instruction set that enables the creation of per-application 'enclaves'. Enclaves reside in isolated memory regions within RAM with accesses mediated by the CPU, which is considered trusted [6]. Secure storage is provided via the sealing abstraction, where data is encrypted to the untrusted world using a key derived from a processor-specific Storage Root Key (SRK). Enclave- or author-specific

---

[1] Available online at: https://cs.gl/extra/wistp18-scripts.zip.

keys can be derived; that is, respectively, binding data to only that enclave, or from an ID string to preserve persistence between enclaves from the same author. Remote attestation enables remote verification of enclaves and secret provisioning using the Enhanced Privacy ID (EPID) scheme [4], which authenticates enclave integrity measurements without revealing the CPU's identity.

GlobalPlatform (GP) TEE with ARM TrustZone maintains two worlds for all trusted and untrusted applications (see Fig. 1). A TEE kernel is used for scheduling, memory management, cryptographic methods and other OS functions, while user-mode TEE Trusted Applications (TAs) access OS functions exposed by the GP TEE Internal API. The GP TEE Client API [9] defines the interfaces for communicating with TAs from the REE. The predominant method for instantiating the GP TEE is with ARM TrustZone, which enables two isolated worlds to co-exist in hardware using two virtual cores for each world per physical CPU core and an extra CPU bit (NS bit) for distinguishing REE/TEE execution modes. TrustZone provides secure I/O with peripherals connected over standard interfaces, e.g. SPI and GPIO, by routing interrupts to the TEE kernel using the TrustZone Protection Controller (TZPC) for securing on-chip peripherals from the REE, and the Address Space Controller (TZASC) for memory-mapped devices. Both TZASC and TZPC utilise the NS bit for access control. The GP TEE implements secure storage using the sealing abstraction described previously, or to TEE-controlled hardware, e.g. Secure Element (SE).

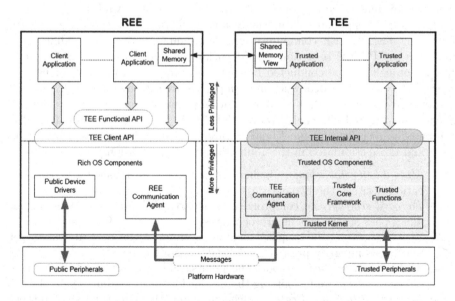

Fig. 1. GlobalPlatform TEE system architecture [22].

Credential Management. Security credentials are the evidence that a communicating party possesses for accessing privileged data and services. Credentials are typically programmed initially into a TEE during the personalisation phase following the procurement of the SoC and TEE software, but prior to deployment. After this, a Trusted Service Manager (TSM) – incorporated into the device manufacturer or outsourced – is responsible for maintaining the TEE, its TAs and on-board credentials thereafter. We define TEE credentials as *the set, C, of key material, certificates and other authentication data issued by TSM that is provisioned into a TA*. TEE credentials may also comprise a key derived from a password-based key derivation function using a password from an operator, or encapsulated by biometrics, e.g. iris and fingerprint, or a behavioural model that maps device continuous data to authentication states [21].

2.1   Credential Management: Security and Functional Requirements

The GP Trusted Management Framework (TMF) does not stipulate particular secure channel protocols, but only that the TSM and TEE should mutually authenticate over a channel that preserves the *"integrity and the confidentiality of the exchanges,"* and addresses replay attacks against a Dolev-Yao adversary [10]. These basic requirements omit desirable features identified in existing literature [2,12,20], such as assurances that the target TEE is authentic and integral. This is typically realised using Remote Attestation (RAtt) where, firstly, system measurements are taken at boot-time or on-demand, which are collected and signed by a trusted measurer under a device-specific key; RAtt protocols subsequently transmit the measurements over a secure channel to a remote verifier, who evaluates the platform's integrity based on these values.

In sensitive deployments, mutually authenticating *both* end-points is useful during TEE-to-TEE communication; for example, between uploading backups from a GP TEE to a cloud-based backup enclave using Intel SGX. Here, RAtt protocols can be conducted independently for each end-point, or using a *mutual attestation* protocol wherein both parties are attested in a single protocol instance. We refer to such mutual attestation protocols, e.g. [20], as providing a Secure and Trusted Channel Protocol (STCP) in this work. We now formalise the baseline security and functional requirements from issues raised in related work and those stipulated in the GlobalPlatform specifications:

(S1) *Mutual key establishment*: a shared secret key is established for communication between the two entities.

(S2) *Forward secrecy*: the compromise of a particular session key should not affect past or subsequent protocol runs.

(S3) *Trust assurance*: the proposal shall allow third-parties to verify the target platform's integrity prior to credential transmission.

(S4) *Mutual trust verification*: both end-points shall successfully attest the state of the other before permitting the establishment of a secure channel.

(S5) *Mutual entity authentication*: each communicating end-point shall authenticate the other's identity to counter masquerading attempts.

(S6) *Denial of Service (DoS) resilience*: resource allocation shall be minimised at both end-points to prevent DoS conditions from arising.

(S7) *Key freshness*: the shared key shall be fresh to the session in order to prevent replay attacks.

(F1) *Avoidance of additional trust hardware*: the protocol shall avoid the need for additional security hardware, e.g. TPMs and SEs, other than the TEE.

(F2) *TEE agnosticism*: the protocols shall remain agnostic of the underlying TEE architecture to facilitate interoperability.

Setup Assumptions. A public-key infrastructure is assumed in which a Certificate Authority (CA) issues certificates to the TSM, TAs, and backup (BA), revocation (RA) and maintenance (MA) authorities used for managing backups, revoking credentials and physically maintaining devices respectively. The TEEs themselves are assumed to be trusted and to possess certified, device-specific attestation and command keys for signing quotes and requests to the TSM. Quotes are a widely-used remote attestation abstraction for TPMs and TEEs, comprising the TEE's identity and the platform integrity measurements collected by a TEE-resident trusted measurer. The resulting quote is signed using the attestation key and transmitted to the remote verifying authority. The credentials are assumed to be securely stored within the TEE, usually performed by encrypting them under a device-specific SRK, as well as secure means of random number generation and key derivation.

3   Migration

TEE migration is the process of transferring and re-provisioning credential data from TA_A to TA_B in distinct TEEs. Migration is crucial in preserving credentials during a device replacement or relocation, where credentials can be remotely transferred without incurring reinitialisation costs. Migrating credentials across TEEs has already attracted some attention in related literature [3,16]. We summarise these schemes and their contributions.

Arfaoui et al. [3] tackle the challenge of credential migration on GlobalPlatform TEEs. The authors introduce a trusted TEE Admin, which possesses a Security Domain (SD) with a TA and key-pair on the source device, to mediate and authenticate the authorisation and migration procedures. Two PKI-based protocols are developed for performing the migration between the target TA and the service provider's TA. Both protocols are subjected to formal verification using the AVISPA analysis tool. While the authors note the importance of remote attestation to verify the target TEE, it is not presented or verified as part of the protocol; it is also omitted during the credential transfer process between the TEEs. Moreover, *mutual* trust assurances between the service provider and TEE is not discussed.

Kostiainen et al. [16] tackle migration for TEE open credential platforms where service providers can provision arbitrary credentials, say, for virtualised access control cards. The authors propose encrypting and backing-up credentials on a trusted server using a tokenised password known only to the user. The credentials are migrated by re-entering the password, which is re-tokenised on the receiver device, and transmitted and verified by the backup server that releases the encrypted credentials. However, like [3], the proposal lacks trust assurances between the TSM and both TEEs, nor is it subjected to formal analysis.

3.1   Proposed High-Level Migration Procedure

Credentials must be deleted on the device from which they are migrated, while transferring them over a secure channel with mutual trust assumptions. In Fig. 2, we show how migration can be performed between remote TAs accounting for the shortcomings in related work, which comprises the following messages:

1. A mutual remote attestation protocol [2,12,20] is executed between TSM and TA_A to bootstrap a secure and mutually trusted channel (STCP).
2. TSM transmits the begin migration command to TA_A.
3. TA_A unseals credentials, C, from its secure storage for transmission.
4. TA_A acknowledges to TSM that the credentials were unsealed successfully.
5. A separate STCP instance is executed between (TSM, TA_B).
6. TSM instructs TA_B to prepare for credential provisioning.
7. TA_B acknowledges to TSM that it is ready to receive credentials.
8. TSM transmits the ID of TA_B to TA_A, e.g. IP address, to which to transmit the unsealed credentials.
9. An STCP is formed using mutual remote attestation between TA_A and TA_B.
10. The credential transfer occurs between TA_A and TA_B.
11. The transferred credential is provisioned into the secure storage of TA_B.
12–13. TA_B acknowledges its provisioning success to TA_A and TSM.
14. TSM instructs TA_A to delete its migrated credential(s).
15–16. TA_A deletes C and acknowledges its success to TSM.

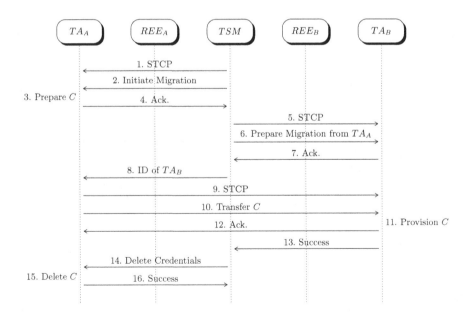

Fig. 2. Proposed TEE credential migration procedure.

The high-level procedure uses three STCPs with mutual attestation between (TSM, TA_A), (TSM, TA_B) and (TA_A, TA_B), thus addressing the absence of bi-directional trust assurances in existing work. The proposal avoids unnecessarily exposing credentials to the TSM by transmitting data directly between the mutually authenticated TAs. Implicitly, the protocol avoids specifying TEE-specific functionalities; rather, for F2 (TEE agnosticism), we abstract the protocol appropriately to allow migrations between heterogeneous TEEs by allowing either a GP TEE application or Intel SGX enclave to act as either TA. For TEE-specific implementation guidance, the reader is referred to existing work such as the GlobalPlatform TMF specifications [10], and the work by Arfaoui et al. [3] for managing and authorising SDs on the GP TEE. In Sect. 7, we specify the protocols and procedures formally, and detail an enhanced mutual attestation protocol for STCP for satisfying the remaining requirements from Sect. 2.1.

4   Revocation

Credentials are typically revoked when they reach the end of their predefined lifespan as part of a key rotation policy; if the OEM discovers a vulnerability in the TA or TEE kernel code, and the credentials were potentially compromised; or the device is retired from service, say, due to obsolescence. Revocation has attracted much attention in related TPM and smart card literature. Chen and Li [5] address credential revocation in TPM 2.0 Direct Anonymous Attestation (DAA). Like conventional group signatures, DAA allows the signer to demonstrate knowledge of its individual private key corresponding to the group's public key; however, this complicates revocation because the signer's identity is not revealed, even to the group manager. The authors review two solutions: *rekey-based*, where the issuer regularly updates its public key (which may or may not include its corresponding secret key), allowing only legitimate non-revoked signers to update their credentials accordingly; and *Verifier-Local Revocation (VLR)*, where the verifier inputs a revocation list (RL), to the DAA's verification function and accepts only signatures from signers $S \notin RL$.

Lueks et al. [18] address revoking attribute-based credentials (ABCs) for smart cards anonymously. Here, the RA possesses an RL of anonymous revocation values, $g_{\epsilon,v}^r$, submitted by the user or verifier (user- and system-instantiated revocation), where r is the revocation value in the user's credential. A revocation 'epoch', ϵ, corresponding to a time period, is used to provide unlinkability by re-computing and re-sending the new valid RLs to the verifiers at each epoch; that is, $RL_{\epsilon,V} = sort(\{g_{\epsilon,V}^r \mid r \in MRL\})$, where MRL is the master revocation list. Using bloom filters, this occupies only 4–8 MB for 2^{21} revoked credentials depending on the chosen probability tolerance.

Katzenbeisser et al. [15] propose revocation for TPM 1.2 using blacklisting and whitelisting. For blacklisting, a list of revoked keys, BL, is ordered into a hash chain and encrypted under the TPM's Storage Root Key (SRK); the final hash chain value is stored in a TPM register to maintain integrity. Before loading a key, k', each $k_i \in BL$ is fed sequentially into the TPM, where it is decrypted, and $k' \stackrel{?}{=} k_i$ is tested. Whitelisting incrementally creates keyed hashes of each permitted key under the TPM's SRK and internal secure counter representing the whitelist's 'version'. A key is valid *iff* the keyed hash counter value matches the TPM's internal counter. Revocation is performed by incrementing the TPM's counter and updating all non-revoked hashes with the new value.

4.1   Proposed High-Level Revocation Procedure

Privacy-preserving credential schemes, e.g. DAA and anonymous credentials, are beneficial in verifying credentials without divulging or linking users' identities. However, to serve as an initial baseline, we scope the focus of this work is scoped to centralised deployments for applications where the concern of violating credential privacy has far fewer consequences than government electronic ID cards or TPMs on consumer devices. As such, we consider Industrial IoT (IIoT), logistics, and public devices in smart cities to serve as three potential application domains. Relaxing this constraint provides us with headway to pursue simpler, PKI-based solutions as a first step for providing TEE credential revocation with mutual attestation. We suggest two approaches for blacklisting and whitelisting using a trusted RA, the procedure for which illustrated in Fig. 3 and described as follows:

1. TSM and TA form a STCP using mutual remote attestation to verify each platforms' integrity and bootstrap a secure channel.
2–3. TSM instructs TA to reveal the current credentials in use, C, which are then unsealed from storage, e.g. encrypted in untrusted storage or an SE.
4. C is transmitted to the TSM over the STCP by TA.
5. The TSM forms a STCP with the revocation authority, RA, who maintains the master revocation list of white- or blacklisted credentials.
6–8. TSM submits C to RA, who returns a list of the revoked credentials in C, i.e. $RC \subseteq C$, from its master revocation list (MRL).
9–11. TSM instructs TA to revoke RC internally; TA performs the deletion and acknowledges its success.

Note that a malicious device may purposefully fail to update the status of RC internally and attempt to reuse revoked credentials. Consequently, the use of revoked credentials should be reported to MA responsible for decommissioning compromised devices, a simple protocol for which is listed in Steps A–E in Fig. 3 based on mutual attestation involving (MA, RA). Like [18], delegating revocation list management to RA removes the burden of potentially multiple verifiers synchronising a single list; the TSM can submit a lookup request to the RA, who queries the blacklist or whitelist in $O(1)$ using an associative array. Either black- or whitelisting can be performed in this model. For blacklisting, the RA maintains a master revocation list (MRL) of revoked credentials that should not be used in any transaction in which the MA submits credentials it wishes to revoke to RA (*maintainer-instantiated revocation*). Here, RA tests the revocation status of C by verifying $C \notin MRL$. Whitelisting, conversely, comprises a list of

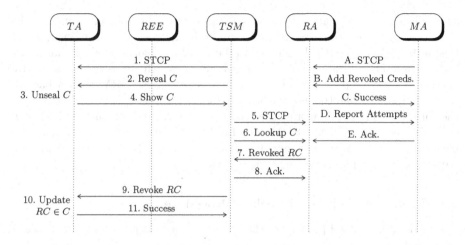

Fig. 3. Proposed credential revocation. *Steps A–E are independent of 1–11.*

only the permitted credentials; a credential is revoked by removing it from the whitelist and, if applicable, updating the list with its replacement. Revocation is tested by verifying $C \in MRL$.

5   Remote Backups

Backup is the process of securely retrieving the set of credentials, C, belonging to a TA for remote storage. In standard practice, backups underpin disaster recovery plans – as stipulated by ISO 27001:2013 [14] – for recovering data from corruption and accidental deletion. Backups may also constitute part of a data retention policy, where device data is used as evidence of regulatory adherence. Secure backup is beneficial when the original credential has non-trivial reinitialisation costs. Next, we examine related work in the backup of remote credentials aboard secure and trusted execution technologies.

Kostiainen et al. [17] address TEE credential backup, restoration and disabling on consumer mobile phones, proposing two solutions. The first uses a SE – a SIM card – in which the TEE credentials are protected under a SIM-specific key provisioned by its provider. This allows the user to uninstall a familiar hardware element, i.e. the SIM, before releasing the device for repairs or to lend to an untrusted user. On reinserting the SIM, an on-board TEE credential manager is used to decrypt and re-initialise the encrypted credentials. The second solution involves the use of a removable microcontroller to counter an honest-but-curious remote server, RS. RS possesses a shared key K_s with the TEE, and stores the backups using a secure counter for rollback protection. To prevent RS reading the credentials, the TEE encrypts them under a separate key, K, derived from a local counter on the microcontroller, and re-encrypts them under K_s.

Akram et al. [1] examine credential restoration for multi-application smart cards on smartphone SEs. The SE's Trusted Environment and Execution Manager (TEM), which dynamically enforces the smart card's run-time security policies, is expanded to facilitate credential backups and restoration. A Backup and Restoration Manager (BRM) is added to the smart card software stack that interfaces with a TEM-resident backup token handler, which stores tokens issued by application service providers. The user first registers the BRM with a backup server (BS) and, when the user wishes to perform the backup, the BRM encrypts the token(s) and communicates them to BS. To restore data, such as to a new card, the user provides the BRM with his/her BS credentials to download the backed-up tokens. A secure channel is formed and the token(s) authenticate the credential restoration from the service provider(s).

5.1   Proposed High-Level Backup Procedure

We introduce a trusted Backup Authority (BA) responsible for storing retrieved credentials. This may be a cloud-based storage provider or Hardware Security Module (HSM) possessed by the credential issuing authority; the precise means by which BA securely stores credentials is out-of-scope in this work. Importantly, we note that credential restoration can be performed by executing the proposed Remote Update procedure in Sect. 6. The proposed procedure between the target TA and BA is shown in Fig. 4, which is described as follows:

1–4. TSM and BA establish a secure and trusted channel with mutual attestation, and TSM requests BA to prepare for backup.
5–6. TSM forms an STCP with TA and commands it prepare the credentials for remote backup; TSM also provides the identity of BA.
7–8. TA unseals the credentials to transmit to BA, and notifies TSM that they were unsealed successfully.

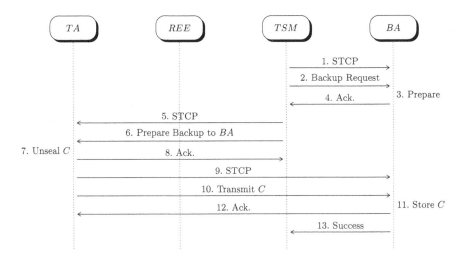

Fig. 4. Proposed high-level remote credential backup protocol.

9–12. TA and BA form a STCP over which C is transmitted to and stored securely by BA. While TSM is considered trusted, a direct connection between TA and BA mitigates the risk of unnecessary credential exposure to TSM.

13. BA notifies TSM that C from TA was backed-up successfully.

6 Remote Updates

Remotely updating credentials is beneficial during routine renewal schedules; for example, with X.509 certificates that reach their validity expiry date, or the device is relocated and the organisational unit to which the credential is issued is no longer valid. Generally speaking, update is the process by which an outdated credential, c_i, is securely replaced by a freshly issued c'_i. Once replaced, c_i should be revoked to prevent reusing obsolete credentials. Little work has been conducted regarding TEE credential updates, which is likely due to the simplicity of a TSM transmitting a new credential over a secure channel or, indeed, the similarity with backup restoration (Sect. 5). Updates can be considered a variation of backup restoration where c'_i is retrieved from an update server; the addition is revoking c_i, achievable using the revocation process proposed in Sect. 4. Next, we describe how this can be achieved with mutual attestation.

6.1 Proposed High-Level Update Procedure

We reintroduce the maintenance authority (MA) from Sect. 4, which issues credential updates as part of a standard rotation policy. If desired, the MA is also responsible for registering obsolete credentials with the revocation authority. The high-level update mechanism is as follows (Fig. 5):

1. MA, who provides the updated credentials, establishes an STCP with TSM.

2–3. MA notifies the TSM of an updated credential. This may include identities of which TEEs need updated or all TEEs.

4–5. An STCP is conducted between (TSM, TA) and an update preparation command is transmitted to TA, along with an optional ID of MA from whom to retrieve the update.

6. TA is locked, i.e. prevented from interacting with the REE, until the update is performed in order to prevent the use of outdated credentials.

7. TA acknowledges to TSM that it is ready to update.

8–10. TA establishes a STCP with MA to receive the credential update; MA transmits the updated credential, c'_i, to TA.

11–12. TA seals c'_i to its secure storage for future use; c_i should be deleted internally before unlocking. TA acknowledges that c'_i was initialised successfully.

13–16. (MA, RA) use an STCP to white- or blacklist the obsolete credential, c_i. Lastly, MA acknowledges completion of the update procedure to TSM.

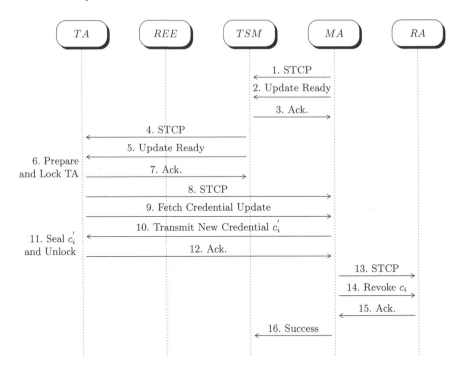

Fig. 5. Proposed credential update procedure.

7   Proposed Protocol Analysis

We now formalise the protocols from the high-level procedures presented previously, which are listed in Protocols 1 to 6 using the notation from Table 1. In Sect. 2.1, we outlined the requirements and assumptions of the protocols, which are referred to throughout. Each proposed protocol is underpinned by an enhancement of the BTP mutual attestation protocol in [20] for establishing the STCP between the TEEs. This protocol (Protocol 6), which establishes a TEE-to-TEE secure channel after exchanging and verifying attestation quotes, is simplified to support authenticated encryption (AE), e.g. AES in GCM mode, rather than a non-AE symmetric scheme with an additional HMAC as in original proposal. This simplification is aimed at reducing protocol implementation complexity and improving performance based on existing benchmarks [13]. The protocol is based on ephemeral Diffie-Hellman key agreement that achieves session forward secrecy (S2), mutual key establishment (S1) and key freshness (S7). Moreover, TEE quotes are mutually exchanged for verifying the integrity of each platform, thus satisfying S3 and S4 (mutual trust verification). The signed attestation values, command instructions, e.g. *Prep_Backup* and *Revoke_Success*, and the shared secret provides mutual entity authentication (S5).

Crucially, the protocols avoid the use of additional trusted hardware, such as TPMs, secure elements and smart cards (F1). The protocols are designed

Protocol 1. Proposed Migration Procedure with BTP (MPBT)

1: Execute BTP (TSM, TA_1)
2: $TSM \to TA_1 : [(Init\_Migrate \parallel X_{TSM})\sigma_{TSM}]_{AE_K}$
3: $TA_1 \to TSM : [(TA_1\_Ack \parallel X_{TA1})\sigma_{TA1}]_{AE_K}$
4: Execute BTP (TSM, TA_2)
5: $TSM \to TA_2 : [(Prep\_Migrate \parallel X'_{TSM})\sigma_{TSM}]_{AE_{K'}}$
6: $TA_2 \to TSM : [(TA_2\_Ack \parallel X'_{TA2})\sigma_{TA2}]_{AE_{K'}}$
7: $TSM \to TA_1 : [(ID_{TA2} \parallel X_{TSM})\sigma_{TSM}]_{AE_K}$
8: Execute BTP (TA_1, TA_2)
9: $TA_1 \to TA_2 : [(C \parallel X''_{TA1})\sigma_{TA1}]_{AE_{K''}}$
10: $TA_2 \to TA_1 : [(TA_2\_Ack \parallel X''_{TA2})\sigma_{TA2}]_{AE_{K''}}$
11: $TA_2 \to TSM : [(TA_2\_Done \parallel X'_{TA2})\sigma_{TA2}]_{AE_{K'}}$
12: $TSM \to TA_1 : [(Delete\_Creds \parallel X_{TSM})\sigma_{TSM}]_{AE_K}$
13: $TA_1 \to TSM : [(TA_1\_Success \parallel X_{TA1})\sigma_{TA1}]_{AE_K}$

Protocol 2. Proposed Revocation Lookup with BTP (RLBT)

1: Execute BTP (TSM, TA)
2: $TSM \to TA : [(Reveal\_Creds \parallel X_{TSM})\sigma_{TSM}]_{AE_K}$
3: $TA \to TSM : [(C \parallel X_{TA})\sigma_{TA}]_{AE_K}$
4: Execute BTP (TSM, RA)
5: $TSM \to RA : [(Lookup \parallel C \parallel X'_{TSM})\sigma_{TSM}]_{AE_{K'}}$
6: $RA \to TSM : [(Revoked \parallel RC \parallel X'_{RA})\sigma_{RA}]_{AE_{K'}}$
7: $TSM \to RA : [(TSM\_Ack \parallel X'_{TSM})\sigma_{TSM}]_{AE_{K'}}$
   If $RC \neq \emptyset$:
8: $TSM \to TA : [(Revoke \parallel RC \parallel X_{TSM})\sigma_{TSM}]_{AE_K}$
9: $TA \to TSM : [(Revoke\_Success \parallel X_{TA})\sigma_{TA}]_{AE_K}$

Protocol 3. Proposed Revocation Procedure with BTP (RPBT)

1: Execute BTP (MA, RA)
2: $MA \to RA : [(Revoke \parallel C \parallel X_{MA})\sigma_{MA}]_{AE_K}$
3: $RA \to MA : [(Revoke\_Success \parallel X_{RA})\sigma_{RA}]_{AE_K}$
4: If reported credentials $(RepC \neq \emptyset)$:
   $RA \to MA : [(Report \parallel RepC \parallel X_{RA})\sigma_{RA}]_{AE_K}$
   $MA \to RA : [(Report\_Success \parallel X_{MA})\sigma_{MA}]_{AE_K}$

Protocol 4. Proposed Backup Procedure with BTP (BPBT)

1: Execute BTP (TSM, BA)
2: $TSM \to BA : [(Prep\_Backup \parallel X_{TSM})\sigma_{TSM}]_{AE_K}$
3: $BA \to TSM : [(BA\_Ack \parallel X_{BA})\sigma_{BA}]_{AE_K}$
4: Execute BTP (TSM, TA)
5: $TSM \to TA : [(Prep\_Backup \parallel ID_{BA} \parallel X'_{TSM})\sigma_{TSM}]_{AE_{K'}}$
6: $TA \to TSM : [(TA\_Ack \parallel X'_{TA})\sigma_{TA}]_{AE_{K'}}$
7: Execute BTP (TA, BA)
8: $TA \to BA : [(C \parallel X''_{TA})\sigma_{TA}]_{AE_{K''}}$
9: $BA \to TA : [(Backup\_Ack \parallel X''_{BA})\sigma_{BA}]_{AE_{K''}}$
10: $BA \to TSM : [(Backup\_Success \parallel X_{BA})\sigma_{BA}]_{AE_K}$

Protocol 5. Proposed Update Procedure with BTP (UPBT)

1: Execute BTP (MA, TSM)
2: $MA \rightarrow TSM : [(Update\_Ready \parallel X_{MA})\sigma_{MA}]_{AE_K}$
3: $TSM \rightarrow MA : [(TSM\_Ack \parallel X_{TSM})\sigma_{TSM}]_{AE_K}$
4: Execute BTP (TSM, TA)
5: $TSM \rightarrow TA : [(Prep\_Update \parallel X'_{TSM})\sigma_{TSM}]_{AE_{K'}}$
6: $TA \rightarrow TSM : [(TA\_Ack \parallel X'_{TA})\sigma_{TA}]_{AE_{K'}}$
7: Execute BTP (TA, MA)
8: $TA \rightarrow MA : [(Fetch\_Update \parallel X''_{TA})\sigma_{TA}]_{AE_{K''}}$
9: $MA \rightarrow TA : [(c'_i \parallel X''_{MA})\sigma_{MA}]_{AE_{K''}}$
10: $TA \rightarrow MA : [(New\_Cred\_Ack \parallel X''_{TA})\sigma_{TA}]_{AE_{K''}}$
11: Execute BTP (MA, RA)
12: $MA \rightarrow RA : [(Revoke \parallel c_i \parallel X'''_{MA})\sigma_{MA}]_{AE_{K'''}}$
13: $RA \rightarrow MA : [(Revoke\_Success \parallel X'''_{RA})\sigma_{RA}]_{AE_{K'''}}$
14: $MA \rightarrow TSM : [(Update\_Success \parallel X_{MA})\sigma_{MA}]_{AE_K}$

Protocol 6. Adapted Bi-directional Trust Protocol (BTP) from [20]

1: $A \rightarrow B : ID_A \parallel ID_B \parallel n_A \parallel g^A \parallel AR_B$
2: $B \rightarrow A : ID_B \parallel ID_A \parallel n_B \parallel g^B \parallel [(X_B)\sigma_B \parallel (V_B)\sigma_B]_{AE_K} \parallel AR_A$
$X_B = H(ID_A \parallel ID_B \parallel g^A \parallel g^B \parallel n_A \parallel n_B)$
$V_B = Q_B \parallel n_B \parallel n_A$
3: $A \rightarrow B : [(X_A)\sigma_A \parallel (V_A)\sigma_A]_{AE_K}$
$X_A = H(ID_A \parallel ID_B \parallel g^A \parallel g^B \parallel n_A \parallel n_B)$
$V_A = Q_A \parallel n_A \parallel n_B$

---

to incorporate abstract TAs, which are verified using the quoting abstraction, whether they be Intel SGX enclaves of GP TEE TAs, thus providing TEE agnosticism (F2). Note, however, that this abstracts away the precision of related work, e.g. Arfaoui et al. [3], which addresses migration specifically in the context of the GP TEE. Such work incorporates GP TEE-specific entites, such as security domains (SDs) and root SDs, which do not exist on Intel SGX or earlier TPM-based TEEs like Intel TXT [11]. As such, users of this work should be aware of the implementation specifics when deploying these protocols; we refer users to [3] and [10] for guidance for GP TEEs, and [6] for Intel SGX.

Formal Symbolic Verification. Scyther by Cremers [7] was employed to verify the correctness of the proposed protocols. A protocol is first specified in the Scyther description language, comprising communicating parties (roles), messages and the desired security properties (claims). Scyther verifies whether the protocol specification satisfies those claims under the 'perfect cryptography' assumption, whereby an adversary learns nothing from an encrypted message unless the decryption key is known, against all possible behaviours of a Dolev-Yao adversary. Despite the challenge of security protocol verification being undecidable in general, many practical protocols can be proven correct; notably, Scyther has been used to verify IKEv1 and IKEv2, and the ISO/IEC 9798 authentication

Table 1. Protocol notation.

Notation	Description
TSM	TEE trusted service manager
BA	Credential backup authority
MA	Device maintenance authority
RA	Revocation authority
TA_X	TEE trusted application on device X
n_X	Secure random nonce generated by X
$H(D)$	Secure one-way hash function, H, on D
$X \rightarrow Y$	Message transmission from X to Y
ID_X	Identity of X
$A \parallel B$	Concatenation of A and B
g^X	Diffie-Hellman exponentiation of X
AR_X	Attestation request on target entity X
Q_X	Attestation quote from TEE X
$(A)\sigma_X$	Signed message A from X under a private-public key-pair (K, P)
$[m]_{AE_K}$	Message m is encrypted using authenticated encryption under session key K derived from the protocol's shared secret
D'	Data specific to a separate session to D

protocol family [8]. We analyse all protocols using Scyther, testing for the secrecy of transmitted quotes from both parties, e.g. (Secret, qta1) and credentials (Secret, c); aliveness (Alive); replay protection, i.e. non-injective agreement (Niagree) and non-injective synchronisation, (Nisynch), defined in [7]; session key secrecy (SKR, K); and the reachability of all entities, e.g. (Reachable, TA). We publicly release the protocol specifications for future research by the community (see Sect. 1). Scyther found no attacks on any protocol.

8   Conclusion

TEEs are emerging as a flexible mechanism for providing a range of assurances regarding the on-device protection of security-critical applications, credentials and related data. In this work, we presented a suite of proposals for remote TEE credential management using mutual attestation for secure *migration*, *revocation*, *backups*, and *updates*. After summarising the features of leading TEE implementations, we formalised the threat model, requirements and assumptions for a typical TEE credential deployment in a centralised setting. Next, we reviewed the state-of-the-art for each credential management challenge, before proposing procedures and protocols for securely realising these notions. The protocols were formalised and subjected to symbolic verification using Scyther, which found no attacks under the Dolev-Yao adversarial model; the protocol specifications are also published publicly for further research. In future work, we aim to incorporate privacy-preserving attestation into our protocol suite, which we considered out-of-scope in this work for centralised deployments, through the use of techniques like DAA and Blacklistable Anonymous Credentials (BLACs). We also wish to address decentralised deployments, where devices have intermittent or potentially no access to a centralised TSM.

Acknowledgements. Carlton Shepherd is supported by the EPSRC and the British government as part of the Centre for Doctoral Training in Cyber Security at Royal Holloway, University of London (EP/K035584/1).

References

1. Akram, R.N., Markantonakis, K., Mayes, K.: Recovering from a lost digital wallet. In: Embedded and Ubiquitous Computing, pp. 1615–1621. IEEE (2013)
2. Akram, R.N., Markantonakis, K., Mayes, K., Bonnefoi, P.F., Sauveron, D., Chaumette, S.: An efficient, secure and trusted channel protocol for avionics wireless networks. In: 35th Digital Avionics Systems Conference. IEEE (2016)
3. Arfaoui, G., Gharout, S., Lalande, J.-F., Traoré, J.: Practical and privacy-preserving TEE migration. In: Akram, R.N., Jajodia, S. (eds.) WISTP 2015. LNCS, vol. 9311, pp. 153–168. Springer, Cham (2015). https://doi.org/10.1007/978-3-319-24018-3_10
4. Brickell, E., Li, J.: Enhanced privacy ID from bilinear pairing for hardware authentication and attestation. Int. J. Inf. Priv. Secur. Integrity **1**(1), 3–33 (2011)
5. Chen, L., Li, J.: Revocation of direct anonymous attestation. In: Chen, L., Yung, M. (eds.) INTRUST 2010. LNCS, vol. 6802, pp. 128–147. Springer, Heidelberg (2011). https://doi.org/10.1007/978-3-642-25283-9_9
6. Costan, V., Devadas, S.: Intel SGX Explained. IACR Cryptology ePrint (2016). https://eprint.iacr.org/2016/086.pdf
7. Cremers, C.J.F.: The scyther tool: verification, falsification, and analysis of security protocols. In: Gupta, A., Malik, S. (eds.) CAV 2008. LNCS, vol. 5123, pp. 414–418. Springer, Heidelberg (2008). https://doi.org/10.1007/978-3-540-70545-1_38
8. Cremers, C.: Key exchange in IPsec revisited: formal analysis of IKEv1 and IKEv2. In: Atluri, V., Diaz, C. (eds.) ESORICS 2011. LNCS, vol. 6879, pp. 315–334. Springer, Heidelberg (2011). https://doi.org/10.1007/978-3-642-23822-2_18
9. GlobalPlatform: TEE Protection Profile (v1.2) (2014)
10. GlobalPlatform: TEE Management Framework (TMF), v1.0 (2016)
11. Greene, J.: Intel Trusted eXecution Technology (TXT): Hardware-based technology for enhancing server platform security. Intel, Inc., Technical report (2012)
12. Greveler, U., Justus, B., Löhr, D.: Mutual remote attestation: enabling system cloning for TPM based platforms. In: Meadows, C., Fernandez-Gago, C. (eds.) STM 2011. LNCS, vol. 7170, pp. 193–206. Springer, Heidelberg (2012). https://doi.org/10.1007/978-3-642-29963-6_14
13. Gueron, S.: AES-GCM for efficient authenticated encryption - ending the reign of HMAC-SHA-1. In: Real World Cryptography (2013)

14. International Standards Organisation: ISO 27001:2013 - Information Security Management (2013). https://www.iso.org/standard/54534.html
15. Katzenbeisser, S., Kursawe, K., Stumpf, F.: Revocation of TPM keys. In: Chen, L., Mitchell, C.J., Martin, A. (eds.) Trust 2009. LNCS, vol. 5471, pp. 120–132. Springer, Heidelberg (2009). https://doi.org/10.1007/978-3-642-00587-9_8
16. Kostiainen, K., Asokan, N., Afanasyeva, A.: Towards user-friendly credential transfer on open credential platforms. In: Lopez, J., Tsudik, G. (eds.) ACNS 2011. LNCS, vol. 6715, pp. 395–412. Springer, Heidelberg (2011). https://doi.org/10.1007/978-3-642-21554-4_23
17. Kostiainen, K., Asokan, N., Ekberg, J.-E.: Credential disabling from trusted execution environments. In: Aura, T., Järvinen, K., Nyberg, K. (eds.) NordSec 2010. LNCS, vol. 7127, pp. 171–186. Springer, Heidelberg (2012). https://doi.org/10.1007/978-3-642-27937-9_12
18. Lueks, W., Alpár, G., Hoepman, J.H., Vullers, P.: Fast revocation of attribute-based credentials for both users and verifiers. Comput. Secur. **67**, 308–323 (2017)
19. Sadeghi, A.R., Wachsmann, C., Waidner, M.: Security and privacy challenges in industrial Internet of Things. In: 52nd Design Automation Conference. ACM (2015)
20. Shepherd, C., Akram, R.N., Markantonakis, K.: Establishing mutually trusted channels for remote sensing devices with trusted execution environments. In: 12th International Conference on Availability, Reliability and Security. ACM (2017)
21. Shepherd, C., Akram, R.N., Markantonakis, K.: Towards trusted execution of multi-modal continuous authentication schemes. In: Proceedings of the 32nd Symposium on Applied Computing. pp. 1444–1451. ACM (2017)
22. Shepherd, C., et al.: Secure and trusted execution: past, present, and future - a critical review in the context of the Internet of Things and cyber-physical systems. In: 15th IEEE International Conference on Trust, Security and Privacy in Computing and Communications. pp. 168–177. IEEE (2016)

Detection of Bitcoin-Based Botnets
Using a One-Class Classifier

Bruno Bogaz Zarpelão[1,3]([⊠]) (ID), Rodrigo Sanches Miani[2] (ID),
and Muttukrishnan Rajarajan[3] (ID)

[1] Computer Science Department,
State University of Londrina (UEL), Londrina, Brazil
brunozarpelao@uel.br
[2] School of Computer Science,
Federal University of Uberlândia (UFU), Uberlândia, Brazil
miani@ufu.br
[3] School of Mathematics, Computer Science and Engineering,
City, University of London, London, UK
r.muttukrishnan@city.ac.uk

Abstract. Botnets have been part of some of the most aggressive cyber-attacks reported in recent years. To make them even harder to be detected and mitigated, attackers have built C&C (Command and Control) infrastructures on top of popular Internet services such as Skype and Bitcoin. In this work, we propose an approach to detect botnets with C&C infrastructures based on the Bitcoin network. First, transactions are grouped according to the users that issued them. Next, features are extracted for each group of transactions, aiming to identify whether they behave systematically, which is a typical bot characteristic. To analyse this data, we employ the OSVM (One-class Support Vector Machine) algorithm, which requires only samples from legitimate behaviour to build a classification model. Tests were performed in a controlled environment using the ZombieCoin botnet and real data from the Bitcoin blockchain. Results showed that the proposed approach can detect most of the bots with a low false positive rate in multiple scenarios.

Keywords: Anomaly detection · Bitcoin · Blockchain ·
Botnet detection · One-class Support Vector Machine

1 Introduction

Botnets are a significant threat to the Internet security. By compromising hundreds or thousands of Internet nodes, attackers can coordinate distributed large-scale attacks, which usually are very aggressive. Botnets are composed of three

We would like to thank Dr. Syed Taha Ali for kindly sharing the ZombieCoin's source code with us, as well as Dr. Hassaan Khaliq for all his help. We would also like to thank the financial support from UKIERI (UK India Education Research Initiative).

O. Blazy and C. Y. Yeun (Eds.): WISTP 2018, LNCS 11469, pp. 174–189, 2019.
https://doi.org/10.1007/978-3-030-20074-9_13

main elements: bots, botmasters, and the C&C (Command and Control) infrastructure. Bots are regular network nodes that attackers compromise to be under their control. Botmasters are malicious users who design the attacks and send instructions to bots for attacks execution. The C&C infrastructure is the logical communication infrastructure that botmasters use to send instructions to bots. C&C architectures have evolved over the years. Attackers have built centralised infrastructures, based on protocols such as IRC (Internet Relay Chat) and HTTP (Hypertext Transfer Protocol), as well as distributed ones, which rely on peer-to-peer networks [1,8].

Attackers have also been investing in C&C infrastructures that explore legitimate applications to keep their operations covered. In these scenarios, bots and botmasters operate as clients of widely used services such as instant messengers [14], online social networks [11] and blockchains [3]. Once these services are designed to share data with as many people as possible, attackers build their C&C structure on top of them. Therefore, they have resilient environments to rely on, which are kept up by the services' owners. Moreover, their actions are harder to detect because their traffic may be mistaken as the legitimate traffic from regular clients of these services. These botnets are also referred to as stealthy botnets [2,14].

In this work, we propose an approach to detect Bitcoin-based botnets. In these botnets, botmasters send instructions piggybacked on Bitcoin transactions to the bots. These botnets are not observable in general traffic features such as packet size, volume of packets, and bit rate, because they use the same Bitcoin network protocols as regular users. Therefore, we assume that, in Bitcoin-based botnets, the systematic behaviour typically found in bots can be observed in transactions attributes such as their values, numbers of inputs, numbers of outputs, and addresses.

The proposed approach makes use of the One-class SVM (Support Vector Machine) algorithm and can be divided into two main steps. First, data about legitimate transactions are collected from the Bitcoin blockchain, which is publicly available, to create a classification model with OSVM. Then, transaction data are retrieved from network packets and compared to the model, allowing the classification of the traffic as legitimate or malicious. To evaluate the approach, we built a controlled environment using the ZombieCoin botnet [3]. The results showed that our approach could detect the most of the bots, keeping a low false positive rate.

To the best of our knowledge, no other work has proposed a systematic approach to detect Bitcoin-based botnets. The key contributions of our study are:

- an approach to detect Bitcoin-based botnets that analyses only transactions attributes. It is independent of traffic features such as packets size, volume of packets, and bit rate;
- design of the detection approach based on the OSVM algorithm, which, unlike supervised techniques, does not require samples of malicious observations to create a classification model.

The remaining of this paper is organised as follows. Section 2 presents the related work. In Sect. 3, we discuss the proposed model. Section 4 shows the evaluation. Finally, Sect. 5 draws the final conclusions.

2   Related Work

Researchers have proposed multiple approaches for botnet detection in recent years. They range from methods that do not aim at any specific type of botnet to approaches designed specifically to Web-based, P2P, or stealthy botnets.

In [13], Wang and Paschalidis proposed a detection method that does not have any specific botnet type as a goal. They assume that activities are more correlated among malicious nodes than among legitimate ones, and botmasters and attack targets present distinguishable network traffic because they communicate with many other nodes. Their approach starts by employing the large deviations principle to detect anomalies in IP flows. It also models interaction graphs from source/destination data in network packets and makes use again of the large deviations principle to detect anomalies in these graphs. The outputs of these two processes are analysed to find out the most active nodes, which are supposed to be botmasters or targets. Then, community detection techniques are used to identify bots from the interactions of the most active nodes.

Sakib and Huang [8] proposed an approach to detect HTTP-based botnets. The proposed solution applies three anomaly detection algorithms in two steps. In the first step, HTTP requests features are analysed using Chebyshev's Inequality, One-class SVM, and Nearest Neighbor based Local Outlier Factor to find out if the requests were generated by human actions or bots (legitimate or malicious). In the second step, Chebyshev's Inequality is used to classify the bot requests as malicious or legitimate. Hsu et al. [4] also analysed HTTP packets to detect HTTP-based botnets. However, unlike [8], they computed metrics based on the number of distinctly accessed servers and the payload size similarity. To detect the bots, they compare these metrics to thresholds.

Wang et al. [12] proposed the BotCluster, a botnet detector that inspects IP flows to detect P2P-based botnets. At first, it combines unidirectional IP flows to turn them into bidirectional flows. Next, the system filters out non-P2P flows using a whitelist and the flow loss response rate. Then, DBSCAN, an unsupervised clustering algorithm, is applied to separate the legitimate P2P flows from the malicious ones. The authors assumed that botnets behaviour presents high regularity, as well as actions from different bots in the same botnet are correlated, the both being observable in IP flows. Zhang et al. [14] proposed to detect stealthy P2P botnets following a similar sequence of two steps. First, they identified all hosts that were part of P2P communications. Next, they analysed the P2P flows to detect the malicious ones. To do so, they selected the more active P2P clients, considering them as bot candidates. Then, they investigated the hosts the bot candidates interacted to. According to the authors, bots usually communicate with the same hosts, which was observed to distinguish them from legitimate clients.

Albanese et al. [2] also proposed a system to detect stealthy botnets. This system explores the periodicity of traffic associated with data exfiltration using periodogram analysis. Additionally, the authors discussed techniques to find the best places in the network to deploy the solution, and the use of moving target defence to neutralise stealthy bots evasion movements. Venkatachalam and Anitha [11] proposed a system to detect Stegobot, a stealthy botnet proposed by [6] that makes use of steganography to leak the target data in images shared on online social networks (OSN). The proposed system extracts features from OSN profiles regarding uploaded images, level of activity, and relationships with other profiles. Then, these profiles are classified into legitimate or malicious by supervised classification techniques such as SVM, k-Nearest Neighbour, Decision Tree, and Naive Bayes.

Unlike the previous work [12–14], in this work we do not rely on IP flow analysis. In Bitcoin-based botnets, once bots communicate with peers to disseminate transactions in the same way regular users do, there are no flow statistics that can disclose bot-related activities. Instead, we analyse transaction attributes such as the number of inputs and outputs, values of outputs, and rates of transactions to detect bot traffic. In this sense, our work follows a strategy similar to that used by [4,8,11], which also make use of information extracted from bots activities on a low-level basis. Nonetheless, it is important to highlight that, to the best of our knowledge, it is the first time a systematic approach has been proposed to detect Bitcoin-based botnets.

3   Proposed Approach

In this section, we present the proposed approach to detect Bitcoin-based botnets. We discuss first the approach rationale, and then the details on the two modules: Model Creation Module and Botnet Detection Module.

3.1   Approach Rationale

Different works on botnet detection assumed that bots present a more systematic behaviour than regular nodes. Depending on the work, this regularity was observed on the correlation between bots behaviour [12,13], features extracted from HTTP packets [4,8], the time the bots kept active [14], and the periodicity of traffic related to data exfiltration [2].

In this work, we explored the regularity of bots behaviour regarding the transactions attributes. Each transaction has different attributes such as number of inputs and outputs, addresses, and values. Figure 1 illustrates a transaction. It contains an identifier, which is the hash of the transaction, and the inputs and outputs with their addresses and values. In the transaction illustrated, a user is transferring $1.0 from its account holding the address "12cb...Tu3S" to the accounts with addresses "1Q2T...Jvm3" and "1bee...Vwq8", which will receive $0.8 and $0.2, respectively. We assumed that bots present a more systematic behaviour for these attributes because they are programmed, and so they may not follow the same behaviour as a human being making Bitcoin transfers.

To be able to compute the evolution of these attributes throughout multiple transactions, we grouped these transactions according to the users that issued them. The blockchain is composed of a set of transactions denoted as $T = \{t_1, \ldots, t_n\}$. Considering the set of users $U = \{u_1, \ldots, u_n\}$ that issued these transactions, we assume that each user u_i has its set of transactions T_{u_i}, where $T_{u_i} \subset T$. Each transaction t is defined by the 3-tuple (ts, I, O), where ts denotes the transaction timestamp, I the set of inputs, and O the set of outputs.

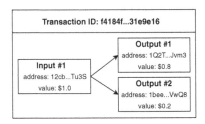

Fig. 1. Example of a transaction.

Having the set of transactions T_{u_i} for a user u_i, we can extract the features to distinguish botnet traffic from regular traffic. Algorithm 1 shows how the features are extracted. In this algorithm, $|X|$ denotes the amount of elements in the set X, e.g., $|t_1.I|$ represents the number of inputs in the transaction t_1.

Algorithm 1. Extracting a feature vector for a set of transactions

Input   : List of transactions $T_u = \{t_1, t_2, \ldots, t_n\}$ for user u, and the timestamp
            $startTime$ referring to the oldest transaction of the dataset

Output: Feature vector f for user u

1 **Function** extractFeatures($T = \{t_1, t_2, \ldots, t_n\}$, $startTime$)
2     $f.inMedian \leftarrow$ median($|t_1.I|, |t_2.I|, \ldots, |t_i.I|$);
3     $f.inIQR \leftarrow$ iqr($|t_1.I|, |t_2.I|, \ldots, |t_i.I|$);
4     $f.outMedian \leftarrow$ median($|t_1.O|, |t_2.O|, \ldots, |t_i.O|$);
5     $f.outIQR \leftarrow$ iqr($|t_1.O|, |t_2.O|, \ldots, |t_i.O|$);
6     $f.lowVMedian \leftarrow$ median(lowestOutput(t_1), ..., lowestOutput(t_i));
7     $f.lowVIQR \leftarrow$ iqr(lowestOutput(t_1), ..., lowestOutput(t_i));
8     $f.iatMedian \leftarrow$ median($t_2.ts - t_1.ts, t_3.ts - t_2.ts, \ldots, t_i.ts - t_{i-1}.ts$);
9     $f.iatIQR \leftarrow$ iqr($t_2.ts - t_1.ts, t_3.ts - t_2.ts, \ldots, t_i.ts - t_{i-1}.ts$);
10   $f.txTime \leftarrow (t_i.ts - startTime) \div (|T_u|)$;
11   $f.addressPerTx \leftarrow (|$inputAddrs($T_u$)$|) \div (|T_u|)$;
12   **return** f
13 **end**

Almost all the features extracted are based on two statistical measures: the median (denoted in Algorithm 1 as the function $median(x_1, \ldots, x_n)$), and the interquartile range (IQR, denoted in Algorithm 1 as $iqr(x_1, \ldots, x_n)$). The median is a measure of central tendency, while the IQR measures the data dispersion. The objective is to determine the central tendency and the dispersion of some transaction attributes for a particular user, modelling its behaviour. All the extracted features are discussed next.

- The median (*inMedian*) and the IQR (*inIQR*) of the number of inputs, and the median (*outMedian*) and the IQR (*outIQR*) of the number of outputs of each transaction. Legitimate users can build transactions with various amounts of inputs and outputs depending on their needs, while bots, being programs, might present a more systematic behaviour.
- The median (*lowVMedian*) and the IQR (*lowVIQR*) of the lowest output value of each transaction. Bot transactions cannot involve high amounts of funds, because their operation must be as profitable as possible to the attackers. This way, it is expected that the lowest output value of bot transactions is usually smaller than the one found in legitimate transactions. Besides, unlike bots, legitimate users are expected to present more variability in these values. In Algorithm 1, *lowestOutput(t)* denotes a function that take as input a transaction and returns its lowest output.
- The median (*iatMedian*) and the IQR (*iatIQR*) of the time intervals between two subsequent transactions. Bots are expected to present more periodicity than legitimate users, since they usually perform some automatic tasks.
- The relation (*txTime*) between the amount of transactions and the time elapsed. Bots may present a high level of interaction with botmasters, particularly when they are receiving instructions to launch attacks. This way, it is expected that they receive more transactions within a particular time interval than a legitimate user.
- The relation (*addressPerTx*) between the number of distinct input addresses and the number of transactions. The decision on how to use (or reuse) addresses is programmed in bots, while legitimate users can change it from one transaction to another. Therefore, the number of distinct addresses can vary from legitimate to bot users. In Algorithm 1, *inputAddrs(T)* represents a function that takes a set of transactions as input and returns the set of distinct input addresses used in these transactions.

To classify the feature vectors as legitimate or malicious, we employed the OSVM technique. In supervised machine learning techniques, usually employed in botnet detection, a classification model is built from data instances representing the different classes the data can be classified into. For example, to detect botnets, samples from malicious and legitimate behaviour should be labelled and presented to the classifier, which would construct a model that could be used to classify future samples as legitimate or malicious. This can be problematic when the labelling process is labour-intensive and error-prone, or samples of some of the classes hardly occur [5].

A solution to address this issue is to use one-class classifiers. In these techniques, only samples of one class are presented to the classifier to build the classification model, e.g., samples of legitimate behaviour. Then, the upcoming samples are classified as belonging or not to this class. Therefore, the labelling process is no longer necessary. The OSVM algorithm is a one-class classification technique that was successfully used in many domains [5]. This technique creates hyperplanes that work as boundaries around the region containing the training data. This way, if an instance is inside these boundaries, it is classified as belonging to the modelled class. Otherwise, it is classified as an anomaly. In our case, we provided data from legitimate Bitcoin users to create the model. Then, all data instances that are outside the boundaries set for this class are classified as bots.

3.2   Model Creation Module

The objective of the Model Creation Module, represented in Fig. 2, is to create a classification model from information available on the Bitcoin blockchain.

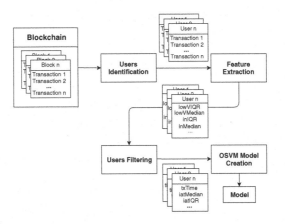

Fig. 2. Creation of classification model from Blockchain data.

The first step for the model creation is to retrieve a set of blocks from the blockchain. All the transactions from the retrieved blocks are extracted to a list denoted as $T = \{t_1, \ldots, t_n\}$. Next, the *Users Identification* step is performed. The objective of this step is to assign every transaction in T to a user u.

As already discussed in Sect. 3.1, a Bitcoin transaction t has a set of inputs and outputs. Inputs and outputs are associated with addresses, which are derived from the public keys of the users involved in the transaction. These addresses are pseudonyms, and a single user can have multiple addresses. When a user wants to send funds to someone, it signs the transference using its private key and informs the public keys of the fund destinations. It is recommended that users generate new keys for every transaction, avoiding that transactions are traced and the users identified [7]. Even so, it is possible to group Bitcoin transactions according to their source. We followed two strategies to do it:

- As many users do not generate new keys to make new transactions, it is possible to explore this fact to group them. Let t_1 and t_2 be two transactions, and $inputAddrs(\{t_1, \ldots, t_n\})$ a function that returns the set of input addresses for a given set of transactions. If $inputAddrs(\{t_1\}) \cap inputAddrs(\{t_2\}) \neq \emptyset$, then we assume that these two transactions were generated by the same user.
- The second strategy explores a heuristic based on multi-input transactions [7,10]. Sometimes, a user does not have enough funds attached to a single address to complete a transaction. To avoid breaking this transaction into smaller ones, the user includes multiple inputs, each one associated to an address, in a single transaction. Therefore, it is possible to assume that all the input addresses of this kind of transaction belong to the same user.

After assigning the transactions to the users, the next step is to extract the feature vectors from them. To do so, all the transactions of each user are ordered by timestamp. Then, for a given user u_i, the transactions in T_{u_i} are processed according to Algorithm 2. The main idea of Algorithm 2 is to generate feature vectors as the transactions were being assigned one by one to the user. For example, let's suppose a user has six transactions $\{t_1, \ldots, t_6\}$ and $minTxs$ is 4. Then, three different feature vectors would be extracted: f_1 extracted from t_1, t_2, t_3 and t_4, f_2 extracted from t_1, t_2, t_3, t_4 and t_5, and f_3 extracted from t_1, t_2, t_3, t_4, t_5 and t_6. The function $extractFeatures(T, startTime)$ present in Algorithm 2 is defined in Algorithm 1.

Algorithm 2. Extracting feature vectors for one user

Input   : List of transactions $T_u = \{t_1, t_2, \ldots, t_n\}$ for user u, the timestamp $startTime$ referring to the oldest transaction present in all blockchain collected data, and the minimum number of transactions per user $minTxs$

Output: List of feature vectors F_u for user u

1 **for** $i \leftarrow minTxs$ **to** n **do**
2 $\quad$ $f \leftarrow$ **extractFeatures**$(\{t_1, t_2, \ldots, t_i\}, startTime)$;
3 $\quad$ *add f to F_u*;
4 **end**

The idea behind this approach is related to the way the Botnet Detection Module works, classifying users every time they have new transactions. If the Botnet Detection Module waits until it gathers a large number of transactions for a particular user to start analysing it, the bot detection might take a long time. Otherwise, if the Botnet Detection Module analyses this user every time a transaction is assigned to it, it might detect a bot quicker, after only a few transactions has been assigned to this user. Once the Model Creation Module is building a classification model for the Botnet Detection Module, it has to emulate the same process followed by the latter one.

After extracting the features, the next step is *Users Filtering*. Users with high dispersion for the number of inputs and outputs and the output values are more likely to be legitimate. Therefore, in this step, we filter this kind of user out. Only legitimate users that may be more similar to bots are included in the OSVM model, since they demand a more sophisticated technique to be differentiated from bots. The filtering process is detailed in Algorithm 3. Three thresholds, t_{in}, t_{out} and t_{low}, are set by computing the first quartile (denoted in Algorithm 3 as the function $firstQuartile(x_1, \ldots, x_n)$) of three features, namely $inIQR$, $outIQR$ and $lowVIQR$. All feature vectors in F are considered to compute these thresholds. Next, all feature vectors that hold values below the thresholds are included in a new list of feature vectors F'. In F', a feature f' is defined by the 5-tuple $(lowVMedian, iatMedian, iatIQR, txTime, addressPerTx)$.

Algorithm 3. Filtering out users with high dispersion

 Input : List of feature vectors $F = \{f_1, f_2, \ldots, f_n\}$
 Output: List of remaining feature vectors $F' = \{f_1, f_2, \ldots, f_m\}$, where $m \leq n$
1 $t_{in} \leftarrow$ firstQuartile$(\{f_1.inIQR, f_2.inIQR, \ldots, f_n.inIQR\})$;
2 $t_{out} \leftarrow$ firstQuartile$(\{f_1.outIQR, f_2.outIQR, \ldots, f_n.outIQR\})$;
3 $t_{low} \leftarrow$ firstQuartile$(\{f_1.lowVIQR, f_2.lowVIQR, \ldots, f_n.lowVIQR\})$;
4 **foreach** f in F **do**
5 | **if** $f.inIQR \leq t_{in} \wedge f.outIQR \leq t_{out} \wedge f.lowVIQR \leq t_{low}$ **then**
6 | | *add f to F'*;
7 | **end**
8 **end**

The last step performed by the Model Creation Module is *OSVM Model Creation*. In this step, firstly, all features for each feature vector are scaled according to their minimum and maximum values between a range from 0 to 1, as defined by Eq. (1):

$$x_f[j] = \frac{x_f[j] - min(x[j])}{max(x[j]) - min(x[j])}, \forall f \in F', \forall j \in J \tag{1}$$

where f corresponds to a given feature vector, F' to all feature vectors extracted, j to a feature in the J feature space, and $x_f[j]$ to the value present in feature j for the feature vector f. The OSVM algorithm receives the normalised feature vectors as input and provide as output a model of the behaviour of the users represented by these feature vectors.

3.3 Botnet Detection Module

The Botnet Detection Module analyses network packets to detect the presence of bots in the monitored network. Therefore, in a real network, this module would be placed in the border between the monitored network and the Internet, being able to analyse all Bitcoin packets exchanged between internal and external nodes. We assume that Bitcoin-based bots are implemented as SPV (Simplified Payment Verification) clients due to their low memory and traffic footprint. Unlike full Bitcoin clients, SPV clients do not receive all the transactions that other clients broadcast, and do not keep a copy of the entire blockchain. They rely on full nodes, which forward to SPV clients the transactions of their interest. An overview of this module is presented in Fig. 3.

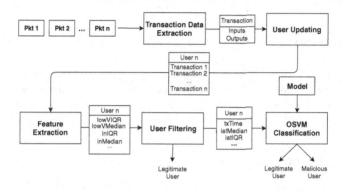

Fig. 3. Botnet detection using data extracted from transactions and the model created previously.

The first step of the Botnet Detection Module is to inspect Bitcoin packets, one by one, and extract transaction data from them. Then, this data is used to update a user profile. The users are determined according to the packets' IP addresses, since SPV nodes only receive transactions of their interest. A user u has a list of transactions $T_u = \{t_1, \ldots, t_n\}$, which were forwarded to the u's IP address. Every time a new t is added to T_u, u is classified again. To classify u, it is necessary to extract its features. The list T_u containing all the transactions that u received so far is passed as an argument to the function $extractFeatures(T, startTime)$ in Algorithm 1. This function returns a feature vector f_u.

With f_u, it is possible to perform an attempt of classification using the thresholds set in Algorithm 3. If the user cannot be classified based on those thresholds, the OSVM algorithm is used. Before applying the OSVM algorithm, the feature vector f_u is scaled following the normalisation step in Eq. (1), except that this time, the $max(x[j])$ and $min(x[j])$ are the same as the ones used when the model was created. As it was done in the Model Creation Module, only the features $lowVMedian$, $iatMedian$, $iatIQR$, $txTime$, and $addressPerTx$ are used in the OSVM classification. Algorithm 4 shows how the classification process works. In this algorithm, the normalisation step is denoted as the function $normalise(x)$, and the OSVM classification algorithm is denoted as the function $OSVM(x)$.

Algorithm 4. Classifying user

Input   : A feature vector f for user u
Output: Classification of u: "legitimate" or "malicious"
1 **if** $f.inIQR > t_{in} \lor f.outIQR > t_{out} \lor f.lowVIQR > t_{low}$ **then**
2 | $classification \leftarrow$ "$legitimate$";
3 **else**
4 | $f' \leftarrow$ normalise(f);
5 | $classification \leftarrow$ OSVM(f');
6 **end**

---

4   Evaluation

In this section, we describe the experiment performed to evaluate the proposed approach. First, some concepts of the ZombieCoin botnet [3] are presented. Next, the details of the experimental design are provided. Finally, the results are presented and discussed.

4.1   ZombieCoin

To evaluate our approach, we built an instance of the ZombieCoin botnet, which was proposed by Ali et al. [3]. This botnet makes use of the Bitcoin network to allow the botmaster to transmit instructions to the bots. Both the botmaster and the bot are developed with the BitcoinJ library as SPV clients. This botnet explores a function in Bitcoin transactions referred to as OP_RETURN. This function allows users to include up to 80 bytes of data into the transaction. It may be used, for example, to add textual information about the transaction like clients usually do in conventional banking transfers. Next, we present an outline of ZombieCoin operation:

– The botmaster has a key pair (public and private keys) that is used to protect its account and sign its transactions. When the botmaster is installed, it provides a command line interface to the user with a list of instructions that can be transmitted to the bots.
– The bot has the public key of the botmaster hardcoded. Using this key, it can request the botmaster transactions to its peers and authenticate them. Once the bot is installed, it can receive transactions with instructions from the botmaster, decode them and perform actions as requested.
– All the communication between bots and botmaster is based on standard Bitcoin protocol specification.

We implemented three commands in the ZombieCoin bot and botmaster: REGISTER, SYN FLOOD ATTACK, and UDP FLOOD ATTACK. When a bot receives the REGISTER command, it generates a file with a unique bot identifier, the current timestamp, and some information about the compromised host such as the number of processors, processor architecture, operating system, and available memory. This file is uploaded to a Dropbox account belonging to the botmaster. Botmasters send this kind of command periodically to enumerate the active bots and have some control and detailed information about the compromised machines [3,14]. When SYN FLOOD ATTACK or UDP FLOOD ATTACK commands are sent, the bot launches the respective DoS attack against the selected target.

4.2 Experiment Design

To emulate the malicious traffic, we built a network with six nodes. An instance of the ZombieCoin botmaster was deployed in an Amazon Web Service (AWS) host. To implement the bots, five Linux containers were created in a host at our laboratory, and each container hosted a ZombieCoin bot instance. Containers are lightweight virtual machines that emulate a machine with its own operating system, but share the host's operating system kernel with other applications. LXC[1] was used to create and manage the containers. The botmaster host had a public IPv4 address attributed by AWS. Private IPv4 addresses were assigned to the bots' hosts. The botmaster and the bots had access to the Internet. The software Wireshark[2] was installed in the machine hosting the bots' containers, being able to capture all the packets the bots transmitted and received.

Bots and botmaster were executed for nearly two hours, and the botmaster sent twelve commands to the bots. The objective was to reproduce a situation with an attacker actively using its botnet to launch DDoS attacks, while checking the status of its bots periodically. These commands will be detailed in the next section, when a particular scenario is discussed to show how the approach detected the malicious commands.

The legitimate behaviour was emulated with 239,495 transactions collected from blocks appended to the main Bitcoin blockchain between 17-06-2018 and 20-06-2018. They were grouped into users, composing a database of legitimate users.

Multiple experimental scenarios were set according to two parameters: the number of legitimate users used to create the model (l_{model}) and the number of legitimate users present in the botnet detection step ($l_{detection}$). The idea behind the first parameter was to observe if the performance proposed by the approach improves depending on the size of the sample of legitimate users used for the model creation. The second parameter was defined to analyse if different numbers of legitimate users could influence the task of distinguishing malicious and legitimate instances. Higher amounts of legitimate users increase the probability of having more diverse legitimate behaviour, which might confuse the botnet detector.

Five different values were assigned to l_{model}: 100, 200, 300, 400, and 500 users. $l_{detection}$ received the values 10, 20, 30, 40, and 50. The combination of these values resulted in twenty five experimental scenarios. Ten rounds were executed

---

[1] https://linuxcontainers.org/.

[2] https://www.wireshark.org/.

for each scenario, and, at each round, the legitimate users were randomly selected from our database. The five malicious users were included in all rounds for all scenarios.

The performance of the proposed approach was evaluated according to the following metrics [9]:

- **TPR**: $\frac{TP}{TP+FN}$ among all feature vectors extracted from malicious users, how many were correctly classified.
- **FPR**: $\frac{FP}{FP+TN}$ among all feature vectors extracted from legitimate users, how many were incorrectly classified as malicious.
- **AUC**: $\frac{1}{2}(TPR + (1 - FPR))$ combines TPR and FPR into a single metric, facilitating the comparison between different experimental rounds.

TP, TN, FP, and FN stand for true positives, true negatives, false positives, and false negatives, respectively. The RBF (Radial Basis Function) kernel was used for the OSVM algorithm. For all tests, $minTxs$ was set to 3 transactions.

4.3   Results and Discussion

Firstly, we searched for a common value for the OSVM hyperparameter ν that could allow the different scenarios to reach a good performance. For each scenario, the proposed approach was executed with ν ranging from 0.05 to 0.95 in steps of 0.05. The ν values that yield the best AUC for each scenario were computed, and Fig. 4 shows the histogram for these values. It is possible to observe that $\nu = 0.05$ is the most frequent value, which was assumed for the remaining tests.

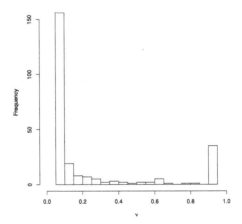

Fig. 4. Histogram for best values of ν considering different scenarios.

Another objective of the evaluation was to investigate how the number of legitimate users selected to create the model (denoted as l_{model}) and the number of legitimate users present in the detection step (denoted as $l_{detection}$) could affect the results. Figure 5 shows the performance of the approach taking into consideration the arithmetic mean of the AUC calculated throughout the ten rounds at each combination of l_{model} and $l_{detection}$. Although most of the scenarios presented good results, with the mean AUC above 0.8, the scenario with $l_{model} = 500$ users was clearly the best one. Different values for $l_{detection}$ did not affect the results in any situation. We assumed $l_{model} = 500$ users for the remaining tests.

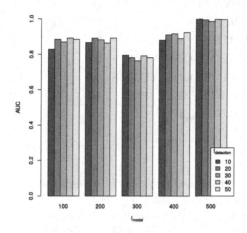

Fig. 5. AUC mean for different combinations of l_{model} and $l_{detection}$.

The next step is to analyse the results for the metrics AUC, TPR, and FPR considering $l_{model} = 500$, $\nu = 0.05$, and $l_{detection} = \{10, 20, 30, 40, 50\}$. The mean (1.00) and the standard deviation (0.00) computed for TPR indicate that this metric was equal to 1.00 for all the rounds. This means that even creating different classification models at each round and changing $l_{detection}$, the proposed approach was able to classify correctly all the feature vectors related to malicious users. The mean FPR was very low (0.01), and its standard deviation (0.02) shows that the values computed for this metric throughout the multiple rounds were not significantly higher than its mean. Once AUC is a function of TPR and FPR, its results were also good, with the mean $= 0.99$ and the standard deviation $= 0.01$.

Finally, we analysed a particular case to observe the characteristics of the true positives and the false positives. To carry out this analysis, we selected the case that presented the closest AUC to the mean for this metric, which was 0.99. The selected case was the sixth round of the experiment with $l_{model} = 500$, and $l_{detection} = 40$. For this case, we had 54 true positives, 248 true negatives, 1 false positive, and 0 false negatives. Table 1 presents the classification of the feature vectors generated from the commands received by the malicious users.

As soon as the proposed approach started analysing the transactions, it detected the bots. $minTxs$ was set to 3, so the approach waited for three transactions of a user to begin analysing it. In our tests, the botmaster sent the third

Table 1. Malicious commands sent and their detection.

Elapsed time (min)	Command	User 1	User 2	User 3	User 4	User 5
0	REGISTER	NA	NA	NA	NA	NA
7	REGISTER	NA	NA	NA	NA	NA
14	SYN FLOOD ATTACK	TP	TP	TP	TP	TP
22	REGISTER	TP	TP	TP	TP	TP
35	SYN FLOOD ATTACK	TP	TP	TP	TP	TP
37	REGISTER	TP	TP	TP	TP	TP
52	REGISTER	TP	TP	TP	TP	TP
54	UDP FLOOD ATTACK	TP	TP	TP	TP	TP
64	UDP FLOOD ATTACK	TP	TP	TP	TP	TP
67	REGISTER	TP	TP	TP	TP	TP
82	REGISTER	TP	TP	TP	TP	TP
97	REGISTER	TP	TP	TP	TP	TP

transaction 14 min after the beginning of the experiment. Table 1 shows that the two first transactions were not analysed ("NA") and, after that, all the analysed transactions sent for the bots were classified as malicious ("TP"). The only false positive was raised to a user that presented a very low dispersion for the number of inputs, outputs, and transferred value. Besides, its number of outputs was unusually high and its transfer value uncommonly low, when compared to other normal users.

Overall, the approach presented a high predictive performance. We evaluated different scenarios with multiple numbers of legitimate users, and the results for true positives and false positives were good for most of them. The scenarios that included more users (500) in the model creation step were the ones with the best results. In these scenarios, all malicious feature vectors were correctly classified as so in all rounds, and there were only a few false positives. Still, in all these scenarios with 500 users for model creation, the proposed approach was able to detect the bots as soon as it gathered the minimum number of transactions that allowed an analysis. This means that, for these cases, the proposed approach detected the bots right after the botmaster sent the third transaction in a row, only 14 min after the experiment had started.

5   Conclusion

Botnets have been the protagonists of severe attacks on the Internet. As attackers started building their C&C infrastructures on top of widely-used services, they became harder to be detected and mitigated. In this paper, we proposed an approach to detect Bitcoin-based botnets. The approach is based on the OSVM classifier, which requires only legitimate samples to build the classification model. To detect the bots, the proposed approach extracts information from different transactions belonging to the same user, aiming to identify whether the traffic belongs to a bot. Tests were conducted using the ZombieCoin botnet and real transaction data from Bitcoin blockchain. The results demonstrated a high predictive performance, with high true positive rates and low false positive rates in several scenarios. The study of a particular case showed that the proposed approach detected the bots after the botmaster had sent only three commands. As future work, we intend to extend the proposed approach to detect botnets based on other blockchain applications such as Ethereum.

References

1. Acarali, D., Rajarajan, M., Komninos, N., Herwono, I.: Survey of approaches and features for the identification of HTTP-based botnet traffic. J. Netw. Comput. Appl. **76**, 1–15 (2016)
2. Albanese, M., Jajodia, S., Venkatesan, S.: Defending from stealthy botnets using moving target defenses. IEEE Secur. Priv. **16**(1), 92–97 (2018)
3. Ali, S.T., McCorry, P., Lee, P.H.J., Hao, F.: ZombieCoin 2.0: managing next-generation botnets using Bitcoin. Int. J. Inf. Secur. **17**(4), 411–422 (2018)
4. Hsu, F.H., Ou, C.W., Hwang, Y.L., Chang, Y.C., Lin, P.C.: Detecting web-based botnets using bot communication traffic features. In: Security and Communication Networks 2017 (2017)
5. Khan, S.S., Madden, M.G.: A survey of recent trends in one class classification. In: Coyle, L., Freyne, J. (eds.) AICS 2009. LNCS (LNAI), vol. 6206, pp. 188–197. Springer, Heidelberg (2010). https://doi.org/10.1007/978-3-642-17080-5_21
6. Nagaraja, S., Houmansadr, A., Piyawongwisal, P., Singh, V., Agarwal, P., Borisov, N.: Stegobot: a covert social network botnet. In: Filler, T., Pevný, T., Craver, S., Ker, A. (eds.) IH 2011. LNCS, vol. 6958, pp. 299–313. Springer, Heidelberg (2011). https://doi.org/10.1007/978-3-642-24178-9_21
7. Nakamoto, S.: Bitcoin: a peer-to-peer electronic cash system (2008)
8. Sakib, M.N., Huang, C.: Using anomaly detection based techniques to detect HTTP-based botnet C&C traffic. In: 2016 IEEE International Conference on Communications (ICC), pp. 1–6, May 2016
9. Sokolova, M., Lapalme, G.: A systematic analysis of performance measures for classification tasks. Inf. Process. Manag. **45**(4), 427–437 (2009)
10. Spagnuolo, M., Maggi, F., Zanero, S.: BitIodine: extracting intelligence from the bitcoin network. In: Christin, N., Safavi-Naini, R. (eds.) FC 2014. LNCS, vol. 8437, pp. 457–468. Springer, Heidelberg (2014). https://doi.org/10.1007/978-3-662-45472-5_29
11. Venkatachalam, N., Anitha, R.: A multi-feature approach to detect Stegobot: a covert multimedia social network botnet. Multimed. Tools Appl. **76**(4), 6079–6096 (2017)
12. Wang, C.Y., et al.: BotCluster: a session-based P2P botnet clustering system on NetFlow. Comput. Netw. **145**, 175–189 (2018)
13. Wang, J., Paschalidis, I.C.: Botnet detection based on anomaly and community detection. IEEE Trans. Control Netw. Syst. **4**(2), 392–404 (2017)
14. Zhang, J., Perdisci, R., Lee, W., Luo, X., Sarfraz, U.: Building a scalable system for stealthy P2P-botnet detection. IEEE Trans. Inf. Forensics Secur. **9**(1), 27–38 (2014)

Internet of Things

A Family of Lightweight Twisted Edwards Curves for the Internet of Things

Sankalp Ghatpande, Johann Großschädl$^{(\boxtimes)}$, and Zhe Liu

CSC and SnT, University of Luxembourg,
6, Avenue de la Fonte, 4364 Esch-sur-Alzette, Luxembourg
{sankalp.ghatpande,johann.groszschaedl,zhe.liu}@uni.lu

Abstract. We introduce a set of four twisted Edwards curves that satisfy common security requirements and allow for fast implementations of scalar multiplication on 8, 16, and 32-bit processors. Our curves are defined by an equation of the form $-x^2 + y^2 = 1 + dx^2y^2$ over a prime field $\mathbb{F}_p$, where d is a small non-square modulo p. The underlying prime fields are based on "pseudo-Mersenne" primes given by $p = 2^k - c$ and have in common that $p \equiv 5 \bmod 8$, k is a multiple of 32 minus 1, and c is at most eight bits long. Due to these common features, our primes facilitate a parameterized implementation of the low-level arithmetic so that one and the same arithmetic function is able to process operands of different length. Each of the twisted Edwards curves we introduce in this paper is birationally equivalent to a Montgomery curve of the form $-(A + 2)y^2 = x^3 + Ax^2 + x$ where $4/(A + 2)$ is small. Even though this contrasts with the usual practice of choosing A such that $(A + 2)/4$ is small, we show that the Montgomery form of our curves allows for an equally efficient implementation of point doubling as Curve25519. The four curves we put forward roughly match the common security levels of 80, 96, 112 and 128 bits. In addition, their Weierstraß representations are isomorphic to curves of the form $y^2 = x^3 - 3x + b$ so as to facilitate inter-operability with TinyECC and other legacy software.

1 Introduction

Elliptic Curve Cryptography (ECC), introduced independently by Koblitz [22] and Miller [26] in the mid-1980s, is nowadays widely considered the most viable alternative to RSA and other traditional public-key cryptosystems [10]. The main attraction of ECC is the absence of a subexponential-time algorithm for solving the Discrete Logarithm Problem (DLP) on a general elliptic curve over a finite field [8,20]. Therefore, elliptic curve cryptosystems can use much smaller groups than their "classical" DLP-based counterparts to achieve a certain level of security. Smaller groups normally implies shorter keys and, in turn, savings in execution time, energy consumption, memory requirements, as well as transmission bandwidth, all of which is important in the embedded and mobile domains. The expansion of the Internet of Things (IoT) in recent years has created a strong demand for lightweight implementations of ECC that can accommodate the stringent resource

© IFIP International Federation for Information Processing 2019
Published by Springer Nature Switzerland AG 2019
O. Blazy and C. Y. Yeun (Eds.): WISTP 2018, LNCS 11469, pp. 193–206, 2019.
https://doi.org/10.1007/978-3-030-20074-9_14

constraints of wireless sensor nodes, RFID tags, and various other kinds of smart devices [31]. According to the Ericsson Mobility Report from November 2017 [16], the number of devices connected to the Internet is expected to grow from roughly 19 billion in 2018 to more than 30 billion by the end of 2023. However, only about one third of these 30 billion devices will be classical computers (PCs, laptops, tablets, smart phones), while the remaining two thirds (i.e. around 20 billion devices) will be related to the IoT. Consequently, in a few years, "things" like machines, meters, point-of-sale terminals, consumer electronics, electrome-chanical sensors, actuators, wearable gadgets, and medical devices will most likely account for far more deployments of ECC than classical computers.

An elliptic curve has to satisfy various security and efficiency requirements to be suitable for cryptographic algorithms [6,9,13,17]. Most importantly, the group of rational points on the curve must contain a (large) subgroup of prime order since this order determines the computational cost of the Elliptic Curve Discrete Logarithm Problem (ECDLP). However, determining whether a curve has a near-prime cardinality requires one to count the number of points on the curve, which is a complicated and computation-intensive endeavor [20]. There-fore, it is common practice to use "standardized" curves that were generated to meet certain security requirements. A multitude of standardization bodies has recommended domain parameters for elliptic curves of different cryptographic strength, in most cases comparable to that of 128, 192, and 256-bit AES. The currently most important and widely-used curves are the ones specified by the US National Institute of Standards and Technology (NIST) [28], which provide security levels in the range of 80 to 256 bits. These so-called NIST curves were allegedly generated by Jerry Solinas in the 1990s, who was an employee of the National Security Agency (NSA) at that time [7]. Five of the NIST curves are defined over prime fields and given by a Weierstraß equation of the form

$$E_W : y^2 = x^3 + a_4 x + a_6 \tag{1}$$

where a_4 fixed to -3 for efficiency reasons [20]. However, the Weierstraß form is performance-wise not state-of-the-art anymore since alternative curve models for special families of curves allow for much faster execution times.

Two examples of special elliptic curves with excellent arithmetic properties are (twisted) Edwards curves [3,15] and Montgomery curves [27]. The addition law of twisted Edwards curves is much more efficient than that of conventional Weierstraß curves and has the further advantage of completeness when certain conditions are met [5]. Also Montgomery curves are attractive for practical use due to an extremely simple, yet very fast, scalar multiplication technique, the so-called Montgomery ladder [27]. In the recent past, a number of new curves in Edwards or Montgomery form, most of them defined over a pseudo-Mersenne prime field, have been published, e.g. [1,4,9,19,29]. Almost all of these curves target security levels of 128 bits and above, which is somewhat surprising given the rapid proliferation of the IoT along with the fact that many applications in such domains as home automation and consumer electronics do not really have high security requirements. The only proposals for smaller curves we are aware of came from Aranha et al., who introduced in [1, Sect. A] Montgomery curves over 159 and 191-bit prime fields, as well as Edwards curves over 157, 168, and 191-bit fields, respectively.

In this paper, we present a set of four twisted Edwards curves over pseudo-Mersenne prime fields that we generated in a transparent and verifiable way to meet common security and efficiency requirements. These four curves, which we call *LiTE curves* (an abbreviation for Lightweight Twisted Edwards), provide security levels of about 80, 96, 112, and 128 bits, respectively, and are suitable for IoT applications running on restricted devices. Using curves that offer less than 128 bits of security allows for large savings in execution time[1] and makes particular sense for applications with low or medium security requirements. The four twisted Edwards curves we present in this paper differ from the Edwards curves introduced by Aranha et al. in [1] in two important aspects. Firstly, we chose the prime fields and generated the curves with the goal of having consistency across security levels, which means they share many basic properties like the group structure. Most notably, all our curves are defined over prime fields with $p = 2^k - c$ elements and have in common that k is a multiple of 32 minus 1 (i.e. $k = 159, 191, 223,$ or 255) and c has a length of at most eight bits. This consistency facilitates a parameterized implementation[2] of the field-arithmetic operations, which minimizes the code size when different security levels are to be supported and has some other benefits like reduced development cost. The second difference is that we aimed for curves capable to reach top performance with the twisted Edwards representation *and* the birationally-equivalent Montgomery representation. Aranha et al. [1], on the other hand, specified two sets of curves, namely Montgomery curves with a small parameter A and Edwards curves with a small parameter d; in both cases the rationale was to improve the arithmetic performance. The four twisted Edwards curves we put forward have a small parameter d and a fixed to -1, which implies the parameter A of the birationally-equivalent Montgomery curves has the property that $4/(A - 2)$ is small. While this contrasts with the usual choice of $(A - 2)/4$ being small, it is possible to perform a point doubling equally fast as on e.g. Curve25519 thanks to a simple modification of the doubling formula.

2   Preliminaries

In 1987, Peter Montgomery introduced a new model for elliptic curves and demonstrated its practical use by speeding up algorithms for integer factorization [27]. Formally, a so-called *Montgomery curve* over a non-binary field $\mathbb{F}_q$ can be described through the equation

---

[1] For example, the results in [25] show that a scalar multiplication on a 192-bit elliptic curve (providing about 96 bits of security) takes less than half of the execution time of a scalar multiplication on a 256-bit curve (128 bits of security).

[2] A parameterized implementation of a field-arithmetic operation can support fields of different order (i.e. fields of different bit length), typically in steps of 32 bits. The parameters include besides the operands (or pointers to operands held in RAM) an additional parameter that specifies the length of the operands.

$$E_M : By^2 = x^3 + Ax^2 + x \tag{2}$$

where $A, B \in \mathbb{F}_q$ and $A \neq \pm 2$, $B \neq 0$ (or, equivalently, $B(A^2 - 4) \neq 0$). Curves of such form allow a full scalar multiplication $k \cdot P$ to be carried out using the x coordinate only, which is clearly more efficient than when both the x and the y coordinate are involved in the point arithmetic. A point $P \in E_M(\mathbb{F}_q)$ given in projective coordinates of the form $(X : Z)$ can be doubled with only three multiplications (3M) and two squarings (2S) in the underlying finite field. On the other hand, a differential addition of two points (i.e. the calculation of the sum $P+Q$ of two points $P, Q \in E_M(\mathbb{F}_q)$ whose difference $P-Q$ is known) requires two multiplications (2M), two squarings (2S), as well as a multiplication by the constant $(A + 2)/4$. The so-called Montgomery ladder for scalar multiplication has an overall computational cost of about 5ℓ multiplications and 4ℓ squarings for an ℓ-bit scalar, i.e. 5M + 4S per bit [2].

Exactly 20 years after Montgomery's discovery, Harold Edwards introduced a normal form to describe certain elliptic curves, which have since then become known as Edwards curves [15]. Bernstein and Lange [5] showed that curves in Edwards form have good cryptographic properties with respect to performance and protectability against side-channel attacks. *Twisted Edwards curves* (in the following abbreviated as "TE curves") were presented in [3] as a generalization of Edwards curves with similarly good implementation properties. A TE curve over a non-binary field $\mathbb{F}_q$ is defined by the equation

$$E_T : ax^2 + y^2 = 1 + dx^2y^2 \tag{3}$$

where a and d are distinct elements of $\mathbb{F}_q^*$. The additive group $E_T(\mathbb{F}_q)$ contains a neutral element $\mathcal{O} = (0, 1)$, which can, under some conditions, be used as an input to the addition formula given in [3]. More concretely, when a is a square and d a non-square in the underlying field $\mathbb{F}_q$, then the addition law from [3] is *complete* and yields the correct sum for any pair $P, Q \in E_T(\mathbb{F}_q)$, including the corner cases $P = \mathcal{O}$, $Q = \mathcal{O}$, and $P = Q$. Hişil et al. presented in [21] extended projective coordinates, the currently fastest means of point addition on a curve in TE form. When $a = -1$, then a "mixed" addition $P + Q$, where P is given in extended projective coordinates and Q in extended affine coordinates, requires seven multiplications (7M) in $\mathbb{F}_q$, while the cost of a point doubling amounts to three multiplications (3M) and four squarings (4S) [12,18].

Montgomery curves and TE curves are closely related due to the fortunate fact that every Montgomery curve over $\mathbb{F}_q$ is birationally equivalent over $\mathbb{F}_q$ to a TE curve and vice versa [3]. Specifically, if a, d are distinct and non-zero in $\mathbb{F}_p$, then the TE curve E_T given by Eq. (3) is birationally equivalent over $\mathbb{F}_p$ to the Montgomery curve E_M given by Eq. (2) with the parameters

$$A = \frac{2(a + d)}{a - d} \quad \text{and} \quad B = \frac{4}{a - d}. \tag{4}$$

Bernstein et al. demonstrated in [3] that also the converse holds. Namely, when $A \in \mathbb{F}_p \setminus \{-2, 2\}$ and $B \in \mathbb{F}_p^*$, then the Montgomery curve E_M given by Eq. (2) is birationally equivalent over $\mathbb{F}_p$ to the TE curve given by Eq. (3) where

$$a = \frac{A+2}{B} \quad \text{and} \quad d = \frac{A-2}{B}. \tag{5}$$

This curve always exists since $A \neq \pm 2$ and $B \neq 0$. In some sense, the TE form and Montgomery form complement each other in an optimal way and facilitate so the implementation of elliptic-curve cryptosystems. The Montgomery shape is well suited for scalar multiplication $k \cdot P$ with a variable base point (i.e. P is not known in advance), but little attractive in settings where P is fixed. Fortunately, such fixed-base scalar multiplication is exactly the domain in which the TE shape excels. Various algorithms for scalar multiplication with a fixed base point, such as the comb method or window method [20], are extremely fast on TE-form elliptic curves due to the high efficiency of the addition law [3,9]. The birational equivalence between these two curve models is particularly useful in ephemeral ECDH key exchange [20], where each involved entity has to perform a fixed-base scalar multiplication (to generate an ephemeral key pair) as well as a variable-base scalar multiplication (to get the shared secret). The former can be efficiently computed on a curve in TE form using e.g. a comb method, while the latter can take advantage of the simple yet fast Montgomery ladder on the birationally-equivalent Montgomery curve (see [25] for details).

3   LiTE Curves

We decided to base our new curves for lightweight ECC on the TE model due to its excellent arithmetic properties that enable fast scalar multiplication and effective protection against (certain kinds of) side-channel attacks. A TE curve over $\mathbb{F}_p$ is fully specified by the prime p and the two coefficients a and d of its defining equation, which is Eq. (3). We fix a to -1 so that implementers can unleash the full performance of the extended coordinates described in [21]. As a consequence, the curve-generation procedure boils down to finding a suitable prime field and second coefficient. For efficiency reasons, it is common practice to use primes of some "special" form that allow one to minimize the cost of the modular reduction operation and to choose the coefficient d to be small since it appears as operand of a multiplication in the addition formulae specified in e.g. [3] (for both projective and inverted coordinates) and [21, Sect. 3.1].

3.1   Selection of Prime Fields

An analysis of recent proposals for new curves shows that the underlying fields are based on three main classes of primes, namely generalized-Mersenne primes [28], pseudo-Mersenne primes, and primes for which Montgomery reduction can be optimized, i.e. "Montgomery-friendly" primes [13]. Pseudo-Mersenne primes seem to be particularly attractive since they were used by the majority of the recent curve proposals, e.g. [1,2,4,6,9,29]. Formally, a pseudo-Mersenne prime can be written as $p = 2^k - c$ where c is small in relation to 2^k. The reduction of a $2n$-bit integer x modulo p requires, in essence, just a multiplication of the upper half of x (i.e. the k most significant bits of x) by c, and then an addition of the product to the lower half of x (see e.g. [2,9] for further details). Besides excellent arithmetic efficiency, these primes offer the virtue of minimizing the surface for side-channel attacks since the reduction can be easily implemented to have constant (i.e. operand-independent) execution time. Pseudo-Mersenne primes also allow for a parameterized implementation of the modular reduction operation so that one and the same reduction function can be used for primes of different length, which is not possible with the generalized-Mersenne primes of the NIST curves. This combination of desirable features led to our decision to use pseudo-Mersenne prime fields for the LiTE curves.

Now that the basic form of the primes is fixed to $p = 2^k - c$, the next step is to determine the actual values for the exponent k and constant c. Since we aim for elliptic curves providing security levels of (approximately) 80, 96, 112, and 128 bits, their cardinalities need to contain a large prime factor of magnitude 2^{160}, 2^{192}, 2^{224}, and 2^{256}, respectively, which requires due to Hasse's theorem [20] that the underlying prime fields have about the same order. This suggests to use $k = 160, 192, 224$, and 256, yielding primes whose bit-lengths are a multiple of 32, similar to the NIST primes [28]. However, choosing the exponents in this way does not necessarily lead to peak performance. Namely, as shown in [2], it can be beneficial to use a prime with a bit-length that is a tad below the "nominal" bit-length for the targeted security level, e.g. a 255-bit prime instead of a 256-bit prime. Having on bit of "headroom" simplifies the implementation of the field arithmetic when one aims for both high performance and resistance to side-channel attacks via constant (i.e. operand-independent) execution time [9]. Therefore, we decided to fix the values of k to 159, 191, 223, and 255.

The concluding step in the process of selecting a pseudo-Mersenne prime is to determine the constant c, which is typically chosen as the smallest integer so that $p = 2^k - c$ is prime [2]. An additional criterion often taken into account is the congruence class of p modulo 4, whereby the two most common choices are $p \equiv 3 \bmod 4$ and $p \equiv 5 \bmod 8$ (which implies $p \equiv 1 \bmod 4$)[3]. In the former case (i.e. $p \equiv 3 \bmod 4$), it is possible to find a TE curve with the property that the curve and its quadratic twist have both a minimal co-factor of 4 [23]. Unfortunately, -1 is always a non-square modulo such a prime and, consequently, the fast addition for TE curves from [21] is not guaranteed to be complete. On the other hand, if $p \equiv 5 \bmod 8$, then -1 is definitely a square in $\mathbb{F}_p$, but either the TE curve or its quadratic twist will have a co-factor of at least 8. However, we consider having a fast and complete addition law clearly more important than minimal co-factors, and thus we chose the values for c as the smallest integers that yielded primes congruent to 5 mod 8. The four primes we obtained in this way are $2^{159} - 91$, $2^{191} - 19$, $2^{223} - 235$, and $2^{255} - 19$. A TE curve over these primes with $a = -1$ can safely use Hişil et al.'s point-arithmetic formulae without compromising completeness [21]. To summarize, the four pseudo-Mersenne primes we put forward share the following three basic features, which facilitate

---

[3] These two choices allow for an efficient computation of square roots in $\mathbb{F}_p$ (which is needed for the decompression of compressed points [8]) through exponentiation.

a "parameterized" implementation of the field arithmetic: (i) the exponent k is a multiple of 32 minus 1, (ii) the constant c is at most eight bits long, (iii) p is congruent to 5 mod 8, i.e. -1 is a square in $\mathbb{F}_p$. The second feature guarantees that a reduction modulo each of our primes can be efficiently implemented on 8, 16, and 32-bit microcontrollers since c always fits into a single register.

3.2 Requirements

State-of-the-art curve-generation procedures, in particular the ones described in [9,17], put a strong emphasis on transparency and reproducibility to help the obtained curves find acceptance and trust in the cryptographic community. An important ingredient of such procedures is a set of well-explained and clearly-specified requirements to convince potential users of the curves that they were generated in a highly systematic and rigid fashion [6]. Our LiTE curves are, in essence, based on four major requirements, namely (i) security, (ii) arithmetic efficiency of operations in both the field and the group, (iii) consistency across security levels, and (iv) inter-operability with "legacy" cryptographic hardware software that supports only the Weierstraß form.

Security requirements for elliptic curves mainly consist of criteria to ensure the hardness of the ECDLP, but may also take certain implementation aspects into account, e.g. to prevent non-obvious side-channel pitfalls [17]. In our case (i.e. TE curve over a large prime field), the ECDLP is generally assumed to be a hard problem if (i) the group of points on the curve E_T contains a large sub-group of prime order ℓ (or, equivalently, the co-factor $h = \#E_T(\mathbb{F}_p)/\ell$ of E_T is small) and (ii) the curve does not belong to some special class of "weak" curves for which discrete logarithms can be computed in less than the $0.886\sqrt{\ell}$ steps required by Pollard's rho method [6]. Like Montgomery curves, TE curves have a co-factor of $h \geq 4$ [3,27]. Fortunately, most standards for ECC accept curves with small co-factors (e.g. $h \leq 8$ as in [23, Sect. A.1]), and some standards even tolerate not-so-small co-factors. For example, the NIST permits implementers of ECDSA to use an elliptic curve with a co-factor of up to 2^{10} if ℓ is between 160 and 223 bits long, while h can become as big as 2^{14} for ℓ lying in the range of 224 to 255 bits [28, Table 1]. When generating new TE curves, it is common practice to discard candidates that enable a multiplicative transfer or feature an efficient endomorphism because these properties would allow an attacker to "shortcut" the computation of discrete logarithms [1,6]. Therefore, one has to check whether a curve candidate has a large embedding degree[4] e and a large Complex-Multiplication (CM) field discriminant D [17]. Some recent proposals for curve generation, e.g. [23, Sect. A], explicitly exclude also curves with trace $t = 0$ (i.e. supersingular curves) and $t = 1$ (i.e. anomalous curves), but this is

---

[4] For a TE curve E_T over $\mathbb{F}_p$ with $\#E(\mathbb{F}_p) = h\ell$, the embedding degree is defined as the smallest positive integer e such that ℓ divides $p^e - 1$.

redundant[5] when targeting TE curves over $\mathbb{F}_p$. An additional requirement often taken into account is *twist security*, which means that not only the TE curve E_T, but also its quadratic twist E'_T, meets the security criteria specified above (i.e. small co-factor and large embedding degree[6]) [6]. Twist security is a useful feature for x-coordinate-only ECDH key exchange based on Montgomery-form curves, such as X25519 [23], because it eliminates the need to check whether an incoming x-coordinate belongs to a point on the curve or on the twist [13]. All LiTE curves are twist-secure since ECDH is one of their main applications.

The second requirement we put on LiTE curves is to enable efficient implementations and facilitate state-of-the-art optimization techniques for both the field and group arithmetic. More precisely, we aim for curves that allow one to reach peak performance not only with the TE model, but also when using the birationally-equivalent Montgomery representation of the curve. A wide range of IoT devices (e.g. wireless sensor nodes) are equipped with small 8-bit microcontrollers whose limited computational capabilities may introduce long delays or high energy consumption when executing scalar multiplications. This makes a good case to take efficiency aspects—at both the field and group level—into account in the curve generation. Our approach of choosing a set of prime fields with good arithmetic properties, even on 8-bit microcontrollers, was explained in Subsect. 3.1. The addition law of TE curves can be fast *and* complete when $a = -1$ is a square in $\mathbb{F}_p$ and d a non-square; ideally, d is a small non-square so that a multiplication by d becomes less costly than an arbitrary multiplication in the field $\mathbb{F}_p$. On the other hand, when generating a Montgomery curve, it is usual practice to fix B to 1 and choose a small A congruent to 2 modulo 4 to ensure a multiplication by $(A + 2)/4$ is fast [2,27]. Unfortunately, a TE curve with "ideal" coefficients (i.e. $a = -1$ and d is small) is birationally-equivalent to a Montgomery curve with coefficients that are far from ideal. Namely, as can be seen from Eq. (4), the coefficient A of the corresponding Montgomery curve is $2(a + d)/(a - d) = 2(1 - d)/(d + 1)$, which is normally not small. We tackle the problem of non-ideal Montgomery coefficients through a small modification of the (projective) Montgomery doubling to minimize its execution time when $4/(A + 2)$ is small instead of $(A + 2)/4$ (see Sect. 4 for details).

Our third requirement is consistency across security levels, which means the curves should share certain properties about the structure of the elliptic-curve groups (e.g. co-factor, sign of trace) and the prime fields. Consistency enables a parameterized software implementation of the group arithmetic (i.e. addition and doubling of points) and the scalar multiplication so that one and the same arithmetic function can be used for curves of different order, e.g. ranging from

---

[5] A TE curve E_T over $\mathbb{F}_p$ can never be anomalous since a co-factor of $h \geq 4$ implies $\#E_T(\mathbb{F}_p) \neq p$ and also $\ell \neq p$. Supersingular curves are implicitly excluded because they do not have a large embedding degree. Concretely, a supersingular TE curve E_T over $\mathbb{F}_p$ has an order of $\#E_T(\mathbb{F}_p) = p + 1$, which means its embedding degree is $e = 2$ since $p + 1 = h\ell$ divides $p^2 - 1$ and, consequently, ℓ divides $p^2 - 1$.

[6] There is no need to check the CM field discriminant of E'_T since E_T and E'_T share the same endomorphism ring and, therefore, have the same discriminant.

159 to 255 bits in steps of 32 bits. Similar to efficiency, also consistency affects both the selection of fields (which we already discussed in Subsect. 3.1) and the generation of curves. The four LiTE curves we introduce in this paper have in common that the coefficient d is positive and small enough to fit into a single 32-bit word, which makes it straightforward to write a parameterized function for point addition. Besides point arithmetic also other operations, such as the generation of secret scalars for x-coordinate-only ECDH key exchange, can be implemented in a parameterized way, provided the set of curves meets certain conditions. If, for example, the bitlength of the underlying prime fields differs by a fixed amount (e.g. 32 bits) and each curve has a co-factor of 8 and a negative trace (like Curve25519), then a single parameterized function[7] suffices to generate scalars for all curves. Implementing or using a parameterized software library for the field/group arithmetic (and other operations) in settings where different levels of security need to be supported provides two major advantages compared to a separate implementation for each curve. First, it allows for substantial savings in (binary) code size, which is an important asset in the realm of the IoT. Second, the software development effort is significantly lower since each arithmetic function needs to be written and tested only once [13].

Finally, the fourth requirement is inter-operability with legacy elliptic-curve hardware and software that only supports the standard Weierstraß model given by Eq. (1). For efficiency, the coefficient a_4 of a Weierstraß curve is often fixed to -3, while the second coefficient a_6 is typically chosen to be a non-square in $\mathbb{F}_p$ in order to prevent the existence of points whose x-coordinate is 0. This is necessary because, as noted in [14, Sect. 3], some legacy ECC implementations encode $\mathcal{O}$ as $(0,0)$, which would cause an ambiguity with one of the two points $(0, \pm\sqrt{a_6})$ when point compression is applied. Our LiTE curves are required to have a Weierstraß-form representation that is isomorphic to a Weierstraß curve with $a_4 = -3$ and a non-square a_6. We clearly prefer an isomorphism over an isogeny to keep the cost of converting points between different representations at a minimum. The need for point conversions between the Montgomery or TE form and the Weierstraß form arises when a state-of-the-art cryptosystem like X25519 [23] or EdDSA has to be implemented on top of some legacy hardware accelerator or software library for scalar multiplication. A well-known example of such legacy software is TinyECC [24], a lightweight ECC library for wireless sensors that supports solely Weierstraß curves with $a_4 = -3$. Another scenario requiring a conversion of points is discussed in [30] and concerns standardized cryptosystems like ECDSA, which use (affine) Weierstraß coordinates as "wire format." Instantiating ECDSA with a TE curve allows an implementer to take advantage of the high performance of the TE addition law for point arithmetic at the (small) expense of a conversion from TE to Weierstraß form during the signature generation, as well as a conversion in the opposite direction (i.e. from Weierstraß to TE form) when verifying a signature.

---

[7] This parameterized function can follow the approach of Curve25519, which means it first generates an array of (pseudo-)random bytes of the same byte-length as the underlying prime field and then "prunes" the first and last byte as in [23, p. 8].

3.3 Curve Generation

Since we have already chosen the prime fields of our LiTE curves and fixed the coefficient a to -1, the final step of the curve generation consists of finding the smallest coefficient d that satisfies all requirements discussed in Subsect. 3.2. In fact, these requirements can be condensed into five basic conditions, which are specified in the following definition of a LiTE curve.

Definition 1. *Let $\mathbb{F}_p$ be a prime field with $p \equiv 5 \bmod 8$. A LiTE elliptic curve is a twisted Edwards curve over $\mathbb{F}_p$ given by the equation*

$$E_T : \ -x^2 + y^2 = 1 + dx^2 y^2$$

where d is the smallest element of $\mathbb{F}_p \setminus \{-1, 0\}$ so that the following five conditions are met

1. *d is a non-square in $\mathbb{F}_p$*
2. *E_T has a co-factor of $h = 8$ and a negative trace (i.e. $\#E_T(\mathbb{F}_p) > p$), while its quadratic twist E_T' has a co-factor of $h' = 4$ and a positive trace*
3. *E_T has an embedding degree of $e \geq (\ell - 1)/100$ and E_T' an embedding degree of $e' \geq (\ell' - 1)/100$*
4. *E_T has a CM field discriminant of $|D| > 2^{100}$*
5. *the Weierstraß representation of E_T is isomorphic to a curve defined by an equation of the form $y^3 = x^3 - 3x + b$ where b is a non-square in $\mathbb{F}_p$*

The first condition is necessary to ensure that Hişil et al.'s "extended" addition formulae from [21] reach maximum performance *and* are complete, which is an efficiency requirement on our LiTE curves. In contrast, the second condition is related to security and to consistency. It guarantees, on the one hand, a basic prerequisite for the complexity of the ECDLP, namely the existence of a large cyclic subgroup of E_T (and of E_T'). Since we use prime fields with $p \equiv 5 \bmod 8$ (which implies $p \equiv 1 \bmod 4$), it is not possible that both the curve E_T and its quadratic twist E_T' have a minimal co-factor of 4 [23]; either h or h' has to be at least 8. We followed the approach of Curve25519 [2] and opted for $h = 8$ in order to prevent the accidental leakage of a bit of the secret scalar in protocols that involve a co-factor multiplication [23, Sect. A.1]. On the other hand, the second condition contributes to consistency because a negative trace means ℓ is always slightly larger than a power of 2, which enables a parameterized implementation of a function to generate secret scalars as discussed in the previous subsection. The third and fourth condition are linked to security; their purpose is to exclude curves with a transfer or a (fast) endomorphism. Both conditions are not new since they can be found in a similar form in [6,14,23]. Finally, the fifth condition guarantees inter-operability with legacy ECC hardware/software that supports only Weierstraß curves with $a_4 = -3$ and ensures the conversion of points through an isomorphism (the conversion of points between isogenous curves would be more complex [11]). An arbitrary Weierstraß curve over $\mathbb{F}_p$ is isomorphic to one governed by the equation $y^3 = x^3 - 3x + b$ when $-3/a_4$ has a fourth root in $\mathbb{F}_p$, which holds in our case for 25% of all values of a_4 [8].

We used the computer algebra system Magma V2.24 to compute the coefficient d according to Definition 1 for each of the four levels of security we consider in this paper. More concretely, we wrote a Magma script that essentially consists of a loop in which d gets incremented in each iteration until all five conditions are satisfied. This script output the coefficients 49445, 141087, 987514, as well as 4998299, which define the four LiTE curves:

$$\text{LiTE-P159:} -x^2 + y^2 = 1 + 49445x^2y^2 \bmod 2^{159} - 91$$
$$\text{LiTE-P191:} -x^2 + y^2 = 1 + 141087x^2y^2 \bmod 2^{191} - 19$$
$$\text{LiTE-P223:} -x^2 + y^2 = 1 + 987514x^2y^2 \bmod 2^{223} - 235$$
$$\text{LiTE-P255:} -x^2 + y^2 = 1 + 4998299x^2y^2 \bmod 2^{255} - 19$$

Our smallest coefficient d (which is the one of the 159-bit curve) is only 16 bits long, whereas the largest coefficient has a length of 23 bits. The execution time of the script on a 2.4 GHz Xeon E5-2407 v2 processor ranged from 11 min (for the 159-bit curve LiTE-P159) to roughly 87 hours (LiTE-P255).

4   Birationally-Equivalent Montgomery Curves

For a LiTE curve (or any other TE curve with $a = -1$), the coefficients A and B of the birationally-equivalent Montgomery curve are

$$A = \frac{2(a+d)}{a-d} = \frac{2(1-d)}{1+d}, \tag{6}$$

$$B = \frac{4}{a-d} = -\frac{4}{1+d} = -\frac{2(1-d) + 2(1+d)}{1+d} = -(A+2). \tag{7}$$

Consequently, the Montgomery representation of a LiTE curve is given by an equation of the form

$$-(A+2)y^2 = x^3 + Ax^2 + x. \tag{8}$$

The Montgomery-coefficient A obtained via Eq. (6) does not correspond to the common perception of efficiency since it is normally not small (and likely also not congruent to 2 modulo 4). In other words, when generating an efficient TE curve (i.e. a TE curve with $a = -1$ and small d), one can not expect that the birationally-equivalent Montgomery curve is also efficient. This problem exists in the opposite direction as well; for example, the TE curve that is birationally-equivalent to Curve25519 does not have a small coefficient d [30]. One way to deal with this issue is to generate, for each targeted security level, a TE curve with ideal coefficients and a distinct Montgomery curve with ideal coefficients (like in [1]). Unfortunately, this approach is not useful in the case of ephemeral ECDH key exchange, where one typically aims to reach maximum performance with the TE shape and the Montgomery shape of one and the same curve (see Sect. 2 and [25]). Bos et al. [9] approached this problem by exploiting isogenies between elliptic curves; concretely, they generated efficient Montgomery curves that are isogenous to efficient TE curves. In this way, they were able to obtain elliptic curves that *simultaneously* feature a small coefficient A in their Montgomery representation and a small coefficient d in the isogenous TE form. Also Curve448 (an efficient Montgomery curve over a 448-bit prime [19]) is specified in [23] together with an isogenous Edwards curve with a small d. However, the conversion of points between isogenous curves is rather costly; for example, the 4-isogeny maps for Curve448 provided in [23, p. 6] are much more complicated than the birational maps for point conversion from [3].

The approach we take in this paper is to generate "ideal" coefficients for the TE model, but compensate the disadvantage of having a large coefficient A in the birationally-equivalent Montgomery representation by a slight modification of the point doubling for Montgomery curves. As pointed out before, when the coefficient a of a TE curve is set to -1, then the resulting coefficient A of the birationally-equivalent Montgomery curve is $2(1 - d)/(d + 1)$, which means the constant $(A + 2)/4$ is not small. However, we found its reciprocal $4/(A + 2)$ to be small when $a = -1$ and d is small. More concretely, due to Eq. (7) we have $4/(A + 2) = d + 1$, and this implies $4/(A + 2)$ is small when d is small.

$$4X_n Z_n = (X_n + Z_n)^2 - (X_n - Z_n)^2 \tag{9}$$

$$X_{2n} = (X_n + Z_n)^2 (X_n - Z_n)^2 \tag{10}$$

$$Z_{2n} = (4X_n Z_n) \left[(X_n - Z_n)^2 + ((A + 2)/4) (4X_n Z_n) \right] \tag{11}$$

Montgomery provided in [27] the above formulae for the doubling of a point in projective $(X : Z)$ coordinates. The computation of $4X_n Z_n$ takes two squarings (2S) in $\mathbb{F}_p$ and, then, the computation of X_{2n} and Z_{2n} requires a multiplication (1M) each, which means the overall cost amounts to $2M + 2S$, plus a multiplication by $(A + 2)/4$. Fortunately, these formulae can be easily adapted for the Montgomery representations of our LiTE curves, whose A coefficients have the property that $4/(A + 2)$ is small. Namely, by simply multiplying both X_{2n} and Z_{2n} by $4/(A + 2)$, we obtain the doubling formulae below, which do not contain a multiplication by the constant $(A + 2)/4$ anymore.

$$X_{2n} = (X_n + Z_n)^2 (X_n - Z_n)^2 (4/(A + 2)) \tag{12}$$

$$Z_{2n} = (4X_n Z_n) \left[(X_n - Z_n)^2 + ((A + 2)/4) (4X_n Z_n) \right] (4/(A + 2))$$

$$= (4X_n Z_n) \left[(X_n - Z_n)^2 (4/(A + 2)) + (4X_n Z_n) \right] \tag{13}$$

This modification does not change the affine x-coordinate $x_{2n} = X_{2n}/Z_{2n}$, and so we can safely use these formulae for the Montgomery ladder. Similar to the original doubling method, $4X_n Z_n$ has to be computed first and, thereafter, the product of $(X_n - Z_n)^2$ and $4/(A + 2)$ can be formed. This product serves then as operand for the computation of X_{2n} and Z_{2n}, respectively, which means the total cost amounts to $2M + 2S$ and a multiplication by $4/(A+2)$. Apart from that, two additions and two subtractions in $\mathbb{F}_p$ have to be executed, exactly as with the original formulae [27]. In summary, performing a scalar multiplication on the Montgomery curves that are birationally-equivalent to our LiTE curves takes exactly the same number of $\mathbb{F}_p$-operations as when a Montgomery curve with a small coefficient A and $B = 1$ is used, e.g. Curve25519.

References

1. Aranha, D.F., Barreto, P.S., Pereira, G.C., Ricardini, J.E.: A note on high-security general-purpose elliptic curves. Cryptology ePrint Archive, Report 2013/647 (2013). http://eprint.iacr.org

2. Bernstein, D.J.: Curve25519: new Diffie-Hellman speed records. In: Yung, M., Dodis, Y., Kiayias, A., Malkin, T. (eds.) PKC 2006. LNCS, vol. 3958, pp. 207–228. Springer, Heidelberg (2006). https://doi.org/10.1007/11745853_14

3. Bernstein, D.J., Birkner, P., Joye, M., Lange, T., Peters, C.: Twisted edwards curves. In: Vaudenay, S. (ed.) AFRICACRYPT 2008. LNCS, vol. 5023, pp. 389–405. Springer, Heidelberg (2008). https://doi.org/10.1007/978-3-540-68164-9_26

4. Bernstein, D.J., Chuengsatiansup, C., Lange, T.: Curve41417: karatsuba revisited. In: Batina, L., Robshaw, M. (eds.) CHES 2014. LNCS, vol. 8731, pp. 316–334. Springer, Heidelberg (2014). https://doi.org/10.1007/978-3-662-44709-3_18

5. Bernstein, D.J., Lange, T.: Faster addition and doubling on elliptic curves. In: Kurosawa, K. (ed.) ASIACRYPT 2007. LNCS, vol. 4833, pp. 29–50. Springer, Heidelberg (2007). https://doi.org/10.1007/978-3-540-76900-2_3

6. Bernstein, D.J., Lange, T.: SafeCurves: Choosing safe curves for elliptic-curve cryptography (2013). http://safecurves.cr.yp.to

7. Bernstein, D.J., Lange, T.: Security dangers of the NIST curves. Presentation given at the 3rd Workshop on International View of the State-of-the-Art of Cryptography and Security and its Use in Practice, Athens, Greece, 30–31 May 2013 (2013). http://www.hyperelliptic.org/tanja/vortraege/20130531.pdf

8. Blake, I.F., Seroussi, G., Smart, N.P.: Elliptic Curves in Cryptography. London Mathematical Society Lecture Notes Series, vol. 265. Cambridge University Press, Cambridge (1999)

9. Bos, J.W., Costello, C., Longa, P., Naehrig, M.: Selecting elliptic curves for cryptography: an efficiency and security analysis. J. Cryptogr. Eng. 6(4), 259–286 (2016)

10. Bos, J.W., Halderman, J.A., Heninger, N., Moore, J., Naehrig, M., Wustrow, E.: Elliptic curve cryptography in practice. In: Christin, N., Safavi-Naini, R. (eds.) FC 2014. LNCS, vol. 8437, pp. 157–175. Springer, Heidelberg (2014). https://doi.org/10.1007/978-3-662-45472-5_11

11. Brier, E., Joye, M.: Fast point multiplication on elliptic curves through isogenies. In: Fossorier, M., Høholdt, T., Poli, A. (eds.) AAECC 2003. LNCS, vol. 2643, pp. 43–50. Springer, Heidelberg (2003). https://doi.org/10.1007/3-540-44828-4_6

12. Chu, D., Großschädl, J., Liu, Z., Müller, V., Zhang, Y.: Twisted Edwards-form elliptic curve cryptography for 8-bit AVR-based sensor nodes. In: Xu, S., Zhao, Y. (eds.) Proceedings of the 1st ACM Workshop on Asia Public-Key Cryptography (AsiaPKC 2013), pp. 39–44. ACM Press (2013)

13. Costello, C., Longa, P., Naehrig, M.: A brief discussion on selecting new elliptic curves. Technical report MSR-TR-2015-46, Microsoft Research, June 2015. http://research.microsoft.com/apps/pubs/default.aspx?id=246915

14. ECC Brainpool Consortium. ECC Brainpool standard curves and curve generation (2005). http://www.ecc-brainpool.org/download/Domain-parameters.pdf

15. Edwards, H.M.: A normal form for elliptic curves. Bull. Am. Math. Soc. 44(3), 393–422 (2007)

16. Ericsson. Ericsson Mobility Report November 2017 (2017). http://www.ericsson.com/assets/local/mobility-report/documents/2017/ericsson-mobility-report-november-2017.pdf

17. Flori, J.-P., Plût, J., Reinhard, J.-R., Ekerå, M.: Diversity and transparency for ECC. Cryptology ePrint Archive, Report 2015/659 (2015). http://eprint.iacr.org
18. Hamburg, M.: Fast and compact elliptic-curve cryptography. Cryptology ePrint Archive, Report 2012/309 (2012). http://eprint.iacr.org
19. Hamburg, M.: Ed448-Goldilocks, a new elliptic curve. Cryptology ePrint Archive, Report 2015/625 (2015). http://eprint.iacr.org
20. Hankerson, D.R., Menezes, A.J., Vanstone, S.A.: Guide to Elliptic Curve Cryptography. Springer, New York (2004). https://doi.org/10.1007/b97644
21. Hişil, H., Wong, K.K.-H., Carter, G., Dawson, E.: Twisted Edwards curves revisited. In: Pieprzyk, J. (ed.) ASIACRYPT 2008. LNCS, vol. 5350, pp. 326–343. Springer, Heidelberg (2008). https://doi.org/10.1007/978-3-540-89255-7_20
22. Koblitz, N.I.: Elliptic curve cryptosystems. Math. Comput. **48**(177), 203–209 (1987)
23. Langley, A., Hamburg, M., Turner, S.: Elliptic curves for security. Internet Engineering Task Force, Internet Research Task Force, RFC 7748, January 2016
24. Liu, A., Ning, P.: TinyECC: a configurable library for elliptic curve cryptography in wireless sensor networks. In: Proceedings of the 7th International Conference on Information Processing in Sensor Networks (IPSN 2008), pp. 245–256. IEEE Computer Society Press (2008)
25. Liu, Z., Wenger, E., Großschädl, J.: MoTE-ECC: energy-scalable elliptic curve cryptography for wireless sensor networks. In: Boureanu, I., Owesarski, P., Vaudenay, S. (eds.) ACNS 2014. LNCS, vol. 8479, pp. 361–379. Springer, Cham (2014). https://doi.org/10.1007/978-3-319-07536-5_22
26. Miller, V.S.: Use of elliptic curves in cryptography. In: Williams, H.C. (ed.) CRYPTO 1985. LNCS, vol. 218, pp. 417–426. Springer, Heidelberg (1986). https://doi.org/10.1007/3-540-39799-X_31
27. Montgomery, P.L.: Speeding the Pollard and elliptic curve methods of factorization. Math. Comput. **48**(177), 243–264 (1987)
28. National Institute of Standards and Technology (NIST). Digital Signature Standard (DSS). FIPS Publication 186-4, July 2013. http://nvlpubs.nist.gov/nistpubs/FIPS/NIST.FIPS.186-4.pdf
29. Scott, M.: Ed3363 (HighFive) - An alternative elliptic curve. Cryptology ePrint Archive, Report 2015/991 (2015). http://eprint.iacr.org
30. Struik, R.: Alternative elliptic curve representations. Internet Engineering Task Force, Light-Weight Implementation Guidance (LWIG) Working Group, Internet draft draft-struik-lwip-curve-representations-02 (work in progress), July 2018
31. Yan, L., Zhang, Y., Yang, L.T., Ning, H.: The Internet of Things: From RFID to the Next-Generation Pervasive Networked Systems. Auerbach Publications (2008)

A Generic Lightweight and Scalable Access Control Framework for IoT Gateways

Juan D. Parra Rodriguez[(✉)]

IT-Security Group, University of Passau, Passau, Germany
`dp@sec.uni-passau.de`

Abstract. Gateways prevail in IoT (Internet of Things) set-ups for connectivity, privacy, and other reasons; however, there has not been a generic and open-source framework offering authentication, identity management, policy administration and policy evaluation as a service for such a scenario. Meanwhile, cloud-based security solutions are available, but they use too much memory and CPU to be deployed in low-cost hardware typically used for IoT gateways such as the Raspberry Pi.

In our work, we identified critical requirements for a generic security framework that could be deployed to low-cost hardware used for IoT gateways. From this point on, we implemented the security framework, and modified a Content Management System (CMS) to rely on the framework for authentication and policy evaluations.

We evaluated our component's runtime performance and computational resource consumption in comparison to a popular attribute-based security framework written in Java. We measured the CPU, memory, and network usage for each security framework, their databases, and the CMS across three different hardware platforms. To ensure our results are not biased towards a particular hardware set-up, we chose hardware with two different processor architectures, different capabilities and vendors. Our results indicate that our framework not only requires less time to complete requests but also makes less intensive use of the processor and the memory, i.e., the most critical capabilities for IoT gateways today.

Keywords: Access control · IoT gateway · Identity management

1 Introduction

Affordable single-board computer hardware equipped with WiFi, Bluetooth, I/O pins, among other features lets developers and makers create applications to

This research has been supported by the EU under the H2020 AGILE (Adaptive Gateways for dIverse muLtiple Environments), grant agreement number H2020-688088. Also, the authors would like to thank Eduard Brehm for the WordPress integration and various updates in the agile-security code-base.

© IFIP International Federation for Information Processing 2019
Published by Springer Nature Switzerland AG 2019
O. Blazy and C. Y. Yeun (Eds.): WISTP 2018, LNCS 11469, pp. 207–222, 2019.
https://doi.org/10.1007/978-3-030-20074-9_15

obtain information from sensors easily[1]. Also, the increasing privacy awareness has influenced users to store sensor data locally instead of delivering it directly to IoT clouds and services[2] when possible.

Keeping data locally is undoubtedly one step towards data privacy; however, in scenarios where gateways need to offer multi-tenant support, there is an additional need to enforce security policies on data stored in the gateway and other services running in the same environment. To support this, we have developed a prototypical implementation of a security framework, called agile-security[3]. Agile-security allows applications running inside or outside the gateway to rely on authentication, identity management, policy administration and authorization as a service. In this way, access to sensors, application APIs, or other security-sensitive assets can be managed centrally by the security framework hosted in the gateway. Agile-security supports a generic attribute-based identity and access control model to remain as flexible as possible.

Despite considerable research towards IoT application security, there has not been an open-source solution to handle the security requirements for gateway-based scenarios in a generic, lightweight and scalable manner. On the one hand, researchers have previously argued for a capability-based approach whereby a certificate referencing a subject, i.e., user, and its access rights is presented to the service provider, i.e., a device [9,15]. However, this requires Certification Authorities (CA)s to sign certificates and assumes that users interact directly with devices. Closer to our research, there have been efforts towards enforcing security policies for brokers or gateways using MQTT, HTTP and CoAP brokers [5,6,12]; however, these integrations with specific protocols fail to provide a generic framework to build security solutions.

From a different perspective, cloud systems rely on centralized components offering authentication, attribute-based authorization and policy management as a service. There are commercially available implementations from Oracle [2], Microsoft [1], and IBM [14], as well as an open-source implementation called WSO2 Balana [3]. However, cloud-based security components require computational resources beyond the capabilities of affordable single-board computers commonly used to host IoT gateways. Instead, our solution can be deployed in smaller single-board computers, and uses less resources than WSO2 and scales[4] to medium cloud-based set-ups with some configuration adjustments.

Our **contributions** can be summarized as follows: (1) we outline requirements and challenges faced while developing of a generic, lightweight, and scalable attribute-based security framework. (2) we explain how we addressed such challenges during the implementation of our security framework. (3) we perform a quantitative comparison between our framework and the WSO2 server in a realistic scenario. To this end, we use automated UI-testing to visit a modified

---

[1] Single-board computers such as the Raspberry Pi, the Beaglebone board or the UPBoards are computers (ARM- or Intel-based) available from 30 to 60 USD.

[2] There are several IoT specific clouds, sich as Xively, Amazon IoT or Thingspeak.

[3] Available at: https://github.com/agile-iot/agile-security.

[4] Scalability means the agile-security can be configured differently depending on the hardware available, e.g., to use more resources and provide responses faster.

CMS using one of the two security frameworks to assess the runtime performance as well as the usage of computational resources.

This paper is structured as follows: We introduce basic terminology used across the paper in Sect. 2. Afterward, we describe the requirements and provide an overview of the security framework in Sect. 3. Section 4 shows an example of how agile-security can implement role-based access control policies. After concluding the conceptual description of the framework, we evaluate it in comparison to WSO2 in Sect. 5. Finally, we present related work and our conclusions in Sects. 6 and 7, respectively.

2   Attribute-Based Access Control Definitions

For clarity, we describe our work using well-established terminology presented in the attribute-based concepts provided by NIST from Hu et al., which states:

*"A logical **object** -sometimes referred to as a resource- is an entity to be protected from unauthorized use.*

*The term **subject** is used to denote a human or non-person-entity requesting access to an object.*

*Privileges represent the authorized behavior of a subject; they are defined by an **authority** and embodied in policy or rules.*

***Digital Policy (DP):** Access control rules that compile directly into machine executable codes or signals. Subject/object attributes, operations, and environment conditions are the fundamental elements of Digital Policies, the building blocks of Digital Policies rules, which are enforced by an access control mechanism.*

***Meta Policies (MP):** A policy about policies, or policy for managing policies, such as the assignment of priorities and resolution of conflicts between Digital Policies or other Meta Policies."* [10]

3   Overview of the Security Framework

We start by listing the requirements addressed by our security framework. Then, we explain conceptually how generic Digital and Meta Policies can be achieved, followed by a description of the policy evaluation process, the identity model and the support for authentication mechanisms. We have used Node JS, a server-side JavaScript runtime, for the development of the agile-security framework.

3.1   Requirements

The security framework must:

R1. Allow users to define entities, i.e., objects and subjects, and security policies with the highest flexibility possible.

R2. Be usable from different kinds of applications (web, mobile, cron-jobs, command line programs, and other applications) and regardless of their location and operating system (running on the gateway or in a server).

R3. Perform efficiently in affordable single-board computer hardware, as well as more expensive servers (cloud).

R4. Be modular and extensible, so developers can add or disable functionality easily to fulfill their particular needs.

R5. Be easy to integrate for developers through libraries, standard interfaces, or rapid prototyping tools used in IoT environments.

3.2 Generic Digital Policies and Meta Policies

To address R1, developers must be able to define their own security policies with the highest flexibility possible. Thus, we need to provide a generic entity model that allows developers to define subjects and objects freely. Agile-security tackles this by letting developers specify *entities to represent subjects and objects in the same way*. Also, there are two key considerations. First, the framework must allow developers to define Digital Policies on the attributes and actions corresponding to entities. Second, the model needs to provide means to specify who is the *authority* for each attribute, i.e., a Meta Policy, generically.

A policy evaluation mechanism is the main building block for a framework for managing identities and access control rules. To represent how we leverage the policy evaluation mechanism across agile-security, Fig. 1 illustrates the relationship between the policy evaluation mechanism, Digital Policies, Meta Policies and the representation of entities in the identity model. First of all, Fig. 1 shows the mechanisms to evaluate and manage Digital and Meta Policies in grey. They are shown in the same color because they use the same policy evaluation mechanism described in Sect. 3.3. Digital Policies enforce access to attributes and actions that can be performed by, or on, entities. Furthermore, the picture illustrates different levels of customization that may be required by specific applications.

The first level, on the left-hand side of Fig. 1, shows a mechanism with enough flexibility to evaluate Digital Policies on attributes and actions of entities. However, in the first level, such a model would not allow users to define who can update Digital Policies. As a result, policies can only be applied to every kind of entity in the same way without giving users the possibility to update policies. This kind of mechanism is commonly referred to as Mandatory Access Control (MAC) because users cannot choose to override security mechanisms applied system-wide.

On the second level, the security model can be extended with the capability to evaluate Meta Policies, i.e., policies enforcing access to Digital Policies. Having fixed Meta Policies creates the opportunity for users to update the Digital Policies. In other words, models implemented with 2 levels or more allow for Discretionary Access Control (DAC), as users can update Digital Policies according to Meta Policies. Similarly, three levels allow to update the Meta Policies.

The result of our work implements a security framework that can evaluate policy hierarchies of level n. Notwithstanding, we do not foresee the need of using any level higher than 3, as this would increase the complexity of the system significantly and make it prone to human errors.

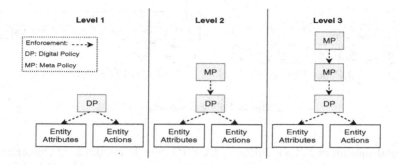

Fig. 1. Policy interactions to realize the security model

3.3 Policy Evaluation Framework

We used the UPFROnt policy evaluation framework[5]. UPFROnt defines policies as a collection of blocks specifying restrictions on reading or writing operations. Users can execute read, or write, operations as long as there is at least one read, or write, block allowing this. Figure 2a shows an example where a read operation would be allowed, while write operations would be denied. Besides, within each block, there can be zero or more locks where each one evaluates to a boolean value. All locks must evaluate to true to allow a block of the policy, i.e., white read block in Fig. 2a. Thus, the evaluation of a block is calculated by joining the boolean value returned by every lock with an and operator. Figure 2b shows two locks: the read block on the left is allowed, while the read block on the right is not allowed. More to the point, in the case of Fig. 2b, the read action would still be allowed overall, as the requirement is to have at least one block allowing the operation. The composition of locks and blocks in this way creates a boolean formula in Disjunctive Normal Form (DNF).

The approach followed by UPFROnt is an extension to the parametrized locks proposed by Broberg and Sands [4]. During policy evaluations, locks receive attributes for both entities, i.e., subject and object, and additional parameters specified in the policy. For example, an `attributeEquals` lock would receive two arguments: the attribute name, and the expected value. In this way, this lock can be used to assert that a user has an admin role by specifying a policy with a block, which contains the `attributeEquals` lock with the arguments "role" and "admin". Similarly, the `isOwner` lock verifying if a subject owns an object does not take any arguments, but compares the "id" attribute of the subject with the "owner" attribute of the object.

A flexibility aspect of the UPFROnt component is that developers can plug in their code to evaluate locks. These locks are executed within the policy framework and can have a state; moreover, the lock implementation can use any API offered by the Node JS framework which contributes to the generic approach

---

[5] UPFROnt has been developed by Daniel Schreckling and is available at https://github.com/SEDARI/UPFROnt.

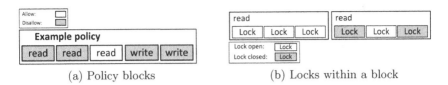

(a) Policy blocks   (b) Locks within a block

Fig. 2. Policy components

(R1) and modularity (R4). Initially, UPFROnt includes the `attributeEquals` and the `isOwner` lock. We have developed new locks to support logging of actions and management of groups.

As shown by Fig. 1, the evaluation mechanism described in this section applies to Digital Policies governing write and read access to attributes and actions that can be performed on entities. Moreover, the policy evaluation based on locks is also used to evaluate Meta Policies enforcing access to Digital Policies.

3.4 Identity Model

Based on the policy evaluation already presented, the identity management component within agile-security lets developers define the entity format, i.e., which fields are required for each type of entity through a JSON schema specification loaded from a configuration file. For example, a developer can specify that he requires a kind of entity called "sensor" with the possible attributes "location", and "dataType". Also, developers can specify which attributes are allowed, their type, and whether they are mandatory. If developers choose so, they can even restrict possible values an attribute can take.

The identity management has privileged attribute names that cannot be used by developers; these are "id", "owner", "entity_type" and "auth_type". We do this to ensure that the identity management system assigns an "id", an "owner", and an "entity type" for every entity during its creation. The owner's identifier is set to match the identifier of the entity's creator except for users. Users own themselves as they are the root of the ownership hierarchy. Further, as agile-security supports several authentication mechanisms, the identity management ensures that users always have the "auth_type" to determine which authentication mechanism must be used.

Identity management handles entities and performs access control on attributes. To achieve this, identity management validates whether the user sending a request can perform the action, e.g., update attribute. If this check is successful, the relevant read or write Digital Policies for each attribute are evaluated. Subsequently, if a user can read an entity but the Digital Policies disallow access to a particular attribute, then the identity management framework removes the attribute from the response. This allows for a simple declassification mechanism and grants access to attributes selectively based on the user's Digital Policies.

Like with the definition of entities, the configuration file for agile-security includes default Digital Policies enforcing access to each attribute. This allows developers to set-up a security model based on their needs. The definition of Digital Policies on attributes specify who is the *authority*, according to the NIST definitions, to update or read the attribute. In addition, the configuration file also specifies the level of Meta Policies supported according to Fig. 1 and default MetaPolicies applied to each Digital Policy. As a result, developers can decide whether they need Meta Policies, how many levels, and how they should rule the access to Digital Policies. Last but not least, we solve the bootstrapping problem by including information in the configuration file to create entities to be created in the first boot, e.g., first administrator of the system.

3.5 Wide Support for Authentication Mechanisms

Applications can rely on agile-security as an OAuth2 Identity Provider (IdP). On the one hand, this tackles ease of integration requirement (R5) because many libraries are implementing OAuth2 clients in many programming languages and operating systems. On the other hand, by implementing every token grant specified by OAuth2 in agile-security, we ensure that all sorts of applications running inside or outside the gateway can rely on agile-security as an IdP (R2). Particularly, as we implemented all the authorization flow grants from OAuth2, we ensure that not only Web applications are supported. Also, command line or even cron-jobs can rely on agile-security. In addition to offering standard OAuth2 interfaces, we developed a JavaScript library encapsulating the authentication, identity management, policy administration, and policy decision for ease of integration (R5). We also provide extensions for Node-RED, a visual development environment used for IoT applications, connecting the policy framework too.

For ease of integration into existing applications that already rely on other IdPs, e.g., Google, agile-security addresses the extensibility requirement R4 by letting developers define passport source files (a Node Js authentication framework) to add new authentication mechanisms besides local users handled by agile-security. To exemplify this, agile-security already contains strategies to rely on authentication from Google, Dropbox, PAM (Linux Pluggable Authentication Modules) and WebID.

4   Digital Policies Example (Role-Based Access Control)

This section illustrates an instance where the security model is used to represent a simple role-based access control model using identity definitions and policies. Even though passwords are not needed when developers rely on external authentication mechanisms, e.g., Google, we show an example of role-based access control where users do have a password attribute. First, the entity schema needs to specify the "role" and "password" attributes.

The policies represented by Fig. 3 rely on the `attributeEquals` and `isOwner` locks from Sect. 3.3 to define the role-based access control model[6]. The left-hand

---

[6] In addition to these policies, a policy allowing everyone to execute an action may also be needed. To this end, a block without any locks lets the user access everything.

side shows a policy allowing only users who own an entity to perform an action the attribute, Digital Policy or Meta Policy. Similarly, the figure on the right-hand shows a policy where only administrators are allowed.

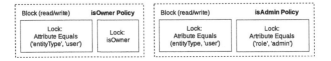

Fig. 3. Policy samples

In addition to the evaluation process presented in Sect. 3.3, UPFROnt has a hierarchical way of evaluating policies for simplicity and efficiency. In particular, entities are objects containing attributes that can be strings, numbers, but also objects. As a result, entities can have nested attributes. To avoid forcing users to set a policy for each nested property, UPFROnt uses the concept of a top-level policy. The top-level policy from any point in the object hierarchy applies to child nodes of a given attribute.

Figure 4 shows a possible agile-security configuration implementing a simple role-based access control model using the policies introduced in Fig. 3 and the top-level concept. To ensure that only administrators can create users, the top level policy for the user entity is set to allow everyone to read, but ensure that only owners or administrators can write to attributes within the entity (unless elements below in the hierarchy override them). As the creation of a user implies writing the attributes of the newly created user to set them, agile-security prevents non-admin users from creating users in this setting.

For clarity, we show light grey policies in front of the attributes when they have been inherited by a top-level policy above them, i.e., id and owner. In addition to this, we show an entity model where only administrators can set the attribute role. This ensures that users cannot upgrade their privileges on their own because there is no writeOwner policy for the role attribute. Conversely, the password attribute can be set by the owner and administrators; however, administrators cannot read the password. The previous example shows how to achieve interesting properties to handle the password and role attribute to balance the authority for a role attribute (set role), and the user's privacy (read password).

In more complex scenarios where Meta Policies are involved, agile-security links them using the tree structure presented in Fig. 1. In this way, the security framework traverses the tree, starting from the entity or action, to validate whether a particular Digital Policy or Meta Policy can be changed. If there is no parent for a Digital or Meta Policy, this means it cannot be updated.

Entity's Attributes	Policies
	[readAll , writeOwner, writeAdmin] ◄ Top Level Policy for Entity
• Id	• Id : [readAll , writeOwner, writeAdmin]
• Owner	• Owner : [readAll , writeOwner, writeAdmin]
• Role	• Role : [readAll, writeAdmin]
• Password	• Password: [readOwner, writeOwner, writeAdmin]

Fig. 4. Role-based access control model example

5   Evaluation

Every system faces a trade-off between using computational resources and providing a good response time. For example, loading all data in memory instead of placing it in a hard drive decreases the response time but may starve other processes of memory. To validate how well our security framework can execute in single-board computers, as well as bigger setups (R3), we perform an extensive quantitative evaluation. This is critical to obtain all aspects related to trade-offs between resource consumption and efficiency.

5.1   Scenario

To obtain a realistic scenario, we modified the most popular CMS[7] currently, i.e., WordPress, to outsource authentication and authorization to an external security framework. We created two branches of WordPress version 4.9.5 overriding security functions validating whether users are allowed to see a particular page or open the administrative dashboard. One branch of WordPress uses the Balana WSO2is server version 5.3.0, and the other one uses agile-security.

A factor motivating us to use WordPress as an example is that it evaluates more than 70 capabilities (mapped to each security framework) while actions are taken by a user; more to the point, each capability is evaluated separately. This sub-optimal setting is not desirable for a production environment because it triggers a separate network request with headers or XML content from WordPress to the security framework. However, this sub-optimal environment provides us a worst-case scenario where an application makes intensive use of the APIs from the security frameworks under evaluation. What is more, if we can establish that our security framework works for this environment, the runtime performance and resource use can only improve after optimizations are applied.

Concerning the software set-up, we always had a modified WordPress relying on one of the two security frameworks (WSO2 or agile-security). However, agile-security can be executed in two ways: either using an external database (MongoDB) or using a database running in the same process (LevelDB). This helps agile-security to remain flexible to the requirements of a given application and execute in less or more resource-constrained environments. Thus, we

---

[7] As of October 2018, WordPress has 59.9% of the CMS market share: https://websitesetup.org/popular-cms/.

evaluate the performance of WSO2 connected to an external MySQL database, agile-security connected to an external MongoDB database, or agile-security using LevelDB (same process as the security framework).

To isolate resource consumption per component, we have deployed Word-Press, the security frameworks and their databases (when they are separate processes) in separate containers. In turn, this allows us to use docker APIs to monitor the amount of memory, network, and CPU used by each component. Also, to ascertain properties for the security frameworks used without relying on a particular hardware implementation, and to obtain a big picture on the performance of the security frameworks, we executed the evaluation on three different hardware devices shown in Table 1. All our experiments use 64-bit processors and use the two most prominent processor architectures.

Table 1. Hardware configurations

Property	Raspberry Pi 3(B)	Upboard(UP-CHT01)	Lenovo T470S
Memory	1 GB	2 GB	16 GB
CPU	Quad Core 1.2 GHz	Quad Core 64 1.92 GHz	Quad Core 2.70 GHz
Storage	SD card size	16 GB	500 GB (Solid state)
Architecture	ARMv7	x86_64	x86_64

Also, we created an automated web test to interact with the WordPress interface to log in a user, open the dashboard, log out and visit the public site, using Cypress (a Web UI automation framework). Figure 5 shows the use of the docker containers, the security frameworks, and the UI testing framework. We recorded resource consumption continuously, while 100 interactions were performed automatically by the UI testing framework. Each interaction from the UI framework had two actions. First, an admin user logged in and then WordPress would forward him to the administrative dashboard page. Afterward, the user would log out and therefore load the public site. We recorded the time to load the dashboard and the public page, i.e., login and log out.

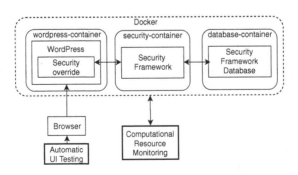

Fig. 5. Evaluation set-up

In the following measurements, there are no results for WSO2 on the Raspberry Pi 3 because WSO2 requires the hardware to have at least 2 GB of RAM to execute. On the contrary, we show that agile-security can be executed in the Raspberry Pi 3, and therefore imposes much less restrictive requirements on the hardware level than WSO2.

5.2 Runtime

We calculated the mean of 100 WordPress interactions, and their standard deviations to assess the response time of WordPress while relying on WSO2 or agile-security to evaluate the policies associated with the capabilities required to render the dashboard or log out the user. Figures 6a and b show the results measured in seconds to load each page. The amount of time measured during the page load is higher than the actual time due to the execution of the automation framework to interact with the UI. Still, this quantitative measure helps to compare the performance of each setting. To represent the results intuitively, we sort the hardware, in ascending order, from less to more powerful.

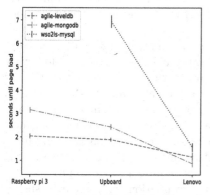

(a) Login and loading of dashboard

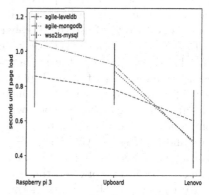

(b) Logout and loading of public stie

Fig. 6. Mean and standard deviation of loading time for 100 visits

From both figures, it can be observed that agile-security has a setting, either with levelDB or MongoDB, that offers better speed than WSO2. Also, in the case of agile-security it is better to use LevelDB, i.e., running the database code within the same process as the security framework, than executing a separate database, i.e., MongoDB, for small single-board computers, e.g., the Raspberry Pi. Notwithstanding, as more hardware is available for the external database, it is more efficient to separate the security business logic from the database to take advantage of the computational resources and achieve a better response. For both actions, login, and log out, the point where one should divide the database from agile-security lies somewhere between the resources available in the Upboard and the Lenovo laptop. The standard deviations represented for both figures show that measurements have stable values across the 100 experiments.

Figure 6a also shows that agile-security provides the same loading time on a Raspberry Pi 3 than the time achieved in the Lenovo laptop for WSO2. Besides, agile-security provides better loading time for the dashboard (log in) than WSO2 for all our experiments. We must also clarify that, although the deviations seem bigger in Fig. 6b, this is a visual effect due to the change of scale, i.e., all logout actions lie below 1.2 s.

5.3   Resource Consumption

It is clear that agile-security provides better runtime performance than WSO2. However, this section assesses the computational resource consumption to validate whether the performance improvement is sustainable in terms of hardware.

We obtained the number of bytes used in memory, the number of bytes sent through the network, and the number of processor ticks used by each component. Even though counting ticks does not have an intuitive meaning, it provides a way to compare the use of computational power in each scenario. We opted for this approach instead of showing percentage of use of CPU, as the latter is inherently biased by the underlying hardware, i.e., 10% of use in the Lenovo laptop is not comparable to 10% of use the Raspberry.

Docker provides one event every second with statistics on resource consumption. Thus, we calculate the average consumption value per second for every resource and then plot it in Table 2. Moreover, we use the same ordering as Sect. 5.2 to improve readability. On top, we represent values in the table as a heat-map showing higher numbers with a darker background. The values are only compared vertically; that is to say, there are separate scales for memory, network and CPU ticks. Also, the agile-leveldb set-up does not contain a database measurement because LevelDB is executed in the same memory space as the agile-security framework and therefore does not require a separate process.

By considering the results of the runtime evaluation, agile-security should be used without the database in both single-board computers because agile-security requires more processing power, network and memory than LevelDB. On the contrary, it is sensible to use agile-security with MongoDB for the Lenovo laptop, where there is a runtime improvement in comparison to LevelDB.

Following this reasoning, the table shows that agile-security and its database make intensive use of the network; especially, if this compared to the network consumption between WSO2 and MySQL. This is clearly due to the transport protocols used, i.e. MySQL is binary and MongoDB uses HTTP. Luckily, intensive use of network between agile-security and its database is not an issue when users deploy the security framework and the database in the same device. Even though communications between agile-security and its database are classified as networking in our experiment, this traffic is routed through the loopback interface, without requiring actual network transmissions.

On the other hand, WSO2 uses more networking between the security framework and WordPress. Unlike in the case of agile-security and its database, WSO2

Table 2. Memory, network and CPU consumption per component

hardware	setup	container	memory (MB)	network (KB/s)	cpu (Mtics/s)
Raspberry-pi3	agile-mongo	framework	75.73	217.44	344.51
		wordpress	63.66	50.24	62.20
		database	73.41	207.44	19.29
	agile-leveldb	framework	41.46	8.86	270.31
		wordpress	64.32	118.85	73.85
Upboard	agile-mongo	framework	90.04	185.23	266.61
		wordpress	77.33	39.47	58.59
		database	65.82	210.54	48.44
	agile-leveldb	framework	94.20	16.31	254.05
		wordpress	112.69	104.79	58.66
	wso2is-mysql	framework	1648.28	90.98	570.23
		wordpress	117.05	76.78	123.14
		database	126.43	45.97	42.40
Lenovo-t430	agile-mongo	framework	89.74	228.63	92.15
		wordpress	95.30	52.36	19.33
		database	33.15	220.53	15.57
	agile-leveldb	framework	82.57	8.45	67.79
		wordpress	109.68	64.17	22.14
	wso2is-mysql	framework	1239.83	157.00	196.97
		wordpress	141.08	160.36	59.94
		database	80.77	112.81	14.69

(or agile-security) and WordPress are more likely to be deployed in separate hardware as WordPress is a relying party decoupled from the security framework. Also, WSO2 makes intensive use of memory and processor in both scenarios where it can be executed, i.e., Upboard and Lenovo. These are resources that are critical to ensuring that additional applications can be deployed in an IoT gateway.

Even though we already established that WSO2 has lesser runtime performance than agile-security for all the hardware we tested, it is particularly problematic to use WSO2 for deployments where the IoT gateway has limited memory capacity. In particular, Table 2 shows that WSO2 consumes 1.6 GB out of 2 GB available to the whole system in the Upboard. Also, the overhead of the eXtensible Access Control Markup Language (XACML) policies can be observed by an increase in the amount of memory and processor required by WordPress in comparison to the settings where agile-security was used in the same hardware.

5.4   Limitations

We performed precise measurements regarding resource consumption and interactions involving the system modified to use the security frameworks, i.e., WordPress. However, we were able to run experiments only to the point equivalent to a medium-sized server, i.e., 16 GB of RAM. So, even though we conclude that our framework is better for IoT gateways and medium-sized set-ups, we do not assert that agile-security replaces the niche where WSO2 is currently used, i.e., bigger cloud set-ups. In this sense, Java technologies are deployable in enterprise servers to form clusters, which lie beyond the capabilities of agile-security.

6   Related Work

Fysarakis et al. described an instance where a centralized ABAC system was used to enforce policies in a Smart Home environment based on the Sun Java implementation of XACML. Although their approach focuses on attribute-based access control, like ours, their contribution is on an architectural level [8]. Also, The approach from Fysarakis et al. requires capabilities beyond affordable single-board computers, i.e., at least 4 GB of RAM to execute the policy decision point.

Colombo et al. [6] and Niesse et al. [12] propose the integration of policies for the IoT directly within MQTT brokers. Although this approach shares the gateway-centric perspective, it goes into details regarding each protocol. Instead, we provide a security component usable from internal and external applications. Hao et al. proposed JACPoL: a simple access control policy language in JSON [11]. Their approach is to provide an attribute-based language more lightweight than XACML. Their evaluation was done using 16 GB memory and a 2.6 GHz and considered only the time required to reply to policy requests. Although we also use a JSON-based policy language, we based our approach on parametrized locks [4] which allows developers to integrate code for the policy evaluation. Also, our evaluation is more concerned with a realistic scenario and provides a better overview of computational resource consumption. There is an analysis of gateway-centric scenarios sharing data with third parties [13] by Parra et al., but their focus considers only architectural aspects and technologies useful to provide access control towards some parties involved. Also, there have been extensions to provide an OAuth2-based architecture for the IoT [5] and to extend the WSO2 server to use flows authenticate devices [7].

7   Conclusion

XACML-based access control is used for enterprise large-scale applications, where there is trained personnel to configure XACML policies, and policy decision points. However, the knowledge required to specify policies and the nuances related to its configuration are baffling to most developers dealing with smaller set-ups. On top, the resource consumption of XACML servers, e.g., WSO2, is prohibitively high for an IoT set-up. Thus, we close the gap where developers need authentication and attribute-based policies deployed in a single-board computer.

To save resources while offering flexibility for the policy definition and evaluation, agile-security loads an entity specification along with default policies applied to new entities of each type such as users, OAuth2 clients, devices, or any other entity defined by developers. Also, agile-security can allow the update of Digital Policies used to enforce access to attributes and other read or write actions on entities. This is achieved through a generic, hierarchical, structure of policies that yield Meta Policies. For clarity, we show a simple scenario where agile-security is used to implement a role-based access control model. In this model, the role attribute is protected from unauthorized writes, yet keeping the user's password secret even from administrators.

The policy framework lowers the entry barrier for developers to use a security framework, in comparison to XACML servers. In particular, agile-security allows the definition of policies based on atomic and simple building blocks, i.e., locks, computed for the policy evaluation. At the same time, security experts and developers can plug-in custom logic in locks achieving extensibility. From the authentication perspective, agile-security can be used as an IdP from a vast set of applications ranging from batch jobs to mobile or web applications because it supports all authorization codes specified in the OAuth2 protocol.

Aside from showing the way to achieve flexibility, extensibility, and ease of deployment, we evaluate the resource consumption and response time of agile-security in comparison to WSO2, a popular open-source Java XACML solution. We establish that our approach saves resources and provides a lightweight framework. Also, our solution scales as more hardware is available after changing the configuration settings and using an external database.

After executing experiments with 100 visits to a modified WordPress instance, we conclude that our framework offers better runtime performance than WSO2 in all scenarios. More to the point, computational resource consumption is also lower as our solution uses more networking in the loopback interface than the WSO2 server, but saves memory and CPU: the most limited resources in an IoT gateway. Still, we clarify that our analysis in the scope of the paper does not claim that agile-security outperforms WSO2 in all set-ups. We believe there is a clear need for services like WSO2; however, such services should not be used for IoT gateways due to their high resource consumption.

References

1. Microsoft Claim-based Identity Model (2018). https://docs.microsoft.com/en-us/dotnet/framework/security/claims-based-identity-model. Accessed 03 Oct 2018
2. Oracle Identity Mgmt. Fine Grained Authorization: Technical Insights for using Oracle Entitlements Server (2018). http://www.oracle.com/technetwork/middleware/oes/oes-product-white-paper-405854.pdf. Accessed 03 Oct 2018
3. WSO2 Balana Implementation (2018). https://github.com/wso2/balana. Accessed 03 Oct 2018
4. Broberg, N., Sands, D.: Paralocks: role-based information flow control and beyond. In: Proceedings of the 37th Annual ACM SIGPLAN-SIGACT Symposium on Principles of Programming Languages, POPL 2010, pp. 431–444. ACM, New York (2010). https://doi.org/10.1145/1706299.1706349
5. Cirani, S., Picone, M., Gonizzi, P., Veltri, L., Ferrari, G.: IoT-OAS: an OAuth-based authorization service architecture for secure services in IoT scenarios. IEEE Sens. J. **15**(2), 1224–1234 (2015). https://doi.org/10.1109/JSEN.2014.2361406
6. Colombo, P., Ferrari, E.: Access control enforcement within MQTT-based internet of things ecosystems. In: Proceedings of the 23nd ACM on Symposium on Access Control Models and Technologies, SACMAT 2018, pp. 223–234. ACM, New York (2018). https://doi.org/10.1145/3205977.3205986
7. Fremantle, P., Aziz, B., Kopeck, J., Scott, P.: Federated identity and access management for the internet of things. In: 2014 International Workshop on Secure Internet of Things, pp. 10–17, September 2014. https://doi.org/10.1109/SIoT.2014.8

8. Fysarakis, K., Konstantourakis, C., Rantos, K., Manifavas, C., Papaefstathiou, I.: WSACd - a usable access control framework for smart home devices. In: Akram, R.N., Jajodia, S. (eds.) WISTP 2015. LNCS, vol. 9311, pp. 120–133. Springer, Cham (2015). https://doi.org/10.1007/978-3-319-24018-3_8

9. Gusmeroli, S., Piccione, S., Rotondi, D.: IoT access control issues: a capability based approach. In: 2012 Sixth International Conference on Innovative Mobile and Internet Services in Ubiquitous Computing, pp. 787–792, July 2012. https://doi.org/10.1109/IMIS.2012.38

10. Hu, V.C., et al.: Guide to Attribute Based Access Control (ABAC) Definition and Considerations (2014). https://doi.org/10.6028/NIST.SP.800-162

11. Jiang, H., Bouabdallah, A.: JACPoL: a simple but expressive JSON-based access control policy language. In: Hancke, G.P., Damiani, E. (eds.) WISTP 2017. LNCS, vol. 10741, pp. 56–72. Springer, Cham (2018). https://doi.org/10.1007/978-3-319-93524-9_4

12. Neisse, R., Steri, G., Baldini, G.: Enforcement of security policy rules for the Internet of Things. In: 2014 IEEE 10th International Conference on Wireless and Mobile Computing, Networking and Communications (WiMob), pp. 165–172, October 2014. https://doi.org/10.1109/WiMOB.2014.6962166

13. Rodriguez, J.D.P., Schreckling, D., Posegga, J.: Addressing data-centric security requirements for IoT-based systems. In: 2016 International Workshop on Secure Internet of Things (SIoT), pp. 1–10, September 2016. https://doi.org/10.1109/SIoT.2016.007

14. Schefenacker, S.: Portal Access Control Attribute Based Security for WCM Content (2018). https://www.ibm.com/developerworks/community/groups/service/html/communityview?communityUuid=8f2bc166-3bdc-4a9d-bad4-3620dbb3e46c#fullpageWidgetId=Wc5d73787a343_444e_a578_049379d72276&file=d898a782-82e5-43a1-86f1-4d983b342256. Accessed 03 Oct 2018

15. Tandon, L., Fong, P.W.L., Safavi-Naini, R.: HCAP: a history-based capability system for IoT devices. In: Proceedings of the 23nd ACM on Symposium on Access Control Models and Technologies, SACMAT 2018, pp. 247–258. ACM, New York (2018). https://doi.org/10.1145/3205977.3205978

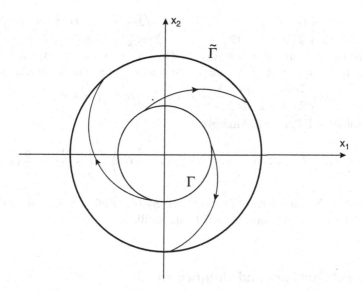

Fig. 8.3 The phase portrait of system (8.4)

Assume that $G = \{(x_1, x_2)| \ 1 < x_1^2 + x_2^2 < 4, \ x_1, x_2 \in \mathbb{R}\}$. A trajectory of the system is seen in Fig. 8.3. One can easily find that $\Phi(x) = x_1^2 + x_2^2 - 1$, $\tilde{\Phi}(x) = x_1^2 + x_2^2 - 4$, $f(x) = (-x_1 - 3x_2, 3x_1 - x_2)$, $J(x) = (2x_1, 2x_2)$. Let us check conditions (C1)–(C6). We have that $\nabla\Phi(x) = (2x_1, 2x_2) \neq 0$. So, condition (C1) is satisfied. Moreover, J, f are continuously differentiable functions and $\det[\frac{\partial J(x)}{\partial x}] = det \begin{pmatrix} 2 & 0 \\ 0 & 2 \end{pmatrix} = 4 \neq 0$, for all x. It is also obvious that $\Gamma \cap \tilde{\Gamma} = \emptyset$. Finally, $\langle \nabla\Phi(x), f(x) \rangle = \langle (2x_1, 2x_2), (-x_1 - 3x_2, 3x_1 - x_2) \rangle = 2 (-x_1^2 - x_2^2) = -2 \neq 0$, for all $x \in \Gamma$, and $\langle \nabla\tilde{\Phi}(x), f(x) \rangle = \langle (2x_1, 2x_2), (-x_1 - 3x_2, 3x_1 - x_2) \rangle = 2 (-x_1^2 - x_2^2) = -8 \neq 0$, for all $x \in \tilde{\Gamma}$. Thus, all conditions (C1)–(C6) are fulfilled.

Example 8.1.3. Let us consider the following system:

$$x_1' = -\frac{1}{3}x_1 - 3x_2,$$

$$x_2' = 3x_1 - \frac{1}{3}x_2,$$

$$\Delta x_1|_{x\in\Gamma} = (2\cos\frac{\pi}{6} - 1)x_1 - 2\sin\frac{\pi}{6}x_2,$$

$$\Delta x_2|_{x\in\Gamma} = 2\sin\frac{\pi}{6}x_1 + (2\cos\frac{\pi}{6} - 1)x_2. \tag{8.5}$$

where $G = \mathbb{R}^2$, and $\Gamma = \{(x_1, x_2)| \ x_1 = x_2, \ 0 < x_1\}$. Let us start to check conditions (C1)–(C6). One can easily find that $\tilde{\Gamma} = \{(x_1, x_2)| \ \sqrt{3}x_1 =$

$x_2, 0 < x_1\}, \Phi(x) = x_1 - x_2, \tilde{\Phi}(x) = \sqrt{3}x_1 - x_2, f(x) = (-\frac{1}{3}x_1 - 3x_2, 3x_1 - \frac{1}{3}x_2), J(x) = (2\cos\frac{\pi}{6}x_1 - 2\sin\frac{\pi}{6}x_2, 2\sin\frac{\pi}{6}x_1 + 2\cos\frac{\pi}{6}x_2).$
Consequently, we have that $\nabla\Phi(x) = (1, -1) \neq 0$, so, condition (C1) is satisfied. It is seen that J, f are continuously differentiable functions and
$\det[\frac{\partial J(x)}{\partial x}] = \det\begin{pmatrix} 2\cos\frac{\pi}{6} & 2\sin\frac{\pi}{6} \\ 2\sin\frac{\pi}{6} & 2\cos\frac{\pi}{6} \end{pmatrix} = 4(\cos^2\frac{\pi}{6} + \sin^2\frac{\pi}{6}) = 4 \neq 0$, for all x. It is
also obvious that $\Gamma \cap \tilde{\Gamma} = \emptyset$. Moreover,

$$\langle \nabla\Phi(x), f(x) \rangle = \left\langle (1, -1), (-\frac{1}{3}x_1 - 3x_2, 3x_1 - \frac{1}{3}x_2) \right\rangle = \left(\frac{-10}{3}x_1 - \frac{8}{3}x_2 \right) \neq 0,$$

for all $x \in \Gamma$. The inequality $\langle \nabla\tilde{\Phi}(x), f(x) \rangle \neq 0$, for all $x \in \tilde{\Gamma}$, can be shown similarly. Thus, all conditions, (C1)–(C6) are fulfilled.

8.2 Local Existence and Uniqueness

Definition 8.2.1. A function $x(t) \in \mathcal{PC}^1(I, \theta)$, where $I \subset \mathbb{R}$ is an interval, $\theta \subset I$ is a B-sequence of discontinuity points, is said to be a solution of (8.3) if:

(i) the differential equation (8.3) is satisfied at each $t \in I \backslash \theta$ and $x'_-(\theta_i) = f(x(\theta_i))$, $\theta_i \in \theta$, where $x'_-(\theta_i-)$ is the left-sided derivative;
(ii) $\Delta x(\theta_i+) = W(x(\theta_i))$ for all $\theta_i \in \theta$.

Theorem 8.2.1. *Assume that conditions (C1)–(C4) hold. Then for every $x_0 \in D$ there exists an interval $(a, b) \subset \mathbb{R}, a < 0 < b$, such that a solution $x(t) = x(t, 0, x_0)$ of (8.3) exists and is unique on the interval.*

Proof. Consider the following alternative cases:

(a) Assume that $x_0 \notin \Gamma \cup \tilde{\Gamma}$. Then there exists a number $\epsilon > 0$ such that $B(x_0, \epsilon) \cap (\Gamma \cup \tilde{\Gamma}) = \emptyset$, and $B(x_0, \epsilon) \subset G$, where $B(x_0, \epsilon)$ is the ball with the center at x_0 and the radius ϵ. Therefore, by the existence and uniqueness theorem [59], $x(t)$ exists and is unique on an interval (a, b) as a solution of the system

$$y' = f(y). \tag{8.6}$$

(b) If $x_0 \in \Gamma$, then $x(0+) \in \tilde{\Gamma}$. There exists a number $\epsilon > 0$ such that $B(x(0+), \epsilon) \cap \Gamma \neq \emptyset$ and $B(x(0+), \epsilon) \subset G$. Hence, $x(t)$ can be continued at the right. Let us consider $t < 0$ now. By condition (C4), there exists a number $\epsilon > 0$ such that $B(x(0), \epsilon) \cap \tilde{\Gamma} \neq \emptyset$ and $x(t)$ can be proceeded at the left.
(c) We can discuss the case $x_0 \in \tilde{\Gamma}$ similarly to the previous one.

The uniqueness of the solution for all cases (a)–(c) follows the theorem on uniqueness of ordinary differential equations [77] and the invertability of J.
   The theorem is proved. □

Since conditions (C1)–(C4) were verified in Examples 8.1.2 and 8.1.3, solutions of systems (8.4) and (8.5) locally exist and are unique.

8.3 Extension of Solutions

In this section, we will prove continuation theorems. The main results claim that every solution of (8.3) is continuable to ∞ and $-\infty$. In other words, $\mathbb{R}$ is a maximal interval of existence of each solution $x(t, 0, x_0), x_0 \in D$ of (8.3). That is, $x(t, 0, x_0) \in \mathcal{PC}(\mathbb{R})$. Illustrating examples are given, where solutions exist on $\mathbb{R}$.

Definition 8.3.1. A solution $x(t) = x(t, 0, x_0)$ of (8.3) is said to be continuable to a set $S \subset \mathbb{R}^n$ as time decreases (increases) if there exists a moment $\xi \in \mathbb{R}$, such that $\xi \leq 0$ $(\xi \geq 0)$ and $x(\xi) \in S$.

The following theorems provide sufficient conditions for the continuation of solutions of (8.3).

Theorem 8.3.1. *Assume that:*

(a) *every solution* $y(t, 0, x_0), x_0 \in D$, *of (8.6) is continuable to either* ∞ *or* Γ, *as time increases;*
(b) *there exists a positive number* $\bar{\theta}$ *such that*

$$\frac{\epsilon_x}{\sup_{B(x,\epsilon_x)} \|f(x)\|} \geq \bar{\theta},$$

for every $x \in \tilde{\Gamma}$ *and all* $\epsilon_x > 0$ *with* $B(x, \epsilon_x) \cap \Gamma = \emptyset$.

Then every solution $x(t) = x(t, 0, x_0), x_0 \in D$, *of (8.3) is continuable to* ∞.

Proof. Fix $x_0 \in D$ and let $x(t) = x(t, 0, x_0)$ be a solution of (8.3). Consider the following two cases.

(A) If x(t) is a continuous solution of (8.3), then it is a solution of (8.6) and is continuable to ∞.
(B) Let $x(\theta_i+) \in \tilde{\Gamma}$ for a fixed i. We set $M_x = \sup_{B(x,\epsilon_x)} \|f(x)\|$. Assume that there exists a number $\xi > \theta_i$, such that $\|x(\xi) - x(\theta_i+)\| = \epsilon_{x(\theta_i+)}$ (otherwise $x(t)$ is continuable to ∞). Then

$$x(\xi) = x(\theta_i+) + \int_{\theta_i}^{\xi} f(x(s))ds,$$

and $\epsilon_{x(\theta_i+)} \leq M_{x(\theta_i+)} (\xi - \theta_i) \leq M_{x(\theta_i+)} (\theta_{i+1} - \theta_i)$, where $M_{x(\theta_i+)} > 0$ (Why?). The last inequality implies that $\theta_{i+1} - \theta_i \geq \bar{\theta}$ for all i. That is, θ_i is a sequence of β-type if $\theta_i \geq 0$. The proof is complete. $\square$

In a similar manner, one can prove that the following theorem is valid.

Theorem 8.3.2. *Assume that:*

(a) every solution $y(t, 0, x_0)$, $x_0 \in D$ of (8.6) is continuable to either $-\infty$ or $\tilde{\Gamma}$, as time decreases;
(b) there exists a positive number $\bar{\theta}$ such that

$$\frac{\epsilon_x}{\sup_{B(x,\epsilon_x)} \|f(x)\|} \geq \bar{\theta},$$

for every $x \in \Gamma$ and all $\epsilon_x > 0$ with $B(x, \epsilon_x) \cap \tilde{\Gamma} = \emptyset$.

Then, every solution $x(t) = x(t, 0, x_0)$, $x_0 \in D$, of (8.3) is continuable to $-\infty$.

Theorems 8.3.1 and 8.3.2 imply that the following assertion is valid.

Theorem 8.3.3. *Assume that*

(a) every solution $y(t, 0, x_0)$, $x_0 \in D$, of (8.6) satisfies the following conditions:

   (a1) it is continuable to either ∞ or Γ, as time increases,
   (a2) it is continuable to either $-\infty$ or $\tilde{\Gamma}$, as time decreases;

(b) there exists a positive number $\bar{\theta}$ such that

$$\frac{\epsilon_x}{\sup_{B(x,\epsilon_x)} \|f(x)\|} \geq \bar{\theta},$$

for every $x \in \tilde{\Gamma}$ and all $\epsilon_x > 0$ with $B(x, \epsilon_x) \cap \Gamma = \emptyset$.
(c) there exists a positive number $\tilde{\theta}$ such that

$$\frac{\tilde{\epsilon}_x}{\sup_{B(x,\tilde{\epsilon}_x)} \|f(x)\|} \geq \tilde{\theta},$$

for every $x \in \Gamma$ and all $\tilde{\epsilon}_x > 0$ with $B(x, \tilde{\epsilon}_x) \cap \tilde{\Gamma} = \emptyset$.

Then, every solution $x(t) = x(t, 0, x_0)$, $x_0 \in D$, of (8.3) is continuable on $\mathbb{R}$.

Other sufficient conditions for the continuation of solutions of (8.3) are provided by the following theorems.

Theorem 8.3.4. *Assume that*

(a) every solution $y(t, 0, x_0)$, $x_0 \in D$, of (8.6) satisfies the following conditions:

   (a1) it is continuable either to ∞ or Γ, as t increases;
   (a2) it is continuable either to $-\infty$ or $\tilde{\Gamma}$, as t decreases;

(b) $\sup_D \|f(x)\| < +\infty$.
(c) $\mathrm{dist}(\Gamma, \tilde{\Gamma}) > 0$.

Then every solution $x(t, 0, x_0)$, $x_0 \in D$, of (8.3) is continuable on $\mathbb{R}$.

Proof. Fix $x_0 \in D$ and let $x(t) = x(t, 0, x_0)$ be a solution of (8.3). According to Definition 2.1.1, we shall consider the following three cases:

(A) If x(t) is a continuous solution of (8.3), then it is a solution of (8.6) and, thus is continuable on $\mathbb{R}$.

(B) Denote by θ_{max} and θ_{min} the maximal and minimal elements of the set $\{\theta_i\}$, respectively. Consider $t \geq \theta_{max}$. By the condition on J we have that $x(\theta_{max}+) = J(x(\theta_{max}-)) \in D$ and the solution $x(t) = y(t, \theta_{max}, x(\theta_{max}+))$, where y is a solution of (8.6) and is continuable to ∞. For $t \leq \theta_{min}$, one can apply the same arguments to show that x(t) is continuable to $-\infty$.

(C) Consider the following three alternatives.

(c_1) If the sequence $\{\theta_i\}$ has a maximal element $\theta_{max} \in \mathbb{R}$, but does not have a minimal one, then by using (B), it is easy to prove that $x(t)$ is continuable to ∞. Let t be decreasing. We have that

$$x(\theta_i+) = x(\theta_{i+1}) + \int_{\theta_{i+1}}^{\theta_i} f(x(s))ds. \tag{8.7}$$

Denote $\sup_D \|f(x)\| = M$ and $\mathrm{dist}(\Gamma, \tilde{\Gamma}) = \alpha$. Then (8.7) implies that $\frac{\alpha}{M} \leq (\theta_{i+1} - \theta_i)$. Hence, $\frac{\alpha}{M}(i - i_0) \geq (\theta_i - \theta_{i_0})$, where i_0 is fixed. The last inequality shows that $\theta_i \to -\infty$ as $i \to -\infty$. Thus, $x(t)$ is continuable to $-\infty$.

(c_2) Assume that the sequence $\{\theta_i\}$ has a minimal element θ_{min}, and does not have a maximal one. Then by the arguments of (B) $x(t)$ is continuable to $-\infty$. For increasing t we have that

$$x(\theta_{i+1}) = x(\theta_i+) + \int_{\theta_i}^{\theta_{i+1}} f(x(s))ds, \tag{8.8}$$

$\frac{\alpha}{M} \leq (\theta_{i+1} - \theta_i)$ or $\frac{\alpha}{M}(i - i_0) \leq (\theta_i - \theta_{i_0})$, where i_0 is fixed. Hence, $\theta_i \to \infty$ as $i \to \infty$. That is, $x(t)$ is continuable to ∞.

(c_3) Assume that $\{\theta_i\}$ has neither a minimal nor a maximal element. The result for this case follows (c_1) and (c_2). The proof is complete. $\square$

Theorem 8.3.5. *Assume that*

(a) every solution $y(t, 0, x_0)$, $x_0 \in D$, of (8.6) is continuable to either ∞ or Γ, as time increases;

(b) there exists a neighborhood S of Γ in D such that

    (b1) $\mathrm{dist}(\Gamma, \partial S) > 0$;
    (b2) $\sup_S \|f(x)\| < \infty$;
    (b3) $\tilde{\Gamma} \cap S = \emptyset$.

Then every solution $x(t) = x(t, 0, x_0)$, $x_0 \in D$, of (8.3) is continuable to ∞.

Proof. Denote $d = \text{dist}(\Gamma, \partial S)$ and $M = \sup_S \|f(x)\|$. For a fixed i one can see that

$$x(\theta_{i+1}) = x(\theta_i +) + \int_{\theta_i}^{\theta_{i+1}} f(x(s))ds.$$

Condition (b3) implies that $d < \|x(\theta_{i+1}) - x(\theta_i +)\| \le M(\theta_{i+1} - \theta_i)$. Thus $\theta_{i+1} - \theta_i \ge \frac{d}{M} > 0$ for all i. Further discussion is fully analogous to that of the last theorem. $\qquad\square$

Exercise 8.3.1. Prove the following theorem.

Theorem 8.3.6. *Assume that:*

(a) every solution $y(t, 0, x_0), x_0 \in D$, of (8.6) is continuable to either $-\infty$ or $\tilde{\Gamma}$, as time decreases,
(b) there exists a neighborhood $\tilde{S}$ of $\tilde{\Gamma}$ in D such that:

    (b1) $\text{dist}(\tilde{\Gamma}, \partial\tilde{S}) > 0$;
    (b2) $\sup_{\tilde{S}} \|f(x)\| < \infty$;
    (b3) $\Gamma \cap \tilde{S} = \emptyset$.

Then, every solution $x(t) = x(t, 0, x_0), x_0 \in D$, of (8.3) is continuable to $-\infty$.

Using the conditions of both Theorems 8.3.5 and 8.3.6, one can formulate the following assertion.

Theorem 8.3.7. *Assume that:*

(a) every solution $y(t, 0, x_0), x_0 \in D$, of (8.6) satisfies the following conditions:

    (a1) it is continuable to either ∞ or Γ, as time increases;
    (a2) it is continuable to either $-\infty$ or $\tilde{\Gamma}$, as time decreases;

(b) there exist neighborhoods S and $\tilde{S}$ of Γ and $\tilde{\Gamma}$ in D, respectively, such that:

    (b1) $\text{dist}(\Gamma, \partial S) > 0$, $\text{dist}(\tilde{\Gamma}, \partial\tilde{S}) > 0$;
    (b2) $\sup_{S \cup \tilde{S}} \|f(x)\| < \infty$;
    (b3) $\tilde{\Gamma} \cap S = \emptyset$, $\Gamma \cap \tilde{S} = \emptyset$.

Then, every solution $x(t) = x(t, 0, x_0), x_0 \in D$, of (8.3) is continuable on $\mathbb{R}$.

Example 8.3.1. Let us consider system (8.5) and study the extension property. The differential equation in the system is a linear one, consequently, each solution of this equation is continuable to ∞, since maximal interval of existence is $\mathbb{R}$. The first condition of Theorem 8.3.1 is satisfied. Let us fix an initial value $x_0 = (x_1^0, x_2^0) \in \tilde{\Gamma}$, that is $\sqrt{3}x_1^0 = x_2^0$. Then, one can easily evaluate the distance between Γ and x_0

$$\text{dist}(x_0, \Gamma) = \frac{|x_1^0 - x_2^0|}{\sqrt{2}} = \frac{\sqrt{3}-1}{\sqrt{2}}|x_1^0| = \frac{\sqrt{3}-1}{2\sqrt{2}}\|x_0\|.$$

Fix

$$\epsilon_{x_0} = \frac{\sqrt{3}-1}{2\sqrt{2}} \|x_0\| \tag{8.9}$$

and take any $x \in B\left(x_0, \epsilon_{x_0}\right)$, then

$$\|x\| < \epsilon_{x_0} + \|x_0\|. \tag{8.10}$$

Substituting (8.9) into (8.10), one can conclude that

$$\|x\| < \left[\frac{\sqrt{3}-1+2\sqrt{2}}{2\sqrt{2}}\right] \|x_0\|.$$

Computing the norm of the function f in this ball, we get that

$$\|f(x)\| \le \frac{\sqrt{41}}{6}\left[\sqrt{3}-1+2\sqrt{2}\right]\|x_0\| = M_{x_0}.$$

By easy calculation,

$$\inf \frac{\epsilon_x}{M_x} = \frac{\frac{\sqrt{3}-1}{2\sqrt{2}}\|x_0\|}{\frac{\sqrt{41}}{6}\left[\sqrt{3}-1+2\sqrt{2}\right]\|x_0\|} = \frac{3\left(\sqrt{3}-1\right)}{\sqrt{82}\left(\sqrt{3}-1+2\sqrt{2}\right)} > 0.$$

We can see, now, that condition (b) is valid. Thus, all conditions of Theorem 8.3.1 are satisfied, and every solution of system (8.5) is continuable to ∞. The continuation of solutions for decreasing t can be shown by using Theorem 8.3.2.

Example 8.3.2. Let us examine system (8.4). The domain of this system is $D = \{(x_1, x_2) | \ 1 \le x_1^2 + x_2^2 \le 4, \ x_1, x_2 \in \mathbb{R}\}$. Manifolds Γ and $\tilde{\Gamma}$ are boundaries of this ring. They are circles with radii 1 and 2, and $\text{dist}(\tilde{\Gamma}, \Gamma) = 1$, respectively.

The differential equation in (8.4) is a linear system with constant coefficients, and one can determine that all solutions are continuable to Γ, as time increases, and are continuable to $\tilde{\Gamma}$, as time decreases. Hence, the first condition of Theorem 8.3.4 is satisfied.

Moreover,

$$\|f(x)\| = \sqrt{(-x_1 - 3x_2)^2 + (3x_1 - x_2)^2} = \sqrt{10}\sqrt{x_1^2 + x_2^2}, \tag{8.11}$$

and

$$\sup_D \|f(x)\| = 2\sqrt{10} < \infty.$$

Since, all conditions of Theorem 8.3.4 are satisfied, every solution of system (8.4) is continuable on $\mathbb{R}$.

Example 8.3.3. Consider the following impulsive autonomous system:

$$x_1' = -2x_1 - 3x_2,$$
$$x_2' = 3x_1 - 2x_2,$$
$$\Delta x_1|_{x \in \Gamma} = (2\cos\frac{\pi}{6} - 1)x_1 - 2\sin\frac{\pi}{6}x_2,$$
$$\Delta x_2|_{x \in \Gamma} = 2\sin\frac{\pi}{6}x_1 + (2\cos\frac{\pi}{6} - 1)x_2, \qquad (8.12)$$

where manifolds of discontinuity are

$$\Gamma = \left\{(x_1, x_2)| \quad x_1 = \sqrt{3}x_2, \quad \frac{1}{2} < x_2 < \frac{3}{2}\right\}$$

and

$$\tilde{\Gamma} = \left\{(x_1, x_2)| \quad \sqrt{3}x_1 = x_2, \quad 1 < x_1 < 3\right\}.$$

Domain $D = \mathbb{R}^2 \backslash \left\{\left(\frac{\sqrt{3}}{2}, \frac{1}{2}\right), \left(\frac{3\sqrt{3}}{2}, \frac{3}{2}\right), \left(1, \sqrt{3}\right), \left(3, 3\sqrt{3}\right)\right\}$. Let us look for sufficient conditions of Theorem 8.3.5 to indicate continuation of solutions of the system (8.12) for increasing t. The differential equation in (8.12) is a linear system and maximal interval of existence is $\mathbb{R}$, so each solution of the differential equation is continuable to ∞ as time increases. Hence, the first condition is satisfied. While dealing with other conditions, we prefer to use both polar and Cartesian coordinates. First, let us define an auxiliary set S in polar coordinates (see Fig. 8.4),

$$S = \left\{(\rho, \theta)| \quad \frac{9}{10} < \rho < \frac{21}{10}, \quad \frac{\pi}{12} < \theta < \frac{\pi}{4}\right\}.$$

One can easily see that $\Gamma \subset S$ and $\tilde{\Gamma} \cap S = \emptyset$. The distance between Γ and ∂S, is the minimum of the following two numbers: the distance between Γ and the arc $\gamma = \{(\rho, \theta)|\rho = \frac{9}{10}, \frac{\pi}{12} < \theta < \frac{\pi}{4}\}$; the distance between Γ and the line $\ell = \{(\rho, \theta)|\frac{9}{10} < \rho < \frac{21}{10}, \theta = \frac{\pi}{4}\}$. One can find that $dist(\Gamma, \gamma) = \frac{1}{10}$. Next, let us write the equation of the line in Cartesian coordinates as

$$\ell = \left\{(x_1, x_2)| \quad x_1 = x_2, \ x_1, x_2 \in \mathbb{R}^+\right\}.$$

To find $dist(\Gamma, \ell)$, it is sufficient to find out the distance between the line ℓ and the points $A\left(\frac{\sqrt{3}}{2}, \frac{1}{2}\right)$ and $B\left(\frac{3\sqrt{3}}{2}, \frac{3}{2}\right)$,

$$dist(\ell, A) = \frac{\left|\frac{\sqrt{3}}{2} - \frac{1}{2}\right|}{\sqrt{1+1}} = \frac{\sqrt{3}-1}{2\sqrt{2}}, \qquad dist(\ell, B) = \frac{\left|\frac{3\sqrt{3}}{2} - \frac{3}{2}\right|}{\sqrt{1+1}} = \frac{3\sqrt{3}-3}{2\sqrt{2}}.$$

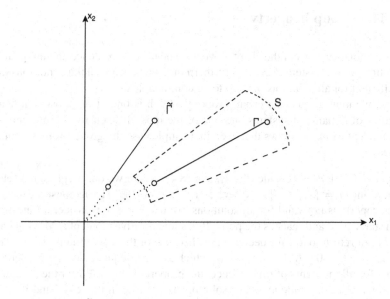

Fig. 8.4 Manifolds Γ, $\tilde{\Gamma}$, and an auxiliary set S

Then, distance between Γ and the surface ∂S is

$$dist(\Gamma, \partial S) = \frac{1}{10}.$$

Now, we take the norm of the function $f(x)$,

$$\|f(x)\| = \sqrt{4+9}\sqrt{x_1^2 + x_2^2}.$$

Since

$$\frac{9}{10} < \sqrt{x_1^2 + x_2^2} < \frac{21}{10},$$

$$\sup_S \|f(x)\| = \frac{21\sqrt{13}}{10}.$$

Thus, all conditions of Theorem 8.3.5 are satisfied, and every solution of system (8.12) is continuable to ∞.

Exercise 8.3.2. Prove, by using Theorem 8.3.6, that all solutions of system (8.12) are continuable to $-\infty$.

8.4 The Group Property

In the previous sections of the chapter, we have dealt with existence and uniqueness of solutions of the system (8.3), and furthermore, we have given the conditions that are sufficient for all solutions of (8.3) to be continuable on $\mathbb{R}$.

Now, we may discuss the group property, which is one of the most significant properties of dynamical systems and one of the most difficult for the present discussion. Next example shows that even in a simple case the group property can be violated.

Example 8.4.1. Let us consider the system (8.4), where we only replace the set G by a new one $G = \{(x_1, x_2) \mid x_1^2 + x_2^2 > 1, \quad x_1, x_2 \in \mathbb{R}\}$. To demonstrate that the group property is not valid for all solutions, we use Fig. 8.5. Consider a trajectory, which starts at x_0 and reaches the point P at some positive moment t. Moving back it could not return to x_0, for decreasing t, because of the discontinuity set $\tilde{\Gamma}$. That is, equality $x(-t, 0, x(t, 0, x_0)) = x_0$, which is a consequence of the property is not true for all moments of time. Hence, the property is not valid for the system. It is obvious, also, that uniqueness of solutions is not true in this case, and it is not surprising, as it is known that the group property and the uniqueness are strongly related to each other.

The last example shows that specific conditions to guarantee the group property should be found.

The following condition is one of the most needed in this chapter.

(C7) (a) for every $x \in \Gamma$ there exists $\epsilon_x > 0$ such that $\text{sign}\Phi(x)$ is a constant function in $[B(x, \epsilon_x) \cap G] \backslash \Gamma$;
(b) for every $x \in \tilde{\Gamma}$ there exists $\epsilon_x > 0$ such that $\text{sign}\tilde{\Phi}(x)$ is a constant function in $[B(x, \epsilon_x) \cap G] \backslash \tilde{\Gamma}$.

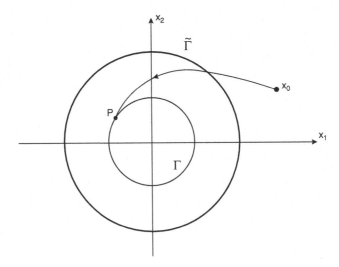

Fig. 8.5 The trajectory of Example 8.4.1

Lemma 8.4.1. *Assume that (C1)–(C7) hold and $y(t) : (-\alpha, \alpha) \to \mathbb{R}^n$, $\alpha > 0$, is a solution of (8.6). Then $y(0) \notin \Gamma$ and $y(0) \notin \tilde{\Gamma}$.*

Proof. Assume, on the contrary, that $y(0) = y_0 \in \Gamma$. We have that

$$\Phi(y(t)) = \Phi(y(t)) - \Phi(y_0) = \langle \nabla \Phi(y_0), y(t) - y_0 \rangle + o(\|y(t) - y_0\|) =$$

$$\langle \nabla \Phi(y_0), f(y_0)t + o(|t|) \rangle + o(\|f(y_0)\||t| + o(|t|)) = \langle \nabla \Phi(y(0)), f(y(0)) \rangle \, t + o(|t|).$$

By condition (C7) function $\mathrm{sign}\Phi(y(t))$ has a constant value for sufficiently small $|t|$, and by condition (C4) the value of $\langle \nabla \Phi(y(0)), f(y(0)) \rangle$ is not zero. This contradiction proves our lemma for Γ. The proof for $\tilde{\Gamma}$ is similar. $\qquad\square$

Lemma 8.4.2. *Assume that (C1)–(C7) hold. Then $x(-t, 0, x(t, 0, x_0)) = x_0$ for all $x_0 \in D, t \in \mathbb{R}$.*

Proof. Consider $t > 0$. If the set $\{\theta_i\}$ is empty, then the proof follows immediately the assertion for continuous dynamical systems [39]. One can see that it remains to check the validity of $x(-\theta_i, 0, x(\theta_i+)) = x(\theta_i)$ for all i, and the condition $x(-\theta_1, 0, x(\theta_1, 0, x_0)) = x_0$. The first one is obvious because of invertability of J. Let us consider the second one. Denote $x(t) = x(t, 0, x_0)$, $\tilde{x}(t) = x(t, 0, x(\theta_1))$. Since $x(\theta_1) \in \Gamma$, then by (C4), the solution $\tilde{x}$ moves along the trajectory of (8.6) for decreasing t, and it cannot meet $\tilde{\Gamma}$ if $t > -\theta_1$. Indeed, assume on the contrary that there exists moment θ, $-\theta_1 < \theta < 0$, where $\tilde{x}$ intersects $\tilde{\Gamma}$. Then $\tilde{x}(\theta+) = x(\theta + \theta_1)$. We have obtained a contradiction to Lemma 8.4.1 since $x(t + \theta + \theta_1)$ is the solution of (8.6) in a neighborhood of $t = 0$. If $t < 0$, the proof is very similar to that of $t > 0$, and the proof with $t = 0$ is primitive. The lemma is proved. $\qquad\square$

Let us continue with the following auxiliary result.

Consider a solution $x(t) : \mathbb{R} \to \mathbb{R}^n$ of (8.3). Let $\{\theta_i\}$ be the sequence of discontinuity points of $x(t)$. Fix $\bar{\theta} \in \mathbb{R}$ and introduce a function $\psi(t) = x(t + \bar{\theta})$.

Lemma 8.4.3. *The sequence $\{\theta_i - \bar{\theta}\}$ is a set of all solutions of the equation*

$$\Phi(\psi(t)) = 0. \tag{8.13}$$

Proof. We have $\Phi(\psi((\theta_i - \bar{\theta}))) = \Phi(x((\theta_i - \bar{\theta}) + \bar{\theta})) = \Phi(x(\theta_i)) = 0$. Assume that $t = \varphi$ is a solution of (8.13), then $\Phi(x(\varphi + \bar{\theta})) = \Phi(\psi(\varphi)) = 0$. That is, $\varphi + \bar{\theta}$ is one of the numbers $\{\theta_i\}$. Let $\varphi + \bar{\theta} = \theta_j$, then $\varphi = \theta_j - \bar{\theta}$. The lemma is proved. $\qquad\square$

Lemma 8.4.4. *If $x(t) : \mathbb{R} \to \mathbb{R}^n$ is a solution of (8.3), then $x(t + \bar{\theta})$, $\bar{\theta} \in \mathbb{R}$, is also a solution of (8.3).*

Proof. From Lemma 8.4.3, it follows that $\psi = x(t + \bar{\theta})$ is a continuous function on the interval $(\theta_i - \bar{\theta}, \theta_{i+1} - \bar{\theta}], i \in \mathbb{Z}$. Fix $i \in \mathbb{Z}$, and consider $t \in \left(\theta_i - \bar{\theta}, \theta_{i+1} - \bar{\theta}\right]$.

We have that $t + \bar{\theta} \in (\theta_i, \theta_{i+1}]$ and one can verify that $\psi'(t) = f(\psi(t))$. That is, (8.3) is satisfied by $x(t + \theta)$.

For fixed i, we have that $\psi((\theta_i - \bar{\theta})+) = x(\theta_i+) = J(x(\theta_i)) = J(\psi(\theta_i - \bar{\theta}))$. Thus, one can see that the jump equations in (8.3) are also satisfied by $x(t + \theta)$, and this completes the proof. □

Lemmas 8.4.2 and 8.4.4 imply that the following theorem is valid. The proof of this theorem is similar to that of continuous dynamical systems [157].

Theorem 8.4.1. *Assume that conditions (C1)–(C7) are fulfilled. Then*

$$x(t_2, x(t_1, x_0)) = x(t_2 + t_1, x_0), \tag{8.14}$$

for all $t_1, t_2 \in \mathbb{R}$.

Remark 8.4.1. Since $x(0, x_0) = x_0$, one can conclude on the basis of Theorem 8.4.1 that $x(t, x_0), t \in \mathbb{R}, x_0 \in D$, defines a one-parameter group of transformations of D into itself.

Exercise 8.4.1. Verify that condition (C7) is fulfilled in Example 8.1.2, and it is not correct in Example 8.4.1.

8.5 Continuity Properties

A dependence of solutions on initial values is a very effective method to investigate various problems of dynamical systems, and we deal with the continuous dependence in this section. It is assumed that all considered solutions are continuable on $\mathbb{R}$. The next example demonstrates that the continuity property should be discussed very carefully when one is busy with nonfixed moments of discontinuity.

Example 8.5.1. Consider the autonomous system

$$\begin{aligned}
x_1' &= 0, \\
x_2' &= 0, \\
\Delta x_1'|_{x \in \Gamma} &= 0, \\
\Delta x_2'|_{x \in \Gamma} &= -1,
\end{aligned} \tag{8.15}$$

where $\Gamma = \{x \in \mathbb{R}^2 : x_1 = x_2\}$. Take solutions $x_0(t) = x(t, 0, (3, 3))$, and $x(t) = x(t, 0, (x_0^1, x_0^2)), x_0^1 > 3, x_0^2 < 3$, and consider them for increasing t. One can easily see that the more points (x_0^1, x_0^2) and $(3, 3)$ are close, the more the distance $\|x_0(t) - x(t)\|, t > 0$, is close to 1.

Fix a point $x_0 \in \Gamma \backslash \partial\Gamma$, and denote by $B(x_0, r)$ an open ball with the center at x_0 and the radius $r > 0$. By condition (C5), if r is sufficiently small, the ball is divided by the surface Γ into two connected and open regions. Denote by $b^+(x_0, r)$ the region, which $x(t, 0, x_0)$ enters as time decreases. Let $c^+(x_0, r) = (\Gamma \cap B(x_0, r)) \cup b^+(x_0, r)$. If $x_0 \notin \Gamma$, then $c^+(x_0, r) = B(x_0, r)$, where the radius r so small that $B(x_0, r) \cap \Gamma = \emptyset$. Similarly, if $x_0 \in \tilde{\Gamma} \backslash \partial \tilde{\Gamma}$ denote by $b^-(x_0, r)$ the region, which $x(t, 0, x_0)$ enters as time increases. Then write $c^-(x_0, r) = (\tilde{\Gamma} \cap B(x_0, r)) \cup b^-(x_0, r)$. We set also $c^-(x_0, r)$ equals $B(x_0, r)$, where the radius r so small that $B(x_0, r) \cap \tilde{\Gamma} = \emptyset$, if $x_0 \notin \tilde{\Gamma}$.

Let $x^0(t) : \mathbb{R} \to \mathbb{R}^n, x^0(t) = x(t, 0, x_0)$, be a solution of (8.3).

Definition 8.5.1. The solution $x^0(t)$ of (8.3) B-continuously depends on x_0 for increasing t, if to any $\epsilon > 0$ and finite interval $[0, b], 0 < b$, there corresponds $\delta > 0$ such that any other solution $x(t) = x(t, 0, \bar{x})$ of (8.3) lies in the ϵ-neighborhood of $x^0(t)$ on $[0, b]$, if $\bar{x} \in c^+(x_0, \delta)$.

Definition 8.5.2. The solution $x^0(t) : \mathbb{R} \to \mathbb{R}^n, x^0(t) = x(t, 0, x_0)$, of (8.3) B-continuously depends on x_0 for decreasing t, if to any $\epsilon > 0$ and finite interval $[a, 0], a < 0$, there corresponds $\delta > 0$ such that any other solution $x(t) = x(t, 0, \bar{x})$ of (8.3) lies in the ϵ-neighborhood of $x^0(t)$ on $[a, 0]$, if $\bar{x} \in c^-(x_0, \delta)$.

Definition 8.5.3. The solution $x^0(t) : \mathbb{R} \to \mathbb{R}^n, x^0(t) = x(t, 0, x_0)$, of (8.3) B-continuously depends on x_0 if it continuously depends on the initial value for both decreasing and increasing t.

Theorem 8.5.1. *Assume that conditions (C1)–(C6) are satisfied. Then each solution* $x^0(t) = x(t, 0, x_0), x_0 \in D$, *of (8.3) continuously depends on* x_0.

Proof. We consider a particular case with a finite interval $[0, b]$, and the points of discontinuity $\theta_i, i = 1, \ldots, m$, of the solution $x^0(t)$ in the interval such that $0 < \theta_1 < \cdots < \theta_m < b$. Moreover, we assume that $t = 0$, and $t = b$ are not the moments of discontinuity. All other cases can be considered similarly.

Fix a positive number α. Let $F_\alpha = \{(t, x) | t \in [0, b], \|x - x^0(t)\| < \alpha\}, G_i(\alpha),$ $i = 0, 1, 2, \ldots, m + 1$, be α-neighborhoods of points $(0, x_0), (\theta_i, x(\theta_i)),$ $i = 1, 2, \ldots, m, (b, x^0(b))$ in $\mathbb{R} \times \mathbb{R}^n$, respectively, and $\bar{G}_i(\alpha), i = 1, 2, \ldots, k,$ be an α-neighborhood of the point $(\theta_i, x^0(\theta_i+))$. Write

$$G^\alpha = F_\alpha \cup \left(\cup_{i=0}^{m+1} G_i(\alpha)\right) \cup \left(\cup_{i=1}^{m} \bar{G}_i(\alpha)\right).$$

Take α sufficiently small so that $G^\alpha \subset \mathbb{R} \times D$. Fix $\epsilon, 0 < \epsilon < \alpha$.

1. In view of the continuity of solutions [77], there exists $\bar{\delta}_m, 0 < \bar{\delta}_m < \epsilon$, such that every solution $x_m(t)$ of (8.6), which starts in $\bar{G}_m(\bar{\delta}_m)$, is continuable to $t = b$, does not intersect Γ, and

$$\|x_m(t) - x^0(t)\| < \epsilon,$$

for all t from the common domain of $x_m(t)$ and $x^0(t)$.
2. By continuity of J there exists $0 < \delta_m < \epsilon$, such that $(\kappa, x) \in G_m(\delta_m)$ implies $(\kappa, x + J(x)) \in \bar{G}_m(\bar{\delta}_m) \cap D$.

3. The continuity theorem yields that there exists $\bar{\delta}_{m-1}, 0 < \bar{\delta}_{m-1} < \epsilon$, such that a solution $x_{m-1}(t)$ of (8.6), which starts in $\bar{G}_{m-1}(\bar{\delta}_{m-1})$, intersects Γ in $G_m(\delta_m)$ (we continue the solution $x_{m-1}(t)$ only to the moment of the intersection) and $\left\| x_{m-1}(t) - x^0(t) \right\| < \epsilon$ for all t from the common domain of $x_{m-1}(t)$ and $x^0(t)$.

Continuing the process for $m-2, m-3, \ldots, 1$, one can obtain a sequence of families of solutions of (8.6) $x_i(t)$, and corresponding numbers $\delta_i, \bar{\delta}_i, i = 1, 2, \ldots, m$. Finally, we find a number $\delta, 0 < \delta < \epsilon$, such that each solution $x_0(t)$, which starts in $G_0(\delta)$ intersects Γ in $G_1(\delta_1)$, if t increases, and satisfies $\|x_0(t) - x^0(t)\| < \epsilon$ if t is from the common domain of $x_0(t)$ and $x^0(t)$. Thus, if one chooses a solution $x(t) = x(t, 0, \bar{x}), \bar{x} \in G_0(\delta)$, of (8.3), then it coincides over the first interval of continuity, except possibly, the δ_1-neighborhood of θ_1, with one of the solutions $x_0(t)$. Then on the interval $[\theta_1, \theta_2]$ it coincides with one of the solutions $x_1(t)$, except possibly, the δ_1-neighborhood of θ_1 and the δ_2-neighborhood of θ_2, etc. Finally, one can see that the integral curve of $x(t)$ belongs to G^ϵ, it has exactly m meeting points with Γ, $\theta_i^1, i = 1, 2, \ldots, m, \left| \theta_i^1 - \theta_i \right| < \epsilon$ for all i, and it is continuable to $t = b$. The theorem is proved. $\square$

8.6 B-Equivalence

In this section, we construct an auxiliary system of differential equations with impulses at fixed moments, a B-equivalent system, for equations (8.3). One have to emphasize that B-equivalence plays less general role for autonomous impulsive systems than for nonautonomous equations. In this part of the manuscript, we specify a B-equivalent system around a solution of equations (8.3).

First, we need to introduce two maps, which will be used throughout the rest of the chapter. Fix $\kappa \in \mathbb{R}$. Denote by $x(t) = x(t, \kappa, x)$ a solution of (8.6), $\tau = \tau(x)$ the moment of the meeting of $x(t)$ with the surface Γ.

Lemma 8.6.1. $\tau(x) \in C^1$.

Proof. Differentiating $\Phi\left(x\left(\tau, \kappa, x\right)\right) = 0$, and using (C5) one can get that

$$\frac{\partial \Phi\left(x\left(\tau, \kappa, x\right)\right)}{\partial \tau} = \frac{\partial \Phi\left(x\left(\tau, \kappa, x\right)\right)}{\partial x} \frac{dx(t)}{dt}\bigg|_{t=\tau} = \frac{\partial \Phi\left(x\left(\tau, \kappa, x\right)\right)}{\partial x} f\left(x\left(\tau, \kappa, x\right)\right) \neq 0$$

Now, the proof follows immediately the implicit function theorem. $\square$

Corollary 8.6.1. $\tau(x)$ *is a continuous function.*

Let $x_1 = x(t, \tau, x(\tau)) + J(x(\tau))$ be another solution of (8.6). Define the map $\Psi(x) = x_1(\kappa)$.

Similarly to Lemma 8.6.1, one can show that the following assertion is valid.

Lemma 8.6.2. $\Psi(x) \in C^1$

Consider a solution $x^0(t) : [a, b] \to R^n, a \leq 0 \leq b$, of (8.3). Assume that all discontinuity points $\theta_i, i = -k, \ldots, -1, 1, \ldots, m$, are interior points of $[a, b]$. That is, $a < \theta_{-k}$ and $\theta_m < b$.

The following system of differential equations with impulses at fixed moments, which are points of discontinuity of $x^0(t)$, is very important in the sequel:

$$y' = f(y),$$

$$\Delta y|_{t=\theta_i} = W_i(y(\theta_i)). \tag{8.16}$$

The function f is the same as in (8.3) and maps $W_i, -k \leq i \leq m$, will be defined below. There exists a positive number r, such that r-neighborhoods $G_i(r)$ of $(\theta_i, x^0(\theta_i))$ do not intersect each other. In view of (C5), one can suppose that r is sufficiently small so that every solution of (8.6) which starts in $G_i(r)$ intersects Γ in $G_i(r)$ as t increases or decreases.

Fix $i = -k, \ldots, m$ and let $\xi(t) = x(t, \theta_i, x), (\theta_i, x) \in G_i(r)$, be a solution of (8.6), $\tau_i = \tau_i(x)$ the meeting time of $\xi(t)$ with Γ and $\psi(t) = x(t, \tau_i, \xi(\tau_i) + J(\xi(\tau_i))$ another solution of (8.6). One should mention that $|\tau_i(x) - \theta_i| = O(r)$. Denote $W_i(x) = \psi(\theta_i) - x$. One can see that

$$W_i(x) = \int_{\theta_i}^{\tau_i} f(\xi(s))ds + J(x + \int_{\theta_i}^{\tau_i} f(\xi(s))ds) + \int_{\tau_i}^{\theta_i} f(\psi(s))ds \tag{8.17}$$

is a map of an intersection of the plane $t = \theta_i$ with $G_i(r)$ into the plane $t = \theta_i$. The functions $W_i, -k \leq i \leq m$, are obtained by using the map Ψ, which has been defined above in this section. Hence, Lemma 8.6.2 implies that all W_i are continuously differentiable maps.

Let us introduce the following sets: $F_r = \{(t, x)|t \in [a, b], \|x - x^0(t)\| < r\}$, and $\bar{G}_i(r), i = -k, \ldots, m$, an r-neighborhood of the point $(\theta_i, x^0(\theta_i+))$. Write

$$G^r = F_r \cup \left(\cup_{i=-k}^m G_i(r)\right) \cup \left(\cup_{i=-k}^m \bar{G}_i(r)\right).$$

Take r sufficiently small so that $G^r \subset \mathbb{R} \times D$. Denote by $G(h)$ a h-neighborhood of $x^0(0)$.

Definition 8.6.1. Systems (8.3) and (8.16) are said to be B-equivalent in G^r if there exists $h > 0$, such that:

1. for every solution $x(t)$ of (8.3) such that $x(0) \in G(h)$, the integral curve of $x(t)$ belongs to G^r and there exists a solution $y(t) = y(t, 0, x(0))$ of (8.16) which satisfies

$$x(t) = y(t), t \in [a, b] \setminus \cup_{i=-k}^m \widehat{(\tau_i, \theta_i]}, \tag{8.18}$$

where τ_i are moments of discontinuity of $x(t)$. Particularly:

$$x(\theta_i) = \begin{cases} y(\theta_i), & \text{if } \theta_i \leq \tau_i, \\ y(\theta_i^+), & \text{otherwise,} \end{cases}$$

$$y(\tau_i) = \begin{cases} x(\tau_i), & \text{if } \theta_i \geq \tau_i, \\ x(\tau_i^+), & \text{otherwise.} \end{cases} \tag{8.19}$$

2. Conversely, if (8.16) has a solution $y(t) = y(t, 0, x(0))$, $x(0) \in G(h)$, then there exists a solution $x(t) = x(t, 0, x(0))$ of (8.3) which has an integral curve in G^r, and (8.18) holds.

The following assertion follows immediately (8.17).

Lemma 8.6.3. $x^0(t)$ *is a solution of (8.3) and (8.16) simultaneously.*

Theorem 8.6.1. *Assume that conditions (C1)–(C6) are fulfilled. Then systems (8.3) and (8.16) are B-equivalent in G^r if r is sufficiently small.*

Proof. Assume that $r > 0$ is small so that W_i, $i = -k, \ldots, -1, 1, \ldots, m$, are defined. Let us check only the first condition of Definition 8.6.1 because that of the second one is analogous. Theorem 8.5.1 implies that there exists a small $h, 0 < h < r$, such that if $\|\bar{x} - x_0\| < h$ and $\bar{x} \in D$, then the solution $x(t) = x(t, 0, \bar{x})$ belongs to G^r. Assume that h is sufficiently small so that $x(t)$ has exactly $m + k$ moments of discontinuity $t = \tau_i, i = -k, \ldots, -1, 1, \ldots, m$. Without loss of generality, we suppose that $\theta_i > \tau_i$ for all i. It is obvious that we need only to prove the theorem for $[0, b]$, because for $[a, 0]$, the proof is similar. Consider the solution $y(t) = y(t, 0, x(0))$ of (8.16). By the theorem on existence and uniqueness [77] the equality

$$x(t) = y(t) \tag{8.20}$$

is valid on $[0, \tau_1]$. Since $(\tau_1, x(\tau_1)) \in G^r$ we see that

$$y(\theta_1+) = y(\tau_1) + \int_{\tau_1}^{\theta_1} f(y(s))ds + W_i(y(\theta_1)) \tag{8.21}$$

is defined and

$$x(\theta_1) = x(\tau_1) + J(x(\tau_1)) + \int_{\tau_1}^{\theta_1} f(x(s))ds. \tag{8.22}$$

Using (8.20)–(8.22) one can obtain that

$$y(\theta_1+) = x(\tau_1) + \int_{\tau_1}^{\theta_1} f(y(s))ds + \int_{\theta_1}^{\tau_1} f(y(s))ds +$$

$$J(y(\tau_1)) + \int_{\tau_1}^{\theta_1} f(x(s))ds = x(\theta_1).$$

Now, defining $x(t)$ and $y(t)$ as solutions of (8.6) with a common initial value $x(\theta_1)$, one can see that $x(t) = y(t), t \in (\theta_1, \tau_2]$. Continuing in the same manner for all $t \in [0, b]$ one can show that $y(t)$ is continuable to $t = b$ and (8.18) holds. Moreover, it is easily seen that for sufficiently small h, the integral curve of $y(t)$ belongs to G_r. The theorem is proved.   □

8.7 Differentiability Properties

Let us consider derivatives of functions $\tau_i(x)$, $W_i(x)$, $i = -k, \ldots, -1, 1 \ldots, m$, which were described in Sect. 8.6. We start with derivatives of $\tau_i(x)$. One should emphasize that $\tau_i, i = -k, \ldots, -1, 1 \ldots, m$ are maps, which are defined by the map τ in Sect. 8.6 with $\kappa = \theta_i, i = -k, \ldots, -1, 1 \ldots, m$. The equalities $\Phi(x(\tau_i(x))) = 0$ imply that

$$\Phi_x(x^0(\theta_i)) f(x^0(\theta_i)) d\tau_i + \sum_{k=1}^{n} \Phi_x(x^0(\theta_i)) \frac{\partial x^0(\theta_i)}{\partial x_k} dx_k = 0.$$

Using the last expression, one can obtain that

$$\frac{\partial \tau_i(x^0(\theta_i))}{\partial x_j} = -\frac{\Phi_x(x^0(\theta_i)) \frac{\partial x^0(\theta_i)}{\partial x_j}}{\Phi_x(x^0(\theta_i)) f(x^0(\theta_i))}. \tag{8.23}$$

Similarly, for W_i the following expression is valid:

$$\frac{\partial W_i(x^0(\theta_i))}{\partial x_j} = f \frac{\partial \tau_i}{\partial x_j} + \frac{\partial J}{\partial x}(e_j + f \frac{\partial \tau_i}{\partial x_j}) - f^+ \frac{\partial \tau_i}{\partial x_j}. \tag{8.24}$$

Thus, formulas (8.23) and (8.24) provide evaluations of the derivatives.

It is known that $x^0(t) : [a, b] \to \mathbb{R}^n$ is the solution of (8.3) and (8.16). Moreover, systems (8.3) and (8.16) are B-equivalent in G^r and there exists $\delta \in R, \delta > 0$, such that every solution which starts in $c^+(x_0, r)$ is continuable to $t = b$. Without loss of generality, assume that all points of discontinuity of $x^0(t)$ are interior points of $[a, b]$. Denote by $x^j(t)$, $j = 1, 2, \ldots, n$, solutions of (8.3) such that $x^j(0) = x_0 + \xi e_j = (x_1^0, x_2^0, \ldots, x_{j-1}^0, x_j^0 + \xi, x_{j+1}^0, \ldots, x_n^0), \xi \in \mathbb{R}$, and let θ_i^j be the moments of discontinuity of $x^j(t)$. By Theorem 8.5.1, a solution $x^j(t), j = 1, 2, \ldots, n$, is defined on $[a, b]$ if $x_0 + \xi e_j$ belongs to $c^+(x_0, \delta)$ and $c^-(x_0, \delta)$ with sufficiently small δ.

Definition 8.7.1. The solution $x^0(t)$ is B-differentiable with respect to $x_j^0, j = 1, 2, \ldots, n$, on $[a, b]$ if for all $x_0 + \xi e_j$, which belong to $c^+(x_0, \delta)$ and $c^-(x_0, \delta)$ with sufficiently small δ it is true that:

A) there exist constants $v_{ij}, i = -k, \ldots, -1, 1, \ldots, m$, such that

$$\theta_i^j - \theta_i = v_{ij}\xi + o(|\xi|); \qquad (8.25)$$

B) for all $t \in [a, b] \setminus \cup_{i=-k}^{m} \widehat{(\theta_i, \theta_i^j]}$, the following equality is satisfied:

$$x^j(t) - x^0(t) = u_j(t)\xi + o(|\xi|), \qquad (8.26)$$

where $u_j(t) \in \mathcal{PC}([a, b], \theta])$.
The pair $\{u_j, \{v_{ij}\}_i\}$ is said to be a B-derivative of $x^0(t)$ with respect to x_j^0 on $[a, b]$.

Lemma 8.7.1. *Assume that conditions (C1)–(C6) hold. Then the solution $x^0(t)$ of (8.16) has B-derivatives with respect to x_j^0, $j = 1, 2, \ldots, n$, on $[a, b]$. Moreover, u_j is a solution of the linear system*

$$\frac{du}{dt} = f_x(x^0(t))u,$$
$$\Delta u|_{t=\theta_i} = W_{ix}(x^0(\theta_i))u(\theta_i), \qquad (8.27)$$

with $u(0) = e_j$, and constants $v_{ij} = 0$, for all i.

Proof. We shall prove the lemma with respect to x_1^0. Let $y_1(t) = y(t, 0, x_0 + \xi e_1)$. By the theorem on differentiability with respect to parameters [77] we have that $y_1(t) - x^0(t) = u_1(t)\xi + \rho(\xi)$, $\rho(\xi) = o(|\xi|)$, for all $t \in [0, \theta_1]$. Particularly, $y_1(\theta_1) - x^0(\theta_1) = u_1(\theta_1)\xi + \rho(|\xi|)$. Then $y_1(\theta_1+) - x^0(\theta_1+) = W_1(y_1(\theta_1)) - W_1(x^0(\theta_1)) = W_{1x}(x^0(\theta_1))[u_1(\theta_1)\xi + \rho(\xi)] + \bar{\rho}_1(\xi)$. Since $\bar{\rho}_1 = o(|\xi|)$, we have that $y_1(\theta_1+) - x^0(\theta_1+) = u_1(\theta_1+)\xi + \tilde{\rho}_1(\xi)$, where $\tilde{\rho}_1 = o(|\xi|)$. Denote by $U(t), U(\theta_1) = \mathcal{I}$, the fundamental matrix of the system $u'(t) = f_x(x^0(t))$. Using the theorem from [60, 77] one can obtain that for all $t \in (\theta_1, \theta_2]$ the following relation is true $y_1(t) - x^0(t) = U(t)(y_1(\theta_1+) - x^0(\theta_1+)) + \rho(y_1(\theta_1+) - x^0(\theta_1+)) = U(t)u_1(\theta_m+)\xi + \rho_2(\xi) = u_1(t)\xi + \rho_2(\xi)$, where $\rho_2 = o(|\xi|)$. Continuing the process we can prove that (8.26) is valid. Formula (8.25) is trivial. The lemma is proved. $\qquad \square$

Theorem 8.7.1. *Assume that conditions (C1)–(C6) are satisfied. Then the solution $x^0(t)$ of (8.3) has the B-derivative with respect to x_j^0, $j = 1, 2, \ldots, n$, on $[a, b]$. Moreover, the derivative $(u_j(t), \{v_{ij}\})$ is a solution of the variational system*

$$\frac{du}{dt} = f_x(x^0(t))u,$$
$$\Delta u|_{t=\theta_i} = W_{ix}(x^0(\theta_i))u(\theta_i),$$
$$v_{ij} = -\frac{\Phi_x u(\theta_i)}{\Phi_x f}, \qquad (8.28)$$

with $u(0) = e_j$.

The last theorem follows immediately Theorem 8.6.1, Lemma 8.7.1, and formulas (8.23), (8.24).

Remark 8.7.1. Higher order differentiability of DDS is considered in [3].

8.8 Conclusion

Let $D \subset \mathbb{R}^n$ be a set, which is described for system (8.3) in the introductory part of this chapter.

Definition 8.8.1. A B-smooth discontinuous flow is a map $\phi : \mathbb{R} \times D \to D$, which satisfies the following properties:

(I) The *group property*:

    (i) $\phi(0, x) : D \to D$ is the identity;
    (ii) $\phi(t, \phi(s, x)) = \phi(t + s, x)$ is valid for all $t, s \in \mathbb{R}$ and $x \in D$.

(II) $\phi(t, x) \in \mathcal{PC}^1(\mathbb{R})$ for each fixed $x \in D$.

(III) $\phi(t, x)$ is B-differentiable in $x \in D$ on $[a, b] \subset \mathbb{R}$ for each a, b such that the discontinuity points of $\phi(t, x)$ are interior points of $[a, b]$.

Remark 8.8.1. One can see that system (8.3) defines a B-smooth discontinuous flow provided that (C1)–(C7) and the conditions of one of the extension theorems are fulfilled.

Let us weaken the smoothness condition to obtain the definition of a discontinuous flow.

Definition 8.8.2. A B-flow is a map $\phi : \mathbb{R} \times D \to D$, which satisfies the property (I) of Definition 8.8.1 and the following conditions:

(IV) $\phi(t, x) \in \mathcal{PC}(\mathbb{R})$, for each fixed $x \in D$, and $\phi(\theta_i, x) \in \Gamma$, $\phi(\theta_i+, x) \in \tilde{\Gamma}$ for every discontinuity point.

(V) $\phi(t, x)$ is B-continuous in x on each finite and closed interval.

Remark 8.8.2. Comparing definitions of the B-differentiability and the B-continuity, one can conclude that every B-smooth discontinuous flow is a B-flow.

Exercise 8.8.1. Use the discontinuous dynamics to arrange a partition of D.

8.9 Examples

Example 8.9.1. Consider the following impulsive differential system:

$$x_1' = \alpha x_1 - \beta x_2,$$
$$x_2' = \beta x_1 + \alpha x_2,$$

$$\Delta x_1|_{x\in\Gamma} = (\sqrt{3}+1)x_1 - x_2$$
$$\Delta x_2|_{x\in\Gamma} = x_1 + (\sqrt{3}+1)x_2, \qquad (8.29)$$

where $\Gamma = \{(x_1,x_2)| \ x_2 = \frac{1}{2}x_1, x_1 > 0\}$, $\tilde{\Gamma} = \{(x_1,x_2)|x_2 = \frac{\sqrt{3}}{2}x_1, x_1 > 0\}$, constants α, β are positive. One can see that $\Phi(x) = x_2 - \frac{1}{2}x_1$, $f(x) = (\alpha x_1 - \beta x_2, \beta x_1 + \alpha x_2)$, $J(x) = (\sqrt{3}x_1 - x_2, x_1 + \sqrt{3}x_2)$. We assume that

$$D = \mathbb{R}^2 \setminus \left[\left\{ (x_1,x_2)| \ \frac{1}{2}x_1 < x_2 < \frac{\sqrt{3}}{2}x_1, \quad x_1 > 0 \right\} \cup (0,0) \right].$$

One can verify that the functions and the sets satisfy (C1)–(C7). Let us check if the conditions of Theorem 8.3.3 are fulfilled. Fix $x \in \tilde{\Gamma}$. Then dist$(x, \Gamma) = \frac{1}{2}||x||$ and

$$||f(x)|| = \sqrt{(\alpha x_1 - \beta x_2)^2 + (\beta x_1 + \alpha x_2)^2} = \sqrt{\alpha^2 + \beta^2}||x||.$$

Thus

$$\sup_{B(x,\epsilon_x)} ||f|| = \sqrt{\alpha^2 + \beta^2}(||x|| + \frac{1}{2}||x||) = \frac{3}{2}\sqrt{\alpha^2 + \beta^2}||x||,$$

and

$$\inf_{\tilde{\Gamma}\times(0,\infty)} \frac{\epsilon_x}{\sup_{B(x,\epsilon_x)} ||f||} = \frac{2}{3\sqrt{\alpha^2 + \beta^2}} > 0.$$

Hence, all conditions of a discontinuous flow are fulfilled.

Example 8.9.2. Consider the following model of a simple neural nets from [123]. We have modified it according to the system (8.3).

$$x_1' = x_2,$$
$$x_2' = -\beta^2 x_1,$$
$$p' = -\gamma p + x_1 + B_0,$$
$$\Delta p|_{(x,p)\in\Gamma} = -p, \qquad (8.30)$$

where $\Gamma = \{(x_1, x_2, p)| \ p = r, \ x_1^2 + \frac{x_2^2}{\beta^4} < 1\}$, $\tilde{\Gamma} = \{(x_1, x_2, p)| \ p = 0, \ x_1^2 + \frac{x_2^2}{\beta^4} < 1\}$, $\Phi(x) = p - r, f(x) = (x_2, -\beta^2 x_1, -\gamma p + x_1 + B_0)$, $J(x) = (x_1, x_2, 0)$, $\beta, \gamma, r > 0$, are constants and $B_0 > \gamma r + 1$. We assume that $D = \{(x_1, x_2, p)|0 \le p \le r, x_1^2 + \frac{x_2^2}{\beta^4} < 1\}$. The variable p is a scalar input of a neural trigger and x_1, x_2, are other variables. The value of r is the threshold. One can verify that the functions and the sets satisfy (C1)–(C7) and the conditions of Theorem 8.3.4. That is, the system defines a B-smooth discontinuous flow.

Example 8.9.3. Let us consider the following system

$$x_1' = \alpha x_1 - \beta x_2,$$
$$x_2' = \beta x_1 + \alpha x_2,$$
$$\Delta x_1|_{x \in \Gamma} = (1 + k)x_1,$$
$$\Delta x_2|_{x \in \Gamma} = (1 + k)x_2, \tag{8.31}$$

where $\Gamma = \{(x_1, x_2)| x_1^2 + x_2^2 = r\}$, $\tilde{\Gamma} = \{(x_1, x_2)| x_1^2 + x_2^2 = kr\}$, α, β, k are constants such that $\alpha, \beta < 0, 1 < k$. Assume that $D = \mathbb{R}^2$. One can see that all conditions (C1)–(C6) are valid for the system. But (C7) is not fulfilled. It is easy to see that a solution $x(t, 0, x_0)$ of (8.31), which starts outside of $\tilde{\Gamma}$, does not satisfy the condition $x(-t, 0, x(t, 0, x_0)) = x_0$ for all t. Thus (8.31) does not determine a discontinuous flow.

Notes

Apparently, T. Pavlidis [123, 124], was the first, who formulated the problem of conditions for autonomous equations with discontinuities, which guarantee properties of dynamical systems. Papers [123, 124, 135, 136] contain interesting practical and theoretical ideas concerning discontinuous flows. These authors formulated some important conditions on differential equations, but not all of them were used to prove basic properties of discontinuous flows. Some ideas on the dynamical properties can be found also in [54, 87, 95, 111].

The chapter embodies results that provide conditions for the existence of a *discontinuous flow* and a *differentiable discontinuous flow*. Concepts of B-continuous and B-differentiable dependence of solutions on initial values are applied to describe DDS and to obtain conditions for the extension of solutions and the group property. Since DF have specific smoothness of solutions we call these systems *B-differentiable discontinuous flows*. The results are due to [1]. Since some conditions of the chapter are sufficient, but not necessary, one can develop them, but we are confident that B-continuity and B-differentiability of a motion cannot be ignored in the future investigations. It is obvious that results of the chapter can be extended for smooth of higher order and analytic discontinuous dynamics.

Chapter 9
Perturbations and Hopf Bifurcation of a Discontinuous Limit Cycle

This chapter is organized in the following manner. In the first section, we give the description of the systems under consideration and prove the theorem of existence of foci and centers of the nonperturbed system. The main subject of Sect. 9.2 is foci of the perturbed equation. The noncritical case is considered. In Sect. 9.3, the problem of distinguishing between the center and the focus is solved. Bifurcation of a periodic solution is investigated in Sect. 9.4. The last section consists of examples illustrating the bifurcation theorem.

9.1 The Nonperturbed System

Denote by $< x, y >$ the dot-product of vectors $x, y \in \mathbb{R}^2$, and $||x|| = < x, x >^{\frac{1}{2}}$ the norm of a vector $x \in \mathbb{R}^2$. Moreover, let $\mathcal{R}$ be the set of all real valued constant 2×2 matrices, and $\mathcal{I} \in \mathcal{R}$ be the identity matrix.

D_0-system. Consider the following differential equation with impulses:

$$\frac{dx}{dt} = Ax,$$
$$\Delta x|_{x \in \Gamma_0} = B_0 x, \tag{9.1}$$

where Γ_0 is a subset of $\mathbb{R}^2$, and it will be described below, $A, B_0 \in \mathcal{R}$.

The following assumptions will be needed throughout this chapter:

(C1) $\Gamma_0 = \cup_{i=1}^{p} s_i$, where p is a fixed natural number and half-lines $s_i, i = 1, 2, \ldots, p$, are defined by equations $< a^i, x >= 0$, where $a^i = (a_1^i, a_2^i)$ are constant vectors. The origin does not belong to the lines (see Fig. 9.1).

(C2)

$$A = \begin{pmatrix} \alpha & -\beta \\ \beta & \alpha \end{pmatrix},$$

where $\alpha, \beta \in \mathbb{R}, \beta \neq 0$;

M. Akhmet, *Principles of Discontinuous Dynamical Systems*,
DOI 10.1007/978-1-4419-6581-3_9, © Springer Science+Business Media, LLC 2010

Fig. 9.1 The domain of the
nonperturbed system (9.1)
with a vertex which unites the
straight lines $s_i, i = 1, 2, \ldots, p$

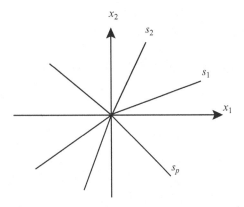

(C3) there exists a regular matrix $Q \in \mathcal{R}$ and nonnegative real numbers k and θ
such that

$$B_0 = kQ \begin{pmatrix} \cos\theta & -\sin\theta \\ \sin\theta & \cos\theta \end{pmatrix} Q^{-1} - \begin{pmatrix} 1 & 0 \\ 0 & 1 \end{pmatrix};$$

We consider every angle for a point with respect to the positive half-line of
the first coordinate axis. Denote $s_i' = (\mathcal{I} + B_0)s_i, i = 1, 2, \ldots, p$. Let γ_i and
ζ_i be angles of s_i and $s_i', i = 1, 2, \ldots, p$, respectively,

$$B_0 = \begin{pmatrix} b_{11} & b_{12} \\ b_{21} & b_{22} \end{pmatrix}.$$

(C4) $0 < \gamma_1 < \zeta_1 < \gamma_2 < \cdots < \gamma_p < \zeta_p < 2\pi, (b_{11} + 1)\cos\gamma_i + b_{12}\sin\gamma_i \neq 0,$
$i = 1, 2, \ldots, p.$

If conditions (C1)–(C4) hold, then (9.1) is said to be a $D_0 - system$.

Exercise 9.1.1. Verify that the origin is a unique singular point of a $D_0 -$ system
and (9.1) is not a linear system.

Exercise 9.1.2. Using the results of the last chapter, prove that $D_0 -$ system (9.1)
provides a B-smooth discontinuous flow.

If we use transformation $x_1 = r\cos(\phi), x_2 = r\sin(\phi)$ in (9.1) and exclude the
time variable t, we can find that the solution $r(\phi, r_0)$ which starts at the point $(0, r_0)$,
satisfies the following system:

$$\frac{dr}{d\phi} = \lambda r,$$

$$\Delta r \mid_{\phi = \gamma_i \, (\mathrm{mod} 2\pi)} = k_i r, \qquad (9.2)$$

where $\lambda = \frac{\alpha}{\beta}$, the angle-variable ϕ is ranged over the set

$$R_\phi = \cup_{i=-\infty}^{\infty}[\cup_{j=1}^{p-1}(2\pi i + \zeta_j, 2\pi i + \gamma_{j+1}] \cup (2\pi i + \zeta_p, 2\pi(i+1) + \gamma_1]]$$

and $k_i = [((b_{11}+1)\cos(\gamma_i)+b_{12}\sin(\gamma_i))^2+(b_{21}\cos(\gamma_i)+(b_{22}+1)\sin(\gamma_i))^2]^{\frac{1}{2}}-1$.
Equation (9.2) is 2π-periodic, so we shall consider just the section $\phi \in [0, 2\pi]$ in what follows. That is, the system

$$\frac{dr}{d\phi} = \lambda r,$$

$$\Delta r \mid_{\phi=\gamma_i} = k_i r, \tag{9.3}$$

is considered with $\phi \in [0, 2\pi]_\phi \equiv [0, 2\pi] \setminus \cup_{i=1}^{p} (\gamma_i, \zeta_i]$. System (9.3) is a sample of the time scale differential equation with transition condition [19]. We shall reduce (9.3) to an impulsive differential equation [4, 19] for the investigation's needs. Indeed, let us introduce a new variable $\psi = \phi - \sum_{0<\gamma_j<\phi} \theta_j$, $\theta_j = \zeta_j - \gamma_j$, with the range $[0, 2\pi - \sum_{i=1}^{p} \theta_i]$. We shall call this new variable ψ-substitution. It is easy to check that upon ψ-substitution the solution $r(\phi, r_0)$ satisfies the following impulsive equation:

$$\frac{dr}{d\psi} = \lambda r,$$

$$\Delta r \mid_{\psi=\delta_j} = k_j r, \tag{9.4}$$

where $\delta_j = \gamma_j - \sum_{0<\gamma_i<\gamma_j} \theta_i$. Solving the last impulsive system and using the inverse of ψ-substitution, one can obtain that the solution $r(\phi, r_0)$ of (9.2) has the form

$$r(\phi, r_0) = \exp(\lambda(\phi - \sum_{0<\gamma_i<\phi} \theta_i)) \prod_{0<\gamma_i<\phi} (1 + k_i)r_0, \tag{9.5}$$

if $\phi \in [0, 2\pi]_\phi$.

Denote

$$q = \exp(\lambda(2\pi - \sum_{i=1}^{p} \theta_i)) \prod_{i=1}^{p} (1 + k_i). \tag{9.6}$$

Applying the Poincaré return map $r(2\pi, r_0)$ to (9.5) one can obtain that the following theorem follows.

Theorem 9.1.1. *If*

(1) $q = 1$, then the origin is a center and all solutions of (9.1) are periodic with period $T = (2\pi - \sum_{i=1}^{p} \theta_i)\beta^{-1}$;
(2) $q < 1$, then the origin is a stable focus;
(3) $q > 1$, then the origin is an unstable focus of $D_0 - $ system.

9.2 The Perturbed System

Theorem 2.4.1 of the last section implies that if conditions (C1)–(C4) are valid, then each trajectory of (9.1) either spirals to the origin or is a discontinuous cycle. Moreover, if the trajectory spirals to the origin then it spirals to infinity, too. That is, the asymptotic behavior of the trajectory is very similar to the behavior of trajectories of the planar linear system of ordinary differential equations with constant coefficients [59,77]. In what follows, we will consider how a perturbation may change the phase portrait of the system.

D-system. Let us consider the following equation:

$$\frac{dx}{dt} = Ax + f(x),$$

$$\Delta x|_{x \in \Gamma} = B(x)x, \tag{9.7}$$

in a neighborhood G of the origin.

The following is the list of conditions assumed for this system:

(C5) $\Gamma = \cup_{i=1}^{p} l_i$ is a set of curves which start at the origin and are determined by the equations $< a^i, x > + \tau_i(x) = 0, i = 1, 2, \ldots, p$. The origin does not belong to the curves (see Fig. 9.2).

(C6)

$$B(x) = (k + \kappa(x))Q \begin{pmatrix} \cos(\theta + \upsilon(x)) & -\sin(\theta + \upsilon(x)) \\ \sin(\theta + \upsilon(x)) & \cos(\theta + \upsilon(x)) \end{pmatrix} Q^{-1} - \begin{pmatrix} 1 & 0 \\ 0 & 1 \end{pmatrix},$$

$(\mathcal{I} + B(x))x \in G$ for all $x \in G$;

(C7) $\{f, \kappa, \upsilon\} \subset C^{(1)}(G), \{\tau_i, i = 1, 2, \ldots, p\} \subset C^{(2)}(G);$

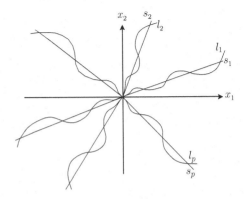

Fig. 9.2 The domain of the perturbed system (9.7) near a vertex which unites the curves l_i associated with the straight lines $s_i, i = 1, 2, \ldots, p$

(C8) $f(x) = o(||x||)$, $\kappa(x) = o(||x||)$, $\upsilon(x) = o(||x||)$, $\tau_i(x) = o(||x||^2)$, $i = 1, 2, \ldots, p$;

Moreover, we assume that the matrices A, Q, the vectors $a^i, i = 1, 2, \ldots, p$, and constants k, θ are the same as in (9.1), i.e.,

(C9) the associated with (9.7) system (9.1) is D_0-system.

If conditions (C1)–(C9) hold, then the system (9.7) is said to be a D-system. If G is sufficiently small, then conditions (C4) and (C8) imply that none of curves l_i intersect itself, they do not intersect each other, and the origin is a unique singular point of the D-system.

Exercise 9.2.1. Using the results of the last chapter, and Example 9.1.2, prove that D-system defines a B-smooth discontinuous flow.

Assume, without loss of generality, that $\gamma_i \neq \frac{\pi}{2} j$, $j = 1, 3$, and transform the equations in (C5) to the polar coordinates so that $l_i : a_i^1 r \cos(\phi) + a_i^2 r \sin(\phi) + \tau_i(r \cos(\phi), r \sin(\phi)) = 0$ or

$$\phi = \tan^{-1}\left(\tan \gamma_i - \frac{\tau_i}{a_i^2 r \cos(\phi)}\right).$$

Now, use Taylor's expansion to get that

$$l_i : \phi = \gamma_i + r \psi_i(r, \phi), \tag{9.8}$$

$i = 1, 2, \ldots, p$, where ψ_i are 2π-perodic in ϕ, continuously differentiable functions, and $\psi_i = O(r)$. If the point $x(t)$ meets the discontinuity curve l_i with an angle θ, then the point $x(\theta+)$ belongs to the curve $l_i' = \{z \in \mathbb{R}^2 | z = (\mathcal{I} + B(x))x, x \in l_i\}$. The following assertion is very important for the rest of the chapter.

Lemma 9.2.1. *Suppose (C7) and (C8) are satisfied. Then the curve l_i', $1 \leq i \leq p$, is placed between l_i and l_{i+1}, if G is sufficiently small.*

Proof. Fix $i = 1, 2, \ldots, p$, and assume that $s_i, s_{i+1}, l_i, l_{i+1}$ are transformed by the map $y = Q^{-1}x$ into lines $s_i'', s_{i+1}'', l_i'', l_{i+1}''$ respectively. Set $L_i = \{z \in \mathbb{R}^2 | z = Q^{-1}(I + B(Qy))Qy, y \in l_i''\}$, $\xi_i = Q^{-1}(I + B_0)Qs_i''$, and let $\gamma_i', \gamma_{i+1}', \zeta_i'$ be the angles of straight lines s_i'', s_{i+1}'', ξ_i. We may assume, without loss of generality, that $\gamma_i' < \zeta_i' < \gamma_{i+1}'$. To prove the lemma, it is sufficient to check whether L_i lies between curves l_i'', l_{i+1}''. Suppose that $0 < \gamma_i' < \zeta_i' < \gamma_{i+1}' < \frac{\pi}{2}$. Otherwise one can use a linear transformation, which does not change the relation of the curves. Let $c_1 y_1 + c_2 y_2 + l^*(y_1, y_2) = 0$ be the equation of the line l_i''. Use the polar coordinates $y_1 = \rho \cos(\phi)$, $y_2 = \rho \sin(\phi)$, and obtain $\phi = \gamma_i' + \rho \psi^*(\rho, \phi)$, where $\psi^*(\rho, \phi) = O(\rho)$ and ψ^* is a 2π-periodic function. If $y = (y_1, y_2) \in l_i''$ then the point

$$y^+ = Q^{-1}(B(Qy) + I)Qy, \tag{9.9}$$

where $y^+ = (y_1^+, y_2^+)$, belongs to L_i. Assume without loss of generality that $y_1^+ \neq 0$. Otherwise use the condition $y_2^+ \neq 0$. If we set $\rho = (y_1^2 + y_2^2)^{\frac{1}{2}}$, $\phi = \tan^{-1}(\frac{y_2}{y_1})$, $\rho^+ = ((y_1^+)^2 + (y_2^+)^2)^{\frac{1}{2}}$, $\phi^+ = \tan^{-1}(\frac{y_2^+}{y_1^+})$ then (9.9) implies that

$$\rho^+ = k_i \rho + \rho \beta^*(\rho, \phi), \tag{9.10}$$

$$\phi^+ = \phi + \theta + \gamma^*(\rho, \phi), \tag{9.11}$$

where β^* and γ^* are 2π-periodic in ϕ functions and $\beta^* = O(\rho), \gamma^* = O(\rho)$. Let $\sigma(y_1, y_2) = c_1 y_1 + c_2 y_2 + l^*(y_1, y_2)$. Then

$$\sigma(y_1^+, y_2^+) = \rho^+(c_1 \cos(\phi^+) + c_2 \sin(\phi^+)) + l^*(\rho^+ \cos(\phi^+), \rho^+ \sin(\phi^+)) =$$

$$\rho^+ \sqrt{c_1^2 + c_2^2} \sin(\theta + \upsilon(\rho, \phi) - \rho \psi^*(\rho, \psi)) + l^*(\rho^+ \cos(\phi^+), \rho^+ \sin(\phi^+)),$$

where $\upsilon(\rho, \phi) = \upsilon(Qy)$. It is readily seen that the sign of $\sigma(\rho^+, \phi^+)$ is the same as of $\sin(\theta)$, if ρ is sufficiently small. Consequently, $\sigma(\rho^+, \phi^+) > 0$. Thus, the curve L_i is placed above the curve l_i'' in the first quarter of the plane $Ox_1 x_2$. Similarly, one can show that it is placed below l_{i+1}''. The lemma is proved.   □

The last lemma guarantees that, if G is sufficiently small, then every nontrivial trajectory of the system (9.7) meets each of the lines $l_i, i = 1, 2, \ldots, p$, precisely once within any time interval of length T.

9.3   Foci of the D-System

Utilize the polar coordinates $x_1 = r \cos(\phi)$, $x_2 = r \sin(\phi)$ to reduce the differential part of (9.7) to the following form:

$$\frac{dr}{d\phi} = \lambda r + P(r, \phi).$$

It is known [38, 59, 107, 117], that $P(r, \phi)$ is 2π-periodic, continuously differentiable function, and $P = o(r)$. Set $x^+ = (x_1^+, x_2^+) = (\mathcal{I} + B(x))x$, $x^+ = r^+(\cos\phi^+, \sin\phi^+)$, $\tilde{x}^+ = (\tilde{x}_1^+, \tilde{x}_2^+) = (\mathcal{I} + B(0))x$, where $x = (x_1, x_2) \in l_i, i = 1, 2, \ldots, p$. One can find that the inequality $||x^+ - \tilde{x}^+|| \leq ||B(x) - B(0)||\,||x||$ implies $r^+ = r + k_i r + \omega(r, \phi)$. Use the relation between $\frac{x_2^+}{x_1^+}$ and $\frac{\tilde{x}_2^+}{\tilde{x}_1^+}$ and condition (C5) to obtain that $\phi^+ = \phi + \theta_i + \gamma(r, \phi)$.

Functions ω, γ are 2π-periodic in ϕ and $\omega = o(r), \gamma(r, \phi) = o(r)$. Finally, (9.7) has the form

$$\frac{dr}{d\phi} = \lambda r + P(r, \phi),$$

$$\Delta r \mid_{(\rho, \phi) \in l_i} = k_i r + \omega(r, \phi),$$

$$\Delta \phi \mid_{(\rho, \phi) \in l_i} = \theta_i + \gamma(r, \phi). \tag{9.12}$$

It is convenient to introduce the following version of B-equivalence.

Introduce the following system:

$$\frac{d\rho}{d\phi} = \lambda \rho + P(\rho, \phi),$$

$$\Delta \rho \mid_{\phi = \gamma_i} = k_i \rho + w_i(\rho),$$

$$\Delta \phi \mid_{\phi = \gamma_i} = \theta_i, \tag{9.13}$$

where all elements, except w_i, $i = 1, 2, \ldots, p$, are the same as in (9.12) and the domain of (9.13) is $[0, 2\pi]_\phi$. Functions w_i will be defined below.

Let $r(\phi, r_0), r(0, r_0) = r_0$, be a solution of (9.12) and ϕ_i be the angle where the solution intersects l_i. Denote by $\chi_i = \phi_i + \theta_i + \gamma(r(\phi_i, r_0), \phi_i)$ the angle of $r(\phi, r_0)$ after the jump.

We shall say that systems (9.12) and (9.13) are B-equivalent in G if there exists a neighborhood $G_1 \subset G$ of the origin such that for every solution $r(\phi, r_0)$ of (9.12) whose trajectory is in G_1 there exists a solution $\rho(\phi, r_0), \rho(0, r_0) = r_0$, of (9.13) which satisfies the relation

$$r(\phi, r_0) = \rho(\phi, r_0), \phi \in [0, 2\pi]_\phi \setminus \cup_{i=1}^{p} \{[\phi_i, \hat{\gamma_i},] \cup [\hat{\zeta_i}, \hat{\chi_i}]\}, \tag{9.14}$$

and, conversely, for every solution $\rho(\phi, r_0)$ of (9.13) whose trajectory is in G_1 there exists a solution $r(\phi, r_0)$ of (9.12) which satisfies (9.14).

We will define functions w_i such that systems (9.12) and (9.13) are B-equivalent in G, if the domain is sufficiently small.

Fix i. Let $r_1(\phi, \gamma_i, \rho), r_1(\gamma_i, \gamma_i, \rho) = \rho$, be a solution of the equation

$$\frac{dr}{d\phi} = \lambda r + P(r, \phi) \tag{9.15}$$

and $\phi = \eta_i$ be the meeting angle of $r_1(\phi, \gamma_i, \rho)$ with l_i. Then

$$r_1(\eta_i, \gamma_i, \rho) = \exp(\lambda(\eta_i - \gamma_i)\rho + \int_{\gamma_i}^{\eta_i} \exp(\lambda(\eta_i - s) P(r_1(s, \gamma_i, \rho), s) ds.$$

Let $\eta_i^1 = \eta_i + \theta_i + \gamma(r_1(\eta_i, \gamma_i, \rho), \eta_i), \rho^1 = (1 + k_i)r_1(\eta_i, \gamma_i, \rho)$ $+ \omega(r(\eta_i, \gamma_i, \rho), \eta_i)$, and $r_2(\phi, \eta_i^1, \rho^1)$ be the solution of system (9.15),

$$r_2(\zeta_i, \eta_i^1, \rho^1) = \exp(\lambda(\zeta_i - \eta_i^1))\rho^1 + \int_{\eta_i^1}^{\zeta_i} \exp(\lambda(\zeta_i - s)P(r_2(s, \eta_i^1, \rho^1), s)ds.$$

Introduce

$$w_i(\rho) = r_2(\zeta_i, \eta_i^1, \rho^1) - (1 + k_i)\rho = \exp(\lambda(\zeta_i - \eta_i^1)[(1 + k_i)(\exp(\lambda(\eta_i - \gamma_i))\rho +$$

$$\int_{\gamma_i}^{\eta_i} \exp(\lambda(\eta_i - s))P(r_1(s, \gamma_i, \rho), s)ds) + \omega(r_1(\eta_i, \gamma_i, \rho), \eta_i)] +$$

$$\int_{\eta_i^1}^{\zeta_i} \exp(\lambda(\zeta_i - s)P(r_2(s, \eta_i^1, \rho^1), s)ds - (1 + k)\rho$$

or, if simplified,

$$w_i(\rho) = (1 + k)[\exp(-\lambda\gamma(r_1(\eta_i, \gamma_i, \rho), \eta_i)) - 1]\rho +$$

$$(1 + k)\int_{\gamma_i}^{\eta_i} \exp(\lambda(\zeta_i - \theta_i - s - \rho\gamma(r_1(\eta_i, \gamma_i, \rho), \eta_i)))P(r_1(s, \gamma_i, \rho), s)ds +$$

$$\int_{\eta_i^1}^{\zeta_i} \exp(\lambda(\zeta_i - s))P(r_2(s, \eta_i^1, \rho^1), s)ds +$$

$$\exp(\lambda(\zeta_i - \eta_i^1))\omega(r_1(\eta_i, \gamma_i, \rho), \eta_i). \tag{9.16}$$

Differentiating (9.8) and (9.16) one can find that

$$\frac{d\eta_i}{d\rho} = \frac{\frac{\partial r_1}{\partial \rho}[\psi_i + r_1\frac{\partial\psi_i}{\partial r}]}{1 - (\lambda r_1 + P)[\psi_i + r_1\frac{\partial\psi_i}{\partial r}] - r_1\frac{\partial\psi_i}{\partial\phi}}, \quad \frac{d\eta_i^1}{d\rho} = \frac{d\eta_i}{d\rho}(1 + \frac{\partial\gamma}{\partial\phi}) + \frac{\partial\gamma}{\partial r}\frac{\partial r_1}{\partial\rho},$$

$$\frac{dw_i}{d\rho} = (1 + k_i)[e^{-\lambda\gamma} - 1] - \lambda(1 + k_i)e^{-\lambda\gamma}(\frac{\partial\gamma}{\partial r}\frac{\partial r_1}{\partial\rho} + \frac{\partial\gamma}{\partial\phi}\frac{d\eta_i}{d\rho})\rho +$$

$$(1 + k_i)e^{\lambda(\zeta_i - \theta_i - \eta_i - \gamma)}P\frac{d\eta_i}{d\rho} +$$

$$(1 + k_i)\int_{\gamma_i}^{\eta_i} e^{\lambda(\zeta_i - \theta - s - \gamma)}\{-\lambda(\frac{\partial\gamma}{\partial r}\frac{\partial r_1}{\partial\rho} + \frac{\partial\gamma}{\partial\phi}\frac{d\eta_i}{d\rho})P - \frac{\partial P}{\partial r}\frac{\partial r_1}{\partial\rho} - \frac{\partial P}{\partial\phi}\frac{d\eta_i}{d\rho}\}ds +$$

$$\int_{\eta_i^1}^{\zeta_i} e^{\lambda(\zeta_i - s)}\frac{\partial P(r_2(s, \eta_i^1, \rho^1), s)}{\partial r}\frac{\partial r_2}{\partial\rho}ds - e^{\lambda(\zeta_i - \eta_i^1)}P(\rho^1, \eta_i^1)\frac{\partial\eta_i^1}{\partial\rho} +$$

$$e^{\lambda(\zeta_i - \eta_i^1)}[-\frac{\partial\eta_i^1}{\partial\rho}\omega + \frac{\partial\omega}{\partial r}\frac{\partial r_1}{\partial\rho} + \frac{\partial\omega}{\partial\phi}\frac{d\eta_i}{d\rho}]. \tag{9.17}$$

Analyzing (9.16) and (9.17) one can prove that the following two lemmas are valid.

Lemma 9.3.1. *If conditions (C1)–(C5) are valid then w_i is a continuously differentable function, and $w_i(\rho) = o(\rho), i = 1, 2, \ldots, p$.*

Lemma 9.3.2. *The systems (9.12) and (9.13) are B-equivalent if G is sufficiently small.*

Theorem 9.3.1. *Suppose that (C1)–(C6) are satisfied and $q < 1$ $(q > 1)$. Then the origin is a stable (unstable) focus of system (9.7).*

Proof. Let $r(\phi, r_0), r(0, r_0) = r_0$, be the solution of (9.12), and $\rho(\phi, r_0)$, $\rho(0, r_0) = r_0$, be the solution of (9.13). Using ψ-substitution one can obtain that

$$
\rho(\phi, r_0) = \exp(\lambda\phi)\{\Pi_{i=1}^m(1 + k_i)\exp(-\lambda\sum_{s=1}^m\theta_s)r_0 +
$$

$$
\Pi_{i=1}^m(1 + k_i)\exp(-\lambda\sum_{s=1}^m\theta_s)\int_0^{\gamma_1}\exp(-\lambda u)Pdu +
$$

$$
\Pi_{i=2}^m(1 + k_i)\exp(-\lambda\sum_{s=2}^m\theta_s)\int_{\zeta_1}^{\gamma_2}\exp(-\lambda u)Pdu + \ldots
$$

$$
\int_{\zeta_m}^\phi\exp(-\lambda u)Pdu + \Pi_{i=2}^m(1 + k_i)\exp(-\lambda\sum_{s=2}^m\theta_s)w_1 +
$$

$$
\Pi_{i=3}^m(1 + k_i)\exp(-\lambda\sum_{s=3}^m\theta_s)w_2\ldots + \exp(-\lambda\zeta_m)w_m\}, \tag{9.18}
$$

where $\phi \in [0, 2\pi]_\phi, P = P(\rho(\phi, r_0), \phi), w_i = w_i(\rho(\gamma_i, r_0)$. Now, applying Theorem 6.1.1, conditions (C4), (C5), and Lemma 9.3.1 one can find that the solution $\rho(\psi, r_0)$ is differentiable in r_0 and the derivative $\frac{\partial\rho(\phi, r_0)}{\partial r_0}$ at the point $(2\pi, 0)$ is equal to q. Since (9.12) and (9.13) are B-equivalent it follows that:

$$
\frac{\partial r(2\pi, 0)}{\partial r_0} = q
$$

and the proof is completed. $\square$

9.4 The Center and Focus Problem

Throughout this section we assume that $q = 1$. That is, the critical case is considered. Functions $f, \kappa, v, \tau_i, i = 1, 2, \ldots, p$, are assumed to be analytic in G. By condition (C8), Taylor's expansions of functions f, κ, and v start with members of order not less than 2, and the expansions of $\tau_i, i = 1, 2, \ldots, p$, start with members of order not less than 3. First, we investigate the problem for (9.13) all of whose elements are analytic functions, if ρ is sufficiently small. Theorem 6.4.2 implies that $w_i, i = 1, 2, \ldots, p$, are analytic functions in ρ and the solution $\rho(\phi, r_0)$ of equation (9.13) has the following expansion:

$$\rho(\phi, r_0) = \sum_{i=0}^{\infty} \rho_i(\phi) r_0^i, \tag{9.19}$$

where $\phi \notin (\gamma_i, \zeta_i], i = 1, 2, \ldots, p, \rho_0(\phi) = 0, q = \rho_1(\phi) = 1$. One can define the Poincaré return map

$$\rho(2\pi, r_0) = \sum_{i=1}^{\infty} a_i r_0^i, \tag{9.20}$$

where $a_i = \rho_i(2\pi), i \geq 1, a_1 = q = 1$. The expansions exist, see Sect. 6.4, such that

$$P(\rho, \phi) = \sum_{i=2}^{\infty} P_i(\phi) \rho^i,$$

$$w_j(\rho) = \sum_{i=2}^{\infty} w_{ji} \rho^i, \tag{9.21}$$

where $P_i(\phi), w_{ji}(\phi), j \geq 2$, are 2π-periodic functions which can be defined by using (9.12). The coefficient $\rho_j(\phi), j \geq 2$, is the solution of the system

$$\frac{d\rho}{d\phi} = P_j(\phi),$$

$$\Delta\rho \mid_{\phi \neq \gamma_i} = w_{ji},$$

$$\Delta\phi \mid_{\phi \neq \gamma_i} = \theta_i, \tag{9.22}$$

with the initial condition $\rho_j(0) = 0$. Hence, coefficients of (9.20) are equal to

$$a_j = \int_0^{\gamma_1} P_j(\phi) d\phi + \sum_{i=1}^{p-1} \int_{\zeta_i}^{\gamma_{i+1}} P_j(\phi) d\phi + \int_{\zeta_p}^{2\pi} P_j(\phi) d\phi + \sum_{i=1}^{p} w_{ji}. \tag{9.23}$$

From (9.20) and (9.23) it follows that the following lemma is true.

Lemma 9.4.1. *Let $q = 1$ and the first nonzero element of the sequence $a_j, j \geq 2$, be negative (positive), then the origin is a stable (unstable) focus of (9.13). If $a_j = 0, j \geq 2$, then the origin is a center of (9.13).*

B-equivalence of systems (9.12) and (9.13) implies immediately that the following theorem is valid.

Theorem 9.4.1. *Let $q = 1$ and the first nonzero element of the sequence a_j, $j \geq 2$, be negative (positive), then the origin is a stable (unstable) focus of (9.7). If $a_j = 0$ for all $j \geq 2$, then the origin is a center of (9.7).*

9.5 Bifurcation of a Discontinuous Limit Cycle

We consider the following system:

$$\frac{dx}{dt} = Ax + f(x) + \mu F(x, \mu),$$
$$\Delta x|_{x \in \Gamma(\mu)} = B(x, \mu)x. \tag{9.24}$$

To establish the Hopf bifurcation theorem we need the following assumptions:

(A1) the set $\Gamma(\mu) = \cup_{i=1}^{p} l_i(\mu)$ is a union of curves in G, which start at the origin and do not include it, $l_i : (a^i, x) + \tau_i(x) + \mu \nu(x, \mu) = 0, 1 \leq i \leq p$;

(A2) there exist a matrix $Q(\mu) \in \mathcal{R}, Q(0) = Q$, analytic in $(-\mu_0, \mu_0)$, and real numbers γ, χ such that $Q^{-1}(\mu) B(x, \mu) Q(\mu) =$

$$(k + \mu\gamma + \kappa(x)) \begin{pmatrix} \cos(\theta + \mu\chi + \upsilon(x)) & -\sin(\theta + \mu\chi + \upsilon(x)) \\ \sin(\theta + \mu\chi + \upsilon(x)) & \cos(\theta + \mu\chi + \upsilon(x)) \end{pmatrix} - \begin{pmatrix} 1 & 0 \\ 0 & 1 \end{pmatrix};$$

(A3) associated with (9.24) systems

$$\frac{dx}{dt} = Ax,$$
$$\Delta x|_{x \in \Gamma(0)} = B_0 x, \tag{9.25}$$

and

$$\frac{dx}{dt} = Ax + f(x),$$
$$\Delta x|_{x \in \Gamma(0)} = B(x, 0)x, \tag{9.26}$$

are D_0-system and D-system, respectively;

(A4) functions $\kappa, \upsilon : G \to \mathbb{R}^2$ and $F, \nu : G \times (-\mu_0, \mu_0) \to \mathbb{R}^2$ are analytic in $G \times (-\mu_0, \mu_0)$;

(A5) $F(0, \mu) = 0, \nu(0, \mu) = 0$, for all $\mu \in (-\mu_0, \mu_0)$.

Additionally, we shall need the following system:

$$\frac{dx}{dt} = A(\mu)x,$$
$$\Delta x|_{x \in \Gamma_0(\mu)} = B(0, \mu)x, \tag{9.27}$$

where $A(\mu) = A + \mu \frac{\partial F(0,\mu)}{\partial x}$, and $\Gamma_0(\mu) = \cup_{i=1}^p m_i$ with

$$m_i : \quad (a^i + \mu \frac{\partial v(0,\mu)}{\partial x}, x) = 0, \quad i = 1, 2, \ldots, p.$$

The polar transformation takes (9.24) to the following form:

$$\frac{dr}{d\phi} = \lambda r + P(r, \phi, \mu),$$

$$\Delta r \mid_{(r,\phi) \in l_i(\mu)} = k_i r + \omega(r, \phi, \mu),$$

$$\Delta \phi \mid_{(r,\phi) \in l_i(\mu)} = \theta_i + r\gamma(r, \phi, \mu). \tag{9.28}$$

The functions $w_i(\rho, \mu)$ can be defined in the same manner as in (9.16) such that the system

$$\frac{d\rho}{d\phi} = \lambda\rho + P(\rho, \phi, \mu), \ \phi \neq \gamma_i(\mu),$$

$$\Delta\rho \mid_{\phi=\gamma_i(\mu)} = k_i \rho + w_i(\rho, \mu),$$

$$\Delta\phi \mid_{\phi=\gamma_i(\mu)} = \theta_i(\mu), \tag{9.29}$$

where $\gamma_i(\mu), i = 1, 2, \ldots, p$, are angles of m_i, is B-equivalent to (9.28).

Similarly to (9.6) one can define the function

$$q(\mu) = \exp(\lambda(\mu)(2\pi - \sum_{j=1}^p (\zeta_j(\mu) - \gamma_j(\mu))\Pi_{j=p}^1(1 + k_j(\mu)) \tag{9.30}$$

for system (9.27). Theorem 6.4.2 of Chap. 6 implies that $q(\mu)$ is an analytic function.

Theorem 9.5.1. *Assume that $q(0) = 1$, $q'(0) \neq 0$ and the origin is a focus of (9.26). Then, for sufficiently small r_0, there exists a continuous function $\mu = \delta(r_0), \delta(0) = 0$, such that the solution $r(\phi, r_0, \delta(r_0))$ of (9.28) is periodic function with period 2π. The period of the corresponding solution of (9.24) is $T = (2\pi - \sum_{i=1}^p \theta_i)\beta^{-1} + o(|\mu|)$. Moreover, if the origin is a stable focus of (9.26) then the closed trajectory is a limit cycle.*

Proof. If $\rho(\phi, r_0, \mu)$ is a solution of (9.29), then by Theorem 6.4.2 we have that

$$\rho(2\pi, r_0, \mu) = \sum_{i=1}^\infty a_i(\mu) r_0^i,$$

where $a_i(\mu) = \sum_{j=0}^\infty a_{ij}\mu^j, a_{10} = q(0) = 1, a_{11} = q'(0) \neq 0$. Define the displacement function

$$V(r_0, \mu) = \rho(2\pi, r_0, \mu) - r_0 = q'(0)\mu r_0 + \sum_{i=2}^\infty a_{i0} r_0^i + r_0 \mu^2 G_1(r_0, \mu) + r_0^2 \mu G_2(r_0, \mu),$$

where G_1, G_2 are functions analytic in a neighborhood of $(0,0)$. The bifurcation equation is $\mathcal{V}(r_0, \mu) = 0$. Canceling by r_0 one can rewrite the equation as

$$\mathcal{H}(r_0, \mu) = 0, \tag{9.31}$$

where

$$\mathcal{H}(r_0, \mu) = q'(0)\mu + \sum_{i=2}^{\infty} a_{i0}r_0^{i-1} + \mu^2 G_1(r_0, \mu) + r_0\mu G_2(r_0, \mu)$$

Since

$$\mathcal{H}(0,0) = 0, \qquad \frac{\partial \mathcal{H}(0,0)}{\partial \mu} = q'(0) \neq 0,$$

for sufficiently small r_0 there exists a function $\mu = \delta(r_0)$ such that $r(\phi, r_0, \delta(r_0))$ is a periodic solution. If conditions $a_{i0} = 0, i = 2, \ldots, l-1$, and $a_{l0} \neq 0$ are valid, then one can obtain from (9.31) that

$$\delta(r_0) = -\frac{a_{l0}}{q'(0)}r_0^{l-1} + \sum_{i=l}^{\infty} \delta_i r_0^i. \tag{9.32}$$

By analysis of the latter expression one can conclude that the bifurcation of periodic solutions emerges if the focus is stable with $\mu = 0$ and unstable with $\mu \neq 0$ and conversely. If $\rho(\phi) = \rho(\phi, \bar{r}_0, \bar{\mu})$ is a periodic solution of (9.29), then it is known that the trajectory is a limit cycle if

$$\frac{\partial \mathcal{V}(\bar{r}_0, \bar{\mu})}{\partial r_0} < 0. \tag{9.33}$$

We have that

$$\frac{\partial \mathcal{V}(r_0, \mu)}{\partial r_0} = q'(0)\mu + \sum_{i=2}^{\infty} i a_{i0}r_0^{i-1} + \mu^2 G_1(r_0, \mu) + 2r_0\mu G_2(r_0, \mu).$$

Let a_{l0} be the first nonzero element among a_{i0} and $a_{l0} < 0$. Using (9.32), one can obtain that

$$\frac{\partial \mathcal{V}(\bar{r}_0, \bar{\mu})}{\partial r_0} = (l-1)a_{l0}\bar{r}_0^{l-1} + Q(\bar{r}_0),$$

where Q starts with a member whose order is not less than l. Hence, (9.33) is valid. Now, B-equivalence of (9.28) and (9.29) proves the theorem. $\qquad\square$

Remark 9.5.1. (a) It is important to notice that the bifurcation theorem can be obtained by applying the results in [83] and theorems of Chap. 6. We follow the approach which is focused on the expansions of solutions [107].

(b) To illustrate that discontinuous dynamical systems may provide more interesting opportunities than continuous dynamics, let us compare the bifurcation diagrams of an ordinary differential equation, Fig. 9.3, and a discontinuous dynamical system of type (9.24), Fig. 9.4. One can see that the first diagram resembles a bud, and the second one a rose. They demonstrate that a theory of differential equations flourishes if a discontinuity is involved in analysis.

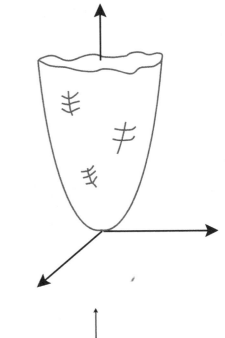

Fig. 9.3 A Hopf bifurcation diagram of an ordinary differential equation

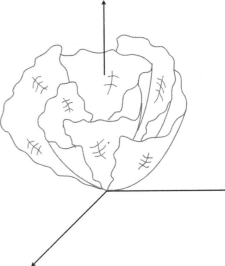

Fig. 9.4 A Hopf bifurcation diagram of a discontinuous dynamical system

9.6 Examples

Example 9.6.1. Consider the following system:

$$x_1' = (2 + \mu)x_1 - x_2 + x_1^2 x_2,$$
$$x_2' = x_1 + (2 + \mu)x_2 + 3x_1^3 x_2,$$
$$\Delta x_1|_{x \in l} = ((\kappa + \mu^2)\cos(\frac{\pi}{6}) - 1)x_1 - (\kappa + \mu^2)\sin(\frac{\pi}{6})x_2,$$
$$\Delta x_2|_{x \in l} = (\kappa + \mu^2)\sin(\frac{\pi}{6})x_1 + ((\kappa + \mu^2)\cos(\frac{\pi}{6}) - 1)x_2, \quad (9.34)$$

where $\kappa = e^{-\frac{11\pi}{6}}$, and the curve l is given by the equation $x_2 = x_1^3$, where $x_1 > 0$. One can define, using (9.30), that $q(\mu) = (\kappa + \mu^2)\exp((2 + \mu)\frac{11\pi}{6})$, $q(0) = \kappa\exp(\frac{11\pi}{3}) = 1$, $q'(0) = -\frac{11\pi}{6} \neq 0$. Thus, by Theorem 9.5.1, system (9.34) has a periodic solution with period $\approx \frac{11\pi}{12}$ if $|\mu|$ is sufficiently small.

Example 9.6.2. Let the following system be given:

$$x_1' = (\mu - 1)x_1 - x_2, \ x_2' = x_1 + (\mu - 1)x_2,$$
$$\Delta x_1|_{x \in l} = ((\kappa - x_1^2 - x_2^2)\cos(\frac{\pi}{4}) - 1)x_1 - (\kappa - x_1^2 - x_2^2)\sin(\frac{\pi}{4})x_2,$$
$$\Delta x_2|_{x \in l} = (\kappa - x_1^2 - x_2^2)\sin(\frac{\pi}{4})x_1 + ((\kappa - x_1^2 - x_2^2)\cos(\frac{\pi}{4}) - 1)x_2, \quad (9.35)$$

where l is a curve given by the equation $x_2 = x_1 + \mu x_1^2, x_1 > 0, \kappa = \exp(\frac{7\pi}{4})$. Using (9.30) one can find that $q(\mu) = \kappa\exp((\mu - 1)\frac{7\pi}{4}), q(0) = \kappa\exp(-\frac{7\pi}{4}) = 1$, $q'(0) = \frac{7\pi}{4} \neq 0$. Moreover, one can see that for the associated D-system

$$x_1' = -x_1 - x_2, \ x_2' = x_1 - x_2,$$
$$\Delta x_1|_{x \in s} = ((\kappa - x_1^2 - x_2^2)\cos(\frac{\pi}{4}) - 1)x_1 - (\kappa - x_1^2 - x_2^2)\sin(\frac{\pi}{4})x_2,$$
$$\Delta x_2|_{x \in s} = (\kappa - x_1^2 - x_2^2)\sin(\frac{\pi}{4})x_1 + ((\kappa - x_1^2 - x_2^2)\cos(\frac{\pi}{4}) - 1)x_2, \quad (9.36)$$

where s is given by the equation $x_2 = x_1, x_1 > 0$, the origin is a stable focus. Indeed, using polar coordinates, denote by $r(\phi, r_0)$ the solution of (9.36) starting at the angle $\phi = \frac{\pi}{4}$. We can define that $r(\frac{\pi}{4} + 2\pi n, r_0) = (\kappa - r^2(\frac{\pi}{4} + 2\pi(n-1), r_0))\exp(-\frac{7\pi}{4})$. From the last expression it is easily seen that the sequence $r_n = r(\frac{\pi}{4} + 2\pi n, r_0)$ is monotonically decreasing and there exists a limit of r_n. Assume that $r_n \to \sigma \neq 0$. Then it implies that there exists a periodic solution of (9.36) and $\sigma = (\kappa - \sigma^2)\exp(-\frac{7\pi}{4})\sigma$ which is a contradiction. Thus, $\sigma = 0$. Consequently, the origin is a stable focus of (9.36) and by Theorem 9.5.1 the system (9.35) has a limit cycle with period $\approx \frac{7\pi}{4}$ if $\mu > 0$ is sufficiently small.

Notes

The present chapter contains mainly results of paper [4], and is based on the perturbation theory, which was founded by H. Poincaré and A. M. Lyapunov [104, 132], and the bifurcation methods [38, 48, 71, 80, 83, 106, 107, 134, 157]. The main result is the bifurcation of a periodic solution from the equilibrium of the discontinuous dynamical system. After the initial impetus of H. Poincaré [132], A. Andronov [38], and E. Hopf [80] this method of research of periodic motions has been used very successfully for various differential equations by many authors (see [66, 71, 83, 107] and references cited there). There have been two principal obstacles of expansion of this method for discontinuous dynamical systems. While the absence of developed differentiability of solutions has been the first one, the choice of a nonperturbed system convenient to study has been the second. The present investigation utilizes extensively the differentiability and analyticity of discontinuous solutions discussed in Chap. 6. The nonperturbed equation is specifically defined. The results of the present chapter can be extended by the dimension enlarging [21] and application to differential equations with discontinuous right side [13]. They are applied to control the population dynamics [14], and can be effectively employed in mechanics, electronics, biology, and medicine [38, 52, 71, 107, 115, 123].

Chapter 10
Chaos and Shadowing

10.1 Introduction and Preliminaries

The proof of the existence of chaotic attractors remains an important and difficult problem, which is still not resolved fully, even for the Lorentz system [49, 72, 84, 150]. In this chapter, a multidimensional chaos is generated by a special initial value problem for the nonautonomous impulsive differential equation. The existence of a chaotic attractor is shown, where density of periodic solutions, sensitivity of solutions, and existence of a trajectory, which is dense in the set of all orbits are observed. That is, we concentrate on the topological ingredients of the version proposed by Devaney [62]. An appropriate example is constructed, where a chaotic attractor is indicated, and the intermittency is observed.

The discontinuous system consists of an impulsive differential equation and of a discrete equation, which generates the moments of impacts.

We suppose that the generator is chaotic while the impulsive system is dissipative for all possible sequences of moments of discontinuities, and we prove that the system has a similar chaotic nature. Similarly, if the generator function has a shadowing property [40,55,76,134], then the system admits an analogue of the property. The shadowing exists if the generator is uniformly hyperbolic on the invariant set of initial moments, or a nonhyperbolic map.

The results of this chapter illustrate that impulsive differential equations may play a special role in the investigation of the complex behavior of dynamical systems.

Finally, one must say that the B-equivalence method is used to obtain main results of this chapter. Thus, we will complete the integrity of the book.

Let us consider a continuous map $H : I \to \mathbb{R}, I = [0, 1]$, with a positively invariant compact set $\Lambda \subseteq I$. Let $\kappa_{i+1} = H(\kappa_i), \kappa_0 = t_0 \in \Lambda$, and the sequence $\zeta(t_0) = \{\zeta_i(t_0)\}$ be defined, where $\zeta_i(t_0) = i + \kappa_i(t_0), i \geq 0$.

One may consider the logistic map $h(t, \mu) = \mu t(1 - t), \mu > 0$, as an example of H. The main object of discussion in this chapter is the following special initial value problem,

$$z'(t) = Az(t) + f(z),$$

$$\Delta|_{t=\zeta_i(t_0)} = Bz(\zeta_i(t_0)) + W(z(\zeta_i(t_0))),$$
$$z(t_0) = z_0, \ (t_0, z_0) \in \Lambda \times \mathbb{R}^n, \tag{10.1}$$

where $z \in \mathbb{R}^n, t_0 \in I, t \geq t_0$.

We shall need the following basic assumptions for the problem:

(C1) A, B are $n \times n$ constant real valued matrices; $\det(\mathcal{I} + B) \neq 0$, where $\mathcal{I}$ is the identical matrix;

(C2) for all $x_1, x_2 \in \mathbb{R}^n$ functions $f(x) : \mathbb{R}^n \to \mathbb{R}^n, W : \mathbb{R}^n \to \mathbb{R}^n$, satisfy

$$||f(x_1) - f(x_2)|| + ||W(x_1) - W(x_2)|| \leq L||x_1 - x_2||,$$

where $L > 0$ is a constant;

(C3) $\sup_{x \in \mathbb{R}^n} ||f(x)|| + \sup_{x \in \mathbb{R}^n} ||W(x)|| = M_0 < \infty$;

(C4) the matrices A and B commute and the real parts of all eigenvalues of $A + \ln(\mathcal{I} + B)$ are negative.

From the previous chapters it implies that under these conditions a solution $z(t) = z(t, t_0, z_0), z_0 \in \mathbb{R}^n$ of (10.1) exists, and is unique on $[t_0, \infty)$.

Consider an unbounded and strictly increasing sequence θ with elements θ_i, $i - 1 < \theta_i < i + 2, i \in \mathbb{Z}$. Let us denote by $Z(t, s)$ the transition matrix of the linear homogeneous system

$$z'(t) = Az(t),$$
$$\Delta z|_{t=\theta_i} = Bz(\theta_i). \tag{10.2}$$

Condition $(C4)$ and the result of Exercise 4.1.8 imply that there exist two positive numbers N and ω, which do not depend on θ, such that $||Z(t, s)|| \leq Ne^{-\omega(t-s)}, t \geq s$. In what follows, we shall denote by $Z(t, s, \xi)$ the transition matrix $Z(t, s)$ if $\theta = \zeta(\xi)$.

We shall need the following additional assumptions:

(C6) $NL[\frac{2}{\omega} + \frac{e^\omega}{1-e^{-\omega}}] < 1$;

(C7) $-\omega + NL + \ln(1 + NL) < 0$.

The solution $z(t) = z(t, t_0, z_0)$ of (10.1) satisfies the following integral equation:

$$z(t) = Z(t, t_0, t_0)z_0 + \int_{t_0}^t Z(t, s, t_0)f(z(s))ds + \sum_{t_0 \leq \zeta_i < t} Z(t, \zeta_i(t_0), t_0)W(z(\zeta_i(t_0))).$$

Using the last formula and technique of Chap. 7 (see Theorem 7.1.5), one can verify that all solutions eventually, as t increases, enter the tube with the radius $M = NM_0[\frac{1}{\omega} + \frac{e^\omega}{1-e^{-\omega}}], t \in \mathbb{R}$. That is, the discussion of this chapter can be made assuming that all solutions are inside the tube. Moreover, if the sequence $\kappa(t_0)$ is periodic with a period $p \in \mathbb{N}$, then there is a solution of (10.1) with the same period, and its integral curve is placed in the tube.

We assume that:

(C8) $Bx + W(x) \neq 0$, if $\|x\| \leq M$.

The last condition implies that periodic solutions are different for different p.

Denote by $\mathcal{PC}$ the set of all solutions $z(t) = z(t, t_0, z_0), t_0 \in \Lambda, z_0 \in \mathbb{R}^n, t \geq t_0$ of (10.1), and denote $\mathcal{PCA} = \{z \in \mathcal{PC} : \|z(t_0)\| < M, t_0 \in \Lambda\}$. In the next section, we define conditions with which $\mathcal{PCA}$ is a chaotic attractor.

10.2 The Devaney's Chaos

Let us assume that the map H admits all Devaney's ingredients of chaos on the set Λ, that is:

1. there exists a positive δ_0 such that for each $t \in \Lambda$ and $\epsilon > 0$ there is a point $\tilde{t} \in \Lambda$ with $|t - \tilde{t}| < \epsilon$ and $|H^i(t) - H^i(\tilde{t})| \geq \delta_0$, for some positive integer i (sensitivity);
2. there exists an element $t^* \in \Lambda$ such that the set $H^i(t^*), i \geq 0$, is dense in Λ (transitivity);
3. the set of period$-p$ points, $p \geq 1$, is dense in Λ (density of periodic points).

Let us define the chaos for the discontinuous dynamics of (10.1).

Definition 10.2.1. We say that (10.1) is sensitive on Λ if there exist positive real numbers ϵ_0, ϵ_1 such that for each $t_0 \in \Lambda$, and $\delta > 0$ one can find a number $t_1 \in \Lambda, |t_0 - t_1| < \delta$, such that for each couple of solutions $z(t) = z(t, t_0, z_0), z_1(t) = z(t, t_1, z_1), z_0, z_1 \in \mathbb{R}^n$, there exists an interval $Q \subset [t_0, \infty)$ with the length not less than ϵ_1 such that $\|z(t) - z_1(t)\| \geq \epsilon_0, t \in Q$, and there are no points of discontinuity of $z(t), z_1(t)$ in Q.

We shall denote $z(t)(\epsilon, J)z_1(t)$, if solutions $z(t)$ and $z_1(t)$ of (10.1), $z(t) = z(t, t_0, z_0), z_1(t) = z(t, t_1, z_1), t_0, t_1 \in \Lambda$, are ϵ-equivalent on J. The concept of the equivalence is described in Sect. 5.4.

Definition 10.2.2. The set of all periodic solutions $\phi(t) = \phi(t, t_0), t_0 \in \Lambda$, of (10.1) is called dense in $\mathcal{PC}$ if for every solution $z(t) \in \mathcal{PC}$ and each $\epsilon > 0, E > 0$, there exist a periodic solution $\phi(t, t^*), t^* \in \Lambda$, and an interval $J \subset [t_0, \infty)$ with the length E such that $\phi(t)(\epsilon, J)z(t)$.

Definition 10.2.3. A solution $z_*(t) \in \mathcal{PC}$ of (10.1) is called dense in the set of all orbits of $\mathcal{PC}$ if for every solution $z(t) \in \mathcal{PC}$ of (10.1), and each $\epsilon > 0, E > 0$, there exist an interval $J \subset [0, \infty)$ with the length E and a real number ξ such that $z_*(t + \xi)(\epsilon, J)z(t)$.

Definition 10.2.4. The problem (10.1) is chaotic if: (i) it is sensitive; (ii) the set of all periodic solutions $\phi(t, t_0), t_0 \in \Lambda$, is dense in $\mathcal{PC}$; (iii) there exists a solution $z_*(t)$, which is dense in $\mathcal{PC}$.

Remark 10.2.1. Definitions of the chaotic ingredients have been worked out in detail issuing from the two reasons: the considered system is nonautonomous and consequently we analyze integral curves, but not trajectories; the system is impulsive and different solutions have different points of discontinuity that necessitates the B-topology.

Theorem 10.2.1. *Assume that conditions (C1)–(C6) are fulfilled. Then the set of all periodic solutions $\phi(t, t_0), t_0 \in \Lambda$, of (10.1) is dense in $\mathcal{PC}$.*

Proof. Fix $t_1 \in \Lambda$ and $E, \epsilon > 0$. The density of periodic points of H and uniform continuity of this map imply that for an arbitrary large number $\tilde{T}$ there exists a sequence $\zeta(t_0)$, defined by a periodic sequence $\kappa(t_0)$, such that $\|\zeta(t_1) - \zeta(t_0)\|_Q < \epsilon$, where $Q = (t_1, t_1 + \tilde{T} + E)$. We shall find the number $\tilde{T}$ so large that solution $z(t) = z(t, t_1, z_1), \|z_1\| < M$, is ϵ-equivalent to $\phi(t, t_0)$ on $J = (t_1 + \tilde{T}, t_1 + \tilde{T} + E)$.

Denote by $Z_1(t, s) = Z(t, s, t_1)$ and $Z_2(t, s) = Z(t, s, t_0), t \geq s$, the transition matrices. We have that

$$z(t) = Z_1(t, 1)z(1) + \int_{c1}^{t} Z_1(t, s) f(z(s)) ds + \sum_{1 \leq \zeta_i < t} Z_1(t, \zeta_i(t_1)) W(z(\zeta_i(t_1))),$$

$$\phi(t) = Z_2(t, 1)\phi(1) + \int_{c1}^{t} Z_2(t, s) f(\phi(s)) ds + \sum_{1 \leq \zeta_i < t} Z_2(t, \zeta_i(t_0)) W(\phi(\zeta_i(t_0))).$$

The difference between $z(t)$ and $\phi(t)$ cannot be evaluated by using the last two expressions since the moments of discontinuities do not coincide. The method of B-equivalence is helpful here. Introduce the following B-maps

$$W_i^1(z) = (\mathcal{I} + B) \left[\left(e^{A(\zeta_i(t_1) - \zeta_j(t_0))} - \mathcal{I} \right) z + \int_{\zeta_j(t_0)}^{\zeta_i(t_1)} e^{A(\zeta_i(t_1) - s)} f(z(s)) ds \right] +$$

$$W((\mathcal{I} + B)[e^{A(\zeta_i(t_1) - \zeta_j(t_0))} z + \int_{\zeta_j(t_0)}^{\zeta_i(t_1)} e^{A(\zeta_i(t_1) - s)} f(z(s)) ds]) -$$

$$\int_{\zeta_j(t_0)}^{\zeta_i(t_1)} e^{A(\zeta_i(t_1) - s)} f(z_1(s)) ds - W(z),$$

where $z(t), z_1(t), z(\zeta_i(t_0)) = z, z_1(\zeta_i(t_1)) = z(\zeta_i(t_1)+)$, are solutions of the equation $z' = Az$. One can easily verify that $M_1 = \sup_{\|z\| \leq M, i \in \mathbb{Z}} \|W_i^1(z)\| < \infty$. Consider the following system:

$$v'(t) = Av(t) + f(v), t \neq \zeta_i(t_0),$$

$$\Delta v|_{t = \zeta_i(t_0)} = Bv(\zeta_i(t_0)) + W(v(\zeta_i(t_0))) + W_i^1(v(\zeta_i(t_0))), \tag{10.3}$$

together with the system

$$z'(t) = Az(t) + f(z), t \neq \zeta_i(t_1),$$
$$\Delta|_{t=\zeta_i(t_1)} = Bz(\zeta_i(t_1)) + W(\zeta_i(t_1)), \tag{10.4}$$

where t_0, t_1 are the numbers under discussion.

Systems (10.3) and (10.4) are B-equivalent. That is, their solutions with the same initial condition coincide on the common domain if only $t \notin (\widehat{\zeta_i(t_0)}, \zeta_i(t_1)], i \in \mathbb{Z}$. So, if $v(t), v(1) = z(1)$, is the solution of (10.3), then $v(t) = z(t)$ for all $t \notin (\widehat{\zeta_i(t_0)}, \zeta_i(t_1)], i \in \mathbb{Z}$. For $v(t)$ we have that

$$v(t) = Z_2(t,1)v(1) + \int_{c1}^{t} Z_2(t,s) f(v(s))ds +$$

$$\sum_{1 \leq \zeta_i < t} Z_2(t, \zeta_i(t_0))[W(v(\zeta_i(t_0))) + W_1(v(\zeta_i(t_0)))].$$

Thus,

$$\|\phi(t) - v(t)\| \leq \|\phi(1) - v(1)\| \|Z_2(t,1)\| + \int_{c1}^{t} \|Z_2(t,s)\| \|L\| \|\phi(s) - v(s)\| ds +$$

$$\sum_{1 \leq \zeta_j(t_0) < t} \|Z_2(t, \zeta_j(t_0))\| \|L\| \|\phi(\zeta_j(t_0)) - v(\zeta_j(t_0))\| +$$

$$\sum_{1 \leq \zeta_j(t_0) < t} \|Z_2(t, \zeta_j(t_0))\| \|W_1(v(\zeta_i(t_0)))\| \leq$$

$$2MN + M_1 \frac{e^\omega}{1 - e^{-\omega}} + \int_{c1}^{t} N e^{-\omega(t-s)} L \|z(s) - v(s)\| ds +$$

$$\sum_{1 \leq \zeta_j < t} N e^{-\omega(t-\zeta_j(t_0))} L \|v(\zeta_j(t_0)) - v(\zeta_j(t_0))\|.$$

Now, applying Lemma 2.5.1, we can find that

$$\|z(t) - v(t)\| \leq (2MN + M_1 \frac{e^\omega}{1 - e^{-\omega}}) e^{(-\omega + NL + \ln(1+NL))(t-1)}.$$

The last inequality implies that $\|z(t) - v(t)\| < \epsilon$ if $t > \tilde{T}, t \notin [\widehat{\zeta_i(t_0)}, \zeta_i(t_1)], i \geq 0$, where $\tilde{T} = 1 + \ln(\frac{\epsilon}{2MN + M_1 e^\omega(1 - e^{-\omega})^{-1}})(-\omega + NL + \ln(1 + NL))^{-1}$, (we may assume that $\epsilon < 2M$). That is why, $z(t)(\epsilon, J)\phi(t)$ if $J = (t_1 + \tilde{T}, t_1 + \tilde{T} + E)$. The theorem is proved. □

Theorem 10.2.2. *Assume that conditions (C1)–(C6) are fulfilled. Then there exists a solution of (10.1), which is dense in* $\mathcal{PC}$.

Proof. Fix positive E, ϵ, and $t^* \in \Lambda$ such that the orbit of t^* is dense in Λ. Set $z_*(t) = z(t, t^*, z^*), \|z^*\| < M$. Let us prove that $z_*(t)$ is the dense solution.

Consider an arbitrary solution $z(t) = z(t, t_0, z_0) \in \mathcal{PC}$. Consider an interval $J_1 = (0, E_1)$, where E_1 is an arbitrarily large positive number. By density of the orbit of t^* and uniform continuity of H, there exists a natural m such that

$$\|\zeta(t_1) - \zeta(t^*, m)\|_{J_1} < \epsilon, \tag{10.5}$$

where $\zeta(t^*, m) = \{\zeta_{i+m}(t^*)\}$.

We have

$$z_*(t + m) = Z_*(t + m, 1 + m)z_*(1 + m) + \int_{1+m}^{t+m} Z_*(t + m, u) f(z_*(u)) du +$$

$$\sum_{1+m \leq \zeta_i(t_0) < t+m} Z_*(t + m, \zeta_i(t_0)) W(z_*(\zeta_i(t_0))) = Z_*(t + m, 1 + m)z_*(1 + m) +$$

$$\int_1^t Z_*(t, u) f(z_*(u + m)) du + \sum_{1+m \leq \zeta_i(t_0) < t+m} Z_*(t + m, \zeta_i(t_0)) W(z_*(\zeta_i(t_0))),$$

and

$$z_1(t) = Z_1(t, 1)z_1(1) + \int_1^t Z_1(t, u) f(z_1(u)) du + \sum_{1 \leq \zeta_i(t_1) < t} Z_1(t, \zeta_i(t_1)) W(z_1(\zeta_i(t_1))),$$

where Z_* and Z_1 are fundamental matrices corresponding to points t_* and t_1, respectively. Now, using the last two formulas, similarly to proof of Theorem 10.2.1, using (10.5) and the B-equivalence technique, we can find a sufficiently large number $E_1 > 2E$, and a natural number m such that $z_*(t + m)$ and $z_1(t)$ are ϵ-equivalent on $J = (E_1/2, E_1)$. The theorem is proved. $\qquad\square$

Let $\overline{m} = \max_{|u| \leq 1} \|e^{Au}\|, \underline{m} = \min_{|u| \leq 1} \|e^{Au}\|$.
Condition (C7) implies that $\eta = \min_{\|x\| \leq M} (Bx + W(x)) > 0$.
From now on we make the assumption:

(C8) $L < \frac{\underline{m}\eta}{2\overline{m}M} \min(1, \frac{\underline{m}\,\overline{m}}{\overline{m}+\underline{m}})$.

Theorem 10.2.3. *Assume that conditions (C1)–(C8) are fulfilled. Then (10.1) is sensitive on* $\mathcal{PC}$.

Proof. Fix a solution $z(t) = z(t, t_0, z_0), t_0 \in \Lambda, z_0 \in \mathbb{R}^n$, and a positive δ. By sensitivity of H there exist $t_1 \in \Lambda, k > 0$, such that $|t_0 - t_1| < \delta, |\zeta_k(t_0) - \zeta_k(t_1)| \geq \delta_0$. Consequently, by uniform continuity of H, there exist numbers δ_1, δ_2, which do not depend on k and $t_0, t_1 \in \Lambda$, such that $|\zeta_{k-1}(t_0) - \zeta_{k-1}(t_1)| \geq \delta_1$,

$|\zeta_{k-2}(t_0) - \zeta_{k-2}(t_1)| \geq \delta_2$. Obviously, one can assume that $k > 3$. Moreover, uniform continuity of H implies that k can be an arbitrarily large number. Take arbitrary $z_1 \in \mathbb{R}^n$ and solution $z_1(t) = z(t, t_1, z_1)$.

Now, let us prove the sensitiveness through the solution $z_1(t)$.

Condition $(C8)$ implies that there exists a positive number ν such that $\frac{2\overline{m}M}{\underline{m}\eta} < \nu < \frac{\underline{m}\eta - 2\overline{m}ML}{\overline{m}}$.

We shall show that constants ϵ_0, ϵ_1 for Definition 10.2.1 can be taken equal to $\epsilon_0 = \min(\underline{m}\eta - \overline{m}(\nu + 2LM), \underline{m}\nu - \overline{m}2LM)$, $\epsilon_1 = \min(\underline{\delta}, \frac{1}{2}(1 - \overline{\delta}))$, where $\overline{\delta} = \max(\delta_0, \delta_1, \delta_2)$, $\underline{\delta} = \min(\delta_0, \delta_1, \delta_2)$. One can easily see that among numbers k and $k - 1$ there exists one , let us say k itself, such that $|\zeta_k(t_0) - \zeta_k(t_1)| \geq \epsilon_1$ and interval $[\zeta_k(t_0) - \epsilon_1, \zeta_k(t_0))$ does not have points of discontinuity from $\zeta(t_0)$ and $\zeta(t_1)$.

Assume that $\|z(\zeta_k(t_0)) - z_1(\zeta_k(t_0))\| < \nu$. Then, for $t \in [\zeta_k(t_0), \zeta_k(t_1)]$,

$$z(t) = e^{A(t - \zeta_k(t_0))}(\mathcal{I} + B)z((\zeta_k(t_0)) + \int_{\zeta_k(t_0)}^{t} e^{A(t-s)} f(z(s))ds +$$

$$e^{A(t - \zeta_k(t_0))} W(z((\zeta_k(t_0)))),$$

$$z_1(t) = e^{A(t - \zeta_k(t_0))} z_1((\zeta_k(t_0)) + \int_{\zeta_k(t_0)}^{t} e^{A(t-s)} f(z_1(s))ds.$$

We have that

$$\|z(t) - z_1(t)\| = \|e^{A(t - \zeta_k(t_0))}[Bz(\zeta_k(t_0)) + W(z(\zeta_k(t_0)))] + e^{A(t - \zeta_k(t_0))}[z((\zeta_k(t_0)) -$$

$$z_1((\zeta_k(t_0))] + \int_{\zeta_k(t_0)}^{t} e^{A(t-s)}(f(z(s)) - f(z_1(s)))ds\| \geq \underline{m}\eta - \overline{m}(\nu + 2LM) \geq \epsilon_0.$$

If $\|z(\zeta_k(t_0)) - z_1(\zeta_k(t_0))\| > \nu$, then, for $t \in [\zeta_k(t_0) - \epsilon_1, \zeta_k(t_0))$,

$$z(t) = e^{A(t - \zeta_k(t_0))} z((\zeta_k(t_0)) + \int_{\zeta_k(t_0)}^{t} e^{A(t-s)} f(z(s))ds,$$

$$z_1(t) = e^{A(t - \zeta_k(t_0))} z_1((\zeta_k(t_0)) + \int_{\zeta_k(t_0)}^{t} e^{A(t-s)} f(z_1(s))ds.$$

and $\|z(t) - z_1(t)\| \geq \underline{m}\nu - \overline{m}2LM \geq \epsilon_0$. The theorem is proved. $\qquad \square$

On the basis of Theorems 10.2.1–10.2.3, we can conclude that (10.1) admits the Devaney's chaos.

It seems natural to consider the chaos only for uniformly bounded solutions on $[0, \infty)$, since the domain of chaos is always assumed to be a compact set, but we consider chaotic properties of all solutions, since the chaotic scenario for these unbounded solutions starts at the moment they reach the region where solutions from $\mathcal{PCA}$ are placed. This set is a chaotic attractor as it is easily seen that $\mathcal{PCA}$ admits defined above all ingredients of Devaney's chaos.

10.3 Shadowing Property

In this part of the chapter, we give definitions of shadowing property for the flow of system (10.1) and prove it for this system if the generator map has the property. A corollary of the result for a map H with the hyperbolic set Λ is obtained.

Assume that the generator map, $H(t)$, is defined in a neighborhood of the unit interval I.

The following definitions are from [55, 122, 131, 134] and are adapted for our system.

A sequence $\{\kappa_i\}_0^N, N \leq \infty$, is said to be a *true* trajectory of H, if $\kappa_0 \in \Lambda$ and $\kappa_{i+1} = H(\kappa_i), 0 \leq i < N$.

A sequence $\{\pi_i\}_0^N, N \leq \infty$, is said to be a κ-*pseudo-orbit*, $\kappa > 0$, of H, if $|\pi_{i+1} - H(\pi_i)| < \kappa$, and $|p_i - \lambda| < \kappa$ for all $0 \leq i < N$, and $\lambda \in \Lambda$.

The true orbit $\{\kappa_i\}_0^N$ δ-shadows the pseudo-orbit $\{\pi_i\}_0^N$ if $|\kappa_i - \pi_i| < \delta$ for all i.

A sequence $\{z_i\}_0^N$ is said to be a *true discrete orbit* of (10.1) if $z_{i+1} = z(\zeta_{i+1}, \zeta_i, z_i)$, where $\zeta_i = i + \kappa_i$ for all $0 \leq i < N$. Let δ be a positive number, and k a positive integer. A sequence y_{ik} such that $0 \leq ik \leq N$ if $N < \infty$, and $i \geq 0$, if $N = \infty$, is said to be a *discrete δ-pseudo-orbit* for the problem (10.1) with associated sequence $\{p_i\}_0^N$ if $\|y_{(i+1)k} - w(p_{(i+1)k})\| < \delta$ for all admissible i, and the solution $w(t)$ of the initial value problem

$$w'(t) = Aw(t) + f(w),$$

$$\Delta|_{t=p_i} w = Bw(p_i) + W(w(p_i)),$$

$$w(p_{ik}) = y_{ik}. \tag{10.6}$$

A discrete δ-pseudo-orbit y_{ik} of problem (10.1) is said to be ϵ-shadowed by a true orbit $\{z_i\}_0^N$ of (10.1) if $\|z_{ik} - y_{ik}\| < \epsilon$, and $|\zeta_{ik} - p_{ik}| < \epsilon$ for all i such that $0 \leq ik \leq N$ if $N < \infty$, and $i \geq 0$, if $N = \infty$. Consider the logistic function $h(x, \mu) \equiv \mu x(1 - x)$ with coefficient $\mu = 3.8$. It is proved in [76] that for $\epsilon = 10^{-8}, N = 10^7, p_0 = 0.4$, the pseudo-orbit $p_i, i = 0$ to N, is ϵ-shadowed by a true orbit, if $\delta = 3 \times 10^{-14}$. Several values of μ were claimed to be proper for the shadowing. Taking into account this result as well as results from [40, 55, 61, 120, 134] the following assertion is very useful.

Theorem 10.3.1. *Assume that conditions (C1)–(C6) are fulfilled. Then, given $\epsilon > 0$, there exists $0 < \delta < \epsilon$ and a positive integer k such that a δ-pseudo-orbit y_{ik} of problem (10.1) is ϵ-shadowed by a true orbit $\{z_i\}_0^N$ of (10.1) if $p_i = i + \pi_i$, and π_i is δ-shadowed by $\{\kappa_i\}_0^N$.*

Proof. Fix positive ϵ and nonnegative integer i. We assume that $\|z_{ik} - y_{ik}\| < \epsilon$, and we will find δ and k, such that $\|z_{(i+1)k} - y_{(i+1)k}\| < \epsilon$. Assume, without loss of generality, that $\zeta_{ik} < p_{ik}$, and let $z(t) = z(t, \zeta_{ik}, z_{ik})$. We have that

$$\|z(p_{ik}) - y_{ik}\| \leq \|z(p_{ik}) - z_{ik}\| + \|z_{ik} - y_{ik}\| = \|e^{A(p_{ik}-\zeta_{ik})}z_{ik}$$

$$+ \int_{\zeta_{ik}}^{p_{ik}} e^{A(t-s)} f(z(s))ds\| + \|z_{ik} - y_{ik}\| \leq$$

$$\|[\mathcal{I} - e^{A(p_{ik}-\zeta_{ik})}]\|\|z_{ik}\| + \delta N M_0 + \epsilon = \delta\phi(\delta) + \epsilon,$$

where $\phi(s)$ is a bounded function.

Similarly to the proof of Theorem 10.2.1, we find that (10.1) is B-equivalent to the following system:

$$\begin{aligned}
v'(t) &= Av(t) + f(v),\\
\Delta v|_{t=p_i} &= Bv(p_i) + W(v(p_i)) + \tilde{W}_i^1(v(p_i)),\\
v(t_0) &= z_0, \ (t_0, z_0) \in \Lambda \times \mathbb{R}^n,
\end{aligned} \tag{10.7}$$

with $M_2 = \sup_{\|z\|\leq M, i\in\mathbb{Z}} \|\tilde{W}_i^1(z)\| < \infty$.

Then we can obtain that

$$\|z(t) - w(t)\| \leq [N(\delta\phi(\delta) + \epsilon) + M_2 \frac{e^\omega}{1-e^{-\omega}}]e^{(-\omega+NL+\ln(1+NL))(t-1)},$$

if $t \notin \widehat{[p_i, \zeta_i)}$. Now, choose k sufficiently large, and δ small for the right-hand side of the last inequality to be less than $\frac{\epsilon}{3}$ at $t = (i+1)k - 1$, and $\delta \max(1, \phi(\delta)) < \frac{\epsilon}{3}$. Then $\|z_{(i+1)k} - y_{(i+1)k}\| < \|z_{(i+1)k} - z(p_{(i+1)k})\| + \|z(p_{(i+1)k}) - w(p_{(i+1)k})\| + \|y_{(i+1)k} - w(p_{(i+1)k})\| < \epsilon$. The theorem is proved. $\square$

Now, by using the Shadowing Theorem [55, 122, 131] one can easily prove that the following assertion is true.

Theorem 10.3.2. *Assume that conditions (C1)–(C6) are fulfilled and H has a compact positively invariant hyperbolic set $\Lambda \subset I$. Then, given $\epsilon > 0$, there exist $0 < \delta < \epsilon$, and a positive integer k such that a δ-pseudo-orbit $\{y_{ik}\}_0^\infty$, of problem (10.1) is ϵ-shadowed by a true orbit $\{z_i\}_0^\infty$ of (10.1) if $\pi_i = p_i - i, i \geq 0$, is a δ-pseudo-orbit of H.*

10.4 Simulations

Consider the following initial value problem

$$\begin{aligned}
x_1' &= 2/5x_2 + l\sin^2 x_2,\\
x_2' &= 2/5x_1 + l\sin^2 x_1, t \neq \zeta_i(t_0),\\
\Delta x_1|_{t=\zeta_i(t_0)} &= -\frac{4}{3}x_1,\\
\Delta x_2|_{t=\zeta_i(t_0)} &= -\frac{4}{3}x_2 + W(x_2),
\end{aligned} \tag{10.8}$$

where $W(s) = 1 + s^2$, if $|s| \leq l, l$ is a positive constant, and $W(s) = 1 + l^2$, if $|s| > l$. One can easily see that all the functions are lipschitzian with a constant proportional to l. The matrices of coefficients

$$A = \begin{pmatrix} 0 & 2/5 \\ 2/5 & 0 \end{pmatrix}, \quad B = \begin{pmatrix} -4/3 & 0 \\ 0 & -4/3 \end{pmatrix}$$

commute, and the eigenvalues of the matrix

$$A + Ln(\mathcal{I} + B) = \begin{pmatrix} -\ln 3 & 2/5 \\ 2/5 & -\ln 3 \end{pmatrix}$$

are negative: $\lambda_{1,2} = -\ln 3 \pm 2/5 < 0$.

The results of the last section make possible the following appropriate simulations.

Choose $\mu = 3.8$ and $l = 10^{-2}$ in (10.8) and consider the solution $x(t) = (x_1, x_2)$ with initial moments $t_0 = 7/9$ and the initial value $x(t_0) = (0.005, 0.002)$.

If one consider the sequence $(x_1(n), x_2(n)), n = 1, 2, 3, \ldots, 75000$, in x_1, x_2-plane, then the attractor can be seen, Fig. 10.1. To approve that the attractor is chaotic, we verify the conditions of the chaotic theorems in the following way. If $|s| \leq l$, then $-\frac{4}{3}s + W(s) = s^2 - \frac{4}{3}s + 1$, and it is never equal to zero. If $|s| > l$, then $-\frac{4}{3}s + W(s) = l^2 - \frac{4}{3}s + 1$. For the last expression to be zero, we need, $s = \frac{3}{4}(1 + l^2)$. From the Figure, it is seen that the second coordinate takes values between 0.32 and 0.42. This is the region where $-\frac{4}{3}s + W(s)$ does not have zeros. All the other conditions required by theorems of this chapter could be easily checked with sufficiently small coefficient l.

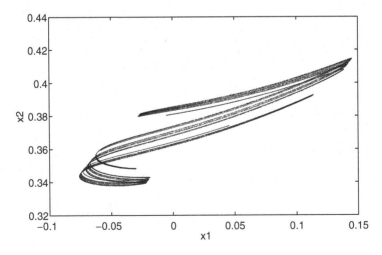

Fig. 10.1 The chaotic attractor by a stroboscopic sequence $(x_1(n), x_2(n))$, $1 \leq n \leq 75{,}000$

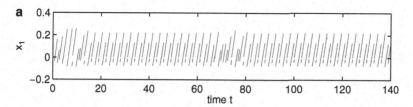

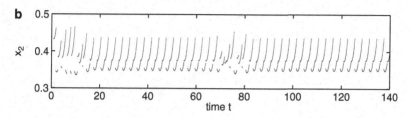

Fig. 10.2 The intermittency of the both coordinates $x_1(t), x_2(t)$ is observable

Now, consider (10.8) with $\mu = 3.8282$. Then the phenomenon of intermittency, i.e., irregular switching between periodic and chaotic behavior, for the solution $x(t)$ can be observed in Fig.10.2. The coefficient's value is such that the logistic map admits intermittency [62].

Notes

The investigation of the last chapter is inspired by the discontinuous dynamics of the neural information processing in the brain, information communication, and population dynamics [70,88,99,100,103,108,160]. While there are many interesting papers concerned with the complex behavior generated by impulses, the rigorous theory of chaotic impulsive systems remains far from being complete. Our goal is to develop further the theoretical foundations of this area of research. The complex dynamics is obtained using Devaney's definition for guidance. The main results of this chapter are published in [11]. There simulations for a pendulum are given. Applications of the present approach to the analysis of the cardiovascular system were considered in [12, 16]. More of our results on chaos excitability can be found in [8–10].

References

1. E. Akalin, M.U. Akhmet, The principles of B-smooth discontinuous flows, Comput. Math. Appl., 49 (2005) 981–995.
2. M.U. Akhmet, On the general problem of stability for impulsive differential equations, J. Math. Anal. Appl., 288 (2003) 182–196.
3. M.U. Akhmet, On the smoothness of solutions of impulsive autonomous systems, Nonlinear Anal.: TMA, 60 (2005a) 311–324.
4. M.U. Akhmet, Perturbations and Hopf bifurcation of the planar discontinuous dynamical system, Nonlinear Anal.: TMA, 60 (2005b) 163–178.
5. M.U. Akhmet, Integral manifolds of differential equations with piecewise constant argument of generalized type, Nonlinear Anal.: TMA, 66 (2007a) 367–383.
6. M.U. Akhmet, On the reduction principle for differential equations with piecewise constant argument of generalized type, J. Math. Anal. Appl., 336 (2007b) 646–663.
7. M.U. Akhmet, Almost periodic solutions of differential equations with piecewise constant argument of generalized type, Nonlinear Anal.: HS, 2 (2008) 456-467.
8. M.U. Akhmet, Devaney's chaos of a relay system, Commun. Nonlinear Sci. Numer. Simul., 14 (2009a) 1486–1493.
9. M.U. Akhmet, Li-Yorke chaos in the impact system, J. Math. Anal. Appl., 351 (2009b), 804–810.
10. M.U. Akhmet, Dynamical synthesis of quasi-minimal sets, Int. J. Bifurcation Chaos, 19, no. 7 (2009c) 1–5.
11. M.U. Akhmet, Shadowing and dynamical synthesis, Int. J. Bifurcation Chaos, Int. J. Bifurcation Chaos, 19, no. 10 (2009d) 1–8.
12. M.U. Akhmet, The complex dynamics of the cardiovascular system. Nonlinear Anal.: TMA, 71 (2009e) e1922–e1931.
13. M.U. Akhmet, D. Arugaslan, Bifurcation of a non-smooth planar limit cycle from a vertex, Nonlinear Anal.: TMA, 71 (2009) e2723–e2733.
14. M.U. Akhmet, D. Arugaslan, M. Beklioglu, Impulsive control of the population dynamics, Proceedings of the Conference on Differential and Difference Equations at the Florida Institute of Technology, August 1–5, 2005, Melbourne, Florida, Editors: R.P. Agarval and K. Perera, Hindawi Publishing Corporation, 2006, 21–30.
15. M.U. Akhmet, D. Arugaslan, M. Turan, Hopf bifurcation for a 3D Filippov system, Dyn. Contin. Discrete Impuls. Syst., Ser. A, 16 (2009) 759–775.
16. M.U. Akhmet, G.A. Bekmukhambetova, A prototype compartmental model of the blood pressure distribution, Nonlinear Anal.: RWA, 11 (2010), 1249–1257.
17. M.U. Akhmet, C. Buyukadali, Differential equations with a state-dependent piecewise constant argument, Nonlinear Analysis: TMA, 72 (2010), 4200–4211.
18. M.U. Akhmet, M. Kirane, M.A. Tleubergenova, G.W. Weber, Control and optimal response problems for quasi-linear impulsive integro-differential equations, Eur. J. Operational Res., 169 (2006) 1128–1147.

19. M.U. Akhmet, M. Turan, The differential equations on time scales through impulsive differential equations, Nonlinear Anal.: TMA, 65 (2006) 2043–2060.

20. M.U. Akhmet, M. Turan, Differential equations on variable time scales, Nonlinear Anal.: TMA, 70 (2009a) 1175–1192.

21. M.U. Akhmet, M. Turan, Bifurcation of 3D discontinuous cycles, Nonlinear Anal.: TMA, 71 (2009b) e2090–e2102.

22. M.U. Akhmetov, On periodic solutions of certain systems of differential equations, Vestn. Kiev. Univer., Mat. i Mekh. (russian), 24 (1982) 3–7.

23. M.U. Akhmetov, Periodic solutions of non-autonomous systems of differential equations with impulse action in the critical case (russian), Izv. Akad. Nauk Kazakh. SSR, Seria Fiz.-Mat., (1991a) no. 3, 62–65.

24. M.U. Akhmetov, On the existence of higher-order B-derivatives of solutions of impulse systems with respect to initial data (russian), Izv. Akad. Nauk Kazakh. SSR, Seria Fiz.-Mat., (1991b) no. 1, 15–17.

25. M.U. Akhmetov, Asymptotic representation of solutions of regularly perturbed systems of differential equations with a non classical right-hand side. Ukrainian Math. J., 43 (1991c) 1298–1304.

26. M.U. Akhmetov, Periodic solutions of systems of differential equations with a non classical right-hand side containing a small parameter (russian), TIC: Collection: asymptotic solutions of non linear equations with small parameter. 1991d, 11–15. UBL: Akad. Nauk Ukr. SSR, Inst. Mat., Kiev.

27. M.U. Akhmetov, On the smoothness of solutions of differential equations with a discontinuous right-hand side, Ukrainian Math. J., 45 (1993) 1785–1792.

28. M.U. Akhmetov, On the method of successive approximations for systems of differential equations with impulse action at nonfixed moments of time (russian), Izv. Minist. Nauki Vyssh. Obraz. Resp. Kaz. Nats. Akad. Nauk Resp. Kaz. Ser. Fiz.-Mat. (1999) no. 1, 11–18.

29. M.U. Akhmetov, R.F. Nagaev, Periodic solutions of a nonlinear impulse system in a neighborhood of a generating family of quasiperiodic solutions, Differ. Equ., 36 (2000) 799–806.

30. M.U. Akhmetov, N.A. Perestyuk, On the almost periodic solutions of a class of systems with impulse effect (russian), Ukr. Mat. Zh., 36 (1984) 486–490.

31. M.U. Akhmetov, N.A. Perestyuk, Almost periodic solutions of sampled-data systems. Ukr. Mat. Zh. (russian), 39 (1987) 74–80.

32. M.U. Akhmetov, N.A. Perestyuk, On motion with impulse actions on a surfaces (russian), Izv.-Acad. Nauk Kaz. SSR, Ser. Fiz.-Mat., 1 (1988) 111–114.

33. M.U. Akhmetov, N.A. Perestyuk, The comparison method for differential equations with impulse action, Differ. Equ., 26 (1990) 1079–1086.

34. M.U. Akhmetov, N.A. Perestyuk, Asymptotic representation of solutions of regularly perturbed systems of differential equations with a non-classical right-hand side, Ukrainian Math. J., 43 (1991) 1209–1214.

35. M.U. Akhmetov, N.A. Perestyuk, Differential properties of solutions and integral surfaces of nonlinear impulse systems, Differ. Equ., 28 (1992a) 445–453.

36. M.U. Akhmetov, N.A. Perestyuk, Periodic and almost periodic solutions of strongly nonlinear impulse systems, J. Appl. Math. Mech., 56 (1992b) 829–837.

37. M.U. Akhmetov, N.A. Perestyuk, On a comparison method for pulse systems in the space $\mathbb{R}^n$, Ukr. Math. J. 45 (1993) 826–836.

38. A.A. Andronov, A.A. Vitt, C.E. Khaikin, Theory of oscillations, Pergamon, Oxford, 1966.

39. D.V. Anosov, V.I. Arnold, Dynamical Systems, Springer, Berlin, 1994.

40. D.V. Anosov, Geodesic flows and closed Riemannian manifolds with negative curvature, Proc. Steklov Inst. Math. 90 (1967).

41. J. Awrejcewicz, C.H. Lamarque, Bifurcation and chaos in nonsmooth mechanical systems, World Scientific, Singapore, 2003.

42. G. Aymerich, Sulle oscillazioni autosostenute impulsivamente, Rend. Semin. Fac. Sci. Univ. Cagliari, 22 (1952) 34–37.

43. V.I. Babitsky, Theory of vibro-impact systems and applications, Springer, Berlin, 1998.

44. A. Balanov, N. Janson, D. Postnov, O. Sosnovtseva, Synchronization: from simple to complex, Springer, Berlin, 2009.

45. D.D. Bainov, P.S. Simeonov, Stability under persistent disturbances for systems with impulse effect, J. Math. Anal. Appl., 109 (1985) 546–563.

46. D.D. Bainov, P.S. Simeonov, Impulsive differential equations: asymptotic properties of solutions, World Scientific, Singapore, New Jersey, London, 1995.

47. D.D. Bainov, V. Govachev, Impulsive differential equations with a small parameter, World Scientific, Singapore, New Jersey, London, Hong Kong, 1994.

48. N.N. Bautin, E.A. Leontovich, Methods and rules for the qualitative study of dynamical systems on the plane (russian), Nauka, Moscow, 1990.

49. M. Benedicks, L. Carleson, The dynamics of the Henon map, Ann. Math., 133 (1991) 73–169.

50. M. di Bernardo, C.J. Budd, A.R. Champneys, P. Kowalczyk, Piecewise-smooth dynamical systems, Springer, London, 2008a.

51. M. di Bernardo, A. Nordmark, G. Olivar, Discontinuity-induced bifurcations of equilibria in piecewise-smooth and impacting dynamical systems, Phys. D, 237 (2008b) 119–136.

52. R. Bellman, Mathematical methods in medicine, World Scientific, Singapore, 1983.

53. I.I. Blekhman, Synchronization of dynamical systems (russian), Nauka, Moscow, 1971.

54. E.M. Bonotto, M. Federson, Limit sets and the Poincaré-Bendixson theorem in impulsive semidynamical systems, J. Diff. Eqs., 244 (2008) 2334–2349.

55. R. Bowen, ω-limit sets for Axiom A diffeomorfisms, J. Diff. Eqs., 18 (1975) 333–339.

56. B. Brogliato, Nonsmooth impact mechanics, Springer, London, 1996.

57. B. Brogliato, Impacts in mechanical systems – Analysis and modeling, Springer, New York, 2000.

58. D. Chillingwirth, Differential topology with a view to applications, Pitman, London, 1978.

59. E.A. Coddington, N. Levinson, Theory of Ordinary Differential Equations, McGraw-Hill, New York, 1955.

60. C. Corduneanu, Principles of differential and integral equations, Chelsea Publishing Co., Bronx, NJ, 1977.

61. E.M. Coven, I. Kan, J.A. Yorke, Pseudo-Orbit Shadowing in the Family of Tent Maps, Trans. Am. Math. Soc., 308 (1988) 227–241.

62. R. Devaney, An introduction to chaotic dynamical systems, Addison-Wesley, Menlo Park, CA, 1990.

63. A.B. Dishliev, D.D. Bainov, Sufficient conditions for absence of 'beating' in systems of differential equations with impulses, Appl. Anal., 18 (1984) 67–73.

64. A.B. Dishliev, D.D. Bainov, Differentiability on a parameter and initial condition of the solution of a system of differential equations with impulses. sterreich. Akad. Wiss. Math.-Natur. Kl. Sitzungsber. II 196 (1987) 69–96.

65. A. Domoshnitsky, M. Drakhlin, E. Litsyn, Nonoscillation and positivity of solutions to first order state-dependent differential equations with impulses in variable moments, J. Diff. Eqs., 228 (2006) 39–48.

66. M. Feckan, Bifurcation of periodic and chaotic solutions in discontinuous systems. Arch. Math. (Brno), 34 (1998) 73–82.

67. M.I. Feigin, Doubling of the oscillation period with C-bifurcations in piecewise continuous systems (Russian), J. Appl. Math. Mech., 38 (1974) 810–818.

68. A.F. Filippov, Differential equations with discontinuous right-hand sides, Kluwer, Dordrecht, 1988.

69. M. Frigon, D. O'Regan, Impulsive differential equations with variable times, Nonlinear Anal.: TMA, 26 (1996) 1913–1922.

70. L. Glass, M.C. Mackey, A simple model for phase locking of biological oscillators, J. Math. Biol., 7 (1979) 339–352.

71. J. Guckenheimer, P.J. Holmes, Nonlinear oscillations, dynamical systems and bifurcations of vector fields, Springer, New-York, 1083.

72. J. Guckenheimer, R.F. Williams, Structural stability of Lorentz attractors, Publ. Math. IHES, 50 (1979) 59–72.

73. V. Gullemin, A. Pollack, Differential topology, Prentice-Hall, New Jersey, 1974.
74. A.M. Gupal, V.I. Popadinets, Notes on formulas of differentiability of 'discontinuous solutions' of systems of ordinary differential equations on initial values and parameters (russian), Kibernetika, 4 (1974) 148–149.
75. A. Halanay, D. Wexler, Qualitative theory of impulsive systems (romanian), Edit. Acad. RPR, Bucuresti, 1968.
76. S.M. Hammel, J.A. Jorke, C. Grebogi, Do numerical orbits of chaotic dynamical processes represent true orbits? J. Complexity, 3 (1987) 136–145.
77. P. Hartman, Ordinary Differential Equations, Wiley, New York, 1964.
78. C.S. Hcu, W.H. Cheng, Applications of the theory of impulsive parametric excitation and new treatment of general parametric excitations problems, Trans. ASME, 40 (1973) 2174–2181.
79. P.J. Holmes, The dynamics of repeated impacts with a sinusoidal vibrating table, J. Sound Vib., 84 (1982) 173–189.
80. E. Hopf, Abzweigung einer periodishen Losung von einer stationaren Losung eines Differential systems, Ber. Math.-Phys. Sachsische Academie der Wissenschaften, Leipzig, 94 (1942) 1–22.
81. F.C. Hoppensteadt, C.S. Peskin, Mathematics in Medicine and in the Life Sciences, Springer, New York, 1992.
82. S.C. Hu, V. Lakshmikantham, Impulsive differential systems and the pulse phenomena, J. Math. Anal. Appl., 137 (1989) 605–612.
83. G. Iooss, D.D. Joseph, Bifurcation of maps and applications, Springer, New York, 1980.
84. M.V. Jakobson, Absolutely continuous invariant measures for one parameter families of one-dimensional maps, Commun. Math. Phys., 81 (1981) 39–88.
85. Qi Jiangang, Fu Xilin, Existence of limit cycles of impulsive differential equations with impulses at variable times. Nonlinear Anal.: TMA, 44 (2001) 345–353.
86. A. Katok, J.-M. Strelcyn, F. Ledrappier, F. Przytycki, Invariant Manifolds, Entropy and Billiards; Smooth Maps with Singularities, Lecture Notes in Mathematics, 1222, Springer, Berlin, 1986.
87. S. Kaul, On impulsive semidynamical systems, J. Math. Anal. Appl., 150 (1990) 120–128.
88. A. Khadra, X. Liu, X. Shen, Impulsive control and synchronization of spatiotemporal chaos, Chaos, Solitons and Fractals, 26 (2005) 615–636.
89. A.E. Kobrinskii, A.A. Kobrinskii, Vibro-shock systems (russian), Nauka, Moscow, 1971.
90. A.N. Kolmogorov, On the Skorokhod convergence (russian), Teor. Veroyatn. i Prim., 1 (1956) 239–247.
91. N.M. Krylov, N.N. Bogolyubov, Introduction to nonlinear mechanics, Acad. Nauk Ukrainy, Kiev, 1937.
92. M. Kunze, Non-Smooth Dynamical Systems, Lecture Notes in Mathematics, Vol. 1744, Springer, Berlin, 2000.
93. M. Kunze, T. Küpper, Qualitative bifurcation analysis of a non-smooth friction-oscillator model, Z. Angew. Math. Phys., 48 (1997) 87–101.
94. Y. Kuramoto, Chemical oscillations, Springer, Berlin, 1984.
95. V. Lakshmikantham, D.D. Bainov, P.S. Simeonov, Theory of impulsive differential equations, World Scientific, Singapore, NJ, London, Hong Kong, 1989.
96. V. Lakshmikantham, S. Leela, S. Kaul, Comparison principle for impulsive differential equations with variable times and Stability theory, Nonlinear Anal.: TMA, 22 (1994) 499–503.
97. V. Lakshmikantham, X. Liu, On quasistability for impulsive differential equations, Nonlinear Anal.: TMA, 13 (1989) 819–828.
98. S. Lefschetz, Differential equations: Geometric theory, Interscience Publishers, New York, 1957.
99. W. Lin, R. Jiong, Chaotic dynamics of an integrate-and-fire circuit with periodic pulse-train input., IEEE Trans. Circuits Syst. I Fund. Theory Appl., 50 (2003) 686–693.
100. W. Lin, Description of complex dynamics in a class if impulsive differential equations, Chaos, Solutions and Fractals, 25 (2005) 1007–1017.
101. L. Liu, J. Sun, Existence of periodic solution for a harvested system with impulses at variable times, Phys. Lett. A, 360 (2006) 105–108.

102. X. Liu, R. Pirapakaran, Global stability results for impulsive differential equations, Appl. Anal., 33 (1989) 87–102.

103. A.C.J. Luo, Global transversality, resonance and chaotic dynamics, World Scientific, Hackensack, NJ, 2008.

104. A.M. Lyapunov, Probléme général de la stabilité du mouvement, Princeton University Press, Princeton, N.J., 1949.

105. I.G. Malkin, Theory of stability of motion, U.S. Atomic Energy Commission, Office of Technical Information, 1958.

106. J.E. Marsden, M. McCracken, The Hopf bifurcation and its applications, Appl. Math. Sci., Vol. 19, Springer, New York, 1976.

107. N. Minorsky, Nonlinear Oscillations, D. Van Nostrand Company, Inc. Princeton, London, New York, 1962.

108. R.E. Mirollo, S.H. Strogatz, Synchronization of pulse-coupled biological oscillators, SIAM J. Appl. Math., 50 (1990) 1645–1662.

109. E. Mosekilde, Zh. Zhusubalyev, Bifurcations and chaos in piecewise-smooth dynamical systems, World Scientific, River Edge, NJ, 2003.

110. A.D. Myshkis, On asymptotic stability of the rough stationary points of the discontinuous dynamic systems on plane, Autom. Remote Contrl., 62 (2001) 1428–1432.

111. A.D. Myshkis, A.M. Samoilenko, Systems with impulses at fixed moments of time (russian), Math. Sb., 74 (1967) 202–208.

112. R.F. Nagaev, Periodic solutions of piecewise continuous systems with a small parameter (russian), Prikl. Mat. Mech., 36 (1972) 1059–1069.

113. R.F. Nagaev, Mechanical processes with repeated and decaying impacts (russian), Nauka, Moscow, 1985.

114. R.F. Nagaev, Dynamics of synchronising systems. Springer, Berlin, 2003.

115. R.F. Nagaev, D.G. Rubisov, Impulse motions in a one-dimensional system in a gravitational force field, Soviet Appl. Mech., 26 (1990) 885–890.

116. Yu.I. Neimark, The method of point transformations in the theory of nonlinear oscillations (russian), Nauka, Moscow, 1972.

117. V.V. Nemytskii, V.V. Stepanov, Qualitative theory of Differential Equations, Princeton University Press, Princeton, New Jersey, 1966.

118. A.B. Nordmark, Existence of periodic orbits in grazing bifurcations of impacting mechanical oscillators, Nonlinearity, 14 (2001) 1517–1542.

119. H.E. Nusse, E. Ott, J.A. Yorke, Border-collision bifurcations: an explanation for observed bifurcation phenomena, Phys. Rev. E, 49 (1994) 1073–1076.

120. H.E. Nusse, J.A. Yorke, Is Every Approximate Trajectory of Some Process Near an Exact Trajectory of a Nearby Process? Commun. Math. Phys., 114 (1988) 363–379.

121. M. Oestreich, N. Hinrichs, K. Popp, C.J. Budd, Analytical and experimental investigation of an impact oscillator. Proceedings of the ASME 16th Biennal Conf. on Mech. Vibr. and Noise, DETC97VIB-3907: 1–11, 1997.

122. K. Palmer, Shadowing in dynamical systems: Theory and Applications, Kluwer, Dordrecht, 2000.

123. T. Pavlidis, A new model for simple neural nets and its application in the design of a neural oscillator, Bull. Math. Biophys., 27 (1965) 215–229.

124. T. Pavlidis, Stability of a class of discontinuous dynamical systems, Inform. Contrl., 9 (1966) 298–322.

125. F. Peterka, Part I: Theoretical analysis of n-multiple $(1/n)$-impact solutions, CSAV Acta Technica, 26 (1974) 462–473.

126. F. Pfeiffer, Multibody systems with unilateral constraints (russian), J. Appl. Math. Mech., 65 (2001) 665–670.

127. F. Pfeiffer, Chr. Glocker, Multibody dynamics with unilateral contacts. Wiley, New York, 1996.

128. N.A. Perestyuk, V.N. Shovkoplyas, Periodic solutions of nonlinear impulsive differential equations, Ukr. Mat. Zh., 31 (1979) 517–524.

129. A. Pikovsky, Synchronization : a universal concept in nonlinear sciences, Cambridge University Press, Cambridge, 2001.
130. V.N. Pilipchuk, R.A. Ibrahim, Dynamics of a two-pendulum model with impact interaction and an elastic support, Nonlinear Dynam., 21 (2000) 221–247.
131. S.Yu. Pilugin, Shadowing in dynamical systems, Springer, Berlin, 1999.
132. H. Poincaré, Les méthodes nouvelles de la mécanique céleste, 2,3, Gauthier-Villars, Paris, 1892.
133. L.D. Pustylnikov, Stable and oscillating motions in non-autonomous dynamical systems, Trans. Math. Soc., 14 (1978) 1–10.
134. C. Robinson, Dynamical Systems: stability, symbolic dynamics, and chaos, CRC, Boca Raton, Ann Arbor, London, Tokyo, 1995.
135. V.F. Rozhko, Lyapunov stability in discontinuous dynamic systems, (russian), Diff. Eqs., 11 (1975) 761–766.
136. V.F. Rozhko, On a class of almost periodic motions in systems with shocks (russian), Diff. Eqs., 11 (1972) 2012–2022.
137. A.M. Samoilenko, N.A. Perestyuk, Second N.N. Bogolyubov's theorem for impulsive differential equations (russian), Differentsial'nye uravneniya, 10 (1974) 2001–2010.
138. A.M. Samoilenko, N.A. Perestyuk, Stability of solutions of impulsive differential equations (russian), Differentsial'nye uravneniya, 13 (1977) 1981–1992.
139. A.M. Samoilenko, N.A. Perestyuk, Periodic solutions of weakly nonlinear impulsive differential equations (russian), Differentsial'nye uravneniya, 14 (1978) 1034–1045.
140. A.M. Samoilenko, N.A. Perestyuk, On stability of solutions of impulsive systems (russian), Differentsial'nye uravneniya, 17 (1981) 1995–2002.
141. A.M. Samoilenko, N.A. Perestyuk, Differential Equations with impulsive actions (russian), Vishcha Shkola, Kiev, 1987.
142. A.M. Samoilenko, N.A. Perestyuk, Impulsive Differential Equations, World Scientific, Singapore, 1995.
143. G. Sansone, Sopra una equazione che si presenta nelle determinazioni della orbite in un sincrotrone, Rend. Accad. Naz. Lincei, 8 (1957) 1–74.
144. S.W. Shaw, P.J. Holmes, Periodically forced linear oscillator with impacts: Chaos and long-period motions, Phys. Rev. Lett., 51 (1983a) 623–626.
145. S.W. Shaw, P.J. Holmes, A periodically forced piecewise linear oscillator, J. Sound Vibr., 90 (1983b) 129–155.
146. Ya. G. Sinai, What is ... a billiard? Notices Am. Math. Soc., 51 (2004) 412–413.
147. A.V. Skorokhod, Limit theorems for random processes, (russian), Teor. Veroyatnost. i Primenen., (1956) 289–319.
148. F.W. Stallard, Differential systems with interface conditions, Oak Ridge Nat. Lab. Rep. ORNL 1876, 1955.
149. F.W. Stallard, Functions of bounded variations as solutions of differential systems, Proc. Am. Math. Soc., 13 (1962) 366–373.
150. I. Stewart, The Lorentz attractor exists, Nature, 406 (2000) 948–949.
151. P. Thota, H. Dankowicz, Continuous and discontinuous grazing bifurcations in impacting oscillators, Phys. D, 214 (2006) 187–197.
152. J.D. Vasundara, A.S. Vatsala, Generalized quasilinearization for an impulsive differential equation with variable moments of impulse, Dynam. Syst. Appl., 12 (2003) 369–382.
153. A.S. Vatsala, J. Vasundara Devi, Generalized monotone technique for an impulsive differential equation with variable moments of impulse, Nonlinear Stud., 9 (2002) 319–330.
154. Th. Vogel, Théorie des systémes evolutifs, Gauthier-Villars, Paris, 1965.
155. F. Wang, C. Hao, L. Chen, Bifurcation and chaos in a Monod-Haldene type food chain chemostat with pulsed input and washout. Chaos, solitons and fractals, 32 (2007) 181–194.
156. G.S. Whiston, Global dynamics of a vibro-impacting linear oscillator, J. Sound Vibr., 118 (1987) 395–429.
157. S. Wiggins, Global Bifurcation and Chaos: Analytical Methods, Springer, New York, 1988.
158. L.A. Wood, K.P. Byrne, Analysis of a random repeated impact process, J. Sound Vib., 82 (1981) 329–345.

159. J. Yan, A. Zhao, J.J. Nieto, Existence and global activity of positive periodic solutions of periodic single-species impulsive Lotka-Volterra systems. Math. Comput. Model. 40 (2004) 509–518.
160. T. Yang, L.O. Chua, Impulsive control and synchronization of non-linear dynamical systems and application to secure communication, Int. J. Bifurcation Chaos Appl. Sci. Eng. (electronic resource), 7 (1997) 643–664.
161. Y. Zhang, J. Sun, Stability of impulsive delay differential equations with impulses at variable times, Dyn. Syst., 20 (2005) 323–331.
162. V.F. Zhuravlev, A method for analyzing vibration-impact systems by means of special functions, Mech. Solids, 11 (1976) 23–27.

Index